# Complete Presidential
# Press Conferences of
# FRANKLIN D. ROOSEVELT

# Complete Presidential
# Press Conferences of
# FRANKLIN D. ROOSEVELT

*Introduction by Jonathan Daniels*

## Volumes 3-4

## 1934

DA CAPO PRESS • NEW YORK • 1972

Library of Congress Cataloging in Publication Data

Roosevelt, Franklin Delano, Pres. U.S., 1882-1945.
  Complete presidential press conferences of Franklin
D. Roosevelt.

  1. United States—Politics and government—1933-1945.
2. Presidents—United States—Press Conferences.
E806.R7424    1972        973.917        78-155953
ISBN 0-306-77500-X

Published by Da Capo Press, Inc.
A Subsidiary of Plenum Publishing Corporation
227 West 17th Street, New York, New York 10011

Manufactured in the United States of America

## PUBLISHER'S NOTE

This edition of the *Complete Presidential Press Conferences of Franklin D. Roosevelt* has been prepared from the original transcripts on deposit in the Franklin D. Roosevelt Library, Hyde Park, New York, and from the indexes to those transcripts compiled by the staff of the Library. Except for correction of unmistakable typographical errors and for slight changes in the alphabetization of the indexes, the text of the transcripts and indexes is unedited and unaltered.

The original twenty-five volumes of double-spaced typewritten transcript are here published in more concise format in twelve physical volumes. However, the pagination of the original volumes is retained throughout, with the page numbers inserted within the text immediately *preceding* the contents of the specified pages in the original transcripts. For purposes of uniform citation, references to particular conferences should be by their dates and by their volume and page numbers within the original transcripts.

The publishers are grateful to Professor Frank Freidel of Harvard University and to Dr. James E. O'Neill, formerly Director of the Franklin D. Roosevelt Library, for their suggestions concerning this publication, and to the staff of the Franklin D. Roosevelt Library for their assistance in gathering the photographs which appear in these volumes. However, it should be emphasized that neither the Franklin D. Roosevelt Library nor the National Archives and Records Service has participated in the preparation or publication of the work, other than to provide the same generous help that is available to any interested citizen or organization. The responsibility for the work in its present format is entirely that of the publisher.

# CONTENTS

# Complete Presidential Press Conferences of
# FRANKLIN D. ROOSEVELT

## Volume 3
## January, 1934 — June, 1934

Press Conference #83
Executive Offices of the White House
January 3, 1934, 10:50 A.M.


THE PRESIDENT: I got to bed at 1:30.

Q: After we wrote the stories that you were going to work all night on your Message?

THE PRESIDENT: Yes. (Laughter)

MR. DONALDSON: All in.

THE PRESIDENT: I don't think there is any particular news. You have a message. I think it speaks for itself. Tomorrow the Budget Message comes out and this afternoon we have arranged for a little party of the financial people who are coming over to the White House, to the Oval Room, and we will sit around and talk figures.

MR. EARLY: 4:30?

THE PRESIDENT: 4:30 in the Oval Room and try not to make it more than thirty of forty people, if you can, because you will all have to sit on the floor.

MR. EARLY: The Budget Director advises that he will have copies available at 3:30.

THE PRESIDENT: The copies will be available at 3:30 so that those who are going to come will be able to go over the copies.

Q: When may we expect that the debt Message will go up?

THE PRESIDENT: I have no idea. There isn't any timetable on that.

On the pay cut thing you were asking about, a draft of Order came to me this morning and, because it did not have all the supporting figures which I want to go into myself, I have sent for the supporting figures and it will probably be some time before

--- [2] ---

I go through all the figures.

So there really isn't any news. Just as a hint, I would go a little slow about talking about large restorations and also I think that you do have to remember that I am bound by law on this thing.

Q: Is that six per cent a good guess?

THE PRESIDENT: I think it is a terrible guess. (Laughter)

Q: Which way?

THE PRESIDENT: (No answer)

Q:   How would you guess?

THE PRESIDENT:  I haven't the figures yet, that is it.

Q:   You said it would be some time. Is that hours or days, several days --

THE PRESIDENT:  (interposing)  I told you it is merely a question of my getting
    time to do it.  It depends on when I get back to the house and when we get
    through with the Budget talk.  I am going to try to get at it today but I
    cannot guarantee it.

Q:   Mr. President, is it permissible to discuss the text of the Message at
    this time?

THE PRESIDENT:  I do not suppose that we had better talk about the details of
    the Message because, in the first place, most of your stories are written.
    What were you going to ask, what particular kind of a thing?

Q:   You said in the Message that some of the sister nations were not ready to
    stabilize. Does that mean that we are?

THE PRESIDENT:  I do not think I need to elaborate on the language at all. It
    is perfectly clear and speaks for itself.

--- [3] ---

Q:   Mr. President, do the other Messages make specific recommendations?

THE PRESIDENT:  I haven't any schedule at all.  I don't know.  There will be,
    of course, during the course of the session, other messages.  I don't
    think that I will adopt the attitude of sending a message up on every spe-
    cific subject.  Some of the legislation will probably originate in commit-
    tees.  In other words, there will be a pretty close liaison between the
    White House and the committees and there will be substantial agreement.  A
    good many things will not be -- will not take the form of messages to
    Congress at all.  There probably will be a message, as I said the other
    day, on tariffs but there isn't any regular schedule of messages or even
    a determination of what things will take the form of messages and what
    won't.

Q:   Tentatively again, isn't every nation going to stabilize if it could name
    the parity figures?

THE PRESIDENT:  If it could name its own figure?  I don't know.  I think you
    had better use this -- I suppose you can use it as background.  There are
    a good many nations whose entire financial set-up is so weak that it makes
    it awfully difficult for them to do anything -- unbalanced budgets, things
    of that kind.  It is a little bit as if you and Stevie and I were to agree
    to enter into a partnership and each put in $100,000.  (Laughter)  And
    then you and I were to discover that while Stevie had $100,000, he was
    living away beyond his means. (Laughter) Well, the chances are that you
    and I would go ahead without Stevie and that is a perfectly good illustra-
    tion of one of the international problems relating to permanent stabiliza-
    tion.

--- [4] ---

You will notice that when I used to word "stabilization," I also used the word "permanent" which is a very different thing than "temporary" and also the term "world-wide." In other words, we are looking a long ways or to the time when we can get it world-wide.

Q:  Are there any countries that just want to stay away from stabilization and stay away from gold and go on a managed currency entirely?

THE PRESIDENT:  For instance, Sweden has a managed currency today.

Q:  Would Sweden have preferred to stay away?

THE PRESIDENT:  Great Britain has a managed currency.

Q:  And there is some sentiment toward keeping it that way?

THE PRESIDENT:  Yes.

Q:  Would you suggest that the N.R.A. be made permanent at this session of the Congress?

THE PRESIDENT:  Well, I think you are a little premature, John (Boettiger). I think if you will read the message, it makes it perfectly clear that certain objectives or certain functions of the N.R.A. -- not necessarily because I very carefully said that there are some things that need readjustment of machinery -- but that certain objectives and purposes must not only be made permanent but are permanent. They are just there. The people who are kicking, they are just out of luck.

Q:  Mr. President, in the Interstate Commerce Commission, in the matter of the appointment of the successor of Brainerd (Mr. Ezra Brainerd, Jr.), has that matter been taken up?

THE PRESIDENT:  I have not had time to take it up at all. Probably the vacancies on the R.F.C. won't be filled. I have to reappoint

--- [5] ---

the Board of the R.F.C. I think on the sixteenth of January, about then, and I will fill the two vacancies. There is one (now) and of course Mr. Couch (Mr. Harvey Couch) is going off until that time.

Q:  In your discussion of your Message, I guess we are bound to keep that until it is released?

THE PRESIDENT:  Oh, I think so. You will have to keep this talk of the Message until it is actually delivered. Don't put anything on the wire until then.

Q:  Don't tell anything about my hundred thousand dollars?

THE PRESIDENT:  No. (Laughter) Right, stout fellow.

Q:  (Mr. Stephenson) Thank you, Mr. President.

Q:  Have you discussed this matter of retiring submarginal lands?

THE PRESIDENT: Somebody wrote the story way back sometime during the summer when we announced the policy that for every acre we would put in by reclamation we would take out an equivalent number of acres that would produce the same crops. It is a perfectly definite policy and has been for months.

Q:  Thank you, Mr. President.

Press Conference #84 - Budget,
Executive Offices of the White House
January 3, 1934, 4:45 P.M.


THE PRESIDENT: Well, Gentlemen of the Senate, (laughter) I am sorry Lew Douglas
   is not here but Mrs. Douglas is not well up in New York and Lew had to go
   up this afternoon, so I haven't anybody to explain the details and I do not
   believe I can. I will do the best I can. I think I can talk about the
   high spots of the Budget Message but when it comes down to details you will
   have to dig into the figures yourselves, as I will have to dispense with
   Lew Douglas.

   By the way, please note that the confidential release means "when delivered
   to the Houses," which will be, I take it, at the opening of the session
   tomorrow morning. They will be there at that time, anyway, so when they
   are handed in at the desk at the Senate and House, either one, let it go.

   In regard to the Message, I suppose if I were writing your stories for you,
   I would say it is the most brutally frank Budget Message ever sent in. In
   other words, I am not mincing words or trying to hide anything. However,
   and this is going to be awfully hard for you to write, there isn't a single
   figure in this, except about a billion dollars in regard to this year's
   Budget -- this year's financial operations of the Government -- that you
   people have not been in possession of since the sixteenth of June and I am
   awfully sorry if you people have not used your own pencils. It is not my
   fault, the figures were there all the time and any one of you could have
   added them up. So I hope you will make it perfectly clear that what may
   appear in this particular fiscal year's

                              --- [7] ---

   figures as being perhaps a bit of a shock is your fault and not mine because, when you come down to it -- let me give you a little philosophy in
   Budget-making -- a legislative body authorizes appropriations. From that
   moment on the authorized appropriation becomes a contingent liability. It
   may not be spent but it may be spent. It may not all be spent this year,
   some of it may be spent next year and some of it the year after; on the
   other hand, all of it may be spent this year, therefore it is a contingent
   liability.

   Now, the authorizations of the last session of the last Congress, in other
   words, the Congress that went out on the fourth of March last, plus the
   authorizations of the special session, make it perfectly clear that we
   might very easily spend this current fiscal year that we are in now
   $10,000,000,000. Now, you ask, "How do you arrive at that figure?" Turn
   to page -- at the bottom of page V. It shows that we expect to spend -- to
   spend, mind you; there is all the difference in the world between expenditure and appropriation -- we expect to spend $9,403,000,000.

   Turn over to the next page and that is itemized in that table into two main
   headings: for the general expenses of the Government, $3,045,000,000, and
   for emergency expenses, $9,403,000,000. (There was a slight pause.) Now,
   that $9,403,000,000 might have been a great deal bigger.

Q:    You mean $6,357,000,000?

Q:   You mean six billion --

THE PRESIDENT:   (interposing)  I mean nine billions, the total of the figures.
The total figures will be, as far as we can tell now,

--- [8] ---

$9,403,000,000.

Now, I say, that should not be a shock.  First, there is a whole lot of
stuff that has not been authorized by the Congress, has not been spent and
is not going to be spent this fiscal year.  For example, the total appropriations for public works, which were $3,300,000,000, we only have gone
in for $1,677,000,000.  We might, if we had allocated it differently,
spend the whole $3,300,000,000.  In the same way, on R.F.C., that big
item, $3,969,000,000, Jesse Jones might have obligated the Government for
the total amount.  As I remember it, that is about $150,000 shy of what
he could have spent or obligated the Government for -- what he could have
spent this fiscal year.  Therefore, and I am taking the offensive here --
therefore, if you people had only added up figures that were in your possession on the sixteenth day of June, you could have figured very, very
easily that the expenditures during this fiscal year could have run beyond
$10,000,000,000.  So, do not blame me for springing things on you.

Q:   Do you know what the emergency expenditures are?

THE PRESIDENT:   I have not got it.

Q:   Do you know whether the Government could spend money as fast as shown in
here?  People have added figures and concluded a deficit between four and
five billion dollars, reckoning that the Government could not spend money
faster than that, even with C.C.C. and --

THE PRESIDENT:   (interposing)  In the first place, this emergency list of
$6,357,000,000 is made up by taking the lowest estimate of what each one
of these agencies expects to spend.  Their estimates that they think they
can spend are higher than these.  We are taking the

--- [9] ---

lowest.

Q:   We added it up to $5,000,000,000 and I cut it and said it was
$4,000,000,000.

THE PRESIDENT:  Well, for example, nobody on the sixteenth of June had the foggiest idea as to how much of the Public Works money could be spent before
the first of July next, 1934.  If we had not reached it the way we had, if
we had just approved every application from every state and community all
through the country, we would have spent it and a great deal besides.  But
it was available for expenditure and the actual rate of expenditure depen-
ded on the administrative methods for spending it.  That amount of
$9,000,000,000 does not represent nearly what we could have spent under
authorizations that were all completed on the sixteenth day of June.  That
is the point I want to make.  Therefore, there should not be anything
suprising in the figures for this fiscal year.

Q:   Is direct relief in here?

THE PRESIDENT:  Yes.

Q:  Under Public Works?

THE PRESIDENT:  As I remember it -- now you are getting me down to details --
as I remember it, part of the relief money came from the R.F.C. and
$400,000,000 of the C.W.A. came from Public Works.  Am I right on that?  I
think that is right.

Q:  Carrying on this question of how fast the money can be spent, I think the
Treasury's last statement showed that the R.F.C. spent $600,000,000 in the
first six months.  This figure would mean that in the coming six months
they would have to spend five times that amount.  Is there any expansion
in the R.F.C. activities which

--- [10] ---

would enable them to do that?

THE PRESIDENT:  I think that means they have spent 600 millions more than their
receipts.

Q:  This is not a net figure then?

THE PRESIDENT:  No, this is a gross figure.

Q:  Is there any figure showing the return to the Treasury by the R.F.C.?

THE PRESIDENT:  I think that is in here but I could not tell you where.  Now
you have me; I do not know.

Q:  On page VI you say that there are certain additional expenditures in that
$1,166,000,000 "shown in a subsequent table herein."  Where is that table?
I have not found it.

THE PRESIDENT:  Maybe it is in the big book.

MR. EARLY:  That is where I think it is.

THE PRESIDENT:  I think it is in the big book.

Q:  Mr. President, just to clear this up, this $9,403,000,000 is the figure
you actually expect to reach in this fiscal year?

THE PRESIDENT:  Yes, the total expenditure.

Q:  That is exclusive of the things that may be spent but that are not going
to be spent?

THE PRESIDENT:  Yes.

Q:  Otherwise it would have totaled ten billions plus?

THE PRESIDENT:  And most of them, if not all, appear in next year's Budget.
For instance, the first item, page VII, (under emergency expenditures) is
for Public Works, $1,089,000,000.  Now, that is all monies appropriated
before the sixteenth of June last, and there will still be some money out
of the $3,300,000,000 that will be spent in the fiscal year 1935-1936.

For example the

--- [11] ---

Triborough Bridge in New York and the building of Government ships and
items of that kind will take three years to complete.

Then on page VI, the next paragraph below the table, the estimated receipts
for the fiscal year are $3,259,000,000. Those, of course, are very dis-
tinctly better than we had any idea of last spring. In other words, taxes
have been coming in in better shape during the last six months than we had
anticipated. Then, leaving out certain additional expenditures over 1934,
(reading from 1935 Budget)

> "On this basis, including, however, certain additional
> expenditures for 1934 which are not included in the Budget
> estimates but which I believe to be necessary and amounting
> to $1,166,000,000 as shown in a subsequent table herein --"

Where that subsequent table is I do not know. I can describe it to you.
Those are amounts which we believe we have to get appropriations for very
soon from the Congress, I mean within the next month, in order to carry us
through on certain operations that are under way, all of it to be spent
before the first of July. The principal item is the one we talked about
the other day for continuing the C.W.A. In other words, we only have
enough money to run the C.W.A. until the fifteenth of February and we believe that these four million people who are on the rolls of C.W.A. ought
to be given work up to warm weather which, on the average of the country --
we set the date as of the fifteenth of April. That means providing the
money for four million people for two months longer. That will come, as I
remember it the last time they wrote the figures, to about $400,000,000.
Then there are certain other items; I think there are four or five of them.
There

--- [12] ---

is money needed for the Home Loan Bank Building, for Farm Credit which is
mostly, as I remember it, not direct loaning for farm credit on farms but
is to take up the older financing of the land banks, the Federal Land
Banks, as I remember it, which is 100 or 150 million dollars. There are
several items of that kind to put the previous legislation into full effect
and it totals $1,166,000,000.

Q:  That will bring the total expenditures for this fiscal year to
$10,500,000,000?

THE PRESIDENT:  $10,569,000,000, yes -- no,no; on this basis, including, however
-- we are wrong there -- including, however, certain additional expenditures for 1934 to the tune of $1,166,000,000 as shown in a subsequent
table, the excess of expenditures over receipts is $7,309,000,000. Now
that figure is arrived at -- you have it right -- the expenditures of
$9,403,000,000 less the income of $3,259,000,000, plus the new expenditure
of $1,166,000,000 -- right?

Q:  Yes, sir.

Q:  But the gross expenditures will be over $10,000,000,000?

THE PRESIDENT: Yes. On the basis of these estimates the total debt, in the strict sense of the term, at the expiration of this fiscal year -- in other words, the debit side of the Government balance sheet -- will therefore amount to approximately $29,847,000,000, or an increase as shown above of $7,309,000,000. (Reading)

> "However, as against this increase in the total debt figure, it is right to point out that the various governmental agencies have loans outstanding with a book value of $3,558,516,189 against which collateral or assets have been pledged.

--- [13] ---

> "In order to make clear to the Congress what our borrowing problem is for the next 6 months, permit me to remind you that we shall have to borrow approximately 6 billion dollars of new money and, in addition, 4 billion dollars to meet maturities of a like amount."

I do not think there is any question of the authority of the Government to borrow that amount of money for the next six months in view of the subsequent pages in this Budget Message, in other words, the proposals for the next two fiscal years.

Q: This credit side of the ledger, this $3,558,000,000, against which collateral or assets have been pledged, does that include the Public Works loans already made, or does it include the R.F.C. loans to banks?

THE PRESIDENT: I could not tell you except -- and this, I must tell you, is part guess on my part -- I do not think that includes any of the Public Works loans except where the collateral is actually in the Government possession at this time, and that is only a very small percentage of the allotments that have been made to self-sustaining public works. In other words, a great deal of it, as you know, is in process of the actual signing up of the contracts with the municipalities and the delivery of the certificates of indebtedness or bonds or whatever it may be. Actually, this figure of $3,558,000,000 is a very conservative figure. It probably runs a good deal more than that and, in these figures, it is also fair to say that of the figures on the expenditures, as I said, we have taken the maximum.

Of course we all know that probably a good deal of this will not be spent this fiscal year but I am taking the worst side of

--- [14] ---

expenditures and the same way on the income side, the revenue end, I am taking the lowest figure that anybody has estimated. I do not want to make the mistake that has been made on certain previous occasions you are all familiar with.

Q: Is there any estimate here on the amount of the processing taxes you were able to collect? I have not been able to find it. On page VI there is an item, "Agricultural Adjustment Administration, $103,000,000" but I have not been able to find any estimate of the processing tax.

THE PRESIDENT: I think they were left out on both sides. There is something about processing taxes a little later on.

Q: Mr. President, on page 21 of the Secretary of the Treasury's Annual Report, the increase in the 1934 estimates makes it (the excess of expenditures over receipts) $6,141,000,000 and the increase in the public debt to $28,679,000,000. I do not quite understand how you reconcile that with the Budget figures, which are more than a billion dollars higher. Is that because the figure $1,166,000,000 is not taken into account?

THE PRESIDENT: I guess so. See if it checks.

Q: It does not quite, to the extent of 30 or 40 million dollars.

THE PRESIDENT: Well, what is that between friends? (Laughter) I guess that is it. Of course when that report of the Secretary of the Treasury was made, he did not know about my $1,166,000,000.

Q: I see.

Q: Mr. President, on page VIII can you break down that $2,000,000,000 for the next fiscal year that you are going to ask for?

THE PRESIDENT: Let me come to that. On the top of page VII you take

--- [15] ---

up the fiscal year 1934.

Q: Mr. President, just one more question before we go on. This sounds very silly: Why is it that the expenditures of this fiscal year, which ends June thirtieth, are taken up in this Budget report? I thought this Budget report dealt with the fiscal year 1934 and 1935.

THE PRESIDENT: Because, in dealing with the fiscal year 1934-5, I have got to tell the country how we started off on the first of July, 1934. If I were to tell the country that we started off on the first of July, 1934, with an estimated public debt of $29,847,000,000, without explanation, it would have been pretty bad.

Now, the fiscal year 1935. (Reading)

> "The Budget estimates of expenditures, exclusive of debt retirement of $525,763,800 and exclusive also of such sum as may be necessary for new and extraordinary recovery purposes, for the fiscal year ending June 30, 1935 amount to $3,960,798,700."

On the expenditures for the fiscal year ending June 30, 1935, under general expenditures, we have for Departmental, Legislative and Independent establishments the total amount of $3,237,000,000.

Then, under emergency expenditures, we have the Public Works Administration, $1,089,000,000 already appropriated for; the Agricultural Adjustment Administration, $5,000,000, which has already been obligated; Emergency conservation work, $65,000,000; the R.F.C., $480,000,000, which is the excess of credits and you will therefore deduct it; the Tennessee Valley

Authority, $31,000,000, which is the balance of the $50,000,000 appropriated to them, already authorized but not expended; and Federal Land

--- [16] ---

Banks, $12,650,000, making the total for the year, not counting any new
emergency expenditures, of $3,960,000,000. (Reading)

> "It will be noted that many of these items such as public
> works fall under appropriations made in 1933, the actual
> expenditures not taking place until after June 30, 1934.
> (For details of above expenditures see Budget Statement
> No. 3, table A.)

> "The above figures do not include additional loans by the
> Reconstruction Finance Corporation. If its loaning authority
> is extended beyond June 30, 1934, it is contemplated that any
> additional loans by it would thereafter be taken from the new
> and additional recovery fund hereinafter referred to."

In other words, what we have done there is in our figures of receipts and
expenditures of the R.F.C., we close them out as of the thirtieth of June,
which means that if their life is extended and they go on for another year,
anything additional they spend in the new year will come out of new appropriations.

Q: Doesn't their lending power expire this January? Don't you have to have it
extended to June thirtieth?

THE PRESIDENT: Part of it does and part does not. I think some of it does have
to be extended.

Now, as against that figure of total estimated expenditures, we get estimated receipts for the next fiscal year, exclusive of foreign debt payments
and, by the way, that does not mean that we have abandoned asking and
trying to get foreign debt payments -- and of increased revenue flowing
from amendments to the existing revenue law, amounting to $3,974,000,000.
(Reading)

> "Therefore, exclusive of debt retirement, these Budget
> estimates for the next fiscal year show a small surplus of
> $13,866,779. But it must be borne in mind that this surplus
> does not include any ad-

--- [17] ---

ditional expenditures for extraordinary recovery purposes."

So you might fairly say that, exclusive of those two, exclusive of foreign
debt, liquor taxes and increased revenue from tightening up on the existing
law, on the credit side of the ledger, we would have a surplus for the next
fiscal year of $13,000,000, without counting any new appropriations towards
recovery.

Then I go on: (Reading)

> "It is clear that the necessity for relief and recovery will
> still be with us during the year 1934-35. Additional relief

funds will be necessary. Further needs of the country
prohibit the abrupt termination of the Recovery Program.
No person can on this date definitely predict the total
amount that will be needed, nor the itemizing of such an
amount."

That is the answer to your question. (Reading)

"It is my best judgement at this time that a total
appropriation of not to exceed 2 billion dollars will,
with the expenditures still to be made next year out
of existing appropriations, be sufficient.

"I shall therefore ask the Congress for appropriations
approximating that amount."

Now, the best way to put it to you is the way I put it to the Senate and
House leaders the other day. I said, "I am going to ask you for
$2,000,000,000 and I don't care, it is up to you gentlemen on the Hill, as
to how you are going to pass that $2,000,000,000. You can either give it
to me as a lump sum, or, if you prefer, you can itemize it according to the
best information and recommendations I can give you at the present time in
regard to those items. But if you do itemize it, I hope that you will give
me the authority to shift amounts from one item to another as may be
needed."

--- [18] ---

Now, roughly speaking, -- I do not see that there is any reason why I
should not tell you now, this is very general -- as to the itemizing, and
it gives a pretty good example too, take the question of relief for next
winter: nobody knows what that will run to. We cannot tell until we know
the conditions next fall. We do not believe that we can cut off Federal
assistance to the states or municipalities altogether. We do not think
there is a possibility of that. We think it may run a minimum around
$300,000,000; we think it may run a maximum of $800,000,000, but we cannot
tell in between those figures. Therefore, if I were asked what amount I
would put in the itemization of the $2,000,000,000 for relief, I would
say "Somewhere around 550 or 600 million dollars." When the time comes,
it may be less or it might be more.

Another item, public works, ought to have some leeway again. We have the
carryover of a little over a billion dollars to spend next year but there
will undoubtedly be certain projects which ought to go on, both because of
their own merit and also in order not to chop off the work in any given
locality. We probably ought to have a comparatively small additional sum
for public works. There again, I could not tell on the second day of
January exactly what the situation would be, or even on the first day of
July, and I would put down as a rough figure $500,000,000 for public works.

Then, the third major item relates to the R.F.C. There probably will be,
next year, certain necessities for Government lending, which is very difficult to forecast at the present time. It may be necessary to use some
additional Public Works -- R.F.C.

--- [19] ---

money, for example to help out weak banks, for the purchase of the assets
of banks. It may be necessary or advisable for the R.F.C. to take care of
certain other financing that has not been cleared up yet and probably --
I think probably you had better treat this off the record because we do
not want to scare people -- we may need, when we come down to it, certain
financing for building and loan associations. There is no legislation to
take care of it. We may be able to work it out this year, before the
first of July. After all, we have insured the savings banks and all the
other banks and even the Morris Plan Bank that came in yesterday, and some
of the building and loan associations that are used for the investment of
savings may need the same kind of assistance we have given to other
savings institutions. I would rather you not say anything about it because it may cause a run on building and loan associations. Take another
instance: The insurance company problem is a good deal better than it was
because, now that the fuss is over, you and I can talk privately among
ourselves and admit that last March there was not a solvent insurance company in the United States. The Federal Government has never gone into the
insurance field in any way. It has always been a state matter. We may
need to strengthen some of the insurance companies next fall. Not that
they are not today technically solvent, all of them. Then some of the
mortgage guarantee companies, which have spread an enormous volume of
securities -- guarantee mortgages -- out through some of the larger centers of the country, we may need to do some financing on some of those.
Therefore, I am putting in $500,000,000 for the R.F.C.

--- [20] ---

That brings you to $1,600,000,000, those three items, $600,000,000 for relief, $500,000,000 for R.F.C., $500,000,000 for public works, which is
$1,600,000,000. Then $300,000,000 for the Civilian Conservation Corps,
because I am going to recommend that that go through another year. That
is $1,900,000,000. The last $100,000,000, I have forgotten now, but I
think it is Farm Credit and Home Loan. But, as I say, I want to have --
I have asked Congress to give me authority to shift from one item to the
other as may be necessary, at least until Congress meets next January.

Q: Will the N.R.A. additional expenditures come out of Public Works?

THE PRESIDENT: I think -- and on this again you had better check it -- I think
I have allocated enough out of Public Works already to tide them over to
the end of their legal life.

Q: Did the off-the-record apply to the mortgage guarantee companies only?

THE PRESIDENT: I would make it apply to the building and loan and insurance
and mortgage guarantee, all three. You might call it the emergency needs
of the R.F.C.

Q: That mortgage guarantee has already been done to a small extent?

THE PRESIDENT: Yes, but we are not out of the woods on it yet. (Reading)

> "This amount is not included in the Budget estimates. If
> appropriated and expended, therefore, it will change the
> small estimated surplus of 13 million dollars into a debt
> increase of nearly 2 billion dollars. It is only fair, of

course, to say that such a debt increase would be partially
offset by loans made against collateral and assets pledged."

That would be so in the case of R.F.C. and Public Works. (Reading)

--- [21] ---

"Therefore, the total debt, if increased by the sum of
2 billion dollars during the fiscal year 1935, would amount
to approximately $31,834,000,000 on June 30, 1935."

Then come what is really these two things, which amount to the most important part of the Budget Message from the point of view of putting the lid
on unlimited Government expenditures. (Reading)

"It is my belief that so far as we can make estimates with
our present knowledge, the Government should seek to hold
the total debt within this amount."

That really is the most significant phrase in the entire Message.
(Reading)

"Furthermore, the Government during the balance of this
calendar year should plan to bring its 1936 expenditures,
including recovery and relief, within the revenues expected
in the fiscal year 1936."

In other words, plan definitely as a part of Government policy during the
balance of this year to bring in a Budget next year that will be absolutely
balanced and with no deficit in it. In other words, a Budget that will
include recovery and relief as well as general expenses of the Government
and have that all covered by revenue. (Reading)

"Let me put it another way: The excess of expenditures
over receipts during this fiscal year amounts to over
7 billion dollars. My estimates for the coming fiscal
year show an excess of expenditures over receipts of 2
billion dollars. We should plan to have a definitely
balanced Budget for the third year of recovery and from
that time on seek a continuing reduction of the national
debt."

Q:  Mr. President, reverting to the top paragraph of the page, you leave out
liquor taxes. Are you saying that the liquor taxes will take care of such
appropriations as Congress will make which you are

--- [22] ---

not contemplating?

THE PRESIDENT: I am not talking about those they are not contemplating at all.
But we certainly will get quite an additional sum, as far as any human
being can tell, from the liquor taxes and the tightening up on the income
taxes, et cetera, yes.

Q:  You speak of that (the continuing reduction of the national debt) from that
time on. Is there to be any annual debt retirement in the interval?

THE PRESIDENT: That is just what I talked about. I said, "Why don't you put debt retirement down?" But, what is the use if you are borrowing more than your debt retirement; why not leave it out? We could very easily put debt retirement in and borrow that much more but, as long as you are running a deficit, it is simpler this way.

Q: Later on in this Message you indicate that the revenues from these sources, liquor and income taxes, will amount in a few years to approximately $400,000,000 and nowhere in the Budget does that show as an offset. If the estimates of revenue from that source prove sound, would that mean that the deficit in two years will be approximately $400,000,000 less?

THE PRESIDENT: Yes but, of course, I cannot take cognizance of that because that is up to Congress.

Q: Are we not abating some taxes, those taxes that were levied for the emergency?

THE PRESIDENT: Yes, they do not appear in this.

Q: Therefore the liquor tax is to take the place of those sources of revenue, is it not?

--- [23] ---

THE PRESIDENT: As I remember it, we abated about $110,000,000 worth of taxes --

Q: (interposing) $227,000,000.

Q: (by a representative of the Budget Bureau) It was $220,000,000.

THE PRESIDENT: Was it $220,000,000 that went out?

Q: (by a representative of the Budget Bureau) Yes, that was the carrying charge on the $3,300,000,000.

Q: By increased taxes you mean all over $1.10?

THE PRESIDENT: All over $1.10, and I can tell you that the gentlemen from the Hill, when I read this the night before last and showed them that I was only estimating $50,000,000 on that, they said, "You are way low." I said, "It is up to you gentlemen." So that might come way up.

Q: You are not including any new taxes on new tax legislation passed this Congress?

THE PRESIDENT: No.

Q: On this $2,000,000,000 emergency and recovery fund you asked for in this 1935, either in a lump sum or specified, plus these points you make about the total public debt, am I right in assuming that your policy or intention is to slough off these public works or emergency activities ---

THE PRESIDENT: (interposing) I said today in the Message to Congress, in a nutshell, that we are engaged in -- you might almost call it rebuilding the the face of the country and that it will be, eventually, a national plan. You take, for example, the Missouri River or the Arkansas River or the Upper Mississippi: what we are doing out of Public Works is some of the obvious work at the major places, some

--- [24] ---

of these big dams. Eventually, as we go through with the entire planning
which, in the case of a river watershed, might run anywhere up to twenty-
five or forty years, my thought is that by another year and a half we will
have those plans pretty well nationalized so that there will be a complete
national picture and that we will proceed on them at a rather definite
yearly rate with the object of getting back as much as we can of that
financing, knowing at the same time that we are increasing general national
values, even if it does not come back to the Treasury, very largely and
doing it in an orderly way and, as we are doing it, paying for it out of
current revenues. In other words, putting it, as far as national planning
goes, on a pay-as-you-go basis. These Public Works programs are taking
care of some of the larger projects first.

What I would like to see -- and this is an expression of what I hope will
happen in another year and a half -- is that we will definitely advocate,
as a national policy, the expending of $500,000,000 a year to restore the
face of nature and that will be paid for, not out of bond issues but out of
current revenues.

Q:    What I had in mind was a certain school of thought which advocates vast
      housing undertakings, not slum clearings but housing, something along the
      lines done in England and Germany, as a measure for restoring the economic
      structure. That probably is not included in this plan.

THE PRESIDENT:  No. It involves a great many difficulties. Of course I have
      belonged to the school of thought that says we ought to clean out our slums
      but it is pretty obscure as to how we are going to do it and nobody has
      yet, not even Brother Sprague, has come

--- [25] ---

forward with a practical method of doing it. The simplest illustration I
know of is that on the East Side of New York, in those worst slum areas,
there are probably two or three hundred thousand human beings living in
rooms that cost $5 per room per month. Now, those families, most of them
foreigners, cannot afford to pay more than that and I do not yet understand
the method of tearing down those buildings and putting up new buildings
that will cost $11 or $12 per room per month because those unfortunate human beings cannot afford that rent.

A lot of people say, "Move them out into the extreme limits of Queens County." Now, that presupposes that we can probably provide it for them at $5
a month and that also presupposes that they have the carfare to get them in
to where they work or the transportation facilities. It means building a
new subway. It is a very difficult problem.

This is strictly off the record: Brother Sprague, the last time he came in
to see me, the last time I went to Warm Springs, I said, "Professor, have
you any real solution?" He said, "I have. Start immediately and spend
$4,000,000,000 for suburban housing." I said, "Where?" "Everywhere." I
said, "Let us see: Take the towns I know. Take Poughkeepsie: There are
about 200 vacant suburban houses that you could pick up for a song today.
Very nice. Take Atlanta, Georgia; Columbus, Georgia; Albany, New York. It
is the same story in the Middle West and the same story, largely, in New

England. It would be fine to spend $4,000,000,000 but you would never get it back and there are a lot of people who could not afford to live in your type of house."

----[26] ---

It is a very difficult problem and I do not know the answer to it.

Q: In lifting the face of Miss America, is it still the same thought to give the St. Lawrence a dip in the cosmetic bags? (Laughter)

(The President indicated the affirmative.)

Q: Mr. President, talking about the emergency expenditures which will expire in 1935, do you think that recovery will have been restored by then to normality?

THE PRESIDENT: I would not say normality or normalcy. I hope we won't have to have large recover expenditures after that.

Q: They are mostly to take care of unemployment and I notice that you use the Federal Reserve index, which is quite high for 1935 and 1936 receipts, which would indicate that there would not be any need for extensive unemployment relief during that year?

THE PRESIDENT: Of course it is anybody's guess. In a nutshell, what we are doing is tapering off from the $7,000,000,000 this year to the $2,000,000,000 next year, which $2,000,000,000 includes well over a billion dollars already authorized, and then, the third year, to cut it out altogether except for such items as we have been talking about for the general rebuilding of the face of nature.

Q: That is what you meant a little while ago when you said there would not be any question about the ability of the Government to borrow $10,000,000,000 in the next few months in view of the subsequent pages?

THE PRESIDENT: Yes. (Reading)

"This excess of expenditures over revenues

--- [27] ---

amounting to over 9 billion dollars during 2 fiscal years has been rendered necessary to bring the country to a sound condition after the unexampled crisis which we encountered last spring. It is a large amount, but the immeasurable benefits justify the cost."

The nature of the table on page IX, I do not understand it myself -- (laughter) it shows the estimate for those past years, based on some kind of an index, and the expected rise in Government receipts on an index basis. Quite a lot of the Treasury people figure a good deal higher than this. We are taking the most conservative estimates by the Treasury.

Then you come down to appropriations. (Reading)

"The Budget estimates of appropriations for 1935, exclusive
of Agricultural Adjustment Administration benefit payments
and refunds of processing taxes, but inclusive of all other
appropriations for regular departments and independent establishments including interest on the debt and debt retirement
are $2,980,293,833.60. When compared with Budget estimates
of appropriations transmitted in the Budget for 1934 they
show a reduction of $684,913,167."

In other words, that is a direct comparison with the Budget that was sent
up in December, 1932, and is the net measure, as I understand it from
Douglas, a net measure of the savings we have made in the cost of running
the regular Government.

Next we have taxes. (Reading)

"The estimates of receipts take no account of the additional
revenue which may be obtained from an increase in liquor taxes
and from the proposed changes in the income-tax law. Since
neither of these tax measures has come before Congress as yet,
no accurate estimate can be made of their yield. However, if
as proposed by the Committee of Ways and Means, the tax on
distilled spirits is increased from $1.10 a gallon to $2 a gal-
lon, and the rates of tax on wines are also increased, the
estimated revenue would be increased by approximately
$50,000,000, --"

--- [28] ---

and, as I told you, the members of the House and Senate say it will probably be a good deal more than that -- (reading)

"-- assuming that consumption is not affected by additional
gallonage taxes imposed by the States."

That is a gentle hint they should not make liquor too expensive. (Reading)

"Considerable additional revenue can also be secured from
administrative changes in the income-tax law, which may
amount to as much as $150,000,000 for a full year.

"The estimates for the Post Office Department are predicated
upon a continuation of the 3-cent postal rate for nonlocal
mail. It is highly important that this rate be continued.
I recommend its continuance.

"ECONOMY LEGISLATION"

"The estimates of appropriations submitted in the Budget are
predicated on the continuation of certain economy legislative
provisions which I ask to be enacted and which are appended
hereto. The most important is that having to do with reduction of compensation of Federal employees."

Therefore, on the actual estimates in the departments we have based the
figures on a restoration by law of five per cent of the cut. In other
words, one-third of the fifteen per cent on the first of July is mandatory
and the other ten per cent will remain, as it is, discretionary depending

on the cost of living figures of the Department of Labor.  (Reading)

> "It is eminently fair that, the cost of living having fallen
> as compared with 1928, the employees of the Government sus-
> tain some reduction in compensation.  This is not inconsis-
> tent with our policy of advocating an increase in wages in
> industry.  For wages there had fallen far beyond any reduc-
> tion contemplated for Federal employees and in most grades
> are even now substantially below compensation paid Federal
> employees under the maximum reduction of 15 percent.

--- [29] ---

> "Among the legislative provisions appended hereto is one
> prohibiting automatic increases in compensation except in
> the Army, Navy, and Marine Corps.  The personnel of these
> three services are engaged in a life service to their coun-
> try.  Some, by reason of the pay freezes, have sustained
> reduction in compensation of more than 25 percent."

As I understand it, if you get promoted you do not get the additional compensation that goes with the promotion.  (Reading)

> "They are, therefore, in a different category from those
> in other governmental agencies.  They should, in 1935, be
> released from the restrictions on automatic increases in
> compsensation.

"CONTROL"

And this is quite an important piece of news.  Listen:  (Reading)

> "Up to now there has been no coordinated control over
> emergency expenditures.  Today, by Executive order, I
> have imposed that necessary control in the Bureau of
> the Budget.

> "Heretofore, emergency expenditures have not been subject
> to audit by the Comptroller General of the General Account-
> ing Office.  Today I am, by Executive order, reposing in
> him the authority to conduct such an audit and to continue
> to audit each such expenditure.  Hereafter, therefore, just
> as in the departmental expenditures, there will be, in
> emergency expenditures, a pre-Budget and a post audit."

And so, it puts the spending of money by all these new agencies exactly on
the same basis that all the old departments are.  You have to go to the
Director of the Budget for the approval of the items of expenditures and,
after that has been done and the orders placed, you have to go to the
Comptroller General before the money is actually paid out.  (Reading)

> "By reason of the fact that the Bureau of the Budget has
> had no control in the past over the various expenditures,
> obligations, and allotments made by the emergency organi-
> zations, the task of preparing the present Budget has been
> the most difficult one

--- [30] ---

since the Budget and Accounting Act went into effect in
1921. These difficulties, in future years, will be
substantially minimized by the control which I have
established.

"It is evident to me, as I am sure it is evident to you,
that powerful forces for recovery exist. It is by laying
a foundation of confidence in the present and faith in
the future that the upturn which we have so far seen will
become cumulative. The cornerstone of this foundation is
the good credit of the Government.

"It is, therefore, not strange nor is it academic that
this credit has a profound effect upon the confidence so
necessary to permit the new recovery to develop into
maturity.

"If we maintain the course I have outlined, we can confidently look forward to cumulative beneficial forces represented by increased volume of business, more general profit, greater employment, a diminution of relief expenditures, larger governmental receipts and repayments, and
greater human happiness.

FRANKLIN D. ROOSEVELT.

"January 3, 1934."

In other words, as we were talking before, through the very definite
Government plan of expenditures in this year which will create a deficit
of seven billions, we believe we can advance a Government plan of reducing
that to two billions next year, balance the Budget the following year and,
from that time on, pay some of the debts.

Q: Is there any thought of changing the present sinking fund requirements in
connection with the reduction of debts beginning in 1936?

THE PRESIDENT: Changing them? How?

Q: It is so very much larger that the present sinking fund would not take it
down fast enough. Therefore, the sinking fund would have

--- [31] ---

to be increased by the next Congress if they are to guarantee a reduction
in 1936.

THE PRESIDENT: I do not know. I never never went into that phase of it at all.
What are the sinking fund requirements for it at the present time? Fifty-
year basis on the average?

Q: About that. It is $2\frac{1}{2}\%$.

THE PRESIDENT: Then it is less than fifty years?

Q: Forty years.

Q:  It is a cumulative arrangement there.

Q:  The 2½% is not on the entire debt.  There are peculiar arrangements.  They take the war debt and deduct the amount that Europe owes us and then set up a sinking fund for the remainder.

THE PRESIDENT:  Yes.

Q:  And then, there is a sinking fund in the National Recovery Act.

Q:  Are we going to go ahead with the sinking fund for the $3,300,000,000?

THE PRESIDENT:  We are, in effect.  We are getting taxes to equal a sinking fund.  Of course, as I said the other day, it does not make any difference whether you actually put your sinking fund in and add it to the total or leave it out.  You get the same total in the long run.

Q:  This reference to taxes seems to indicate that, aside from plugging up the loopholes in the income tax, that you do not plan additional legislation.  Is that a correct inference?

THE PRESIDENT:  I think it is a pretty good inference for this year and the reason for it is that I am very hopeful that the actual tax receipts will run a good deal higher than the estimates we have here.  I think it is better to plug the loopholes rather than get

--- [32] ---

into a discussion of taxes at this session.

Q:  Can you give us a concrete and definite illustration of how the new Accounting Office control is going to work for emergency expenditures?

THE PRESIDENT:  No. 1, it will mean that all purchases by N.R.A. or Public Works will have to go through the centralized purchasing bureau before the money is spent.  No. 2, on any question of pay, salaries, et cetera, -- well, as a concrete illustration, before General Johnson fixes anybody's salary, he will have to go to Lew Douglas.  (Laughter)

Q:  This is not retroactive, is it?

THE PRESIDENT:  No; have a heart.  (Laughter)

Q:  Would he have to go to General McCarl or Lew Douglas?

THE PRESIDENT:  He will have to go to Lew Douglas in the first instance.  And then, before the check is made out, he has to go to General McCarl.

Q:  He is going to have a hard time of it.

Q:  They will have to go through the same procedure, step by step, that the old organization went through?

THE PRESIDENT:  Yes.  Of course you could not do that during organization but the time has come where we should not exercise the same powers we have in the past.

Q:  You do not contemplate any restoration of pay of the Government people between now and July first?

THE PRESIDENT: You are a little ahead of time. I have not finished reading the various documents yet.

Q: I noticed it has one from July first on.

--- [33] ---

THE PRESIDENT: Yes.

Q: Is the five per cent mandatory provision included?

THE PRESIDENT: Yes, it is included in the actual estimates in each department for pay of personnel. The additional ten per cent restoration does not appear in figures but would be accomplished through authorizing me to incur a deficit if the cost of living went up sufficiently.

Q: Does not $3,900,000,000 for R.F.C. include about a billion for which you have to get new authority?

THE PRESIDENT: You mean authority from the first of January on?

Q: Yes.

THE PRESIDENT: I think so. In other words, as I understand it, their total borrowing capacity is, roughly, $4,000,000,000, and if we extend their borrowing capacity up to the first of July, they will be able to loan out again certain payments that will be made, repayments, between now and the first of July so that on the first of July they will have actually loaned out practically all that they are authorized to lend out. Is that right? I think that is correct.

Q: The effect of the Budget on public works is for carrying out existing commitments?

THE PRESIDENT: For carrying out existing commitments and carrying out a general plan which, after that, would be carried out through current revenue.

To avoid any misunderstanding, anything said today is confidential until the Budget is released tomorrow.

--- [34] ---

Q: Is it background?

THE PRESIDENT: Background, except for R.F.C.

Q: How about the illustration?

THE PRESIDENT: Yes. (Laughter) Stevie (Mr. Stephenson), you would ask that. (Laughter)

Q: In the event that between now and July first you restore to the Federal employees one or two or three per cent of that cut, what is the situation after July first? Does that add to the five per cent?

THE PRESIDENT: No; then it depends on the new figures on the first of July.

Q:  I still do not think you could spend money this fast.

THE PRESIDENT:  I hope not.  But, as I said, I think we have gone the limit.

Q: There was a lot this week, Mr. President, but the boys seem anxious for more.

THE PRESIDENT: Yes. Fred Storm suggests that you are bears for punishment, that you had an awful lot of news this week and are just coming back for more.

Q: Was there any news in the report of the Appropriation Committee Chairman?

THE PRESIDENT: No, just talking about various aspects of the total picture and I told them I thought they should live within the total picture, that I regard it as of very great importance that they should live within the picture, and they all agreed.

Q: Have you received Mr. Peek's report yet?

THE PRESIDENT: I do not know. I think I have, but I have not read it.

Q: You cannot tell us whether it recommends the establishment of a foreign trading corporation?

THE PRESIDENT: I think it does but the thing is only in a very preliminary stage yet. We haven't got to the point of working the thing out. As I say, I have not even read it yet.

Q: Mr. President, have you in mind any recommendations for the reforming of N.R.A.?

THE PRESIDENT: No; you mean what we were talking about the other day?

Q: I mean that and perhaps there are some other things such as preventing exorbitant profits and protecting the consumer.

THE PRESIDENT: No. The only thing that happened was that we talked

--- [36] ---

about the use of the Federal Trade Commission for certain perfectly obvious things that they are charged by law to do. In other words, the theory is this: When you come down to unfair trade practices, the complainant would go in the first instance to the N.R.A. organization and the N.R.A. organization would try to settle the matter, sitting around the table, without formal proceedings. If, for example, the matter involved let us say a labor question, it would go to Senator Wagner's labor committee. If it involved a violation of the Sherman Anti-Trust Law or a similar unfair trade practice within the jurisdiction of the Federal Trade Commission, it would be referred, via me, to the Federal Trade Commission for determination.

You see, in that way you get a more or less formal decision by an existing agency which is fitted to handle it. But that does not mean that it takes the jurisdiction away from the N.R.A. as the first place to lay your

complaint. What we are trying to do is handle it on a practical basis --
settle it, if we can, around the table and if we cannot settle it then
send it to the official body for an official ruling.

Q:   Would that take care of the complaint of the little fellows that they have
to bring their complaints before a Code Authority which is originally
hostile to them?

THE PRESIDENT:  If they felt that they had been badly treated by the Code Authority, the first thing they would do would be to go to the N.R.A. and that
body would try to straighten it out without formal or court action and
then, if they could not straighten it out, that matter would be referred
to the Federal Trade Commission.

--- [37] ---

Q:   You spoke of a special board in the N.R.A. that might be set up to hear
these complaints?

THE PRESIDENT:  No, I don't know what the details will be.

Q:   Anything new on the Newspaper Code?

THE PRESIDENT:  No, I have not looked at it.

Q:   Any changes contemplated in the child labor provisions?

THE PRESIDENT:  I think I am going to make some inquiry about it.

Q:   Mr. President, today Secretary Wallace indicated that he is working out an
official solution for the jurisdiction over the code of the N.R.A. and
A.A.A.

THE PRESIDENT:  I thought that was done.  I did not know it had not been done.

Q:   He said it was being done at the time.

THE PRESIDENT:  I do not know; I have not heard a word about it.

Q:   Have you picked a successor to Senator Wagner?

THE PRESIDENT:  Not yet.

Q:   Would you say that something in the nature of a trading corporation is a
good guess?

THE PRESIDENT:  I would not guess because, as I said, I have not read any of
the reports, either the Committee report or Peek's suggested setup.

Q:   Mr. President, the other day Phillips, Acting Secretary of State, said he
was going to refer -- ask you about a report which he said was not complete
concerning the Foreign Policy Committee.  Can you discuss that?

THE PRESIDENT:  I have got three, in that basket, different things, none of
which I have read.  One is from the State Department and another

this Joint Committee and another from Peek.  I do not know what is in them.

Q:   May we look today for the order on the pay restoration, or part of it?

THE PRESIDENT:  I doubt it.  I haven't got to that yet.  I have got to act very
soon on account of the fifteenth of January checks.

Q:   Can you amplify what you said about your conference with the Committee
Chairman?

THE PRESIDENT:  We just talked about various phases.  No news in it.  Going over
lots of different kinds of appropriations.

Q:   Anything on the Interstate Commerce Commission and Mr. Brainerd?

THE PRESIDENT:  No, not yet.

Q:   In view of the amount of money that you recommend for public works in the
year 1935, does that indicate that you see the end of public works allocations at some definite time?  In other words, the amount is comparatively
small, $500,000,000.

THE PRESIDENT:  Were you there at the Budget discussion?

Q:   No.

THE PRESIDENT:  We took that up at that time and it is a pretty long story.  The
general situation I outlined was this:  That, in line with national planning, we would probably, as a Federal Government, go ahead on a very large
national plan which would take in all parts of the country, that is watersheds, etc., with perhaps -- I would hate to call it a 25-year or 50-year
plan because that sounds too much like some other country -- a long-range
plan for public works.  Such a plan would, in a sense, take into consideration the economic and, to a certain extent, a good many social

--- [39] ---

features in preventing waste, better land use, prevention of soil erosion,
prevention of floods, and so forth and all the various elements that go
into forestry.  The idea of that is that eventually the National Government
would work out a plan by which it would spend a certain definite amount
towards that program every year with a definite objective, but that that
amount would be cared for out of the current annual revenue so that it
would not get the Government into any more debt.  That amount might run
four or five hundred million dollars a year as a perfectly definite thing.

Q:   Mr. President, will there be any more new money for public works during
this fiscal year, prior to July first?

THE PRESIDENT:  I have not got that table.  You mean within the $1,166,000,000?

Q:   Yes, sir.

THE PRESIDENT:  Gosh, I haven't the table; I do not know.

Q:   That was not broken down in the table.

Q:   I think you named Civil Works as one item in that.

THE PRESIDENT: Civil Works. I cannot remember the amount, it was either 350 or 400 millions for Civil Works.

Q: Can you tell us something about the R.F.C. funds, what they are going to be used for?

THE PRESIDENT: Which?

Q: The increased funds for the R.F.C. How they are going to be allocated?

THE PRESIDENT: I think Lew Douglas is the only man in the world who has the table and he is in New York.

--- [40] ---

Q: For the gold policy, for instance?

THE PRESIDENT: And I think there was an item in there for additional gold purchases but I couldn't tell you the amount.

Q: Was the discussion of the land buying program a part of this general plan you speak of? Would that be a part of it?

THE PRESIDENT: Yes.

Q: Was there anything definite arrived at today when Secretary Wallace spoke with you?

THE PRESIDENT: We did not talk about that; we talked about liquor.

Q: I thought you talked about the land plan?

THE PRESIDENT: You see, there is nothing new on the land purchase thing. That was decided way back August or September, somewhere along there.

Q: What can you tell us about liquor?

(The President did not answer.)

Q: What don't you know about liquor? (Laughter)

THE PRESIDENT: I got a darned good story about Scotch whisky but I cannot tell you. Go to the British Embassy and ask them.

Q: Going to be cheaper Scotch?

THE PRESIDENT: No, less.

Q: How about Canadian Rye?

THE PRESIDENT: Well, we are letting quite a lot of that in.

Q: Have the British come forward for any other request for additional quota?

THE PRESIDENT: I might tell you this, off the record. I cannot tell you the results but I can tell you off the record entirely what the situation is. We are trying, quite frankly, to get rid of

--- [41] ---

certain agricultural surpluses, especially hog surpluses and butter surpluses and our good friends, the British, are not getting about sixty-five per cent of all their hogs and a good part of their butter from Denmark and, out of the kindness of their hearts, they have been allowing us to send in six per cent of their consumption. They, very generously, have offered to raise that to seven and a half, and they think it is very generous, but we have not yet decided how much Scotch whisky we are going to allow in. And, for the story itself, I am only going to give you a lead as to where to go. For the story itself, consult the British Embassy and the State Department.

Q: So there won't be any misunderstanding, the International News had it in their story this morning.

THE PRESIDENT: That is all right. (Laughter)

Q: May we have it as background or off the record?

THE PRESIDENT: Off the record, because it is not in my jurisdiction yet.

Q: Would you care to discuss the subject of the French wine and liquor quotas in connection with the same thing?

THE PRESIDENT: I think that is all settled up.

Q: I thought there were still some matters in connection with the wine to be settled?

THE PRESIDENT: I do not know; I had an idea it was settled up.

Q: When do you intend to make your tariff proposals to the Congress?

THE PRESIDENT: Probably not for some time.

Q: Can you tell us anything about war debts?

THE PRESIDENT: About war debts?

Q: Yes.

--- [42] ---

THE PRESIDENT: I am going to say something to Congress later on but I do not know when.

Q: Have you anybody preparing material for you on the subject?

THE PRESIDENT: Not for me. I think the Senate passed a Resolution; they wanted the data from the Treasury Department to be given them.

Q: Have you any specific message to be sent at the early date for any specific legislation?

THE PRESIDENT: No. In all probability, as background. But only as a probability, and that is that next week there will be some kind of a recommendation -- I don't know whether a message or a letter to the Committee -- in
relation to the Farm Credit Administration bonds.

What I would like to do is to consolidate the gains we have already made.
You know, last spring we actually took nine money-lending organizations and
put them together in the Farm Credit Administration. Now, the last special
session authorized them to issue up to two billion dollars in bonds, on
which the Government guaranteed the interest but not the principal. Now
the question comes up as to whether we should not be honest and face the
fact. The fact is that the public and the Congress at some future date, in
case these bonds, the principal of these bonds, showed a slight deficiency,
the public and the Congress would undoubtedly feel that it was a moral
obligation on the part of the Government to make good that deficiency.

There is a very interesting parallel on that. In the State of New York and
a number of other states, the state governments created what they called
authorities or quasi-public corporations

--- [43] ---

affecting some particular district. These authorities are run by individuals who are named by the state governor and they market out their own securities. They are quasi-public only in the sense that they are created by
the state and the state runs them through its own appointee.

Two or three years ago there was in the State of New York what was called a
river-regulating district that had been so created to prevent floods in one
of the tributaries to the Mohawk River. Theoretically, this river-regulating district corporation was self-liquidating through taxes and assess-
ments on the property benefited. Actually they made a miscalculation and
the receipts of the Corporation were not sufficient to pay the interest and
retire the annual amount of funds. Thereupon an individual bondholder
brought suit against the State and the Court of Appeals of the State of New
York held that while the bondholder could not obtain a judgment against the
State that there was a moral obligation -- not a legal obligation but a
moral obligation -- on the Legislature to make good the deficiency on the
bonds. The Legislature recognized that dictum on the part of the Court of
Appeals and appropriated the money, thereby making the principal of the
bonds good.

Now, as I see it in the case of these Farm Credit bonds, there is the same
moral obligation on the part of the Federal Government to make them good in
case there is a deficiency. Now, if there is that moral obligation which
might arise twenty years or thirty years from now, why, in all common
sense, should we not recognize it now. In other words, why not guarantee
the principal and the interest of these bonds now. The net result of doing
that would

--- [44] ---

actually save the Government a great deal during the present period. It
would mean, in effect, that the Farm Credit bonds would be a direct obligation of the Government. They would be just as good and perhaps better than
the ordinary Government bonds because they would have real estate behind
them besides the Government credit. Of course, that is a thing that I
would not emphasize but in any event they are just as good and they would,

at the same time, give you the right to go to the bank with them and borrow 100 per cent on them just the same way that you can go to the Federal Reserve Bank and borrow 100 per cent on a Government bond. Immediately they would have a value commensurate with Government bonds, which is around par. Immediately, also, people would take these bonds in lieu of cash. It would mean also that the Farm Credit Corporation can finance itself instead of having to go to the Treasury and getting the Treasury to finance them.

So, in all probability, next week there will be either a letter or a message along that line.

Q:    Would that apply to Home Loan bonds too?

THE PRESIDENT:  I have not taken that up to the point where I can say "Yes" but I think the chances are that it will also apply to Home Loan bonds.

Q:    The principle is exactly the same?

THE PRESIDENT:  The principle is the same, As a matter of fact, the Home Loan bonds carry this interesting statement, I am told -- I never saw one -- that the Government guarantees the interest on these bonds until they are paid. That means, of course, that if it is a 30-year bond and the principal was not paid at the end of

--- [45] ---

thirty years, the Government would keep on paying interest. So, you can see that it is tantamount to a Government guarantee of the principal.

Q:    There are two billion dollars of Home Owners Loan, are there not?

THE PRESIDENT:  Yes, and, as I said in one of my Messages, the way the applications are coming in we think the Congress made a pretty darn good guess as to the total amount that would be needed. We hope there won't be a call for more than the two billion. We think that is the upper limit to meet the needs of the case.

Q:    Both?

THE PRESIDENT:  Both Farm Credit and Home Loan.

Q:    Congress seems to feel it ought to get together with you on the question of inflation to see if they cannot bring the two factions there more closely together. How does the idea strike you?

THE PRESIDENT:  Will you act as the go-between and arrange the meeting?  (Laughter)  I'd be delighted.

Q:    One more question about these bonds: Will that extra $4,000,000,000 added in the commitments make any difference in the financing program?

THE PRESIDENT:  Not at all.

Q:    Cannot those bonds be put into the Treasury and currency issued on them under this plan?

THE PRESIDENT:  You've got me, Stevie (Mr. Stephenson), I do not know. What --

currency issued against them?

Q:   I thought they might be.

THE PRESIDENT:  What?

Q:   Discounted by the Federal Reserve?

--- [46] ---

THE PRESIDENT:  You borrow on them, that is a different thing.  That is not
issuing currency on them.  You talk like Senator Thomas.  (Laughter)

Q:   Mr. President, would you explain to a person who does not understand just
exactly what you mean by saying that by this guarantee of principal as well
as interest the Farm Credit Administration would be able to finance itself
instead of going to the Treasury?  The point is not quite clear to me.

THE PRESIDENT:  For instance, suppose you are the holder of a mortgage on a
farm and the farmer wants it refinanced.  You have been charging him seven
per cent and the farmer thinks it is too darned high and so does everybody
else.  You are willing to have the mortgage paid off.  At the present time
the only way in which it can be paid off is to have the Farm Credit Administration take its bonds and go to the Treasury and say, "Give me the
money?"  That means the Treasury has to raise that money some way.  Then
the Farm (Credit) people do not give you the actual cash.  Under this method you would be entirely willing to accept these good bonds because you
can always borrow on them up to one hundred per cent at the bank.

Q:   In either case, do these bonds constitute a part of the regular debt of
the United States?

THE PRESIDENT:  Yes and no.  It depends on a legal decision that has never been
rendered.  At the present time it is certainly a moral obligation, from my
point of view, on the Government.

Q:   Would you guarantee all principal for the bonds already outstanding, as
well as those to be issued?

--- [47] ---

THE PRESIDENT:  Well, this plan involves creating the machinery of a separate
corporation under the Farm Credit Administration.  That is merely a pure
technicality and that new corporation will actually issue the bonds and
take up all those now outstanding.  It would mean that the R.F.C. would be
repaid whatever it is that they have loaned up to the present time; I think
it is $150,000,000.

Q:   That means taking up all land bank bonds out now?

THE PRESIDENT:  Oh, no.

Q:   These are land bank bonds, these two billions?

THE PRESIDENT:  No -- are they land bank bonds?

Q:   Yes.

THE PRESIDENT: I could not tell you.

Q: There are a lot of old bonds out and the new two billions?

THE PRESIDENT: This only applies to the new two billions.

Q: Mr. President, do you care to say anything about your plans for raising this $10,000,000,000 in the next six months that you speak of in the Budget Message?

THE PRESIDENT: I will take care of it in normal course.

Q: The Home Loan bonds under this proposition would put an end to all objection now by people who are objecting to taking those bonds and would put that outfit right on its feet?

THE PRESIDENT: Yes.

Q: Thank you, Mr. President.

> (One of the newspaper correspondents asked the President a question about the St. Lawrence River, to which the President did not respond. Another correspondent asked the President about Bob Gore and the President replied that he had not seen him yet.)

CONFIDENTIAL
Press Conference #86
Executive Offices of the White House
January 10, 1934, 10:45 A.M.

Q:   (Mr. Storm)  You have got a full house this morning.

THE PRESIDENT:  There isn't any news.

Q:   (Mr. Stephenson)  We will find out.

THE PRESIDENT:  I tried to invent something but could not do it.

Q:   (Mr. Young)  You did the same thing Friday and it was pretty good.

THE PRESIDENT:  Yes, Friday I had a happy thought.

Q:   (Mr. Stephenson)  You told us no news Friday and we filled up the paper.

THE PRESIDENT:  Yes, I know it.

MR. DONALDSON:  All in.

THE PRESIDENT:  Somebody is sure to ask the question --

(interrupted by the noise of a falling object)

who died?

Q:   Just a bottle of rye fell down.  (Laughter)

THE PRESIDENT:  Only a bottle of rye?  (Laughter)  Charlie (Mr. Hurd), are you all set?

Q:   (Mr. Hurd)  Go right ahead, sir.

THE PRESIDENT:  Somebody is sure to ask a question about the Home Loan bonds. Mr. Fahey was over here yesterday and we agreed that we would say the following:  that, obviously, the home bonds will have to be treated on a basis of substantial equality with the farm bonds although they are not in today's Message, which relates only to farm bonds.  The Home Loan Board is now preparing for me a recommendation as to methods of handling some form of guarantee and also certain additional legislation on the Home Owners'

--- [49] ---

Loan Corporation needs.  Mostly, it is clarification stuff.  Nothing very important but they think they need a few small amendments in the law.

Q:   Mr. President, will the Home Loan bonds be guaranteed as to principal?

THE PRESIDENT:  That is what they are working on at the present time.  All he said is that they should be treated on a basis of substantial equality with the farm bonds.

Q:    Will there be a Message on that, Mr. President?

THE PRESIDENT:  I do not know, Fred (Mr. Storm).  I suppose so.  It might origi-
    nate in the Committee, however.

Q:    How are you coming on the St. Lawrence Message?

THE PRESIDENT:  I haven't written the Message as yet.  I have to write it right
    away because I hope to get it up this afternoon if the Senate sits in ses-
    sion long enough.

Q:    Are you going to take up the diversion of water in Chicago?

THE PRESIDENT:  Yes, John (Mr. Boettiger).

Q:    Can you tell us what it is?

THE PRESIDENT:  Yes, I can tell you what it is.  You had better hold this until
    after the Message goes up there, if you don't mind.  With that understand-
    ing, I would put it this way, generally: That the War Department feels,
    and everybody else who studied it feels, that the Treaty in its existing
    form provides for enough water to maintain the flow of Chicago sewers and
    also such navigation as is desirable between Chicago and the Mississippi.
    And then, of course, in regard to the lower Mississippi -- this is back-
    ground stuff for after the Message goes in -- there is a certain amount of
    what might be called local opposition on the southern end of

--- [50] ---

Mississippi and around Missouri.

It is not equitable or fair that we should divert water out of the Great
Lakes.  It can only be done, as a matter of justice, by agreement with Canada.  The water is not ours.  It belongs to Canada and to us.  There is
no getting around that fact.  We cannot go ahead bluntly and take all the
water we want out of the Great Lakes and divert it into a different watershed.  It is not a square thing to do to a neighboring country.  Whatever
diversion we take must come by agreement with Canada, Chicago to the contrary notwithstanding.  The general problem of the Mississippi navigation,
which is an entirely different watershed, we believe can be solved through
this rather broad national planning which I have talked about.  It can be
solved within the Mississippi watershed itself by the control of waters
at the headwaters.  That would be by flood prevention and the construction
of reservoirs so that we can have a continuous and natural flow through the
Mississippi Valley with enough water for adequate navigation purposes.

When it comes down to a question of shipping the products of the Middle
West and Northwest, it is very largely a question of mileage.  Suppose you
want to ship a thing from St. Louis to London, let us say, what is the
straight line?  Well, the straight line is down to the Great Lakes and out
through the Great Lakes to the Atlantic Ocean and then across the Atlantic
Ocean.  I suppose it might help New Orleans if we went around three sides
of the square instead of going straight, but it is "agin" nature.  You
would have to go down the Mississippi to the Gulf and then you would have
to go east through the Cuba channel, and then you

--- [51] ---

would head north to get up to the latitude of London. In other words, it is going around three sides of a square instead of one. Obviously that would apply to wheat from Montana or the Dakotas. The logical outlet is the straight line. It is against nature to have that wheat shipped down to Galveston or Houston and then go around three sides of the square instead of going straight.

That is the of the principal answers to some of the objections to the Treaty. It is the rule of common sense.

Q: May we use this for background?

THE PRESIDENT: Yes.

Q: Mr. President, does this mean that the Treaty ratification will be advocated on the basis of the present form, then? Do they want any reservations?

THE PRESIDENT: I don't know of any reservations.

Q: I think that the Engineers' report showed there has to be more water through the Chicago Canal and the Illinois River, otherwise they will have backwater of the thing?

THE PRESIDENT: There is a new War Department report which covers that pretty well.

Q: Is it the one out last month?

THE PRESIDENT: Yes, that one. Has that been released? Have you had it?

Q: Yes, sir.

THE PRESIDENT: What does it say?

Q: It says that the District and Division Engineers and the Board of Engineers feels that the question should be left with the Chief of Engineers to increase the diversion, if it becomes necessary,

--- [52] ---

and the Chief of Engineers disagreed with all the subordinates.

THE PRESIDENT: I think that is provided for in the Treaty. In other words, the chief objection on the part of the Engineers, even the Sanitary Engineers, is that at certain times of the year there might be a necessity of taking quite a large volume of water over a very short period in order to flush out the Chicago sewage system. Now, in effect, that is provided for in the Treaty.

Q: That would take quite a lot of water, wouldn't it?

THE PRESIDENT: I imagine it would. (Laughter) But I think the Canadians would take that into consideration. (Laughter) They know Chicago, too, you know. That is not background. (Laughter)

Q: Do I understand, Mr. President, we can use this as background now?

THE PRESIDENT:  No, after the Message goes up.

Q:  Anything further about publication of income taxes?

THE PRESIDENT:  I have not thought about it at all.  I suppose that will come up in conference with some of the House people and Senate people.

Q:  Can you tell us the status of the proposed Navy-Coast Guard measure?

THE PRESIDENT:  I have not heard anything more about it.  I heard in the paper something of a report made.

Q:  Our trade negotiators are telling us that, as far as they know, after March we shall abandon the liquor embargo system and go to the old system of unrestricted flow?

THE PRESIDENT:  I do not know anything about it.

Q:  The liquor quota system, as far as they know, was only temporary, to end March thirty-first.

THE PRESIDENT:  I would be very leary of that.  (Laughter)

--- [53] ---

Q:  Mr. President, in this milk strike out west there some of the strikers, within the last twenty-four or forty-eight hours, have stopped or waylaid a train, which was interstate commerce, and dumped about 12,000 gallons of milk.  That was night before last.  Has that been called to your attention?

THE PRESIDENT:  No, where was that?

Q:  It was on the Soo Line between Mundelein, Wisconsin (Illinois?), and a Minnesota town.

THE PRESIDENT:  Was it headed for Chicago?

Q:  Yes, sir; it was between two stops in one state and another.

THE PRESIDENT:  I had not heard about it.  Who do you suppose would know about that, the Department of Commerce?

Q:  I imagine it would have been called to their attention, sir.

Q:  Mr. President, do you favor the amortization of railroad debts through sinking funds as recommended by the Interstate Commerce Commission in its annual report to the Congress?

THE PRESIDENT:  Yes, absolutely.  One of the chief troubles, of course, with the whole railroad financial problem has been the fact that such a very large proportion of the capital structure has been in the form of a mortgage debt rather than stock.

Last spring, without naming any names of roads, a number of the largest and most important carriers that had been solvent for a great many years were faced with receivership and if the conditions of the first three months had continued they would probably, as we know now -- I don't think there is any particular reason why it should not be stated as a fact that six months would have seen receiverships for a number of the major roads of the United States.

--- [54] ---

Of course, that would have been caused by their inability to meet the interest on their mortgage debts, which, in many cases, ran as high as 50 to 60% of their entire capital structure. It has been the history of railroading in this country -- it is the old school of thought -- that when a mortgage becomes due, when the life of a bond issue came to an end, instead of paying it off out of a sinking fund or instead of amortizing it over a period of years, the railroads would refund the debt by borrowing an equal amount of money and extending the debt for thirty years or fifty years, or something like that.

One of the best illustrations is the road running past our place in Hyde Park, built in 1841. They issued, for the construction of the Hudson River Railroad, seven per cent gold bonds. I think they were thirty-year bonds, but they never established a sinking fund and, when 1871 came along, they refunded by another issue of thirty-year bonds, and when those came due they refunded that with another issue, and then finally, when the market was good, around 1911 or 1912, they refunded with a new issue which, if I remember it correctly, was due in the year 2001.

In effect, there was a debt for the construction of a railroad which was incurred in 1841, and they never paid off a cent of it, and it has now been extended so that it may be paid in the year 2001. In other words, it is just borrowing from John in order to pay Paul, or something like that. Most people today feel that the Interstate Commerce Commission is dead right in demanding, as a broad principle, that the railroads, as fast as it is financially possible for them to do so, should set up sinking funds for annual

--- [55] ---

payments of some kind out of earnings, so as to pay off an incurred mortgage obligation when it falls due.

Going back again to the situation last spring which I was talking about, these major railroads faced difficulties because they had not made enough money to pay the interest on their mortgage debts. In most cases, if their mortgage debt had been a great deal lower in proportion to their capital, they would have had enough money to get by with. In other words, if stock has replaced that mortgage debt, assuming that the total capitalization was correct, if stock had replaced that mortgage debt, all they would have done would be to pass the dividend on to stocks. That does not throw any corporation into bankruptcy.

So I think the tendency is going to be -- and I think it is from the viewpoint of sound financing of public utilities -- that from now on they will make every effort to set up some fund for amortization.

Now that means, to be fair to the railroads, that regulatory bodies like the Interstate Commerce Commission and other utility commissions of states, ought to seek in their decisions and orders to make it possible for the utilities to earn enough to set up this sinking fund or amortization fund. That is only fair.

Q: Would you set up the amortization out of earnings or out of operating expenses?

THE PRESIDENT: That is a technical question which I cannot answer; I don't know. It is about as long as it is short, isn't it?

Q: The railroads favor it to come out of operating expenses.

Q: In view of what you said about railroads, does the same thing apply

--- [56] ---

to public utilities?

THE PRESIDENT: On public utilities?

Q: Telephones and everything?

THE PRESIDENT: Yes.

Q: On the liquor situation, is it a good guess that we shall continue to insist on concessions from countries abroad in return for imports into this country?

THE PRESIDENT: I do not know. We are going ahead on the present basis for a three-months period, or something like that --

Q: (interposing) It is a four-months period.

THE PRESIDENT: And we have not taken up what we will do at the end of the period.

Q: Any comments on the situation with Russia? Could you lead us in any fashion in our United States-Russia stories which are coming to the front all the time?

THE PRESIDENT: I don't think there is any news outside of receiving the Ambassador. You had better go and see Bill Bullitt.

Q: He is quite quiet.

THE PRESIDENT: The only thing I have talked to Ambassador Bullitt about is what we are going to do about housing.

Q: Mr. President, is there any progress in setting up some corporation or other organization to trade with Russia?

THE PRESIDENT: No. There is nothing more on that. I do not believe there will be very much in the way of news of any export corporation or export plan until the Secretary of State gets back. We want him back here before we get any very definite plan.

Q: When do you expect him?

--- [57] ---

THE PRESIDENT: About the twenty-fifth.

Q: Comptroller Tremaine (Morris S. Tremaine) of New York State conferred the other day with the Tax Board on making warrants and certain securities of states and cities discountable with the Federal Reserve Board.

THE PRESIDENT: Who did, Broderick?

Q: Tremaine, of the New York State Board.

THE PRESIDENT: New York City and other cities?

Q: I believe the proposition is that where the taxes had been in arrears in previous years, they would still have a certain percentage discountable with the Federal Reserve System, which would unfreeze a lot of notes now lying around in banks.

THE PRESIDENT: I had not heard anything about it. As a matter of fact, the tax arrear payments are coming along pretty well in most of the New York cities.

Q: This would not apply only to New York but all over the country.

THE PRESIDENT: Yes, even over the country they are beginning to pay arrearages.

Q: Where can I get any figures on that, do you know?

THE PRESIDENT: I do not know.

Q: There was a suggestion at Mr. Ickes' conference yesterday that you might ask Congress for further appropriations on the Public Works program. Can you enlighten us a little on that?

THE PRESIDENT: Only what I told you before, the $1,166,000,000. that will be going up sometime soon and the $2,000,000,000. fund, the allocation of which we are not certain about yet, for the following fiscal year. That is as far as we got.

--- [58] ---

Q: Coming back for a moment to this question of setting up a sinking fund, you said that as far as possible regulatory bodies should seek to make possible such payments. Does that involve the idea that in specific instances it might be advisable or necessary to increase rates to make possible such payments? Do you think that would be possible?

THE PRESIDENT: Let's put it the other way around: In the reduction of rates, they should not be reduced so as to make it impossible.

MR. EARLY: Let's go.

CONFIDENTIAL
Press Conference #87
Executive Offices of the White House
January 12, 1934, 4:12 P.M.


THE PRESIDENT: The only news is that the duck season is coming to an end. Mr. Early has left and at his suggestion we had better put the lid on until Monday or somewhere along that.

Q: Mr. President, did you have a conference today on the Weirton case with the Attorney General and others?

THE PRESIDENT: Just one for the facts in the case. Nothing decided.

Q: No decision?

THE PRESIDENT: No.

Q: Mr. President, is there anything new on the monetary situation?

THE PRESIDENT: Not a thing. We continue to discuss it as usual.

Q: Has the Attorney General submitted an opinion as to whether legislation will be necessary to take the gold from the Federal Reserve Banks in the event of deflation?

THE PRESIDENT: I have not had an Attorney General's opinion on that subject since the silver purchase.

Q: There has been a report around Capitol Hill that some of them are expecting you to address a joint session on Monday on a topic undefined?

THE PRESIDENT: Nothing at all.

Q: Also a report that you plan to issue a monetary statement? (Laughter)


(The President did not answer the question.)


Q: Mr. President, is there anything to say about the proposed reduction of the forty-hour week that General Johnson has been saying a little about?

--- [60] ---

THE PRESIDENT: I meant to ask him about it when he was here this morning and I forgot.

I think if you were to go and see Assistant Secretary Moore you could get a story out of him. I got this at the Diplomatic Dinner last night. You know there has been some discussion between us and Great Britain about swapping pork for liquor, and apparently Mr. Moore sent a very, very good Virginia ham to the British Ambassador and he got back a bottle of Scotch. (Laughter)

Q: Mr. President, have you sufficient authority under the Thomas Amendment to withdraw this Federal Reserve gold?

THE PRESIDENT:  Oh, I think so.

Q:   What was the answer to that?

THE PRESIDENT:  I think -- I do not think there is any question of the Executive authority to take all the gold in the country.

Q:   Through the Secretary of the Treasury?

THE PRESIDENT:  Yes, I think so.  I do not remember the exact method; I suppose it is the Secretary of the Treasury.

Q:   Do you intend to do that?

THE PRESIDENT:  Oh, heavens!  (Laughter)

Q:   In regard to the question about the possibility that you will address the Joint Congress, does that apply over the week end to any radio addresses?

THE PRESIDENT:  I am not making any speeches over the week end; in fact, I do not think I have any speeches listed for any date in the future.

Q:   Do you care to tell us anything about the Congressional delegation that came up here to save the Coast Guard from the Navy merger?

THE PRESIDENT:  I told them that nothing had been decided about it.

--- [61] ---

Q:   Nothing decided?

THE PRESIDENT:  No.

Q:   Mr. President, have you had any conferences with Senator Wagner?  Is there anything you can tell us on that subject regarding making the Labor Board permanent by legislation?

THE PRESIDENT:  We have not got to that.  We only talked about the facts in the Weirton case this morning.

Q:   The Senator has some bills?

THE PRESIDENT:  He told me he was working on the legislative end of the thing.

Q:   Any thought of recommendations?

THE PRESIDENT:  No, because he is not ready yet.

Q:   Have you heard from John Fahey about the Home Owners' Loan recommendation he was going to prepare for you?

THE PRESIDENT:  No, not a word.

Q:   What is the situation in the bituminous coal controversy -- the Captive Mine situation?

THE PRESIDENT:  I do not think that has come up at all.  You see, the Weirton case is under the Steel Code.

Q: Mr. Lane and his assistants were in yesterday and I thought something new had developed.

THE PRESIDENT: I did not see them.

Q: They were here while you were out.

MR. McINTYRE: They were here to extend an invitation to you to attend their Annual Convention next month, that is all.

THE PRESIDENT: Did Mac say that with a straight face? (Laughter)

Q: Is a sugar conference in contemplation?

--- [62] ---

THE PRESIDENT: No, that is something I cannot tell you, even as background. You will have to find out from the State Department. I can only give you a suggestion as to what it is about because I don't remember who it was that sent the proposal in here. They wanted to have -- I don't know whether it came from England or France or somewhere across the ocean -- but they suggested a preliminary conference that would not be final for anybody, just to discuss the general world sugar situation. You had better find out from the State Department about it. I don't see any reason why it should not be made public. We said we would be glad to talk things over with anybody. It is only a preliminary thing to see whether it is worth while having a later conference looking towards an agreement.

Q: Mr. President, there are widespread reports to the effect that the Administration is considering the establishing of a central bank. Can you tell us anything about that?

THE PRESIDENT: That is a new one on me. I think it is a rotten guess.

Q: Mr. President, --

THE PRESIDENT: (interposing) I would be doing the opposite of Andrew Jackson. He abolished it.

Q: Are you planning any conferences on the 30-hour week with the advocates of it in Congress.

THE PRESIDENT: No. It has not come up at all. I meant to talk to Hugh Johnson about it this morning and forgot to talk about it.

Q: I meant the Congressional end?

THE PRESIDENT: No.

Q: Can you tell us anything about your war debt message?

--- [63] ---

THE PRESIDENT: No. It will go in sometime -- I haven't even got any idea of whether it will be in the next two weeks or the next two months.

Q: What about your tariff Message?

THE PRESIDENT: I think you could make a pretty good guess on the tariff Message, that there won't be anything done on tariff until the Secretary of State gets back, which will be inside of two weeks. He ought to be here by the twenty-fifth.

Q: Any consideration of opening postal deposits to checking accounts?

THE PRESIDENT: Only what you read in the paper. We have not discussed it at all.

Q: There is a lot in the papers these days. (Laughter)

Q: Mr. President, can you tell us anything about the Japanese landing tuna fish under the N.R.A. label? (Laughter)

THE PRESIDENT: I forgot to ask about that too. I read that in the paper.

Q: Would you care to make any comment on the flight to Hawaii by the Navy planes?

THE PRESIDENT: I sent them a message of congratulations.

Q: Have you heard anything, Mr. President, from the Senate on the St. Lawrence Treaty?

THE PRESIDENT: No, what happened to it?

Q: They talked all day.

Q: They recessed until Monday, Mr. President.

THE PRESIDENT: Fine.

Q: Have you seen Hiram Johnson's Resolution?

THE PRESIDENT: I have not seen it. I sent for it and I do not know

--- [64] ---

which one it was. He had two.

Q: This one is to bar the purchase of securities from countries which have not paid their debts.

THE PRESIDENT: I have not seen it.

Q: Thank you, Mr. President.

THE PRESIDENT: I am sorry there isn't any more news.

Press Conference #88
Executive Offices of the White House
January 15, 1934, 10:40 A.M.

> (This Press Conference was held for the
> financial experts in order to explain the
> President's Message of January 15, 1934,
> to the Congress)

THE PRESIDENT: Are these the only people out of all the White House correspondents who know anything about finance? (Laughter)

Q: We are the only ones who admit that we do not. (Laughter)

THE PRESIDENT: The easiest way, I think, is for me to read this release to you.

MR. EARLY: They already have it.

THE PRESIDENT: I just want to say one or two things. In the first place, Steve
(Mr. Early) wanted me to stress that all this is in confidence until the
Message is released and nothing is to be said in advance of the release.

Q: By the way, when will the release be made?

THE PRESIDENT: As soon as it gets up there to Congress. I don't know whether
it is released up there before it is read by the Clerk or not, but I see
by the heading "until its reading has begun in the Senate or in the House."

Now, in a nutshell, the first portion of this, down to the first line,
might be called philosophical. In other words, it merely goes into the
general theory that the issuance of money or currency or any medium of
exchange is solely a government prerogative and always has been since the
days of Babylon or the time they used sea shells or coral shells in the
South Sea Islands. In

--- [66] ---

theory, coral shells are a perfectly good medium of exchange, perfectly
good money as such, provided there is control over them. It becomes a
question of control and because of the lack of assurance of control
throughout history, it has always been, for the sake of stability, advisable to have some basis behind the currency which, as a matter of practical
fact through the ages, has been the precious metals, gold and silver. We
do not have to go on further with that.

Q: Might we assume that that is an argument against greenbacks? What you have
just stated?

THE PRESIDENT: It certainly is an argument against starting of the printing
presses. On the other hand, of course, as you know, there has been a very
great difference of opinion as to what is a greenback and what is not a
greenback. If we were to start tomorrow, this is the easiest illustration,
to pay off the deficit of this year just by printing greenbacks, that would
be greenbacks, there is no question about that.

On the other hand, a limited amount of non-interest bearing five and ten dollar bonds to retire an outstanding debt and with provision for retirement of those new non-interest bearing bonds would not be greenbacks.

What people fear about greenbacks is, of course, that some future Congress may take off the limit -- take off the lid.

Then we come down to the next point which is the taking of the title of the gold in the Government and that follows out logically the theory that the Government is entitled to control the basis behind all currency.

----[67] ---

Then the third point is the establishment of an upper limit within which I have to act. By that I mean that I could not stabilize at above 60 if this is put through. This does not stabilize at 60. It still leaves me free to stabilize between 50 and 60.

And -- this is just for information because I have noted one or two stories -- there has been absolutely no doubt from the legal point of view of the authority under the previous act to stabilize more than once and to put it at 50 or 60 or anything alse I want, as often as I want.

Q: What act is that?

THE PRESIDENT: Oh, last spring; the Banking Bill.

Q: Yes.

Q: This is a 40 per cent deflation by enactment of Congress?

THE PRESIDENT: No, it is not. That is exactly what it is not. Congress has said that I may devalue as low as 60. Now I am asking them to give me authority to devalue by not less than 40.

Q: This is a further limitation on your power but does not require you to do anything?

THE PRESIDENT: Today I can revalue between 100 and 50 and I am asking them to limit my power so that I can only revalue between 50 and 60.

Q: Then, until you devalue you merely do not have to revalue at all?

THE PRESIDENT: No, but if I revalue I won't be able to revalue higher than 60 or lower than 50. This is a 10-cent leeway.

Then the third point in that same paragraph, it would set up a fund of two billion dollars for the purchase and sale of gold, foreign exchange and Government securities.

--- [68] ---

Q: Might that be called a stabilization fund?

THE PRESIDENT: Well, that is only part of it.

Q: Isn't that, Mr. President, the commodity dollar feature.

THE PRESIDENT: It is the tieing in of certain powers that we have at the present time. For instance, the buying of gold and silver through the R.F.C., it is to simplify that procedure. It is to keep this fund intact in the Treasury so as to stabilize, insofar as possible, foreign exchange.

Q: The point I had in mind was this, that this would permit you to deal with foreign exchange without definitely fixing, permanently, the value of the dollar.

THE PRESIDENT: Let me give you a little background on this particular thing, because I think it is important. Last spring things went up much too fast in this country. Wheat went up to $1.25 which, undoubtedly, was altogether too high. That was caused by speculation and a great many manufacturers overproduced, the steel companies overproduced, the textile people overproduced, for various reasons, trying to get in under the wire before the Code went into effect. The result was a perfectly natural one. There was quite a big drop in commodity prices of all kinds around the middle of July. That was a perfectly healthy thing. But a little bit later on, somewhere around September, there began a very definite drift of commodity prices downward. That was caused by a great many factors. It was caused by people who did not approve of N.R.A. Codes, it was caused by some of our foreign friends who were deliberately trying to increase the exchange value of the dollar and decrease the exchange value of the franc -- there were a good many

--- [69] ---

foreign elements that entered into it.

The result was that by the tenth or fifteenth of October we were in a definite downward drift which, if carried out, would have been a serious thing. Wheat, which should have a normal value of 85 or 90 cents had gotten down to 60. Cotton had gotten down to below 9 cents a pound and there was a rather determined drive against prices. The whole line was down. That was when we took action on gold. I have forgotten what gold was at that particular point, it was around 4.60 as I remember it. It was around 4.60 and the tendency was for it to go to 4.50, 4.40 or 4.30 and, perhaps eventually because of the pressure on the other side, if left alone might have gone back to the figure that the British Treasury and the Bank of England, away back last May and June, were taking as the stabilization figure, about 3.90 to the pound.

We then started to purchase gold. There are various ways of maintaining foreign exchange. You can either purchase bills of exchange, et cetera, or actually buy the gold. This move today was in prospect at that time and obviously it was to the interest of the United States to buy gold. So we bought gold and have been buying it ever since in fairly large quantities and the result has been that the exchange has gone up to well over five dollars and has maintained itself there largely because of the American purchase of gold.

It has, I think, been felt by people on the other side as well as here that if we had not pursued the gold purchase policy, the actual exchange value rate on gold would be 4 and something instead of 5 and something.

--- [70] ---

The other result of maintaining the dollar-pound and dollar-franc ratio as high as it has been has shown itself in our ability to get rid of a great many of our export surpluses. Cotton has been moving out. Of course, you know our objective is to eliminate the very large surplus which has been overhanging the domestic prices. The same thing applies to wheat and everything else. Our one objective was to get rid of the surpluses. We got rid of a great deal of cotton and we got rid of a great deal of copper, for instance. At the same time the import trade has increased enormously during the past three months since the dollar has gone down in terms of pounds. The result has been a very excellent one from a general economic domestic point of view.

This revaluation of not more than 60 per cent and not below 50 per cent should enable us to maintain a fairly reasonable exchange ratio with other nations. The reason it has to be done this way is what I said in the Message to Congress, that there is at the present time no willingness on the part of the other nations to go ahead and go back on a fixed basis. In other words, to put in the other way around, Great Britain has been pursuing what you call the Professor Warren theory for perhaps two and a half years. That is the thing that some of our people forget very definitely. They have a managed pound, absolutely managed, far more so than we have ever thought of managing the dollar.

Q: Does that indicate that an open gold market in the United States will be established? It talks about --

THE PRESIDENT: I don't know. Of course there has been talk about an open gold market. That is one of the mechanics of the situation.

--- [71] ---

I don't know. There is no immediate prospect.

Q: What is the purpose of purchasing Government securities along with gold and exchange?

THE PRESIDENT: I suppose the easiest way to answer that, the purchase of Government securities, is to ask the question, "Is it right or proper that a handful of people who did not happen to like what was going on or who wanted to use a club in order to get something of their own through -- that such private individuals should have the right, without check, at their own sweet will, to dump Government bonds into the market and artificially depreciate the price of Government bonds? Is it moral that private individuals should have that right?"

Q: Was there short selling of Government bonds?

THE PRESIDENT: I couldn't tell you whether it was short selling or not but there were, undoubtedly, certain individuals -- this does not by any means apply to the overwhelming majority of the bankers in the United States -- but there were individuals who recommended to their clients that they should get rid of Government bonds and in most of those cases there were ulterior motives.

Now, the fact that the Government would be given the right to purchase Government bonds means that a private effort of that kind could be check-

mated right away.  This is protective armor for any Government and we
ought to have it.

Q:  Does the setting up of that two billion dollar fund depend on the profits
of revaluation?

THE PRESIDENT:  Yes.

Q:  Until you definitely revalue, there will be no profits, however?

--- [72] ---

THE PRESIDENT:  No, it is out of the profits.

Q:  When do you need the fund?

THE PRESIDENT:  No, we haven't gotten to that yet.

Q:  Do you contemplate, as soon as this bill is passed, very promptly thereafter, immediately, issuing a revaluation proclamation?

THE PRESIDENT:  We haven't come to that yet.

The last part relates to silver -- expresses the thought that silver has
also been used from time immemorial as a metallic base and that it is still
used by half the population of the world as such; that it is used by us and
is a crucial factor in international trade and that it cannot be neglected.
Further on I say that Governments can well employ silver as a basis for
currency and I look for a greatly increased use.  I also describe the
existing situation with respect to the agreement among the sixty-six nations and the fact that we have put our part into effect.  I also say that
I am withholding any recommendations to the Congress at this time for further extension because I want to know the results of the London agreement
and the results of the rest of our monetary measures.

Q:  Can you tell us anything about the legislation that is to be offered in
connection with this?

THE PRESIDENT:  There has been drafted what might be called a purely tentative
method of arriving at the things recommended in the Message.  I am perfectly frank in telling you that I haven't even read it.  In other words, it is
to save the committees trouble and give them something to chew on in order
to carry out the recommendations.  It is not an Administration bill.  It is
just to help the committees.

--- [73] ---

Q:  On this gold policy, there is no thought in mind of the Treasury, with its
gold stocks, issuing money on the basis of 40 per cent reserve?

THE PRESIDENT:  No.  The idea is, of course, that for this money turned in the
Federal Reserve Banks are given certificates that there is gold in the
Treasury, dollar for dollar, and that on those certificates the Federal
Reserve Banks can issue their own currency to their member banks.

Q:  Do you look for any immediate effect on domestic prices from the mere passage of this legislation?

THE PRESIDENT:  I don't know; I have no idea.

Q:    The profit from this operation clearly is to go to the Treasury?

THE PRESIDENT:  Yes.  Right on that point, there has been a divergence of
     opinion amongst some of the bankers -- not by any means all -- and on the
     part of a few politicians who have wondered whether the Government had any
     right to take this profit or whether the profit should accrue to the stock-
     holders of the banks.  Of course, so far as I can see, there is no ques-
     tion on that at all.  We asked individuals to turn in their gold and get
     paper money on it.  We also asked all the corporations to do it and sub-
     stantially all came across and did as requested.  I cannot see a great
     deal of difference between a bank and a private corporation.  The consti-
     tuent bank is owned by private individuals and if we were to pursue that
     policy of letting the stockholders of the banks take this profit, it would
     mean that the Government was handing them a great big Christmas present.

     I was very careful to point out in this message that such

--- [74] ---

     legislation places the right, title and ownership of our gold reserves in
     the Government itself.  It makes clear the Government's ownership of any
     added dollar value of the country's stock of gold which would result from
     any decrease of the gold content of the dollar which may be made in the
     public interest.

     But, in order to be fair, I pointed out that the Government would lose such
     dollar value if the public interest in the future should require an in-
     crease in the amount of gold designated as a dollar.

Q:    It is your idea to have a permanent policy, retaining the limits within the
     50 and 60, revaluing within those limits from time to time?

THE PRESIDENT:  As far as any human being can say "permanent."

Q:    And to continue to hold all the gold?

THE PRESIDENT:  Certainly, to hold all the gold.

Q:    If you issue dollar for dollar, that is, under the old Gold Certificate
     Act--

THE PRESIDENT:  (interposing)  No, it would be under the new act.

Q:    Well, it is similar to that.  Isn't the gold, in effect, then left in the
     Federal Reserve and their profits -- that it is still within the Federal
     Reserve System as profits of the bank?

THE PRESIDENT:  Oh, no.  They get a piece of paper under this which says that
     there is in the Treasury, say on a $10 certificate, that there is in the
     Treasury $10 worth of gold.  It does not say how much gold or grains or
     anything like that.

     Now, on that certificate which will be held by the Federal Reserve Bank on
     behalf of the member banks, the banks will issue

--- [75] ---

currency on the 100 to 40 basis.  Is that right, Henry?

SECRETARY MORGENTHAU:  Yes.

Q:    Then the Federal Reserve Banks would have authority to issue their notes
      against that gold?

THE PRESIDENT:  It depends on what you revalue at.

Q:    This would not increase the currency issuing power of the Federal Reserve
      at all?

THE PRESIDENT:  The thing to remember is that every bank statement -- the state-
      ments of the member banks, the state banks, and the twelve Federal Reserve
      Banks, their statements are in terms of dollars and there is absolutely no
      change in their statements.  It does not give them less reserve or more.
      They have the same number of dollars.

Q:    Would you mind phrasing in words of one syllable to millions of unlettered
      people, to most of whom this would be Greek, how the Government would de-
      rive these profits that there is so much talk about?

THE PRESIDENT:  Let's put it this way:  We have been trying to bring the pur-
      chasing power of the dollar back, approximately, to the level in which the
      average of the debts of the country were incurred so that the average of
      people can pay off those debts in a dollar that has approximately that
      same purchasing power.  Because of that, one method -- the most practical
      method of doing it, is to cut the theoretical gold content of the dollar.
      Now, you can only make that practical and fair if the Government has all
      the gold.  The number of dollars in the banks of the country will be exact-
      ly the same as they were before and the Government will have -- as the cur-
      rency issuing power, will have the same weight of gold in the Treasury

--- [76] ---

but actually, in terms of dollars for the Treasury, that will represent 80
per cent more or 100 per cent more depending on what we revalue at.

Q:    Have you estimated the profits in terms of dollars?

THE PRESIDENT:  There will be, therefore, a nominal profit to the Government of
      somewhere between 3 billion 400 million and 4 billion 200 million depending
      on what we revalue at.  Is that about right?

SECRETARY MORGENTHAU:  Yes, sir.

Q:    That is between 50 and 60 per cent?

THE PRESIDENT:  Yes.

      Now, there is one other thing.  Of course, in terms of foreign exchange,
      the dollar is today, in terms of gold, worth only about 63 cents.

Q:    How much?

THE PRESIDENT:  About 63 cents.

Q:   Can you make any use of this profit other than the two billion dollar fund you set up?

THE PRESIDENT:   That is for the future.

Q:   Have you any authority to issue currency against it?

THE PRESIDENT:   No.

Q:   And the profit does not represent a base of currency in the Federal Reserve?

THE PRESIDENT:   No.   We keep it in the Treasury.

Now, off the record, just for your information -- I have to keep it off the record because it involves another branch of the

--- [77] ---

Government -- we do not intend to encourage Congress to spend the billions of the profit.   (Laughter)

Q:   If anything like that were done, it would be up to Congress to take action?

THE PRESIDENT:   We asked them to take action on the two billions.

Q:   Congress would have to pass further legislation if you wanted to make use of the profit?

THE PRESIDENT:   Yes.

Q:   Do you hope that this will encourage international stabilization?

THE PRESIDENT:   I hope so.

Q:   If you use a bullion system --

THE PRESIDENT:   (interposing)   This is a bullion system.   We will not coin any gold coins except such as might be necessary to make up small amounts less than a bar of gold.   Loose change.

Q:   In other words, I don't see how you can make an artificial gold price effective unless exchangeable in some form.

THE PRESIDENT:   The bullion and small change would be used for foreign settlements.   Those take place every six months or a year.

Q:   Did you say that the export embargo was removed?

THE PRESIDENT:   No, no.   Of course, after the whole system gets into bullion, obviously the export embargo would be removed to the extent that if we do have an unfavorable trade balance at the end of the period, we would ship out bullion to pay unfavorable trade balances.

Q:   There is no relaxation of the order, then?

THE PRESIDENT:   No.

Q:   Everybody in the country is wanting to know how it is going to affect

--- [78] ---

him.

THE PRESIDENT:  How?

Q:   He wants to know whether it is going to increase his buying power or
     increase his wages -- how much it is going to be felt.

THE PRESIDENT:  Probably very little.  Probably certain commodity prices will
     go up to a certain extent and it will enable people, knowing that Congress
     has said between 50 and 60, it will enable people to make contracts ahead
     with far greater assurance than at the present time, because today it is
     between 50 and 100.

Q:   And now it will be definitely between 50 and 60?

THE PRESIDENT:  That bill makes it between 50 and 60.

Press Conference #89
Executive Offices of the White House
January 17, 1934, 10:45 A.M.


THE PRESIDENT: Too much musicale last night.

Q: (Mr. Storm) Have a crowd?

THE PRESIDENT: No, had a boy violinist and a lady who recited. Acute indiges-
tion most of the night. (Laughter) I don't know whether it was cause and
effect or not. (Laughter)

Q: Looks like a clear desk this morning, Mr. President.

THE PRESIDENT: The way they keep coming on one would think there was some
news. There isn't any. (Laughter)

MR. DONALDSON: All in.

THE PRESIDENT: All right, go ahead and ask questions. It is a dull day and I
think it may rain. That is all I know.

Q: The sun is shining out there.

Q: You are unduly optimistic.

THE PRESIDENT: Anything doing for the District of Columbia?

Q: I don't know.

THE PRESIDENT: What vacancies have I got left?

Q: The Public Utilities Commission and Judge of the Municipal Court.

THE PRESIDENT: Is that the lady I appointed and she could not take office?

Q: No, that is another one.

THE PRESIDENT: What has happened? (Laughter)

Q: Her time expires January twenty-second.

THE PRESIDENT: I will make a note of it.

Q: And the Public Utilities Commissioner?

--- [80] ---

THE PRESIDENT: I am trying to find somebody right now. Have you any ideas?

Q: I have indeed. (Laughter) A very good man and a very good lady, too.

Q: Mr. President, do you care to discuss public reaction to your gold message?

THE PRESIDENT: I have not read the papers yet. (Laughter)

Q:  Mr. President, there seems to be considerable complaint around the country
that wages paid to C.W.A. workers in some instances are considerably higher
than wages paid under the codes and prevailing wages paid. Has there been
any discussion or consideration of a revision or anything of that sort, or
have those complaints come to you?

THE PRESIDENT:  Only from Harry Hopkins. He told me about them and he said
there have been complaints from certain parts of the country, as you say,
and he is working on the possibility of cutting the number of hours where
the existing scale does give more than the going rate in the locality. I
do not know whether he has worked out the plan yet and is putting it into
effect but the result would be to give a slightly smaller total for the
week's work by working less hours. He was working on it. I do not know
whether it is done or not.

Q:  We have heard complaints of people who quit jobs in private industry and
laid off for a week or two and got on the C.W.A.

THE PRESIDENT:  There have been things of that kind and because the C.W.A. is
handled entirely by local relief organizations so far as names go, there
are difficulties in places where there are

--- [81] ---

no local relief organizations. For example, you take the State of Georgia,
there are quite a lot of counties in the State of Georgia that have no
relief organizations and, therefore, no relief rolls.

Q:  On that same question, how about the compensation of war veterans who are
on the C.W.A. pay roll?

THE PRESIDENT:  You mean as to the legal conflict of their getting two pays?

Q:  Two pays, yes. I understand you have an Executive Order more or less prepared on that subject.

THE PRESIDENT:  It has not come back. There is one in preparation.

Q:  Mr. President, quite a few of us have been writing stories about the activities of National Committeemen practicing before the Departments, and
some have gone so far as to say that it is embarrassing the Administration.
Have you anything to say on that?

THE PRESIDENT:  I think if we can avoid reference to individuals, it is all
right to talk about the general principle. I have felt all along that it
is not quite in accord with the spirit of the Administration that any individual who holds a high Party position, such as National Committeeman,
should earn a livelihood by practicing law, because, in a sense, he holds
himself out as having access to the back door of the Administration. It
just is not done. That is strictly true. It has been done and it ought
not to be done.

Q:  Mr. President, is there anything you can tell us in connection with the
Iowa situation that seems to be heading up today? The Public Works Administrator was fired out there.

--- [82] ---

THE PRESIDENT: The Attorney General -- I asked him on the telephone -- the
District Attorney is arriving here to talk it over with the Department (of
Justice) and I imagine the Department (of Justice) will be largely guided
by the recommendation of the District Attorney.

Q: He was ready to lay it before the Grand Jury when he was called down here.
He had eighty witnesses.

THE PRESIDENT: I understand there are two stories on that. I do not know the
actual facts as to whether he was ready or wanted to talk it over with us
first. I think you had better check on it over there.

Q: Mr. President, can you tell us anything as to when the war debt Message
will be ready?

THE PRESIDENT: I will make a pretty long guess on that. I should say not for
a month.

Q: Mr. President, did you inquire specifically into the constitutionality of
the so-called compensation law before?

THE PRESIDENT: Which one?

Q: The matter that the Senate Committee took up yesterday?

THE PRESIDENT: The due process of law thing?

Q: Yes.

THE PRESIDENT: Oh, yes; the Attorney General is perfectly definite on that.

Q: He has already given you his opinion?

THE PRESIDENT: He gave us an oral opinion on it as far back as the time we
went off gold, last April. I do not know whether he gave a written
opinion at that time or not -- I think he did -- so far

--- [83] ---

as private individuals or corporations went. He has been perfectly clear
on the thing all the way through.

Q: How about the Newspaper Code, Mr. President?

THE PRESIDENT: I have not got to it yet. It is sitting beside my desk in the
White House.

Q: Mr. President, is it a good guess that the war debt Message will contain
a recommendation for reduction of armaments?

THE PRESIDENT: I have no idea. I have not taken it up at all.

Q: Mr. President, can you tell us the status of negotiations with England?

THE PRESIDENT: I have not talked with Phillips (Under Secretary of State) about
it for ten days. I do not know exactly how far they have got.

Q:   Are you seeking any understanding with Great Britain on the currency and monetary program?

THE PRESIDENT:  No.

Q:   Or on trade?

THE PRESIDENT:  No.  The only thing I know about is the big whiskey deal.
     (Laughter)

Q:   Is the whiskey coming in?

THE PRESIDENT:  Yes, and the pigs are going out.

Q:   There have been reports published this morning to the effect that the Administration has undertaken conversation with Great Britain to avoid any sort of possible conflict of stabilization funds?

THE PRESIDENT:  No, nothing on it.  No communications at all.

Q:   Mr. President, is there anything you can tell us in the way of new developments in the Weirton case on which you had a conference just prior to the last Press Conference?

--- [84] ---

THE PRESIDENT:  I do not think there is anything can be printed on that.  I saw Weir on that other day and had a talk with him about it, more along the broad line of some effort on his part to eliminate the present feeling on the part of some people who claim that the election was not fairly held.  They are going to have further conferences.  There isn't anything more than that at the present time.

Q:   Did he indicate he would accede to a second election?

THE PRESIDENT:  No, hadn't got as far as that.  Talked about the particular objective.

Q:   Ireland is sending over the head of its Department of Commerce to talk the possibility of reciprocal trade agreements with us.  Can such an agreement be drawn by you or must there be a tariff Message to the Congress?

THE PRESIDENT:  I do not know.  That is the first I heard of it.

Q:   I wonder if the Administration has any objections to the State Department going ahead with it?

THE PRESIDENT:  No.  Tell me, can we enter into a trade agreement with Ireland without the consent of Great Britain?

Q:   I think so.  Ireland claims they can.  (Laughter)

Q:   Would you care to discuss Senator Johnson's bill for trading with countries who are in debt with us?

THE PRESIDENT:  I think you had better lay off that for a while.  (Laughter)

Q:   What will be the subject of your next special Message to the Congress?

THE PRESIDENT: I haven't any Messages in mind at the present time, not a single one.

Q: I wondered what you are working on in preparing this legislative

--- [85] ---

program?

THE PRESIDENT: I imagine the next thing that will go up will be that appropriation of $1,166,000,000. to carry us through until the first of July, because there is real need of getting that through before the tenth of February. Hopkins' appropriation will be exhausted on the eleventh of February. He won't have any more money.

Q: Has Secretary Dickinson's report on the regulation of stock exchanges reached you?

THE PRESIDENT: I spoke to Dan Roper and he expected to have it in two or three days.

Q: Have you had a chance to talk about a new governor for Hawaii?

THE PRESIDENT: No. Off the record, for your information, we had a man picked and he could not take it, so we are just where we were before.

Q: Will you favor legislation for the regulation of motor vehicles on the highways at this session, such as the Rayburn Bill?

THE PRESIDENT: I don't know. I frankly haven't gone into it at all. It is a difficult subject, and Commissioner Eastman is not ready to report. I asked him yesterday in the Council meeting to come in some time in the course of the next week and talk over legislation. He said he is not ready to make any recommendations as yet.

Q: That means legislation?

THE PRESIDENT: On the whole transportation problems, transportation of all kinds. Remember we had it in mind. There is no particular secret about it. It follows the Salt Lake City speech. It is to try to consolidate control of all transportation into probably the

--- [86] ---

Interstate Commerce Commission. That would include motor buses and trucks and waterways and railroads.

Q: Waterways in and outside the country, like the Panama Canal?

THE PRESIDENT: No, not the Panama Canal. I would not say that categorically. I suppose it might include the Panama Canal, since it competes with railroads on U.S. shipping from one port to the other. I guess it would.

Q: Any phase of the Cuban mess you can discuss?

THE PRESIDENT: No, it moves too fast for me. I haven't heard this morning.

Q: Thank you, Mr. President.

Press Conference #90
Executive Offices of the White House
January 19, 1934, 4:18 P.M.


THE PRESIDENT: I will have to confess that I was entirely ignorant of the fact
    that you were outside. I was talking to the Secretary of the Interior
    about the Ogdensburg Bridge, one of my old favorites. Do you remember,
    Fred (Mr. Storm)?

Q: (Mr. Storm) Yes, I do.

MR. DONALDSON: All in.

THE PRESIDENT: I think you all got this veterans release. It has been in ef-
    fect these last three months and it is just carrying out what we have been
    doing ever since last spring, correcting under the Executive Order what
    seemed to be inequalities. I have got the totals. I think Steve (Mr.
    Early) has given the breakdown of the $21,000,000. of additional cost to
    some of you; if not, they are all here in the tables. The increase from
    $90. to $100. a month is about $8,000,000. The liberalization of the
    eligibility roll on hospital treatments amounts to about $8,000,000. The
    $15. a month Spanish War is about $2,000,000.; there are a very small num-
    ber of the Spanish War people left and they were only sixteen or seventeen
    years old when they enlisted. There are only seven or eight thousand of
    them left, and the burial and funeral allowance is about $1,250,000. The
    war veterans coming under the ninety-day service clause, $204,000. The
    widows, $470,000. The Federal employees clause, $1,250,000. The renounce-
    ment of pensions, no cost. The total is $21,000,000., all of which come
    within the terms of the policy outlined in the Chicago speech and do not
    go

--- [88] ---

beyond it. I think you can make a pretty good guess that I won't go beyond
it. In other words, we will stay tight on the Chicago policy.

Q: What about Federal employees? There has been a lot of talk in the local
    papers about it.

THE PRESIDENT: I do not know what has been happening up there on it.

Q: Mr. President, can you tell us what progress has been made on the guaran-
    teeing of Home Loan bonds?

THE PRESIDENT: I have not heard anything since Tuesday and, on Tuesday, Mr.
    Fahey said it probably would not be ready until the end of this week or the
    beginning of next week.

Q: Any appointments for us?

THE PRESIDENT: No. These (indicating) are all affirmations by the Senate.

Q: Mr. President, is there anything to be said yet about the Los Angeles post-
    master? They are getting nervous out there. It seems that three people
    out there are all mentioned.

THE PRESIDENT: I did not even know there was a vacancy. It is very careless
on my part. (Laughter)

Q: Anything further on the Weirton Steel case?

THE PRESIDENT: Not a word. Nothing has come in at all.

Q: (Mr. Boettiger) How does this veterans program line up with the four-point
program?

THE PRESIDENT: I do not know, John (Mr. Boettiger); you will have to compare
it.

Q: Mr. President, what do you think of today's president in Cuba?

THE PRESIDENT: Well, I think if I were writing the story -- just a

--- [89] ---

background story, let us say -- I would put it this way: That we do hope
that the election -- don't bring me into this at all -- of Mr. Mendieta
looks very hopeful towards a realization of the two points that we have
hoped would be fulfilled. The first was a government in Cuba which would
have the substantial backing of the Cuban people; and the other, a government that would be able substantially to maintain law and order.

Of course, you cannot, within twenty-four or forty-eight hours, determine
that this new government will be able to fulfill those hopes. I do not
call them conditions, I call them hopes. I think you can make it a guess
that if in perhaps a week from now or ten days from now there seems to be
a carrying out, a fulfillment of those hopes -- in other words, if things
go along all right -- that probably I will converse with some of the American republics and have an interchange of views in regard to recognition,
making it clear that recognition would not be in any way dependent on an
agreement in any way between the various American republics; but, having
talked things over with them before, I think that probably we should have a
general talk about the situation as we hope it will be a week or ten days
from now.

Q: Mr. President, will any of our ships be withdrawn in the meantime, or will
things stay as they are?

THE PRESIDENT: It depends entirely. I couldn't tell you yet. If the people
down there seem to think that things are quite normal the thing to do would
be to withdraw the ships, but we have no report on that yet.

Q: Mr. President, reports are current in California that you are con-

--- [90] ---

templating a trip to the West Coast via the Canal after you get rid of
Congress. Is that true?

THE PRESIDENT: I do not think there is anything particularly new. I said all
along that if Congress went home fairly early in the spring and, if everything else was quiet, that I would like nothing better than to get on a
ship and go to California through the Canal. I also expressed the hope
that I could visit Puerto Rico, the Virgin Islands and Hawaii. But it is

still in the form of a hope.

Q:   Will you make any speeches in California?

THE PRESIDENT:  Oh, no.  (Laughter)  I hope I won't have to make any speeches anywhere.  (Laughter)

Q:   Do you expect before that time to have a new governor in Hawaii whom you might visit?

THE PRESIDENT:  I hope so.

Q:   There will be a new governor?

THE PRESIDENT:  What?

Q:   Excuse me.

THE PRESIDENT:  I don't know, Stevie (Mr. Francis Stephenson of the A.P.)

Q:   Will you ask again for legislation permitting you to appoint as governor of Hawaii some other than a Hawaiian resident?

THE PRESIDENT:  Not at this session.

Q:   One of the Press Associations had a story this afternoon that the Administration was going to favor the Vandenberg Bill along political lines. Anything to tell us about that?

THE PRESIDENT:  I think I can tell you off the record in this particular instance because I have not seen the bill but I have talked to a

--- [91] ---

number of very serious gentlemen, some of them from the Hill.  The question has been raised:  If we are going to treat a condition like that that the Vandenberg Bill is aimed at, if we are going to seek to correct the situation by legislation instead of by general ethics, why not go the whole hog? Why not take in everybody in the employ of the Government, including Senators and Congressmen?  (Laughter)

Q:   Aren't the Senators and Congressmen already in?  They are not practising before departments now?

THE PRESIDENT:  No, they are not allowed to practise before the Government departments but of course you and I -- mind you, this is off the record -- you and I know there are an awful lot of Senators and Congressmen who are getting paid for political influence.  I am just saying that in the broad and what has hitherto been accepted as the proper sense with respect to the use of the words "political influence."

Q:   You mean they are practising law while still serving in Congress?

THE PRESIDENT:  Yes.  As the Vice President suggestively remarked a little while ago; he said it is perfectly proper for any Congressman or Senator to do political favors which would result in a political reward as long as it is not a financial reward.  There is all the difference in the world between those two.  Naturally, every member of the legislative body, and I have been one myself, will go out of his way to do favors for people in the hope that that is going to reelect him. It is perfectly all right. That is an inherent part of our Government political system. But, when he does political favors for pay, that is a horse of a different

--- [92] ---

color and I think that is where the distinction should be drawn.

Q:  Isn't there a good deal of that?

THE PRESIDENT:  There always used to be when I was in Washington before. Of course I have not been able to circulate as freely during the last year or two. (Laughter)

Q:  That would not apply to practice before the courts, would it?

THE PRESIDENT:  It depends entirely on the individual case.

Q:  For example, a man who is elected to Congress and has some law practice hanging over and the cases come up while he is in Congress?

THE PRESIDENT:  What kind of cases? Cases in which the Government is in no way involved?

Q:  A civil suit?

THE PRESIDENT:  And the Government involved?

Q:  No.

THE PRESIDENT:  If the Government is not in any shape, way or manner involved, that is all right. It is only a question where the fact that he is a Congressman or a Senator or a member of the National Committee is going to help him in that suit.

Q:  Will that include contributions to the campaign funds in return for favors done?

THE PRESIDENT:  By whom?

Q:  Favors done, political favors?

THE PRESIDENT:  Yes, I think so. Generally the only thing on the campaign fund element is the old difficulty of finding enough rich men to go as ambassadors to foreign countries. Almost of necessity you do go into the realms and ranks of those who have contributed. It is a very difficult problem, that question of ambassadors, be-

--- [93] ---

cause almost every rich man has contributed.

Q:  I was thinking about votes for tariff bills and other things from which contributions might come, things of that kind.

THE PRESIDENT:  Votes?

Q:   Votes on tariff bills and legislation from which contributions come to members of Congress or to the political committees?

THE PRESIDENT:  Give me an example.

Q:   I mean to say, when they put tariff rates in, you can expect that those who benefit will contribute to the political campaign funds.

THE PRESIDENT:  It is the same thing as if they were doing it for political favors.  It is awfully difficult to draw a hard and fast line, but the principle is apparently clear.

Q:   Mr. President, do you think this law will prevent public officials of either party from holding an office in the party?

THE PRESIDENT:  Oh, you mean Jim Farley?  (Laughter)

Q:   Not particularly, Mr. President.  (Laughter)

THE PRESIDENT:  I do not know why party officials should hold public office except, in the case of the Chairman of the National Committee, your Postmaster General might be called the political Pooh-Bah of the party.  I do not think it is good and -- this is still off the record -- Jim (Mr. Farley) has felt all long that he ought to get out as Chairman of the National Committee.  It has been a question of finding someone to take his place.  The chief reason for having that particular assignment to the Post Office is that in the old days the postmasterships were the principal things in patronage that the Government had.  I do not think it is a good thing.  I think it is one of the things we should get rid of as

--- [94] ---

soon as we can.  That does not mean that Jim should get out.

Q:   Senator Borah has introduced a bill which would prevent Senators and Representatives from representing a client in any court if that client had business before the Government.  For instance, he says that if a Representative or Senator is retained for $10,000. in one particular case, it is much easier for him to vote for something that affects a client, although that particular case had nothing to do with it.  Your idea would include something like that?

THE PRESIDENT:  Yes.

Q:   Can you tell us anything about the Johnson Bill that would prevent the issuance of bonds of a defaulting country?

THE PRESIDENT:  Yes.  That question came up Wednesday.  I am not ready to shoot on it.  I am studying the bill with great care.

Q:   There is a report around -- I don't know where it originated -- that you favor handling the stabilization funds on the basis of a three-year operation.

THE PRESIDENT:  I think we are a little ahead on that story.  You had better wait until the bill comes out of the Committee, and I think you will see that there is a perfectly satisfactory clause in it.  In other words, on this question of stabilization fund -- and I think you had better wait

because I am telling stories on it out of school, since it should wait until they make their report -- there has been a feeling that the actual
operation of the fund should be secret without any question. But, at the
same time, there should be some thought of making a report to Congress at
some future date on the status of the fund. That is not the operation of
the

--- [95] ---

fund, but the status. When that report is made to Congress on the broad
status of the fund, they would then be in a position to determine whether
they wanted to terminate the fund or not. I think you will find that the
amendment which they bring in to the bill as it was originally drawn will
carry that thought out. We will have a report a little bit later on and I
think three years is a pretty good guess.

Q:    Obviously, there would not be any publicity given to the operation; that
      would defeat the whole purpose?

THE PRESIDENT: Yes, but it is perfectly all right that Congress should get a
      report on the general status and then have the right to say that they are
      going to cut it off.

Q:    How many people would share the secret of the fund operation? It will be
      controlled by the Secretary of the Treasury, and of course he would report
      to you?

THE PRESIDENT: Yes.

Q:    Would there be a board set up to handle it in addition to the Secretary of
      the Treasury.

THE PRESIDENT:  I don't know. That is a matter of mechanics as to how many peo-
      ple? The fewer the better, from the publicity viewpoint.

Q:    In that connection, did you read Walter Lippmann this morning?

THE PRESIDENT: Yes.

Q:    What do you think of control by a high monetary court instead of by the
      Congress or the President?

THE PRESIDENT:  I don't think any human being can tell what ought to be done
      until we get some experience on it. It may be a perfectly pious idea of
      Walter's, but I don't think we can tell until we see

--- [96] ---

how the working of the fund is carried out. It may come to something like
that.

Q:    Mr. President, is there anything to be said about the Finance Committee?

THE PRESIDENT:  I am talking to the Secretary of the Treasury on Monday evening
      about it, not until then.

Q:    On the stabilization fund, will its operations as to purchase and sale of
      Government bonds also be a secret, or will that be made public?

THE PRESIDENT: That, frankly, I don't know.

Q: The use of funds of other Government agencies is made public.

THE PRESIDENT: I don't think it would be of necessity. It may be decided to make it public, but I don't think it is provided for.

Q: Mr. President, are you still of the opinion that only 5% of the 15% pay cut should be restored?

THE PRESIDENT: At this time. In other words, we are basing the thing on the determination by the Congress last year that the cost of living should enter into consideration. The cost of living figures, as you know, indicate that there has been a very slight increase and that increase has not brought it up to the minus 15%. It is still 21% minus.

Q: Anything on the extension of C.W.A. beyond May first?

THE PRESIDENT: The bill will be ready on -- oh, you mean May first?

Q: Yes, sir.

THE PRESIDENT: No. The bill will be ready on Monday.

Q: Any developments in sugar, Mr. President?

THE PRESIDENT: No sugar today.

--- [97] ---

Q: Mr. President, is it your idea that after February fifteenth or after February tenth, if the money is given by Congress, that they will go back to the 30-hour work week in C.W.A.?

THE PRESIDENT: I think it depends largely on the district or locality.

Q: There might be a readjustment with respect to localities, depending on the condition?

THE PRESIDENT: Depending on the condition at the time.

Q: Does that mean as between urban and rural or by locality?

THE PRESIDENT: It depends entirely on the locality. In some cases it would be urban and in some cases rural.

Q: Has Roper presented his report on stock exchange regulations?

THE PRESIDENT: He is bringing that in Monday, also the Securities Bill.

Q: Mr. President, will that include the Communications report at the same time; I think that is ready?

THE PRESIDENT: I don't know; I did not ask him about that.

Q: Mr. President, did you say that there will be a Securities Bill?

THE PRESIDENT: No, I did not. But his Committee has been studying not only the stock exchange end but the securities end and the problem of the investment banker. For instance, a firm which is engaged in buying and selling securities, in other words, as a broker, is, at the same time, an investment banker, and at the same time runs an investment corporation. Now that kind of a firm has three functions and the question has come up as to how one firm can conduct all three functions at the same time without letting his right hand know what his left foot is doing.

Q:  Mr. President, can you tell us anything about your talk today with Whitney and the other railroad men? They were very silent when

--- [98] ---

they went out of here today.

THE PRESIDENT: We talked about two things. One was, tentatively about the 10% railroad pay reduction, which does not come to a head until sometime in the spring. We just talked about it in very general terms. The other subject was the St. Lawrence. I pointed out, in the case of the St. Lawrence, that whether the Treaty was ratified or not the seaway without any question would be built, and that it could be built by Canada without entering into United States territory at all and without building a dam. All they would need would be some locks.

Q:  Thank you, Mr. President.

CONFIDENTIAL
Press Conference #91
Executive Offices of the White House
January 24, 1934, 10:45 A.M.


MR. DONALDSON:  All in.

THE PRESIDENT:  I think I can save time by telling you what is not news.  The
    Secretary of Commerce gave me yesterday the report of the Committee which
    has been studying stock exchange regulations.  I have not read it yet but
    as soon as I have I am going to send it up to the proper Committees in the
    in the Congress for their information.  That does not mean that it is an
    Administration proposal or policy or anything else.  I say that before I
    have read it, so it is perfectly safe.  It may be all right and it may not.
    It is merely for the information of the Committees and I will tell them
    that after they have read it and have gone over the suggestions made by
    their own people, I will be glad to see them and talk over the whole sub-
    ject before we come to a determination of policy.  The same thing applies
    to communications.  That report also came from the Secretary of Commerce
    and I am sending it on in exactly the same way for the information of the
    Congressional Committees.

    The liquor bill for the District of Columbia is sitting here on my desk.
    I have not taken it up as yet.

Q:   Are you going to do it today?

THE PRESIDENT:  I hope to do it today.  If I get a free afternoon, I hope to
    make the basket look more respectable.

Q:   The sooner the better on that, Mr. President.

Q:   Do you have any ceremony?

THE PRESIDENT:  No.

                          --- [100] ---

Q:   Any new developments in the pay cut situation?

THE PRESIDENT:  No, Count (Rudolph De Zappe), I do not think there is another
    thing.

    Then, on the currency bill, Mr. Morgenthau just this moment handed me the
    bill marked with the Senate Committee amendments and I have not had a
    chance to read it yet, so I cannot say anything about it as I have not read
    the amendments.

Q:   Did the Secretary make any comment on them?

THE PRESIDENT:  No, just gave me the bill.

Q:   Yesterday Senator Tydings, after his Committee had acted on the Hawes-Cut-
    ting Bill, issued a statement favoring the extension of seven months on
    the Hawes-Cutting Treaty.

THE PRESIDENT:  There again, it is first in the basket.  I have a written memorandum from Manuel Quezon, who is, I think, talking with the Secretary of War about it this week. And I won't do a single thing until I have talked with the Secretary of War. I haven't said yes or not to any proposal. I have not even talked to Senator Tydings about it except that I did talk to Senator Cutting last week in regard to extending the life before last Wednesday, the day it was to expire, and we both agreed it was not necessary to extend the life before last Wednesday, that it would be done later if we decided to do it.

Q:   Among other things that Senator Tydings said yesterday was that after the new election if the Legislature again failed to take action, or action adversely, it would be notice to Congress that the Filipinos do not desire independence and would be willing to continue under the present status.

--- [101] ---

THE PRESIDENT:  No, nothing to say.

Q:   Does the Stock Exchange regulation include the Grain Exchange?

THE PRESIDENT:  I have not read it.  I wish I could tell you.

Q:   Do you anticipate any Congressional action on that matter this session?

THE PRESIDENT:  On which?

Q:   The Stock Exchange regulation?

THE PRESIDENT:  I hope so.  It is one of the planks of the Democratic platform which has not yet been fulfilled.

Q:   Mr. President, can you tell us anything as yet as to when you will be ready to talk over the Platt amendment with Cuba?

THE PRESIDENT:  No, because there has not been time since four o'clock yesterday afternoon to talk that over at all.  Nothing has been done on it.

Q:   Is there anything you can tell us about the Newspaper Code?

THE PRESIDENT:  That is sitting on my other desk.

Q:   Is that likely to be reached at all?

THE PRESIDENT:  I hope to get at it this week if I get out of this jam a bit.

Q:   In that connection, the Newspaper Guild has protested against Ralph Pulitzer as the administrator of the Code.  Have you received that?

THE PRESIDENT:  No.

Q:   Care to comment on it?

THE PRESIDENT:  No,  What is it based on?

Q:   I do not know; I did not get a chance to read it.  I just know they have.

--- [102] ---

Q:    Dispatches from Tokyo indicate the Japanese Government has approached our
      Government with a view to settling disputes which will occur in the next
      two years, meaning the naval question.  Have you received any information
      to that effect?

THE PRESIDENT:  Nothing done on the preliminaries of the naval conference at all.

Q:    Can you tell us anything more about the proposed guarantee of the Home Loan
      Bank bonds?

THE PRESIDENT:  Yes.  They were in yesterday afternoon and the bill for the guar-
      antee of the bonds will be substantially the same as the Farm Credit guar-
      antee bill.  They also have another question under consideration and that
      is the need that the Home Loan Board feels for additional lending power to
      finance improvements in homes, the rebuilding of existing homes, with the
      thought that it would take up quite a good deal of slack in the building
      trades and put a good many people to work.  That is being studied now as to
      the necessity for it and also as to where the money would come from, wheth-
      er it would be an expansion of the two-billion-dollar borrowing power or
      bond issuing power or whether it should be done through some other form of
      financing.

Q:    Has any figure been mentioned?

THE PRESIDENT:  I think $250,000,000.

Q:    Additional?

THE PRESIDENT:  Yes.

Q:    Mr. President --

THE PRESIDENT:  (interposing)  It is merely in the study stage.

Q:    Any change in the decision to stop the C.W.A. on May first?

--- [103] ---

THE PRESIDENT:  No.

Q:    You are going to ask for additional funds?

THE PRESIDENT:  Additional $350,000,000.

Q:    Does that go up today?

THE PRESIDENT:  Lew (Lewis Douglas, Director of the Budget) said yesterday after-
      noon he would have it today, and $500,000,000 for the following fiscal year.

Q:    For C.W.A.?

THE PRESIDENT:  No, for relief which, of course, could be used through a C.W.A.
      method, at least in part.  In other words, we are not going -- on the re-
      lief question we cannot determine at this time what the necessities and
      needs will be next autumn and next winter.  We have got to have a certain
      amount of flexibility in there.

Q:    In that connection, have you any reports that might throw any light on the expected absorption of these C.W.A. workers during this spring?

THE PRESIDENT: Only such a vague figures at this time that it is awfully hard
to put them down. I would put it this way: that we hope, through the
actual operation of the P.W.A. funds and also through the hoped for pickup
in industry, and also through the seasonal reemployment as, for instance,
in the South, crop planting, and in the West, general farming operations
to take up a large portion, at least a majority, of the people who are on
the C.W.A. That does not mean that all of them will be taken up through
those other methods. I hesitate to use figures because

--- [104] ---

it is still in the guess stage.

Q: Mr. President, would you comment on Coordinator Eastman's conclusions that,
if possible, Government ownership would be the best solution of the railroad problem?

THE PRESIDENT: I do not think I had better because he has -- how many more?

Q: Two more.

THE PRESIDENT: Two more reports coming in. I think I had better wait.

Q: He has not been over to see you since last week?

THE PRESIDENT: No, he has not been over to see me since last week.

Q: On the C.W.A., have these stories of graft been called to your attention?

THE PRESIDENT: I suppose ever since the first week it was organized we have had
an average of several hundred letters a day, most of them political protests that the local agencies, which, of course, means local government,
have been using the C.W.A. funds to build up political machines or to favor
people belonging to one party or the other. I should say those protests
are equally divided between Republican and Democratic politicians, and if
I have had two or three hundred a day, probably Harry Hopkins has had two
or three thousand a day. We are getting after them as soon as we possibly
can.

Obviously, on the C.W.A., the actual operation of the thing is in the hands
of the local government and the keeping out of graft in the actual administration, the keeping out of politics, depends on the quality of the local
government. We are doing everything we can not only to run down specific
cases

--- [105] ---

but also to get the idea abroad in different communities that the thing
ought to be kept out of politics.

Q: Mr. President, is there any undermining of the Federal Reserve System in
giving the Secretary of the Treasury central banking powers?

THE PRESIDENT: No. What do you mean, central banking powers?

Q: This bill is supposed to give banking powers to the Secretary of the

Treasury?

THE PRESIDENT: Oh, no; it does not give the Secretary of the Treasury any central banking powers and it does not undermine the Federal Reserve System.

Q: Any comments on the downfall of Huey Long?

THE PRESIDENT: No. (Laughter) Stevie (Stephenson), the only thing I can say is that it is a local matter. (Laughter)

Q: So far. (Laughter)

THE PRESIDENT: That is not for the record.

Q: On those Home Loan bonds, will provision be made for guaranteeing the principal of bonds already outstanding as with the Farm bonds?

THE PRESIDENT: I think so, but I would not swear to it; I think so.

Q: Some of those bonds are already in the hands of the investing public. Will those be guaranteed?

THE PRESIDENT: I don't see how we can discriminate between them.

Q: Your statement, issued at the time the German Ambassador was here, mentioned the German trade. Can you explain that for us?

THE PRESIDENT: Only as a matter of theory. I told them just what I told a great many other people, that the ultimate ideal, the ultimate objective was for every nation's trade to be on a

--- [106] ---

balanced basis, so that the total income from foreign ports equalled the total outgo to foreign ports, with the world objective of eliminating these large favorable or unfavorable trade balances that have to be paid in gold from time to time. That being so, in the case of Germany, for example, we would be perfectly willing to discuss with them the question first as to whether the trade between Germany and America, both ways, is out of balance or not. The thing has never been studied. We don't know until we actually make a complete study whether we actually export more goods to Germany than we receive from Germany. We have never explored the other side of the picture -- the invisible exports of money from this country to Germany through the tourist trade, remittances by immigrants, and so forth.

The first step is to get figures along that line and then, if it appears that there is a balance, favorable or unfavorable, one way or the other, the time will come to try to correct that through purchases on the debit side of the ledger.

Q: Mr. President, is the Government giving its support to the American representatives to the Debt Conference?

THE PRESIDENT: Yes and no. They are private individuals; one of them is a classmate of mine. They are private individuals but, at the same time, we have said perfectly clearly to the German Ambassador and also to our Ambassador on the other side that we are anticipating the same kind of

treatment, without discrimination, that other nations are getting. There
has been a great deal of complaint, as everybody knows, about discrimination. Switzerland and Holland are being paid approximately 100% on the

--- [107] ---

debts that are due their citizens by German municipalities and states and
corporations, as against other nations that are getting only 50% in cash
and scrip for the other 50% which, when you come to cash it, only works
out at 25%. We were disturbed, Great Britain was disturbed, and other
nations, by the suggestion from Berlin that this 50% cash payment would be
further reduced to 30 or 35%. That is all we have done.

Q:  Mr. President, the special treatment to Holland and Switzerland followed
    threats of retaliation by them. Have we gone as far as that?

THE PRESIDENT:  No.

Q:  Can you tell us what the German Ambassador said in reply to your represen-
    tations concerning discrimination against Americans?

THE PRESIDENT:  I think you had better ask him.

Q:  We did, Mr. President. (Laughter)

THE PRESIDENT:  Of course, off the record -- I think you had better use it as
    background as long as you do not attribute it to me in any way -- the
    theory of the German Ambassador and German Government is a theory which
    is somewhat difficult to understand. It goes along this line: That if
    they pay 100 cents on the dollar to Switzerland and Holland creditors,
    eventually, some day in the future, the general economic situation will be
    so much better that they will be able to pay 100 cents on the dollar to
    other people. The best word to use is an unbalanced theory that does not
    bring much cash into one's pockets.

Q:  In that connection, is there anything to be said on the rumor that the
    German Government is buying bonds at the present low prices?

--- [108] ---

THE PRESIDENT:  That has been stated. It has been stated that as high as five
    hundred million dollars of German bonds in this country have already been
    bought up at away below par. I don't know whether that is true or not. I
    don't know whether anybody has checked.

Q:  It has been checked, and the statement has been found to be accurate. In
    the last year, 1932, they are supposed to have bought up a good deal more
    than the equivalent interest payments would have been had they met their
    various payments due on obligations.

THE PRESIDENT:  Yes?

Q:  In connection with the debts, Secretary Morgenthau, at the hearing, is
    quoted as saying that the responsibility has been transferred back from
    the Treasury to the State Department. Is there any significance in that?

THE PRESIDENT:  No.

Q:  Your communication to Congress on C.W.A. will take the form of a message or letter to the Committee?

THE PRESIDENT:  I don't know, Fred (Mr. Storm).  I don't know that I will send anything up myself.  In other words, it was in the budget, and I think probably everybody knows all about it.  Probably Lew Douglas will just go up there and explain it to them.  Possibly I may have to send a letter of transmittal to the Committee.

Q:  Did you get a chance to read Prime Minister MacDonald's speech this morning in which he suggested stabilization of the currencies?

THE PRESIDENT:  Off the record, I have read it; on the record, I have not. (Laughter)

Q:  Thank you, Mr. President.


(The Press Conference adjourned at 11:00 A.M.)

Press Conference #92
Executive Offices of the White House
January 26, 1934, 4:05 P.M.

Q:  Stevie (Mr. Stephenson) was almost killed in the grand rush, Mr. President.

THE PRESIDENT:  I think I ought to assign a Marine guard to him.

Q:  I think he can take care of himself, Mr. President.

THE PRESIDENT:  You think so?

Q:  I think so; he can carry the ball right along.

THE PRESIDENT:  He is getting to be a smart guy.  (Laughter)

MR. DONALDSON:  All in.

THE PRESIDENT:  I have a rather important piece of news:  The ladies have been
in to see me and they want a special stamp for Mother's Day.  All the
sportsmen of the country are united behind a duck stamp bill.

Q:  What is this, stamp day?

THE PRESIDENT:  No, you stamp the duck.

Q:  Try to do it.  (Laughter)

THE PRESIDENT:  That is all I know.

Q:  Have you any comment on controlling cotton at the gin -- the production of
cotton?

THE PRESIDENT:  No.  I think that the Department of Agriculture is sending out
a questionnaire to try to get the general sentiments of the cotton growers
as to whether there should be a more specific control over acreage and if
so what form that control should take.  If any other further control is
adopted, there arises the question of which of two forms should be followed.  I talked to Senator Bankhead and the others about this.  One

--- [110] ---

form is the method of licensing the individual farmer to a certain, definite amount.  The other form is arriving exactly at the same result through
taxation at the gin, with a rebate to the quota amount.

I think it is largely, as between those two methods, a matter of legal
opinion and a good many people feel that the taxing method would stand up
more readily in court than a straight licensing proposition.  I think that
Senator Bankhead is entirely willing to have that position taken, perhaps
as an amendment to his bill.  You arrive at the same result.  It is merely
a matter of difference in machinery.

Q:  Do you believe that some action along that line is necessary?

THE PRESIDENT:  There again it is a bit too early to tell.  I am inclined to

think we may have to come to it.  But, if we do come to it, we want to come
to it, if possible, with the general approval of the cotton growers themselves, which I think we will get.  There are two reasons for it and because of the two reasons, it is not yet clear.  The first is that the man
who restricts his acreage may put in more fertilizer and get as much cotton
as he did before.  The other is the factor of new acreage which has never
been planted to cotton being brought in.

Q:  The taxation plan will not take cotton out of production, will it?  The
farmer can grow as much as he wants to if he is merely taxed for the over-
supply?

THE PRESIDENT:  Well, he is not going to grow a lot of cotton if he has to pay
a tax on it.

Q:  How about wheat and the others?

--- [111] ---

THE PRESIDENT:  Well, that is too far off.  In other words, we are feeling our
way on the general theory of trying to bring total production within the
limits of total consumption.

Q:  Reports are printed today that you have named or will name individual
experts for virtually each major country on foreign exchange when the stabilization fund becomes operative.

THE PRESIDENT:  That is a new one on me.

Q:  It is on the front pages of the papers today.

THE PRESIDENT:  Probably what that story arose from was that somebody was down
here a couple of days ago and wanted to know about the proposed monetary
commission and I think I casually remarked that of course we would have
people to keep us in touch with the actual facts on exchange in probably
a dozen different centers of exchange including, I think I used the words,
"including Shanghai."  And probably whoever I told it to -- I have forgotten who it was -- announced that I was going to have fifty experts centered
all over the world.

Q:  Can you tell us when you are going to ask for money for the recovery agencies for the rest of this year, the $1,166,000,000. or part of it?

THE PRESIDENT:  The situation is, I think they are up on the Hill today, trying
to find out whether the leaders in the House and Senate would rather have
the appropriation bills in the form of one bill or two bills or a multi-
plicity of bills.  It is largely a question of the jurisdiction of the
different committees.  A general bill would have so many different matters
that would fall under the jurisdiction of so many different committees
that we want to find out really what they want to have on the bill before
we decide on the form of the bill or bills.  Lew (Mr. Douglas)

--- [112] ---

will probably let me know about it tonight or tomorrow morning.  The bill
or bills will go up in the next few days.

Q:  The amount is still the same, regardless?

THE PRESIDENT:  $1,166,000,000. plus $2,000,000,000.

Q:  The liquor trade negotiators tell us that they believe the liquor quota system will be continued after March first.  Is that correct?

THE PRESIDENT:  I do not know anything about liquor.

Q:  I understand under Section 5 of the Economy Act, you have powers to modify or cancel the airmail contracts.  Has that possibility been discussed?

THE PRESIDENT:  The first time was at lunch today when Hugo Black was down here and told me I had that authority.  I did not know it.

Q:  Are you glad you have it?

THE PRESIDENT:  Yes.

Q:  Did you discuss the airmail situation with the Postmaster General?

THE PRESIDENT:  No, I talked it over wtih Senator Black.

Q:  Have you decided whether you will send that Special Message for grazing control legislation?

THE PRESIDENT:  What did happen on that was that I talked with the Secretaries of Interior and Agriculture about that yesterday and I have forgotten what we decided.  (Laughter)  There is, as I remember it, there is a bill up there, the Taylor Bill.

Q:  Right.

THE PRESIDENT:  And they both agreed that that is a pretty good bill and I asked the two of them to give me a letter on the subject and undoubtedly it will result in a letter from me to whatever Committee is in charge of that bill.

Q:  Is there anything further in the Weirton case?

--- [113] ---

THE PRESIDENT:  I have not heard a word, not a word.

Q:  Is there anything new in the C.W.A. charges of graft in that situation?

THE PRESIDENT:  No, I have not heard anything more.  They are investigating every charge and it costs quite a lot of money too.

Q:  There is a bill providing for the control of exchanges, providing for the Administration's views, that is being drawn up, providing for control by the Federal Trade Commission?

THE PRESIDENT:  The control of exchanges?

Q:  The issuance of securities?

THE PRESIDENT:  I don't know; I never heard of it.

Q:  Mr. Landis, I believe, is supposed to be working on it?

THE PRESIDENT: I do not believe there is any bill. I know he has been working on the thing and these various reports of Roper's committees were sent up without recommendation -- we just put them in.

Q: Have the Newspaper Codes been signed as yet?

THE PRESIDENT: I have not looked at it since I saw you last.

Q: Any recent developments in the Administration's sugar program?

THE PRESIDENT: No; haven't taken that up at all.

Q: Anything you can tell us about today's patronage meeting?

THE PRESIDENT: We had a very nice hour. (Laughter)

Q: They left here smiling.

Q: Jim Farley said it was a great social success. (Laughter)

THE PRESIDENT: I suggested a number of things to do. The first was that they should continue and not disband. They should act as a clearing house and, secondly, on the question of complaints, that the complaints should be made as specific as possible. It is

--- [114] ---

impossible to investigate a perfectly general complaint but, as to a specific complaint, we would be quite willing to go into it.

Q: The recognition of Salvador has started talk of the possibility of the United States going into Pan America and recognizing revolutionary governments as set up in --

THE PRESIDENT: (interposing) There isn't anything on that at all. The only thing, as I remember it, is that the three Central American Governments, which were still bound by the old non-recognition treaties -- you see, Costa Rica had withdrawn and Salvador practically had taken itself out, and the three that were still bound decided to make this recognition of the present Salvador Government immediately, and then call together a conference of the five republics in order to discuss a new agreement relating to recognition. Of course, our policy there has been to go along with the Central American policies. We were not a signatory of that previous treaty but we said as long as that is the general rule in Central America, we would adopt the same policy. That is all that happened.

Q: No change.

THE PRESIDENT: No. There is, as I understand it, going to be a meeting of the five governments after recognition of Salvador.

Q: Are you any nearer the tariff Message to the Congress?

THE PRESIDENT: No.

Q: How about war debts?

THE PRESIDENT: The only thing we are nearer on is that I have to ask the

Secretary of State to bring himself up to date on the reports that were made during his absence.

--- [115] ---

Q:   I have one more inquiry on money here. The dollar, you know, is getting stronger every day and closed at 4.94 to the pound in London today. Is there anything of special significance on our monetary program?

THE PRESIDENT:  Not that I know of.

Q:   We have reports that unusually large amounts of foreign money are coming into this country presumably for investment purposes and there is a report that one company is offering $60,000,000. in securities on the London market. Has that any particular connection?

THE PRESIDENT:  I think probably you had better ask Henry Morgenthau about it. I think that some of the gold that we have been purchasing on the other side is coming back to this country in the form of bars.

Q:   Paris is clearing out fifteen millions a day, mostly sent to this country.

Q:   Have you any ideas about unifying the military air forces of the Government under one separate Air Corps command?

THE PRESIDENT:  Haven't thought of it.

Q:   Can you give us any details on Senator Black's visit?

THE PRESIDENT:  No. We talked over the general work of his Committee and he told me he hoped to be able to make a preliminary report within a month. He also told me that they would not have covered all the ground by that time and I told him I hoped very much that he would cover all the ground before he got through.

Q:   In that connection, do you think it is necessary to use the authority you have over these airmail contracts that you found out about

--- [116] ---

today?

THE PRESIDENT:  Well, as I say, I did not hear about it until lunch-time. I do not know any details. He told me that in his judgment, most of the present inequalities and troubles with the airmail as well as the ship mail could be corrected by Executive Order but probably some legislation will be needed -- that most of the trouble could be corrected by Executive Order.

Q:   That would indicate the cancellation of contracts here and there?

THE PRESIDENT:  Yes.

Q:   I suppose you are looking into the matter of making a further examination of it, sir?

THE PRESIDENT:  I am sort of waiting for the report of the Black Committee because we haven't any report of recommendations on it at all. And, of course, tied up with that is the general subject that came up way back in the 1932 Campaign, that some effort be made on the part of Government to coordinate the transportation end.  If you will read the Salt Lake City speech, you will see what the object is, to coordinate all transportation, which means railroads, air, canals, waterways and shipping under some directing body, which would possibly mean the giving of added jurisdiction to the I.C.C.; in other words, building up the I.C.C.  Whether we will be ready for the legislation at this session of the Congress, I do not know. In other words, I do not know whether we can carry it all through this year or through the winter.  It is a pretty big and complicated subject.

Q:  I understand the Postmaster General is making an investigation and report to you on aviation.

THE PRESIDENT:  He isn't through.

--- [117] ---

Q:  Mr. President, you told us about Douglas (Lewis Douglas, Director of the Budget) being on the Hill on a number of bills relating to emergency appropriations for P.W.A. or C.W.A.  Can you tell us anything further?

THE PRESIDENT:  We are waiting to find out today.  The first form that came to me on it was a draft message and a different bill for each item and I think we can save time and trouble if we cut it down to a smaller number of bills.

Q:  Mr. President, any progress on trade talks with Russia?

THE PRESIDENT:  With Russia?

Q:  Anything on it?

THE PRESIDENT:  I think that is rather a separate thing.

Q:  Any talk at all?

THE PRESIDENT:  No.

Q:  Mr. President, would you care to tell us what you told the Democrats today at this patronage conference?

THE PRESIDENT:  They were here about an hour and they talked fifty minutes and I talked ten.

Q:  Mr. President, have you done anything with respect to the vacancy on the Power Commission?

THE PRESIDENT:  Power Commission?  No, I have not.  They were down the other day and I asked them to make suggestions and I have not heard anything further.

Q:  Thank you, Mr. President.

THE PRESIDENT:  Put the lid on until Monday.

Q:  The last time you put the lid on we had to stand out in front of the White House until twelve midnight.

Press Conference #93
Executive Offices of the White House
January 31, 1934, 4:15 P.M.


Q:  Mr. President, did you have a good birthday?

THE PRESIDENT:  Louis (Mr. Howe) isn't up yet.  (Laughter)

Q:  (Mr. Stephenson)  Steve (Mr. Early) can't say a whole lot.  (Laughter)

MR. McINTYRE:  I gave Steve the cigar this morning.

THE PRESIDENT:  I am glad you smoked it.  I thought you were a little green
    around the gills.

MR. DONALDSON:  All in.

THE PRESIDENT:  Will you please not go out for five minutes.  It will be a very
    short conference because I would very much like to have you all get this
    on the wires as soon as possible.  The reason for this haste is that the
    gold market over here stays open until five or half-past and it will pro-
    bably be advantageous for the American gold market to be open instead of
    having this operate only on the European gold market tomorrow morning.
    Therefore, the quicker you get it out the better I will be pleased.

    We have fixed at 3:10 this afternoon, by proclamation, the weight of the
    gold dollar at 15 5/21 grains of gold, nine tenths fine.

Q:  Is that 15.5/21?

THE PRESIDENT:  No, it is 15 5/21.  This is the equivalent of 59.06-plus.  In
    other words, it figures on a mathematical basis to 59.06-plus of the for-
    mer weight of 25 8/10 grains.

    The new gold content of the dollar became effective the moment I signed
    the proclamation at 3:10 P.M.

                    --- [119] ---

We will have a mimeographed statement for you later on, but this is just
a flash.

Number two, the Secretary of the Treasury with the approval of the President, has issued a public announcement that beginning on February first,
tomorrow, he will buy through the Federal Reserve Bank of New York, as
fiscal agent for the account of the United States, any and all gold --
that is not just American-produced, that is any and all gold -- delivered
to the United States mint or the Assay Offices in New York or Seattle at
the rate of $35 per fine troy ounce, less the usual mint charges and less
one-quarter of one per cent for handling charges.

The purchases are to be in compliance with the regulations and are to
continue until further notice.

Then there are a lot of more details in here which you can keep for your
main stories.  Steve (Mr. Early) will have them for you very soon.  I don't

think there is any other important news.

Q:   There is something of importance to Washington in the report that the
     Senate Committee is putting in the five per cent pay restoration on
     February first?

THE PRESIDENT:  I have not heard a word on it.

Q:   That would be the independent appropriation bill.

THE PRESIDENT:  I have not heard a word about it.

Q:   Mr. Farley said the other day that he thought you would discuss the atti-
     tude towards National Committeemen?

THE PRESIDENT:  I am going to have a talk with Jim Byrnes and Norris and
     Vandenberg and one or two others in the next few days.

Q:   Can you tell us about your flood control conference you had here?

--- [120] ---

THE PRESIDENT:  It was preliminary; we are going to meet again.  We talked
     about flood control from the point of view of national planning with the
     general thought that we would try to work out a national plan in the
     larger aspect that would list the various rivers and flood control pro-
     jects in the order of their necessity; that is, on the order of damage
     done, human beings affected, property affected, et cetera.  But that is
     as far as we got, discussing national planning for flood control and all
     the things that go with it, power, reclamation, submarginal lands and
     everything else.

Q:   Can you tell us anything of the Newspaper Code?  Has that been signed?

THE PRESIDENT:  No.

Q:   Have you received protest from the Guild relative to Mr. Pulitzer, et
     cetera?

THE PRESIDENT:  Yes; it is on my desk still.

Q:   In view of this gold action, do you contemplate any discussions with the
     British or other countries on stabilization?

THE PRESIDENT:  There have been absolutely no discussions at all and Henry
     Morgenthau is correct in saying that any questions on this won't be
     answered.

Q:   Does that apply here also?

THE PRESIDENT:  Yes.

Q:   Now that Secretary Hull is back, is there anything to say on the foreign
     trade plans?

THE PRESIDENT:  No; they are all working there on the various reports that have
     been made -- the State Department, the Department of Commerce, George Peek,
     et cetera, Agriculture -- and I have not seen him yet.

--- [121] ---

Q:  Is there any provision in the Secretary's regulations for purchasing gold, providing that gold illegally held under these hoarding orders will not be bought, or will it be bought?

THE PRESIDENT:  You will have to ask him.  There are so darned many that I could not tell you intelligently.

Q:  It is reported that you are going to send a Message to Congress on Home Owners' Loan Corporation.  Can you tell us when?

THE PRESIDENT:  Soon.  I do not know whether it will be Monday or not.  We have not anything drafted.  I talked to them yesterday.

Q:  Can you tell us anything about the Weirton steel situation?

THE PRESIDENT:  There is going to be some kind of an Executive Order from either NRA or the Labor Board or both, which I think will clarify the situation very much.

Q:  Will that come out today?

THE PRESIDENT:  I asked General Johnson to get it out as soon as he could.  I do not know whether it will be today or tomorrow morning.

Q:  What is the status of the Tariff Message?

THE PRESIDENT:  That also is being studied by the Secretary of State.  That goes along with the other thing, the general foreign trade.

Q:  Will there be a Tariff Message?

THE PRESIDENT:  I think so.

Q:  Is there anything further to be said regarding that German private debt situation?

THE PRESIDENT:  I have not seen a single report from the other side since their first meeting on Wednesday last, was it?

Q:  Thursday.

THE PRESIDENT:  Yes.

--- [122] ---

Q:  It is reported from Berlin that they have agreed not to reduce cash payments any more without conferring with the creditors, and also says that they will put it on a contractual basis.  Wasn't it our complaint that they were reducing cash payments without compensation?

THE PRESIDENT:  Our chief objection was that they were discriminating against creditors of one country against another.

Q:  That would not completely satisfy us?

THE PRESIDENT:  I do not know.  It depends on where they have the thing and whether they make the same terms with respect to all.

Q:   Mr. President, are there any further Executive Orders to place the stabilization fund in operation?

THE PRESIDENT:  I think it is all done.

Q:   It is all done with the signing of the Proclamation?

Q:   Do you care to add anything on the discussions of the Stock Market bill?

THE PRESIDENT:  Just discussing it, that is all.  I think they will be down to
talk from the Hill.  I asked them to confer.

Q:   Did any statisticians happen to figure out what the Treasury profit was
on the basis of this new figure?

THE PRESIDENT:  They haven't got to that yet.

Q:   That is just a bit over 40 per cent, isn't it?

THE PRESIDENT:  Yes.  40.94

Q:   Mr. President, will you tell us just why that particular figure was arrived
at?

THE PRESIDENT:  Purely because of higher mathematics.  We were faced with the
question of fixing it at some particular point which would

--- [123] ---

bring it out to a round figure per ounce of gold.  Thirty-five dollars an
ounce works out to 59.06.

Q:   In other words, you started out at $35 and worked backwards?

THE PRESIDENT:  Yes.

Q:   Was there any relaxation on the embargo on the export of gold?

THE PRESIDENT:  There again you have to read through the various orders.  Some
were Treasury orders and some were mine.

Q:   Has the order been signed creating the stabilization fund of two billion
dollars?  I suppose that goes with this.

THE PRESIDENT:  I don't think it has, but you had better check with Henry.
Maybe it doesn't have to be.

Q:  Thank you, Mr. President.

(The Press Conference adjourned at 4:25 P.M.)

Press Conference #94
Executive Offices of the White House
February 2, 1934, 10:50 A.M.


THE PRESIDENT: I think there is absolutely no news today.  It is a very good
Friday.  We will put the lid on again until Monday.  The last time I asked
you to put the lid on somebody thought that we had issued a national press
censorship.  (Laughter)

Q: I have just one question to ask:  Senator Byrnes, according to this
morning's Herald, said that you were in favor of the five per cent pay
restoration February first and July first but would object to the restoration of ten per cent on July first.

THE PRESIDENT: I have not said one thing about it one way or the other.  It is
still a pending matter up there (on the Hill).  I have not said a thing.

Q: Can you tell us something about the conversation late yesterday with Mr.
Jones (Jesse H. Jones, Chairman of the R.F.C.) and Mr. Bullitt (William
C. Bullitt of the State Department)?

THE PRESIDENT: I do not think I can.  I think you are a little ahead of time.
The machinery -- we have not decided on what kind of machinery we are
going to use for a certain purpose yet.

Wait a minute, I think I can -- I don't know, you had better see Jones
about it but I can tell you what it is about.  There is no reason why I
should not tell you, off the record, what it is about.  Don't print the
thing until you have seen Jones.  We are probably going to organize some
kind of corporation, which may be a District banking corporation, in order
to establish certain -- I cannot think of what the word is -- endorsements
of loans to Russia.

--- [125] ---

It is not straight credit.

Q: Confined entirely to Russia?

THE PRESIDENT: That is the primary purpose.  But you had better get that from
Jesse because there was not a final decision on the form of the corporation
yesterday afternoon.

Q: Do you mean by that endorsement of loans a Government guarantee of the
loans to the American exporters?

THE PRESIDENT: Portions, yes.  It means, of course, the American exporter
would take some of the risk himself.  That is the general theory.

Q: Would that entail an amendment to the R.F.C. Act with respect to export
credits?

THE PRESIDENT: I do not think so.

Q: Mr. President, how much credit is contemplated, exactly?

THE PRESIDENT: That has not been discussed.

Q: Would it come under the Federal Reserve System? There is a provision in there?

THE PRESIDENT: I should think so. I think it is the kind of bank that the R.F.C., if I remember it, can take stock in. But, as I say, you must check with Jesse Jones on that first because I do not know enough about the actual details.

Q: In view of the fact that they are trying to get unanimous consent to vote on the St. Lawrence, is there anything you can say with reference to it?

THE PRESIDENT: Only that Senator Robinson told me yesterday that they are trying to get a unanimous consent vote in about a week. That is all right, so far as I am concerned.

Q: Norman H. Davis is in town studying disarmament over at the State

--- [126] ---

Department. In view of the fact that the British and Italians have made proposals, have you anything to say?

THE PRESIDENT: So far as I know, there has been no date set for the reconvening of the conference. There is a committee meeting which will decide on a date. I think that committee meeting is to be held on the fourth of February, day after tomorrow.

Q: The thirteenth.

THE PRESIDENT: It has been put off? Ask Davis.

Q: In connection with that, both the British and the Italian proposals provide that -- our position as outlined by Secretary Hull is that we are opposed to any rearmament by any nation at the present time but in view of these other proposals, is it a safe proposition that if Europe agrees to let Germany rearm, we won't object?

THE PRESIDENT: I cannot say anything about it for the reason that since Geneva adjourned there heve been at least six different proposals and you can never tell whether they are coming through as definite and final proposals, and also the fact that they seem still to be in the realm of European politics rather than world disarmament. We made our position pretty clear on that. We draw the line and distinction between European political adjustments and world disarmament.

Q: Now that you have recognized Cuba, is there anything you can tell us on sugar?

THE PRESIDENT: I am talking with several people about that this afternoon. Of course the Philippine situation is also somewhat involved. We have not made any decision or found any plan different from the one we had a month ago or a week ago.

--- [127] ---

Q: Are you will working on the idea of quotas?

THE PRESIDENT: Yes, in general.

Q: Can you tell us with whom you are going to talk?

THE PRESIDENT: I think I am talking with -- I am having two talks, one with the Secretary of War around noon and with Senor Quezon around fifteen minutes later and, this afternoon, I think I am talking with Secretary Hull and Sumner Welles. This is just developing, that is all.

Q: To return to Russia, will this banking corporation handle any arrangement for mutual exchange of goods as well as credit?

THE PRESIDENT: That I do not know; I have not got as far as that at all.

Q: To clarify that a little bit more, is this along the lines of the plan suggested by Peek to you in his report?

THE PRESIDENT: It all ties in together.

Q: We still do not know what the Peek report is. That is the reason for the question.

THE PRESIDENT: That was only a very preliminary report, that is all. It ties in with so many departments, Agriculture, Commerce, State, et cetera. Probably over the week end or early in the week we will get to it.

Q: Have you had any conversations about Stock Exchange regulations?

THE PRESIDENT: No.

Q: Have you had any protests from the Japanese or others on the naval situation?

THE PRESIDENT: No, I have not heard a word.

Q: In that connection, Pan Pacific asks that you come to Tokyo when and if you go to Hawaii?

--- [128] ---

THE PRESIDENT: That is still perfectly vague. It depends on Congress and a lot of other things.

Q: I think he was saying that you have an invitation to go to Japan when you go to Hawaii.

THE PRESIDENT: No. It is a very grave question as to whether I can take enough time to go to Hawaii. You have to go straight up from the Canal to San Diego.

Q: This morning I noticed that in London the gold price has gone to $34.85. In view of that and the fact that they have substituted the American dollar in place of the French franc --

THE PRESIDENT: (interposing) Now you are getting on the subject we called "verboten," Fred (Mr. Storm).

Q: Do you care to say whether we are having any negotiations with Great

Britain -- (Laughter)

THE PRESIDENT: Stevie (Mr. Stephenson), we will consider that question as duly
asked and a "No" answer made from now on.

Q: (Mr. Stephenson) The sky is the limit.

Q: Mr. President, just before Congress was adjourned last summer, you appointed Huston Thompson on the question brought up by Senator Norris on the
power at Muscle Shoals. Has any report been made or is there anything
available to the Press? We have heard nothing of it since.

THE PRESIDENT: Gosh, it was so long ago that I have forgotten. Huston
Thompson made a report and, as I remember it, there was switching of power.

Q: Did that involve culpability on the part of the Army Engineers?

THE PRESIDENT: I do not think so but I think the methods have been

--- [129] ---

completely changed down there. Now that is just recollection on my part.

Q: Is there any way in which that might be made available to us, or is it
such a thing that we cannot get?

THE PRESIDENT: I do not know whether we are going into it further or not.

Q: The Army was much involved and one paper --

THE PRESIDENT: (interposing) So far as I know, there is no culpability fixed
on anyone. The best thing would be to ask the Attorney General or Huston
Thompson about it.

Q: So many of us have asked Huston and he refuses to say anything.

THE PRESIDENT: Ask Homer Cummings. I have not heard of it for three months.

Q: The term of the Quartermaster General expires tomorrow. Have you named
anyone to succeed him?

THE PRESIDENT: Have I, Steve? Steve (Mr. Early) says no.

Q: Have you determined whether or not you are going to give P.W.A. any more
than the $500,000,000.?

THE PRESIDENT: No. The allocation of those two sums, $1,166,000,000. and
$2,000,000,000., I am asking that they be left elastic as to the specific
allocation to items, depending on how the conditions develop next fall.
We cannot tell.

Q: Mr. President, when the Retail Food and Drug Act was introduced, it was
understood to be an Administration measure. After hearings, it was introduced in revised form. Now I understand it is to be revised again.

THE PRESIDENT: I think the only source of information should be the two

--- [130] ---

gentlemen, Dr. Copeland and Dr. Sirovich. Between the two of them I think
they have three or four bills and what will come out from them I do not
know.

Q:   What do you want?  (Laughter)

Q:   Is there any time when you will send up the tariff Message?

THE PRESIDENT:  No.

Q:   That has not been drawn completely?

THE PRESIDENT:  Not a bit.

Q:   Anything to say on the political aspects of the Philippine independence
     question?

THE PRESIDENT:  No.  I had a long memo -- I suppose that is the correct word
     for it -- from Senor Quezon.  Of course it is not a public memo, it just
     represented his own views.  I talked to the Secretary of War and the
     Bureau of Insular Affairs about it today and then we are talking, all of
     us, with Senor Quezon about it.  I have not had a chance to talk to
     either of them yet.

Q:   On tariff, do you intend to send a Message?

THE PRESIDENT:  On tariff?

Q:   Yes.

THE PRESIDENT:  I think there will be a Message.

Q:   You spoke about the allocations of these funds:  you are staying within
     the limits, that is $1,166,000,000. --

THE PRESIDENT:  (interposing)  Yes.

Q:   You won't go beyond that?

THE PRESIDENT:  Not if we can possibly help it.

MR. YOUNG:  Thank you, Mr. President.


                    (The Press Conference adjourned at 11:05 A.M.)

Press Conference #95
Executive Offices of the White House
February 7, 1934, 10:40 A.M.


Q:   How is Louis (Mr. Howe), Mr. President?

THE PRESIDENT:  Louis is better.  He was up yesterday, wandering around.

MR. DONALDSON:  All in.

THE PRESIDENT:  I don't think there is any news.  I have been having a spring
house cleaning with my basket at the White House for two days.

Q:   I would like to ask a question, Mr. President.

THE PRESIDENT:  Yes, Count (Rudolph De Zapp).

Q:   The West Virginia delegation, according to newspaper accounts, seems to
feel satisfied that their candidate has the inside track for appointment
as a member of the Public Utilities Commission.

THE PRESIDENT:  Ask Mac (Mr. McIntyre, Secretary to the President).  I have not
heard a word about it, not a word.  The last I did was about ten days ago
when I said to Mac, "I think we ought to do something about it," and that
is as far as we got.  We have not done a thing and have not discussed it
since then.

Q:   If you want to know a good man, I have --

THE PRESIDENT:  (interposing)  That is all right.

Q:   -- a very good man.

THE PRESIDENT:  Write it down on a slip of paper and fold it over twice and put
it in a hat.  (Laughter)

Q:   Mr. President, do you care to say anything about the announcement in the
Post (The Washington Post) this morning that your Emergency Council has
approved a larger appropriation for C.W.A. and direct

--- [132] ---

relief?

THE PRESIDENT:  Elliott Thurston gives me real information.  I had not heard a
word about it and have not yet.

Q:   Any publicity on income tax returns?

THE PRESIDENT:  That is unfinished business; I have not heard a word about it.

Q:   Any more agitation about the Securities Act?

THE PRESIDENT:  Has anything happened on it?  I have not heard a word.  I have
been practically out of the news the last two days and I have not seen
anybody about particular information.

Q:   That is it and we are trying to get back in.

THE PRESIDENT:   I have not heard a word about the Securities Act.

Q:   How about the Dickinson report?

THE PRESIDENT:   The one I sent up?  No, I have not seen the other one.

Q:   Are you going to issue a statement on sugar?

THE PRESIDENT:   I think maybe; I cannot tell you when.  It might even come this
    afternoon.  In other words, that is the top of the pile.  I want to do
    something about it.

Q:   Will there be a Message to the Congress or a statement?

THE PRESIDENT:   No, just a statement.

Q:   What will that statement say?  (Laughter)

THE PRESIDENT:   I have to take it off the top of the pile first.

Q:   Will that be accompanied by a bill?

THE PRESIDENT:   I do not think so.  Of course there is the bill to make sugar
    one of the basic commodities.

Q:   That is Costigan's (Senator Costigan) amendment?

THE PRESIDENT:   Yes.

--- [133] ---

Q:   I understood it might be necessary to introduce it in the House as the
    point of origin?

THE PRESIDENT:   I do not know yet.  I do not think anybody has decided on that
    yet.

Q:   That seems to be Joseph Robinson's (Senator Robinson) opinion on it the
    other day.  They think it should start there.

THE PRESIDENT:   You see, if it is made a basic commodity, we could put on a
    processing tax without any further legislation.

Q:   Can you make it a basic commodity under the terms of the Agricultural Ad-
    justment Act?

THE PRESIDENT:   No, we have to have legislation in order to make it a basic
    commodity.

Q:   Can you make it a basic commodity on the same terms as other crops of
    which we produce an exportable surplus?

THE PRESIDENT:   I think so.

Q:   Have you had any conferences with the leaders on the Hill on Stock Exchange
    regulation?

THE PRESIDENT: No, have not talked at all.

Q: They seem to be very much perturbed as to whether it will be in this session.

THE PRESIDENT: I have been for legislation in this session right along. It is in the platform. That Stock Exchange legislation has all been held up until the Senate Committee is ready to talk with me about it and we have not discussed it at all.

Q: I heard you might send in a bill Thursday or Friday?

THE PRESIDENT: Probably somewhere around the end of this week and the beginning of next week we will have a talk.

--- [134] ---

Q: Do you expect them to talk to you before they put the bill in?

THE PRESIDENT: That I do not know.

Q: Have you had any talk with Jesse Jones about the District banking corporation?

THE PRESIDENT: The Export-Import Corporation?

Q: Yes.

THE PRESIDENT: Well, it is in process.

Q: Is 2,000,000 tons a good guess for this Cuban sugar quota?

THE PRESIDENT: I won't start guessing. Just wait until this afternoon. I think I can get it out this afternoon.

Q: Mr. President, certain radical elements have adopted a recent article by Mr. Woodring as substantiation of their claim that the C.C.C. is what they call a "pacifist" army. In view of that, do you care to restate or say anything about the Administration's attitude toward the C.C.C., or comment on the Woodring article?

THE PRESIDENT: I have not. I have been very careful not to read it.

Q: It puts the C.C.C. as a great military achievement.

THE PRESIDENT: I heard about it and Steve (Mr. Early) got a large stack of petitions and things as a result of it. I think Steve and Harry Woodring are having a little conversation but I have not read the article. Of course it is perfectly obvious that the C.C.C. is not in the slightest degree militaristic. Anybody who sees them knows they are not.

Q: Can you give us any background on the events leading up to the Woodring and Silverman thing?

THE PRESIDENT: The only background I can give you -- I cannot give you anything definite because I do not know anything about it -- but

--- [135] ---

complaints came in from at least three or four different sources and they
seemed worthwhile investigating, so the whole thing was turned over to the
Department of Justice and, I think, the Senate Committee -- who was it had
them yesterday?

MR. EARLY:  The Department of Justice only -- the Grand Jury.

THE PRESIDENT:  They have had various people up there to ask questions and I
imagine, from what I hear from subterranean sources, that there is going
to be action pretty soon.

Q:  The investigation was ordered from the White House?

THE PRESIDENT:  It was not ordered from the White House.  I think some had already gone to the Department of Justice.  I told the Attorney General to
go ahead, naturally.

Q:  What was the character of the complaints?

THE PRESIDENT:  All sorts of allegations about the improper letting of contracts.

Q:  Mr. President, can you tell us anything about silver now that Morgenthau
is taking an account of stock?

THE PRESIDENT:  No, he is just checking up.

Q:  You don't care to say whether that presages anything?

THE PRESIDENT:  No.

Q:  As a result of your conversations with Bullitt, have you anything further
to say on Russian relations?

THE PRESIDENT:  There isn't any news on that except this new Import-Export Bank
which is in process of organization.  We have not even discussed the people to run it yet.

Q:  Have you anything to say about the Home Owners' Loan Corporation?

--- [136] ---

THE PRESIDENT:  That is now in the Treasury Department and we expect a report
tomorrow afternoon on it.

Q:  Mr. President, Mr. Woodring, in his article, advocated turning the C.C.C.,
the complete control, over to the Army.  Can we say there is no intention
of doing that?

THE PRESIDENT:  I think so.

Q:  Mr. President, you are going to read that article yet.  (Laughter)

Q:  (Mr. Storm) Anything further on the proposed tariff Message, Mr. President?

THE PRESIDENT:  No.  That is Stevie's (Mr. Stephenson) question, is it not?

Q:  (Mr. Stephenson) Yes, what is the idea?  (Laughter)

Q:  Have you had an opportunity to prepare your letters to the Congressional Committees on the Taylor Bill regarding control of grazing lands?

THE PRESIDENT:  No, I have not.  I will probably take action on that in the next two days.

Q:  Any further discussion of the possibility of an Executive Order with-drawing those lands pending such an investigation?

THE PRESIDENT:  I signed an Executive Order yesterday withdrawing a very large area and I couldn't tell you where that is, whether that is it or not, or whether it is part or the whole of it.  I signed an Executive Order yes-terday withdrawing 1,200,000 acres and you will have to check up and find where it was.

Q:  Have any other complaints come in to you about contracts in any other branch of the Government?

THE PRESIDENT:  Not that I know of.  There might be complaints in the

--- [137] ---

Department of Justice.  Of course we are going to follow them up, every one.

Q:  In connection with the alleged improper letting of War Department con-tracts, does that go back to past administrations?

THE PRESIDENT:  I think so; it goes all the way back -- how far, I do not know. But I think it comes right up to date.  I do not think it is only in the previous administration.

Q:  Senator Wagner suggests you tack $600,000,000 in gold revaluation onto C.W.A. in addition to the items given out on the Hill.  Have you given any consideration to that?

THE PRESIDENT:  No.

Q:  Mr. President, would you be willing for Congress to increase the amount of C.W.A.?  The proposal now is to increase it to two and a half billion.

THE PRESIDENT:  I believe in resting on the Message which went up.

Q:  Mr. President, I am writing something, generally, about the New Deal and there are four questions to which nobody has been able to give me answers. (Laughter)  Will you kindly give me something?  Namely, was America, after all, discovered, manufactured, deducted or invented?  (Laughter)

THE PRESIDENT:  I should say that America is in process of being perfected.

Q:  Thank you very much.

Q:  Mr. President, do you think it would aid the credit situation -- in other words, do you subscribe to this discussion in favor of capital instead of having an interest rate of six per cent, to reduce it to five per cent?

THE PRESIDENT:  What kind of capital?

--- [138] ---

Q:  The theory of reducing the general rate -- instead of having a basic six
per cent rate, reduce it to five?

THE PRESIDENT:  There isn't any six per cent rate.

Q:  The accepted rate of six per cent.

THE PRESIDENT:  Of course that is such a broad question, when you come to rates
of interest on money.

Q:  That is the topic.

THE PRESIDENT:  Perhaps I had better give you this as background, if you want.
The theory in the past has been that the rate varied with the security,
but, of course, that has not by any means been carried out in practice.
For example, in certain portions of the country -- the rural districts --
you cannot get a small mortgage loan on a farm for less than nine or ten
per cent, even if it is perfectly good security.  That means, immediately,
that your rule has gone overboard.  That is true, too, to a large extent
on real estate loans.  On perfectly good first mortgage loans, in some
sections and especially in rural districts, the interest rate will be infinitely higher than that on a city mortgage on a new building where the
security is not nearly as good.

On a great many of these new buildings that have gone up over the country
in the last ten years, the first mortgage was written at five, five and a
half per cent, and the security is not anywhere near as good as the small
town or farm mortgage where the interest charge is eight or ten per cent.

Of course, where you come down to other forms of lending money, you run
into the field of short-term and long-term.  Yesterday the Treasury borrowed money, I think it was at sixty-six hundredth of

--- [139] ---

one per cent, that is .66.  They borrowed that money yesterday at less
than one per cent for six months.

I think we are gradually getting a better understanding of interest and
it will come out through this whole reorganization procedure.  Excess of
interest ought to be eliminated as far as we possibly can eliminate it.
At the same time, we have the problem of reducing the debt structure and
the reduction of interest will automatically reduce the debt structure
because there will be more money in the hands of the mortgagor which can
then be applied to amortization.

Of course, I am talking theory now.

You take, for instance, the railroad financing.  Speaking generally -- and
this does not apply to every road but to the majority of roads -- the
interest structure, the fixed charges, bear too large a proportion to the
capital of the road, and if, in our refunding operations, we can set up
the principal of lower interest and a larger amortization fund, we will
reduce the fixed charges and in time of depression will make it less likely

that the railroad will have to go through the process of receivership.

Of course, on other debts, I think everybody is working towards the same end. You take, for instance, foreign debts. Let us take foreign debts of foreign governments that are owed to American citizens. Let us take them from the practical point of view. Suppose, for the sake of argument, I had bought ten bonds of some other government a few years ago. They are eight per cent bonds. I know of quite a lot of eight per cent bonds. It is an unconscionable rate. Now, what I do want is to get my $10,000. back and, in order to get

--- [140] ---

it back, I ought to be entirely willing to reduce that eight per cent to four or five per cent if, in so doing, it will enable the foreign government to pay me back my $10,000. What I want is my principal back and certainly it would be very foolish on my part to insist on eight per cent if that jeopardizes the $10,000. I think that is the easiest way of putting it.

Now, that applies all the way through. If we can reorganize the debt structure -- foreign, private, agricultural, real estate, industrial, everything else -- by reducing interest, we automatically make the payment of the principle more probable and we reduce the fixed charges of the country at the same time, thus increasing the probable value of the equities.

Of course, that is all theory and you will find a great many exceptions to it in individual cases.

Q: Is there any way you have in mind of going about that, or would it be a voluntary proposition rather than a government proposition?

THE PRESIDENT: Of course, it can be worked out in various ways, either by consent, which is the voluntary method, or else by the new form of receivership, the short receivership, which enables a substantial proportion of the security owners, by agreeing to a reduction, to compel the non-assenting security holders to do the same thing that they have agreed to. That was the bill that went through last year.

Q: Can you apply that to municipalities as well?

THE PRESIDENT: I think, frankly, it should be. There are a great many municipalities -- for example, when I was in Albany there were a great many municipalities whose credit was absolutely sound but, because of market conditions, they had to borrow money at six per cent

--- [141] ---

and, from my point of view, that is unconscionable. They ought to have been able to borrow money around four per cent.

Q: Do you think there ought to be some procedure for reaching an agreement on debts, such as the Wilcox bill?

THE PRESIDENT: I don't know that bill.

Q: That permits them to come into courts in order to get a debt reduction agreement.

THE PRESIDENT:  I don't know; I could not answer it.

Q:   The Wilcox bill provides that seventy-five per cent of the creditors must agree before they can do anything.

THE PRESIDENT:  What is the ratio in the bill passed last year?

Q:   I think it is 66-2/3 per cent.  That is on the corporations.  It is two-thirds.

THE PRESIDENT:  Yes.  I think, as a matter of principle, somewhere between sixty-six and seventy-five per cent would be a perfectly proper figure.

Q:   Have any of the foreign nations indicated their willingness to pay up if you reduce the interest payments?

THE PRESIDENT:  No.

Q:   Could you reduce those interest charges much further?  (Laughter)

Q:   Thank you, Mr. President.


(The Press Conference adjourned at 11:02 A.M.)

Press Conference #96
Executive Offices of the White House
February 9, 1934, 4:20 P.M.


        (The Postmaster General was present at this Conference.)


THE PRESIDENT:  Well, I suppose somebody is going to ask me about air-mail
    contracts.

Q:    You took the words right out of our mouths.

THE PRESIDENT:  The Postmaster General is about to issue an order cancelling
    all mail contracts -- air-mail contracts.  Further details are not yet
    ready.  The ground of cancellation is what is believed to be sufficient
    evidence of collusion or fraud.

    I expect to issue, almost immediately, I have not got it in final form
    yet, an Executive Order directing the Postmaster General, the Secretary
    of War, the Secretary of Commerce, with the officers and the officials of
    their respective departments to cooperate to the end that necessary air-
    mail service be afforded.  Furthermore, that the Secretary of War is to
    place at the disposal of the Postmaster General such airplanes, landing
    fields, pilots and other employees and equipment of the Army of the United
    States as are necessary for the transportation of mail during this emer-
    gency by such air routes and on such schedules as the Postmaster General
    may prescribe.

    So much for that.

Q:    Does the word "emergency" there indicate that later on you may award the
    contract to private lines again?

THE PRESIDENT:  I don't know.

Q:    Will that be effective immediately?

                     --- [143] ---

THE PRESIDENT:  We have not worked out the details but very, very soon.

Q:    Will that bar these people from bidding again?

THE PRESIDENT:  I think it does under the law.

Q:    Five years?

THE PRESIDENT:  Five years.

Q:    Domestic and foreign both?

THE PRESIDENT:  Only domestic.

Q:    It means, in effect, that the Army is taking over the air-mail service
    temporarily?

THE PRESIDENT: Only where it is necessary. In other words, we haven't the details on all of them yet.

Q:   Did I understand that applies to all air-mail contracts?

THE PRESIDENT: All domestic.

Q:   That does not apply to Pan American?

THE PRESIDENT: No.

POSTMASTER GENERAL FARLEY: Not in this instance, it does not.

Q:   May some of the lines be discontinued?

THE PRESIDENT: I think so.

Q:   May not this result in permanent return to direct carrying of the mails by the Post Office Department?

THE PRESIDENT: I said we have not got to that yet.

Q:   Mr. President, reports are circulating this morning that you also intended to cancel all bids received so far on the $10,000,000 motorization project for the Army. Is that correct?

THE PRESIDENT: I do not know; I have not heard anything about it.

Q:   Do you intend to ask Congress for C.C.C. funds to carry through the C.C.C. beyond June thirtieth next?

--- [144] ---

THE PRESIDENT: C.C.C.?

Q:   Yes.

THE PRESIDENT: Yes. I have forgotten whether it is $275,000,000 or $300,000,000 that is going to go in. It is one of those -- somewhere between those two figures.

Q:   For the fiscal year 1935?

THE PRESIDENT: You had better check on whether it is to the end of the fiscal year or to the first of May. In other words, the next two periods. I could not tell you.

Q:   Mr. President, have you a successor for Russell Hawkins of the Home Loan Bank Board?

THE PRESIDENT: Not yet; I do not think I have.

MR. EARLY: No, sir.

THE PRESIDENT: How about it?

MR. EARLY: You haven't the Home Loan.

THE PRESIDENT: Are you sure it did not go up?

MR. EARLY: No, sir.

THE PRESIDENT: It is all made out but it has not gone up.

Q:    Would you care to state your attitude toward the Wagner Unemployment
      Insurance Bill?

THE PRESIDENT: No, only that we have discussed it a good deal. I think I can
      put it this way on the Wagner Unemployment Insurance Bill, that both Mrs.
      Perkins and I are very sympathetic with the general theory of the bill
      but it is not a bill that I have to send a Message on. There is that
      distinction.

Q:    Mr. President, can you tell us what progress is being made on the guaran-
      tee of the principal of the Home Owners' Loan Corporation

--- [145] ---

bonds?

THE PRESIDENT: Still talking with the Treasury about it. It has not come to
      me yet.

Q:    And no progress, no reports come to you on the procedure for setting up
      a modernization fund to be used for direct loans? There was an announce-
      ment made that they intended to ask for authorization to make loans for
      new building?

THE PRESIDENT: That is part of the plan. It is a comparatively small amount
      and would not require any additional budget financing.

Q:    Authorization?

THE PRESIDENT: Yes.

Q:    To go back to this Wagner Bill for a minute, does your statement mean that
      you are very sympathetic toward the objectives?

THE PRESIDENT: Yes, I could not tell you the details of the bill myself.

Q:    Is your waterways Message going up in the next few days?

THE PRESIDENT: Oh, that will be as soon as the Home Owners' -- you mean in
      response to that resolution?

Q:    Yes.

THE PRESIDENT: Oh, it will be six weeks. We have an interdepartmental commit-
      tee working on it. It will take a long time.

Q:    Has any consideration been given to the contributions to be made to
      state highway construction during the next year? This allocation of
      Public Works funds is about used up, I understand.

THE PRESIDENT: No. Of course you have to remember one thing and that is that
      the peak of last year's appropriation won't be reached probably until

next summer.

Q: The actual work, you mean?

--- [146] ---

THE PRESIDENT: Yes.

Q: Senator Dill said today that he is going to introduce a Communications Commission bill. Do you care to outline your views on that?

THE PRESIDENT: No, except that he came down this morning and we talked it over, and the next step is for him to show me his proposed bill.

Q: Mr. President, is there anything to be added to what Colonel Roosevelt (Colonel Theodore Roosevelt, who had been Governor of the Philippines under the previous administration) told us today with respect to your discussion of the Philippine independence question?

THE PRESIDENT: No, I was just getting background.

Q: Mr. President, is there going to be any further conference at the White House with Congressional leaders on stock market regulations?

THE PRESIDENT: I don't think so. On that stock market, as a general thing, I think for background it would be useful for you to read the Democratic platform in regard to this whole subject because it is very, very clear and something that should not be entirely forgotten.

We are really trying to carry out the purpose of the platform and we have already carried out a good portion of that purpose. The platform says, "We advocate protection of the investing public by requiring to be filed with the Government and carried in advertisements of all offerings of foreign and domestic stocks and bonds true information as to bonuses, commissions, principal invested, and interests of the sellers."

Of course, the Securities Act is intended to cover that.

Then the next is, "Regulation to the full extent of Federal power of (a) Holding companies which well securities in interstate

--- [147] ---

commerce." That has not yet been completely taken care of.

"(b) Rates of utility companies operating across State lines." That has not yet been taken care of.

"(c) Exchanges in securities and commodities." My Message yesterday covered that phase.

And then, the rest relates to the banking end of things that has been pretty well carried out all right through last spring's Banking Act.

Q: Are the details of the Bill which went in today satisfactory to you?

THE PRESIDENT: I have not read them. I don't know them.

Q:  In light of the Securities Bill, do you contemplate one of a similar
nature for the commodity exchanges?

THE PRESIDENT:  Yes.  I recommended that yesterday and it is up to them on the
Hill as to whether they want it in one bill or in two separate bills.

Q:  Thank you, Mr. President.


(The Press Conference adjourned at 4:30 P.M.)

Press Conference #97
Executive Offices of the White House
February 14, 1934, 10:40 A.M.


THE PRESIDENT: Good morning, Fred (Mr. Storm). Was he (meaning Mr. Stephenson)
    up late last night?

Q:    (Mr. Storm) Yes, sir.

THE PRESIDENT: You ought to take better care of him. I will lend you the
    Marines, if you want.

Q:    We need somebody to take care of us.

THE PRESIDENT: Grand. I have not made that appointment for you yet.

Q:    Are you going to?

THE PRESIDENT: I have not done anything about it.

Q:    (Mr. Stephenson) Better ask Miss LeHand to watch out. We may ask her a
    question or two today.

Q:    (Mr. Storm) They are complaining about my size. They can't see. I told
    them I'd fill them in.

THE PRESIDENT: I do not think there is anything in particular this morning.

Q:    Anything new on the air-mail situation, Mr. President?

THE PRESIDENT: Not that I know of. There is a letter going up from the Post-
    master General and I think one from the Secretary of Agriculture to the
    Agricultural Committee. I do not think it is done yet.

Q:    Mr. President, are you planning on a Cabinet Commission to handle inland
    waterway problems or inland waterway commissions?

THE PRESIDENT: Both Houses passed resolutions about two weeks ago asking for
    some kind of a comprehensive plan. It originated from the fact that we,
    frankly, had no real plan that would take care of

--- [149] ---

rivers and harbors and reclamation and forestry and so forth. There is
a Cabinet committee at work on that at the present time. They probably
won't get a report out for another three weeks because it is so big.

Q:    Who heads that up?

THE PRESIDENT: Let me see, there is Agriculture, Interior, Commerce, War -- I
    don't know whether Labor is on it or not but I think so.

Q:    Would this have anything to do with the St. Lawrence Waterway Development,
    for example?

THE PRESIDENT: No, merely as one of the watersheds. The general idea is this:

That we have been going ahead year after year -- you can use this as background -- going ahead with rivers and harbors bills and various other
pieces of legislation which were more or less dependent, as we all know,
on who could talk the loudest. There has never been any definite planning
and the general thought is that we will try, out of this report, to get
a permanent planning commission.

This commission will be non-political, non-partisan and this commission
will study the whole area of the United States, and the easiest way to do
that is by watersheds.

For example, they will study the needs of all of the territory affected
by the water that flows into the Atlantic Ocean and then they will list
the projects within that watershed in the order of their importance from
two points of view: First, the point of view of danger and damage to
life and property which includes soil erosion and things like that. Secondly, from the point of view of economics as to whether a new canal is
needed or something of similar character. Then there is a third point
of view which might be called the social

--- [150] ---

point of view as to whether a territory should have land eliminated from
cultivation or whether it could support a greater population.

Then, another survey would cover the watersheds of the rivers that flow
into the Gulf, directly into the Gulf, excluding the waters from the
Mississippi River which really form a problem all themselves. Then there
would be a further study of the waters flowing into the Pacific Ocean.

On each of these watersheds, the idea is that this commission which probably eventually will become permanent, will list the projects in the
order of their importance and, having so listed them, recommendations
would be made to the Congress with, of course, full authority in the
Congress to change the recommendations. They could change them any way
they wanted because that is, essentially, a legislative prerogative.

This permanent long-range planning commission could plan ahead for twenty-five or fifty years, subject of course to changing conditions as time
went on. Then, every year -- and this carries out what I was talking
about a couple of weeks ago -- the National Government would plan to
spend some more or less regular sum which, in a sense, would take the
place of the public works money and would be used primarily to relieve
unemployment which we will always have with us in one form or another.

This plan would put the physical development of the country on a planned
for the first time. Of course it would include a great many factors. It
would include flood-control, soil erosion, the question of sub-marginal
land, reforestation, agriculture and the use of the crops, decentralization of industry and, finally, trans-

--- [151] ---

portation.

Q:     And water power?

THE PRESIDENT: And water power.

Q:    This can be called your land plan?

THE PRESIDENT:  Yes.  Land and water.  Of course it is based, in a sense, on
      water -- on watersheds -- because this whole thing ties around the prob-
      lem of the watersheds rather than other types of geographical lines.

Q:    Do you still have an idea of taxing the use of the water highways?

THE PRESIDENT:  That is being studied at the same time.  In other words, so far
      as possible, with all these developments, they ought to be put on a self-
      sustaining basis, if it is a possible thing to do it.  The Government
      spends at the present time on mere maintenance of existing rivers and
      harbors and channels, etc., somewhere between 60 and 70 million dollars a
      year which is an out-of-pocket expense for which the Government is prac-
      tically not compensated at all.  We are studying the possibility of get-
      ting back at least the cost of upkeep.

Q:    Is there any reason why the St. Lawrence Waterways action should be with-
      held pending the development of this general plan?

THE PRESIDENT:  No.

Q:    Will you go further on the decentralization of industry, what is meant by
      that?

THE PRESIDENT:  Well, the general thought is that there are large areas of the
      country where farming, by itself, will only provide perhaps a bare sub-
      sistence so far as food goes.  In other words, the farmer won't bring in
      a cash crop, and people have to have a certain amount

--- [152] ---

of cash to live on.

Therefore, the idea is to try experiments on the decentralization of industry so that the people living in those parts of the country where they
cannot make a profit on farming will be able to do some farming and get
a cash crop in the way of wages for part-time work during the year.  One
thing they are studying, which is not quite parallel, is in connection
with the forestry organization.  In some of our forest areas which are
primarily used for timber, I think we can well adopt what they have done
in certain places in Europe where the population of that area lives on
small farms, getting their food off the farms.  However, it is such moun-
tainous country that they cannot make a profit, they cannot get cash in
addition to food, and therefore, during the wintertime, that population
as, for instance, in the Hartz Mountains and Black Forest has an average
of one person out of each family working in the forests during the winter
for cash wages.  In that case your forestation or timber cutting is an
industry.

Q:    Then you don't mean taking out factories where they are pretty close to-
      gether?

THE PRESIDENT:  Oh, no.  Of course there is probably too much centralization in
      some areas, but the law of economics will take care of that.  This is no
      wild-eyed idea of moving millions of people overnight.

Q:    A project by the Rivers and Harbors Board, will it first go to the

Cabinet Board before Congress?

THE PRESIDENT: Now you are talking about mechanics.  I don't know how it would
work out.  Essentially the Committee is getting all the

--- [153] ---

information from the Board of Engineers of the Army.

Q:    Does this mean there would be any more allocations from Public Works at
all for river projects?

THE PRESIDENT:  Oh, heavens, no.  This is a gradual conversion of the theory
of public works into an orderly annual process.

Q:    Would it be --

THE PRESIDENT:  (interposing) And the elimination of the old methods of river
and harbors bills.

Q:    Do you think that the allotments made by the Public Works would be revised
to fit this plan after the report is in?

THE PRESIDENT:  Yes, I think that is true.  I will give you an example on that.
As you know, there are a great many projects that come in.  Take this
Trans-Florida Canal.  There is no reason why it should not be known.  I
personally have been very keen about the Trans-Florida Canal and I believed that it was possible to build one for a price that would return
at least the cost of upkeep and perhaps a small margin toward the retirement of the cost.

The Army Engineers made preliminary surveys last spring of two or three
routes and figured out $110,000,000  to $125,000,000  as the cost.

We had no board, no central committee, to which we could refer it, to
which we could refer the general necessity for a Trans-Florida Canal, so
I had to more or less handle it myself.  I had a very careful recheck
made by the Army Engineers on the cost of it and the probable use of it,
if built.  Well, the recheck was very discouraging.  They figured out
that it would cost $175,000,000  to $200,000,000  and that the use of it
would not be as great as we

--- [154] ---

had expected.

So, until something else turns up or we get new figures or increased
traffic, the Trans-Florida Canal is unfortunately overboard, much to my
disappointment.

Q:    Was an allotment made for it?

THE PRESIDENT:  No.

Q:    The House today takes up the tax bill and, among other things, there will
be a controversy over there about depreciation charges.  There has been
something said about depreciation charges on the barns on your farm.  Have
you thought about that problem of depreciation?

THE PRESIDENT: Yes, a great deal.

Q:   What can you tell us about it?

THE PRESIDENT:   The story of my barn is a very simple one. I bought the back
      farm at Hyde Park about 1910 or 1912, as I remember it, and I sent for
      an insurance appraiser to tell me how much I could insure the house and
      the chicken coop and the barn for. He said, "I can insure the house for
      $4,000. and I think the barn for $4,000." In making up the income tax
      every year, I took what everybody else took -- I have forgotten whether
      it was 2½ or 3 per cent depreciation on these old wooden buildings. Ac-
      tually the barn was built in 1790, so I started 110 or 112 years later
      to take depreciation on that barn and I took it at the rate of 2½ or 3
      per cent a year on a building 120 years old. The barn burned down in
      1928, I got my $4,000. and the farm was worth exactly as much without the
      barn as with the barn.

Q:   That so clearly demonstrates this depreciation. May we use it?

THE PRESIDENT:   I think so. I don't know enough about the technicalities

                        --- [155] ---

      of law to tell you what ought to take its place, but I do know the law is
      wrong in some way.

Q:   Do you know whether it ought to be changed by administrative changes or
      in the law itself? The House Committee at one time wanted depreciation
      charges reduced by twenty-five per cent and now they hope to do something
      about the situation through administrative channels.

THE PRESIDENT:   I don't care which way, as long as it is done.

Q:   One of the papers this morning said that the Federal Reserve Board is
      about to set up twelve regional banks to make loans to industry?

THE PRESIDENT:   I know that Governor Black is coming in to lunch with me tomor-
      row and says he has three or four things to talk over with me.

Q:   We have a report that Peek is leaving the Government service this week?

THE PRESIDENT:   Not that I know of. There has been no conference.

Q:   What is the status of his plan and that of the others?

THE PRESIDENT:   I don't know. They have had the Committee working on it and I
      am going to see them tomorrow or the day after, the Secretary of State,
      George Peek, the Secretary of Commerce, et cetera.

Q:   There is a report this morning that the American Minister to Austria, up
      in Philadelphia, is coming down to see you today?

THE PRESIDENT:   Is he coming?

MR. McINTYRE:     (Mr. McIntyre at first indicated affirmation.)

No, I am confused; I was thinking of George (Governor Earle of Pennsylvania).

Q:     Can you comment on the C.W.A. tapering off starting tomorrow, the fifteenth?

THE PRESIDENT:  I do not know; you will have to ask Harry Hopkins.  I imagine that in certain of the agricultural sections down south, where they started plowing, it will start to taper off.

--- [156] ---

Q:     There is a report around Wall Street that the Administration is not going to press for legislative action at this session on Stock Exchange regulation.  Has there been any change of policy?

THE PRESIDENT:  It sounds like a Wall Street report.  I believe that we should take action, not only on Stock Exchange regulation but also on commodity markets regulation, for the very simple fact that it is in the platform, both of them.

Q:     Do you favor the bill in its present form?

THE PRESIDENT:  I still am able to say truthfully that I have not read it.

Q:     Secretary Morgenthau intimated that you are about to do something on silver?

THE PRESIDENT:  Not that I know of.

Q:     The morning papers have stories to the effect that you plan to restore some of the contracts (air-mail contracts) before the end of this week.  Have you any plans with regard to air mail that you might throw light on for us?

THE PRESIDENT:  I don't suppose I ought to talk about it at all because it is primarily a matter for the Postmaster General and the Attorney General.  I think, however, off the record, so you don't get any bum steers, the general situation is that all of the lines, with one exception, are in trouble because of the conference which the former officials of the Post Office Department took part in in 1930.  That one exception is the National Parks Airways and it does not seem wholly clear, although their man was present in this famous meeting, it does not appear clear that they obtained any wrongful advantage out of the subsequent lettings.  I think that is, as far

--- [157] ---

as I know, the whole story when you come down to the details of what happened in the meeting.

Q:     Are there any grounds for action against individuals?

THE PRESIDENT:  I haven't any idea; I do not know.

Q:     In view of the fact that these contracts have been cancelled, do you care ⌐o outline what you have in mind for the future of air mail?

THE PRESIDENT:  I am not ready on that either.  The Executive Order was, of
course, based merely on the emergency, the necessity of carrying the
mails, caused by the termination of the contracts and that is, literally,
as far as we have gone.  What will be the permanent method of carrying
the mails, I do not know.  We have not come to it yet.

Q:   Can you give us any indication of what will happen in the case of the
ocean mails?  Black's Committee is talking about very questionable practices there although precisely not of the same nature.

THE PRESIDENT:  That is being studied and Black isn't through with his work up
there.  I think he is doing very good work.

This is perfectly true, too, under the ocean-mail contracts:  In the first
place, they have been called "mail contracts" in a great many instances
where they ought to be called straight subsidies.  We ought to call them
by their right name.  Let us take a line, for example, from Texas to London, that carries perhaps ten pounds of mail in the course of a year.  If
we are giving them subsidies for the obvious purpose of keeping that line
of American flag ships going it should be called a subsidy rather than a
mail contract.  It was silly to pay them $75,000  to $100,000  for carrying ten pounds of mail.

--- [158] ---

In the same way probably, through this subterfuge, we have been giving
mail contracts to a whole lot of lines that ought not to have carried
mail.  Take a very simple example.  It would be silly for a line of
freight ships from Norfolk, taking three or four weeks to perform a voyage, to carry the mail.  It would be much easier and quicker and, in the
long run, cheaper to send the mail to New York and cross the ocean in a
fast ship.

So there undoubtedly will be a complete reorganization of the ship-mail
subsidies.  I want to call it by its right name, a "subsidy" and I do
believe, in the case of ship subsidies, that we should give ship subsidies in this country because of the higher wages and better conditions
that we are giving to American sailors.  Without some form of Government
help, a subsidy, those conditions would in large part drive the American
flag off the ocean.

Q:   To go back to the air mail for a moment, the National Parks Airline is,
unfortunately, one of the lines not operating now.

THE PRESIDENT:  Is it?  (Laughter)

Q:   I mean it is one not restored and yet you made an exception by saying it
is one to be restored.  Which is it?

THE PRESIDENT:  It is just out temporarily or for the winter.  Doesn't it run
during the summer and then is cut down in the winter?

Q:   The correspondence showed that it operates in June, July and August.  This
last year they finally barred that out.

THE PRESIDENT:  I think it is a season line.

Q:   Yes, sir; largely through the summer and fall.

Q:    Thank you, Mr. President.

(The Press Conference adjourned at 11:10 A.M.)

Press Conference #98
Executive Offices of the White House
February 16, 1934, 4:10 P.M.


THE PRESIDENT: What is the news?

Q:    (Mr. Stephenson) I don't know.

THE PRESIDENT: Being Friday, we might just as well put the lid on tomorrow and
      the next day. Everything is quiet.

Q:    Can you tell us anything about this heavy industries bank?

THE PRESIDENT: Export-Import Bank?

Q:    No, the A.P. story yesterday about the creation of a new intermediate bank
      to loan money to heavy industries, as I understood it.

THE PRESIDENT: My, my! I did not read the story, but there isn't anything like
      that in contemplation. The nearest thing is that Governor Black has been
      checking with Secretary Morgenthau and with me about the possibility of
      setting up some method of facilitating loans to industries as a whole.
      That does not mean heavy industries. One of the several suggested ways
      of setting it up might be called intermediate credit banks, one in each
      Federal Reserve District. You know, at the present time, under the law,
      if a concern wants to borrow money on commercial paper, for instance, and
      it cannot get accommodations at its local bank, it has the right to borrow
      from the Federal Reserve Bank of its District. But, actually, there is no
      practical machinery set up for carrying that through, and it is only in a
      very few Federal Reserve Districts -- Atlanta is one of them -- where any
      loans have been made by the Federal Reserve Banks. The theory is merely
      to

--- [160] ---

      facilitate the extension of credit of that kind, and it is in a very, very
      tentative stage.

      I don't think there is any particular story because that is only one of a
      number of particular ways that is being talked over. There is no agree-
      ment on whether that would be the way or not.

Q:    The reason I said heavy industries was because the loan would be perhaps
      of five years' period, which would suggest buildings or something of that
      kind?

THE PRESIDENT: Yes, it would be a little bit more than a current order.

Q:    Mr. President, can you tell us who you have in mind for the presidency of
      the Export-Import Bank?

THE PRESIDENT: I do not know. There is some legal question in that whole
      thing.

Q:    There are reports published this morning that you had abandoned sending
      your Message up on debts. Is that correct?

THE PRESIDENT: It is not ready yet.

Q:  On the Export-Import Bank what are the legal difficulties?  Can you go into that?

THE PRESIDENT: No.  It is some question that has arisen.  It is too technical to explain.

Q:  Is the tariff Message going up?

THE PRESIDENT: Nothing yet.

Q:  Have you heard anything from the railroad people about the wage dispute?

THE PRESIDENT: No, nothing on that.

Q:  Do you feel there is a very serious friction?

THE PRESIDENT: What was the hypothetical question?

--- [161] ---

Q:  I want to know if you felt the friction.

THE PRESIDENT: It is in many lines, yes.

Q:  Do you feel there is still a great need for the Government to extend credit?

THE PRESIDENT: I would say there is a great need in many lines for a greater extension of credit.

Q:  Will you tell us what will be the next steps in the Philippine independence question?

THE PRESIDENT: I think you will have to get that up on the Hill.  In other words, I think that up there they are working out something and I am not yet in a position to say anything myself until I find out a little bit more about it.  But it does look as if they are getting somewhere.

Q:  Are you working on either the debt or tariff Message now?

THE PRESIDENT: No.

Q:  Mr. President, have you heard from Whitney, the railway man?

THE PRESIDENT: No, not for three days or four days.  He was in either on Monday -- I told him that I had not had a chance to talk with any of the railroad executives but, after talking with them, I probably would send that letter and I did talk with Gray (Mr. Carl Gray) and did send a letter to both of them.

Q:  Did they say anything about a strike?

THE PRESIDENT: No.

Q:  Do you hope to see a Senate vote on the St. Lawrence Treaty this session?

THE PRESIDENT: I hope so.

Q:  What is the indication?

--- [162] ---

THE PRESIDENT: I don't know. I hope it will come up and get voted on.

Q:  They seem to be waiting on you?

THE PRESIDENT: No, I do not think so.

Q:  At Mr. Hopkins' Press Conference this morning, he suggested certain other devices for meeting the C.W.A. needs after May first through other Government agencies. I wondered if you --

THE PRESIDENT: (interposing) Unless he was talking about the taking on (of men) by P.W.A. around that time.

Q:  This Cabinet meeting on planning, was it that?

THE PRESIDENT: No, that has nothing to do with it. That is long-range planning.

Q:  He was talking about long-range planning, where the future of these people would be laid down.

THE PRESIDENT: After this year. This long-range plan would not affect this year.

Q:  He referred to a gradual absorption of it.

THE PRESIDENT: In future year. That is an entirely different subject itself. It had nothing to do with what will happen this spring.

Q:  The question was, What would happen after May first and he mentioned this long-range plan in connection with that?

THE PRESIDENT: Had nothing to do with this year, obviously.

Q:  Putting the question another way, what will be done with the C.W.A. workers in the cities that will be let off May first?

THE PRESIDENT: I think that we took it up, it must have been about a month ago, and we talked about the general results with respect to the C.W.A., as you know. I think you had better use this just

--- [163] ---

as pure background and nothing else.

Obviously, when C.W.A. was put in, the whole country had underestimated the actual unemployment. You will remember that we all went on figures of around twelve million people. This is all old stuff, I have talked about it before. We figured that through the general pickup in business, N.R.A., et cetera, somewhere around four million of them had gone back in industry and probably a good many more had gone back who had been actually earning something on the farms. That would have cut down the total of those figures to under eight million and then, if we put four million to work under C.W.A. during the winter months, it would reduce it to below four million.  But actually, when we came to the checkups, there were a good many more than three or three and a half million unemployed, so we went back to the original figures, the estimates of twelve or thirteen million, and we had to revise them.  It was apparent that there were a good many more people out of work than shown by the very best figures obtainable through 1933.

To come down to the question of what happens this spring.  Of course this is still a hope and nobody can do more than make an intelligent guess. We hope that a good many of these people laid off will go back into industry, that a good many will go back into agriculture, and that a good many will go into public works which will be fairly well in its stride by that time.  Now, that does not mean that all four million people will be actually in a position to get employment during the summer.  Some will go into industry, some into agriculture and some into public works, and

--- [164] ---

probably there will be some left over during the summer months.  But we do hope that with the general pickup that condition will get better as the summer goes on, and even more so in the fall.

But we are not going to bind ourselves as to what will happen next winter.  We are not going to tell people stories.  We hope we won't have to reconstitute C.W.A. on a scale like this year, but we are not going to let people starve.  However, that is a problem for the future, and one which we cannot determine in February or March.

Q:    Are you planning a conference on air-mail legislation?

THE PRESIDENT:  I do not think so.  I do not think there is anything coming up.

Q:    There is a report up on the Hill that Secretary Hull had suggested that the United States Government take some -- make some representations to the Dollfuss Government about conditions over in Vienna.  Is there anything you can tell us about that?

THE PRESIDENT:  Not that I know of.  That is the first I had heard of it.  I guess there is nothing in that.

Q:    There are two vacancies on the Mediation Board.  Are they going to be filled?

THE PRESIDENT:  No.

Q:    Does that mean you are contemplating some reorganization of that Board and the Act under which it functions?

THE PRESIDENT:  Yes.  As far as we got on that is this:  Eastman is checking up on the proposed legislation and it is possible that the Board of Mediation will be, in some way, reconstituted.  You are probably familiar with the legislation.  I do not know the details

--- [165] ---

of the legislation except in general terms it would provide for simplitying the mediation machinery and, pending the outcome of that, I am not filling those places.

Q:    Mr. President; does this all link in with Eastman's recommendations for changing the labor provisions under the Emergency Act?

THE PRESIDENT:  Yes, it is all tied in together and all one bill, probably.

Q:    Do you expect that to go up soon?

THE PRESIDENT:  I think Eastman ought to be ready on it in a week.

Q:    I do not think you mentioned it in your letter to the railway presidents. Is that another reason why they should hold off?

THE PRESIDENT:  No, I did not use that as a reason.

Q:    What is the status of the Newspaper Code and particularly the Graphic Arts Code?

THE PRESIDENT:  The status is myself.  It is actually -- I have got it off my desk and got it into the basket so it will be acted on, I hope, over the week end.

Q:    How far does your endorsement of the revised Bankhead Bill go -- on compulsory cotton control?

THE PRESIDENT:  I wish you would let me not answer that question now.  I think something is going to happen and I would rather it break the other way. You can make a pretty good guess on it.

Q:    Have you read the Stock Exchange regulation bill yet?

THE PRESIDENT:  It is not even on the desk yet.

Q:    There is a report on the Hill that either in the war debt Message or in a separate Message you are expected to ask legislation in order to make a concession to Finland because it has kept up its

--- [166] ---

payments.  Anything to that?

THE PRESIDENT:  You are two months ahead of time.

Q:    Does that mean a debt Message is not going up in two months?

THE PRESIDENT:  Maybe.  Frankly, I have not given any consideration either to the tariff Message or the debt Message, any more than I had two months ago.

Q:    You received the new Japanese Ambassador this week and exchanged greetings in which you said that you thought that any problems should be settled amicably.  Do you care to go into that at this time?

Q:    Are there any discussions coming up on that?

THE PRESIDENT:  Not that I know of.  The State Department is the place to ask.

Q:   We noticed he told you that anything done in the Far East would be in the interests of peace.

THE PRESIDENT:   (The President did not answer.)

Q:   Thank you, Mr. President.

THE PRESIDENT:   I do not think there is a single conference on over the week-end.

Q:   That is good.

Q:   The problem in Detroit regarding C.W.A. is a little different than in some other places because there was a surplus of labor before on account of overexpansion of industry there.   Even if industry picks up one hundred per cent in Detroit, there would be a good many people there who would be left unemployed and the number left unemployed would be a rather staggering figure.

THE PRESIDENT:   Of course there are all sorts of things that Detroit

--- [167] ---

has been working on.   They are even working on the possibility of moving a lot of people out back to their own states, to where they came from.

Q:   Would it be a bad thing to speculate on that?

THE PRESIDENT:   That is a local thing.   I am simply telling you what happened in Detroit.   Frank Murphy had all sorts of ambitious plans to move out 25,000 people.

Q:   Thank you, Mr. President.

(The Press Conference adjourned at 4:30 P.M.)

Press Conference #98-A
With Members of the National Conference
    of Business Paper Editors
Executive Offices of the White House
February 16, 1934, 4:30 P.M.


      (Mr. Paul Wooton, Washington correspondent of the McGraw-Hill
      Publications, introduced Mr. Anderson, President of the
      Association)

Q:   (Mr. Wooton) They have a few questions they want to ask.

THE PRESIDENT: Fine.

    Well, I will consider that Mr. Wooten has introduced everybody representing
the people behind the business of the country, so if you have any thoughts
I hope you will consider this one of the old-fashioned Press Conferences.
We will go ahead.

Q:   (Mr. Anderson) I do believe this represents a pretty good bellwether of
business because, if you will remember, the last time we were here there
were just a few of us sounding the blues. Now we are an aggregation. With
that I will let Mr. Ed Warner talk.

Q:   (Mr. Warner) Mr. Anderson has asked me to say a word on behalf of the
group about one or two of our special interests. We cover a diversity but
there are some points on which we are all confused. In particular, we are
a puzzled unit trying to assist and advise our industries in cooperating to
help you to succeed in your economic program. But, beyond that, we have
interests that affect all our fields.

    In particular, we are, of course, deeply concerned with any technological
advance. We believe, of course, from our background that the only hope of
a steady improvement in the standard of living and a steadily increasing
ability of industry to give better

               --- [169] ---

services at lower costs lies in the further promotion of technological
devices in the improvement of equipment and machinery. We are deeply concerned, however, with what appears to be the alarming slowing down of re-
equipment of industry at the present time. Of course, almost everyone is
familiar over the past few months with the fact that the capital group of
industries have suffered a loss of seventy per cent of their pay rolls at
the bottom and the consumer goods industries have also suffered but have
recovered substantially. We know our industries badly need new equipment.

    We find our industries sound. But, beyond the recognition of the need and
before that dammed-up purchasing power that has been deferred can be released, we must first regain confidence and, secondly, some devising of
appropriate methods of financing. I am sure if we had canvassed the entire
business world on the one subject that was of greatest interest, that would
have been the one selected. I know that is a matter of vital concern to
you. I think it is on that subject we most of all desire your special
counsel, as has been indicated by the subjects laid before you.

THE PRESIDENT: That is one of the questions with respect to the capital goods industry that I have been devoting a lot of time to since last March and April, and there are a great many crosscurrents. Insofar as equipment and re-equipment, replacing and improving the technological methods go, I think we can all be absolutely at one. We want to do everything we possibly can to encourage re-equipment, to encourage the bettering of machinery. I have not given the slightest indication of saying that our Government is

--- [170] ---

going to scrap machinery and go back to plain man power. I do think there has been such a complete lack of planning in the past in regard, not to equipment, but in regard to the total capacity of production that we have fallen into our own trap. There are a great many examples that you can bring up. For instance, you know, a couple of months ago I had a question up with the four companies that make steel rails in regard to the price that they were asking and, being half Dutch and half Scotch, I got a pretty good bargain out of them. But, in the course of the conversation, I said to them, "How much can you turn out in the way of steel rails a year?"

Well, there was U. S. and Bethlehem and Inland and Colorado Fuel and Iron -- those were the only four companies who make steel rails. They said, "We can turn out 4,000,000 tons a year." I said, "I have checked with the railroads and there isn't a Chinaman's chance that the railroads are going to need, on the average, over the next ten years, more than one million tons a year. How did it come that you fellows went ahead and built a plant capacity of four million tons when the railroads only need one million tons?" They said, "It was lack of planning."

That is an illustration that brings up one of the absolutely unsolved problems of the future. We do not want for a moment, and nobody wants to prevent John Smith, who has never been in the shoe business in his life from going ahead and going into the shoe business, if he wants to. On the other hand, ought not we to tell John Smith before he goes into the shoe business that if all the shoe factories in the United States were to produce, they would

--- [171] ---

turn out between eight and nine million pairs of shoes, and the country uses only three million pairs of shoes? Therefore, John Smith, be warned. If you have a new method of turning out shoes, go to it but remember, when you set up a new factory and turn out shoes, you are going to put another factory out of business. If you employ a thousand new people, you are going to put another thousand out of business.

One of the things we all of us have to give more consideration to than we ever have before is facts and figures to present to people who are about to go into a large capital investment which would result in overproduction in some particular individual industry where there is, already, overproduction.

In other words, every time you merely increase the units which make for additional overproduction, you drive somebody else out of business and, every time you do that, you have a loss and it is a capital loss as well as a loss of actual employment. Frankly, we have not the answer to it yet. I do not know what it is and you people have more time to study it because you are more or less specializing in one particular field. I have -- I think somebody brought the figures yesterday -- 215 different fields of action to run the United States. You people have only got to have ten or twenty, so I wish very much you would set your minds on that particular problem so that we can avoid the waste of capital in new industries, new plants, which we have been subjected to in the past because of lack of planning.

Now I agree absolutely that we would not want to prevent or check techno-logical improvement. I am all for it just so long as

--- [172] ---

it is done with our eyes open, and if somebody comes along with a techno-logical improvement which we know is going to drive some old fellow out of business, we want to take care of that old fellow and find something for him to do.

Q: We are particularly concerned with the devices which the old, established shoe factories may acquire and put into service in their old plants and scrap the obsolete and uneconomical machinery.

THE PRESIDENT: Frankly, you and I know that while some of the old stories about the strike on the part of some of the bankers are exaggerated, there is some fire behind the smoke and that capital has not been provided as much or as readily as it should have been provided for technological im-provements and the scrapping of outworn machinery. We are doing every-thing we can to encourage the lending machinery of the country to put the money out for legitimate purposes. They have used all kinds of excuses before, up to the present time. They said that we did not have a monetary standard, but they are finding out over a period of months that the dollar is not so very different and that, undoubtedly, we must increase the gene-ral values as a whole to make the payments of the debts of the country, which were incurred under a different dollar on the average, to make the payment of those debts more easy. But we are not going through what Ger-many went through by dilution or even England went through by dilution. We are doing it very gradually and we have not an awful lot further to go. We have gone along part of the way already. So the lending sources have not the same excuse for holding back that they had before and if there

--- [173] ---

is any way we can help in the putting out of additional credit, we are going to do it.

I was telling the White House Press just now -- we were discussing the pos-sibility of creating a device which the Chairman of the Federal Reserve Board, Eugene Black, has suggested, of creating some form of what might be called an intermediate credit bank for every one of the twelve Federal Reserve Bond districts -- that is one of the suggestions, there have been half a dozen other suggestions -- so that the Federal Reserve Board in each district would, in a sense, be responsible for a direct loan to an indivi-dual industry instead of having to come down here to the R.F.C.

If there is anything we can do along that line, I hope you will let us know.

Q: That subject of shoes is rather interesting to me. I happen to have a shoe trade paper and I have always challenged Stuart Chase's nine hundred

million or eight hundred million because the actual published figures within the industry indicate that it has a plant capacity of five hundred and
fifty million and we are subject to these tremendous peaks and valleys of
the public demand. They will not have shoes that are not in fashion at
the time they want them, and the natural result is that shoe machinery has
been a thriving business, even during the worst period -- and the last
month was during August (in 1933) -- due to the fact that we had obsolete
forms of machinery to make the old and everybody wants the new. It seems
to me that we have solved the difficulty because of the whims of fashion
and the woman.

THE PRESIDENT: Yes, the ladies are responsible for much. (Laughter)

--- [174] ---

(At this point Mr. Early handed the President a memorandum
which had been prepared in connection with this conference.)

I had not seen that. (Reading)

"1. To date the administration program to promote relief
and recovery has consisted largely of government spending.
Isn't the next step in the recovery program to open up
channels for financing industrial developments from private
sources?"

Well, I was just talking about that. (Reading)

"This money can come only from --

"(1) Profits from improved industrial operations - either
from increased volume at present efficiency or from the
same volume at increased efficiency

"(2) Accumulated surpluses now held by a few companies"

Well, of course, in addition to that we have a very large volume of excess
bank credit which exists today. It is no secret that probably excess bank
lending capacity is bigger now than it has been at any time in the last
fifteen or twenty years. (Reading)

"2. How far can the government assist in the financing
of capital-goods purchases to meet the needs of private
industry, in order to take up the added slack in the
capital-goods industries when expenditures for public
construction slow down?"

As I said before, I do not want to put the R.F.C. into the business of
making direct loans to individual firms if we can possibly help it. You
know what would happen if you centralized that business in one board in
Washington: One would come in with a perfectly good demand or a request
for a loan and would get it and somebody would come in the next day with a
request not based on sound

--- [175] ---

financing and he would start to get turned down and then his Congressman
and Senator would come around and it is going to be terribly hard for one
central body in a political capital to discriminate between individuals
and corporations seeking loans.  Therefore I think it is a far better
thing to work out a perfectly fair banking institution which will be more
local in its scope, like the Federal Reserve Districts or something of
that kind, and which will be controlled insofar as its policies are concerned by businessmen rather than bankers.

I think that is a pretty sound differentiation to make; in other words,
making the directors of that corporation the leading businessmen and industrialists of the Federal Reserve Districts rather than the leading
bankers of the Federal Reserve Districts.  The industrialists themselves
know better than the bankers do what firms should get loans and what should
not.

And then, (reading)

> "3.  Is it the administration policy that recovery cannot
> be permanent until job security has been attained by com-
> pulsory unemployment insurance; sickness, accident, and
> death benefits; old age pensions and other social legis-
> lation?"

Well, the answer to that is that we are headed right that way and we have
been for twenty years and we have not stopped.  There is not question
about it, we will have to have some form of unemployment insurance.  But
on all of these plans I think we are all agreed, business and Government,
that we want to keep away from the dole method, that it ought to be put on
an actuarial basis insofar as we possibly can; in other words, that it
should not be

--- [176] ---

a straight handout by Government.  It ought to be on a contribution basis,
whether it be unemployment insurance or sickness or accident insurance or
old age pensions or anything else.  What I have always said when I was
Governor of New York was that it was probably a great mistake for Government to do more than pay for the overhead and administration costs, that
they might be considered a legitimate Government function but that the
actual fund should be set up and maintained through the contribution system, roughly half from the employer and half from the employee.

Now, the country is not educated up to all of those things yet.  It is, in
some states.  Some states run away ahead of others in that regard.  For
instance, you have workmen's compensation in the State of New York and you
haven't got it on the other side of the line in Pennsylvania.  Gradually
we are coming to it, in my judgment, and the more that we can educate
towards uniformity in that respect, the better it will be for everybody
because it is unfair to the manufacturer in, let us say, New York and Massachusetts which are pretty far advanced in that type of legislation, to
have to compete with the manufacturer in another state, down in Georgia,
that hasn't any legislation of that kind.  It ought to be made as uniform
as possible.

On the other hand, the Federal Government cannot go ahead with it all alone

because there are grave questions as to whether the Federal Government has
the constitutional right to enter into all of these insurance plans. The
suggestion has been made, and I think probably some of you know about it,
what is known as the Wagner-Lewis Bill, which is only, so far, in tentative
form, but

--- [177] ---

the general principle of that bill is that there should be a Federal tax
put on, say at the end of a couple of years, on every employer, all over,
who employs -- I have forgotten what it is -- ten people or more, and
thereupon any employer who takes out unemployment insurance in acceptable
form, either under a state plan or private company plan, would have that
tax remitted. In case the employer did not do it, the tax would go to the
Federal Government and, in effect, would be used as the basis for unemployment relief, and that would be the source of unemployment relief funds.

Now, that method is well known in Government. In other words, the Federal
Government in effect says to the states, "Go ahead and set up something
like this. If you don't, then we will put a tax on." It is an incentive,
or some people would call it a bribe to the states to go ahead and enact
some form of legislation. Of course the chief purpose, as I said before,
the chief purpose and objective of all this is to get a uniform system
over the United States. If every state does the same thing, it is not
going to hurt the individual employer because he would have exactly the
same conditions no matter where he happened to have his factory and his
competitor would have the same conditions. (Reading)

> "4. Looking forward to the time when recovery can be con-
> sidered as complete, upon what principle should the line
> be drawn between publicly and privately operated business
> enterprise?"

Now, that is too broad a question. I don't quite get it. What, for instance? Give me an example.

Q:    I will undertake it. Assuming we get out of an emergency condition

--- [178] ---

where everything has to do with recovery. There are certain lines of
activity which have been Government, some private and some on the line
between. Now, we are all thinking along new lines. To what extent does
it appear that the line ought to be shifted and that local government or
state government, with Federal cooperation, should take over the lines
that have been private?

THE PRESIDENT: I do not think we should change very much one way or the other.
Of course the only change we have made is in regard to certain forms of
electric utilities where I have come out with a stick, but the necessity
of wielding a stick over the utilities has been apparent for a long time.
We could not get into their books and, if we did, they took us to court
for twelve years. So, eventually, the Government had to do something to
protect itself.

Now, there are some lines of industry that have a public character besides
utilities but not an awful lot. If the steel corporations, the four of
them that turn out steel rails, won't let me go into their books and find

out whether they are making 75% or 3%, the Government has to do something about it because, after all, a steel rail goes on a railroad, which is a public utility, and I cannot sit here and let the railroads of the country pay a profit when I do not know what the profit is. That is all and that is perfectly simple. If they will let me go into their books, I am perfectly willing to let the four steel rail companies earn a profit, but I want to know what it is. If they deny me access to the books, the Government has to act. I do not want to go into the steel rail business.

--- [179] ---

MR. WOOTON: Thank you so much for giving us this time. It is mighty fine.

(The Conference adjourned at 4:53 P.M.)

CONFIDENTIAL
Press Conference #99
Executive Offices of the White House
February 21, 1934, 10:40 A.M.


THE PRESIDENT: When do they start counting the ballots? (Referring to the election of a new president for the White House Correspondents' Association)

Q: Monday, at six o'clock.

THE PRESIDENT: Is it a secret ballot?

Q: Very much so.

THE PRESIDENT: Has Truly Warner (Albert Warner) got thoroughly organized yet?

Q: Thoroughly organized -- ask me. (Laughter)

Q: There is other propaganda against Stevie (Francis Stephenson) though. The Senator is the campaign manager of the White House Correspondents, Mr. President. (Laughter)

THE PRESIDENT: I hope you find it easier to raise funds than the Democratic National Committee does. (Laughter) We get plenty of offers of funds. The problem is the source. We have to be awfully careful on that.

Q: We are not concerned with the source; all we want is the money.

Q: We are still worried about a Senate investigation.

THE PRESIDENT: This is merely conversation in the front row; it is not for publication.

I do not think there is any news. Several members of the Cabinet had to to be away Friday, so we are meeting today instead. It is just a regular Cabinet meeting.

Q: Why did they have to be away Friday?

--- [181] ---

THE PRESIDENT: Washington's Birthday; double holiday.

Q: Anything further on Governor Black?

THE PRESIDENT: No, I have not heard another thing since he was here last week.

Q: I presume you read the morning papers. The Federal Advisory Council wants to open up heavy industries.

THE PRESIDENT: What is the Federal Advisory Council?

Q: The Federal Reserve Board Advisory Council.

THE PRESIDENT: They want to open up what, loans to heavy industries?

Q: Yes.

Q: Anything more on the air-mail situation?

THE PRESIDENT: No. No, you are a little ahead of time. I hope there will be soon.

Q: Are you planning to send a tariff Message to Congress soon?

THE PRESIDENT: Sometime before they adjourn.

Q: What shall I say about the bonus?

THE PRESIDENT: I said all I could say. I said it to Speaker Rainey yesterday by telephone.

Q: Anything for the local democracy?

THE PRESIDENT: Count (Rudolph De Zapp), Homer (Attorney General Cummings) and I are talking about it today.

Q: I understand that Mr. Starbuck's (William D. L. Starbuck) appointment on the Radio Commission expires tomorrow night. Have you given any consideration on that?

THE PRESIDENT: Mac (Mr. McIntyre) told me about that last night and I have not thought about it at all. I did not realize it was expiring.

--- [182] ---

Q: Is that likely to stay vacant until some action on the communications problem is taken up on the Hill?

THE PRESIDENT: I have not thought about it. I do not know how far they got on that communications bill.

Q: Mr. President, will recognition of Manchukuo by foreign powers change our own point of view regarding that country?

THE PRESIDENT: I will have to talk to the Secretary of State about it before answering that question. It is fraught with dynamite.

Q: On the bonus, would you care to give us your reasons for being opposed to the bonus?

THE PRESIDENT: No, I do not think at this time I had better go into it any further. Just let it rest at this time on what I said to the Speaker yesterday.

Q: On the Johnson Bill that has to do with the right of public utilities to appeal to the court on rate decisions, which comes up in the House pretty soon, are you taking any attitude?

THE PRESIDENT: I have not, except that there is a long history. In 1929 I was in Albany and the United States -- I do not know whether it was the Supreme Court or the Circuit Court of Appeals, handed down a decision in the New York Telephone case after seven years. The whole State of New York got considerably exercised about that situation. The New York Telephone Com-

pany was solely an intra-state company and the State Public Service Commission had sought, seven years before, to reduce the telephone rates within
the State. They were taken to the Federal Court and there it rested for
seven years before there was a determination. Now, of course that sort of
thing is an impossible situation.

--- [183] ---

I very strongly advocated, as I remember it -- you will have to check on
this -- as I remember it, I recommended to the Legislature and they put
through a resolution calling for exactly what this Johnson Bill provides
for. I am very strongly in favor of removing the jurisdiction of the Federal Courts over purely intra-state utilities of that nature. I hope it
will go through. I am not sending any Message on it.

Q:   Mr. President, during the last two or three days Mr. Hopkins has indicated
that some sort of program will be worked out between now and May first to
take care of possible overflow of unemployment which will not be absorbed
by private industry or in our public works program.

THE PRESIDENT:  No, except we are all doing the best we can to find employment
for as many people as we can.

Q:   Have you received a letter from the railroad managers in response?

THE PRESIDENT:  Yes, one came in yesterday. I don't see there is any particular reason why it should not be given out, Steve (Mr. Early).

MR. EARLY:  I have not seen it.

THE PRESIDENT:  It said in effect that they had communicated with the railway
labor executives and they are having a meeting on the fifteenth of March.

Q:   Do you see anything more that can be done to bring the price of liquor
down to a reasonable level? (Laughter)

THE PRESIDENT:  Who has been stinging you?

Q:   This is more than an academic question. (Laughter)

THE PRESIDENT:  That is why I said, "Who has been stinging you?"

Q:   No, seriously. (Laughter)

--- [184] ---

It seems to me that in the long run the Government itself is going to lose
on this basis because the bootlegger can undersell the legitimate --

THE PRESIDENT:  (interposing) Absolutely. It is the thing we are all worried
about. As I understand it, Joe Choate is concerned over the fact that the
imports are not coming in nearly as fast as we expected them. He is looking into it at the present time but is not yet ready to report. But the
fact is that the liquor is coming in from outside the country in comparatively small volume.

Q:   Of course there is a seven dollar tax on it before you get it.

THE PRESIDENT: Yes, and this you will have to keep off the record, as an indication of it a Congressman came down to see me and he wanted the R.F.C. to finance the import companies on the ground that they could not pay, that they could not find the money to finance this large tax. There is a lag between the time the tax is paid and the time the importing company gets paid by the wholesalers and retailers. Of course I do not think the R.F.C. can do anything about it but that is an indication.

Q: Cannot we say for you that you are for more and cheaper liquor? (Laughter)

THE PRESIDENT: I might say that at the dinner on March third. (Laughter)

Q: Did you sign the crop reduction loan bill?

THE PRESIDENT: No, and I asked for it last night. I haven't had it on my desk. It has probably gone somewhere for checking.

Q: To go back to this for a minute, is it possible that we will have to lower the tariff or the combined tariff and income tax?

THE PRESIDENT: I won't express an opinion because Joe Choate is looking

--- [185] ---

into the question at the present time.

Q: Has any consideration been given to the proposition originally suggested to have a Government corporation that will do all importing and distribution of liquor?

THE PRESIDENT: Not that I know of. We are getting on very well with the Virgin Islands rum proposition. Have you had that yet?

Q: Yes, sir. You allowed unrestricted imports.

THE PRESIDENT: I think we had allotted a million dollars to set the corporation up.

Q: Are there any others of the Dominions that figure in the rum business? Puerto Rico or --

THE PRESIDENT: (Interposing) Puerto Rico has made some rum; not very much, I think.

Q: Does the liquor tariff situation tie up with your general tariff Message? You proposed originally to set up a liquor tariff that would give lower rates to those countries taking farm goods and other stuff from us, but that was dropped by the Ways and Means Committee and they are awaiting further recommendations from you on general tariff policies.

THE PRESIDENT: That does not mean that the policy is out of the window entirely. It means that all along we were faced with the liquor shortage problem and it has not been so much a question of tariff bargaining at that time as getting enough liquor to put the bootlegger out of business.

Q: Have you figured out about what the prices ought to be in order to get rid of the bootlegger?

THE PRESIDENT: It depends on the brand. (Laughter) I will to into a

--- [186] ---

secret conference with you on that afterwards. (Laughter)

Q:  May we experiment with the different brands? (Laughter)

Q:  On this financing proposition, wouldn't that come under the functions of this proposed Import and Export Bank?

THE PRESIDENT: I do not know enough about the problem of raising money on a shipment of liquor to raise the tax. I should not think it would be a difficult thing to finance it offhand. After all, liquor is a changeable asset and once in the bonded warehouses it has pretty good value. I should think that almost any bank would lend money on it.

Q:  Some of us are getting queries on the Newspaper Code and particularly how it affects Washington correspondents. We might have a five-day week, with vacation on the sixth day, or use the last day as cumulative time for vacations. If you add that to your vacations, then you have to hire somebody and that would work as your reemployment.

THE PRESIDENT: My thought was that probably there ought to be. This is rule of thumb shot in the dark -- there ought to be some leeway but not very much. In other words, it ought not to be possible to work people sixty-five or seventy hours a week and then accumulate a large vacation, too large a vacation at the end. There ought to be a rule of reason on it.

Q:  I mean a forty-hour week and then accumulate time and in that way you help reemployment because you have to hire somebody during a vacation.

THE PRESIDENT: Of course the main objective is to work it out so there will be more people taken on. That is the objective we have in

--- [187] ---

mind.

Q:  Have you signed the Fisheries Code yet?

THE PRESIDENT: Fisheries Code?

Q:  National Fisheries Code.

THE PRESIDENT: I have not heard of it. (Laughter)

Q:  Will there be a separate code for Press Associations? (Laughter)

THE PRESIDENT: I think A.P. came under the Country Club Code. (Laughter)

Q:  What are you talking about? (Laughter)

THE PRESIDENT: I don't know what the other Associations came under but, as I understand it, they are voluntarily under one of the codes for the graphic arts.

Q:  I don't recall but they will do whatever is right.

Q:   I checked up on that last night with General Johnson's office and when he asked the Press Associations to submit a code, their answer was they would probably come under the Newspaper Code, but nothing has been heard of them since.

THE PRESIDENT:  We had better make them reply.

Q:   You expect them to come in under the Newspaper Code?

THE PRESIDENT:  Some code.  I do not know what code but some code.

Q:   The Stock Market regulation bill, have you read it yet?

THE PRESIDENT:  No, not yet.

Q:   Thank you, Mr. President.

MR. DONALDSON:  All in.

THE PRESIDENT:  On the forty million dollar emergency crop production loan bill, I am signing it this afternoon.  I haven't done it yet but will do it in the next five minutes.  I am going to sign it with the following explanation, that in signing this bill I do so only on the theory that it is proper to taper off the crop loan system rather than cut if off abruptly. They got this year something like eighty million dollars and it is forty for the coming year.

A useful purpose will be served by aiding certain farmers who cannot yet qualify for crop production loans from the newly established production credit associations.  Of course, such credit associations have been formed to take care of these crop loans.  However, where farmers have security to offer this year, they should be required to obtain their loans from the associations which have been established to give farmers a permanent source of production credit.

The record in the past of these crop production loans is very bad.  Unfortunately, previous crop loans show a large loss to the Government.  In prior years, that is on the return of the loan, it runs sixty and seventy and seventy-five per cent.  In other words, the return shows a big loss and also in prior years the administrative costs have actually exceeded the interest collected.  That is bad business.

--- [189] ---

The amount appropriated this year is far below the appropriations of previous years.  I think this is less than half of what it was last year, but this 1934 loan by the Government ought to be considered as a tapering-off loan, and should be the last of its kind.  In other words, I do not want any more bills along this line next year.  I was rather horrified by the returns that came in.  For instance, in loans made in 1933 so far, up to the first of the year, only 73% has been repaid.

Q:  The first of which year?

THE PRESIDENT:  1933 (1934 ?).  Only 73% had been repaid up to the first of the year.  There will be a material loss.

Q:  What was the total of the loan for 1933, do you happen to know?

THE PRESIDENT:  Either eighty or a hundred million dollars, I have forgotten which.

Q:  A hundred million dollars.

Q:  Would you care to state whether or not the crop reduction plans have anything to do with cutting of production loans?

THE PRESIDENT:  No, an entirely different thing.  The new associations being formed are intended to take care of crop loans.

Q:   Have you had a return on the fifty thousand questionnaires that went out
     in reference to the advisability of making compulsory or voluntary reduc-
     tions?

THE PRESIDENT:   The last I heard from the Department of Agriculture was 95% in
     favor.

Q:   That was on cotton, was it not?

Q:   Was that in favor of the tax idea?

THE PRESIDENT:   No.  It was put out in three different ways and split

--- [190] ---

roughly three different ways.  The 95% was split three different ways, but
the whole of the 95% were in favor of some kind of more compulsory system
than the old method.  I thought those figures were given out.  I thought
that they had been given out by the Department of Agriculture.

Q:   Mr. President, the Army seems to be having a difficult time of it on the
     mails.  Would you care to make any comment on that situation?

THE PRESIDENT:   No, except, of course, that everybody deplores any accident in
     the air.

Q:   Has the Army got the equipment, do you think, necessary for this?

THE PRESIDENT:   They seem to be flying the mails.

Q:   Do you care to discuss the visit you had from the Reforestation people
     today?

THE PRESIDENT:   Who?

Q:   The lumber people.

THE PRESIDENT:   Yes.  They came in to give me a preliminary report on what
     amounts, really, to an extension of the lumber code that was signed last
     fall, developing it into what might be called a conservation code.

     There was a clause in the original lumber code that provided a meeting,
     of which today's meeting is a result, between the private owners of forests
     and the state and Federal forestation services, with the idea that we
     would cooperate, the Government and state-owned forests and forest systems,
     with private ownership, which amounts to four-fifths of the total, in a
     general plan which would cover reforestation.  It is a thing that has been
     worked out, that form of cooperation, in almost every European country with

--- [191] ---

very great satisfaction and very great success, and there is no reason why
we should not work it out over here.  It depends for its success, of
course, on enforcement.  It means that either a large company or a small
private owner who does not live up not only to the provision for hours of
work and pay per hour, but also to provisions for cleaning up after he has
lumbered off his property by reseeding or planting, whether a big company
or a small company, if they do not live up to it it means the whole thing

falls down. Therefore, it becomes largely a matter of private practice and it must be almost 100% perfect in carrying out the agreement. Like so many other things, about 5% of the operators, if they chisel, the whole thing falls down. But the lumber companies who are represented -- I should say the industry itself -- feel that proper enforcement can be obtained not only through their own efforts, but also through the assistance of the state and Federal forestry services. It looks as if they are really getting somewhere.

I am particularly interested because away back in 1911 I got through the Legislature the first definite effort to bring the private companies into a spirit of conservation. We passed what was called the "top lopping" bill up in the Adirondack section. Up to that time, when they would cut down a spruce or a pine, they would work out the power part, the stick, and leave the upper part of the tree sticking up in the air. If you had a fire where that had been done the whole section would burn out over night. The top lopping provided that all branches should be laid back and that would all work into the ground in the course of a couple of years and would present no longer the fire hazard which the former

--- [192] ---

method of working it did.

Q:  Does the code provide that they must reseed after they cut off the timber? Is that in the code?

THE PRESIDENT: Of course that depends entirely on the kind of land. For instance, you take down in the yellow pine belt. Nobody plants yellow pine. If, after you have lumbered a yellow pine area, you clean the ground, you will get a reseeding from the trees that are left -- so many trees to the acre left for reseeding purposes -- you will get a natural reseeding in two or three years. On the other hand, in certain parts in the North, if you cut clean or even if you leave only a small number of seed trees, according to the character of the land, you do not have to replant. Taking it by and large, in lumbering operations, the percentage of land that has to be replanted is almost infinitesimal. It is one or two per cent because, in almost all forest land, if you leave seed trees, two or three seed trees to the acre, you get an annual reseeding without any cost if you prepare the ground for it by cleaning up.

Q:  Have you anything on the Bank?

THE PRESIDENT: Nothing further. Have not a word about it the last three or four days.

Q:  Do you regard it as a hopeful development, having the bankers participating in the sixty million dollar New York Central refinancing, although the R.F.C. will put up twenty million dollars and the bankers forty million dollars?

THE PRESIDENT: You mean private bankers?

Q:  Yes. What is your reaction to the private bankers' participation in the New York Central refinancing?

--- [193] ---

THE PRESIDENT: It looks to me, from the way the darned thing is going that the Government won't have to put up one red cent.

Q: Isn't it indicative of --

THE PRESIDENT: (interposing) What is it selling, 111 and 112?

Q: 113.

THE PRESIDENT: And yet people came down with tears in their eyes, saying that nobody would take it. It proves what I said was right.

Q: Anything new on the tariff Message today?

THE PRESIDENT: No.

Q: Returning to air mail, can you say whether any plans are being formulated to open the bidding for lines again?

THE PRESIDENT: We are working on plans. We have not got it out yet.

Q: Anything you can tell us about the Russian Ambassador's visit today? He told us he had a small, small commission.

THE PRESIDENT: It was a very small matter.

Q: Nothing about debts?

THE PRESIDENT: No.

Q: Anything on your buying land with the proceeds of the processing tax?

THE PRESIDENT: I don't know where that is now. It is kicking around somewhere. I do not know where it is. It is going between departments.

Q: Do you care to comment on Sirovich's (Representative Sirovich, of New York) bill for an exporting corporation?

THE PRESIDENT: I do not know it. What is it?

Q: It was noticed on the fifteenth of February and provided for a three hundred million dollar corporation to engage in foreign trade and

--- [194] ---

other business, et cetera.

THE PRESIDENT: Why is a bill necessary?

Q: Well, he seemed to consider it was; he put it in. (Laughter) Maybe he heard about what the White House planned to do. (Laughter)

Q: You recently told us, or did you, about National Committeemen practicing as lawyers. I have an inquiry from Chicago asking if that applies to National Committeemen who bid on municipal contracts where P.W.A. funds are involved.

THE PRESIDENT: If you just leave it in general form and do not talk about the gentleman himself. Just leaving it as a matter of broad general princi- ple, I am inclined to think that a National Committeeman within a state ought to choose. If he wants to bid on public contracts that have any relationship at all with the National Government, if he is the low bidder he should get it, but I don't think he should continue to be National Committeeman at the same time. It is a question of ethics. He ought to choose.

Q: There seems to be a little distinction there. Do you mean, holding his job, it would be suitable for him to make a bid and then, if he does get the project itself, --

THE PRESIDENT: No, I don't think he should engage in that work. (Laughter)

Q: Have you read Whitney's (Richard Whitney, of New York) idea on how the Stock Exchange should be regulated?

THE PRESIDENT: The story that came out today?

Q: Yes.

THE PRESIDENT: I do not think I read it. I think Ray Moley told me about it before it came out.

--- [195] ---

Q: His statement before the House?

THE PRESIDENT: No, I have not read it.

Q: Do you consider filling the vacancy on the Tariff Commission?

THE PRESIDENT: Not at the present time.

Q: There is a rumor that one of the Justices of the Supreme Court is about to retire?

THE PRESIDENT: No comment.

Q: Is Mr. Peek (Mr. George Peek) expected to take the presidency of this new intermediate Export-Import Bank?

THE PRESIDENT: Not that I know of.

Q: He says he is waiting to see you on it.

THE PRESIDENT: No. That whole thing, as I told you before, is really awaiting a meeting on the general foreign trade question. I think we are going to hold it on Monday.

Q: There are little differences of opinion developing in the House Committee over the matter of sugar. Do you care to discuss it?

THE PRESIDENT: The only thing coming to my attention the last couple of days -- I am not quite clear what I thought about Brother Weaver's testimony the other day, and I got a telegram from the Governor of Hawaii in which he quoted the Associated Press -- (laughter)

Q:    (Mr. Stephenson interposing)  It must have been right, then.

THE PRESIDENT:  -- and saying the Islands are all up in the air because the
     A.P. story said that we were taking the position that Hawaii was not a
     portion of the United States, and that they felt very much hurt.

     Now, I wired him back, or Mac (Mr. McIntyre) did, that the

                      --- [196] ---

     position in this quota theory is, we think, a perfectly fair one.  We took
     the quota for continental United States beet sugar, continental United
     States cane sugar and Hawaii and Puerto Rico and the Virgin Islands on the
     basis of the three-year average.  We applied the same rule to all four
     places.  I also said at the end of the telegram that it was perfectly true
     that the beet sugar people here in Washington are trying to suggest that
     Hawaii and Puerto Rico and the Virgin Islands are not parts of the United
     States, and that, therefore, the beet sugar people should have preferential
     treatment.  But those quota figures were honestly based on a three-year
     average.

Q:    In respect to Mr. Weaver's testimony, Dr. Tugwell the next day, in a state-
     ment, said it was the Administration's intention to prevent any further
     expansion of the sugar beet industry, and that seems to be the source of
     trouble with the Committee.

THE PRESIDENT:  If the Committee would just use a little horse sense and read
     what I said to the Congress, they would be out of their troubles.  I re-
     commended a quota system based on the amount of consumption of sugar, and
     that consumption is divided up on a quota basis.  Now, what would happen
     if we ate twice as much sugar four years from now, I am not able to say.

Q:    Once you get the agricultural end of that bill through, what about the
     dogfight between the refiners on the official quotas?

THE PRESIDENT:  On the refiners, we are applying the same principle; in other
     words, to allow the refiners to refine the same proportion that they have
     refined over the last three years.  Use exactly the same yardstick on
     everybody.

                      --- [197] ---

Q:    On this Hawaii thing, I want to get that straight.

THE PRESIDENT:  I did not see the story that went out.

Q:    I did not either, but you are standing by your statement, the original
     sugar statement, and on that Hawaii was given a quota?

THE PRESIDENT:  Absolutely, based on a three-year average.

Q:    Do you regard Hawaii --

THE PRESIDENT:  (interposing)  As part of the United States, very definitely.
     (Laughter)

Q:    You mentioned this foreign trade meeting.  Can you give us a little more
     on that?

THE PRESIDENT:  The thing we have been talking of holding the last three weeks.

Q:   It is going to be held, when?

THE PRESIDENT:  Sometime Monday or Tuesday.

Q:   The Secretary of State, undoubtedly?

THE PRESIDENT:  The Secretary of State, Commerce, Agriculture and one or two others, Tariff Commissioner O'Brien and somebody else.

Q:   Anything you can tell us about your meeting with Mr. Walsh (Frank Walsh, of New York) today?

THE PRESIDENT:  That was on the St. Lawrence Treaty, that is it.  It is just more information on the St. Lawrence Treaty, which I hope will go through.

Q:   Will Mr. Peek be among those present on Monday?

THE PRESIDENT:  I do not know.  I imagine he will but I do not know whether he is down on the list or not.

Q:   He is taking part in that, generally?

THE PRESIDENT:  The Interdepartmental Committee that has been working.

--- [198] ---

I don't know who there is -- Dickinson, Frank Sayre --

Q:   (interposing)  I believe he made the interdepartmental report?

THE PRESIDENT:  -- but I think Peek will be there too.

Q:   To discuss the foreign trade policy?

THE PRESIDENT:  And of course -- lest you ask the question, I will forestall it -- tariff is involved in it too.

Q:   Does that involve legislation too?

THE PRESIDENT:  Yes.

Q:   Can you tell us whether there are any developments in Russian exports?

THE PRESIDENT:  Won't be until next week.  Nothing until we have a meeting.

Q:   Can you tell us anything about the proposed legislation guaranteeing the bonds of the Home Owners' Loan Corporation?

THE PRESIDENT:  I am just about ready to send it to Congress.  I should think that by Monday that could go to the Congress.

Q:   On Monday?  Thank you.

Q:   You are not going up to Oyster Bay on March third, to the wedding?

THE PRESIDENT:  I cannot.  I have to go to a dinner here that night.

Q:    There is another report out that you are going to Maryland in the near future for some tercentenary?

THE PRESIDENT:  It happens later on.  The reason I cannot go is that I have to go for the fiftieth anniversary of my old school on the first of June.  It clashes with the Fleet review on the thirty-first of May.

Q:    Anything you can tell us about Vice President Garner's visit up here today with Senator Byrnes?

--- [199] ---

THE PRESIDENT:  Just talking politics.  (Laughter)

Q:    Can you elaborate on that a little bit?

THE PRESIDENT:  No.

Q:    Anything new in the railroad situation on wages?

THE PRESIDENT:  No.

Q:    Have you any assurances from either side on that proposition?

THE PRESIDENT:  Have to wait until after the fifteenth of March.

Q:    Any developments on the Weirton situation?

THE PRESIDENT:  I do not think so.  I talked to Bob Wagner about it two or three days ago.  I do not think there is anything since then.

Q:    Mr. President, there seems to be developing a new -- a theory of national defense, to separate the Air Corps from the Army and Navy.  Are you taking an active interest in that?

THE PRESIDENT:  I have not heard of it.

Q:    Thank you, Mr. President.

(The Press Conference adjourned at 4:35 P.M.)

CONFIDENTIAL
Press Conference #101
Executive Offices of the White House
February 28, 1934, 10:55 A.M.


THE PRESIDENT: Why so shrinking?


            (The President was speaking to Francis Stephenson,
            new president of the White House Correspondent's
            Association)


Q:   (Mr. Stephenson)  The weight of responsibility, Mr. President.

THE PRESIDENT:  Wait until next year at the dinner.  It will give me an oppor-
    tunity I have been awaiting for years.

Q:   Give it to him good, Mr. President.

THE PRESIDENT:  I am sorry I have to wait for a whole year to do it.

Q:   (Mr. Stephenson)  I will go to work on you in the meantime.

THE PRESIDENT:  I had hoped, speaking in the family, that Jim Hornaday would be
    in today.

Q:   Here he is.

THE PRESIDENT:  Let him come up here and shake hands on his fiftieth anniver-
    sary.


            (The President shook hands with Mr. Hornaday
            to the accompaniment of applause.)


Congratulations and I think the nicest thing and truest thing I can say
is that you are a gentleman of the Press.  (Applause)

I have got a handout for you, which Steve (Mr. Early) will give you as you
go out, in regard to unemployment.  It covers the general lessons and the
general experience that we learned things from in the past few months and
might be called the first part of the new procedure after the first of
May.  You will get it so I won't read the whole thing to you but, in general, in case you want to ask questions, the experience of the Emergency
Relief organization shows

                        --- [201] ---

now that we ought to separate the relief problem into three parts.  The
first is the proof that you cannot apply the same methods and means to
rural areas that you apply to city areas and therefore we set up as the
first group the problem of distressed families in rural areas.  We found
from experience that their security must be identified with agriculture
and that, in many parts of the country, this calls for a change from commercial farming, that does not pay, and dependence on a single cash crop,

that only pays one year out of four or five, something like that, to the raising of various commodities needed to maintain the family. Therefore relief funds for the rural areas will have to be spent in rather a different way. Work for wages is not for them the same kind of an essential that it is in the city because some of the expenditures by Government -- and by Government I mean state, local and national -- must go to make them self-sustaining.

Well, the simplest illustration I know of is what we tried to do in Georgia a few years ago, the hog, home and cow campaign, where the Government aided them to get the cow and let them pay for it over a period of years. In the long run that is cheaper than buying milk for them.

At the same time (under this program) we would try to get a certain amount of cash for these families in rural areas that need help by distributing the local public works among them. For example, the highway work that goes on in every rural community every year, give that highway work to the people who need it, again coming down to the essential element of need.

Then, the second category is something that has also developed because of the experience in the last few months. It is a problem of

--- [202] ---

the stranded populations. In other words, families in communities -- the easiest example is the community that used to be a one industry town and has lost that industry and the people cling to their towns, hoping against hope, year after year, that the industry is going to start up again and it never does. One example is the coal mine that has run out and the people stay there, year after year. It is a stranded community -- stranded families. In that case we have to adopt a means of relief which eventually looks to taking the people off relief.

Q:   May I ask a question? Is that population large?

THE PRESIDENT:  Fairly large. We haven't any definite figures on it. I asked yesterday at the Council meeting how large it was and Harry Hopkins said that his very, very rough guess was it was 300,000 families. One or two other people from the Labor Department and one or two others thought it might run as high as half a million families. Those people, obviously, have got to be given the opportunity, at least given the offer of moving to some small community where, either through farming operations of their own or through a combination of farming and industry, they can make themselves self-supporting.

Then, the third category relates to urban areas, the cities and suburbs of the larger cities. There again we are definitely taking the position that we don't want them to go on a dole. We want to remove, as far as we possibly can, what we used to call home relief, that is to say, cash, and substitute for it work relief.

In regard to these urban areas, the plan is, from the spring on, to work with the communities and put the public bodies on notice that they have got to devise properly organized work programs and that the federal contribution would go in carrying out these work programs al-

--- [203] ---

most one hundred per cent, you might say, for wages and that the federal contributions would be confined to needy persons.

The $950,000,000 appropriation will have been reduced by May to a little over $600,000,000 and by the end of the fiscal year probably to the $500,000,000 for the following year. That will be used and we hope will be sufficient to carry us through the greater part of the next fiscal year, without any question, in this program, this threefold program of helping the rural population, the stranded families and the urban population. In other words, we are now using the experience we got in the past few months.

Q: Mr. President, did you get any report as to the total number of families on relief at present?

THE PRESIDENT: Yes. You mean on CWA, or on relief as a whole?

Q: Both, if you can give them.

THE PRESIDENT: I haven't it for the whole thing. Harry Hopkins can give you the number on CWA. It is about 3,200,000 at the present time.

Q: The urban program to be carried out through the CWA organization?

THE PRESIDENT: Yes, by putting more responsibility on the locality to see that only families in need get that money, get those wages, because it is wages for work.

For instance, one very simple figure, the only one I remember out of this mass, is that out of the 4,000,000 individuals on CWA there are only 2,000,000 of them that have come from relief rolls. Now, that is rather an amazing thing. The other 2,000,000 were people out of work who came and said they were out of work. Because of the need for hurrying last fall, very, very careful checkups were impossible. Now we have plenty of time to turn around before next fall and every case will be looked into to see whether they are the most proper subjects for this

--- [204] ---

employment.

Q: Did you mean 3,200,000 families or individuals?

THE PRESIDENT: Individuals.

Q: Mr. President, you said that the federal aid would be immediately -- you mean the old people, the unemployed?

THE PRESIDENT: What?

Q: You said the federal aid would be for needy people. Do you mean by that the old people who are unemployed?

THE PRESIDENT: You mean old people? That is a different thing. You have to take care of them through what amounts to the dole system.

Q: Do you mean the Federal Government will control the highway construction so as to give work to the local people?

THE PRESIDENT: No, certainly not, but what we are going to devise in the case of the rural population is to persuade the local authority. For instance, as an example, in any township in the State of New York, the State Government, in the average township in the State of New York, employs a highway gang on the State road that runs through their township, and they have probably five or six people on the highway gang. In addition, there is the Town Superintendent of Roads, who employs sporadically perhaps eight or ten other people on the town roads. In North Carolina it is all one system, so it is all one agency that does the hiring but in the average township there are fifteen or twenty people on the highways. In a great many cases those people are not the needy people in the community and an effort will be made, through local government, to take on the needy people on all kinds of Government public works, rather than those who do not need it as much.

The same problem comes up in the case of two or three people in one family who are employed. We are going to spread the employment

--- [205] ---

so that only one person in the family will get the employment if there is nobody in the family working.

Q: Is the Federal Government going to contribute in the same proportion?

THE PRESIDENT: It will depend on the need condition as it develops during the spring and summer.

Q: What will be done in the case of certain localities unable to take their part?

THE PRESIDENT: There we will have to bear an additional cost.

Q: I presume that the Federal Government may have to bear the whole cost?

THE PRESIDENT: There are very few, like the drought areas in the Dakotas or Oklahoma, but it is a comparatively small number.

Q: Does the subsistence homes bill stay in the big city picture?

THE PRESIDENT: I should say, offhand, that the subsistence homes program will be used more largely in the future for the stranded family classification.

Q: Is this program going to be carried out in connection with Dr. Wilson's office?

THE PRESIDENT: They are all tied in together now.

Q: We were given to understand the other day by Hopkins that the present plan, which included carrying baskets of food to the farmers, and this farm road relief had not worked out very well.

THE PRESIDENT: It has not put nearly as many people to work as we expected on the road thing.

Q: Is this a continuation of the same plan? I mean, using the highways as a method of work, is that a continuation of the same scheme?

THE PRESIDENT: Of what scheme?

Q:   Of using highway employment in the rural areas?

THE PRESIDENT: That will fit into the picture in the proper place.

--- [206] ---

Q:   Hopkins said it had not worked out satisfactorily.

THE PRESIDENT: What he meant was that out of the total amount of money, it did not put as many people to work as we expected.

Q:   Do you have a new highway appropriation in mind for next year?

THE PRESIDENT: I think not. You see, on the highway appropriation -- I do not know the actual figures but I think probably they could tell you in the highway bureau -- but just as a guess on my part, I should not say that more than half of it would have been spent by the spring. It means that the other half will be actually paid out in wages during the balance of this year.

Q:   Will the CWA wage scale continue or will it change in the cities?

THE PRESIDENT: I do not know yet; we have not got to that.

Q:   Will it include the waterway projects as well as highways?

THE PRESIDENT: No, not under Hopkins. The waterways projects will go forward like the Fort Peck Dam, et cetera. That will come out of whatever additional money we get for public works, but the thing will tie right in together.

Q:   Has any estimate been made of the cost of this new relief program as compared with CWA work?

THE PRESIDENT: No. What I said before is that we hoped that the $950,000,000 will carry us through, certainly until next spring but of course that is subject to the reservation that no human being can tell what the conditions will be late in the fall.

Q:   Have any of the details of the methods for handling the stranded population or relief been worked out?

THE PRESIDENT: No, we have set up the three groups. This is merely the preliminary of the announcement of the general policy.

--- [207] ---

Q:   Can you divide the things by a rough figure of the people stranded in the city and in the country?

THE PRESIDENT: No.

Q:   Does the stranded population include transients or floaters or people that have moved into the cities that do not properly belong there?

THE PRESIDENT: I do not think it does. I think the figures we talked about with respect to relief applied to the families that were still in the community where they got stranded.

Q: I was thinking about the Southern California situation.

THE PRESIDENT: Of course that Southern California situation just sticks out by itself as a sore thumb.

Q: Is it contemplated that the Federal Surplus Relief Corporation will be part of this work for the stranded families, colonizing them on submarginal land?

THE PRESIDENT: I do not think that comes out of surplus relief, but am not certain.

Q: Are there any developments in prospect concerning National Committeemen who have been doing law business -- some of those who have not resigned as yet?

THE PRESIDENT: Who are you talking about, which one?

Q: Arthur Mullen.

THE PRESIDENT: Arthur Mullen. I have not heard a word about any of them or anybody else for the last week. Have you heard any?

Q: Except I understand that Mullen is going around indicating he had no intention of resigning. (Laughter)

Q: Is it still your view that the railroads are not subject to NRA Codes?

THE PRESIDENT: Yes. We have specifically put them off on one side as a separate problem, with the consent of everybody.

--- [208] ---

Q: Have you asked General Johnson to do anything in that connection?

THE PRESIDENT: No.

Q: Going back to the Southern California situation, have you read the special report of the National Labor Board Commissioners?

THE PRESIDENT: Have they got one? I did not know that; I must get it.

Q: The conferences on the St. Lawrence Waterway, anything new with reference to that?

THE PRESIDENT: Yes, I said at the last Press Conference that I hoped they would take a vote sometime.

Q: On foreign trade, various things have been going on in that line?

THE PRESIDENT: Not quite ready to shoot on that; pretty soon.

Q: Will there be more Public Works money likely to be appropriated and made available in addition to the amounts already in?

THE PRESIDENT: Oh, yes; we are sending up that request for -- I do not know
what the total is -- it is around $2,000,000,000 for various things. You
see, that appropriation has not gone up as yet. Public Works is included
in that.

Q:    That is the original $500,000,000 estimate?

THE PRESIDENT: Yes. But always remember the classifications on that
$2,000,000,000 are intended to be highly elastic. In other words, any
subdivision of the amounts in this bill are subject to reallocation at any
time. There is not any hard and fast amount. It is an estimate. I will
probably send it up as an estimate. It might run more.

Q:    This $2,000,000,000 is an addition to the $3,300,000,000 ?

THE PRESIDENT: Yes. It was in the Budget.

Q:    Isn't this $500,000,000 for the continuation of relief next year in your
Budget? Wasn't that included in the $2,000,000,000?

--- [209] ---

THE PRESIDENT: That has gone in.

Q:    Does that cut this other bill by a half billion? I thought it was probably
part of the next year's money.

THE PRESIDENT: But you will have to figure as to exactly what they have appropriated. The total amounts in the Budget were $1,166,000,000 for the ba-
lance of this year and $2,000,000,000 for next year. That makes a total
of $3,166,000,000 , all of the items to be interchangeable. Now, I do not
know how much they have passed already -- I have forgotten -- but what they
have passed you deduct from $3,166,000,000 and you will find out how much
more is due from Congress.

Q:    Any requests for PWA outside of the Budget?

THE PRESIDENT: Not that I know of.

Q:    Is it fair to ask if you think that the margin requirements in the pending
Stock Exchange Bill are wise?

THE PRESIDENT: I cannot talk about it. While it would be absolutely fair to
say that I have not read the bill -- I have not read it but I pretty well
know what it has in it. But because it is in the stage of discussion, I
think I had better not go into the details any more than I should go into
details at the present time about what happened yesterday.

Q:    I was just going to ask you about it.

THE PRESIDENT: I just knew you would. (Laughter)

Q:    How about the announcement today about the Commission (D.C. Commission)
vacancy? Keech or any other candidates?

THE PRESIDENT: They may have seen Mac.

Q:    I am taking care of the citizens of Columbia (The District of Columbia).

The local citizenship associations are engaged in a membership drive --

--- [210] ---

that is, every ten years -- and they are very anxious, of course, to have the President of the United States to become a member of the local Citizens' Association.

THE PRESIDENT: Would I lose my voting residence at Hyde Park if I did that?

Q: You know they don't vote here.

THE PRESIDENT: That is all right.

Q: President Woodrow Wilson was a member of the local Citizens' Association and if the President can see his way clear to become a member, they would feel, naturally, highly honored.

MR. McINTYRE: You have a delegation coming later today to offer you the invitation.

THE PRESIDENT: How much does it cost?

Q: You will get a free membership.

Q: With regard to the establishment of these three banks to finance the development of foreign trade, can we say what you have in mind with regard to what the Government would be willing to guarantee the railroads?

THE PRESIDENT: I do not think we have come anywhere near talking about that, even Peek himself. It would depend on the individual case.

Q: With regard to this bank, it was mentioned twenty million dollars as a possible credit we will extend to the American silver producers to ship silver down there. Is that figure correct?

THE PRESIDENT: You had better check with Sumner Welles. My general impression is that it was ten.

Q: The Secretary said a few million and we thought twenty was rather high.

THE PRESIDENT: I think it was ten. You had better check on it.

Q: In connection with this passage of additional legislation regulating securities, utilities, et cetera, do you see any need for a uniform

--- [211] ---

federal incorporation law such as you have a uniform bankruptcy law?

THE PRESIDENT: The only thing that has happened on a federal corporation law is that there is a committee studying it. There are all sorts of problems involved and the committee has made one or two reports on details, on portions of the general problem. I do not think they are ready to make a report that would be really worthwhile at this time and therefore, in talking to some of them yesterday, we all thought it was better to let that go over to another session of Congress, pending more study of it, so we will know better where we stand.

Q:   What committee is that?

THE PRESIDENT:   I could not tell you who is working on it. There is somebody --
    the Federal Trade Commission, the Department of Commerce, the Attorney
    General.

Q:   That was on the subject of securities?

THE PRESIDENT:   On the subject of the possibility of providing for a voluntary
    federal incorporation law.

Q:   Thank you, Mr. President.

Q:   Is there anything new in the air mail situation?

THE PRESIDENT:   Not yet; soon.


(The Press Conference adjourned at 11:25 A.M.)

CONFIDENTIAL
Press Conference #102
Executive Offices of the White House
March 2, 1934, 4:07 P.M.


THE PRESIDENT: How is he (referring to Mr. Francis Stephenson)?

Q: He is finding himself. He is taking his new duties very seriously.

THE PRESIDENT: By God, he needs to. (Laughter) Says one President to another.
(Laughter)

Q: (Mr. Stephenson) O.K., Mr. President.

Q: (Mr. Storm) This place was overrun with presidents this morning. We had
Stevie in here and Bill Murphy from the Press Club and George Durno, all
at one time.

THE PRESIDENT: That is going some. It is a good combination. (Laughter)

MR. DONALDSON: All in.

THE PRESIDENT: Somebody was asking the other day about the spending of the
highway money and I have two large volumes from the Secretary of Agriculture which I am going to ask Steve (Mr. Early) to look through and dig
out the information for you from those two volumes as to how much money
has been spent up to the present time. The only figure I can find is that
seventy-three per cent of the total money handed out by the Department of
Agriculture has been obligated by the state governments. Now, how much
has been actually spent in labor, I do not know. That is a job for you.

MR. EARLY: Don't give it to me. (Laughter)

Q: There is a story in the paper this morning that an article that was being
prepared by the National Committee, reviewing the first year of the Administration, had been killed because you did not want to get into any controversy. Is there any possibility that you will give us a

--- [213] ---

statement?

THE PRESIDENT: No. Steve (Mr. Early) brought me the memo that was sent out to
the editors killing it. I think that states the fact very simply and very
truthfully, that this article was prepared at the request of the Press,
outlining the history of the past year. As our good friend Charlie
Michelson honestly admitted, he wrote the article without any effort to
make it a part of an article, but the National Committee decided that the
very fact of publication of it, sending it out over the name of the National Committee, might be construed as pursuing the same tactics as -- this
is off the record -- as the Republican National Committee, and they did
not want to be placed in that position, either by editors or the public.
In other words, they believe that the people in this country go along with
the idea that they are trying to run this party for the good of everybody
and not for the good of the party.

Q: Is there anything you can tell us about the mission of Mr. Norman Davis to

London?

THE PRESIDENT: Norman hasn't any mission in London. He is going over on some private business, purely as a lawyer, as I understand it. He has got no messages, no work to do. I think he is going to Sweden. Is he going to London?

Q: He is in London now.

THE PRESIDENT: I suppose he is on his way to Sweden.

Q: I understand there are dispatches from London indicating that we are submitting some sort of formula regarding armaments.

THE PRESIDENT: Norman Davis is going over purely and solely in a private capacity. He is not on the Government payroll and he won't have anything to do with the Government work until and unless there is a meet-

--- [214] ---

ing in Geneva, and Lord knows when that will be.

Q: We understand a communication has been sent to the British Government concerning disarmament. Can you tell us anything about that?

THE PRESIDENT: There was one went off a couple of weeks ago. I think it is going to be given out this afternoon by the State Department at the request of various people.

Q: It was not a special message sent by you?

THE PRESIDENT: No. There is nothing in it that in any way changes the attitude. It shows polite and real interest in the progress -- any progress that they can make over there in the European political situation, with the hope that it will bring things around to the point where we can again discuss world disarmament.

Q: That will be given out by the State Department?

THE PRESIDENT: There or here?

MR. EARLY: Immediately following your Conference, by the State Department.

THE PRESIDENT: There is no story in it because it is merely a reiteration of what we have said half a dozen times before.

Q: Does that go over with your signature?

THE PRESIDENT: No.

Q: Can you tell us whose signature?

THE PRESIDENT: I don't know. I think I saw it at the time; it is one of the regular State Department dispatches.

Q: Wasn't it a reply to the British memo sent to us about that time?

THE PRESIDENT: That I do not know. I do not know that they sent a memo.

Q: They presented one to us. It was the regular British note, which was sent around to all the powers about a week ago.

THE PRESIDENT: Yes?

Q: The belief had been, until the bill was made public up on the Hill, that

--- [215] ---

you were asking emergency powers to last three years. The bill that Senator Harrison gave us this afternoon indicates that these agreements are terminable within three years but that they may be renewed for any number of years in addition to that.

THE PRESIDENT: I don't think it makes any difference one way or the other.

Q: Some persons recommended the adoption of a permanent tariff policy?

THE PRESIDENT: You will see the word "emergency" very distinctly in the Message.

Q: I was speaking about the bill.

THE PRESIDENT: I do not care what the bill is so long as I get the authority. If they make it a three-year authority, that is perfectly all right.

Q: You expect to terminate the authority within three years?

THE PRESIDENT: It is an emergency power, distinctly asked for as that. The agreements can only be made over a period of three years. Congress can terminate them at that time, if they want. In other words, it is a purely academic discussion. The intent is quite clear.

Q: Mr. President, have you taken any action on wild life restoration?

THE PRESIDENT: I do not know where it is now. Do you know?

Q: It is supposed to be here. It came back night before last.

Q: Have you discussed the Weirton case with the Attorney General lately?

THE PRESIDENT: I have not heard anything about it for a week or ten days.

Q: Can you give us any information on Panama's refusal to accept our check, preferring to have gold?

THE PRESIDENT: Not yet. The Secretary of State is conferring with various other people, the Treasury and the Attorney General.

Q: Hasn't the Attorney General rendered an opinion yet?

--- [216] ---

THE PRESIDENT: No, not that I know of.

Q: Mr. President, are you discussing with House leaders the Independent Offices Bill?

THE PRESIDENT: No.

Q: Sir, is your debt Message any nearer? Any time soon?

THE PRESIDENT: You are right, it is nearer. (Laughter)

Q: Is it coming any time soon?

THE PRESIDENT: I do not think as a matter of fact that there is anything much more in prospect of sending up to Congress except minor matters. Pretty nearly everything is completed with today's action except the war debts and we are nearer that.

Q: How about public utilities holding companies, Mr. President?

THE PRESIDENT: Public utilities? I do not know what happens on that.

Q: You mentioned some weeks ago about an unfulfilled plank in the platform.

THE PRESIDENT: I do not know. To tell you the honest truth, I have not thought about it at all. Is there anything about holding companies in the Stock Exchange bill?

Q: The Communications Bill has holding companies in it.

THE PRESIDENT: Frankly, I have not taken it up at all.

Q: Under the Home Loan legislation, do you contemplate the financing of new home construction or just refinancing?

THE PRESIDENT: I don't know. We had been talking about the desirability of getting financed, preferably by private means, a large program of home improvement and also home building. That goes rather into the subject which is still under discussion about agencies to improve the credit situation, like, for instance, the suggestion of the twelve regional banks which is still in suggestion form.

We believe that there is a great deal of money that is needed to

--- [217] ---

be applied for the building of new homes and for putting in bathrooms and furnaces, etc., improving the old home, and it is largely a question of working out a plan for getting the credit for it. We haven't got beyond the discussion stage in regard to those twelve banks.

Q: Any further progress on the intermediate credit banks?

THE PRESIDENT: No, still talking about it. In fact, I think they have a conference this afternoon on it.

Q: Senator Vandenberg was here today, and he told us that he had discussed plans for demonetizing politics. Can you tell us anything further on it?

THE PRESIDENT: Right. (Laughter) No, because it is in the conference stage and we brought in a good many people from the Senate and the House. We had Senators Byrnes, Norris, King, Judge Sumners, Senator Vandenberg, and one or two others, and they are continuing the conference with the idea of

getting a bill which they could get through Congress which would have two
applications, as a general proposition. One would be in connection with
practicing before departments or with departments on any monetary matters
by Congressmen, Senators, members of the National Committee, etc., etc.
The other phase of it, the regulation part of it, has to do with who they
would allow to appear before them with the objective of the elimination of
people who make their livelihood by such representations and receive large
sums for it under what amounts, in many cases, to false pretense. They are
trying to get somebody agreed on some bill up there.

Q:  Mr. President, would practicing before departments be broad enough to prevent contracts going to National Committeemen under PWA?

THE PRESIDENT:  Yes, but that is not practicing before departments, that is the
political angle of it.

Q:  Have you seen the proposed amendments to the Agricultural Adjustment Act?

--- [218] ---

THE PRESIDENT:  No. I think the Secretary (Secretary Wallace) said there were
a number of amendments but they were all rather technical in character and
merely clarifying. There would be no trouble about them one way or the
other. I have not seen them.

Q:  There is a report that the air mail lines are going to be turned back
Saturday at midnight?

THE PRESIDENT:  Oh, no.

Q:  Anything new on that situation?

THE PRESIDENT:  Not yet, but very soon, we hope.

Q:  Mr. President, do you care to say anything about Senator Wagner's new
bill?

THE PRESIDENT:  No, I have not seen the bill. Apparently there are quite a
number of different subjects in it. The only thing I knew about was the
general thought of making the National Labor Board more practical. But I
understand there are other things. I have not seen it.

Q:  Can you tell us anything about the Japanese problems that Prince Tokugawa
took up with you?

THE PRESIDENT:  Not at all.


(The Press Conference adjourned at 4:22 P.M.)

Press Conference #103
Executive Offices of the White House
March 7, 1934, 10:55 A.M.


Q:    (Mr. Storm)  Good morning, Mr. President.

THE PRESIDENT:  Good morning, Mr. President (Mr. Stephenson).

Q:    (Mr. Stephenson)  Good morning, Mr. President.

Q:    The president (referring to Mr. Stephenson) issued his first executive order yesterday.

THE PRESIDENT:  Did he, really?

Q:    He authorized the purchase of a new chessboard for the press room.

Q:    (Mr. Stephenson)  And also no more Monday morning speeches by the President.

THE PRESIDENT:  How about backgammon?  Have you taken it out there?  You ought to do it.  I play it on the NOURMAHAL all the time.  You can play a whole game in about four minutes.  And, by doubling, you can lose your shirt on it too.  (Laughter)

I do not think there is any news at all except I am feeling quite chipper because I finished all the work on the forthcoming book at midnight last night.

Q:    When will it come out?

THE PRESIDENT:  About the middle of April, I think.

Q:    How long is it?

THE PRESIDENT:  About 300 pages.

Q:    Is the title still to be, "On Our Way?"

THE PRESIDENT:  You will have to ask the publisher.  I don't know.  I think it was announced as that.  That is a thing over which the author has no control.

Q:    What is the nature of the writing?

THE PRESIDENT:  Mostly compilation.

--- [220] ---

Q:    Can you tell us anything about the strike situation in the automobile industry -- collective bargaining?

THE PRESIDENT:  I have not heard a word about it.  Johnson has been too busy the last three days to talk to me about it at all.

Q:    Have you had much reaction to your speech on Monday on N.R.A.?

THE PRESIDENT: There was a flock of telegrams that afternoon. I did not see any yesterday. Did any more come in?

MR. EARLY: I gave them out, sir.

Q: There is some confusion about Senator Robinson's speech on the state of the Union, and particularly the Stock Market Regulation Bill. Is he speaking for himself or --

THE PRESIDENT: (interposing) I have got to be frank and off the record, I haven't read it.

Q: The House Ways and Means Committee is holding hearings on the free ports. I think it is understood you were in favor of it?

THE PRESIDENT: I did not know they had any legislation up there at all. I have always been interested in the possibility of free ports, but nothing specific. It is a perfectly fine idea and they do have free ports in certain parts of the world that work very, very well.

Q: Do you think it would help our foreign trade?

THE PRESIDENT: Yes. Where they have free ports it seems to work out very well. It encourages trade.

Q: Mr. President, the mayors of the Great Lakes cities are coming in tomorrow about St. Lawrence. Anything you can tell us?

THE PRESIDENT: I understand they are coming here to endorse it.

Q: We thought they were going to put the heat on. (Laughter)

THE PRESIDENT: That would not be a bad idea either. (Laughter)

--- [221] ---

Q: Mr. President, are you going to ask for an extension of the licensing provisions of the NRA? I think they run out in June.

THE PRESIDENT: I think they do and, Stevie (Mr. Stephenson), I have not talked to anybody about it yet. I think it would be a pretty good guess to say we would, but I have not talked about it and I cannot answer yes or no. It is something I have got to do fairly soon.

Q: Also there are some reports you are planning executive action to bring about the shorter work week, which you suggested to the NRA meeting the other day, in the event that they do not do it themselves?

THE PRESIDENT: That is very premature. We will let them finish their conversations this week.

Q: Mr. President, will you soon be able to give attention to the local appointments, the Justice of the Municipal Court and the Public Utilities Commissioner?

THE PRESIDENT: I think that is a very good idea. I think, for your sake, I will try to take it up this week. Are we ready to shoot on that?

MR. McINTYRE:  What is that?

THE PRESIDENT:  Municipal Court and Public Utilities?

MR. McINTYRE:  I do not think so.

THE PRESIDENT:  Keep after Mac.  (Laughter)

Q:  Is your Message on war debts about ready to go up?

THE PRESIDENT:  No.  It is nearer than it was last week.  (Laughter)

Q:  Is there any change in the sugar situation that has caused such a furor out west?

THE PRESIDENT:  No.  Has there been some furor out there?

Q:  Over limiting domestic production.

THE PRESIDENT:  They have had furors in Hawaii and Puerto Rico and the Philippines too.  They are all having them.

--- [222] ---

Q:  The Inter-American Highway, do you favor its extension beyond Panama to Buenos Aires?

THE PRESIDENT:  No.  The general thought is that if we can get all the Central American Republics to go along with the building of it, then the South American Republics can take it up of their own accord.  Eventually, if we can link North America and South America, it would be a great achievement.

Q:  Anything new in the railroad legislation?

THE PRESIDENT:  No, they are meeting on the fifteenth.

Q:  You have not heard anything of the position of Labor, whether they will go along?

THE PRESIDENT:  No.

(The Press Conference adjourned at 11:00 A.M.)

Press Conference #104
Executive Offices of the White House
March 9, 1934, 4:08 P.M.


Q:   It looks like you have got a lot of business there (indicating the desk,
     piled high with papers).

THE PRESIDENT:  I don't think there is a blessed bit of news.  My basket is al-
     most empty and I am almost up to date on everything.

Q:   What are the prospects tomorrow?  Put the lid on again?

THE PRESIDENT:  Yes.

Q:   Anything you can tell us, sir, about the matter of liquor quotas and the
     letting down of the bars in the matter of liquor importations?

THE PRESIDENT:  Yes, I can.  We talked it over in the Cabinet meeting and the
     general feeling was that we should let down the bars and, at least, for
     a temporary period, thirty days or sixty days, temporarily let up on the
     quota system.  We will let liquor come in because it is obvious that it is
     not being sold at a low enough price in this country.

     Then, there was one other phase I talked with Choate about yesterday.  He
     has applications from quite a number of distilleries, most of them -- this
     is American liquor, Rye and Bourbon -- which did not get in within the time
     limit for setting the domestic manufacturers' quotas.  Most of them are
     comparatively small distilleries, most of them old, that were owned by old
     families in Kentucky, Tennessee, et cetera, and did not get their applica-
     tions in in time.  To give them permits at this time will undoubtedly in-
     crease the possible total of manufactured liquor in this country to a total
     maximum on a 24-hour basis of 44 million gallons a year.

Q:   Increase it to that?

--- [224] ---

THE PRESIDENT:  No, by that.  That is the maximum possible running on a 24-hour
     basis, and Mr. Choate recommended and I approved going along with the idea
     of giving them permits.

Q:   These late fellows?

THE PRESIDENT:  These late fellows, in order to again bring down the price of
     United States made, tax paid liquor.

Q:   Is there any discussion on decreasing the duty on imported liquor?

THE PRESIDENT:  Not at this time.

Q:   Mr. President, does that mean that any American importer now may get a per-
     mit for any amount he wishes for the next thirty or sixty days?

THE PRESIDENT:  Yes, as I understand it.

Q:   When does it go into effect?

THE PRESIDENT: At the end of the present quota period, whenever that is. I think you had better check on that.

Q: That means there won't be any restrictions whatever on imports during that period?

THE PRESIDENT: Yes, it means there won't be any restrictions on imports during that period.

Q: There won't be until April thirtieth?

THE PRESIDENT: I don't know whether right away or wait until the end of the quota period.

Q: Did you discuss a definite period?

THE PRESIDENT: No, but it will only be a trial period.

Q: Is there any considerable amount of protests coming in from small businesses to the effect that they cannot stand reduced hours?

THE PRESIDENT: You mean the liquor business?

Q: No, sir; reduced hours in general.

THE PRESIDENT: I do not know; I have not been to the NRA meetings. I suppose

--- [225] ---

there have been some protests, the same way there have been some protests from large companies that could not stand it.

Q: One of the morning papers today ventured the opinion that you had decided to shelve the debt issue because it was not included in the list which Senator Robinson brought to the White House.

THE PRESIDENT: I think you have answered your question, "They have ventured the opinion."

Q: Do you still intend to send a Message up?

THE PRESIDENT: Yes, and it is nearer than it was two days ago.

Q: Is it likely that the Message will have any legislation?

THE PRESIDENT: I have not thought about it at all.

Q: The same paper ventured the same opinion about the Pure Food and Drug Bill.

THE PRESIDENT: Not that I know of. Frankly, I have not heard of it the last ten days. I do not know what has happened to it.

Q: They have been having hearings on it in revised form and now they are waiting to see whether Copeland (Senator Copeland) will make any changes.

THE PRESIDENT: I have not approved any revised form. I did not know they had got to that.

Q:   Senator Copeland said it was satisfactory to you in the revised form.

THE PRESIDENT:   I have not seen any revised form and it is news to me that
     Copeland and Tugwell (Assistant Secretary of Agriculture Rexford G. Tug-
     well) were together on it.

Q:   Any possibility of your taking action regarding legislation or other steps
     to control the operation of chain stores?

THE PRESIDENT:   I have not heard a word about it.   Any talk in the NRA?

Q:   No, sir, not yet; but there has been some recent action in conference on
     the same subject and there are rumors, not very definite.

THE PRESIDENT:   I have not heard a word about it.

                           --- [226] ---

Q:   We have had a pretty difficult winter here.   Any chance of going south, do
     you think?

THE PRESIDENT:   I do not know.   I have been looking at some people -- I think
     you need Florida for a few days.

Q:   Yes, indeed.

THE PRESIDENT:   So, just out of consideration for the Press, I am really think-
     ing of -- depending on Congress, of course, and it is really tentative --
     going off with Vincent Astor on the NOURMAHAL, going off the end of this
     month sometime, the last week of this month, to catch some fish off the
     coast of Florida.   We will send in a radio to the Florida coast every
     morning and every evening.

Q:   At Miami, Mr. President?

THE PRESIDENT:   So you will be all right.   (Laughter)

Q:   At Palm Beach?

Q:   You are going to board the NOURMAHAL at Miami, did you say?

THE PRESIDENT:   I do not know where.

Q:   Can you tell us anything about your conversation with Sumner Welles?

THE PRESIDENT:   Oh, that was about starting a Cuban bank.   That is all ready to
     be signed this afternoon, the Executive Order.

Q:   Can you tell us anything about your conversation with Green (William Green
     of the American Federation of Labor)?

THE PRESIDENT:   Green came in to recommend a gentleman for appointment to some
     office and I have forgotten which one it was.   He and some Senator came in
     today.   (Laughter)

Q:   In connection with the Cuban bank, has it not been definitely decided to
     extend $10,000,000  of credit for silver purchases?

THE PRESIDENT: No, the bank, as organized, will have $250,000 in common stock and two and a half million dollars in preferred stock. Of course

--- [227] ---

that can always, at any time later, be amended but that is the way it will be organized.

Q: And the purpose of the bank, Mr. President, is to finance trade?

THE PRESIDENT: The immediate purpose of the bank is to make it possible for Cuba to obtain silver currency, of which there is a shortage.

Q: How much will Cuba take at the beginning, sir?

THE PRESIDENT: I do not know.

Q: To whom will this stock be sold, the RFC?

THE PRESIDENT: Yes.

Q: Can you comment on legislation pending in Congress to appropriate anywhere from a billion and a quarter to two billion dollars to have the RFC take over the assets of all closed national and state member banks and pay the deposits one hundred per cent?

THE PRESIDENT: The only comment will be, off the record, that the bill won't go through and, if it goes through, it will get vetoed.

Q: Have you given any consideration to establishing a new agency to administer the proposed Stock Market Regulation Bill?

THE PRESIDENT: No; I read in the paper they had a new bill. Is that right?

Q: They are drafting it now.

Q: In connection with the Cuban bank, can we understand that the credit granted will be granted to American exporters of silver?

THE PRESIDENT: I have no idea what the latest details are. I think it is a straight transaction with the Cuban Government, but I am not sure.

Q: Will it involve a cash loan to the Cuban Government?

THE PRESIDENT: No, it is a banking transaction.

Q: Speaking of vetoes, do you care to offer any comment on the veterans' bill?

THE PRESIDENT: No, not at all.

Q: I understand Ray Stevens has withdrawn from the Foreign Bondholders' Pro-

--- [228] ---

tective Council and there are charges that the Council has been doing business with some of the issuing houses of the Latin American securities, something which you warned against. Is there any chance, under these conditions, that you will revive Section II?

THE PRESIDENT: Ray Stevens was in bad need of a holiday, which he had not had since his return from Siam. As I understand it, he got out temporarily in order to be entirely free during the balance of the winter and, as I understand it, he hoped to be able to go back in the spring sometime. What the details are, I do not know.

Q: There is no plan to revoke under Section II?

THE PRESIDENT: No.

Q: There have been several reports lately that despite the promises made by Litinov, when you recognized the Soviet Government, the Communists have continued their propaganda in the United States?

THE PRESIDENT: I have not heard anything about it at all. Have you any reports, specific ones?

Q: Quite a few.

THE PRESIDENT: Ask the State Department; I haven't any.

Q: Would you care to comment on the suggestion of General Johnson for a ten per cent increase in wages?

THE PRESIDENT: Still in the discussion stage over there.

Q: There is a revival of the report that Farley intends to get out as National Chairman?

THE PRESIDENT: I guess it is true, as soon as we can find anyone to succeed him.

Q: How about the group on St. Lawrence?

THE PRESIDENT: They left a three-page full and complete endorsement, which they say came from practically every city in the whole Great Lakes area,

--- [229] ---

in favor of the St. Lawrence Treaty. I sent them up to the Hill.

(The Press Conference adjourned at 4:20 P.M.)

Press Conference #105
Executive Offices of the White House
March 14, 1934, 10:35 A.M.


THE PRESIDENT: I think I have only one suggestion and that is that you should
get your accommodations at Miami as soon as possible because they say
there is hardly a bed to be had down there.

Q: We had better work today?

Q: That is where you will keep headquarters, will you, Mr. President?

THE PRESIDENT: No, that is where you will make your headquarters. (Laughter)

Q: How soon are you going down?

THE PRESIDENT: I hope the beginning of the week after next or the middle of the
week after next, I don't know the exact date. It will be somewhere around
the twenty-seventh, depending a little bit on what Congress does in the
meantime.

I haven't any news for you this morning.

Q: That is all right; you will have some before you go away.

THE PRESIDENT: I think so.

Q: Mr. President, yesterday Senator Robinson of Arkansas said that he was for
a unified air force. I was wondering whether that is a reflection of the
Administration's viewpoint or just his own. Can you tell us anything
about that?

THE PRESIDENT: Only this, for background: We have by no means solved permanently the general aviation policy of the Government. It has been kicking
around, as you all know -- you have to use this as background -- and the
present board that has been reconstituted will take it up from the point
of view of the Army Air Service. It is primarily limited to that. Now,
of course, that only covers a part of the story. You have

--- [231] ---

still got all the other relationships of government to aviation. You have
got the Customs Service, the Internal Revenue Service, and the Department
of Commerce and its relationship to civilian aviation. You have the Navy
and the Marine Corps. There has never yet been worked out a satisfactory
complete Government policy. It is a thing you cannot work out immediately.
The only thing you can say is that we are all studying it and hope to work
out a complete Government policy. That will be the objective. The appointment of the Board is only in relation to the Army Air Service. I
think we will be able to work something out. We may eventually appoint a
board or an individual, but the object will be to get a complete Government
policy.

Q: Can you tell us anything about General Mitchell's visit yesterday?

THE PRESIDENT: Only that he came in and gave me a great deal of information

from his point of view. He is a very old friend of mine and there is no
question, of course, but that he has had a great deal of experience in
aviation. I am trying to get every angle.

Q:  There are stories to the effect that he may take charge of aviation for
the Government.

THE PRESIDENT:  That is just a story. Anything of that kind is just nonsense.
You have to have a policy first.

Q:  When you spoke of board or individual, did you mean to make a further study
or to be in charge of the whole situation?

THE PRESIDENT:  We are making a study at the present time. Whether it needs a
board or ten boards or an individual or fifty individuals, that is a matter
to be worked out. You have to try a new Government policy because the old
one has not worked for twenty years.

Q:  Are you going to recommend to Congress legislation regulating motor and
water carriers?

--- [232] ---

THE PRESIDENT:  You mean the Eastman report?

Q:  Yes.

THE PRESIDENT:  I think all that has been done is the transmittal to Congress,
like the first report was.

Q:  Mr. President, they are about to vote today on the St. Lawrence Treaty,
and it looks like the vote is against you. I was wondering if you would
care to offer any comment on that.

THE PRESIDENT:  No. However, there is one phase of it -- in fact, two phases
of it. One is perfectly simple to mention and the other is a bit more
difficult.

The first phase of it is that whether the thing goes through this afternoon or not makes no difference at all because the St. Lawrence Seaway
will be built. That is perfectly obvious. And it will be built at a
very, very low cost as things go today. You have left only the International Rapids Section and the Lachine Rapids Section. You can visualize
the whole navigation problem; it is so obvious that man is going to follow
the lead of Nature. Whether the thing goes through today or next year
makes, on the whole, very little difference -- it is going through.

You see, you have got today a seaway practically from the top end of Lake
Superior down through the Sault Ste. Marie locks, which are big locks, down
through Lake Michigan and Lake Huron, then through the Detroit River into
Lake Erie, through the Welland locks, which are big locks, and then through
Lake Ontario to the St. Lawrence River. And of course the St. Lawrence
River runs to the sea.

Now, there are three waterfalls -- rapids, actually. One of them, the middle one, at Beauharnois, has already been built -- they are nearly finished
with it. Some of you were up there with me about three years

--- [233] ---

ago. They have already practically completed the power development and,
as a part of that power development, for just a very small sum, they can
add locks. The Canadian Government is also proceeding with plans for the
last waterfall, the Lachine, and there they can do one of two things.
They can either build a dam and put locks in the dam, or they can dig the
old Lachine Canal and deepen it from twelve to thirty feet without building a dam. That leaves only the top or western waterfall called the International Rapids. Canada already has a twelve-foot canal around the International Rapids.

Now, it is not the least bit necessary to develop power which, of course,
calls for a dam. It would be a perfectly proper thing and a perfectly
possible thing for Canada to enlarge the International Rapids Canal on
the Canadian side of the River without ever building a dam. Canada isn't
so crazy to have water power; they have an awful lot of it. If Canada
were to do that on the Canadian side of the River, there would be a Canadian seaway. Mind you, the amount necessary to do that Canal over would
be less than one hundred million dollars, so you see what a small amount
it is. There would then be a Canadian seaway from salt water up the St.
Lawrence River, past the Lachine, Beauharnois, and the International Sections, and then you would be in the Lake. That seaway would be one hundred per cent under the control of Canada.

And if Canada wanted to be mean -- and lots of governments and people are
mean to their neighbors -- so far as treaties go, Canada has an absolute
right -- not a moral right, but a legal right -- to let British and Canadian ships use that Canadian seaway free of charge and to charge a toll to
American ships. In other words, if you look at it purely from the national point of view, the United States on one side and Canada on the other
side, without looking at it from the broader

--- [234] ---

point of view of commerce and humanity, if we don't go along with Canada
in the development of this seaway, we open ourselves, without any question,
to the Canadian right to build a Canadian seaway and discriminate against
all American ships. If Canada were to do that, British and Canadian ships
could use that seaway free of all charge and it would be prohibitive for
American ships to use it. That is a distinct and definite legal right
that Canada would have if we do not go along with her and do it jointly.

Now, one other phase of it -- and I will tell you a story. A certain
Senator said that he was going to vote against the treaty because of the
Mississippi and the taking of water out of Lake Michigan. I asked him if
he thought we had any right to divert water over and above the need for
drinking and health purposes from one watershed into another. Then I told
him a story about an old case in up-State New York. A fellow had a piece
of property on a river but, at that particular point, there was practically
no drop in the river -- it was practically a flat river. He was most
anxious to put up a grist mill and he didn't have any water power. People
down in the stream below him had grist mills. Suddenly he had a bright
thought one night. He said to himself, "by cutting a little ditch through
a little hill on my property I can run this water over into the watershed
of another little river and I can get a 50-foot drop. I can take the water
out of this river and carry it through the ditch, drop it down over a wheel
and put it into another river." Of course, it was a grand idea. But,

unfortunately, he ran up against what is known in the common law as the riparian right of the man further down the stream. Well, the mills down the stream at once brought suit and said that ever since 1450 when the first case came up in England the rule has been on a watershed, on a river, that you have

--- [235] ---

the right to use the water but you have to put it back into the river. You cannot divert it into some other watershed.

Well, this Senator, who is a good lawyer, admitted all that and finally said that international law is different. I said, "There aren't any cases of international law that are different from the old rule based on common sense." He said, "Never mind whether international law is different or not, we are going to try to take all the water we want out of Lake Michigan and put it into the Mississippi, no matter what anybody else says."

So that is a perfectly clear-cut issue. The Government of the United States believes in the common law and believes that we have no right to injure our neighbor, Canada, by diverting water out of the Great Lakes into another watershed, any more than the fellow upstream a hundred years ago in New York had a right to divert water from one creek into another. Chicago is absolutely entitled, under the common law and under common decency, to all the water they want to drink, to all the water they need for sewage purposes and Canada has even gone further; they have given them enough water by treaty to give them, in all probability, pretty decent navigation down to the Mississippi and down from there to the Gulf. Of course, not ocean-going steamers but probably nine-foot draft, which is the same as the upper Mississippi.

And so, the thing is going through, perhaps not today but the St. Lawrence Seaway is going to be built just as sure as God made little apples. The only difference is that I would like to see it done by joint action of two neighboring nations. If we don't go along, Canada has a perfect right to build an all-Canadian seaway and discriminate against us, if they so desired.

Q:   In other words, this treaty will go back again?

--- [236] ---

THE PRESIDENT:  It will go back in some form. How soon, I don't know but it will go back as soon as it can.

Q:   Can we use this?

THE PRESIDENT:  As background, I think it is all right.

Q:   What did the Senate leaders tell you about the bonus?

THE PRESIDENT:  I haven't talked to them about the bonus at all.

Q:   Will you say anything on the House action on the bonus?

THE PRESIDENT:  No. I never comment on that. There is an article in this morning's Wall Street Journal by Bernard Kilgore that really anybody who writes about finances and bonuses and currency issues and so forth ought to read because it is pretty darn good. I don't agree with the story all the way through, but it is a good story. It is an analytical story on an exceedingly difficult subject -- on the question of issuing currency to meet Government obligations. I think that Kilgore could have gone just a little bit further than he did. Of course this is all background.

It was along the general line that almost everybody who has studied -- well, I will tell you a story; Paul Warburg a good many years ago, ten years ago, who had a very great mind, talked over with me one day the proposition of issuing Government currency to retire Government debts. In other words, they were what might be called baby bonds to retire outstanding Government debts. As he put it, there is nothing wrong about it except the opportunity that it gives to a legislative body in the future to pay the running expenses of Government by printing paper. Now, there is all the difference in the world between paying the running expenses of the Government by issuing paper and retiring the outstanding interest-bearing obligations by the issuance of paper, provided always that the paper is amortized and retired year by year as the bonds would

--- [237] ---

have been. But the one fear is that is a legislative body gets into the habit of it that they will just run wild year after year, and if they once started to run wild they would pay off the veterans this year and then to-morrow they would say to the people in this country who, in 1917 and 1918, worked on munitions, who had rather unhealthy conditions, long hours and not much sanitation, good patriotic men and women who probably came out of the war physically rather worse off than they went in, certainly far worse off than the men in uniforms who spent their time in camps a few miles away from them -- they would say, "Why shouldn't you come in for a bonus on the ground that you have worked overtime and under difficult conditions for two horrible years?" And then, if you paid them, you would find another class in the community entitled to the same treatment. Then take Government employees, why shouldn't they get better treatment, get 25% more than anybody else?

And so you would start paying with paper and you would keep on paying with paper. In other words, this bonus bill comes down to a fundamental -- you might say two fundamentals: One is the method of payment, and the other is whether the Government is going back on its contract. The Government has a contract. Kilgore's article is well worth reading.

Q:   Mr. President, did you talk to Senator Harrison about sugar yesterday in the course of your conference?

THE PRESIDENT:  I do not think we did. Yes, we did, at the very end, just a mention. I said, "How is the sugar thing coming on?" and he said, "We are going to try to work it out."

Q:   Members of the Judiciary Committee of the Senate say they are expecting some word from you on the Municipal Bankruptcy Bill that has been reported on. I understand you have some change?

--- [238] ---

THE PRESIDENT:  Has it been reported on?

Q:   Yes, sir; by the Committee.

THE PRESIDENT: No, I am not proposing any changes but Judge Sumners of the House is working on an amendment to meet certain objections to the bill as it passed the House. Don't let this come from me because it is entirely a matter on the Hill. I am simply telling you what you can find out from Sumners. The thought is this, that the bill as reported out allows 66 per cent of the creditors to agree with the city on a complete revamping of the debt. Now, that applies not only to interest rates and the maturity dates -- in other words, extension of time of payment -- but also extension of principal and the insurance companies and savings banks have objected to that feature for fear that the principal would be cut down. Judge Sumners was working on an amendment which would make it necessary for 80 per cent of the creditors to agree if the principal amount of the debt was cut down, leaving it 66 per cent for the interest rates and the date of maturity.

Q: Does that same provision apply to the private debts of corporations? Van Nuys has a bill on that.

THE PRESIDENT: All private debts.

Q: In bankruptcy? These buildings, et cetera, corporations and bankruptcy?

THE PRESIDENT: They have that right now.

Q: In bankruptcy, but to cut down their fixed charges?

THE PRESIDENT: Wait a minute, Stevie (Mr. Stephenson) has a bright thought.

Q: The other day the Department of Justice gave notice that they were going to seek proceedings against Mellon and others on tax evasion. Can we look for others on that?

THE PRESIDENT: I will give you something off the record on that, if you wish.

Q: Yes.

--- [239] ---

THE PRESIDENT: The income tax prosecutions are not exactly prosecutions. Here is the real problem that was put up and, frankly, it is a problem of Government. I think the reason there was an announcement of names the other day -- and of course there are a great many other names -- was because if there had not been an announcement from here the story about these particular names would have broken in each of the districts very shortly and therefore it was easier to announce them from here. Now, these actions are by no means confined to the names announced. There are several hundred cases in exactly the same category.

Here is the Government problem, and I will put it up to you. The Government finds, in going over income tax records, that there are a certain number of people who have failed to include certain income. Putting it the simplest way, they have done that or, in working out their returns, they have made the amount owing a great deal less than the Government thinks it ought to get. Immediately there arises the question of motive. If the motive was to cheat the Government, it is a criminal offense. If, however, the motive was a perfectly honest mistake, it is not a criminal offense but the Government has a civil suit to recover. Now, who is going to determine what the motive was in filing a return that lacked either the

proper amount of the inclusion of certain income? Who is going to determine whether the motive was to cheat the Government or not?

If you leave that determination to some individual in the Department of
Justice or in the Internal Revenue Bureau and he lets off a very prominent
man, you know what the people of this country will say. If he decides to
prosecute the little fellow and let the big fellow off, you know what the
country will say. On the other hand, if he decides

--- [240] ---

to prosecute the big fellow, you know what some people will say. They will
say that it is persecution and not prosecution.

It puts the Government action up to some Government individual in Washington. Well, they are human and it is a mighty difficult thing to put up to
them. We have, in our laws, a system of determining motive. It is called
a grand jury. Now, the policy that has been adopted is based not only on
justice as we have it, but on common sense. If we were to determine these
matters here and say, "Why no; Mr. Jones did not intend to cheat the
Government, he merely followed his highly paid lawyers' advice," every
other Mr. Jones in the country would thereupon go to his high priced
lawyer and would be open to the temptation of putting in a return that was,
in effect, cheating the Government, with the assurance, mind you, that two
years later or three years later all he would have to do would be to go to
Washington and say, "I did not intend to cheat the Government; I merely
took the advice of my lawyer," and he would get a clean bill of health.

In other words, it is a definite invitation to people to cheat the Government and then come back afterwards and say, "I did not cheat the Government. I did not intend to." Therefore, what we are doing is taking all
of these cases, sending them to the District Attorneys of the respective
districts and saying to them, "Put these up to the grand jury." If the
grand jury does not think that the man or his lawyer were trying to cheat
the Government, it is perfectly all right. In that case we will bring a
civil suit and recover our money. If the grand jury does think there was
a motive there, to avoid the payment of taxes, then the grand jury will
indict." And so you have got a panel of twenty-three men under an American
system who determine the question of motive. Now, that is all there is to
any of these income tax cases. It catches the

--- [241] ---

big fellow and the little fellow and we apply the same rule to the big
fellow and the little fellow, and we are going to put them all up to the
grand jury.

Q: Is that off the record, Mr. President?

THE PRESIDENT: You can make it background. Don't write the story around the
    Mellon case because it applies just as much to the man with an income of
    $3,000 a year as it does to the man whose income is very high, or to Mr.
    Mellon. It is a matter of principle.

MR. STEPHENSON: Thank you, Mr. President.


(The Press Conference adjourned at 11:07 A.M.)

Press Conference #106
Executive Offices of the White House
March 16, 1934, 4:10 P.M.


THE PRESIDENT: Have the accommodations been taken (at the hotel where the temporary White House is to be established)?

Q: The first steps have been taken.

THE PRESIDENT: Good.

Q: The reporters will go back to Miami from the ship, won't they?

THE PRESIDENT: Will they go back?

Q: To Miami?

THE PRESIDENT: It depends a little bit. Do you know how to figure out latitude and longitude?

Q: If necessary, we can learn.

THE PRESIDENT: I will bet you can, in Miami. You can learn almost anything there. Sometimes people forget where they are.

Q: We can learn anything to justify the end.

THE PRESIDENT: I foresee that a radio message will come in signed, "Stevie," "Please send me my latitude and longitude."

Q: (Mr. Stephenson) Eddie (Roddan) is getting out of control again.

THE PRESIDENT: The only news I have is off the record -- literally off the record -- my income tax was paid yesterday and I did not know I had that much money in the world. I hope the check is good but I don't know yet.

Q: There are a lot of people that feel the same way. (Laughter)

THE PRESIDENT: They take 15 per cent off of you and an income tax on top of that. It is an awful lot.

Q: Have you had any estimates as to how much income taxes they are going to get?

--- [243] ---

THE PRESIDENT: Henry (Morgenthau) said this morning on the telephone that it is running ahead of their estimates. Up to last night, while it was not very much ahead, it was definitely ahead of the estimates and of course the estimates were away ahead of last year.

Q: Mr. President, the hearings before the Senate Interstate Commerce Committee developed that the main opposition to the Dill Communications bill was the going beyond the bare recommendation which you made for transfer of existing authority. Would you care to express your attitude on that?

THE PRESIDENT: I do not know. I have not read the bill. In what way does it go beyond?

Q: Providing for effective regulation of rates, interlocking directorates and intercompany transactions.

THE PRESIDENT: Not having read the bill, I cannot talk about it intelligently. The only thing I talked with -- who was it put in the bill, Sam Rayburn -- the only thing I talked with him about was the general thought that we ought to provide for control of communications between this country and other countries by any company which is foreign owned, that that ought to be an American controlled company. In other words, I only talked about the principle and I do not know what the actual details of the bill are.

Q: The president of the I.T.& T. (International Telephone and Telegraph Company) said 9 35/100 per cent of the stock was foreign owned.

THE PRESIDENT: Only 9 per cent?

Q: Just about.

THE PRESIDENT: Then the company would not have any trouble. It means 100 per cent control.

Q: Twenty per cent foreign is the limit.

THE PRESIDENT: I will have to tell you this off the record. The general

--- [244] ---

thought on that was this; that there is a tendency on the part of foreign companies which are either Government controlled or quasi Government controlled, like the British Communications, Ltd., which is actually privately owned but the policy of it is dictated by the British Government, to interfere in our communications with foreign countries and it is our thought to prevent such interference. Well, one simple example is the feeling we have had that the dissemination of news by the Havas Agency in South America has been, as practised, very distinctly anti-United States. There is no particular secret about that. I have complained to the Havas people about it and of course the Havas Company is subsidized by the French Government. We won't be able to get United States, American news, and especially press news out of this country in such a way that foreign newspapers will get proper news.

Q: Did you complain to the Havas news agency?

THE PRESIDENT: Entirely unofficially. I did not do it myself.

Q: Is that in the dissemination of news from the United States through South America?

THE PRESIDENT: Yes.

Q: Is this on the record?

THE PRESIDENT: Oh, no. I think you had better treat that off the record, this last part about foreign news agencies, because that is a thing that concerns all of us rather than the general public in this stage of the game.

Q: I understand on these bids for the $10,000,000 worth of motor trucks, they say the decision rests with you as to whether it is to be accepted or rejected or an extension of time.

THE PRESIDENT: I have not the foggiest idea. It has not come to me yet.

Q: A bill was brought up on the Hill today, both Houses, that would give the

--- [245] ---

RFC authority to lend money to industry. That is the description I get but, technically I do not know whether it is correct or not. Does this conflict with the proposition to put up credit banks or is it supplementary? Our office is rather excited. It is said to be sponsored by Jones (Jesse Jones). It is an Administration measure.

THE PRESIDENT: I have not the faintest idea. I never saw it. I think probably the plan for the intermediate credit banks will go through. It will be asked for.

Q: But that will have a Federal Reserve action and not RFC?

THE PRESIDENT: Yes.

Q: You will need legislation on that?

THE PRESIDENT: On the intermediate banks? Yes.

Q: Tell us about your talk with Governor Lehman today.

THE PRESIDENT: It is a question of finding about sixty or seventy million dollars. In other words, the Governor gave the estimates of what New York State and the communities could raise and what the total amount necessary was for the next ten months and then Harry Hopkins told me how much we could contribute definitely, I mean the minimum amount we could contribute, and that still left the State of New York about sixty or seventy million dollars short of what they thought they needed. What they are doing now is conferring as to where they can save a portion and where they can get it another way.

Q: Will you tell us the proportion that Hopkins said the Federal Government may be able to contribute?

THE PRESIDENT: On the plan as laid out, it will be one-tenth of $600,000,000 or $60,000,000.

Q: From the Federal Government?

THE PRESIDENT: Yes. You see, the State of New York gets, on a basis of

--- [246] ---

population and also based on need, about 10 per cent of the entire Federal Government relief monies.

Q: Is the treasury of New York State depleted to the point where they cannot raise this money?

THE PRESIDENT: No. Their present bond issue still has in it -- you had better not take my figure -- it is about $35,000,000 and they undoubtedly will probably ask for an additional bond issue but, of course, that could not be voted on until November. You had better not say "undoubtedly" because the Governor did not say "undoubtedly." He said they were still considering it.

Q: Isn't that thirty-five million, forty-eight million?

THE PRESIDENT: Thirty-five, I think.

Q: Did the City (City of New York) Economy bill enter into the discussions?

THE PRESIDENT: Yes. (Laughter)

Q: Did you give any advice on it?

THE PRESIDENT: I did.

Q: What was it? (Laughter)

THE PRESIDENT: Well, I told the Majority Leader in the Senate and the Minority Leader in the Assembly that the quicker the City of New York was put into a proper financial status the quicker they would get Federal funds, and that we could not wait all year, that some other city might balance its budget and be entitled to it.

Q: General Johnson seems to have written another letter to the railroads on the code proposition. Would you care to say anything?

THE PRESIDENT: To the railroads?

Q: Yes, March eighth.

THE PRESIDENT: What about?

Q: February twenty-first and March eighth.

--- [247] ---

THE PRESIDENT: What about?

Q: Suggesting they confer on a matter about bringing certain employees under a code -- certain classes of their employees.

THE PRESIDENT: What kind of employees?

Q: Probably maintenance of way and white collar workers, particularly maintenance of way.

THE PRESIDENT: I do not know; I have not talked to him at all.

Q: Thank you, Mr. President.

THE PRESIDENT: I think we had better put the lid on tomorrow. There is nothing doing. What happened last week?

Q: On Saturday morning we had the air mail statement.

THE PRESIDENT:  I forgot it was Saturday; I won't do it tomorrow.

(The Press Conference adjourned at 4:20 P.M.)

CONFIDENTIAL
Press Conference #107
Executive Offices of the White House
March 21, 1934, 10:50 A.M.


THE PRESIDENT: I hear you all had a late night last night.

Q: It was a tough day, too.

Q: Can't you pull in your neck?

Q: (Mr. Storm) It is the first time I have been hearing so many complaints (about his size).

THE PRESIDENT: You look a little pale this morning -- overwork?

Q: We need the sun, Mr. President.

Q: You can't go (to Florida) too soon.

THE PRESIDENT: I hope we can get off. I do not know now, with all these things popping.

Q: There is a full house today (meaning the attendance).

MR. DONALDSON: All in.

THE PRESIDENT: I cannot see you people at the back but all the people in the front look awfully tired and overworked. (Laughter)

Q: That is repeal. (Laughter)

THE PRESIDENT: I got a telegram last night -- I do not think you have it; Steve (Mr. Early) will give you copies afterwards -- from Collins (William Collins), National Representative in Detroit of the American Federation of Labor. In it he states that:

> (Reading) "The conference of the officers of Federal Labor Unions of the United Automobile Workers affiliated with the American Federation of Labor, held at Pontiac, Michigan, on Tuesday, March twenty, nineteen thirty four, at five P.M., whose case has been presented to the National Labor Board, Washington, D.C., do hereby declare our complete sympathy with your efforts to bring the country out of the depression. We speak for the employees in the automobile industry in expressing our sincere admiration of your high leadership in the

--- [249] ---

> problems that face the country. Therefore, as the responsible officers of these unions, we pledge to you our undivided support in every attempt to bring about in the spirit of the New Deal the cooperation of labor and capital under the machinery of the National Recovery Act. We, therefore, are prepared to place our case before you confident that in the interpretation of Section Seven A of the National Recovery Act, the right of free choice of representatives will be maintained.

We therefore are appointing a committee to meet with you
at your invitation. The strike is held in abeyance pending
the outcome of your conference at Washington, and we further ask your indulgence in granting the conference that in
addition to William Green, President, American Federation
of Labor; William Collins, national representative; Arthur
Greer and John Bailey, that you give each chosen representative of the thirteen unions an opportunity to attend the
conference."

And I wired back:

(Reading) "I greatly appreciate your decision and will be
glad to receive representatives of the thirteen unions as
suggested. I appreciate the good spirit of your telegram
and am looking forward to seeing you on Thursday."

So they will be in tomorrow afternoon about 2:00 or 2:30 and I think this
afternoon -- we haven't definite word -- sometime this afternoon I am
seeing the representatives of the manufacturers, and that is about as far
as we can go in prognostication.

Q: Will the manufacturers also sit in in your conference on Thursday?

THE PRESIDENT: In other words, I am seeing the manufacturers today and the
others tomorrow. I shall ask the manufacturers to stay here until after
I have seen the labor people tomorrow and what the next step will be I do
not know.

Q: Have the manufacturers advised you that they will refuse to sit with the
employees?

THE PRESIDENT: I have not heard from them at all.

Q: Somebody in the Tribune intimated as much.

Q: Can you tell us anything about the conference with Senator Couzens (of
Michigan) this morning?

THE PRESIDENT: No, no particular news in it. We discussed the details of

--- [250] ---

Section 7 (a), that is about all.

Q: Do you have a specific plan proposed for this conference?

THE PRESIDENT: No. The first thing to do is to listen to it. I am having all
sorts of thoughts but the first thing to do is to listen.

Q: Mr. President, there has been considerable publicity the last few days in
the local papers about the plan to reorganize the government of the District of Columbia. It seems to be sponsored by Senator King of Utah and
his plan is in detail -- it is very comprehensive. Are you familiar with
it?

THE PRESIDENT: No.

Q:   Are you in favor of reorganization?

THE PRESIDENT:  I have no idea; I have not thought about it.  You have only one more place to fill, haven't you?

Q:   That is all.  (Laughter)

THE PRESIDENT:  That we will take up as quickly as possible.

Q:   Have you heard from the railroad labor side on this wage matter?

THE PRESIDENT:  No, you have given out nothing since yesterday.  What was that?

Q:   That is from the management.

THE PRESIDENT:  I don't think we have had anything from the unions.

Q:   Are you going to extend the licensing act of the recovery program for another year?

THE PRESIDENT:  I have not discussed it at all.

Q:   The substitute postal employees have been complaining bitterly, particularly in New York, about their lot.  Has that been given any particular consideration by you?

THE PRESIDENT:  A great deal.  The real story behind the one-day a month furlough is something that I don't think has been brought out.  From

--- [251] ---

the strictly business point of view, what might be called the good management point of view, if it were merely a question of dollars and cents, we have about 15,000 more postal employees than we need.  In other words, there is an excess.  That has been caused by the very large falling off in mails as of a year ago although they have begun to pick up in the last six months.  You are faced with the problem, "Shall we think of the dollars and cents or shall we think of the human end of it?"  Now, we ought to have fired 15,000 from the dollars and cents point of view.  We did not do it.  Rather than let them go or put them on relief rolls, we kept them as far as we could.  This furlough, as far as I understand it, is one day a month and we hope that the postal business will pick up by April so that we can restore that one day a month.  I don't think that phase of it has been brought out.  Strictly speaking, we ought to have discharged 15,000 and did not.

Q:   One of the points they have made up there is that in some weeks some married men would make three or four dollars a week.

THE PRESIDENT:  The point was that so far as business went we did not need them at all.

Q:   Are you asking any railroad legislation at this session along the lines of those bills submitted?

THE PRESIDENT:  That is part of this railroad conference we are going to hold and I really ought not to say anything about it until we have had the railroad conference.  It will undoubtedly come out of the present conference that Eastman is holding.

Q:   Mr. President, will you be good enough to comment on the Norris Amendment
     to the Home Owners Loan Corporation Bill?

THE PRESIDENT:  What is it?

Q:   The one that barred politics from consideration in the selection of per-

--- [252] ---

sonnel.

THE PRESIDENT:  I will have to see it.  What does it do?

Q:   It is intended to eliminate political considerations in the building up
     of this organization.  It was adopted by a one-vote majority in the Senate.

THE PRESIDENT:  I'm in favor of a general principle of administration.  I sup-
     pose we have had more protests over the fact that Republicans are in con-
     trol of the Federal Farm Credit Administration and, in many sections, of
     the Home Owners Loan than we have had with respect to Democrats.  We are
     trying to keep politics out of it.  I cannot comment on the particular
     amendment because I have not read it.  We have had all sorts of kicks from
     both sides in almost every State of the Union and about equally divided.

Q:   Mr. President, can you throw any light on the exchange of notes between
     the Japanese Foreign Minister and the Secretary of State, Mr. Hull?

THE PRESIDENT:  I do not know anything about it.

Q:   He wrote Mr. Hull a letter on the twenty-first of February and he answered
     it on March third.

THE PRESIDENT:  Nothing on that now.

Q:   Mr. President, may I ask whether you can comment on the Administration
     policy of giving relief to strikers?  Mr. Hopkins, the other day, said he
     would give relief to strikers unless advised by the Department of Labor
     that the strike is unjustified or unwarranted.

THE PRESIDENT:  Only one policy.  It does not relate to strikers any more than
     to anybody else.  People who are in dire want -- lack of food -- the
     Government is going to try to keep them from starving.  It is just a repe-
     tition of the old thing.

Q:   Hopkins has said that in only one case has he given relief to strikers

--- [253] ---

and then withdrawn it and that was when the Bituminous Board advised him
the strike was unjustified.

THE PRESIDENT:  It is just a simple rule to try to keep human beings from
     starving.

Q:   Any comment on the Federal Trade Commission's report on the Steel Code?

THE PRESIDENT: It is an exceedingly interesting document. I think I can give you, as background, the general thought of the thing. That is that there are two phases of it. The first is the price fixing phase which is in a very unsatisfactory condition. The filing of prices by one steel company with the Steel Institute can, as it is being handled now, very easily result in a fixed price by agreement -- a thing the Government could not stop because there is no way of obtaining proof that there is collusion. It is practically impossible and we have to work out some other method of assuring competition.

The other phase of it relates to cost. We don't know yet what it costs to make steel rails in this country and yet steel rails go to utilities and we have got to work out some method of finding out whether the utilities are paying too much for steel rails or whether they are not. There has been a general opposition on the part of steel rail companies to any disclosure or investigation of what it costs them to make steel rails. We don't know. The general suspicion is that it costs a great deal less than the price we arrived at last Fall, but we don't know. Somebody, some day, has got to find out what it costs to make steel rails.

Q: Are you making such an investigation or study just now?

THE PRESIDENT: No.

Q: Mr. President, on this railroad thing, did you say you were going to hold conferences on the railroad situation?

--- [254] ---

THE PRESIDENT: Mr. Eastman is holding the conferences.

Q: Now?

THE PRESIDENT: I may take part in them, but I don't know. There is no set arrangement.

Q: What is the purpose of the Eastman conferences, as you understand it?

THE PRESIDENT: The purpose is to get a six months' extension of the present schedule.

Q: Mr. President, have you filled the vacancy on the Federal Power Commission?

THE PRESIDENT: No, I have not; and I have not thought about it.

Q: Is it coming soon?

THE PRESIDENT: Give me some names. (Laughter)

Q: Any extension of the Federal Coordinator of Transportation? By proclamation that expires --

THE PRESIDENT: (interposing) No; none of them have been taken up at all.

MR. STEPHENSON: Thank you, Mr. President.

(The Press Conference adjourned at 11:05 A.M.)

Press Conference #108
Executive Offices of the White House
March 23, 1934, 4:08 P.M.


Q:  How is it, Mr. President?  Feeling rather weary these days (referring to
    the hoped for Florida trip)?

THE PRESIDENT:  You are.  (Laughter)

Q:  I am afraid it is going to be bad weather for a long while.

THE PRESIDENT:  So they say.  (Laughter)

MR. DONALDSON:  All in.

THE PRESIDENT:  Well, I do not think I know anything at all except about the
    weather.  It makes Florida look more attractive but not necessarily any
    closer.

Q:  Say not so.

Q:  Steve (Mr. Early) asked us not to ask you that question.

THE PRESIDENT:  If I can only get away with the challenge that Arthur Krock
    gave me this morning.  I could not leave unless I batted a thousand per
    cent four times to the bat before Tuesday.  He is about right, as a matter
    of fact, just about.  Eddie Roddan is looking awfully sad.

Q:  Five hundred is good hitting for anybody.

THE PRESIDENT:  I have not any late news from the automobile conference.  Steve
    (Mr. Early) told me that the information from you people is so far all
    right.  I just came out of the Cabinet meeting so I have not talked to
    Johnson (General Hugh Johnson) since noon.

Q:  Can you tell us what the General reported at noon?

THE PRESIDENT:  Nothing since last night because General Johnson had not started
    to talk with them.

Q:  The French, in a note sent to Great Britain and made public today, declared

--- [256] ---

    that the willingness of other powers to consult in case of treaty viola-
    tions is not sufficient guarantee of their security and they must have
    guarantees of effective action, particularly by groups of nations.  That
    is a bit further than we are prepared to go?

THE PRESIDENT:  What do they want?

Q:  They want Great Britain to come to their aid if Germany violates any of
    the treaties, but they do not specify Great Britain, they say the community
    of nations should come to their aid.

THE PRESIDENT:  Of course we cannot change what we said last year.

Q:  And that still stands?

THE PRESIDENT:  Yes.

Q:  While we are on foreign affairs, we have a report that Ambassador Dodd
    arrives in New York today.  Any significance in his return?

THE PRESIDENT:  No.  He wrote me about a month ago and said it would be a good
    thing to get a little holiday and, at the same time, to report and tell us
    the situation.  I did not know he was landing today.

Q:  Stock Market bill -- anything to say?

THE PRESIDENT:  I have not read it.

Q:  Do you still favor a bill?

THE PRESIDENT:  I favor a bill with teeth in it.

Q:  Have you appointed any kind of committee to study and make reports?

THE PRESIDENT:  No.

Q:  Have you heard of any?

THE PRESIDENT:  No, I have not heard of any.

Q:  Do you care to comment on the veterans' pay allowances voted yesterday by
    the House, which is still in conference?

THE PRESIDENT:  The less I say on that subject the better.  (Laughter)

Q:  Mr. President, have you heard from Eastman on the railroad wage negotia-
    tions?

--- [257] ---

THE PRESIDENT:  I have not heard today at all.  Does anybody know how it is
    getting on?

Q:  He is going to confer with the labor crowd in the morning.  He saw the
    management group twice today and he is seeing the labor group tomorrow
    morning.

THE PRESIDENT:  Right.

Q:  Are you planning to notify the House on your views on the unemployment
    insurance bill through a letter?

THE PRESIDENT:  On the Wagner-Lewis Bill?

Q:  That is the one.

THE PRESIDENT:  I have an idea that I either have sent a letter to the Chairman
    or I am going to.  I do not know whether I have signed it or not.  There
    is no reason it should not be given out as soon as it gets up.  I think I
    signed one yesterday but it may still be in the basket.

Q:   Mr. President, is it favorable to the bill?

THE PRESIDENT:   This is not the NRA bill, this is the unemployment insurance
bill?

Q:   Yes.

THE PRESIDENT:   Yes, it is favorable to the general principles of it.

Q:   Mr. President, have you heard anything new since your telegram last night
from the West Coast notifying that they would call off the longshoremen's
strike?

THE PRESIDENT:   No.  The only other thing is picking the names for the Board of
Mediation.   I probably will have them by tonight.

Q:   Are you picking them here?

THE PRESIDENT:   I think we are, aren't we, Steve (Mr. Early)?

MR. EARLY:   We are, sir.

Q:   What is your attitude toward the Wagner Bill?

--- [258] ---

THE PRESIDENT:   You are a little previous on that.  Hold it until Miami.

Q:   Did you tell the automobile --

THE PRESIDENT:   (interposing)  In other words, do not construe that as being
holding off on it, but from the point of view of timing it is better to
wait until we get some of these very immediate questions on automobile
troubles and longshoremen a little bit further along before I say anything.
There will be something said all right.

Q:   For background I thought we might inject that into the situation, that that
was a sort of hammer over the heads of the industrialists.

THE PRESIDENT:   I don't think you could put it that way.  (Laughter)

Q:   Put it subtly.  (Laughter)

THE PRESIDENT:   If I were writing the story on my own hook, I would say that
the cupboard door is still closed.  We have not made a gesture toward the
cupboard.

Q:   No telling what is inside?

THE PRESIDENT:   No.

Q:   Will you be having conferences direct, either with the automobile manufacturers or the men this afternoon or tonight?

THE PRESIDENT:   I do not know.  I told Johnson (General Johnson) that I would
hold myself in readiness to see either or both at any time.

Q:   Mr. President, there is a delegation of steel officials at the NRA conferring with General Johnson and there is considerable secrecy around their negotiations. Do you know anything?

THE PRESIDENT: I cannot imagine anything unless it is caused by the report of the Federal Trade Commission. It might have been. It created quite a commotion.

Q: Have you any observations on that report?

THE PRESIDENT: No, except as background. It goes back -- I think I talked

--- [259] ---

to you about this before -- it goes back to the question of, this open price posting and of course in practice that almost necessarily results in one price bidding because everybody else follows the first one to post and posts exactly the same price and then they will bid on exactly the same, identical price. Of course, that is not free competition and the thing is not working. We have to find some method of restoring competitive bidding which seems to be pretty well precluded by this open-price posting method that exists. How we are going to go about it we don't know, but we have to do something about it.

Q: Mr. President, have you anything to say about the bill to make cattle a basic commodity?

THE PRESIDENT: I am not familiar enough with the details.

Q: A $150,000,000 amendment was added by Senator LaFollette to finance the reduction of tuberculosis.

THE PRESIDENT: Of course, it is in the legislative stage. I might say, as background, that somebody has to find the $150,000,000 if it stays in. I haven't got it.

Q: Mr. President, are any new slum clearance plans being considered?

THE PRESIDENT: No. On the slum clearance, as a whole, the general thought is this: Our difficulty in giving Federal aid to the major cities that need slum clearance arises out of the real estate values which are very largely fictitious. In fact, in many cases the assessed valuations themselves are fictitious. There are many cases in the slum areas in New York where the city assessment is way above what the owner of the property would be willing to sell the property for. There are a great many tenement house owners that would be tickled to death if they could get 75 per cent of the assessed value in cash. Obviously, just so long as in clearing slum properties you have to pay exhorbitant real estate

--- [260] ---

prices, you cannot put up any new buildings on a sufficiently sound basis so that you will be able to get your money back.

What we would like to see is some method of getting lower real estate costs and, if we get that, it means we would be able to put up buildings in the City of New York that would rent for $6 or $7 instead of $10 or $12 a room a month. We are being held up by the real estate problem. That is the answer. If we can get around that and purchase real estate at a lower

price so that we can put up buildings with low rents, the Federal Government stands ready, out of its next year's appropriation, to increase very
greatly its slum clearance allotment.

Q:  Subject to that condition?

THE PRESIDENT:  Subject to that condition.

Q:  You mentioned New York.  Does that hold good elsewhere?

THE PRESIDENT:  Yes, except that in other places the scale of real estate is a
different one, of course.  For example, in a smaller, a great deal smaller
city, one that still has a slum problem, $6 or $7 a month per room is too
high.  In a city of that kind you want $4 or $5 a month per room.

Q:  Have you signed the Vinson Bill yet?

THE PRESIDENT:  No, it has not come down.  It does not come down until tomorrow.
If I do sign it and if I have time and do not get taken up too much with
automobiles and things like that, I will file with it a memorandum for
your information.  Perhaps you had better not break the story at all and
make this off the record.  It will be a memorandum which will point out the
distinction between an appropriation and an authorization.  It is time that
the public was informed of the difference.  It is not the fault of the
press, because we have all used a word that we understand, but the reading
public does not understand when they read a

--- [261] ---

story in the newspaper that Congress has authorized the building of 102
new ships.  The public assumes that they are going to start building those
102 new ships right away.  So I have to point out in a memorandum that
this bill is really, in its essentials, nothing more than a resolution
that it is still the policy of the United States to build up to the London
Naval treaty limits and, having passed that resolution, it depends on the
action of future Congresses as to whether the ships will be actually
started or not.  I have to do that because I have had so many appeals from
pacifist organizations which do not understand it.

Q:  Are you coming up to the Press Club tomorrow night, Mr. President?

THE PRESIDENT:  What happens?

Q:  The dinner.

THE PRESIDENT:  Do I have to make a speech?

Q:  I don't know about that.  We will let you off on the speech, if you come.

THE PRESIDENT:  All right, if you will do that I will come.

MR. STEPHENSON:  Thank you, Mr. President.

(The Press Conference adjourned at 4:15 P.M.)

Press Conference #109
Executive Offices of the White House
March 27, 1934, 10:50 A.M.


THE PRESIDENT:  Is it true about your shopping expedition?

Q:  (Mr. Stephenson)  Yes, absolutely.

THE PRESIDENT:  We know everything about you here.  Have you been buying, too?

Q:  (Mr. Storm)  Yes, sir; got a new pair of shoes.  Stevie got himself a lot of new white clothes.

THE PRESIDENT:  We will just make it under the wire.  I don't know but I think so.

MR. DONALDSON:  All in.

THE PRESIDENT:  Well, last night it was pretty definite that we would not leave this afternoon but I heard that Fred (Mr. Storm) had been buying white clothes, so I decided to really make a go of it at five o'clock this afternoon.  I am only doing it because of the white clothes.

Q:  (Mr. Stephenson)  Much obliged.

THE PRESIDENT:  Twelve o'clock noon I am going to sign the Vinson Bill with a little statement.  Shortly thereafter we are going to send a Message to the Congress with regard to the Independent Offices bill.

At 12:20 the railroad labor people are coming in.  At 2:00 o'clock we have Council and at 2:30 I am going over the Post Office Department proposals for bids by the air mail during a temporary period.  I don't know when that will come out.  It may come out this afternoon or, if not, tomorrow.

Q:  What about the Board for the automobile industry?

THE PRESIDENT:  I hope to get that out also between now and 12:00 or 1:00 o'clock.

--- [263] ---

Q:  Kind of a light day?

THE PRESIDENT:  Light day, yes.  (Laughter)  And the mail is up to nine P.M. last night.  I haven't done today's mail but expect to do it before I leave.

Q:  Would you care to give us any indication of your attitude toward the Bankhead Bill in the Senate?

THE PRESIDENT:  Oh, heavens!  Didn't I write a letter on that?  I think so.  I think I wrote a letter in favor of it once upon a time.

Q:  On the bids for the air mail, do I understand that there will be temporary bids let?

THE PRESIDENT: Yes.

Q: Until the permanent legislation is passed?

THE PRESIDENT: Yes.

Q: That will be done right away?

THE PRESIDENT: They will be asked for right away.

Q: Are they companies whose contracts --

THE PRESIDENT: (interposing) I cannot tell you anything more about it. You will have to wait until that story breaks.

Q: How can you legally let contracts of this kind when the law prevents any½ of these companies bidding for contracts for the next five years under the Section used in annulling their contracts?

THE PRESIDENT: You will have to wait -- that is the same question -- until you see who can bid. That will be in the proposals.

Q: Have you been informed whether these companies changed their officers?

THE PRESIDENT: No, I haven't heard at all.

Q: Sort of expecting them to do that, aren't you?

THE PRESIDENT: I have not heard. That is a leading question.

Q: Mr. Wirt? (Laughter)

THE PRESIDENT: Have you, too, been hearing from your office on that? That is one of the things that we can just keep among ourselves but of course

--- [264] ---

I know and you know some of the orders that have been received down here by the press from the home office on this Wirt matter. (Laughter) That is just in the family, because it would violate the ethics of the profession, of course, if anybody were to talk about it.

Of course, as a matter of fact -- this is entirely off the record -- the thing goes back and is best illustrated by a story. A great many years ago I had a talk with Charles W. Eliot, President of Harvard University, a very wise old gentleman. Somebody -- this is about 1908 or 1910, along there -- somebody was very radical and was advocating the abolition of the Senate of the United States. A lot of the papers were saying that the man and the people advocating that were bolshevists and communists, etc. Old man Eliot put it rather well. He said, "Under our form of Constitution it is neither unconstitutional nor illegal to advocate a constitutional change of government by constitutional means. But it is absolutely illegal from every point of view to advocate a change of government by force or by unconstitutional means."

Therefore, to boil the thing down on this particular episode, somebody told somebody some kind of a story which may or may not affect some employee of the government. If that employee of the government, on the fact,

not on the supposition but on the fact, was seeking to overthrow the
government, of course that is an offense, very definite. On the other
hand, any employee of the government as well as any citizen has a right to
advocate a constitutional change. Well, you are all familiar with what
happened.

For instance, and I think, as a matter of fact, Dr. Eliot was talking
about using that as an example, in England, up to about that time, they
had two houses, the House of Commons and the House of Lords, with equal
powers. Legislation had to pass the both houses and for

--- [265] ---

years and years, principally on the Irish Home Rule Bill, the Commons would
pass it year after year and the House of Lords would turn it down. It
could not get anywhere. So they put through a constitutional change in
England by which the House of Lords would have the right to veto a bill
one time after it had been passed by the House of Commons but if, after a
reasonable length of time, the House of Commons put through that bill a
second time, the House of Lords had nothing to do with it, they had nothing
to say about it. In England of that period, the people advocating that
change which went through without upsetting the democratic form of government in England, the people advocating that were called wild-eyed radicals.
Yet they were merely seeking to change the constitution by wholly constitutional means.

So it seems to me that, outside of what I first mentioned, the effort to
create a story out of pretty slim pickings, there is not very much to be
said in the matter one way or the other. I shall go away fishing and
shall not give Dr. Wirt very much thought. I don't think anybody else
would. (Laughter)

Q:  Mr. President, are those last two sentences on the record?

THE PRESIDENT:  Not at all. (Laughter)

Q:  Can you tell us whether you have in mind any new thoughts in our relations
with Germany, as a result of your talk with Dodd (Dr. William E. Dodd,
Ambassador to Germany)?

THE PRESIDENT:  No.

Q:  Anything you can tell us about commercial or financial relations there?

THE PRESIDENT:  I do not think so. All that happened was that he was giving
me a general picture of things as he had seen them over there. We did not
talk any more than that.

Q:  Any background on the railroad situation?

--- [266] ---

THE PRESIDENT:  Not yet.

Q:  Do you expect to put this automobile strike settlement in the form of an
Executive Order or will it stand as an informal agreement or amendment to
the Code?

THE PRESIDENT: Just keep it the way it is, just an informal agreement.

Q:   Can you tell us that you are going on this fishing cruise in spite of Dr. Wirt?

THE PRESIDENT: No.

Q:   Are you considering the appointment of an engineer for the District of Columbia and a judge of the Municipal Court?

THE PRESIDENT: Again I think I have something on it.

MR. EARLY: There is something in the making.

THE PRESIDENT: There is something in the making. You shall have it -- I hope so.

Q:   For the morning papers?

THE PRESIDENT: It is for whenever the Count (Rudolph de Zapp) wants it.

MR. STEPHENSON: Thank you, Mr. President.


(The Press Conference adjourned at 11:00 A.M.)

Press Conference #110
Held on the stern seat of the NOURMAHAL
April 9, 1934, about 1:00 P.M.

        (The Press had come out sixty miles in Mr. Gar Wood's express
        cruiser to meet the President at a rendezvous off Bemini Islands.)

THE PRESIDENT: I have got one job for the crowd. I haven't time to prepare
    my speech for the Gridiron Club Dinner.

Q: You promised to make it?

THE PRESIDENT: Yes, I promised to make it.

Q: Save those reports (referring to the pouches of mail and official reports
    which had been brought out) and read them at the Gridiron Club Dinner.

Q: They would not understand them.

Q: It might shock them.

THE PRESIDENT: This has Florida beat a mile, off the record, on this side,
    climate and everything else.

Q: Is this still part of the Bahamas?

THE PRESIDENT: Yes.

Q: Are all the islands around the region part of the Bahamas?

THE PRESIDENT: Yes. When you get down to the Cuban Channel, the Gulf Stream
    swings around, coming west, and comes up this way. Shooting off, straight
    along the north coast of Cuba, is a very deep channel only about thirty
    miles across. That is where we were until last night. That is Anguilla
    Island, various shoals, Elbow Cay, et cetera. That is great country.
    Nobody goes there. I don't think anybody has fished Anguilla Island.

Q: You don't think the fish know the tricks about being caught?

--- [268] ---

(Laughter)

Q: I was told by a fisherman that up to ten years ago nobody had caught a
    sailfish.

THE PRESIDENT: That is right. Nobody with a rod and line under six or eight
    years ago caught a swordfish -- less than that, five or six years ago.
    But now they do it all along.

Q: What is the name of the chap who caught that fish?

THE PRESIDENT: That is Lytell Hull. We call him "Mr. Secretary" on board.

MR. McINTYRE: Why?

THE PRESIDENT: Hull.

Q:   (Mr. Stephenson)  Write it out for him.

> (Only a few minutes were consumed by the Press Conference.  The
> members of the Press had spent most of their visit in looking
> over the specimens of various fish caught, also in inspecting
> the NOURMAHAL.  The principal purpose of the visit of the Press
> was to determine the state of health of the President.  There
> had been rumors that he was very ill, et cetera, and they desired
> to disaffirm these rumors by eye-witness accounts.)

(End)

Press Conference #111
Aboard the Presidential Special Train,
  en route from Miami to Jacksonville
April 12, 1934, 9:45 A.M.


Q:   Is there any news?

THE PRESIDENT:   I do not think there is a blessed thing.  I have not seen any
     mail since what you brought out (to the NOURMAHAL anchored off Bemini
     Islands).

Q:   General Johnson is on board.  Have you anything in particular?

THE PRESIDENT:   No.  I am going to try to make him get off at Palm Beach and
     get three more days holiday.

Q:   Are you, really?

THE PRESIDENT:   I do not see why he has to try to go back.  He might just as
     well stay a little longer.

Q:   Have you looked at the McLeod Bill for the payment of depositors in closed
     banks?

THE PRESIDENT:   No, I never heard about it until I read it in the paper.

Q:   The Frazier Bill either?

THE PRESIDENT:   I do not know what they did with it.

Q:   Do you want new taxes to make up for that?

THE PRESIDENT:   I have no idea how much they got in all told.  I do not know
     the details.  They have up to a hundred or a hundred and fifty million
     dollars for the Department of Agriculture but I do not know the details.
     Exclusive of the ten per cent, they added something.  I cannot talk about
     it because I do not know what is there.

Q:   The Securities Act, any chance of modification?

THE PRESIDENT:   That I do not know.  I do not know what the status of

                          --- [270] ---

     that is.  The last thing that happened was a month ago.  I think it was
     the Trade Commission (the Federal Trade Commission) that was going to
     suggest one or two what might be called minor amendments, and the only one
     I remember is the one which would limit the liability of the house of
     issue to the total of the amount of their own underwriting instead of the
     total of the issue.  That is the only one I remember.

Q:   You approve of that, Mr. President?

THE PRESIDENT:   That is perfectly all right.

Q:   You don't care for any general revision of the Securities Act?

THE PRESIDENT:  No.

Q:   General Johnson told us the other day at the hotel (the Miami-Biltmore
     Hotel in Coral Gables, Florida) that he was content to let the licensing
     provision of the N.R.A. die because he thought there were enough provisions
     in the law to take care of its enforcement.  He said whether it would be
     extended would be up to you.

THE PRESIDENT:  Probably I will talk to him today about it.

Q:   They have a national propaganda on to defeat the Fletcher-Rayburn Bill.

THE PRESIDENT:  Which is that?

Q:   The Stock Market bill.

THE PRESIDENT:  I said that in my letter to him about three weeks ago, so that
     is not news.

Q:   Well, it always helps to say that you are still for it.

THE PRESIDENT:  Yes.  But when you come down to the details of these bills,
     naturally I say nothing at all because they change in the

--- [271] ---

Committee from day to day.  I do not know what the status is today.  I
have no idea.

Q:   Are you counting on Congress going out?

THE PRESIDENT:  I have not any idea.  Are all the appropriation bills through?
     I think they are.

Q:   Most of the big ones are.

THE PRESIDENT:  I wonder what is left in the way of appropriation bills.

Q:   Did the Navy go through?

THE PRESIDENT:  Yes, and Agriculture went through.

Q:   And State and Commerce.

Q:   Have you any new legislation to propose?

THE PRESIDENT:  I do not think there is another thing.

Q:   How much relief legislation is there still to go through?

THE PRESIDENT:  The big bill.

Q:   That will just about wind it up?

THE PRESIDENT:  As far as I know, that is the only appropriation bill left
     except the deficiency bill that goes through the last day just to pick
     up all sorts of odds and ends.

Q:   That is routine.

Q:   The war debt Message is somewhat nearer?

THE PRESIDENT:  Yes, two weeks nearer.  (Laughter)

Q:   How about that?

THE PRESIDENT:  Two weeks nearer.  (Laughter)

Q:   Did you have a good time on the water?

THE PRESIDENT:  Perfectly marvelous; I got a real rest.

Q:   Can we quote that?

THE PRESIDENT:  The first two days I think I slept and then caught a

--- [272] ---

little cold in my nose.  Oh, I fished the first two days, caught a cold
in my nose, slept a couple of days and then fishing some more and lazying
around.

MR. McINTYRE:  I hope you slept last night more than some of us did.

THE PRESIDENT:  Off the record, we stayed up late, about midnight, and had a
little razzing party last night.

Q:   How much did you win?

THE PRESIDENT:  No, razzing.  We did not play anything.  We were razzing the
Commodore last night.

Q:   He can take it.

THE PRESIDENT:  He took it all right.  Strictly between ourselves, we razzed
him about his little dog.

Q:   May we quote you on this, that you said it was perfectly marvelous and
that you got a real rest, that the first two days were spent fishing, and
then a couple of days sleeping, then fishing some more and lazying around?

THE PRESIDENT:  Yes.

Q:   We did a little lazying around, too.

(End)

MR. DONALDSON: All in.

THE PRESIDENT: Well, how are the palefaces?

(The President had just returned from Florida.)

I have not found out anything yet. I have been here just a short time so, if there is any information I can give you I will be grateful.

Q: I see you gave the Congress a little talk today (referring to the President's brief address to the people assembled at Union Station).

THE PRESIDENT:: Yes.

I really do not know a thing yet. I am beginning to learn.

Q: They want to know what you speech meant?

THE PRESIDENT: It was what they call an allegory. (Laughter)

Q: Mr. President, one of your constituents wants to know when the cherry blossoms are going to bloom?

THE PRESIDENT: What time have they set for the party, the nineteenth? I think so.

Q: Mr. President, have you made any engagement with the Premier of Japan to talk things over out in Hawaii?

THE PRESIDENT: No. (Laughter)

Q: That story was in the paper this morning from Hawaii, that something like that might happen.

THE PRESIDENT: What was it, relayed out from Washington? (Laughter)

Q: I think from Japan.

MR. EARLY: Stevie (Mr. Stephenson) is checking up on one of his own

--- [274] ---

stories. It was A.P.

THE PRESIDENT: I thought so, yes.

Q: (Mr. Stephenson) What is this?

Q: Do you expect to take any steps which may obviate the opening on the twentieth of temporary air-mail bids?

THE PRESIDENT: No.

Q: Can you comment on what your policy would be with respect to contractors whose air-mail contracts were cancelled being given six months to reorganize as per the terms of the House bill?

THE PRESIDENT: I never heard of it; I don't know.

Q: Mr. President, since you went away the Senate has added some $150,000,000 to the tax bill. Any preference as to whether that should stay in or not?

THE PRESIDENT: We have not discussed that yet. I do not know what all the items are.

Q: How about the Stock Market bill?

THE PRESIDENT: I do not know what is in it at the present moment. It shifts every day.

Q: Not very much. (Laughter)

THE PRESIDENT: I am asking a number of Senators to come down tomorrow afternoon at 2:30 to give me a lot of information and Sunday, sometime in the evening, probably a number of the people in the House will be down to give me the same information from the House.

Q: Is that on the Stock Exchange bill?

THE PRESIDENT: Everything in the world.

Q: Will you then decide on your program, how long Congress may stay?

THE PRESIDENT: Will we decide how long? I asked them to stay all

--- [275] ---

summer. It is all right with me.

Q: Allegorically? (Laughter)

THE PRESIDENT: I was not very kind to the Washington climate.

Q: Our readers are probably kicking us.

THE PRESIDENT: That line about the humidity, of course that is the real important thing.

Q: You should not call attention to it.

Q: That ought to be good for an editorial. (Laughter)

Q: Have you signed the Johnson Bill?

THE PRESIDENT: This morning.

Q: Can you interpret whether that would apply to those countries making token payments -- in other words, whether those countries making token payments would get their loans?

THE PRESIDENT: I had better talk to the Secretary of State before answering that question; I don't know.

Q: Who will administer that bill, Mr. President?

THE PRESIDENT: I do not know. I suppose the Federal Trade Commission, the Federal Reserve, the State Department -- quite a number.

Q: Mr. President, have you endorsed the Wagner labor disputes bill?

THE PRESIDENT: I have not heard about it for the last two and a half weeks at all.

Q: Some stories indicated you endorsed the general principles of the Supreme Court for labor, or something of that sort?

THE PRESIDENT: No.

Q: How about the silver agitation?

THE PRESIDENT: We are still talking about it.

Q: On the nationalization of silver, they say they have enough votes

--- [276] ---

to pass.

THE PRESIDENT: The Secretary of the Treasury told me there are five bills.

Q: Speaker Rainey announced today they would try to combine the silver bills in the House and try to make an effort to get one of the combined bills through. Have you talked with him about it?

THE PRESIDENT: I have not; I will tomorrow.

Q: Anything to say about the new Code eagle?

THE PRESIDENT: What?

Q: The new drive for the N.R.A. Code eagle?

THE PRESIDENT: Get a new bird?

Q: Yes. (Laughter)

THE PRESIDENT: I think all that is happening on that is that we will have another extension from the fifteenth of April, just as we had it from the first of January, on practically the same terms. Anybody is entitled to use the blue eagle if they conform with the Code provisions.

Q: How long is the extenstion?

THE PRESIDENT: I don't know; it has not come over yet.

Q: Mr. President, have you had an opportunity to look over the pending McLeod Bill since you got back at all?

THE PRESIDENT: Which is that?

Q: It provides for the payment of depositors who had money in all closed banks which are members of the Federal Reserve System.

THE PRESIDENT: I've got quite a lot of claims myself. I lost $300 in a closed bank in 1921. Some of my family lost some money in a closed bank in the 1907 panic and my father lost money in the 1893

--- [277] ---

panic in a closed bank. Do they all come in?

Q: They probably would like to amend it to that effect.

Q: It provides for the payment of depositors in all banks, public and private and what not, up to $2500.

THE PRESIDENT: Are they going to take care of all other bad debts?

Q: It involves only four billion dollars at the present time.

THE PRESIDENT: Only four billion dollars? Why, that is nothing. I lost money in a lobster industry about eight years ago. See if you can't get that in, too.

MR. STEPHENSON: Thank you, Mr. President.

Q: That was more allegory, Mr. President.


(The Press Conference adjourned at 4:22 P.M.)

Press Conference #113
Executive Offices of the White House
April 18, 1934, 10:52 A.M.


Q:  Good morning, Mr. President.

THE PRESIDENT:  Good morning, Fred (Mr. Storm).  How is the seasickness this
    morning?

Q:  (Mr. Storm)  Feeling fit as a fiddle today.

Q:  (Mr. Stephenson)  Did I tell you that I bet on Sea Fox down at Tropical
    Park?

THE PRESIDENT:  What happened?

Q:  It won in the NOURMAHAL handicap.  That is where I got this suit.

THE PRESIDENT:  Pick the nautical names every time.  They are good.

    Count (Rudolph de Zapp), how are you this morning?  Still got any vacan-
    cies?

Q:  (Count de Zapp)  Oh, yes.

THE PRESIDENT:  I do not know why everybody is coming in this morning.  There
    is no news.

Q:  They are very hopeful this morning, Mr. President.

MR. DONALDSON:  All in.

THE PRESIDENT:  I don't know why I am being honored by such a large crowd
    today.  There is no news at all.

Q:  Mr. President, has your attitude on the McLeod Banking Bill changed?

THE PRESIDENT:  Which one?

Q:  The McLeod, the bank depositors bill, has it been changed since his visit
    yesterday, since his conference with you?  (Referring to the conference
    on April 17 with Congressmen McLeod and Palmer at which Mr. Merriam and
    Mr. Crowley were present)

--- [279] ---

THE PRESIDENT:  No.

Q:  You are against it?

THE PRESIDENT:  Yes.  Necessarily, of course.  I think I can talk to you about
    the McLeod and similar bills.  You had better make it halfway between off
    the record and background.  (Laughter)  That is, if you can get that nice
    shade; I don't know where it is myself.

    On any bill of that kind, it is almost impossible to do justice.  For

instance, as an example, I said to Palmer yesterday and to McLeod, "What
are you going to do about this kind of case? Two banks fail at the same
time. They are on opposite corners. One goes into the hands of the receiver and so does the other. One receiver is able to clean up his receivership in the course of a year and thereupon they pay off the depositors,
say, 60 cents on the dollar. Now, those depositors have got their 60
cents on the dollar. The episode is closed -- it is finished business.
The assets have been sold, you cannot reopen it. That is not taken care of
in the McLeod Bill and all they have got is 60 cents on the dollar.

The other bank is only able to pay 30 cents on the dollar but because of
the difficulty of liquidation it is still in the hands of a receiver. The
depositors in that bank, instead of getting 30 cents on the dollar, would
get 100 cents on the dollar under the McLeod Bill.

There is a perfectly good illustration of the impossibility of giving justice in individual cases under any blanket bill. How far back are you
going? Are you going back to the money my father

--- [280] ---

lost in 1893? I don't know. How are you going to fix a date?

Of course, the actual fact of the thing is that we are trying to take care
of a tremendously complicated situation. There are thousands and thousands
of closed banks, state banks and national banks, and we have been lending
money and buying assets. There is an administrative question as to whether, in the carrying out of that process, we are being liberal enough in
the money we are loaning or the money we are paying, and the R.F.C., the
Comptroller, the Federal Deposit Insurance, and the Treasury Department
are all working on the re-examining of every closed bank in order to make
more certain that we have adopted a liberal policy in lending money on
assets or purchasing assets. Now, that is about as far as you can go.

Q: Mr. President, are you impressed with the argument that the anti-hoarding
campaign of a year and a half ago laid an obligation on the Government to
thaw out these frozen deposits?

THE PRESIDENT: You mean under the Hoover Administration?

Q: Yes.

THE PRESIDENT: No, I don't see what that has to do with it all. After all a
bank is a bank.

Q: What was the question, Mr. President?

THE PRESIDENT: He was asking about some kind of a moral obligation on the part
of the Government because the Government kept a bank open. My Lord, we
try to keep every bank in this country open. Some of them we kept open
too long but it did not hurt the assets of the bank, keeping them open.
It probably helped.

Q: Mr. President, do you care to discuss the condition in Japan yester-

--- [281] ---

day in which it is stated that the Japanese Government made objection to foreign loans?

THE PRESIDENT: I have not talked to the State Department at all. I do not think they have heard anything.

Q:   How about the debt Message to the Congress?

THE PRESIDENT: Yes, yes, we are three days nearer.

Q:   What is the railroad situation?

THE PRESIDENT: I have got them coming in, I think it is this afternoon.


(Looking at schedule)


Yes, this afternoon at 3:00 o'clock.

Q:   Who will be in?

Q:   Do you see both sides?

THE PRESIDENT: I do not think so. It is management this afternoon. I will undoubtedly see the others later on.

Q:   Have you any comment on Britain's very splendid financial condition and her action in not taking any cognizance of debt payments to us in her new budget?

THE PRESIDENT: No; wait until the debt Message.

Q:   In that connection, have you had an opportunity to discuss with the Secretary of State the Johnson Bill and its attitude toward token payments?

THE PRESIDENT: No.

Q:   Do you care to offer any comment on the silver legislation? There seem to be several bills and some anxiety.

THE PRESIDENT: The less comment I make at this particular moment, the better.

Q:   Are you willing to have an independent agency administer the proposed Stock Exchange control law instead of the Federal Trade Commission,

--- [282] ---

as proposed in the House bill?

THE PRESIDENT: I am not changing my position publicly from what I have said before. The Message went to Congress and it has been stewing around and they are considering it every day. I do not know what the official decision of the two houses will be. Just a little previous, that is all.

Q:   How about the adjournment of Congress and the legislative program to be enacted before they adjourn?

THE PRESIDENT: No, because that is a little bit like saying we have got to have such and such definite bills. It is a little bit like the difficulty of writing a story that such and such proposal or piece of legislation is conservative or radical. You have to characterize and I do not think the time has come to characterize yet.

Q:  Yesterday, after the conference with you, Senator Wagner indicated that the pending Labor Board Bill and the Unemployment Insurance will both be enacted this session, with some modification?

THE PRESIDENT:  I am having a conference with Wagner and the Secretary of Labor and Harry Hopkins and N.R.A. tomorrow or the next day on the general subject. Of course I would like very much to see something carried out by this Congress in the way of the creation of some form of permanent mediation by Congressional action instead of merely by Executive action. That is about as far as we have got.

Q:  Anything on the attitude toward publicity on income tax returns?

THE PRESIDENT:  No, because that is still in conference and involves not only legislative action but also Executive action and the

--- [283] ---

Executive action might dovetail into Congressional action because, you see, I have the power under last year's bill to make the returns public. I think we will be able to straighten that out without trouble.

Q:  Have you read Colonel Roosevelt's (Colonel Theodore Roosevelt) speech last night?

THE PRESIDENT:  No, did he make a speech?

Q:  T.R., your distant cousin.

THE PRESIDENT:  No. I read Harry's (referring to the Assistant Secretary of the Navy). (Laughter)

Q:  Are you going on the radio?

THE PRESIDENT:  Not that I know of.

Q:  May I ask whether your reference to permanent mediation means that something in the nature of the Wagner Bill should be put through?

THE PRESIDENT:  No, I would not say that, because it might be some different form to carry out the same principle, that is to say a permanent mediation body and possibly a permanent arbitration body. But that does not mean, necessarily, a complete change from the proposal of Senator Wagner. That is a matter I do not know about yet.

MR. STEPHENSON:  Thank you, Mr. President.

Press Conference #114
Executive Offices of the White House
April 20, 1934, 4:05 P.M.


MR. DONALDSON:  All in.

THE PRESIDENT:  I suppose you would like to know about what happened at the
  railroad conference today.  As you know, I held a conference before I went
  off on the trip and then I took with me a trunk full of papers that went
  into all the phases of railroad employment.  Then, after I got back, I saw
  the management the day before yesterday and the employees today.

  I am sending a letter to Commissioner Eastman this afternoon which Steve
  (Mr. Early) will prepare for you so that you may have a copy of it.

  Probably the easiest way is to read the letter because it explains rather
  fully the general railway labor situation and, if you want to ask any questions afterwards, you can base them on the letter.  (Reading)

       "My dear Mr. Eastman:

       "As you know, I have recently conferred with representatives of
       both the railroad managements and the railroad employees in re-
       gard to the wage controversy, and have given this matter further
       consideration.  No one who knows the facts can fail to be moved
       by the suffering which the depression, in combination with the
       great increase in competition from other forms of transportation,
       has inflicted on the employees.  The 10 per cent deduction from
       basic wage rates, which the employees voluntarily conceded in
       1932 for the good of the industry, has not been the major cause
       of this suffering.  Furloughs, part-time employment, demotions
       and pay below a reasonable minimum have been more important
       factors.  Wage rates tell only a part of the story; the whole
       story is told by what a man has in his pay envelope at the end
       of the week or month."

                          --- [285] ---

In other words, just explaining, it has not been the 10 per cent cut that
has caused, by any means, most of the suffering.  There are so many employees who have been employed only one day or two days or three days a week.
Then there were a great many who were employed a month or two and then fur-
loughed for two or three months.  That has been the major cause of the suffering in the ranks of the railroad labor employees.

       "Realizing this suffering, as I do, I have felt that the welfare
       of the employees, and particularly the welfare of those at the
       bottom of the heap, is the vital thing to have in mind in this
       wage controversy.  The question is whether the elimination, in
       whole or in part, on July 1 of the 10 per cent deduction from
       basic wage rates is the thing which their best interests de-
       mand.  If it is necessary to choose between some measure of
       relief from furloughs, part-time work, demotions, and low mini-
       mum pay and the elimination, in whole or in part, of the wage
       deduction the choice should certainly favor the first of these
       alternatives.  The traffic and earnings of the railroads are

improving, but they are still below the 1931 level, a very
large amount of deferred maintenance exists, and maintenance
expenditures are still on a sub-normal basis."

Actually, they are cut in half. Maintenance in 1929, I think it was, ran a
little over two billion dollars. In 1932 and 1933, each of those, the
maintenance ran less than one billion dollars.

"I cannot avoid the conclusion that during the remainder of
this year, it is very important that increased earnings should
be used in the rehabilitation of the properties and in providing such added and improved service as the increased traffic
may demand. This will not only decrease part-time employment
but it will add materially to the total number of men employed."

I said that because there was a good deal of discussion on the part of the
employees of how railroad families have had to double up. One family that
was still employed on the railroad would take

--- [286] ---

another family that was not being employed or was only employed one day a
week or something like that. Therefore the idea is to add materially to the
total number of men employed as well as to increase the part-time.

"An increase in wages will help men now at work, but it will be
of considerably less advantage to the employees as a whole, and
it will also operate to defer the rehabilitation of the properties and the provision of good service which are essential to
the good health of the railroad industry. The employees are
part of the railroad industry and are tied to its future. It
is essential that the railroads should be able to meet effec-
tively the severe competition by which they are now faced, and
inability to do this will inevitably react on the men. The
railroads need the next few months to put their houses in order for this purpose.

"After careful consideration of existing conditions, therefore,
I am fully persuaded that the position which I took in my letters of February 14 and March 20, addressed jointly to the
railroad managements and the labor executives, was sound, and
that an extension of the present wage status for at least six
months is what the welfare of the railroads, of their employes,
and of the entire country demands as the immediate and temporary disposition of this matter. This includes, of course, the
recommendation in my letter of March 20 that the minimum wages
of railroad employees should be brought into conformity with
the standards followed by the National Recovery Administration.

"I shall be glad, therefore, if you will undertake to effect a
settlement between the employees and the managements along
these lines. In that connection, however, I desire to emphasize three things:

"(1) Everything practicable should be done to see to it that
increased earnings of the carriers during the period of the
extension are used to help the more unfortunate employees who
have suffered from unreasonably low minimun pay, furloughs,

part-time, and demotions.  I cannot too strongly urge upon the
managements the necessity of devoting any increased earnings
to the rehabilitation of their properties, better service, and
additional employment.  That will be good business for them.
Whatever safeguards are feasible to assure such use of

--- [287] ---

funds should be applied.  It must be frankly recognized that
there is little prospect that the railroads will be able to
employ in the future the number of men they have employed in
the past, and that they must operate with the utmost efficiency
and economy; yet unemployed and part-time work can be reduced
materially.  It must also be recognized that certain classes
of employees will be affected more than others by rehabilitation and improved service; but all will benefit as the health
and efficiency of the industry are restored.

"(2)  Provision should be made, so far as practicable, to
avoid the renewal of the controversy next August or at any
other time during the period of the extension.  I see no
reason why the deduction should not be put upon the same basis as it was on originally, so that further controversy may
be deferred until at least January 1.  I make only the one
exception that it may be desirable to provide for a reopening
of the matter before that date, in the event that increased
earnings are not put, within reasonable limits, to the use
which I have indicated above.

"(3)  Negotiations should be brought to an end, one way or
the other, without delay, so that if a present settlement
should prove impossible, which I sincerely trust will not be
the case, there will be opportunity for a thorough investigation by a fact-finding commission prior to July 1.  In
order that there may be no apprehension as to possible bias
in such an investigation -- "

I have to appoint the commission.

" -- I may say that I shall make appointments to any such
commission upon the definite understanding that no regard
shall be paid to personal opinions that I may have expressed,
and that the conclusions shall rest solely upon the facts
developed.  Such a commission would, I presume, examine into
the merits of the wage rates of the different classes of
employees, a subject which I have not considered.  I have
considered only the wise disposition for a temporary period
of the immediate issue."

Then there is one other thing I suppose I can give you as background.  As
you know, we have had the problem in the railroad

--- [288] ---

situation of very, very high fixed charges.  In other words, the problem of
the capital structure of the railroads.  One reason for it is the very
large amount of fixed charges that were incurred between 1915 and 1916 and
1929, double tracking, new stations, et cetera, which were paid for in many

instances by bond issues which carried with them large interest charges.

I do not know whether it is a fair way of putting it, but here is a good illustration. Suppose a railroad, during the 1920's, four-tracked its lines and today only needs two tracks. It is still paying interest on those other two tracks and finding it almost impossible to come out even. Now that raises a serious question as to whether a bad guess on the part of the railroads in the 1920's as to future traffic conditions should become a penalty on the capital structure of that railroad for a great many years to come. It raises the question as to whether there should not be some form of reorganization by which unused and unnecessary property should not be capitalized by stock, for the sake of argument, instead of bonds. In other words, that if at some future date it turned out that the guess was a bad guess or that there was a falling off in general railroad use as to whether that should not be a charge on the stockholder, the owners of the road, instead of the mortgagees of the road.

In other words, the railroad situation is so serious that we come pretty close to being faced with two alternatives. One is a policy by which the capital structures of the railroads of the country could be so reorganized that there would never be, even in bad times, a question of meeting fixed charges; something that

--- [289] ---

would eliminate, insofar as possible, the constant threat of receiverships that we have had now for 100 years, continuously, in the country. It would be a reorganization of the capital structure which would leave the control and the management of the railroad in private hands with a fairly definite assurance, first, that they keep out of the hands of receivers, and, secondly, that this whole problem of employment and wages could be put on a fairly permanent and satisfactory basis.

The other alternative, which none of us favor unless the first fails to work out, is Government control.

There does not seem to be any third alternative, which is not exactly grammatical, but expresses the idea.

Q: Right on that point, Mr. President, the railroad people say that the third alternative is super-consolidation. Would you care to touch on that as embraced by the principal plan?

THE PRESIDENT: Yes. That is really not an alternative because nobody has yet brought in a plan for consolidation which takes care of the human element. Every plan that has been brought in for consolidation involves the throwing out of work of somewhere around 30 to 33 per cent of the present number of railroad employees. And the present number of railroad employees who are employed is only a little over 50 per cent of the total number. In other words, 50 per cent of them are still employed and, unfortunately, in railroading it is like coal mining. Once a railroad man always a railroad man. You cannot become a politician or a newspaperman if you have once served as a railroad man. And these plans of consolidation do not take into consideration the human element.

--- [290] ---

Q: Would consolidation solve the matter of capital structure to any degree?

THE PRESIDENT: Only in this way, that it would bring the reorganization of general structure to the point of negotiation and you might be able to get an agreement on the cutting down in that way. But, even then, under the present law on reorganization of capital structure, there are only two ways of doing it. One is by unanimous consent, which is almost impossible to get. For example, a fellow has what he was told is a bond when he bought it. Actually it is not, it is a debenture. Actually he bought it as a bond but he hoped to trade it in for the common stock some day at a profit, even though the common stock has not paid a dividend for ten years. The other method is receivership.

So, the principal thing is to simplify the method of reorganizing the capital structure. The only thing I have done on this is to call it to the attention of the Cabinet and I have asked two or three members of the Cabinet to study the question informally, to talk with the Interstate Commerce Commission, with the Coordinator of Railroads and other people, employees, managers, et cetera, and in the course of the next month or two to see if we cannot have something that is fairly definite to serve in a discussion of future national policy. It is a thing which won't come to a head probably before the summer.

Q: Can you tell us the names of the Cabinet officers?

THE PRESIDENT: The Secretary of Commerce, the Secretary of Labor and the Attorney General.

Q: Have you given any thought to the proposal of the House Ways and

--- [291] ---

Means Subcommittee for a forty per cent horizontal reduction in tabacco taxes?

THE PRESIDENT: I don't know a thing about it, only what I read in the papers. Why a forty per cent reduction in tobacco taxes?

Q: On manufactured products.

THE PRESIDENT: You mean instead of a six-cent stamp on my Camels there will be only a two-cent stamp?

Q: Yes, sir.

THE PRESIDENT: Why, my Lord in Heaven, we need the revenue.

Q: They claim the increased sales would make up for the loss of taxes by reudcing it to ten cents.

THE PRESIDENT: I don't think I will smoke two packs a day instead of one.

There is one interesting thing on the Hill in regard to tobacco taxes I have a good deal of sympathy in -- I have not taken part in any way -- and that is the opposition of people who pay ten cents to soaking them a six-cent tax, when the fellow who pays twelve or thirteen cents only pays six cents. There is a great deal of merit, but as I understand it, it will never come out of committee.

Q: How about the Bankhead Cotton Bill? I understand that there is apprehension that a lot of manufacturers in other countries will increase their production comparably to our reduction?

THE PRESIDENT: Those are the five per cent of the growers?

Q: Yes. Is that a serious problem at all?

THE PRESIDENT: No.

Q: You are not considering any agreements or anything?

--- [292] ---

THE PRESIDENT: No.

Q: May we anticipate that your debt Message to the Congress will be more than merely a report on the debt situation?

THE PRESIDENT: All I can tell you is that it is two days nearer.

Q: There are a couple of new developments in the air-mail situation. The first is that in your message (released to the Press) explaining the conference you held last week with the two Senators and Mead (Representative Mead) of the House Committee you expressed the desire for one year competitive bidding. The Post Office Department has opened temporary contracts which, under the old law, will permit three months' operation with two similar extensions, making it nine months. Can you comment on whether or not it is your desire for them to go ahead with the temporary bids?

THE PRESIDENT: Yes, because I do not know what the Congress will do with even one year permanent bids.

Q: And the other is that the House Committee voted at a meeting to strike out the ban which will prevent contractors having contracts cancelled from bidding?

THE PRESIDENT: I don't know; I will have to see exactly what they said and did because it is a legal question. If they struck out the ban, did they repeal the old law? I don't know.

Q: Could you tell us anything about your conference today with Senator Wagner, Secretary Perkins and Johnson?

THE PRESIDENT: Only that they are conferring in regard to a Wagner Bill. In other words, so much water has gone over the dam -- I think I can say this off the record -- Senator Wagner realizes that certain provisions of the bill -- for instance, the settle-

--- [293] ---

ment of the automobile strike -- changed the character, so they are working on an amended bill.

Q: Mr. President, can you tell us about silver?

THE PRESIDENT: About silver? What about it?

Q: Can you tell us your views on it?

THE PRESIDENT:   I think it is an awfully long subject.  Suppose we wait until
   after tomorrow's meeting.   In general I think you can use this talk as
   background, if you want to write a silver story, that we have learned from
   experience that even if you have all the known facts, a panacea does not
   always cure the patient as expected.  As, for example, in the case of
   gold.  We undoubtedly did put up the price level in this country through
   the purchase of gold and the increase in price.  We did not put it up as
   much as we expected to.  The effect of putting it up and getting more gold
   and increasing prices was all to the good but there we were operating under known facts.  We knew where all the gold in the world was.  We knew
   practically within a billion dollars' worth who owned the gold and where
   it was, -- central banks, governments et cetera.

In the case of silver, we are dealing with absolutely unknown factors all
   the way through.  No two people agree on how much silver there is in the
   world.  Some people believe there is probably two or three billion dollars
   worth of silver hidden away.  Silver was mined before Christ was born.  In
   the case of gold we were buying not only a known quantity in relation to a
   known quantity but we were buying a very large part of the total gold supply of the world.  In the case of silver, some guesses are that there are
   eleven or twelve billion ounces of silver in the world.  A very small pro-

--- [294] ---

portion of that is held by governments or banks.  It is mostly in private
   hands.  Probably, as a minimum guess, there may be fifteen or eighteen billion ounces.  Nobody knows.

For us to undertake to buy 50 million ounces a month is such a drop in the
   bucket that instead of bringing the world price of silver up to $1.29, it
   might not raise it more than 15 or 20 cents.  You will find a very good example if you will refer back to your files, I think it was December 21 last
   when we undertook by Executive Order to buy American-mined silver at,
   roughly, 20 cents above the world price.  As I remember it, it was selling
   at 43 or 44 cents at that time.  We offered to buy it at 64½ cents an
   ounce.  Some of our silver friends on the Hill threw up their hats and
   cheered lustily and gave you people stories to this effect.  "This is the
   most glorious and far-reaching event in American history.  When the market
   opens tomorrow morning the world price of silver will be 64½ cents an
   ounce."  Now, that was the best judgment of people who believe in silver.
   Actually it went to 46 cents and is now back at 44½ cents an ounce.  Enough
   said.

Q:   The Darrow Board is supposed to have its report in?

THE PRESIDENT:   I have either got an appointment or am getting an appointment
   with Darrow (Clarence Darrow of Chicago) to come in and have a talk with
   me about it.

Q:   Do you know whether it will be made public or not?

THE PRESIDENT:   I guess we had better see it first.

Q:   Did you say before whether that amended Wagner Bill would be on the program?

THE PRESIDENT:   We are not quite ready.  Let us see first how it is

--- [295] ---

amended.  The general thought is, as I said the day before yesterday, we
all believe there should be some more permanent body for mediation and arbitration of labor disputes, something that would become a more central
body than our present method.  Today we have the Department of Labor mediating, we have the National Labor Board mediating, we have Hugh Johnson
mediating and father mediating.  So what we want to do, what we would like
to do, is to have one central body doing most of the mediating.  That automobile business took a lot of my time, just about a whole week.  I want to
avoid that kind of thing in the future, if I can.

Q:  Are you going to sign the cotton bill?

THE PRESIDENT:  Tomorrow.

MR. STEPHENSON:  Thank you, Mr. President.

Press Conference #115
Executive Offices of the White House
April 25, 1934, 10:45 A.M.


Q:   Just as well you did not stay at the ball game.  They got licked.

THE PRESIDENT:  My record is still pure.  I have never seen them lose.  What is
    the news this morning?  I do not know a thing, really not a thing.

Q:   About Japan?

THE PRESIDENT:  Japan?  Don't know a thing.

Q:   Haven't you heard anything about it?

THE PRESIDENT:  No, I have not seen the Secretary of State since he got back.

Q:   Any sort of background on the situation?

THE PRESIDENT:  I think I had better not today because there are an awful lot of
    cross currents and cross wires.

Q:   You said you were going to see the Secretary of State today.  Are you going
    to discuss the Japanese situation or just see him?

THE PRESIDENT:  See him.  I suppose he has got a great many other things.

Q:   Are you considering making any suggestions in connection with the Fisher
    Body strike in Cleveland and St. Louis?

THE PRESIDENT:  That has not come to me at all.  Of course, on the Fisher Body
    strike, as I suggested the other day, I am trying to avoid having all of
    these strikes come up to me.  Take the case, for instance, of the coal sit-
    uation in Western Kentucky.  Some of our good Senators and Congressmen from
    Kentucky would like to have me jump in.  I would be doing nothing else but
    arbitrating if I took cognizance and jurisdiction over all of

--- [297] ---

these.

Q:   How about the Wagner Bill?

THE PRESIDENT:  I have not heard anything further.  They were going to have a
    conference, Wagner, Miss Perkins and NRA.  I have not heard anything since
    then.

Q:   You think that is the solution, do you, to take that off your back?

THE PRESIDENT:  It will help.  It may not be a permanent and final solution, but
    it will help.

Q:   How about unemployment insurance legislation?

THE PRESIDENT:  I am not quite ready on that.  You mean the insurance?

Q:   Yes.

THE PRESIDENT:   I think you had better let me thing it out a little more; anoth-
        er few days.  Of course, I am tremendously in favor of unemployment insur-
        ance.  I guess you had better wait and let me talk off the record on Friday
        on that.  I can be a little bit more coherent then.

Q:   Are you going to make public the Darrow report on the N.R.A. Codes?

THE PRESIDENT:   I suppose so, when it is written.  It has not been written yet,
        as far as I know.  Mr. Darrow did not say it had (been written).  When it
        is written he is going to come up here with the members of that committee
        and talk things over.  I mean, when they have a preliminary draft of it.

Q:   Any decision on a Message on the debt due from Finland and other foreign
        nations?

THE PRESIDENT:   Not yet.  It is three days nearer.

Q:   Both Governor General Murphy and Governor Winship of Puerto Rico telegraph-
        ed into the War Department protesting some provisions

--- [298] ---

        of the Costigan sugar bill, saying that that bill, when put into effect,
        would create a great deal of unemployment in the Islands.

THE PRESIDENT:   It has not come down yet and I frankly do not know the language
        in the conferee's report.  It has been approved?

Q:   Only by the House.

THE PRESIDENT:   Only by the House.  I do not even know the language in it.

Q:   Murphy suggested that instead of having the bill become retroactive to Jan-
        uary first, it be made effective with our fiscal year, as of July first, so
        that it will enable the Philippines to dispose of a great deal of their
        1933-1934 surplus.

THE PRESIDENT:   I will take that up today.  I don't know anything about it.

Q:   Anything new on the railroad negotiations?

THE PRESIDENT:   I have not heard a word.

Q:   In the event that the State Department finds that one of the assenting par-
        ties to the Nine-Power Pact had violated that pact, would we consider it
        our duty to make protest?

THE PRESIDENT:   That is a very, very "iffy" question.

Q:   Do you care to offer any observations on the silver question?  It has been
        constantly popping up.

THE PRESIDENT:   Which one?

Q:   Just in general.

THE PRESIDENT: No, I don't think so.

Q:   Are you going to see the silver bloc committee?

THE PRESIDENT: Not that I know of.  I told them I would be glad to see them any
time they come down.

--- [299] ---

Q:   In your recent talks with Senate leaders, have you taken up or decided
whether you want the bonus bill brought on the floor?  It has been in committee for quite a while.

THE PRESIDENT: I am not saying anything about it.  I think you can make a good
guess on it.

Q:   I understand you spent an hour on this Public Works of Art Project.  What
do you think of it?

THE PRESIDENT: I was awfully keen about it.  I think the best line of the whole
exhibit is what the Director of the Corcoran (Art Gallery) said to me and
that is that of all these six hundred pictures there isn't a single one,
without one possible exception, that shows despair or despondency.  Taking
it by and large, those pictures are hopeful pictures, and that is a very
remarkable thing when you think that the people who did them were actually
on relief.  And, more than that, they are honest pictures; in other words,
they depict American life in an American way.  There is very little of what
some of the committee call decadent foreign art.  You can tell right away
what the picture is intended to be.  (Laughter)

Q:   Mr. President, have you approved any definite plan for the enlargement of
the offices here?

THE PRESIDENT: No, not yet.

Q:   Is it contemplated?

THE PRESIDENT: It is contemplated.  Of course, it is a very difficult proposition.  I hate to put any more buildings into the White House grounds, but,
on the other hand, you know the situation among the employees of this office at the present time.  It is

--- [300] ---

cruel and inhuman and everything else the way they are housed at the present time.  The way it works out, it is almost impossible to maintain offices in the State, War and Navy Building.  It is too far away.  There are
things we need all the time.  So it looks as if we will have to put into
the next appropriation bill an authorization for adding to these offices
out this way (indicating), directly south, and along Executive Avenue, not
a great distance, a matter of sixty feet.

Q:   Would that give you a new office?

THE PRESIDENT: Yes, it would push my office down to the south end.

Q:   Can we take this over for the Press Room, then?

THE PRESIDENT:   I was thinking about that.   (Laughter)

Q:   Have you any information on the German Government or German agencies making an attempt to secure loans from the Export-Import Corporation [Bank?]?

THE PRESIDENT:   No.   What I read this morning in the papers is the first I heard of it.   George Peek is coming in today but it is not on that, it is a talk we have been arranging for two weeks.

Q:   Don't you expect to do this (fix the offices) this summer?

THE PRESIDENT:   Yes, it will be an authorization in the next appropriation.

Q:   What do you think it will cost, rough figures, two or three hundred thousand dollars?

THE PRESIDENT:   I think a great deal less than that.   Oh, yes, I remember, a hundred and twenty thousand dollars.

Q:   Would that take in the Cabinet Room too?

THE PRESIDENT:   Yes, and if I leave this room for the Press, I will leave the fish up there to inspire you.

--- [301] ---

Q:   Any plans for carrying on these Public Works projects?

THE PRESIDENT:   Well, it is though of -- it hasn't got into the definite stage as yet.   There is no reason why you should not know what we are discussing. That is the possibility, in these public buildings which are going up, post offices, custom houses, etc., all over the country -- I'm not talking about Washington, I'm talking about government buildings all over the country -- as things are now, we make an estimate on the cost of the building, as you know, and in most cases the actual contract price works out somewhere below that estimate.   Say it is a $75,000 building and the lowest bid is sometimes $70,000 or $71,000 and we find we have got a definite saving on the appropriation because of the fact that the bid is below the estimate. Then, in addition to that, we have done a good deal in our designs in the past, in the hallways of those buildings, in the way of fairly expensive curlicues, scroll work, cornices, etc., and a certain amount of gold, all expensive decoration, and we are talking about the possibility of eliminating this more expensive decoration such as gold leaf and fancy cornices and fancy ceilings and devoting some of that money to the decoration of the building by artists who are on the relief rolls.   It does not get very much beyond that.   In other words, it would be a small percentage of the saving over the estimated price.   It looks like a perfectly legitimate thing to do, or perfectly legal, and the total amount would be extremely small.

Q:   Do you feel, in view of the character of the painting, that it would be safe?   Is their ability sufficient?

THE PRESIDENT:   I think it would have to be checked into in some cases.

Q:   Isn't gold out anyway?

--- [302] ---

Q:   Do you care to discuss that suggestion made by Vinson (Representative Vin-
     son of Georgia, Chairman of the Naval Affairs Committee of the House) to
     take PWA funds to start building a new Navy?

THE PRESIDENT:  You are a little previous.  That will appear, probably, in the
     estimate -- somewhere around, a little short of a billion and a half dol-
     lars -- that will go up as soon as the revenue bill has finally passed
     both Houses.

Q:   With the prospect of passing it at this session?

THE PRESIDENT:  Oh, we have to have the billion and a half.  Oh, my, yes.

Q:   And there will be funds for starting this naval program?

THE PRESIDENT:  There will be an authorization, as there was in last year's
     bill.  That means it leaves it up to me to decide how many ships, if any,
     we would start.

Q:   Anything to say on the Russian-American debt negotiations?

THE PRESIDENT:  No.

Q:   Will you take that matter up with Peek -- that Russian matter up with Mr.
     Peek?

THE PRESIDENT:  No.

Q:   Did you sign any important bills this morning?

THE PRESIDENT:  Three bills for Alaska.  I am going to sign them now.

Q:   Thank you, Mr. President.

Press Conference #116
Executive Offices of the White House
April 27, 1934, 4:10 P.M.


THE PRESIDENT: I do not think there is any news except that I am extending --
the final form is not complete yet -- extending Title I of the Emergency
Railroad Transportation Act for another year, in other words, to June 18,
1934 (1935?), which extends Mr. Eastman for one more year. We are all very
much gratified over the settlement of the railway wage controversy.

Q: Mr. President, what about -- don't you expect Eastman to submit a report
on railroad legislation? It was contemplated last year.

THE PRESIDENT: He has got a lot up there on the Hill.

Q: In that connection, do you have any assignments for Eastman?

THE PRESIDENT: Good Lord, man, he has three men's jobs now. How do you mean?

Q: New ones?

THE PRESIDENT: He has got plenty to work on.

Q: He says he still has lots left to accomplish.

THE PRESIDENT: Yes.

Q: Speaking of June sixteenth, have you decided whether you will or will not
ask for a renewal of licenses under N.R.A.?

THE PRESIDENT: I have not done a thing about it in the three weeks since I got
back.

Q: Have you changed your views on the tobacco taxes?

THE PRESIDENT: I have asked various people to look it over. The situation, of
course, depends a good deal on the amount of money or revenue the Government is going to get. I am perfectly willing

--- [304] ---

to have the tobacco tax restudied but we have to have the same number of
dollars come into the Treasury from one source or another.

Q: You asked us to remind you to say something about the Wagner-Lewis unemployment insurance bill?

THE PRESIDENT: I do not think there is anything more to say. I have written in
favor of it. I hope it will pass.

Q: How about the labor disputes bill?

THE PRESIDENT: No, they have a committee at work on it, Senator Wagner, Miss
Perkins, Johnson, Richberg and Hopkins. They are still working.

Q: As a result of your luncheon with the Secretary of State, can you comment on the Far Eastern situation?

THE PRESIDENT: No.

Q:   Will you comment on Davis' report on disarmament?

THE PRESIDENT: We only had time to talk fifteen minutes and he is coming back
     to lunch tomorrow with the Secretary of State. We have only begun to talk
     about it.

Q:   How about the sugar bill?

THE PRESIDENT: That has not come to me yet.

Q:   Have you made up your mind?

THE PRESIDENT: It has not come to me yet.

Q:   Are you in favor of one-year or three-year contracts on the air-mail bill?
     There is some difference up there on each side.

THE PRESIDENT: You will first have to tell me the situation on the Hill. I
     don't know.

Q:   I believe in the Senate bill it is three years and Chairman Mead

--- [305] ---

put one year in the House bill. I understand it was one year up here.

THE PRESIDENT: I think you had better let them talk with each other on the Hill
     a little more.

Q:   Has any progress been made to carry out the conservation section of the
     Lumber Code?

THE PRESIDENT: Charlie (Mr. Hurd, of the New York Times), I don't know. I have
     not heard a word about it.

Q:   It is said that the lumber people are getting a little bit discouraged and
     are hoping that the Government would carry out their part. Others said
     they were attempting to go ahead.

THE PRESIDENT: Frankly, I do not know anything about it. I suppose the Govern-
     ment's part will be carried out partly through the Forestry Bureau and
     partly through CCC and partly through Public Works. I don't know who is
     handling it.

Q:   The way they (the lumber people) talked, a big appropriation was held up
     and that is what is holding it. They said the Government is expecting to
     spend $68,000,000.

Q:   They have asked for a $200,000,000 revolving fund. Anything in that?

THE PRESIDENT: They certainly cannot have it this year; we have not got it.

Q:   Reports from Hawaii say that the Costigan-Jones Sugar Bill is discrimina-
     tory so far as the Island is concerned in sugar production. Can you tell

us anything about that?

THE PRESIDENT:   I cannot until it comes down.

Q:   Have you made any decision on the Beck conservation report?

THE PRESIDENT:   I don't know.  We have given them a million dollars.

Q:   Yes.  That is separate from the report on conservation.

--- [306] ---

THE PRESIDENT:   As far as the principle goes, of course it is a grand report.
When you come down to the question of financing it, we have to do it only
as fast as we can.

Q:   Some time ago you said that if the post office business picked up, as you
thought it might, you would be able to aid some substitute postal employees.  I understand that today the postal employees' unions are asking you
to sign that bill?

THE PRESIDENT:   The bill came in before I went into Cabinet meeting and all I
know is that there is a recommendation for veto.  I have not looked at it
so I do not know what I am going to do.  It has come with a recommendation
for veto from the Post Office Department.

Q:   In the Comptroller General's report on War Department contracts, he criti-
cized them for the manipulation of their specifications.  Have you discussed that?

THE PRESIDENT:   No, only what I read in the papers.

Q:   Any planning in progress in regard to mineral policies?

THE PRESIDENT:   You will have to let me check up on that.  Something has been
done.  We are working on -- I cannot tell you, I cannot remember -- I have
talked with Secretary Ickes about it and the Bureau of Mines and various
other people quite a long time ago.  In other words, we have in mind starting the machinery towards getting a national mineral policy.  I cannot tell
you any more because that is literally all there is.  Ickes may have studied it.

Q:   Have you done anything about the housing stimulation bill that Frank Walker
is preparing?

--- [307] ---

THE PRESIDENT:   Yes, and I think we will have a story in the course of two or
three days.  The thing is tying in pretty well together.

Q:   Do you expect any legislation will be required?

THE PRESIDENT:   The thing that is holding it up is that we are trying to do it
without legislation.  There are one or two obscure points.  The Attorney
General is trying to work out the establishment of certain forms of insurance for home building credit and home repair credit and if we can set up
that kind of insurance without legislation, we are certainly not going to
ask for it.

Q:   Will that be done through the R.F.C.

THE PRESIDENT:  Yes.

Q:   Have you enough information to decide whether the token payment governments
come within the purview of the Johnson Act?

THE PRESIDENT:  No.  Henry Morgenthau and the Secretary of State are working together on that now, trying to work out somebody in Washington that will be
able to say "Yes" or "No."

Q:   Another air-mail question:  Senator Black said it would turn regulation over to the ICC six minutes after the bill was passed?

THE PRESIDENT:  I cannot tell you anything about that bill because it changes so
often.

Q:   Do you intend to ask Congress for a Joint Resolution changing the cocoanut
oil tax?

THE PRESIDENT:  You had better let that come down to me first.

MR. YOUNG:  Thank you, sir.


(The Press Conference adjourned at 4:15 P.M.)

CONFIDENTIAL
Press Conference #117
Executive Offices of the White House
May 2, 1934, 10:50 A.M.

(Harry Hopkins and Frank Walker were present.)

THE PRESIDENT: I don't think there is any particular news. I think you can be
fairly certain that there will be either a message to Congress or letters
to the appropriate Chairmen fairly soon on the housing matter. But I have
not got around to writing it yet. I may have it in the course of the next
couple of days. I think all you can say now is that it is perfectly clear,
from the surveys we have made over the last couple of months, that there is
a real need, all over the country, practically every part, for better housing and new housing; that in taking active steps to encourage better housing and new housing we will be doing a great deal to alleviate unemployment, especially in certain trades that have come back slower than almost
any other trades, in other words, building trades. Also that we will raise
the general standard of American housing.

I cannot tell you the details of the plan yet because that, I suppose, I
ought to hold for either the letters to the Committee; but you will have
the details very shortly. The plan is just about ready.

Q: The fact that you are going to send a letter or a message indicates that
you need legislation?

THE PRESIDENT: We do. We hoped to get by without legislation but we do require
very, very simple permissive legislation, which is practically along the
same lines as existing law applying to other things. In other words, it is
carrying out, as a broad principle,

--- [309] ---

the methods we have applied to other needs.

Q: Will you ask for a special appropriation for housing?

THE PRESIDENT: I do not think so.

Q: Is Mr. Hopkins going to be in charge of the housing?

THE PRESIDENT: I haven't any idea; I haven't taken it up. Obviously, we cannot
start an organization until we have the authority.

Q: The price of labor and materials for building have gone up so greatly during the past few months. How will that affect those prices?

THE PRESIDENT: We hope to keep them down to a reasonable amount.

Q: About how much money do you think will be expended in this program?

THE PRESIDENT: I don't know; I have no idea at all.

Q: At the present time could you tell us whether you expect to form a special
corporation?

THE PRESIDENT: I cannot tell you that. Probably won't know that until after the legislation goes through. There are lots of ways of carrying out the mechanical end of it.

Q: In this morning's paper there was a big story in connection with the annual meeting of the Chamber of Commerce of the United States that the Government was preparing to relax its restrictions against business and also not planning to ask for a renewal of the licensing provisions of the N.R.A.

THE PRESIDENT: That was just Elliott Thurston, wasn't it?

Q: No, it was just Teddy Wells.

THE PRESIDENT: I guess Teddy and Elliott combined together.

Q: I did not see the Post; it might have been in there too.

Q: Can you tell us about the sugar bill?

THE PRESIDENT: Not yet. I am seeing the Virgin Islands about it sometime this morning, I am seeing Puerto Rico sometime this

--- [310] ---

morning, and I am seeing the Secretary of Agriculture sometime this afternoon.

Q: Is there any possibility of a reduction in the liquor tax?

THE PRESIDENT: I do not know. I have not checked with Joe Choate about that. I should say probably, as a good guess, that there isn't much possibility of a reduction in the tax this session.

Q: Does that apply to the tariff too?

THE PRESIDENT: We are going ahead with the opening up of the quotas, the removal of the quotas, so as to bring in all we can in the next few months.

Q: Any chance of action on the tariff in connection with the quotas?

THE PRESIDENT: I do not think I have got the right under the present legislation to cut it down.

Q: I was more interested in whether you thought it was advisable than whether you had a right to do it.

THE PRESIDENT: I do not think I have the right to do it.

Q: But you could, after this tariff law passed?

THE PRESIDENT: That is almost in the realm of an "if" question.

Q: Steagall (Representative Henry Steagall), in connection with the deposit insurance bill, has had a provision that would permit the Deposit Insurance Corporation to largely increase its funds for buying assets in closed banks and lending money on assets in closed banks. Have you looked into it at all?

THE PRESIDENT: What bill is it on?

Q: On the bill that would continue the present temporary --

THE PRESIDENT: (interposing) No, I have not seen that at all.

Q: With reference to the air-mail situation, could you indicate your

--- [311] ---

preference to the Senate bill which contains provision for early transfer of control to the ICC or to the House bill which merely provides for a commission?

THE PRESIDENT: I imagine they will iron that out between themselves.

Q: The conference with Darrow yesterday, can you tell us anything?

THE PRESIDENT: I had better not.

Q: Has his report come in?

THE PRESIDENT: Just between us girls, there was a certain disagreement in that Darrow committee which will probably come to a head.

Q: How is it going to come to a head?

THE PRESIDENT: I do not know yet.

Q: As a result of your conversation with the Soviet Ambassador early this week, do you share his belief that the prospects are bright for an early settlement of the debt question?

THE PRESIDENT: The whole problem, do you mean, or the Soviet?

Q: All debts, yes.

THE PRESIDENT: I hope so, that is all I can tell you.

Q: Anything on the Wagner Bill?

THE PRESIDENT: No, Miss Perkins and Bob Wagner (Senator Wagner) are lunching with me today.

Q: Do you understand they have a bill ready to submit?

THE PRESIDENT: I don't know.

Q: A short time ago you wrote letters to the heads of the Senate and House Committees on the Howard Bill (the Wheeler-Howard Bill affecting Indian rights) --

THE PRESIDENT: (interposing) In other words, my letter distinctly said that I was primarily interested in the principles of the

--- [312] ---

bill. When you come to the details, that is different. I think that Senator Wheeler has quite a number of amendments which he proposed himself to the bill as originally introduced. What they are, I do not know.

Q: We have a constantly recurring rumor that Mr. Straus (Ambassador to France) is coming home and that Morgenthau is going to France and that Baruch (Bernard M. Baruch of New York) is going to replace Morgenthau (Secretary Morgenthau) in the Treasury?

THE PRESIDENT: It sounds like Drew Pearson. Getting very personal this morning.

Q: I understand that you have been looking at some reports on Puerto Rico and that you saw the Governor yesterday. Have you any plans or hopes?

THE PRESIDENT: No. You have been there, you might give me some suggestions. Pretty difficult, isn't it? That whole problem is one of the most difficult things in the world.

Q: Speaking of Puerto Rico, do you have any views as to including Puerto Rico in the Union, as a state?

THE PRESIDENT: No, which party favors that?

Q: That has been currently agitated.

Q: That is the Republican Party, if I may answer his question.

Q: There continues to be a lot of discussion of your views on silver. I was wondering if you care to say anything about it at this time?

THE PRESIDENT: There is no use going into a long discussion on silver but I think, just as a sort of tip, if you will read all the way back for a long, long time, over a year, what has been said, mostly by me I guess, about a monetary or, rather, a metal base

--- [313] ---

for currencies, in other words, if you get a complete picture of the general line we have taken, I think you can get a better story out of it than coming to the conclusion that we are either one hundred per cent one way or the other. It does date back quite a long ways and it is a perfectly consistent policy.

Q: Do you think anything can be done?

THE PRESIDENT: Hope springs eternal.

Q: The District National Guard is without a Commanding General.

THE PRESIDENT: What happened?

Q: The old one died. I wonder whether the War Department has made any suggestions to you or submitted any names to fill the place?

THE PRESIDENT: Do I appoint?

Q: Yes, you do.

THE PRESIDENT:  I did not know that.  I am becoming a regular dictator, Count
(Rudolph de Zapp).  I will have to find out about it.  I did not even know
that I appointed.

MR. YOUNG:  Thank you, Mr. President.

MR. DONALDSON: All in.

THE PRESIDENT: The only news is still in a package. The package is not opened.
It is the report of the Darrow Board. I shall try to read it tomorrow and
Sunday and if it is not too profane, I shall probably release it on Monday
or Tuesday.

Q: Did Mr. Darrow give you a digest of it?

THE PRESIDENT: No.

Q: Mr. President, will you be able to go to Secretary Woodin's funeral?

THE PRESIDENT: I had hoped to go but it is absolutely impossible. I have so
many things on that I do not see any way out of staying here. I have the
sugar bill and the silver conference tomorrow morning and I have the revenue bill, which probably will call for a Message on my part.

Q: You mean the revenue bill?

THE PRESIDENT: Yes. I think you can make a pretty good guess but I am very,
very much dissatisfied with the provisions in regard to cocoanut oil products of the Philippines in the revenue bill but it is a bill that contains
a very large number of other matters and I do not see my way clear to veto
it for that reason but I do expect to send a Message to the Congress explaining my feeling that the Congress has been unfair to the Philippines in
that regard and suggesting that the Congress restudy those provisions.
That is about the best I can do.

Q: Any other objectionable features to the bill you might mention in

--- [315] ---

that Message?

THE PRESIDENT: None that have been called to my attention yet but probably will
be tomorrow and the next day.

Q: Is it a fair guess that publicity of returns --

THE PRESIDENT: (interposing) Fred (Storm), what does it actually say in the
bill as it passed?

Q: (Mr. Storm) You have me now. (Laughter)

Q: I have written about it a great many times, sir, but immediately after
reading it the bill would be changed.

Q: When you file your income tax return, you file a separate sheet giving your
gross and deductions and net.

THE PRESIDENT: Yes?

Q: And then that part is to be made public, but not the returns.

Q: And also all credits as well as the tax itself.

THE PRESIDENT: What do you mean, credits?

Q: It is to give gross income, deduct any income and credits against net income and finally the tax. That is the formula.

THE PRESIDENT: I never had any credits against net income. Anyway, it sounds pretty good that way.

Q: That is the way it was explained to us.

Q: Has the Attorney General ruled yet on the application of the Johnson Bill to token payers?

THE PRESIDENT: He is going to, pretty soon.

Q: In that connection, are we any nearer the debt Message?

THE PRESIDENT: I should think so. I think as a guess, within a couple of weeks.

Q: Suppose Congress adjourns in the meantime?

--- [316] ---

THE PRESIDENT: That is an impossible suggestion. What odds do you give me?

Q: Do you mean we may have it in a couple of weeks?

THE PRESIDENT: I think so. That is on the theory --

Q: (interposing) Do you propose to sign the revenue bill tomorrow?

THE PRESIDENT: It means I have to have the Message ready when I do sign it to go up at the same time.

Q: Do you expect to sign the sugar bill today or tomorrow?

THE PRESIDENT: Probably not until Monday. There again there will be some kind of a statement which has to cover a great many things, Puerto Rico and Hawaii, Cuba, the Philippines, et cetera.

Q: Have you given any thought to asking the Congress for authority to accept some payments from the debtor nations on June fifteenth at your own discretion?

THE PRESIDENT: No.

Q: In connection with the silver conference tomorrow -- that is my old subject -- there are reports in Wall Street of a lot of buying of silver and there is some speculation that that might be done by the Government?

THE PRESIDENT: I would probably tell you if I knew anything about it but I don't, one way or the other.

Q:   Your intention to send a debt Message to Congress this late in the session, does that mean you will not ask for Congressional action on the war debts?

THE PRESIDENT:   You are about two weeks ahead of time on that.

Q:   Mr. President, do you favor the promulgation of a code for the anthracite industry?  They haven't a code yet.

THE PRESIDENT:   What is the status?

Q:   They have been negotiating since September.  It was first deferred to

--- [317] ---

await promulgation of the Soft Coal Code.

THE PRESIDENT:   Where is it now?  Who is it before?

Q:   Before Mr. Ellis of N.R.A.

THE PRESIDENT:   As I remember it, the last word was two or three weeks ago when General Johnson said it was pretty nearly ready.  I have not heard anything since then.  The Aluminum Code is in the same status.  It is a little more difficult because it is a monopoly code.

Q:   Have you any plans to give a report over the radio?

THE PRESIDENT:   No.

Q:   Can you tell us anything about the future of the Darrow Board, whether it will be transferred or wound up?

THE PRESIDENT:   Mr. Darrow told me this morning that this report is based on hearings on eight industries and I think he told me they would have hearings on four or five more which they are not yet ready to report on.  He saw no reason why they should not be all ready to make a supplementary report and go home before the end of the month.

Q:   It seemed in that report that Mr. Sinclair (a member of the Board) neglected to sign the report of the Board.  I wonder --

THE PRESIDENT:   (interposing)  It is all in here, in carefully sealed envelopes and I have not opened them yet.  I will have to use tongs.

Q:   "The Darrow Board would be ready to go home," does that mean the end of the Board?

THE PRESIDENT:   Yes, so I understood.  As far as I know, there is no reason to continue after they make their report.

Q:   Has Sinclair resigned or is he technically --

THE PRESIDENT:   (interposing)  The status is not changed.

--- [318] ---

Q:   Anything special up before the Cabinet today, any one subject?

THE PRESIDENT: Everything under the sun.

Q:   Any price studies?

THE PRESIDENT:  No.

Q:   Is that Darrow report a majority report or are there several reports there?

THE PRESIDENT:  I think there is a majority report and I think there is a minority report of one, but that is only a guess.

Q:  Thank you, Mr. President.


(The Press Conference adjourned at 4:20 P.M.)

Press Conference #119
Executive Offices of the White House
May 9, 1934, 10:43 A.M.


Q:   It looks like you are going to sign a bill today (referring to a bill on
     the President's desk which had quite a number of pens attached to it).

THE PRESIDENT:   I am going to start charging (for these pens).   Twenty-five
     cents apiece.   (Laughter)

MR. DONALDSON:   All in.

THE PRESIDENT:   I am going to sign the sugar bill at eleven o'clock and a large
     number of pens are requested.   It is a very costly procedure for the Gov-
     ernment and I am going to charge twenty-five cents apiece for all pens used
     in signing bills from now on.

Q:   Cheap at half the price.

Q:   Can you tell us whether you consider now that the debtor nations can escape
     the penalties of the Johnson Act?

THE PRESIDENT:   You are going to anticipate that famous Message going to the
     Congress.   It is nearer now than last week.

Q:   Will an explanation of that be contained in the Message?

THE PRESIDENT:   Maybe; I do not know.

Q:   Can you give us any clarification on the debt Message at all?

THE PRESIDENT:   No, because all these stories being written -- I do not know
     where they come from.   I believe that the position of this Government is
     what it has been all along.   There has been no change --

Q:   (interposing)  Mr. President, --

THE PRESIDENT:   -- no applications made by any other nations or revisions.

                         --- [320] ---

Q:   There seems to be a great deal of opposition, according to the newspapers,
     against the appointment of Scott, the colored lawyer here, as Judge of the
     Municipal Court.   Can you tell us something about it?

THE PRESIDENT:   All I can tell you is that I read about the opposition and sent
     the whole thing over to the Attorney General to give me a report on it.
     That was about a week ago.

Q:   As I understand it, if they do not ask for a revision of war debts, we are
     not offering any?

THE PRESIDENT:   The position is exactly the same.   In other words, for over a
     year and three months we have said very definitely that if a person owes
     money and feels he cannot pay it, it is up to him to go to his creditor and
     tell him the story.

Q:   That means that no negotiations with England at all?

THE PRESIDENT:  None.

Q:   Didn't Britain come and tell us the story last November?

THE PRESIDENT:  Yes, came and told us the story and made a suggestion as to terms, which was not satisfactory.

Q:   Have they come back again?

THE PRESIDENT:  No.

Q:   You say the position of the Government has not changed.  Doesn't the Johnson Act change it as regards partial payments?

THE PRESIDENT:  No.

Q:   It raises the question, can we still accept the partial payments and declare they are not in default?

THE PRESIDENT:  That question came up last year just about this time.  I took the position at that time, under all the circumstances, that I

--- [321] ---

personally did not consider it in default.  Then they came back last November and we canvassed the situation as of that time and again thought it over very, very carefully, and decided again that from my own personal point of view it did not constitute a default.  Now, the question has not come up in regard to the general payment yet.

Q:   You do not wish to say anything regarding --

THE PRESIDENT:  (interposing)  That would be prognostication without facts.

Q:   Do you have something to say on silver this morning?

THE PRESIDENT:  I think yesterday's statement covers it all right.

Q:   Is the silver bill now on the list of "must" legislation?

THE PRESIDENT:  No.  As far as I know there isn't any silver bill yet.

Q:   If they get one along the lines outlined yesterday --

THE PRESIDENT:  (interposing)  That is an "if" question, Stevie (Mr. Stephenson).

Q:   Would you have any thought of exempting P.W.A. from the application of the municipal bankruptcy bill?

THE PRESIDENT:  I do now know enought about it to answer that question.  I haven't even talked with Secretary Ickes about it.

Q:   He expressed himself as feeling that P.W.A. should be exempted.

THE PRESIDENT:  I do not know enought about the status of loans made to municipalities and the conditions of municipalities to which the loans were made really to have an opinion on it. I am glad you mentioned it. I am going to take it up.

Q: Do you have any ideas of filling the vacancy up at the RFC?

THE PRESIDENT: Lots of them but they have not crystalized as yet.

Q: They are drawing a bill up on the Hill providing for the national-

--- [322] ---

ization of silver -- a 25% ratio.

THE PRESIDENT: I think, for background, the easiest way to put it is this; that on the question of increased metallic reserves of silver, there is nothing new in that. That is an old, old thing. We have had much larger silver metallic reserves in a great many other periods of history. We had them during the McKinley Administration, the T. R. Administration, and it is only in comparatively recent years that the silver metallic reserve has been brought down as low as it is now, around 12% at the present time.

As you know, last year we talked in London about trying to get all the nations to increase the ratio of their silver metallic reserves to gold. There is nothing new and startling in it in any way. Half of the world, after all, is on silver, so that part of the story is not exactly new in any way.

The only thing that is new is the canvassing that we are doing as to the desirability or the necessity of giving to me or the Treasury Department the same authority to take over silver stocks in this country that we already have and have carried out in the case of gold stocks. The difference really would be that in taking over the silver stocks we would take over only the silver bullion stocks. In other words, we would not put the silver coins out of general circulation. People would still be allowed to hold them for circulation but not for hoarding purposes.

Q: Have you the power to do that under the existing Thomas Act?

THE PRESIDENT: We don't think so. We don't think we have the right to commandeer silver in the same way we did to commandeer gold.

Q: On the war debt, I understood you to say that the Johnson Bill does not change the Government's position. Does that mean that the question will be decided on its own merits each time?

--- [323] ---

THE PRESIDENT: Yes.

Q: Can you comment on the Darrow Report?

THE PRESIDENT: Yes. (Laughter) Remember, I said I was going to look into it. Finally, I did cut the string and unwrapped and started to read it and I decided, in the first place, that it was a thing we could not possibly brief unless we put two or three people on it and it is a thing you people couldn't have read unless you appointed a committee to read it, section by section. The result is that I am referring it to three people, the Attorney General, the Federal Trade Commission and the NRA, to digest it for me, that report and the minority report.

Q: Can you tell us anything about the Wagner Bill?  I understand it has gone back to the Senate Committee.

THE PRESIDENT:  I cannot talk about it intelligently because we are all agreed on the general principle of the bill but it is the kind of measure that ought to be discussed in committee up there and it is in the legislative stage.

Q: Are there any developments in your water conservation program -- flood control?

THE PRESIDENT:  I probably will have the Message for Congress by the end of this week.  I am sending up the report they asked me for.

Q: Was that committee to include this work projected some months ago?

THE PRESIDENT:  Yes.

Q: Is there any comment on the Mullen verdict?

THE PRESIDENT:  No, except we did with him as we did with everybody else.  We made no exception one way or the other.

Q: You say the question of token payments will be decided on their own

--- [324] ---

merits.  Does that mean if the debtor nation should offer a substantial payment we might except them from default?

THE PRESIDENT:  You cannot answer that categorically because it would depend entirely on the circumstances when they arose and they have not arisen.

Q: Getting back to the Darrow Report, can you tell us the status of Sinclair?

THE PRESIDENT:  Why, yes; there is no particular reason you should not know it because you know it already.  He has tendered his resignation.

Q: Have you accepted?

THE PRESIDENT:  No.  I have not done a thing about it except to refer the package to those three departments.

Q: Have you had a report on the desirability of a uniform Federal incorporation law?

THE PRESIDENT:  No.  I think there was a committee that started to study it about six months ago and they were terribly busy and felt that at this session of the Congress nothing should be asked.  They will go ahead with the study of it during the recess.  Whether they will recommend something or not, I do not know.

Q: Have you decided on the revenue bill, just when that will be signed?

THE PRESIDENT:  I think I will get to it tomorrow.

Q:   On the silver, are you considering anything beyond the possible acceptance
of authorizations with respect to silver?   Is there any talk of mandatory
legislation in any form?

THE PRESIDENT:   No.

Q:   That was given out generally in some circles on the Hill?

--- [325] ---

THE PRESIDENT:   Now, wait a minute.   You get to a very fine distinction.   In
that second thing, we did mention and we did discuss yesterday the possibility of Congress either stating an ultimate objective or a national policy as a declaration of the Congress.   Now, of course, in a sense a declaration of the Congress is mandatory but if the method and time of carrying
it out is not put down in the bill, that part of it is permissive.   So you
get two factors right away.

Q:   That is the point I was thinking of.

THE PRESIDENT:   In other words, what I was talking about yesterday is both mandatory and permissive.   The policy becomes a mandatory policy but the method of carrying it out remains permissive.

Q:   Nationalization would be mandatory, would it not?

THE PRESIDENT:   No.

Q:   It would give you authority?

THE PRESIDENT:   Yes.

Q:   And so far as that goes, that would be acceptable to you?

THE PRESIDENT:   I am still studying it.   I have not said that yet; you nearly
had me.   (Laughter)

Q:   Has Russia made any offer to us?

THE PRESIDENT:   No; nothing has come in at all.

Q:   They are supposed to have offered, I think, one hundred million dollars?

THE PRESIDENT:   No.

Q:   Do you expect to send a Message to the Congress about the housing program
soon?

THE PRESIDENT:   Yes.

Q:   This week?

--- [326] ---

THE PRESIDENT:   I hope within the next couple of days.

Q:   Do you favor law control legislation this session?

THE PRESIDENT: Yes, I think we ought to do it.

(The Press Conference adjourned at 10:55 A.M.)

CONFIDENTIAL
Press Conference #120
Executive Offices of the White House
May 11, 1934, 4:15 P.M.


MR. DONALDSON: All in.

THE PRESIDENT: I do not think I have any news. Has anybody got any?

Q: Mr. President, we understand that the State Department has been notifying the representatives of the debtor nations that their governments will not be exempt from the penalties of the Johnson Act if they continue to make token payments. The State Department refuses to say anything officially. Can you tell us whether that is so?

THE PRESIDENT: I think you will have to get it from the State Department. I hate to cross wires.

Q: Is it not conceivable that if the debtor nations were to offer us a substantial payment, considerably higher than the token payment --

THE PRESIDENT: (interposing) That is the same question that Stevie (Mr. Stephenson) asked the day before yesterday. In other words, exactly what I said the other day, that I cannot give an answer to any specious case until I know the case.

Q: What puzzles us is whether or not you are going to hold them liable to the Johnson Act unless they make full payments or whether you might be willing to find some means of getting around the Johnson Act if they made substantial payments along the lines of their capacity or desire to pay.

THE PRESIDENT: There you are running into the same thing. We cannot say anything about these things until some nation makes a proposition.

--- [328] ---

Q: Then that is still an open matter?

THE PRESIDENT: Yes.

Q: Has any nation asked new negotiations?

THE PRESIDENT: I do not think so.

Q: The British today seemed to express the feeling that if you could call a general debt settlement conference, they would appreciate it very much. (Laughter) How does the Administration feel about that?

THE PRESIDENT: Just what we felt for a year and two months; exactly the same thing. In other words, no such thing as a general debt conference. Each nation is a debtor and talks with its creditor.

There has been a general effort to -- this has to be off the record -- there has been a general effort, every since I have been here, ever since I was elected in November, 1933, to gang me, this is off the record, into saying that we would have a general conference. I said, "No, we will talk anything over with any individual debtor at any time." We have not changed that position.

Q:     May we point out that our position in dealing with them individually still remains unchanged?

THE PRESIDENT:  Yes.

Q:     How far off is our debt Message?

THE PRESIDENT:  Well, I should think I ought to be able to get it in inside of the next ten days.  In other words, what I am planning for is to get it up the week after next, the early part of the week.

Q:     What are you going to say in that, Mr. President?  (Laughter)

Q:     Will that be a sort of general report on conditions as they are?  (Laughter)

Q:     What is the latest on the selection of the Public Printer?

--- [329] ---

THE PRESIDENT:  I do not know.

Q:     There has been a name mentioned?

THE PRESIDENT:  I have not, frankly, been handling it myself.  I have two or three other people looking into it and, as I understand it, they came down to two or three names a week or ten days ago, but I have not heard.

Q:     Do you know anything about the drought in the Middle West?  (Laughter)  You know Clint Mosher once referred to you as "The Rainmaker?"

THE PRESIDENT:  I do.

Q:     When does the relief appropriation Message go up, that billion and a half?

THE PRESIDENT:  Monday.  By the way, it is less than a billion and a half because they have been chipping it away.  I can tell you that the amount left now looks about a billion, 322 million dollars.

Q:     Can you tell us whether that boring has been in the Public Works, whether that reduction has been in the Public Works?

THE PRESIDENT:  Oh, no.  It has been all sorts of -- I will see if I cannot give you enough of a hint on it to give you an idea.

Q:     Mr. President, is there any plan to help the drought sufferers out West?

THE PRESIDENT:  Yes, we talked all about it in Cabinet.  This is something you cannot use yet, it has got to be off the record.  We have been working on it for a whole year and I think I have talked informally here about the general theory of it.  This has got to be off the record because I am a month away from a story on it.  With crop control, in those crops in which there is a surplus of production over consumption, where we are trying to bring production within the general field of consumption in order to prevent

--- [330] ---

abnormally low price levels, at the same time you have to recognize the element that you may have a year of bumper crops and another time you may have a year of serious crop shortage.

Over a year ago we began discussing the principle of establishing what might be called a reserve granary which would contain a large carryover, which would amount to a larger carryover than we have been carrying in normal years. That reserve emergency granary could be used to put surpluses into in the bounteous years, and then we could draw on that granary in years of drought in order to prevent any starvation or anything like abnormally high prices, so that it would work both ways. In other words, in years of plenty it would prevent abnormally low prices and in years of drought it would prevent abnormally high prices.

The thing has been, more or less, in a very tentative stage, a very tentative study stage, for the past year, and they are working on it at the present time. We hope to have something along that line worked out during the course of the next few weeks, not as a message to be presented to this Congress, but as something to be studied as rather an essential component part of the general agricultural program.

Q:   Do you care to tell us what feature of the drought was discussed in the Cabinet meeting?

THE PRESIDENT:  Just the localities, the different localities which came out in the report.

Q:   Was there any discussion of making funds available for some of the farmers who complain that their crops are going to be ruined?

THE PRESIDENT:  No. Of course that would be handled out of the general relief funds if it came to the point of necessity.

--- [331] ---

Q:   Was there any discussion as to how large a fund is now available for that purpose?

THE PRESIDENT:  That you will find in the Monday appropriation bill. I cannot tell you now but somebody was asking about how the total of $3,166,000,000 had been chipped away up to the present time. Well, just a few items, for instance, crop loans, $40,000,000, necessarily reduced that original amount by that much. Then farm mortgages, $40,000,000 -- that is additional capital; veterans' benefits, $22,000,000; Army Air Corps, special appropriation, $5,000,000; Mississippi flood control, $29,000,000; Independent Offices' Act, $228,000,000. Those are the principal items and there are miscellaneous supplementary items which I would leave out because they always go in at the end of the session. Those items I gave you are the principal ones which might be called unexpected reductions from the total amount of $3,166,000,000. If the financial writers would like, before I send this bill up on Monday, would like to come in and have a talk over it, the way we did on the general Budget bill, I would just as soon do it. Talk with Steve (Mr. Early) about it and we can have just another little informal talk about the items in this big appropriation bill so that we will have some background for writing the stories.

MR. EARLY: You don't know when you will send it?

THE PRESIDENT: I thought I would send it up on Monday afternoon.

MR. EARLY: Then we can have a Monday morning conference?

THE PRESIDENT: Yes.

Q: Governor Green of Rhode Island is in town. Has he been in to see you?

THE PRESIDENT: I saw him about a week or ten days ago.

Q: He is not coming in at this time?

THE PRESIDENT: Not that I know of.

--- [332] ---

Q: On these figures, I am not clear -- those are --

THE PRESIDENT: (interposing) Those are unexpected amounts which we did expect
would be appropriated last January and of necessity, if the Budget balanc-
ing is to be maintained, they have to be deducted from the $3,166,000,000
because there is no other place to deduct them from.

Q: On the $288,000,000 Independent Offices?

THE PRESIDENT: Yes.

Q: Under the Mississippi flood prevention, does that include the Wabash and
White Rivers?

THE PRESIDENT: I don't know; you have me there.

Q: Mr. President, do you favor the six-hour day for railroad labor at this
time? The movement seems to be gaining headway in the House.

THE PRESIDENT: I don't know anything about it.

Q: They floated a petition in the House today to force a vote on the six-hour
bill for railroad labor.

THE PRESIDENT: It is news to me.

Q: Have you heard anything from the analysts of the Darrow Report?

THE PRESIDENT: No, only except some perfectly fool stories (laughter) -- the
suggestion that it was not going to be made public. It will, as soon as
somebody can read through and digest it for the Press.

Q: You won't make the text available to the public?

THE PRESIDENT: Oh, yes; you can have the full text and take it to bed with you.

Q: Is silver legislation unchanged?

THE PRESIDENT: No, still talking up there. Morgenthau was up there this morning.

--- [333] ---

Q:   No change in your attitude in relation to monetary legislation?

THE PRESIDENT:   No.

Q:   Have you heard the latest on silver?  They very nearly got to terms up there today on something but that has not been called to your attention?

THE PRESIDENT:   No.

Q:   Do you favor the reelection of La Follette for Wisconsin?  (Laughter)

THE PRESIDENT:   I am not taking any part in any primary or election.

Q:   You say you will be able to make public the Darrow Report sometime next week?

THE PRESIDENT:   The early part of the week.

Q:   Has Thorpe resigned?

THE PRESIDENT:   Yes, and while I have not actually written the letter, it is going out this afternoon, accepting it with great regret.

Q:   Who is that?

THE PRESIDENT:   Thorpe.

Q:   Are you going to appoint a State Marshal in South Carolina?

THE PRESIDENT:   I do not know yet.

Q:   On the matter of that drought, do I understand there was some information about relief in the appropriation?

THE PRESIDENT:   No.  Whatever has to be done will be included in the general relief fund, which is quite a large fund.

MR. EARLY:   Harry Hopkins is making announcements on those things.

Q:   Is any item on naval construction in there?

THE PRESIDENT:   No, it is not in here.

Q:   Thank you, Mr. President.

CONFIDENTIAL
Press Conference #121
Executive Offices of the White House
May 14, 1934, 12:10 P.M.

(This was a special financial Press Conference
called to discuss the President's Message to
Congress of May 15, 1934.)

THE PRESIDENT: I won't make any remarks about the financial knowledge of the
Press, newspaper men and sailors; they have the same general reputation.
(Laughter)

Q: All goes out and nothing comes in.

THE PRESIDENT: Yes. I think the easiest way is to read the Message that is going up to the Congress.

Q: When is it going up?

THE PRESIDENT: Tomorrow. Do not use it until it does go up. (Reading)

"TO THE CONGRESS OF THE UNITED STATES:

"In my budget message to the Congress of January 3, 1934, I
said to you:

'It is evident to me, as I am sure it is evident
to you, that powerful forces for recovery exist.
It is by laying a foundation of confidence in the
present and faith in the future that the upturn
which we have so far seen will become cumulative.
The cornerstone of this foundation is the good
credit of the government.

'It is, therefore, not strange nor is it academic
that this credit has a profound effect upon the
confidence so necessary to permit the new recovery
to develop into maturity.

'If we maintain the course I have outlined, we can
confidently look forward to cumulative beneficial
forces represented by increased volume of business,
more general profit, greater employment, a diminution of relief expenditures, larger governmental
receipts and repayments, and greater human happiness.'

"The budget which I submitted to the Congress proposed expenditures for the balance of this fiscal year and for the coming
fiscal year which, in the light of expected revenues, called
for a definite deficiency on June 30, 1935, but, at the same
time, held out the hope that annual deficits would terminate
during the following fiscal year.

--- [335] ---

"It is true that actual expenditures since January have proceeded at a slower rate than estimated; nevertheless, it
must be borne in mind that, even though the actual deficit
for the year ending June 30, 1934, will be below my estimate,
appropriations are still in force and the amounts actually
to be extended during the following fiscal year will, therefore, be increased over and above my estimate for that fiscal year."

There have been a lot of editorial writers who have gone absolutely cuckoo
on that particular subject, as you know.  In other words, they have said,
"Oh, the Government is not going to spend within three billions of what
they thought they were going to spend, therefore there is going to be that
much saving."  Of course, that is nonsense, because that money has been appropriated and will be spent and most of what is not spent this fiscal year
we are in now will be spent in the next fiscal year, so that by the end of
June, 1935, we will have expended, as far as we can now tell, most or almost all of the appropriations that either are in force or will be in force
when Congress adjourns this year.  The money will be gone.  There are very,
very few items where the actual expenditure will not have been made.  They
will be certain items of public works, long-term works, where there is a
three-year job to do.  There may be some recovery on those items, but the
total will be very, very small.  I should say, just as a rough guess, that
a total of those items of public works that have already been approved and
allotted which won't be spent until after June 30, 1935, will not run to
perhaps more than three or four hundred million dollars which, against the
total, is almost nothing.  (Reading)

"In this connection it is relevant to point out that during
the fiscal year 1935 it is estimated that there will be actually expended on public works $1,500,000,000 out of ap-
propriations heretofore made."

--- [336] ---

In other words, we reach the peak of expenditures on public works, P.W.A.,
some time in August this year, and most of the old three billion three hundred million will have been actually expended by the 30th of June, 1935,
except for that lag that I spoke to you about, things which take three
years to build.  (Reading)

"In my budget message of January 3, 1934, it was pointed out
that there could be no abrupt termination of emergency expenditures for recovery purposes, that the necessity for
relief would continue, and that appropriations amounting to
$3,166,000,000 in addition to the appropriations contained
in the budget itself would be requested for the two fiscal
years ending June 30, 1935."

That is the famous sum of $3,166,000,000.  (Reading)

"The present Congress has already made appropriations out of which,
for the two fiscal years in question, it is estimated there will be
expended the following sums:"

Now, this list contains items which did not appear in other parts of the

budget. In other words, they have got to be taken out of the
$3,166,000,000 if we are to stick within that figure. Those items are,
Relief, $950,000,000, already appropriated. That, in itself, ran a good
deal higher, as you know, than our January 3rd relief estimate, and that
was because of the additional money that we felt was necessary to put into
the C.W.A. during the winter and also the fact that, during the course
of this summer, we will not be able to slow up as much as we expected to.

The next item is Crop Loans, $40,000,000, and Farm Mortgages, $40,000,000.
Now, on the farm mortgages, that is a capital expense because it is providing capital for the farm loan banks and intermediate credit banks.

R.F.C. $500,000,000, Veterans Benefits, $22, 000,000, Army Air Corps,
$5,000,000. Flood Control, Mississippi River, etc.,

--- [337] ---

$29,000,000. Well, of course, that last item in one sense is a relief ex-
penditure, but it has been earmarked.

Independent Offices Act, $228,000,000. That contains the additions on the
Government employees and veterans.

Miscellaneous Supplemental Estimates, $30,000,000.

That all makes a total of $1,844,000,000 which has to be taken away, de-
ducted, from the $3,166,000,000.

This leaves a balance of $1,322,000,000, and out of this balance it is nec-
essary first, to take specific items that have to be appropriated for Federal Land Banks, which are subscriptions to paid-in surplus, $75,000,000,
and reduction in interest payments -- that was when they cut it from five
to four and a half, or four and a half to four per cent, $7,950,000.

We also have to appropriate for the emergency bank act and gold transfer
$3,000,000; for the Internal Revenue Service $10,000,000 -- which is the
effort to stop bootlegging; for salaries in the office of the Secretary of
the Treasury $100,000, and for the Secret Service $45,000, making a total
of $96,095,000, which has to be deducted from the balance of $1,322,000,000.

That leaves available -- and this figure you want to put down --
$1,225,905,000, which is available for the following purposes: (Reading)

> "Civilian Conservation Corps Camps, Public Works, and Relief
> Work, in addition to amounts already appropriated, and in-
> cluding aid to the dairy and beef cattle industries."

Now, taking that sum of $1,225,905,000, it is estimated that the minimum
requirements -- using this process of elimination all the way down -- the
minimum requirements of the CCC Camps will be $285,000,000. You deduct
that from the $1,225,905,000, and the

--- [338] ---

amount available for public works and relief is $940,905,000. A very sim-
ple checkup of these figures shows that they total -- in other words, putting it the other way around and leaving out the odd figures, taking
$940,000,000 for public works and relief, $285,000,000 for CCC Camps, and

$96,000,000 for the small items that I mentioned, and taking the amount already appropriated, $,1,844,000,000, a simple checkup shows that they total $3,166,000,000 to which reference was made in the budget message of January 3rd.

It was my thought in January, and it is my thought now, that this sum should be appropriated to me -- in other words, this sum of $1,225,000,000.

"under fairly broad powers because of the fact that no one could then, or can now determine the exact needs under hard and fixed appropriation headings. In furtherance of this thought it seems appropriate to provide that any savings which can be effected out of certain appropriations made for emergency purposes shall be available for emergency relief purposes.

"In my judgment an appropriation in excess of the above amount would make more difficult if not impossible an actual balance of the budget in the fiscal year 1936, unless greatly increased taxes are provided. The present estimate should be sufficient as a whole to take care of the emergencies of relief and of orderly re-employment at least until the early part of the calendar year 1935. If at that time conditions have not improved as much as we today hope, the next Congress will be in session and will have full opportunity to act."

Now, I am also making a recommendation that out of this lump sum there be made certain specific allocations of $48,000,000 for T.V.A. that being a public work, $35,000,000 for Federal buildings, $100,000,000 for public highways, $40,000,000 for increase of the Navy, and $325,000 for the Executive Office Building. That last item is to give us some room to work in.

By the way, if we get a new building I am going to get an oval room, but it is going to be two feet longer. I am adding

--- [339] ---

that for the Press.

Q:    Can we get a bar in there?

THE PRESIDENT:   Sure. I am going to have steps going up to the mantel piece so the short fellows can sit on the mantel piece. (Laughter)

Then for the inter-American Highway, $5,000,000. That is to provide materials for those countries all the way down to Panama that cannot make their own materials.

Q:    Is that for the survey or the actual construction of the highway?

THE PRESIDENT:   No, I think it is for materials to be bought in this country and donated to those highways. Of course, in a sense, it works in under the relief plan because it puts people to work. It is our contribution.

And then the rest, roughly and broadly, goes into relief and P.W.A.

And then there is one other clause, and that is the clause that would allow me to transfer certain items, certain appropriations if they were not used, to transfer them to relief deficits. For instance, Jesse Jones has already got $500,000,000 and while he does not know and I do not know, nobody knows, whether the RFC will find it necessary or advisable to spend that whole additional $500,000,000, the idea is that if, when we come to it in the fall, he does not need to spend it and we need more money for Harry Hopkins, we will be able to transfer it from Jesse's appropriation to relief work.

Well, that really covers the whole thing.

Q:    Mr. President, does the Department of Justice get anything in its work under the coming plan?

--- [340] ---

THE PRESIDENT:  I think they got it in the deficiency part of this bill -- Internal Revenue gets $10,000,000 -- I don't think it is in the bill, but I talked with Lew Douglas about it and it is going in somewhere. I forget how much they want, I think it is two or three million dollars. I don't think it is physically in there, but it will be asked for all right. It is a comparatively small amount.

Q:    There is some talk on the Hill as to the right to use this money in a discretionary way.

THE PRESIDENT:  Well, the answer is two things. No human being can tell what the situation is going to be on the first of October. Congress won't be back until January and we don't want Congress back for a special session. Further, they don't want to come back for a special session. And nobody, on the whole, will be able to tell as well as myself what the actual needs will be.

There will be, of course, a certain amount of effort to earmark it for one purpose or another.

Q:    Of course every dollar they earmark takes away from the money you may need next November?

THE PRESIDENT:  Absolutely. On the highway thing, people have to realize certain very simple facts. In the first place, money that goes into highways is not as immediately effective as money that goes into what might be called a reorganized or planned CWA. Of course, last fall when we went into CWA it was not a planned thing. We had to trust to the localities, and a lot of localities did certain things and a few localities allowed graft and political preference to enter into it. On the whole, 80 or 90% of it was well spent, remarkably well spent, considering the fact that it was set up in the course of two or three weeks. Now, CWA money is the most effective in

--- [341] ---

that it goes out in direct proportion to people who need it. On the other hand, highway money takes a long time to plan for. We got the highway money last June and the peak of the expenditure won't occur until some time this summer. The bulk of last year's highway money will be spent in 1934. And there will be some left over for 1935.

I am not against going ahead with highways. The pre-depression appropriation for Federal aid to highways ran to $100,000,000. But to go ahead at
this time with a very much larger expenditure, runs up into the difficulty
of taking it out of more direct and quicker relief. It brings us into the
difficulty of having a large portion of the expenditure go to overhead and
to people outside of the particular area as, for example, the contractors
in the State of New York who came from Bridgeport, Connecticut. Then,
there is also the fact that a great deal of this highway work benefits
country communities where the actual unemployment, the actual relief need,
are less serious than they are in the congested centers.

Now, of course, there is going to be an effort made without any question to
earmark more money for this, that or the other thing. The only thing we
can do is hope to work it out in some way.

Q:   From now on the problem with respect to communities is going to be the actual condition, their specific needs, rather than this equal --

THE PRESIDENT:   (interposing) That is true today. There are a good many communities in the country where distress has been reduced 50 or 75%. Then
there are other communities where distress conditions have not been very
much relieved because of families that have been able to hang on without
relief up to this time but have come to the end of their rope.

--- [342] ---

Q:   How about this highway bill of $400,000,000?

THE PRESIDENT:   That is an authorization.

Q:   Does that fit into this picture in any way at all?

THE PRESIDENT:   I don't see where the money for $400,000,000 for highways is
coming from unless we have more taxes.

Q:   They also appropriated money for beef and dairy cattle?

THE PRESIDENT:   That is included in here.

Q:   It comes out of public works in addition to relief?

THE PRESIDENT:   It comes out of relief, yes.

Q:   When you say that the economies should be left to your discretion, does
that mean that in any of the appropriations which are made --

THE PRESIDENT:   No.

Q:   -- you might take that saving and decide in your own mind where to spend
it?

THE PRESIDENT:   No. It is very definitely limited. Any savings or un-obligated
balances in existing appropriations or any savings which can be effected
out of certain appropriations made for emergency purposes shall be available for emergency relief purposes.

Q:   Would that permit cancellation of existing PWA projects and shifting of the
funds?

THE PRESIDENT: No.

Q: Are you planning to have more activity in housing as part of this public works program in the next fiscal year?

THE PRESIDENT: Well, of course there is quite a lot of PWA money in here. And then, there is also some that is left over. A large portion of it will go for housing projects. And then in addition -- I did not have time to talk about it this morning -- the message

--- [343] ---

that went up today called for setting up a Corporation which can be obligated for $200,000,000, but I don't think that that is included in the budget, one way or the other. In other words, it is on the same basis as the $2,000,000 on farm loans and the $2,000,000 on home loans. It is what might be called a contingent liability of the Government which does not figure in the regular budget. You must remember that after the regular budget went up the Government guaranteed four millions of home and farm credit bonds. It is a guarantee and will appear in the annual statement as as a contingent liability. But there isn't much chance of any of it being lost. It looks pretty good, and I think it is Lew Douglas' idea to include this $200,000,000 insurance corporation in the same category.

Q: Have you decided yet on who is going to administer the new corporation?

THE PRESIDENT: Which one?

Q: Housing.

THE PRESIDENT: No, I haven't taken it up at all.

Q: On this new appropriation for relief, does that mean that the CWA is going to be revived?

THE PRESIDENT: No, there is no new corporation. Hopkins continues to run relief and Secretary Ickes Public Works. It simply means that if Hopkins gets short of relief money in the Fall and Ickes has some or Jones has some, that I will be able to transfer either from Ickes or Jones to tide Hopkins over.

Q: Last April the CWA was discontinued and the new process of administering relief was in effect. Now, is it contemplated that this appropriation of $400,000,000 is to re-establish the CWA in the winter time as a Federal project?

--- [344] ---

THE PRESIDENT: There again, I cannot tell; it is too soon. If we do re-establish CWA, it will be done along new lines. They have some fancy term for the new CWA.

Q: E.W.D.?

THE PRESIDENT: That is it. It will be done that way.

Q: You are still, of course, shooting for a balanced budget in 1936?

THE PRESIDENT: Yes. But, of course, there again we don't know. Now this program, if things go extraordinarily well, ought to be enough to last us through, but if things do not go well we will have to have more money, especially for relief work in January or February, immediately available. If things go very badly, I will have to transfer some funds to carry us through until Congress comes back. That is the main point.

Q: The financing of the deficit for this fiscal year, there will be nothing extraordinary about that? You will continue the sale of securities?

THE PRESIDENT: That is going along very well.

Q: Has anybody brought to your attention the amount or the percentage of Government securities that now form bank assets? That is to say, the banks have an extraordinary percentage of Government securities among their assets. Presumably, if those securities are going to be sold through the next fiscal year, that percentage will become considerably higher.

THE PRESIDENT: No, it will work out all right if the banks start to push out credits based on those securities. That is largely up to the banks. If the banks will only do their bit. Those securities, the sum of them, immediately form the basis of three or four times their face value in the form of credit.

--- [345] ---

Q: About twenty billion dollars?

THE PRESIDENT: Yes. In other words, the banks, if they will only push the money out and start things going, will help the situation materially. Here is the thing which has got to be more or less off the record, sort of halfway between background and off the record. There has been all this howl about how the banks are doing their work. On the other hand, we get in here, constantly, protests because banks won't lend on good security. A man came in the other day to see me. He lives in a town of 50,000 people. He said, "My wife and I, about four years ago, bought a little piece of land in the suburbs and paid a thousand dollars. I have got two children. All my taxes have been paid up to date. I have a job and never lost a job, and am making $125 or $150. I have saved up $1,500. We want to build a $3,000 house. In other words, when the house is completed, the property will have cost me $4,000 all together. Now we have that $1,500 in the bank and want to build the house. We need to borrow $1,500, which is a comparatively low percentage and give a mortgage on the property worth $4,000. But there is not a bank in town which will lend it to us. We went to the building and loan association and they said, 'No, nobody is investing.'"

Well, this bill going up today takes care of that because it provides for partial Government insurance for building and loan associations and it ought to enable them to get more savings in in order to enable them to push it out in the form of loans. That will take care of that typical case of the man who wanted to borrow $1,500 to build a $4,000 house.

Q: Was that refusal because of the type of the loan?

--- [346] ---

THE PRESIDENT: I will tell you the real reason. The little banker -- and this is off the record -- the little banker in this little town is in touch by telephone once a week with the Guaranty Trust Company in New York. The Guaranty says, "Our policy is to remain 100% liquid." The little banker takes his cue from the Guaranty Trust Company. If the Guaranty Trust Company and one or two of the other big banks in New York adopt a policy, that spreads all over the country, and in about a week every banker on the crossroads knows that the policy of the big bankers is to remain liquid. It centers right up in New York City, let's be frank. It is psychology, and the little fellow follows the banker in the big city.

Q:    A leading banker said that if a man owned a lot in Detroit worth $2,000 and wanted to build an $8,000 house that he did not know of anybody in Detroit to whom that man could go to get the additional $2,000 with a $10,000 place offered as security.

THE PRESIDENT:  Yes, and the banks are loaded with money.

Q:    We would be glad to write this.

THE PRESIDENT:  Keep it in the back of your heads. You can color your stories that way.

Q:    Have you estimated the amount which will be appropriated for your discretion if the Congress accepts your proposal? Is it something around two and a half billion dollars?

THE PRESIDENT:  Oh, no. The discretionary? You mean on the transfers?

Q:    Yes.

THE PRESIDENT:  On the transfers, there is a possibility of transferring out of Jesse Jones' five hundred million dollars whatever he does not need. There is the possibility of withdrawing from Ickes such

--- [347] ---

balance as he has not allocated out of his un-earmarked PWA fund which is only about two hundred and fifty million dollars. And those amounts can only be transferred for relief purposes and nothing else.

Q:    The discretionary amount, then, is about $750,000,000?

THE PRESIDENT:  Yes, total. And, of course, it really, actually, will be a good deal less than that because Jones will use some of his and Ickes some of his.

Q:    Mr. President, can you tell us about this $40,000,000 for the Navy?

THE PRESIDENT:  That has already been done.

Q:    Secretary Swanson said the other day that he wanted $32,000,000, of which $27,000,000 was for ships and $5,000,000 for aircraft. I wondered where the other $8,000,000 was going to go.

THE PRESIDENT:  I don't know. The figure I got down here is $40,700,000 for the Navy, aircraft, equipment and facilities.

MR. EARLY:  Let us make it clear that all this is in confidence.

THE PRESIDENT:   All in confidence until the message goes up.

Q:   When will copies of the message be available?

MR. EARLY:   Tomorrow morning at ten-thirty.   It goes up at noon.

Q:   These appropriations are supposed to run to June, 1935?

THE PRESIDENT:   Yes, June, 1935.

(The Press Conference adjourned at 12:40 P.M.)

CONFIDENTIAL
Press Conference #122
Executive Offices of the White House
May 16, 1934, 10:40 A.M.


MR. DONALDSON: All in.

THE PRESIDENT: I do not think I have any news. Somebody was asked to ask me a question in regard to this Securities and Exchange bill, a question of who is going to run it, and the answer is a very simple one, that I was very, very scrupulous in keeping my hands off the bill when it was in the House and in the Senate and I told Congressman Rayburn's Committee that of course we had to have some machinery to enforce it and it was up to them to decide what they thought was best. They decided on the Federal Trade Commission and I told Senator Glass that I would interpose no objection if his Committee wanted to put it in as a separate commission, which they did.

Now it is in the point in conference where they have asked me my own feeling and I very carefully did not make up my mind until the bill had passed both Houses because I wanted to keep an open mind and decide honestly what I thought was the best thing for the administration of the bill. After what you call careful consideration, there are a lot of reasons that make me feel, personally, that it would be better to have the bill administered by the same agency that is administering the securities bill, in other words the Federal Trade Commission. That is my own personal feeling about it.

The Federal Trade Commission, in the first place, has a great many -- has existing machinery which would be, to a certain extent, duplicated by another commission, a separate commission; in the second

--- [349] ---

place, it saves money to add two commissioners to the Federal Trade Commission rather than appoint five -- the overhead won't be as great if it stays in the Federal Trade Commission; and then there is the other reason, which I have to make off the record, and that is that, thinking into the future, if it is put into the Federal Trade Commission as one of many duties, it will be less liable to political change in future years. In other words, it would be a more permanent part of our Government.

So I told that to the House Committee and I am telling it this morning at eleven o'clock, by telephone, to the Senate Committee so that they would know just where I stand on it. It is not a frightfully important thing, one way or the other, but so long as they have asked my views, there they are.

Q: How about your views on minimum margin requirements? That is the other point.

THE PRESIDENT: The definite provision in the House bill should stand.

Then there was one other question in regard to that bill which was brought up yesterday. Under the Senate bill providing for a separate commission, the question of the banking credits for brokers' loans was divided in a rather complicated way between the Federal Reserve Board and the proposed separate commission. It seems to me that the question of banking credits should be either one way or the other. I suggested that they should remain in the Federal Reserve Board.

Q: Mr. President, the Senate made some modifications in the Securities Act. Are those O. K. by you?

THE PRESIDENT: It was one of those frightfully complicated things. I have not gone into the details of it but, so far as I know, they

--- [350] ---

are all right.

Q: Anything on the cocoanut oil tax?

THE PRESIDENT: I just haven't got to that. I am a bit behind, about three days behind on things at the present time. It will be going up just as soon as I can get it written.

Q: Anything on the Darrow report yet?

THE PRESIDENT: Oh, I am getting the mimeograph started on it and I think you will have it this afternoon or tomorrow and also I got a report last night which again I have not read as yet. It is the question of physical time -- it is from Johnson (General Johnson) -- and that will be released too, but I have got to have time to read it first. I only got it last night.

Q: Are you considering ordering an investigation of the various shootings and strikes in Los Angeles?

THE PRESIDENT: No, I have not heard anything. I have not seen that telegram from Governor Rolph. All that I know is what I read about it this morning.

Q: No, the shooting in the last ten days.

THE PRESIDENT: I do not know anything except what has come out in the paper. I know nothing about it so far; in fact, it has not been brought to me so far.

Q: What was your attitude on the labor bills pending?

THE PRESIDENT: Still in the conference stage.

Q: Are you going to talk to the silver Senators today?

THE PRESIDENT: Yes, they are coming in after three o'clock.

Q: Have you anything to say about Governor Black?

THE PRESIDENT: It is a perfectly simple thing. Governor Black has been

--- [351] ---

pleading for the last six months to go back to his business in Atlanta and I have been begging him to put it off. He says he cannot afford to stay here. He came originally with the idea of staying three months and has been here for a year. I am going to keep him here just as long as I physically can. I told him yesterday I will have to order out the Marines.

Q:   Have you a successor in mind?

THE PRESIDENT:   No, I have not talked about it yet.

Q:   Is Ambassador Davis taking over any suggestion from you in connection with the disarmament situation?

THE PRESIDENT:   No.  I can say no to that but there is no particular reason why you should not know that Norman Davis has been writing a speech.  In other words, he has been writing a statement to make and we are going over it at the present time.  I cannot tell you what it contains because that will have to wait until he gets to Geneva.

Q:   It is a safe assumption that it outlines our policy?

THE PRESIDENT:   Yes.

Q:   Does it propose any new schemes or plans?

THE PRESIDENT:   Wait a minute -- I will be giving it away.

Q:   Can you tell us anything about the conference on the Steagall Bill yesterday?

THE PRESIDENT:   The only thing I asked them was please, for heaven's sake, to take a vote and get the bill out.  So I think some kind of a bill is going to come out.

Q:   Mr. President, in connection with the disarmament, can you tell us anything yet about the Naval Conference for next year?

THE PRESIDENT:   There hasn't been a single thing done on that yet.

--- [352] ---

Q:   In connection with the Darrow Report, there has been a suggestion that you will have a conference with Darrow and Johnson to talk this over.

THE PRESIDENT:   No.

Q:   Is your debt Message ready?

THE PRESIDENT:   No.  What time did I say, last Friday?  Ten days -- I have not looked at it.

Q:   That was last Wednesday.

THE PRESIDENT:   I still hope to get it up next week.

Q:   Have you found anybody for the Federal Power Commission and RFC vacancies yet?

THE PRESIDENT:   No, I have to do something about it because Congress will go home.

Q:   Anything on the Soviet trade credit situation?  The Soviet Ambassador talked to you about it.

THE PRESIDENT: No, that is still in negotiation here and in Moscow.

Q: In connection with the debts, various dispatches state that the French may be considering sending over a debt mission to us. Have we heard anything officially?

THE PRESIDENT: No.

Q: Have any of the nations made overtures for relief on debts?

THE PRESIDENT: Not so far as I know. I have not talked with the State Department since the day before yesterday so it is subject to check with them.

Q: On the silver, anything on that subject as far as this Conference is concerned?

THE PRESIDENT: No, I have not heard a word from the group. I think they saw Secretary Morgenthau day before yesterday. I have not talked

--- [353] ---

with any of them.

Q: There has been some talk that an international conference may be called on silver.

THE PRESIDENT: No; have not even got to the discussion stage of that.

Q: Have you any message planned to go to Congress in the near future besides that war debt Message and the one on cocoanut oil?

THE PRESIDENT: I do not think so. Yes, I have got another one but I cannot tell you about it yet. I will tell you what it relates to. I might just as well tell you the subject of it -- I might not send it -- but it relates to munitions makers. That is all I can tell you.

Q: Mr. President, the announcement that we are going to make a new statement at Geneva undoubtedly is going to arouse widespread interest in Europe.

THE PRESIDENT: I don't think they may have any interest in it at all.

Q: They may have new hope. (Laughter)

Q: Will this Message you have just mentioned be concerned at all with the report of the War Policies Commission, or the recommendations?

THE PRESIDENT: What is the War Policies Commission?

Q: A commission interested in the advisability or possibility of an amendment to the Constitution -- war without profit --

THE PRESIDENT: (interposing) I have not thought about that at all. It is germaine but it is not tied in with that particular report.

Q: I mentioned that because there was a resolution on munitions makers in it.

THE PRESIDENT: Yes, and then there is the Nye Resolution that went through.

Q:   Will it have any connection with the Nye Resolution?

--- [354] ---

THE PRESIDENT:  You will have to read it.

Q:   In connection with the disarmament, will it be a safe guess that it is a restatement of our policy rather than a new statement?

THE PRESIDENT:  I guess it would not.

Q:   You are receiving the Belgian Mission today?

THE PRESIDENT:  Yes.

Q:   Do you expect to take up any international subjects with them?

THE PRESIDENT:  No, I do not think so.  It is just a formal party.

Q:   In connection with the housing program, building costs are only nine per cent under 1929 as compared with other costs.  Has the Administration planned to compensate for that?

THE PRESIDENT:  I think you had better talk to Frank Walker about it because that is one of the things discussed a great deal and undoubtedly some building material costs are too high, without any question.

Q:   Have you signed the crime bill yet, the new one?

THE PRESIDENT:  No, it has not come to me yet.  I signed one a couple of days ago.  Those passed yesterday have not come in.

Q:   Thank you, sir.

Q:   Can you tell us your reactions on the Pennsylvania Primaries?

THE PRESIDENT:  No.  I will tell you the honest truth, I have been conferring since I started breakfast this morning and I have not even read the morning paper.

(The Press Conference adjourned at 10:55 A.M.)

Press Conference #123
Executive Offices of the White House
May 18, 1934, 4:25 P.M.


MR. DONALDSON: All in.

THE PRESIDENT: Steve (Mr. Early) and the Attorney General have just put into my mouth the powerful statement on signing the crime bills that you will receive today. I call your attention particularly to the clause that Steve (Mr. Early) did not like but I think is grand: (Reading)

> "Law enforcement and gangster extermination cannot be made completely effective so long as a substantial part of the public looks with tolerance upon known criminals, permits public officers to be corrupted or intimidated by them or applauds efforts to romanticize crime."

I think Steve will remember the fact that he was writing for the papers once. (Laughter)

Q: Was that cut out?

THE PRESIDENT: That was off the record. No, I left it in. My remarks are off the record.

Q: On the Munitions Message today, any background on that?

THE PRESIDENT: No, except that we want to do everything that we possibly can on that.

Q: Does it apply to Paraguay and Bolivia?

THE PRESIDENT: That is a different thing. I cannot talk to you about that yet, except off the record, because here is the story. It only came up just within the past twenty-four hours. We would very much like to stop the shipment of any munitions to either Paraguay or Bolivia but we have treaties with them that go back to 1856 or something like that and to put a resolution through the Senate that would forbid the export would be in violation of those treaties.

--- [356] ---

You see, they are inland countries and those treaties were made on the basis of their being inland countries and therefore it would not be sufficient for the nations around them to say, "We won't allow shipments to go in," because we have treaties with them that allow goods through by the Rio Plate. The Secretary of State is consulting at the present time -- that is the reason we have to keep it off the record for the moment -- with Key Pittman or the Chairman of the Foreign Affairs Committee in the House, and discussing with them the possibility of a resolution which will authorize me to stop the sale of any munitions destined for them within the United States. In a sense it is getting around those old treaties but we do not want to act in a way that would be definitely violative of those treaties. We want to accomplish the same end and the language is being worked out now.

Q: The Senator pointed out this treaty this afternoon.

THE PRESIDENT: On the Chaco thing, don't say anything yet because Cordell will probably tell you when he has talked with Key Pittman.

Q: Does the 1925 treaty set up the treaty as you desire, that is to stop the sale by the licensing clause?

THE PRESIDENT: Not if it is in contravention of existing treaties.

Q: But if you get the resolution, you can use it in stopping the sale?

THE PRESIDENT: Stop the licensing because it is going out of the country -- I think so. It is so long since I have looked at it.

Q: How vital do you consider enactment at this session of amendments to the (Agricultural) Adjustment Act?

THE PRESIDENT: I think they are pretty important. I would like very much to have them go through because those amendments, in principle,

--- [357] ---

not the detailed language but in principle, they make clear certain things in the A.A.A. that are not perfectly clear at the present time. That is the main objective of them (to clarify), where there is doubt. I have got a memo on it somewhere. They relate to the three primary methods of aiding agriculture set up in Section 8 of the Act. One is the licensing authority and, after a year's experience in the administration of the Act, it has become clear that the language used in the original Act is not free from doubt. The proposed amendments make clear the Secretary's authority in this respect beyond doubt. In other words, there was not much question as to the original intent but there was whether the language carried out the original intent.

Q: Do you know whether or not the N.R.A. has any regulations in mind for the automotive industry?

THE PRESIDENT: No.

Q: To turn back to the Chaco for a moment, stories have already been printed that the United States will stop the sale of American war supplies. Is there any objection to saying such plans are going forward?

THE PRESIDENT: If you do it in very general terms. I don't want to have anything said that would anticipate the conversation between Cordell Hull and the two Chairmen.

Q: Mr. President, how about raising the deficit.

THE PRESIDENT: No.

Q: The Democratic deficit, I do not mean the Government deficit. Both of them seem very large.

THE PRESIDENT: Both of them the same status as the foreign debts.

Q: In that connection, some time ago you indicated you did not want members

--- [358] ---

of the Democratic National Committee to hold other jobs in the Government and Farley, in amplifying the statement, said you were particularly anxious that no Internal Revenue agent should collect campaign funds.  In Detroit yesterday some officials of the Packard Motor Car Company made a statement that a member of the Democratic National Committee of Michigan, Mr. Abbott, had asked them for $50,000, $30,000 of which was to go to the Democratic Committee.

THE PRESIDENT:   I should say that was highly, highly improper, as you put it.

Q:   Can that have any effect on the rumor of Abbott's resignation?   (Laughter)

THE PRESIDENT:   From which, the Democratic National or the Internal Revenue?

Q:   Either.

THE PRESIDENT:   I don't know; I have not heard the rumor.

Q:   You won't accept funds from large companies?

THE PRESIDENT:   Unfortunately we cannot do it under the law.  Corporations cannot give.  (Laughter)  Charlie (Mr. Hurd of the New York Times), you phrased your question all wrong.

Q:   You answer it your way then.

THE PRESIDENT:   You struck out.  Sorry.

Q:   Has an action been taken on the report of the forty per cent horizontal cigarette tax reduction?

THE PRESIDENT:   I suppose, when you really come right down to it, it is not proper for me to comment because it is a matter distinctly before the Congress.  But I think I can tell you, off the record, just so you know how to write the story, that any tax legislation of any kind at this stage of any session especially where it relates

--- [359] ---

to something that has not been pretty thoroughly discussed beforehand, presents a pretty difficult problem.  We have had very little time to discuss new tax legislation and I think Pat Harrison feels that way about it.  But don't use me in any way on this; get it from the Hill.

Q:   Can you tell us your attitude on R.F.C. loans to schools as provided in the Sabath Bill?

THE PRESIDENT:   I don't know; there are so many bills on the school question.

Q:   This would allow up to seventy-five millions of R.F.C. funds to be loaned to school districts.  The presumption is that Chicago might get twenty millions of the seventy-five.

THE PRESIDENT:   I think that is one of those things we are not going to take any attitude on down here.  Jesse Jones is talking officially on the Hill about it.  They all have been running up to see me.  I think you had better leave it as a matter between Congress and Jesse.

Q:    London reports that the British Ambassador's visit yesterday was to ascer-
tain or make certain the status or a token payment on the fifteenth.

THE PRESIDENT:  That is very interesting.

Q:    Anything about your talk with the British Ambassador?

THE PRESIDENT:  No, I cannot comment at all.

Q:    Mr. President, is the Ickes oil bill "must" legislation for this session?

THE PRESIDENT:  I don't know who invented that term "must legislation." You
see, they get the impression up on the Hill that there are certain definite
things that have to be done.  There has never been any expression out of
the White House on that.  We are as innocent as a newborn

--- [360] ---

babe.  Once can express an interest in legislation or a hope that a certain
thing would go through, but this word "must" is a terrible word.  I would
not use "must" to Congress.  I never have, have I?  (Laughter)

The oil legislation is a little bit like the agricultural legislation.
There are certain words, clauses, language in the old Oil Administration
law, the section of last year, which are not particularly clear so far as
legal purposes are concerned but which are fairly clear as to the original
intent of the Congress and the situation arises on the oil question a
little bit in this way, [that there are some states on the quota basis
which have not got any local state laws for enforcing either quota bases
or hot oil runs, things of that kind, such, for instance, as California.
The intent, of course, was that in those states that the Oil, the Federal
Oil Administrator should be able to act in those states to enforce quotas
that the large majority had agreed on in the absence] of a state law.

Then you come to the second clause, on state taxes, where you have got
machinery.  There the obvious intention of Congress, I think, last year
was that the local machinery should be used for enforcement up to and until such a point as it became clear that the local machinery was not effective, where, in spite of local machinery, large amounts of hot oil were
being run over and above a quota.  Now, obviously, in a case like that the
Federal Government ought to have authority to step in and see to it that
the general theory of a quota on hot oil should be enforced.

Now, as I understand it, the purpose of these amendments is to

--- [361] ---

carry out that general principle and they are very desirable in clearing up
weaknesses of language.

Q:    Mr. President, can you tell us who will succeed Harry New as Federal Commissioner of the World's Fair (at Chicago)?

THE PRESIDENT:  Is Harry New out?

Q:    It was announced yesterday.

THE PRESIDENT: I did not know that; I did not even know.

Q: I understood he sent his resignation to you this morning.

THE PRESIDENT: I did not know it at all. I don't know who is going in his place.

Q: You will have a hard job finding a man for that, won't you?

THE PRESIDENT: By the way, has the Federal appropriation passed yet?

Q: I think it has.

Q: No, it has not. The Federal Commissioners were supposed to O.K. it this afternoon and it goes to the Federal Budget tomorrow and then, if you O.K. it, it goes to the Appropriations Committee.

THE PRESIDENT: It opens (the Fair) next week, does it not?

Q: Yes.

Q: This amount of money to be spent on the conservation program immediately, the report of that Committee, I understand you had a conference on it?

THE PRESIDENT: I think we have allocated $5,000,000 to that. Isn't it $5,000,000? I think so. Then, out of the acquisition of submarginal lands, they will get an amount, as yet undetermined, and whether they will get any more out of relief, I do not know yet. It is a little early. Then they will also get an amount of assistance from C.C.C. camps.

The combination of all these things will give them enough money

--- [362] ---

in the course of the coming year to do a pretty good job. It comes from four sources.

Q: On the tobacco tax, did your committee make a report?

THE PRESIDENT: Which one?

Q: Secretary Wallace and Secretary Morgenthau and Tugwell. They were investigating it.

THE PRESIDENT: Investigating what?

Q: The tobacco tax reduction?

THE PRESIDENT: I do not think they did. I think they were to talk it over with the finance chairman. I have not heard from them. But that background I gave you on it is enough.

Q: Can you tell us anything on silver?

THE PRESIDENT: Silver? What about it?

Q: Will that go up Monday or Tuesday?

THE PRESIDENT:  I think a pretty good guess is a Message on silver on Monday.

Q:  What time are you going down the river?

THE PRESIDENT:  Either seven or nine, I don't know which.  I have not consulted the White House.  I am not the doctor.

(The Press Conference adjourned at 4:33 P.M.)

Press Conference #124
Executive Offices of the White House
May 23, 1934, 10:40 A.M.


MR. DONALDSON: All in.

THE PRESIDENT: Steve (Mr. Early) suggested that I might give you a general
    slant on additional messages to the Congress and I have been trying to
    think over the various ones I have had in the back of my head. I can
    only think of three that are going to go up. One is -- and you will be
    pleased to hear it -- the debt message.

Q:   When?

THE PRESIDENT: Soon. The other is the cocoanut oil message and the third is
    transmitting the reports that have been made to me pursuant to the resolu-
    tion, I think it was the McCarran resolution of the Congress in regard to
    water use. Of course, that will be a fairly broad message. Water use in-
    cludes so many other things such as soil erosion and forestry and marginal
    lands and so forth.


                    (Mr. Early spoke to the President)

Steve suggests that is why some people confuse it with the so-called social
message. I never mentioned any social message.

Q:   What is this water thing?

THE PRESIDENT:  I cannot remember the wording of it but Congress asked me for a
    report on the general policy of the Government in relation to all forms of
    water use which includes the Mississippi channel, the Tennessee, Arkansas,
    Upper Missouri, Ohio, etc., all rivers. It is broad enough to include
    other public works such as channel deepening for harbors and of course, as
    I have said, soil erosion, forestry and marginal lands. It is a tremen-
    dously big subject.

Q:   That is an announcement of policy?

                    --- [364] ---

THE PRESIDENT:  Yes, but it will not call for legislation at this time.

Q:   Will you recommend specific projects in it?

THE PRESIDENT:  I think you will have to wait for the message. I think not.  It
    is the huge stack over there (indicating) in the basket and some of the
    engineering reports have reported on specific projects but this does not
    recommend any specific projects.

Q:   Is that the "pay-as-you-can" proposition -- both using rivers and so
    forth?

THE PRESIDENT:  That might be a phase of it. I have not begun to draft it yet.
    There might be a paragraph on it.

Q:    Will they go up in the order named?

THE PRESIDENT:   I have no idea.

Q:    Am I to understand that you will not send up a message on social reform?

THE PRESIDENT:   Depends on what you call social reform.  Isn't water use social reform?  (Laughter)

Q:    Will that include the St. Lawrence?

THE PRESIDENT:   It will include everything in the way of a river in the United States, as far as policy goes.

Q:    Will that tie up with the Sub-Committee of the Cabinet you spoke of some time ago?

THE PRESIDENT:   That is the one.

Q:    In that connection, do you intend sending a Message to Congress which will deal with pending so-called social legislation which, under my understanding, would embrace unemployment insurance and legislation of that type?

Q:    Old age pension?

THE PRESIDENT:   As a separate Message, no.  Not as a separate Message.  I might say something in other Messages about it.

--- [365] ---

Q:    What Messages?

THE PRESIDENT:   I might put it in cocoanut oil, you can't tell.

Q:    Is that an indication of a veto of the proposed bill?

THE PRESIDENT:   Of course those are bridges we are coming to.

Q:    You do not think there will be legislation this session?

THE PRESIDENT:   Not on the water (use).

Q:    What relation would this board have to subsequent things coming before P.W.A. and to flood control projects?

THE PRESIDENT:   This is a much broader theme.  If you will read the Senate and House Resolution and the Message which is going up, you will see the answer. It does not relate to specific projects.

Q:    It will not stop P.W.A. from granting special projects?

THE PRESIDENT:   That depends entirely on future legislation.  You cannot tell. There is no more money for new projects under the old appropriation.

Q:    Do you anticipate passage of the Wagner National Labor Board Bill at this session?

THE PRESIDENT:   I don't know; I really don't know.

Q:    What about the unemployment insurance?

THE PRESIDENT:    That again, I do not know.  I have not heard for the last four
or five days what the situation is.

Q:    How about the Pure Food and Drug Bill?

THE PRESIDENT:    That I don't know either, except that Senator Copeland mentioned
yesterday he hoped to get it through the Senate.

I am sending up a letter today, in fact it has gone up to the Chariman of
Mines and Mining, Senator Logan, and Congressman Rayburn of the Interstate
and Foreign Commerce Committee, in regard

--- [366] ---

to this oil situation, which is just calling their attention to a letter
that I had from the Administrator for the Petroleum Industry, the Secretary
of the Interior -- Steve (Mr. Early) has copies for you on this -- inform-
ing me of the (reading)

"...continued daily production of oil in excess of the maximum amount determined on by the Administrator pursuant to
authority under the Petroleum Code.

"The Administrator states that the records of the Bureau of
Mines during the first three months of this year show a
daily average production of "illegal" oil of 149,000 barrels.
Technically speaking, this may not all have been "hot" oil,
but in a real sense it is, since it is oil produced in excess
of the allowable.  While the final figures of the Bureau of
Mines are not available for the months of April and May, it
is unquestionably true that there is growing disregard for
production orders issued under the Petroleum Code and that
the trend of hot oil produced is upward.  For example, it
is stated on reliable authority that the daily excess production in the East Texas field alone is running at 60,000
to 75,000 barrels per day.  Other estimators say that this
figure should be much higher.  The Oil and Gas Journal recently estimated that there was illegal production in the country
as a whole of 198,475 barrels per day during the week ending
May 12th.

"If the principle of prorating production under a code is
to be maintained, it seems necessary that the existing law
should be strengthened by the passage of the Bill which has
been introduced in the Senate by Senator Thomas and in the
House by Congressman Disney and supported by the Oil Administrator.

"It is a simple fact that as a result of the work of the
Oil Administrator definite progress has been made both in
eliminating unfair practices and in raising the price of
crude petroleum to a reasonable level, which has brought
added employment and more fair wages to those engaged in
oil production.

"I am frankly fearful that if the law is not strengthened,

illegal production will continue and grow in volume and result in a collapse of the whole structure. This will mean a return to the wretched conditions which existed in the Spring of 1933.

"I hope therefore that the proposed legislation can be enacted. I do not want to see this important American industry reduced to the condition under which it was operating before the Oil Administration started its work."

So that is merely calling their attention up there to what may hap-

--- [367] ---

pen if we do not get additional legislation. Of course, a year ago oil in a good many places was selling at twenty cents a barrel. We know what happened, what the condition of the industry was at that time.

Q:   Mr. President, has the War Department submitted any recommendation as to the appointment of a Commanding Officer of the National Guard for the District of Columbia, or is that place to be filled by Major General Rekord of Maryland, who was appointed yesterday?

THE PRESIDENT:   Count (Rudolph de Zapp), I do not know. I asked somebody to look into that. Will you look into it, Steve (Mr. Early)? Our War Department expert will look into it.

Q:   How about the appointment of a Judge for the Municipal Court?

THE PRESIDENT:   I have not heard from the Attorney General on that. I sent word to him yesterday, asking for it.

Q:   There is word that Frank Walker is planning to resign in the near future and go back to New York. Anything to tell us about that?

THE PRESIDENT:   Frank has been trying to get back to New York for the last six months. I told him to have the summer off and plan to bring him down here in the fall. I need him here in Washington. He said he would have to consult his wife. I told him he might just as well start looking for a house right now.

Q:   Do you mean that the "consult his wife" is off the record?

THE PRESIDENT:   Yes. (Laughter) It is not off the record if you check with him first.

Q:   Anything on the report of the Darrow Board?

THE PRESIDENT:   I have not heard anything more than what I told you about two weeks ago, that Darrow told me he hoped to be able to wind up by the end of May, and that is the last I heard.

--- [368] ---

Q:   Do you contemplate any action to deal with the growth of strikes in the country?

THE PRESIDENT:   We are doing the best we can; that is about the only answer.

Q:   Can you make any comment on the resignation of Mr. Abbott of Detroit?

THE PRESIDENT:   No, except that I knew about it just about the same time that
    it was announced over at the Treasury Department, and not until then.

Q:   That place will have to be filled before Congress adjourns?

THE PRESIDENT:   Not necessarily.

Q:   Isn't there a rule that you cannot make a recess appointment with respect
    to a position vacant during Congress?

THE PRESIDENT:   You can make a recess appointment, but the fellow takes a chance
    of drawing his pay later on.  There will probably be a good many appoint-
    ments of that kind.

Q:   He (Abbott) is of the Democratic Committee?

THE PRESIDENT:   I do not know.

Q:   Can I go back to this Darrow matter?

THE PRESIDENT:   I do not know if it was the end of May, but I told you about it
    about two weeks ago.

Q:   More recently he said that now they have hearings scheduled to later than
    the last of May.  Would you have any comment on that?

THE PRESIDENT:   Not a thing.

Q:   Would you care to comment on the Darrow Report?

THE PRESIDENT:   Res ipsa loquitur.

Q:   Say it again.

THE PRESIDENT:   I doubt if even the A.P. would carry that.

Q:   I don't know; we might interpret it.

                    --- [369] ---

Q:   Did General Johnson speak to you in that connection?   (Laughter)

Q:   Do you contemplate any changes in N.R.A. policy re small business after
    Congress adjourns?

THE PRESIDENT:   Oh, there will probably be weekly changes as there have been in
    the past -- constant changes.

Q:   You said you were referring that report to the Trade Commission (Federal
    Trade Commission) and the Department of Justice.  General Johnson said that
    Chairman Ferguson and the Attorney General were to meet as a committee.
    Can you tell us anything as to getting action from the other two depart-
    ments?

THE PRESIDENT:   I do not know.  I sent the report to all three of them.  I do
    not know what happened.

Q:   Have you done anything to expedite action on grazing legislation this session?

THE PRESIDENT:   I talked to some of the grazing Senators yesterday.   (Laughter)

Q:   Is that off the record, Mr. President?

THE PRESIDENT:   I suppose that ought to be off the record.   (Laughter)   Ruby Black shakes her head; she wants it on the record.   You cannot get the consent of the Senators and it is all right.

I would like to see action on the bill this session.   Their objection to the bill, as was proposed by the Interior Department and the Department of Agriculture, was that in certain cases, as I understand it, there is the summer range up in the National Forest for one man's bunch of cattle and then winter range down in the public domain, and that the owner of that bunch of cattle has to go to two different departments.   What these Senators are afraid of is that they would be thrown out of the forest reserve on a given

--- [370] ---

date and the public domain would not be open to them until a couple of weeks later, and the unfortunate cattle would have nowhere to go.   What I talked over was the definite coordination on the issuing of permits between the Forestry and the Public Domain so they can go to one place and one man and get a permit covering both pieces of territory.

Q:   Do you think the war debts Message will be up today or tomorrow?

THE PRESIDENT:   No; it has not been written.

Q:   Should the Darrow Board find it necessary to go on until after the end of May, would you interpose an objection?

THE PRESIDENT:   I have not the faintest idea.

Q:   There is a report that you are going to draft Owen D. Young and bring him down here to reorganize the N.R.A.?

THE PRESIDENT:   That sounds like a New York report.

Q:   That is too bad.   (Laughter)


(The Press Conference adjourned at 10:55 A.M.)

Q: How do you do, Mr. President? We had a nice time at your party.

THE PRESIDENT: Did everybody survive?

Q: Yes, we all succeeded in pulling through. Still an old football player. That forward pass!

MR. DONALDSON: All in.

THE PRESIDENT: What is the news?

Q: That is what we want to know.

THE PRESIDENT: I almost called the Conference off; I haven't any.

Q: Let us make some.

Q: Mr. President, the French Ambassador told us that he touched slightly on the debts, that is, during his visit. Will you tell us how lightly he touched?

THE PRESIDENT: Very lightly.

Q: Anything further?

Q: Did you only touch lightly on it also?

THE PRESIDENT: Yes, very lightly. What the French call "l'aisement."

Q: Mr. President, anything you care to say about the strike situation?

THE PRESIDENT: I don't think so. I think I had better not. It is awfully difficult to say anything without going into details and differentiations. I think it is probably better I should not. We are all working on it, as you know.

Q: You still need legislation of the type of the Wagner Bill dealing with this?

THE PRESIDENT: It would be very helpful. There is no question about it

--- [372] ---

but it would be very helpful because it would clarify administrative procedure and at the same time would create methods that were perfectly clear under the law. In the individual strike cases people would know on both sides exactly the procedure, who they come under and to whom they go and what authority there is in any given case.

Q: Is it fair to assume, then, that you want this legislation this Session?

THE PRESIDENT: I would like to have it very much. I think it would be helpful.

I think you had better put this off the record.

Q:   What you are saying now?

THE PRESIDENT:  Yes, what I am saying now.  It would be perfectly all right to
     say I am in favor of this legislation and hope it will go through but, off
     the record, you all know that in any period of this kind you are bound to
     have, with a return of prosperity and a return of reemployment and an in-
     crease in values, more strikes.  I look for a great many strikes in the
     course of this Summer, a good many more.  It is a normal and logical thing.
     I think I have said this before at a strike conference.  They are brought
     about by a great many causes.  For instance, keeping this again entirely
     off the record, in this Toledo case, the strike originated with only 400
     employees in one factory but there are a lot of other factors involved.
     They had pretty serious political trouble where a lot of graft and mis-
     government, etc., was shown in the city.  The result was that the popula-
     tion as a whole got sore.  It wasn't just these 400 men.

     Yesterday, when this crowd of between 5,000 and 10,000 people started, they
     were, as a body, sore at certain definite people.  As they got along,
     throwing stones, they would throw stones at one particular factory or shop
     and then they would go along past

--- [373] ---

several other factories or shops they were not sore at and then they would
pick out the next fellow at whom they were sore.

Charlie Taft telephoned to Miss Perkins about two hours ago and made the
point that it is not an indiscriminatory strike, it is a strike against
people they are sore at and it is not just the 400 strikers, it is a very
large element of the population.

So each case really has to be taken up on the merits of that particular,
individual case.  There is no general statement that can be made relating
to it.  Miss Perkins used a parallel which, of course, has got to be
entirely off the record.  She said in conference today that it is not a
general revolutionary feeling but a feeling against certain old-line politicians and a feeling against certain industrialists.  It is a pretty discriminating opposition.  It is based on reason of some kind.

In the Toledo situation, of course, the one thing that all of us ought to
appreciate and write about is that there are methods of settlement and that
the attitude of employers in many cases has been so autocratic.  Take, for
instance, the man in one of the papers this morning who said that he would
consider that he was demeaning himself if he sat in the same room with
William Green.  Now that kind of autocratic attitude on the part of a steel
company official does not make for working things out.  On the other hand,
there are people on the other end of the camp, the labor end, who are just
as autocratic.

Q:   One objection raised to the Wagner Bill is that they have a local board
     out there that is getting along pretty good and they thought that the ac-
     tion of the new board would largely destroy the author-

--- [374] ---

ity of the men working out there.

THE PRESIDENT:   I think under the Act this particular board would keep on functioning.

Q:   Have you had any report from the Williams Board as to what they have accomplished?

THE PRESIDENT:   I think I have one or two of the members next week to talk to me.

Q:   Will that be your first report from them?

THE PRESIDENT:   I have not had merely the one report.  Williams was here nearly three weeks ago and we went into it for half an hour.

Q:   You say you are working on this strike.  Can you tell us what the Federal Government can do or is doing?

THE PRESIDENT:   Well, we have out staff out there acting as mediator for the Department of Labor.

Q:   Have they given any late reports?

THE PRESIDENT:   No, not since the telephone (call).

Q:   Is this Taft report out?

THE PRESIDENT:   No, it has not got to the making of a report stage.

Q:   Have you reached a definite decision as to whether you want the licensing power under the Recovery Act extended?

THE PRESIDENT:   I have not talked to anybody about it; have not mentioned it.

Q:   Mr. President, did you make any statements concerning American naval policy in view of the preliminary talks in London?

THE PRESIDENT:   No.  Anything that comes out will come out from the State Department.

Q:   Have you signed the Japan Resolution as yet?

THE PRESIDENT:   It has not come down yet.

--- [375] ---

Q:   Not down yet?

THE PRESIDENT:   Not down yet.

Q:   Is the debt Message going up next week?

THE PRESIDENT:   I hope so.  It is not written yet.

Q:   The licensing provision of the N.R.A. seems about to lapse and at the same time the proposal is to strengthen the licensing provisions of the A.A.A. under the new bill?

THE PRESIDENT:   It is not necessarily inconsistent.

Q:   I know, but what is the reason for the difference?

THE PRESIDENT:   I do not know enough about it to answer the question fully.

Q:   But there is a difference there, isn't there?

THE PRESIDENT:   Yes.   I do not know enough about the details, frankly.

Q:   What is your attitude on the Costigan-Wagner Anti-Lynching Bill?

THE PRESIDENT:   It is a terribly difficult subject.   I have been talking about
    the theory of it with Costigan and Bob (Wagner) and various other people
    for quite a long while.   I don't think I had better give you an attitude
    because I frankly haven't got sufficient clarity in my own mind as to
    whether that particular method will work and also as to the constitutional-
    ity of it.   I think there is a question.   I am absolutely for the objective
    but am not clear in my own mind as to whether that is absolutely the right
    way to attain the objective.   However, I told them to go ahead and try to
    get a vote on it.   It would be a useful thing to try to get a vote on it in
    the Senate.

Q:   With reference to Chaco, now that you have the authority, do you intend to
    use the authority to prohibit the shipments (of arms, etc.)  immediately,
    or wait for the League of Nations?

THE PRESIDENT:   I haven't any idea at all.   It depends on what Secretary

--- [376] ---

Hull says.

Q:   Any new developments in the Russian credit and trade situation?

THE PRESIDENT:   I have not heard a word.   I don't think there has been anything.

Q:   Have you had an opportunity to study the banking and insurance bill passed
    by the House?

THE PRESIDENT:   No, I have not even seen it.

Q:   What was the idea of dressing up on us last night?  (Laughter)

THE PRESIDENT:   I will tell you off the record.   There was a dispute as to what
    I should wear with the Missus, and my wife was wrong.  (Laughter)   There
    is one case where I was right.   It won't happen in another year.

Q:   Have you heard from the Cabinet Committee on the railroad study they are
    supposed to make as yet?

THE PRESIDENT:   No; I do not believe they will report for some time.

Q:   Thank you.   We are sorry there isn't any more excitement today.

(The Press Conference adjourned at 4:25 P.M.)

Press Conference #126
Executive Offices of the White House
May 30, 1934, 10:45 A.M.


THE PRESIDENT: You are not going to Gettysburg?

Q: (Mr. Young) I am sorry, I am not.

Q: Is that a new suit?

THE PRESIDENT: Yes. (Laughter)

MR. DONALDSON: All in.

THE PRESIDENT: I do not think there is any news and it is a rather horrid [re-
ferring to the weather] morning. The Secretary of State is coming in at
eleven o'clock and I am going to talk debt Message and it is nearer to going up than it was last week. In other words, I do not know about the actual date yet. It may be Friday. Everything from not on is in a sort of a
movable phase, including the trip through the [Panama] Canal; that has been
movable right along. I do not know where I am going. Nothing has ever
been said on definite dates and locations. You can't tell. I might not go
until the beginning of July. It is perfectly movable .

Q: That late?

THE PRESIDENT: Possibly; cannot tell.

Q: Any hope of California?

THE PRESIDENT: I do not think so. There are so many Californians. (Laughter)

Q: Are you going to Hawaii?

THE PRESIDENT: Oh, I hope so.

Q: Are you still going to Puerto Rico?

THE PRESIDENT: Yes, that is sure.

Q: Mr. President, there was a report in the morning paper that Harry Hopkins

--- [378] ---

would be selected to head the housing activities.

THE PRESIDENT: I haven't any more idea than I had when the bill went in. Of
course we still want the bill very, very much.

Q: At this session?

THE PRESIDENT: Very much.

Q: And the Wagner Bill also?

THE PRESIDENT: Yes.

Q:   Will the Steel Code be ready today?

THE PRESIDENT:  Yes.  They are bringing it in at 11:30.  I have to go over one or two clauses in it before I actually decide on it.  I have until tomorrow night but I hope it will be in shape so I can sign it before I go away.

Q:   I notice in the morning papers that the two French flyers are coming down.

THE PRESIDENT:  11:30, also.

Q:   Are they bringing the Steel Code?  (Laughter)

THE PRESIDENT:  Yes, we are pressing everybody into service.

Q:   Do you still stand pat in your decision not to have a general conference for debts with all debtor nations?

THE PRESIDENT:  Somebody suggested that was the policy of the Hoover Administration, also this Administration.  (Laughter)

Q:   Any Message requiring legislation?

THE PRESIDENT:  No.  I think you can all guess on that fairly well.

Q:   There is a report from London that the British are making an offer on debts.  Have you received it yet?

THE PRESIDENT:  No.

Q:   Provided there is a general conference --

--- [379] ---

Q:   (interposing)  Has any nation indicated their intention about the June fifteenth installment?

THE PRESIDENT:  Not so far as I know, unless something came in the State Department yesterday.

Q:   Mr. President, do you care to comment on the court decision in the Weirton case?

THE PRESIDENT:  No, I have not read it so I cannot comment on it.  I have only seen the excerpt.

Q:   Any background on what is going on on the labor front?

THE PRESIDENT:  I don't think any more than what I said last week.  All these various strikes and threats of strikes in various places, we hope we will be able to iron out as many as we possibly can.  Of course we have ironed out a large number.  I suppose you saw that report of the Department of Labor showing a large number of strikes but showing a small number of working hours cut out?  That is pretty significant.  In other words, mediation has been more successfl than at any time in the past.  The length of time they stayed out has been distinctly shortened in a great majority of cases and, of course, it is the total number of hours out that count rather than the actual number of walkouts.

Q:   Can you tell us about any of the appointments to the Power Commission or
the R.F.C.?

THE PRESIDENT:   No.   I am going to try to do that on the train going and coming
during the next three days, all the various appointments.

Q:   Does that include the local appointments?

THE PRESIDENT:   Right.   But, Count (Rudolph de Zapp), I won't release anything
until I get back.

--- [380] ---

Q:   The two vacancies on the Mediation Board have been taken care of?

THE PRESIDENT:   Yes.

Q:   Are they going to be filled?

THE PRESIDENT:   That is something I have to go over.

Q:   When do you intend to make the appointment of Chief of Staff?

THE PRESIDENT:   I have not seen it.

Q:   In connection with the debts, does the fact that you aren't going to ask
any legislation mean that the new agreement with Finland is going to be
postponed?

THE PRESIDENT:   I do not know; I have not taken it up at all.

Q:   Can you tell us something about the sugar quotas for the Islands?

THE PRESIDENT:   Sugar quotas are going to be announced -- I think it is tomorrow.
We decided on them yesterday.   I guess I had better not anticipate the story
which you will get tomorrow.   I can tell you off the record, subject to the
announcement that the Department of Agriculture will make, that we have
had, of course, this shortage in allotments to divide around, which amounts
to a hundred thousand tons, because the Congress supplied us with an extra
one hundred thousand tons for the beet sugar people.   That means that based
on the same estimates of consumption, I have got to divide that one hundred
thousand tons around among Puerto Rico, the Philippines, Hawaii, and that
is an awful thing to do because it has got to be done on some concrete basis of previous production, and it will work a hardship on all of those
countries.   On the other hand, there is a distinct hope that during the
course of this sugar season we can give larger quotas to all of those five
outside places, outside the Continental limits, because of the reduction in
the actual beet sugar crop in this country.   Because of the drought there
has been quite a

--- [381] ---

shortage.   It does not run as high as fifty per cent, as some of the people
in Utah and Idaho and Wyoming claim, but it is a little bit early for us to
make a definite estimate.   It will probably be short of the 1,550,000 tons
allocated and the amount of that shortage -- my general thought in talking
with Agriculture yesterday was that we could divide that shortage and apply
half of it to a reduction of the carryover, which would be a good thing,

and the other half of it to increased allocations to Hawaii, Puerto Rico, etc. So the point I think you can make is that these allotments that will come out tomorrow are not necessarily final, that they are minimum, and that we hope to be able to increase them.

Q: You said this is off the record?

THE PRESIDENT: I think you had better hold it until the statement comes out tomorrow. I would rather have it break from the Department of Agriculture; they have all the figures.

Q: Have you had an opportunity to read Litvinov's proposal at Geneva for the establishment of a permanent security organization to which the nations --

THE PRESIDENT: (interposing) Only the headlines; we have not had the text of it yet.

Q: We cannot induce you to comment on it?

THE PRESIDENT: No.

Q: In connection with the debts, there seems to be an impression in Great Britain and also in France that if their Governments come forward with substantial token payments, some way may be found to dodge the Johnson Act?

THE PRESIDENT: That is hard to talk about until we have the whole proposi-

--- [382] ---

tion, because any proposition would have to be referred to the Attorney General if it related to the Johnson Act.

Q: Thank you, Mr. President.

THE PRESIDENT: I will be back Monday morning.

Press Conference #127
Aboard the Presidential Special Train at Worcester, Massachusetts
June 1, 1934


THE PRESIDENT: Look who we have here! What do you know?

Q: We are looking for a story, Mr. President.

THE PRESIDENT: My story would not even pay your expenses.

Q: Not here -- here we need an overcoat.

THE PRESIDENT: Everything is all quiet. I will have a few things for you tomorrow night.

Q: Will the debt Message go down today?


(The President did not hear the question.)


Q: Any chance of the war debts Message going down?

THE PRESIDENT: It is a very good story. Whenever they meet, both Houses.

Q: It has been completed?

THE PRESIDENT: Oh, yes.

Q: What did you think of that full-bearded sailor (at the Fleet Review)?

THE PRESIDENT: No, I did not see him.

Q: He looked exactly like the advertisement for cigarettes.

Q: How did you like the Review?

THE PRESIDENT: It was grand.

What are we going to do about the scoop the photographers made? Mac (Mr.
McIntyre) is terribly upset. They dropped plates overboard into a speed-
boat.

Q: Oh, yes; I saw that. (Laughter)

THE PRESIDENT: Mac did not sleep all night. We sent the others up [to New
York] with a destroyer or 32-footer.

Q: Still too late?

--- [384] ---

THE PRESIDENT: Still too later.

Q: Smart boys.

THE PRESIDENT:  You know what I said at Gettysburg?

Q:  Chiselers?

THE PRESIDENT:  Yes.  (Laughter)

Q:  Will you meet us here at the train tonight?

THE PRESIDENT:  I will get back when things are through [at Groton].

Q:  Have you received any word about this textile strike?

THE PRESIDENT:  Not a word.

Groton at 11:00, class exercises, luncheon at 1:00 and then after that, I may take a little drive and go down to the river and watch the Crew.  I cannot tell just what I will do.

Q:  Thank you, Mr. President.

THE PRESIDENT:  Well, have a good day.

Press Conference #128
Executive Offices of the White House
June 6, 1934, 10:45 A.M.


Q:   How about the District?

THE PRESIDENT:   I haven't a thing but I expect to have something by tomorrow on
     judgeships -- I hope so.

MR. DONALDSON:   All in.

THE PRESIDENT:   I would be very grateful if you would include in your stories
     this afternoon and tomorrow the announcement that the Corporate Bankruptcy
     Bill is going to be signed actually on the dot of noon tomorrow.  There
     are reasons why it should be known beforehand that it is going to be signed
     at a specific time on account of applications by corporations, etc., to
     various courts.  If it is given out ahead of time it prevents any one cor-
     poration from getting ahead of any other corporation.  So, at 12 noon to-
     morrow, on the dot, it will be actually signed and will become a law.

Q:   Are there any large companies among those?

THE PRESIDENT:   I haven't any idea.  It is a legal technicality but it is to
     prevent anybody from getting an advantage over anybody else.  Mac (Mr.
     McIntyre) says it is all right for me to read to you -- I do not know
     whether it should be off the record or not -- the following telegram which
     Mac received this morning:  (Reading)

          "Marvin McIntyre, Secretary to President, White House, Washing-
          ton, D. C.  Just received telegram from friend of Yale varsity
          who says that David Livingston rowing number four on junior
          varsity cannot go to New London to race against Harvard because
          of ROTC Engineering Camp.  Apparently no Senators have been
          able to excuse him and they wish father to intervene as soon
          as possible if anything can be done.  See you at the races I
          hope.

                                             Franklin Roosevelt, Jr."


                            --- [386] ---


So this unfortunate fellow, apparently having failed through Senatorial influence to get anywheres, it at last reaches the White House.

Q:   Are you going to let him go?

THE PRESIDENT:   I have turned it over to Steve, (Mr. Early) who is very high in
     the War Department, as you know, to let Steve see what he can do.

Q:   Do you mind if we use this?

THE PRESIDENT:   I think you can use it, if you want.  It is rather amusing,
     especially about the Senators.  It would be awful if Steve didn't get the
     poor fellow off.  (Laughter)

I don't think there is any particular news.  The drought message, you all
know about.  There has been nothing since yesterday morning's conference.
I think, just for your information, I might explain one thing to you and
that is what I said to the Senators and Congressmen yesterday.  Of course,
in a very real sense, this is more than a drought.  It comes pretty close
to reaching the proportions of a disaster because of the number of people
affected and affected in a way which -- well, the burning of a great city
might affect just as many individuals but on the other hand, work, if a
city burns up, is immediately available and it is a great deal of work to
clear the ruins.  These poor people on these farms have no work available
for them and in a large portion of this area, even if it rains from now
on, there will be a great many thousands of families who won't be able to
raise anything out of the ground or keep the cattle going.  In other words,
they won't be able to sustain themselves until 1935.

--- [387] ---

As far as the money end of it is concerned, I said to the people from the
Hill yesterday morning, "Of course, the Government has to take care of a
disaster of that size."  We have two ways of going about it.  One is to use
the authority to switch funds, which is in the Appropriations Bill.  In
other words, without asking for any more money by direct appropriation, we
probably could have taken the amount, somewhere around half a billion
dollars -- we don't know the exact amount yet, out of R.F.C. because R.F.C.
under the law, has the authority to raise the money itself.  In other
words, it is totally available and we could transfer it to relief purposes.
But the more I thought it over the more I thought that R.F.C. was frankly
organized for a rather different purpose and it would be a much cleaner
and honest thing to do to make a straight appropriation.  Actually, of
course, the amount of money which it obligates the Treasury to pay is
exactly the same.  If we took it out of R.F.C. it would be disguised
whereas, in this way, it appears in the open and it is much better to do
it in the open.  The total amount of the Government debt under either
method would be exactly the same.

I don't know yet whether I will send the message up today or wait a few
days for further information and we don't know yet whether it will be a
separate bill or whether it will be put on as an amendment to the existing
Deficiency Appropriation Bill.  You will probably know that in the next
twenty-four hours.

Q:   This won't increase the spending program?

THE PRESIDENT:  Oh, my, yes.

Q:   It will be besides the budget, in other words?

THE PRESIDENT:  It will be in addition to the budget, no question of that.  Of
     course the budget was done when nobody had any idea that this

--- [388] ---

major catastrophe was going to happen.  If it came out of R.F.C. borrowing
power it would appear in expenditures and not in appropriations.  This way
it appears in both expenditures and appropriations.

Q:   You won't have a balanced budget in 1936 then?

THE PRESIDENT: Let us cross that bridge when we come to it. If it is not balanced, then it will be balanced by an amount necessary to take care of an unforseeable major calamity. Therefore, in writing the story, I think you should write the whole story, not just a lead saying that a balanced budget is overboard.

Q:    Can you tell us anything about the conference of the automobile men on the Wagner Bill yesterday?

THE PRESIDENT: We didn't talk about the Wagner Bill especially, we talked about the general subject. They thought things were working out pretty well in their industry.

Q:    They seemed to think that the Wagner Bill had upset their Labor Board out there.

THE PRESIDENT: Well, that is a question about which I don't know.

Q:    Is there anything on the legislative situation?

THE PRESIDENT: No, I don't think I had better discuss the individual bills up there because, after all, the thing is up there. All of these various bills are up there and the leaders are doing their best to get as much through as they can. I don't want, at this particular time, to label bills in classes A, B or C because the situation changes from hour to hour and primarily, at the present time, it is the responsibility of Congress.

The only thing I have sent up is that message, to which I don't think there will be any opposition, about turning over some second-

--- [389] ---

hand rifles and a few old shacks down in Haiti but I sent up word that if there is any opposition to that great act of generosity on our  part, not to hold up the Session on account of that.

Q:    Could I go back for a moment to the drought situation?  Are there any estimates of the number of people affected?

THE PRESIDENT: At the present time, in the emergency drought areas -- in other words, the ones that are marked red on the chart, on the map -- there are probably 125,000 families.

Then, in the blue area, from which we are taking a certain number of counties almost every day and adding them to the red area because it is getting worse, that blue area covers such a very large territory that I don't think we have made any check-up on the number of families. Of course, the blue area has a bit of hope of being able to raise some supplies the balance of the season.

Another thing that is tremendously important -- I have spoken about it before but in spite of that there have been some stories -- there is no danger of human famine. Let us get that and repeat it and repeat it. I am going to repeat it this week again and again until I go away. There is no danger of human famine.

There will be probably several million head of cattle which have got to the point where it is cheaper to kill them and can them than it is to try to

bring food in from long distances, especially because of the fact that in
a great many areas there is not enough water for those cattle and it is
almost impossible to bring water in by rail.  But there is no danger of
human famine.  There is plenty of carryover.

Q:     Mr. President, with reference to that report you sent up the day before

--- [390] ---

yesterday, concerning the survey of the drainage areas of the United
States, I notice the one dealing with the Great Lakes presupposes the
building of the St. Lawrence Seaway.  Anything you can tell us about that?
Are they going to negotiate a new treaty or anything of that sort during
recess?

THE PRESIDENT:  All I can tell you is off the record on the St. Lawrence.  It
has got to be off the record because I have not done anything on it.  Dur--
ing the course of the summer probably I will be in touch with the Canadian
Government and also with our own people in the Senate here and see what we
can do.  The only thing we have to bear in mind, very firmly, is that we
haven't by any means abandoned the St. Lawrence Seaway.  We are going ahead
with it but as to the time and method, as to whether there will be any
amendments to the Treaty, I cannot say, because I have not taken it up.

Q:     Can you tell us anything about the application of Chemical Foundation for
funds to develop pine pulp paper in Georgia?

THE PRESIDENT:  I haven't heard.  Was it applied for?

Q:     Dr. Ezekiel made a rather adverse report on it when it was referred to the
Agricultural Department.

THE PRESIDENT:  I did not know it was referred.  What was the name of my friend
down there?

Q:     Dr. Herty.

THE PRESIDENT:  All I have seen was a delightful pamphlet telling about the experiments but, as I remember it, that pamphlet gave the suggestion that
there ought to be another year or two before going ahead on a large commercial basis.

Q:     I understand they are asking $4,000,000 to develop it, that is, to

--- [391] ---

produce commercial paper in a limited way?

THE PRESIDENT:  I do not believe that Public Works funds can be used for purely
development experiments.  I rather doubt it.  If they had something that
was practical, something to go ahead with, it would be a bit different, but
I don't think they are ready to go ahead on a commercial sized plant.

Q:     That is one point that Dr. Ezekiel raised.

THE PRESIDENT:  I am tremendously keen about the thing.  Herty has been down to
the Springs [Warm Springs] and talked to me about it.

Q:     It was announced that Robinson [Senator Joe Robinson] and McNary [Senator McNary] would come up and see you sometime relative to the legislative program.  Is there anything on that?

THE PRESIDENT:  (turning to Mr. McIntyre)  You have not heard anything?

MR. McINTYRE:  No, sir.

Q:     Have you anything on the threatened steel strike?

THE PRESIDENT:  Nothing, except that Hugh Johnson told me yesterday he was still negotiating.

Q:     Have you had a report from the West Coast, from Mr. McGrady [Assistant Secretary of Labor McGrady] in connection with a dock workers' strike out there?

THE PRESIDENT:  No, the only thing I got was that Miss Perkins showed me yesterday a telegram which sounded a bit hopeful, but I think you will have to get it from her.  It looked like better news than we had yesterday morning.

Q:     When you sign the Stock Market Bill, will you be ready to announce the membership of the Commission?

THE PRESIDENT:  No, sir.  It really is true that I have given absolutely no consideration to it.  I suppose I have had fifty or a hundred

--- [392] ---

names submitted and I put them all into a folder and I suppose I will dig it out after Congress goes home.  But I really have not thought about it, despite the fact that New York has announced the membership.

Q:     Anything in the report that Senator Blaine is going to be selected to the R.F.C. before Congress goes home?

THE PRESIDENT:  Yes -- wait a minute -- I haven't got anybody yet, but I am going to send up a name for the Federal Power Commission today.

Q:     In spite of the fact that we have repeatedly told Great Britain that we are willing to listen, they insist that it is up to us to make the first move?

THE PRESIDENT:  I think the only thing to do is to read the Message I sent to the Congress.

Q:     Is it likely you will have any time to receive any European debt missions before you leave?

THE PRESIDENT:  Are any coming over?  They will have to hurry.

Q:     Thank you, Mr. President.

Q:     Can you mention the name of the appointee to the Federal Power Commission?

THE PRESIDENT:  Just as soon as it comes up.

Steve (Mr. Early) suggests if you want to write that St. Lawrence story on your own responsibility, it is all right.

Q:   In connection with that watershed report?

THE PRESIDENT:   Yes.

Q:   Has anything definite been settled on the drought area, the section that is suffering?

THE PRESIDENT:   The only way I can answer that is this way.   I do not know yet how much free money we will have in Public Works in the coming

--- [393] ---

fiscal year and how much will be necessary to carry on existing projects like the Upper Mississippi and Fort Peck, et cetera.   We have not yet discussed how much balance there will be for new projects, but undoubtedly if some of those Upper Missouri projects look pretty good and do not cost very much and will help in this drought area, we may spend some of the Public Works money on that, but we have not got to the point of any decision.

Q:   I understand you have been conferring with some of the Naval officers about the forthcoming talks in London.   Can you give us any intimation of what the attitude of the United States will be?

THE PRESIDENT:   The only thing is that some officers are going over very shortly for preliminary conversations.   That is all.   We won't have any announcement to make at all as to what the policy is.   It will probably come out of London, not here.

Q:   Who is going over?

THE PRESIDENT:   Admiral Leahy -- ask the State Department if there is any reason why the personnel, as to who is going over, should not be --

Q:   (interposing)   It has been made public.

Q:   Are we going to have any platform?

THE PRESIDENT:   No, just conversations.   (Laughter)

Q:   What are the chances on [visiting] Green Bay [Wisconsin]?

THE PRESIDENT:   I hope to get there but it is not definite.

Q:   Will there by any chance of going anywhere else in the State [of Wisconsin]?

THE PRESIDENT:   No.   I hope to do it just at the end of July.

Press Conference #129
Executive Offices of the White House
June 8, 1934, 4:00 P.M.


THE PRESIDENT: Remember that white clothes are much cheaper in Puerto Rico and Panama than here.

Q: We will remember that, Mr. President.

Q: We will need them much more there than here.

Q: I think it will be cheaper for us to buy a couple of suits of dungarees before we leave.

THE PRESIDENT: They are supplied free of charge by the Navy.

Q: You have to pay for them.

THE PRESIDENT: You do? I did not know that.

Q: You can put it on the expense account. (Laughter)

MR. DONALDSON: All in.

THE PRESIDENT: I do not think there is any news except I suggested to The Three Musketeers that white suits are cheaper in Puerto Rico and Panama than here.

Q: That suits us.

Q: We will travel light, then, until we get there.

Q: We may send some back, duty free, for those that don't go.

THE PRESIDENT: I should think so; they are going to charge them to the expense account.

Q: Have you any comment to make on the selection of Fletcher as the new Republican leader?

THE PRESIDENT: No comment on the record but off the record entirely I can repeat to you what I said to Steve (Mr. Early) about it. I said, "De mortius nil nisi bonum." (Laughter)

--- [395] ---

Q: I think it is safe to put that on the record.

THE PRESIDENT: Steve (Mr. Early) said, "Is that a compliment or not?" (Laughter)

I do not think there is any particular news.

Q: What did you really say there?

THE PRESIDENT: I will tell you about the middle of the Pacific Ocean. (Laughter)

Q:     In the Message you say you hope to present a plan to the next Congress.
       That means you will have a commission to study the problem during the sum-
       mer months?

THE PRESIDENT:  I do not know that I will dignify it by the name of a commis-
       sion.  I will do most of the work myself on it.  I have nothing to do this
       summer.  In other words, I will have quite a lot of conferences with the
       War Department, the Reclamation Service, etc, and it may develop into some
       kind of a reviewing commission.  I will handle most of it myself.  That is,
       the land and water, the big drought thing.

Q:     When do you sign the Tariff Bill?

THE PRESIDENT:  I do not think until Monday because there is some kind of com-
       plication about the sugar allotments.  They want to get that out of the way
       first.  I approved that today.

Q:     Mr. President, is there anything you can tell us further about the steel
       situation?  Did you discuss it with Miss Perkins today?

THE PRESIDENT:  The only thing I know is what came out of the ticker [the United
       Press ticker in Mr. Early's room] about three or five minutes ago.  They
       announced something.  I have not heard since then.

Q:     When will you sign the Air Mail Bill?

--- [396] ---

THE PRESIDENT:  That has not come down yet.

Q:     Mr. President, did you get a protest from Senator George and others about
       the attitude of Dr. Ezekiel toward the Chemical Foundation's application
       for money to develop wood pulp paper in Georgia?

THE PRESIDENT:  Oh, yes; I do not know whether you could call it a protest or
       not because I have not seen what Dr. Ezekiel said.  Anyway, I wrote a letter
       on it to somebody, saying I was very much interested in wood pulp made from
       yellow pine.

Q:     Can we have a copy of it?

THE PRESIDENT:  I think it has to be released down there.

MR. EARLY:  You remember the statement you made about the forest conservation.
       That was announced earlier.

THE PRESIDENT:  You did that?

MR. EARLY:  Yes, sir.

THE PRESIDENT:  Steve (Mr. Early) handed out something earlier that took care of
       it.

Q:     I thought what they objected to was that the Chemical Foundation was rais-
       ing the point that seventy per cent of the paper stock was imported and
       Dr. Ezekiel said it was not altogether an evil, that the foreign countries
       used that money to buy American exports, and they construed it as throwing

cold water on this application.

THE PRESIDENT: I do not know what he said but of course the real answer is this: that to make pulp as a general proposition out of an American wood supplied in the North, that supply of wood is decreasing at such a fast rate already that there won't be any woods left. It is obviously the economic thing to do if we can use this yellow scratch pine in the South, which is not being used for anything else, to make

--- [397] ---

paper. That will be all to the good, as long as we replace it as fast as we can. That is the catch to it.

Q: Would you care to say anything about the luncheon today with the Japanese Prince?

THE PRESIDENT: Just a luncheon of courtesy and a visit of courtesy. Very nice time.

Q: Nothing political?

THE PRESIDENT: No.

Q: Did the Labor Board go through?

THE PRESIDENT: I do not know.

Q: Is the Ickes Oil Controll Bill as necessary as it was two weeks ago?

THE PRESIDENT: I have complete ignorance on the subject.

Q: I thought perhaps you might know.

THE PRESIDENT: I have not heard what is happening in Congress since the Vice President got here at 2:00 o'clock.

Q: That is a long while ago. (Laughter)

Q: I understood you to say that the Wagner Bill was not slated to go through?

THE PRESIDENT: I have not heard anything about it since 2:00 o'clock.

Q: Anything about Harry Newton as a member of the Federal Home Loan Board?

THE PRESIDENT: No; I do not think his time is up until July twenty-first. I have not done anything about it.

Q: Any Tariff Commission appointments in mind?

THE PRESIDENT: No. Frankly, on the Tariff Commission, until I have had a chance to have a general talk about it, I do not know whether I am going to fill those two vacancies or not. The thought, as I think I told you all about six months ago, is that four people on the Tariff Commission may not be necessary. I have not discussed the

--- [398] ---

details of it since then.  I suppose, after the Tariff Bill is signed and Congress goes home we will have a general conference on the tariff situation with this Interdepartmental Foreign Trade Committee that is operating and the Tariff Commission to determine whether we should fill those two vacancies or not.

Q:  There is a third vacancy coming up this month, isn't there?

THE PRESIDENT:  I did not know that; who is it?

Q:  Dr. Porter.

THE PRESIDENT:  I did not know that.

Q:  How about the R.F.C. appointment?

THE PRESIDENT:  R.F.C ?  No.  I hope soon.

Q:  Mr. President, have you had any personal part recently in the trade and credit discussions with the Russian people?

THE PRESIDENT:  I have not heard a word on it for a couple of weeks.

Q:  On the tariff, how soon do you think you can get any actual bargaining on that under this new Bill?

THE PRESIDENT:  I think you will have to ask the State Department for details. As I understand it, they have got at least half a dozen nations that they are holding preliminary discussions with already.

Q:  Mr. President, in view of the fact that an agreement has been reached on the Communications Bill in conference, is there anything you can tell us with reference to the plans in reference to that Commission?

THE PRESIDENT:  No, I have not even thought about who is to go on it.  Do you happen to know whether that goes into effect immediately or does it go into effect --

Q:  (interposing)  July first.

THE PRESIDENT:  July first?  Then I won't think about it until after Congress

--- [399] ---

goes home.  I am putting off everything I can until Congress goes home.

Q:  Do you think they will go?

THE PRESIDENT:  Oh, I think so.

Q:  Do you plan to put the Housing Bill through?

THE PRESIDENT:  I think so, very much.  That is an essential thing.

Q:  What instructions are our delegates carrying to London with respect to this Conference preliminary to the Naval Conference?

THE PRESIDENT: That will break from London rather than from here.

Q: Will there be any surprises?

THE PRESIDENT: I do not know.

Q: Are you going to allow your secretary (Mr. Early) to go through with that golf match?

Q: He ought to give Lew Douglas some ideas.

THE PRESIDENT: There is a catch. Lew Douglas is to keep score so Steve (Mr. Early) is perfectly safe. It will be a low score.

Q: Any further reports from the drought area?

THE PRESIDENT: No. Acting Secretary Tugwell gave us a very interesting picture of it in the Cabinet meeting. Of course a great many people are going to be affected who are not on farms. That will be one reason why this Bill that goes in tomorrow is going to carry the provision for putting on relief the people in cities who are thrown out of work because of lack of cattle and wheat coming into the cities. The preliminary, tentative estimate for that is about fifty million dollars more which is to take care of city people thrown out of work. The general thought, in taking care of these drought areas, is that we are doing everything possible to get people to plant, try-

--- [400] ---

ing to get seed to them, to plant any kind of a crop that has a chance of frowing from now on. Of course in certain areas you can plant -- it we get a good deal of rain -- you can plant certain crops up to the first or tenth of July and they will mature sufficiently to take care of the soil, the ground, and provide a certain amount of forage. The chief problem, in general, is the question of forage for livestock, and that is very serious.

Q: Should this drought make any difference in the crop production loans?

THE PRESIDENT: In what?

Q: Your attitude toward crop production loans?

THE PRESIDENT: No.

Q: How about the seed loans?

THE PRESIDENT: Oh, you mean that. Of course those seed loans are primarily cotton loans, not affected by the drought one way or the other. Nearly all of it is cotton.

Q: Do you know whether they plan to handle that as a separate piece of legislation?

THE PRESIDENT: The latest is that it will be tacked on as an amendment in the Senate.

Q: That is fifty million more? What is the total?

THE PRESIDENT: Five hundred and twenty-five million.

Q: Have you heard anything on the Pacific longshoremen's strike?

THE PRESIDENT: I have not heard anything since yesterday, when it looked pretty favorable.

Q: Is there any steel conference scheduled for the week end, or in sight?

THE PRESIDENT: I have no idea. The thing changes from minute to minute.

Q: What is your view on the crop curtailment in the light of the drought?

--- [401] ---

THE PRESIDENT: How do you mean, what is the view on it?

Q: Do you still think it is a desirable thing?

THE PRESIDENT: Has nothing to do, one way or the other; no connection.

Q: The drought affects the crop.

THE PRESIDENT: Which means that next year, if there isn't any carryover on a given crop, you increase the amount of crops that may be sown so as to provide for the estimated annual consumption plus a surplus.

Q: Any further -- (interruption)

THE PRESIDENT: In other words, let us take a very good example of what you might call the eastern city point of view that does not know the difference between barley and wheat. People are apt to jump at the conclusion that there is a connection between a drought and crop curtailment. Of course, there is absolutely no connection whatsoever. The whole theory of crop curtailment is to prevent excessive surpluses. That is because excessive surpluses or carryovers force down the price to such an extent that the farmer cannot make both ends meet. If you have an adequate surplus to take care of a crop failure one season, that is all you need. Only it ought to be absolutely sufficient to take care of a failure, as it will be this year. There is enough food in the country. Now, the next year, you not only plant to grow enough crop to take care of the demand, the consumption, for the following year but also enough to establish a surplus.

Q: Would it be a surplus that the farmer or the Government might own?

THE PRESIDENT: We haven't got to that stage yet in determining that. Of course, it has been under discussion for four or five years as to whether surpluses should be owned or controlled by the Government.

Q: Mr. President, on this loan, is your attitude toward the Three A amendments unchanged?

--- [402] ---

THE PRESIDENT: I think they are advisable.

Q: You still wish to see them go through?

THE PRESIDENT:  Yes.

Q:   What is your attitude on the Ickes oil control?

THE PRESIDENT:  Unchanged.  I hope we will get it because, as I understand this decision down in Louisiana, it is pretty good but only covers the particular case before the court and we are dependent, without the oil bill, on whatever the courts may decide between now and next January.

Q:   Can you throw any light on the conference with Perkins?

THE PRESIDENT:  What did we talk about?

Q:   Steel, by any chance?

THE PRESIDENT:  Only for a minute, that is about all.  I do not know whether -- we talked about various departmental matters.

Q:   It was not only the steel industry?

THE PRESIDENT:  No.

Q:   Have you any more plans for the social service?

THE PRESIDENT:  We will have to keep on studying.  We have been at it now for six months.

Q:   No commissions or anything like that?

THE PRESIDENT:  No.  Probably handle it myself like the other one.

Q:   What did Mr. Eastman have up the other day?

THE PRESIDENT:  To tell you the truth, I have forgotten.  We did talk about the bills up there and he hopes to get some of them through.  Which ones, I could not tell you.  You will have to ask him.  He still thinks there is a chance.

(The Press Conference adjourned at 4:25 P.M.)

MR. DONALDSON: All in.

THE PRESIDENT: I do not believe there is any news today at all.

Q: Tell us about the 22 billions. [Referring to the report by George Peek]

THE PRESIDENT: You have this [indicating printed report]. This is George Peek's story, given out on foreign trade. I do not know whether you are familiar with it but apparently it is the first time it has ever been done. This is something already given out by George Peek's office so I suppose you are all familiar with it. It is what might be called a preliminary estimate and subject of further studies, but it is the first thing of its kind that has been attempted, showing the total of American exports and imports from 1896 down and through 1933. In other words, it is a thirty-seven or thirty-eight-year period.

I suppose most people have the idea that during that period, because we had an apparently favorable export balance, that this country has made a lot of money out of its foreign trade. Well, these figures that George Peek's office has been working out, which have been at least partly checked by the Department of Commerce, rather disprove the theory that the United States makes a lot of money out of its so-called favorable balance. You will have to read the letter to me to get the details of it. The rough figures are that during this whole period we sold to the world goods to the amount of 121 billions -- that is billions, don't make it millions -- and we bought from the world goods valued at 84 billions, so there

--- [404] ---

is an apparently favorable balance to the United States of 36 billion dollars, which means that, in another way of putting it, our imports were only seventy per cent of our exports.

But, as against that apparently favorable balance of 36 billions, George Peek says that we ought, in fairness, to deduct the amount that good Americans spent on their trips to Paris, in other words the tourist money, which amounts to 19 billions, so with that deduction it leaves an apparently favorable trade balance of only 17 billion dollars.

Then, you have two other amounts that you have to take into consideration. First, the services rendered by us to the world in shipping and freight services, interest and dividend payments, interest and principal payments of various debts, etc., which add to the amount owed us 26 billions, making a total owed us of 46 billions. Of course, if you do that, you have to charge off the other side of the picture and deduct the services rendered to us by the world shipping and trade services, interest and dividend payments on all foreigners' investments in the United States, things of that kind, and net gold imports, which would reduce the world debt of 43 billions by 21 billions, which would show that during this 38-year period the net amount owed to the United States is about 22 billion dollars.

And then, Peek makes the point that that 22 billion dollars, which is the

net profit -- the easiest way of putting it -- the net profit of all of our
foreign dealings, that that 22 billion dollars has not been paid us, that
we have only got evidences of indebtedness, so that if those evidences of
indebtedness are paid, then we will be 22 billion dollars better off for
this 38-year period.

--- [405] ---

Now, of course, that is a very interesting thing and I suppose all of you
people who know more of these things then I do will be able to write some
fascinating stories; then you will turn it over to the headline man and he
will do some more editing. However, it is a fine subject to go into because, as far as I know, this is the first time there has ever been what
might be called a serious attempt to estimate these figures and perhaps a
lot of people will dispute them.

Q:  Does it mean that the world welshes on their debts?

THE PRESIDENT:  Oh, no.

Q:  How do they owe us 22 billion dollars?

THE PRESIDENT:  Well, they have not paid us the favorable balance of trade in
cash.

Q:  What are the evidences of indebtedness?

THE PRESIDENT:  I will have to study it some more before I answer that question.
Well, there are balances that various American firms have in Europe, which
they cannot bring back here.  The whole foreign exchange situation is involved in that.  Then there are notes of foreign corporations, bonds of
municipalities, their notes and bonds of all kinds of foreign corporations
that are held here, not only by investors but by companies.  If the General
Electric (for example) sells a lot of equipment to some private concern in
Italy, it takes notes of that private concern over a period of years,
part cash and part notes.  In other words, it is all the various mercantile
type of debts.

Q:  A good part of that is liquid short-term stuff?

THE PRESIDENT:  Yes.

Q:  Is it true that the whole 22 million dollars, none of it has been paid in
cash?

--- [406] ---

THE PRESIDENT:  22 billions.  That is the net part that has not been paid in
cash.  In other words, all the rest has been paid, just the same as we paid
for what we bought.

Q:  Is it true that goods and services of foreign countries must be accepted by
us if this country is to be paid off?

THE PRESIDENT:  That, of course, is much too definite a statement because goods
and services are one form of payment, only one form.  Just the same way as
the reply the Secretary of State made.  For example, there are large headlines in the papers which would give the average layman who reads those

papers -- it is the headline fellow's fault, not yours -- the idea that we
had definitely made an offer to Great Britain that they could pay all their
debt by sending us goods. That is what the layman gets from reading that
type of headline in the morning papers. If you will read Hull's reply carefully, you will see that that kind of headline was unjustified.

Q:    In that connection, the London dispatches state that the British are a
little puzzled by what we mean. Do we mean we would be willing to open our
markets here sufficiently to permit them to accumulate dollar balances
here?

THE PRESIDENT:  We would be willing to discuss that with them as they has suggested on several previous occasions, in order to avoid the obstacle they
raised, which was the payment in cash. We would be entirely willing to go
along and talk about what they had suggested, which was partial payment in
kind, but very partial. Obviously, you cannot transfer the whole -- what
did they agree to pay us, 350 or 400 million dollars? Of course that could
not be paid in kind.

Q:    Isn't it a safe guess we are not going to open our markets to permit

--- [407] ---

them to accumulate dollar balances here?

THE PRESIDENT:  That is a perfectly impossible question to answer. You cannot
answer yes or no unless you start beating your wife. In other words, suppose we had agreed to take some tin. I just take that out of the air because I saw it in the paper this morning. Suppose we agree to take a certain amount of tin which we do not produce, does that open the markets in
this country or not?

You can't write a definitive story on any of this stuff; that is the real
answer. I could not if I tried.

Q:    Isn't the main purpose of this note to keep the debt question open?

THE PRESIDENT:  No, the main purpose is to answer the British note.

Q:    Coming back to the Peek Report for a moment, he says in his report that the
figures show that the international trade has been cumulatively disadvan-
tageous to us and he says we have to make a new approach. Has he made any
definite suggestions to you as to what the new approach might be?

THE PRESIDENT:  No. As I say, this is the first time these figures have been
worked up. Then, too, he divides them into a series of periods which are
quite interesting: 1896 to 1914; 1914 to 1922, which is really the war
period; 1923 to 1929, which is really the madness period; and 1930 to 1933,
which is what might be called the reconstruction period.

Q:    What, if any, moral might be drawn from the figures?

THE PRESIDENT:  None, absolutely none. That is exactly what I am trying to drive
home, that nobody is trying to point any moral or do anything more about it
except to give out these figures for people to think about and get interested in.

--- [408] ---

Q: What effect on your policy in negotiating reciprocal trade agreements will that report have?

THE PRESIDENT: I have not any idea, any more than you have.

Q: You signed a bill of great importance to the District -- I am spokesman here for the District --

THE PRESIDENT: (interposing) Right.

Q: That is the Alley Improvement Bill and in that it says that an agency is to be appointed to take the matter in hand. Have you decided who is to be appointed?

THE PRESIDENT: No. I asked the Commissioners and Mrs. Hopkins to talk over the formation of an agency and to come in and talk to me about it before I go away, because I would like to have something started.

I also told them another thing which, for the District, I suppose has some news value, which was that they have got $500,000 to start this work and I am very keen to see if we cannot increase that sum, how much I do not know, but I do not think that $500,000 is enough on the first year of the operation of this Bill.

Q: How about public works? Where will that come from?

THE PRESIDENT: Public works? Another thing I told the Commissioners is what my position is -- it has always been the same -- I would like to see Washington, D. C., as the best residential city in the United States. But, on the other side of the picture, I do not think the capital of the United States should ever become an industrial or manufacturing city. It would be a shame. It involves all sorts of difficult problems. Let's keep it the best residential city of the United States and stop there.

--- [409] ---

Q: Has the Tariff Bill been signed or are you giving it any further thought immediately?

THE PRESIDENT: No.

Q: The labor disputes compromise -- is there anything on that?

THE PRESIDENT: We are not ready on that because they are talking about it up on the Hill and I suppose I will hear something about it at two or three o'clock this afternoon.

Q: Can you comment on the Goldsborough Bill, parts of which were drawn by the General Motors Acceptance Corporation and the Johns-Manville Acceptance Corporation?

THE PRESIDENT: No, except that everybody is making allegations up there. Some are saying that the Building and Loan Associations are behind the effort to give them more money and eliminate other forms of guarantees. Frankly, I do not know anything about the cat fight going on up there in the Committee.

Q:   Do you want to comment on the House amendments to the Bill?

THE PRESIDENT:   I think it is pretty well known I am not for them.

Q:   How about the new Senate Bill to put it on an administrator?

THE PRESIDENT:   I do not know enough about it.  What are they going to do?

Q:   There is a substitute bill before the Senate Committee which would set up a Federal Housing Administration and put everything in the hands of the Administrator.

THE PRESIDENT:   What did the original bill set up?

Q:   Very much like the House bill, in different sections.

THE PRESIDENT:   What kind of an administration.

Q:   I think all under the R.F.C. in the House bill.  I haven't analyzed that.

THE PRESIDENT:   I don't know enough about the details.

--- [410] ---

Q:   There is a new bill up there.

THE PRESIDENT:   Where?

Q:   In the Committee.

THE PRESIDENT:   In the Senate?

Q:   Yes.

THE PRESIDENT:   How does it differ?

Q:   It puts everything under the Federal Housing Administrator.

THE PRESIDENT:   I do not think it makes a lot of difference who administers it.

Q:   It is an entirely different bill.  I am not familiar with the details.

THE PRESIDENT:   It is a terribly complicated bill.  I read the original through and have not looked at the substitute or amendments or anything else.

Q:   Should the Bill finally come down here so messed up that it is unworkable, is it likely you will veto it?  (Laughter)

THE PRESIDENT:   If it is unworkable, I certainly will.

Q:   Have you any comment to make on Mr. Tugwell's victory before the Senate Agricultural Committee?

THE PRESIDENT:   I think I had better not.

Q:   Have you a Latin comment on that?

THE PRESIDENT:   There is a certain restraint one must exercise.

Q:   Are you in favor of convict labor on roads?

THE PRESIDENT:  Where?

Q:   In Virginia.

THE PRESIDENT:  I haven't any idea; that is a state matter.  We did use them in the State of New York in winter camps.

Q:   In view of the numerous and sundry reports and the changes made on

--- [411] ---

N.R.A., can you give us an outline of your own ideas on the ultimate setup? Does it appear to be shaping up?

THE PRESIDENT:  When I do, it will take forty-eight hours to explain it.

Q:   What are the prospects of adjourning?

THE PRESIDENT:  You will have to ask them up there, I do not know.  Ask John Garner; he is a pretty good guesser.

Q:   Going back to your stand that Washington should not be an industrial city, does that entail greater financial responsibility on the Federal Government for its maintenance?

THE PRESIDENT:  Why should it?

Q:   Industrial development might bring more money.

THE PRESIDENT:  Yes, but good housing conditions bring good receipts too.

Q:   There is a story printed today to the effect that there is a new relief plan whereby unemployed will be put in closed factories and start canning our surplus goods.

THE PRESIDENT:  I read it.  Did that come from Hopkins?

Q:   I do not know where it came from.

THE PRESIDENT:  I guess that probably was a hot weather story.

Q:   I believe the morning story is that they are going to take over a couple of factories and run them.

THE PRESIDENT:  I saw the headline and read the lead; that is all.

Q:   The story seemed to put it rather definitely as the plan of the Federal Emergency Relief?

THE PRESIDENT:  That is new to me.  I never heard it.

Q:   What are the prospects of Governor George White, of Ohio, being given a Federal position?

THE PRESIDENT:  I haven't the faintest idea.

--- [412] ---

Q:   Are you considering a cut in the Canadian whiskey duty?

THE PRESIDENT:   I have not heard about it.  Does it have to come from me?


(The Press Conference adjourned at 11:15 A.M.)

Press Conference #130
Executive Offices of the White House
June 15, 1934, 4:10 P.M.


Q:    That is Stevie's (Mr. Stephenson) presidential suit.

THE PRESIDENT:  Is it his presidential suit.  Looks to me as if he has outgrown
      it in front.  He will lose a lot of that on the destroyer.

Q:    Yes, leaning over the rail.

MR. DONALDSON:  All in.

THE PRESIDENT:  I think all the news is up on the other end of Pennsylvania
      Avenue today.  Things are happening up there and you know more about it
      than I do.

Q:    Is it going fast enough?

THE PRESIDENT:  Oh, I think so; going along all right.

Q:    When does it look like you are going to get it?

THE PRESIDENT:  I have not heard within the last hour.

Q:    What did you hear then?

THE PRESIDENT:  Fifty-fifty.

Q:    Can you tell us whether you are contemplating any action with regard to
      Germany's latest moratorium, that is anything in the nature of representa-
      tions to them?

THE PRESIDENT:  I do not know.  The Secretary of State mentioned in Cabinet
      Meeting that they are studying the effect of the German action.  I do not
      know whether they have taken it up with the German Ambassador yet or not.

Q:    In the absence of our friend, the Count (Rudolph de Zapp), are you getting
      anywhere near that judgeship appointment in the Municipal Court?

                          --- [414] ---

THE PRESIDENT:  God!  You know, I had entirely forgotten it.

Q:    The Attorney General thought he would send a name over here?

THE PRESIDENT:  Will you make a note of that to ask about it?  It will have to
      go up fairly soon.

Q:    The term of Frank McNinch (Chairman of the Federal Power Commission) expires
      next week.  Have you definitely decided --

THE PRESIDENT:  (interposing)  When does it expire?

Q:    The twenty-third [the term actually expired on the twenty-second].

THE PRESIDENT: I have not done anything about it at all.

Q: Isn't there another vacancy on that Commission?

THE PRESIDENT: No, I filled that the other day, Mr. Seavey.

Q: Mr. President, is the Mediation Board going to be filled, Railroad Mediation?

THE PRESIDENT: I doubt it. Something might happen between now and tomorrow night, but I doubt it.

Q: What about a new Public Printer?

THE PRESIDENT: Won't be anything until after the session anyway.

Q: Any more Tariff Commission appointments?

THE PRESIDENT: I do not think so.

Q: Have you signed the Communications Commission Bill today?

THE PRESIDENT: Has it come down to me yet? I do not think it has. It has not got in here yet. The only bill I have on my desk, not acted on, has to do with the Cherokee Indians.

Q: Do you intend to appoint the members to the Communications Commission before you go?

THE PRESIDENT: Yes.

Q: The New York Evening Post carries the story today that Mayor Hague has

--- [415] ---

invited the New York manufacturers to come over to his town with their plants and that there would be no strike trouble. The Chief of Police issued an order forbidding picketing and the National Labor Board said it was powerless. Anything submitted to you yet?

THE PRESIDENT: I think that is the usual attempt of Jersey City to steal New York's business.

Q: The matter has not been laid before you?

THE PRESIDENT: I never heard of it.

Q: Inasmuch as it is [war] debt payday, can I induce you to comment on the generosity of the debtors?

THE PRESIDENT: No.

Q: Can you tell us anything about your plans for the summer other than --

THE PRESIDENT: (interposing) I suppose you would like to know, Fred (Mr. Storm). Well, the only thing that is definite is that the actual date of departure is indefinite. In other words, I do not know what day we are going to push off. I might put it off three or four days to give me a little bit more time to go up to New London and then come back here for three or four days just to clear up odds and ends and then push off from Annapolis instead of New York. But the date is on a moveable basis, some time, we hope, between the twenty-sixth of June and the fourth of July. That is as near as I can give it.

Q:   Have you given any thought to touching at any ports?

THE PRESIDENT:   Yes, I hope very much to be able to go to Cartagena, Colombia, and pay a call on the President of the Republic of the United States of Colombia. It is about fifty miles -- less than that, about forty miles out of the way of the straight course from St. Croix to Panama, so all it would involve would be spending one extra day and

--- [416] ---

go in there if the President of Colombia comes down to Cartagena. We would spend the day together and that would be the first time that any American President has ever visited any nation in South America during his term of office.

Q:   What is the occasion of this official visit?

THE PRESIDENT:   What?

Q:   What is the occasion of the visit to Colombia?

THE PRESIDENT:   Just to say, "How do you do?" It is on the way.

Q:   Any celebration?

THE PRESIDENT:   No, we get there on the Fourth of July if we leave on the twenty-sixth.

Q:   Would that involve landing on their soil?

THE PRESIDENT:   Oh, yes; there would be nothing new in that.

Q:   I thought they might come out to your boat.

THE PRESIDENT:   I am going to lunch with the President of Panama. That has been done on many occasions.

Q:   Mr. President, I am not sure whether there is a map out there in the Press Room. Do you mind spelling the name?

THE PRESIDENT:   Well, anglicized it is C-a-r-t-a-g-e-n-a and it takes you quite a while to practise the pronunciation of the "g."

Q:   On the steel situation, it has been intimated that you might consider calling both parties to Washington. Is that a fact?

THE PRESIDENT:   No, I have not heard anything about it.

Q:   Tomorrow is the sixteenth and the present tenure of the N.R.A. Licensing Act does expire tomorrow. We heard from some people on the Hill that there might be a possibility that you might want to extend that. Can you give us any idea on that?

--- [417] ---

THE PRESIDENT:  It is a long time between now and tomorrow.

Q:  Thank you.  (Laughter)

THE PRESIDENT:  Frankly, I do not know; anything might happen.

Q:  Do you care to comment, or has your attention been called to the statement up there at Pittsburgh proposing that you appoint an arbitration board?

THE PRESIDENT:  Yes, Steve (Mr. Early) told me about it.  Of course I could not comment until I see the whole thing.

Q:  Have you received the Shipping Code?  What has happened to it?

THE PRESIDENT:  I got it quite a while ago and it has been going the rounds.  I think I can intimate that I am not satisfied with it but I have not had time to put down why I am dissatisfied with it.  The same way, I do not like the provisions of the Utilities Code.

Q:  What are the objections?

THE PRESIDENT:  I was just saying I have not got to the point of setting them forth in detail.

Q:  That means you probably won't sign either one?

THE PRESIDENT:  Probably not as submitted.

Q:  Mr. President, on this German moratorium business, Germany complains that she has not been permitted to pay in goods on these obligations.  In view of the fact that we have more or less invited partial payment of war debts in goods, would it not be possible for Germany to come here with goods for payment on these other debts?

THE PRESIDENT:  I don't know.  In other words, we have not considered it one way or the other at all.  They have never offered to pay in goods, have they?

Q:  No, sir; not that I know of.

--- [418] ---

Q:  Did you tell Senator Robinson, sir, that you wanted labor legislation this session, before adjournment?

THE PRESIDENT:  Yes, quite a while ago.

Q:  Have you agreed on a substitute form?

THE PRESIDENT:  That you will have to find out up there on the Hill.  In other words, the real situation is this.  We have been trying to get some form of legislation which would not greatly delay the termination of the session, and there have been at least a dozen different drafts of legislation, and it is a matter, and has been for the last two days, a little over two days, of discussion between Senator Robinson and Senator McNary. That is really what it comes down to.  I haven't heard anything since this morning when various other suggestions were made.

Q:  Mr. President, can you comment on those three or four principal objections
to the terms, such as limiting it to one year and restricting power?

THE PRESIDENT:  There is no objection to restricting it to one year.  There was
definite objection to eliminating the word "organization" from the principle of representation.  In other words, 7-A.  This might just as well be
made absolutely clear once and for all.  About 120,000,000 people out of
125,000,000 understand plain English, and there seems to be a very, very
small minority that do not understand plain English.  7-A says that the
workers can choose representatives.  Now if they want to choose the
Ahkoond of Squat they have a perfect right to do so.  If they want to choose
the Royal Geographic Society, they can do that.  If they want to choose a
Union of any kind, they can do that.  They have free choice of representation and that means

--- [419] ---

not merely an individual or a worker, but it means a corporation or a union
or the Crown Prince of Siam, or anybody.  And that has got to be made absolutely clear in this legislation.

Q:  How do you feel on the point of minorities?

THE PRESIDENT:  The question of minorities is not a tremendously serious one
because that has to be worked out in each individual case.  If there is a
substantial minority, it seems fair and equitable that that minority should
have some form of representation, but that is a matter of detail depending
on the individual case.  In some industries it is possible that neither
side may want to have it.

Q:  Suppose they do choose the National Geographic Society, then do the employers have to trade with them?

THE PRESIDENT:  Absolutely.

Q:  About this Crown Prince of Siam, how is he going to get over?  (Laughter)

THE PRESIDENT:  If he is anything like the King of Siam, he will be pretty good.

Q:  Are you going on the radio before you leave Washington?

THE PRESIDENT:  If I have time.  I don't know whether before I leave Washington
or before I sail.

Q:  With reference to the vacation, have you any plans for touching on the
Pacific Coast?

THE PRESIDENT:  Well, I am going to land on the Pacific.

Q:  On the return?

THE PRESIDENT:  Where I am going to land, I do not know, but of course I would
like to go up the whole length of the Coast although it seems very doubtful
that I would have time at the present time because, as we all know, the
Pacific Coast is exceedingly hospitable and if you

--- [420] ---

go to one place, you have to go to all, and I have to get back to Washington so that the length of time I can be on the Coast will have to be limited. On the way back I am going to specialize, you might say, in going to some of the big projects, like the two Columbia River projects, the Fort Peck project and some of those. Those individual places are not by any means certain but I will go to three or four projects on the way back; it might not be those.

Q: Assuming you get away on the twenty-sixth, at what time will you get to the Coast?

THE PRESIDENT: Somewhere around the end of July.

Q: About four weeks?

THE PRESIDENT: Yes; the total length of time away would be less than five weeks; about four weeks, four days.

Q: On this possible radio speech, will that be a general report of your stewardship?

THE PRESIDENT: I have no idea; none at all. There is one other thing which I noticed somebody had already started to write a piece about, as they say. During the summer -- in case I forgot to mention it -- it looks probably now as if Congress is going to give us some money in order to have a bit more room in the Executive Offices -- this room, too -- and we have, after fifteen or twenty different designs were made, we seem to have arrived at a pretty good design which will have the entire approval and sanction of the Fine Arts Commission and which would at the same time not destroy the general White House plan. There are certain tricks involved in it. A portion of the new space would be undergound, hidden entirely by hedges and things like that, with a sunken courtyard and all sorts of tricks, and another portion

--- [421] ---

of the addition would be up over this [indicating the ceiling] with practically no change except making the attic livable. Then, the third portion would carry a little one-story portico out on that side [indicating] of the Cabinet Room and in that sort of portico effect would be my new office. My new office would be substantially the same design [as this office] but two feet longer and two feet wider. I did that on account of the Press.

Q: Just two feet? (Laughter)

Q: May I offer a suggestion that you have some bleacher seats for those little guys in the back? (Laughter)

THE PRESIDENT: We are going to have it designed. Did you ever see an operating room in a medical school? We are going to have tiers running all around the wall, almost up to the ceiling, so that you can all see the carving.

Q: Are you going to the World's Fair on your return?

THE PRESIDENT: No.

(The Press Conference adjourned at 4:20 P.M.)

Press Conference #131
Executive Offices of the White House
June 19, 1934, 10:50 A.M.


THE PRESIDENT: I do not think there is any news at this end. The news is on
the way down from the Capitol to the White House -- it hasn't got here
yet -- several hundred bills.

Q: Do you plan to sign the Farm Credit Bill?

THE PRESIDENT: I have no idea; I have not read it. I cannot tell you about any
bills as nothing has come down yet. My basket is clean. I am right up to
date on everything there is.

Q: Have you taken notice of the House Committee's report on General Foulois,
Chief of the Air Corps?

THE PRESIDENT: I did not have time. The Secretary of War was in yesterday and
I did not even mention it to him. I was on the end of a telephone most of
the day and most of the night and cleaning up correspondence in between.

Q: There was some starting evidence with regard to the Port Newark Army Supply
Base.

THE PRESIDENT: Was there?

Q: Are you going to settle the judgeship of the District of Columbia before
you go, or after you come back?

THE PRESIDENT: It has been referred back to the Attorney General three separate
times and has not come through yet.

Q: How about the Alley Cleaning Commission [Alley Dwelling Commission]?

THE PRESIDENT: Oh, I do not know. There was a recommendation from some kind of
a board with various -- I do not remember who was on it -- the Planning
Board was represented and then these Alley people who

--- [423] ---

worked for the Bill were to have people on it, but anyway that was
the recommendation. It was a committee.

Q: You have not appointed anybody?

THE PRESIDENT: No, it was a committee of six or seven people with various organizations.

Q: Have you decided whether the Wagner Labor Board will administer this new
Resolution?

THE PRESIDENT: I do not know; we have not taken it up.

Q: Have you decided when you will appoint the Stock Exchange Commission?

THE PRESIDENT: Before I sail.

Q:   How about the Housing Administrator?

THE PRESIDENT:   Before I sail.   I do not think there will be any appointments
announced until I get back here next Tuesday morning.   I do not think
there is a chance.

Q:   Have you any setup ready under the Housing Act?

THE PRESIDENT:   No, not a thing; I have not even mentioned it.

Q:   When do you expect to sail?

THE PRESIDENT:   Somewhere between the thirtieth and the Fourth of July.

Q:   Still?

THE PRESIDENT:   Yes, still.

Q:   There are still some departmental objections to the Taylor Grazing Bill.
Have those been communicated to you yet?

THE PRESIDENT:   I have only a memorandum asking that they be heard from the
Department of Agriculture.   I do not know yet what they are.   I think it
relates to a constitutional question, that is some question of law as
to whether easements to water holes are permanent easements or temporary.
In other words, if it is a permanent easement, it is

--- [424] ---

a vested right and the Taylor Bill, as I remember it, does recognize it as
a vested right.   The Department of Agriculture, I think, says they are not
vested rights but purely temporary easements and there are some Supreme
Court decisions that I am not familiar with and it will hinge largely on
that.

Q:   How about the Coast Guard Pay Bill?

THE PRESIDENT:   No, did it pass?

Q:   Yes, sir.

THE PRESIDENT:   I did not know that.

Q:   Do you intend to visit the Republic of Panama as well as the Canal Zone?

THE PRESIDENT:   I am going to lunch with the President of Panama.

Q:   In Panama?

THE PRESIDENT:   Yes.

Q:   The British and the French Governments have threatened to impound some of
the trade profits on credits affected by the debt moratorium.   Is there
any action along that line that we can take?

THE PRESIDENT:   I do not know.   If I said, "Yes," you would probably say we
were going to do it.   I have not the faintest idea on it but three days
ago I asked the Secretary of State whether legislation was necessary be-

fore Congress went home and he said no, that the legislation was not necessary because the control over the foreign exchange in last year's bill
seems sufficiently broad to cover it if we wanted to do it. I have no
idea what the State Department feels about what we should do. You had
better check up there. We have the power to do it.

Q:   Do you intend to select a chief for your prospective Bureau of Insular
Affairs before you go away?

--- [425] ---

THE PRESIDENT:   I do not know. I spoke to the Secretary of Interior about that
a week ago and we just put off discussing it. When does that go into effect?

Q:   July twenty-eighth.

THE PRESIDENT:   Then we won't do it until I can get back.

Q:   The adjournment of Congress has no effect?

THE PRESIDENT:   Sixty days after it goes in?

Q:   Anything new you can tell us on the steel situation? Do you plan to see
any of the steel people before you go away tonight?

THE PRESIDENT:   Absolutely no plans. I will talk to Perkins [The Secretary of
Labor] about it this afternoon.

Q:   Has anything new come to you recently concerning the drought situation, any
report?

THE PRESIDENT:   Yes; I got a report up to the minute yesterday. I am afraid I
have filed it. I will have to tell you from recollection. Of course, in
the wheat country the sections where there was going to be a total loss
still remain a total loss. There is very little improvement in wheat. In
corn, the situation is a little better but is menaced to a certain extent
by the cinch bug in a good many areas, and we won't know how fast and how
far the cinch bugs will go for another week or ten days.

Taking it by and large the general drought situation is certainly no better, but I don't think it is any worse than it was a couple of weeks ago.
It will depend a good deal on July weather, especially in corn.

The first bale of cotton was picked yesterday somewhere in Texas.

Q:   Mr. President, in connection with the tariff bargaining, do you expect

--- [426] ---

to organize this third Export-Import Bank very soon under Peek?

THE PRESIDENT:   I do not think so; there has been no talk about it.

Q:   What have the existing banks been doing, if anything, so far?

THE PRESIDENT:   The first bank is not doing anything. That was the Russian
[pronouncing it Roossian] Bank. Ever hear of it?

Q:    That is how it is pronounced in Pennsylvania.

THE PRESIDENT:   On the second bank, we are discussing extending its operations
    to take care of the necessary loans to Puerto Rico and the Virgin Islands.

Q:   Thank you.

THE PRESIDENT:   It seems a logical place to fit them in.

Q:   Mr. President, when do you sign the silver bill?

THE PRESIDENT:   Tonight, at 8:45.

Q:   Any proclamation in connection with the silver bill?

THE PRESIDENT:   Not that I know of.

Q:   What is the nature of the loans to Puerto Rico and the Virgin Islands?

THE PRESIDENT:   They have got some pretty ambitious plans worked out.  You had
    better wait until you get down there and I will tell you more about it.

Q:   Rum?

THE PRESIDENT:   No, in Puerto Rico it is largely a question of homesteading and
    taking over quite a large amount of marginal lands.  Of course you are not
    precluded from growing sugar cane for your own consumption, if you want to.

Q:   Will this Export-Import Bank handle the marketing of coffee in other coun-
    tries?

THE PRESIDENT:   No.

--- [427] ---

Q:   They sell their coffee to other countries and not here and they lost their
    market because they lost their supply in a hurricane.  That would supply
    some work.

THE PRESIDENT:   I don't know.  That would be a logical thing.  I signed yester-
    day the Joint Resolution approving of the ten per cent coffee tax for
    Puerto Rico.

Q:   When do you think you will sign the major bills coming down today?  Before
    you get away tonight?

THE PRESIDENT:   I doubt it very much.  There are between two and three hundred
    and the normal course for those bills, of course is to go to the depart-
    ments and agencies they involve for recommendation and they will be drift-
    ing in here in the course of the next four or five days.

MR. EARLY:   There are about 125 of those out in the departments.

THE PRESIDENT:   Steve (Mr. Early) says there are about 125 of those out in the
    departments.  Then of course there was quite a lot of stuff went through
    yesterday that has not got to the departments yet and, well, I will just
    act on them as they come along.  I am having a bunch of them sent up to the
    SEQUOIA Thursday morning and will probably act on those on the high seas

of New London Harbor and have another batch reach me at Hyde Park on Saturday. There won't be any particular order. I will just work on them as
they come along.

Q:  In view of the labor situation, can you give us a background sketch as to
policy in that connection?  What is going to happen to the National Labor
Board?

THE PRESIDENT:  I do not know.  I do not know what the details of the administrative setup would be at all.  The real problem is when it

--- [428] ---

comes down to a question of elections in different plants as to how that
machinery of elections will be conducted.  If they make an effort to hold
practically simultaneous elections in all steel plants, for example, it
would be a tremendous strain on personnel because you have to have people
to conduct the elections who will have some knowledge of the work.  About
the best guess you can make is that we will go ahead with the holding of
these elections as fast as practicable but it does not mean we can do them
all simultaneously or in ten days.

Q:  Is it your desire to set up a national board or industrial boards for each
industry?

THE PRESIDENT:  I do not know yet.  We have not talked about it at all.

Q:  Thank you, Mr. President.

THE PRESIDENT:  I will see you next Wednesday, a week from tomorrow.

(The Press Conference adjourned at 11:02 A.M.)

Press Conference #132
Held aboard the "SEQUOIA" in the harbor of New London, Connecticut
June 22, 1934, 11:45 A.M.


THE PRESIDENT: What paper do you represent [addressing Miss Roberta Barrows]?

MISS BARROWS: The New York Times. (Laughter)

Q: How do you like the races?

THE PRESIDENT: I will have some news for you tomorrow, something really interesting.

Q: Any Commissions there [referring to the official papers being signed by the President]?

THE PRESIDENT: Not yet. Everything is all quiet.

Q: Can you give us a word on the races?

THE PRESIDENT: Both awfully good races.

Q: The freshmen race was much closer than the other.

THE PRESIDENT: Yes, a good race. Here is the Committee's boat.

MRS. ROOSEVELT: Good morning, Stevie (Mr. Stephenson). How are you?

Q: (Mr. Stephenson) Just fine.

Q: Mr. President, are you having a good time?

THE PRESIDENT: Fine. I have to go to work now.

Q: We are having a delightful time over at Henry Morgenthau's Naval Academy [referring to the fact that the Press had been quartered at the Coast Guard Academy near New London].

THE PRESIDENT: Where are you, at the Academy?

Q: Yes, sir; and we are having one grand time.

THE PRESIDENT: That is marvelous. You know, I have never been there.

Q: Goodbye, Mr. President.

Press Conference #133
Executive Offices of the White House
June 27, 1934, 11:00 A.M.


Q: Good morning, Mr. President.

THE PRESIDENT: Good morning, Fred (Mr. Storm). Good morning, Stevie (Mr. Stephenson). This is what is left, plus what is coming in. There are about ten more out.

Q: They are all bills, Mr. President?

THE PRESIDENT: Yes.

Q: Those plus ten?

THE PRESIDENT: Those plus ten that are still out. I did 124 last night and this morning. No, I had 124 last night and 15 this morning.

Q: The Commissioners for the District of Columbia, giving them authority on the --

THE PRESIDENT: (interposing) I cannot tell you yet. They will be with the others.

Q: Is that the District tag, Mr. President?

THE PRESIDENT: Yes.

Q: I hear Roy Vernou [the Naval Aide to the President] says he is arranging for that cruiser to shoot a 16-inch shell through my back. (Laughter)

THE PRESIDENT: It would take a 14-inch shell. (Laughter)

MR. DONALDSON: All in.

THE PRESIDENT: I think the only news I have this morning is that I have been presented with tag license No. 1 for the District of Columbia. So now we are all set up.

The bill position is this, that last night I worked until 1:00 A.M. and did 124 bills; I did 15 more this morning and there are only left

--- [431] ---

six bills on my desk plus about 10 which Steve (Mr. Early) says are still out around the departments. So there are only about 16 more to be acted upon. I hope to finish them up tonight.

Q: The 16 includes the Farm Mortgage Bill?

THE PRESIDENT: I cannot tell you anything about that. There will be a list this afternoon and I think by process of deduction you can find out what bills are among those 16 yet to be acted upon.

Q: How about the Railroad Pension Bill?

THE PRESIDENT: You will have to use deduction methods on it again.

Q: How about the Housing Bill?

THE PRESIDENT: The same thing. I am not going to tell you. It would break Steve's (Mr. Early) heart if I did it now.

Q: Can we look for some pretty big stuff then this afternoon, Mr. President?

THE PRESIDENT: Not this afternoon; not until tomorrow morning. I have some people to see during the course of the day.

Q: Have you seen the election proposal of the Sheet Steel Union?

THE PRESIDENT: No, I have not. Miss Perkins is coming in this afternoon.

Q: What is the status of your appointments that you have to make in the next day or two?

THE PRESIDENT: They will come along after the sixteen bills. I have done nothing on them yet, on any appointments.

Q: Mr. President, while you were away there was a story carried that Sykes [Mr. Sykes, of the Federal Radio Commission] is going to be the only member of the present Federal Radio Commission to be appointed [to the Federal Communications Commission].

THE PRESIDENT: It is literally true that I have not thought of anything.

Q: Do you intend to appoint the Aviation Commission before you leave?

--- [432] ---

THE PRESIDENT: I hope to but it is not definite and I still hope to get off. If I do not do it before I go, I will do it by radio. I still hope to get off on Saturday but I am not going to crowd myself too much. If staying another couple of days will help, I will wait until Monday.

Q: How about the agency for the alley cleaning problem in the District of Columbia?

THE PRESIDENT: I think they are having a meeting today.

Q: They have not been appointed yet?

THE PRESIDENT: I think it is today that they are having a meeting. I sent some kind of a letter yesterday suggesting they have a meeting.

Q: Will the appointments of the Municipal Court (Judges) be announced too?

THE PRESIDENT: I forgot to speak to Jim Farley about that. Steve (Mr. Early), will you remind me to do that?

Q: The British are discussing our naval plans in order to come to a level ratio. Can we say we are through seeking to disarm by one-sided sacrifices?

THE PRESIDENT: That sounds pretty good. Will you write that out for me? (Laughter)

Q:    Isn't it on for discussion?

THE PRESIDENT:   I haven't heard a single thing in the dispatches from Davis
(Ambassador Norman Davis) and anything on that has to come from the other
side.

Q:    We cannot even induce you to comment on the British plans?

THE PRESIDENT:   No.

Q:    Since she left you yesterday [the previous evening] there have been no reports definitely from Miss Perkins [the Secretary of Labor] on the

--- [433] ---

longshoremen's strike.  Is there anything she reported to you which you can
tell us?

THE PRESIDENT:   Was that announced last night?  The only thing that happened
last night was the appointment of the Board.  I think you have that.

Q:    In the morning papers.

Q:    Mr. President, the figures from the Treasury Department indicate that
liquor is being withdrawn at only a rate of a third of what was anticipated.
Choate [Chairman Joseph H. Choate, Jr., Federal Alcohol Control Adminis-
tration] recommended a tariff reduction in duties on that.  Is there anything to be done in that line?

THE PRESIDENT:   I might do it by radio.  The thing is still being studied.

Q:    It looks as if two gallons of bootleg liquor is being drunk to every one on
which tax is being paid.

THE PRESIDENT:   Yes; I have not the figures on it.

Q:    About being drunk, you mean?  (Laughter)

THE PRESIDENT:   What is that?  Stevie (Mr. Stephenson), you had better wait until you get to the Virgin Islands before you do it.

Q:    Are you going to speak in Puerto Rico, Mr. President?

THE PRESIDENT:   I hope not.  I hope I will never have to make another speech.

Q:    Do you plan to appoint people, similar to the longshoremen's strike, in the
steel strike?

THE PRESIDENT:   I do not know, because I have not talked to Perkins.  We did the
longshoremen's last night and might do something today, but I cannot tell
you.

Q:    Since the Labor Bill has been signed, there has been a lot of speculation
with respect to the labor boards that exist and there has been comment that
you intend to abolish them.

--- [434] ---

THE PRESIDENT:  I have not gotten to it yet.

Q:   Mr. President, can you enlighten us on the attitude of the Administration toward LaFollette?

THE PRESIDENT:   No, I could only talk to you off the record about it.  It would have to be off the record because I cannot take part in these things officially or, really, in any other way.  As far as I go, personally, I would love to see Bob LaFollette back here because he is a very old friend of mine and has been very helpful.  But, as you appreciate it, I cannot go ahead and the National Administration cannot go ahead and compel some party organization in a particular state to do something at the command of the National Administration.  It just cannot be done.

My own personal hope is that they will find some way of sending Bob LaFollette back here.  That is about the whole story.  But I cannot compel the democracy of Wisconsin to go ahead and nominate him.  As I say, I have to keep that off the record.

Q:   Does that apply to New Mexico?

THE PRESIDENT:   To tell you the honest truth, I don't know the situation in New Mexico.  Of course, Bronson Cutting is also a very old boy friend of mine, but I understand that Chavez is going to run and Chavez is a pretty good Congressman.  I am trying to get across the idea that if we have the right kind of people, the party label does not mean so very much.  I have to keep that off the record, too.  (Laughter)

Q:   How about Minnesota?

THE PRESIDENT:   I do not know much about it.  Who is running on the Democratic ticket, Hoidale [Representative Einar Hoidale]?

--- [435] ---

Q:   Yes, sir.

THE PRESIDENT:   He is a very good friend of mine and Shipstead [Senator Shipstead] is too.  I am in a sory of quandary there.

Q:   Have you the same difficulty, sir, in Pennsylvania?  (Laughter)

THE PRESIDENT:   There is no difficulty in Pennsylvania at all.  (Laughter)

Q:   Mr. President, before they take you all over the country, let us to to Alaska for a moment about the possibility of establishing a United States Naval Base or Navy Base of some kind up there.

THE PRESIDENT:   I never heard of it.  Is there any talk of it?

Q:   The Army and Navy are sending squadrons as a sort of training fleet and there has been talk of a survey for a base of some kind.

THE PRESIDENT:   I never heard of it.

I do not believe there is anything else in particular.  We will have a conference on Friday afternoon and maybe it will be the last one in some time.

Q:   Thank you, Mr. President.

(The Press Conference adjourned at 11:10 A.M.)

Press Conference #134
Executive Offices of the White House
June 29, 1934, 4:10 P.M.


THE PRESIDENT: [Turning the papers on his desk face down] This is to see that
everything is properly hidden. (Laughter) I wasn't looking at Russell
(Mr. Young); it is all right.

Q: Are you all ready to go this evening?

THE PRESIDENT: All I need is some sleep.

Q: So say we all.

Q: You had a long session of it last night, didn't you?

THE PRESIDENT: I sat up and drank beer with Barney Baruch and Joe Kennedy. I
did not do any work at all. It was awful -- two o'clock and I have no excuse for it.

Q: They hung a thermometer out here a while ago and it only got up to 129½.

THE PRESIDENT: Wait until you get to Cartagena. That is nothing, the mercury
boils down there.

MR. DONALDSON: All in.

THE PRESIDENT: I think the only news at the present moment is an order which I
signed this morning to see if we could correct a very difficult situation
in regard to the purchases of various articles by the Government. You
know, we have been getting a series of identical bids on the plea from the
bidders that they are precluded from putting in competitive bids by their
filed prices with their respective Code Authorities. We are going to try
something new to see if we can break that down. The Executive Order provides -- you can get a copy of it after the Press Conference so that you
can tell what it provides -- that any bidder for a Government contract of
the United

--- [437] ---

States or a state or municipality or other public authority, in other words
any kind of a Government contract for goods on which the bidder has filed
prices with his Code Authority, these bids from now on will be held to have
complied with the Code requirements on two conditions. First, if the bidder quotes a price to the Government agencies not more than 15 per cent
below his filed price and, secondly, if he does quote a lower price than
the filed price, he shall file that lower price with the Code Authority.

In other words, he gives the public the advantage of the same reduction
that he offers to the Government.

The second part of it is that if any other member of the Code believes
that this lower bid is made possible only by unfair practices, that he has
the right to complain to the Administrator of Industrial Recovery who shall
thereupon make a finding as to whether the complaint is justified or not.

We hope by this means to restore competition on Government bids and, incidentally, as a result of that, in a very large line of actual prices to consumers, private consumers, and at the same time to prevent unfair trade practices.

Q:   In other words, Mr. President, if they bid on a Government contract now they do not have to file their prices with the Code Authority?

THE PRESIDENT:   Actually at the present time they all bid the same price with the Government on the excuse that that is the price they have filed with the Code Authority.

Q:   Was this situation true of the Fort Peck Dam Project where they all bid the same price?

THE PRESIDENT:   Literally dozens of cases where we have been getting identical bids.

--- [438] ---

Q:   How could this react on the public?  How could they share if the bids are for the Government?

THE PRESIDENT:   Because they have to file.  When they file bids on the Government contracts, they have to file the same price with the Code Authority.

Q:   Won't that still be uniform?

MR. EARLY:   Fifteen per cent.

Q:   It limits competition within a fifteen per cent range?

THE PRESIDENT:   Yes.  It enables them to have competition to within fifteen per cent below the filed price.

Q:   They could offer the same prices to the public?

THE PRESIDENT:   As to the Government, yes.  When they bid on the Government thing it automatically cuts their filed price with their own Authority [Code Authority].

Q:   That breaks the fixed price?

THE PRESIDENT:   Yes.

Q:   Isn't the result likely to be that anything that one of their competitors will cut fifteen per cent on, they will cut the same amount?

THE PRESIDENT:   We cannot tell; we do not know what the effect is going to be.

Q:   How would this affect the basing point system, if any?

THE PRESIDENT:   I don't know; it is too complicated a question.  I haven't the faintest idea.

Q:   Mr. President, didn't you sign the Railroad Pension Bill?

THE PRESIDENT:   I have acted on the Railroad Pension Bill and the Frazier-Lemke

Bill and the only reason I haven't told you of my action is that I want to file -- to give out a memo or statement at the same time and those are, neither of them, written.

--- [439] ---

Q:   Will we get them tonight?

THE PRESIDENT:   I hope so, but I cannot guarantee it.

Q:   Mr. President, do you care to comment on the volume of work that is likely to flow from the Housing Bill, the Housing Act?

THE PRESIDENT:   Oh, no, I have no idea yet.  There has been no survey of the situation.

Q:   It will certainly be very large?

THE PRESIDENT:   We hope so.

Q:   Can you give us an idea of the setup you supply under that bill, or do you work that out in detail?

THE PRESIDENT:   No.  I have asked -- I had better not even say that.  I have not got to the point of that.

Q:   Will the arrangement be made before you leave?

THE PRESIDENT:   I hope so.

Q:   Are you ready to give us the names of the Stock Market [Commission]?

THE PRESIDENT:   I hope so.

Q:   Today?

THE PRESIDENT:   Tomorrow or Sunday, and the same thing on Communications and the same thing on pensions.  I hope to get most of them done before I do.

Q:   How about the Archivist?

THE PRESIDENT:   I am not appointing anybody yet.  The building won't be finished until next summer and I do not see why I should spend ten or twelve thousand dollars a year.

Q:   Hopkins (Harry Hopkins) said he was definitely out as Housing Administrator.

THE PRESIDENT:   He has never been definitely in or indefinitely in.  (Laughter)

--- [440] ---

Q:   Is it possible on this order for Government bids for a bidder on two successive bids to make two successive fifteen per cent cuts?  That is, he cuts fifteen per cent on the first one and then files it and then --

THE PRESIDENT:   (interposing)  And then there is another opening the following day?  I do not see why not.  It is perfectly all right.

Q:  Mr. President, does he file this price after the bid has been delivered to the Government?

THE PRESIDENT:  Yes.

Q:  It is secret until --

THE PRESIDENT:  (interposing)  Secret until the Government bid is actually opened.

Q:  And if he does not get the contract, he is not bound by that bid price to the public?

THE PRESIDENT:  Yes, he is.  Everybody, every bidder.

Q:  If he doesn't get the bid?

THE PRESIDENT:  I suppose so, from this language.  He shall have been held to comply adequately with the requirements of the Code of Fair Competition, (a) if he quotes a price or prices not more than fifteen per cent below his price or prices filed in accordance with the requirements of the Code and (b) if, after the bids are opened, each bidder quoting a price or prices below his file price shall immediately file a copy of his bid with the Code authorities, with which he is required to file prices.

Q:  In other words, whether he gets the Government's bids or not, that price stands?

THE PRESIDENT:  Yes.

I think Steve (Mr. Early) told you about my going off.  We are

--- [441] ---

going on Sunday evening at six or seven o'clock and getting away during the course of the night and stopping off at Hampton Roads at about seven o'clock the next morning to put off fond farewell messages and to send a report to Fred (Mr. Storm) and Stevie (Mr. Stephenson) and Eddie (Mr. Rodden).

Q:  (Mr. Stephenson)  Say a little about that.

THE PRESIDENT:  To say how they have stood the angry waters of Chesapeake Bay and about half an hour later I hope we will be out of sight of land.  I hope, in the meantime, that you will have, all of you, a pleasant and happy holiday, with no news out of Washington.

Q:  What is this they say about the destroyer?

Q:  I am hearing a lot of tales about how those destroyers ride.

THE PRESIDENT:  Why, they are fine.  (Laughter)

Q:  Oh, yeah?  (Laughter)

THE PRESIDENT:  They are well broken.

MR. EARLY:  That is why they call them destroyers.

Q:   We hope you have a very nice trip.

Q:   Thank you, Mr. President.

# Complete Presidential Press Conferences of
# FRANKLIN D. ROOSEVELT

## Volume 4
## August, 1934 — December, 1934

Press Conference #135
Executive Offices of the White House
August 15, 1934, 10:50 A.M.


MR. DONALDSON: All in.

THE PRESIDENT: I think the only plans that I can announce is that at the request of Messrs. Storm, Stephenson and Roddan we are going back to Honolulu
next summer.

Q:  Why wait?

Q:  Can't we make it sooner than that?

THE PRESIDENT: Well, it is very difficult to see everybody in this room.  I
do not think I have any particular news.

Q:  Mr. President, did you get a request from Minneapolis this morning to take
some action in the strike?

THE PRESIDENT: Not that I know of.

Q:  I understand the employers' committee and the citizens' committee sent a
joint message to the White House last night.

MR. EARLY:  I have not seen anything of it.

THE PRESIDENT: We haven't got it.

Q:  Mr. President, anything new on the drought?

THE PRESIDENT: No.  I mentioned to the Secretary of Agriculture the other day
that when you came in today if you wanted to ask me about drought I would
talk to you about it.  Out of that came this delightful theory that I was
going to issue a statement on drought which, of course, is not true.  I
will be glad to answer any specific questions you may want to ask about
the drought area.  We saw something of the area, as you all know.  You also
have seen the reports of the Department, of the decline in certain crops.

--- [2] ---

Q:  Mr. President, the food prices are going up already.  Can you tell us the
policy on that?

THE PRESIDENT: The food prices, according to headlines in the newspapers, are
going up so fast that it might be called an unconscious effort to instill
fear.  I say, of course, "an unconscious effort."

There is plenty of food in the country, which is what I have been saying
for the last three months, and there will be plenty of food to go around
next Winter.  I have no doubt that the great majority of people engaged
in the food business will not attempt to profiteer on food but in every
profession and business there are chiselers and, of course, we will do the
best we can and use whatever methods are needed to get after chiselers and
profiteers.  However, the great majority of people, being decent Americans,
are not going to try to profiteer in food.  As a matter of fact, food

prices have gone up very, very little. The element of the cost of living that goes into food -- I think you can get it from the Labor Department -- as I remember it, it has gone up 6 per cent in the past year which is very, very little.

Q:    What, exactly, can you do to these so-called chiselers?

THE PRESIDENT:  Each case can be taken up as it comes along. You cannot start at this time of a year and say that if this happens we are going to do thus and so.

Q:    I am just wondering as to the possible means.

THE PRESIDENT:  Oh, there are lots of ways.

Q:    Is there authority under existing law to meet that situation or will you require new legislation?

THE PRESIDENT:  No, I have plenty of authority.

--- [3] ---

Q:    Do you think this $525,000,000 for drought relief is going to be sufficient to last to January?

THE PRESIDENT:  I hope so. I think it will all be spent but I anticipate it will last through.

Q:    Can you augment that in any other way?

THE PRESIDENT:  That I do not know. I frankly do not know the answer to that question yet. It is one of the things I am going to check up on but I do not think we will need to spend more than $525,000,000, certainly before Congress meets.

Q:    Can you tell us anything about the cotton trade agreement?

THE PRESIDENT:  I have got a synopsis of it in my basket and have not read it yet. It is only in tentative form and has not been agreed to.

Q:    Wallace [Secretary of Agriculture Wallace], when he left here yesterday, said the agreement might be considered in a state of suspended animation. Can you tell us what that means? Will it be held up for the time being?

THE PRESIDENT:  I do not know what he meant by that. As I understand it, it was that the great majority of the items that had been discussed had been agreed to but there were still a very small number under discussion.

Q:    Anything you can tell us on the primary?

Q:    On the results reported in this morning's paper?

THE PRESIDENT:  I have not even read them.

Q:    Do you want to hear about them?  (Laughter)

THE PRESIDENT:  I have not even read or heard about them.

Q:  Burke is leading out in Nebraska against Charlie Bryan and Donahey is
    leading White.

--- [4] ---

THE PRESIDENT:  Unfortunately for the people who have written stories on it, I
    cannot help you crawl back from the limb but the fact remains that I have
    not taken part in any primaties and do not intend to.

Q:  Mr. President, we are glad you are back home with us again; we missed you
    very much.  Have you given any consideration to the local management ap-
    pointment of an Engineer Commissioner and a Justice of the Municipal Court?

THE PRESIDENT:  The Engineer Commission -- I think we are going to have some-
    thing in a couple of days.

Q:  How about the Judge of the Municipal Court?

THE PRESIDENT:  No, I have not taken that up at all.

Q:  And the location of the Tuberculosis Hospital?

THE PRESIDENT:  The location of the Tuberculosis Hospital -- I think I have it.

Q:  Any particular site?

THE PRESIDENT:  I suggested to the Secretary of Interior yesterday that in view
    of the fact that this hospital is going to be a pretty important thing for
    patients from the District of Columbia, that the one thing to consider was
    the good of the patients.  There seem to be several different schools of
    thought and several different opinions as to where it should be and I sug-
    gested to the Secretary of Interior that he should get two or three people
    from outside the District to give us a very quick survey and report on it.
    I suggested two or three names of very eminent specialists in tuberculosis
    to come down and look over the situation.

Q:  Can you mention those names?

THE PRESIDENT:  I suggested Dr. Brown up at Saranac.

Q:  Do you know his first name?

--- [5] ---

MR. EARLY:  Dr. Lawrason Brown.

THE PRESIDENT:  I do not know whether he could come down or not, but somebody of
    that type.

Q:  Have you a successor for Governor Black yet?

THE PRESIDENT:  He is going to lunch with me to beg to be allowed to go home
    again.  I have kept him going, just babying him along, kidding him, and
    he is still here.

Q:  Mr. President, I understand you are going to be surprised by the receipt of
    three grains [kernels] of corn today from Fort Erie.  Are you going up?

THE PRESIDENT: No, I cannot go. They are coming in with the three grains.

Q: Mr. President, to go back to the drought, there have been a great many stories to the effect that this organization which is under Hopkins and also Secretary Wallace, has been pretty much working with the two departments, the Emergency Relief and the A.A.A. Have you any intention of setting up a separate outfit?

THE PRESIDENT: No, they are working very well together.

Of course, there is one thing I did not mention before on the drought thing that also has to be watched. That is the speculative end of things. I think it is fair for you to assume that the operations on the produce markets, the grain exchanges, are being watched. There is a good deal of information coming in to show that a lot of what might be called pure speculators -- pure is not a very good adjective -- have transferred their operations from stocks to grain. We all remember what happened a year ago in July, when a very small number of men as, for instance, the dentist from Louisiana ran a 40 or 50 thousand dollar shoestring on the Chicago Grain Exchange

--- [6] ---

up to about 20 million bushels of various kinds of grain. He and half a dozen other very large speculators forced the price of wheat at that time, just as an example, up to $1.25 which was absolutely out of line with the economic wheat situation and then, of course, there was a perfectly terrific smash after that and it dropped in one or two days from $1.20 to $.95, wiping all those fellows out. That, of course, very definitely hurt the farmer who was producing grain and selling it at that time. We have a good deal of authority over Produce and Grain Exchanges and we want to avoid that kind of speculation in grain by people who would not know wheat from rye if they saw it in a field. And, just in the same way, we want to avoid speculation in food supplies after processing.

Q: Who would handle that general surveillance work?

THE PRESIDENT: Agriculture.

Q: Just the Agriculture Department?

THE PRESIDENT: Yes.

Q: On the Cuban trade agreement, are you going to give that back to the State Department with your approval. Can you tell us when?

THE PRESIDENT: It won't come to me for approval.

Q: It will not come to you for approval until it gets to the final form?

THE PRESIDENT: This memo is just to keep me in touch.

Q: Have you had time to study the Russian debt situation?

THE PRESIDENT: I have not had time to talk about it at all.

Q: Do you expect to go into that?

THE PRESIDENT: I suppose so. Of course all of these people are coming in to see me, have come in to see me in the last three days more to bring me up to date than anything else.

--- [7] ---

Q: Anything from Secretary Hull on the status of the debt?

THE PRESIDENT: The general debt situation?

Q: No, Russian?

THE PRESIDENT: No, not yet.

Q: On the drought, could you comment at all on the effect of the drought on the agricultural control?

THE PRESIDENT: Only to comment in this way, that it does not affect the thing at all, one way or the other, but the point of view of the principle. It does not affect the principle. It is a perfectly simple, practical policy that was adopted a year and a half ago, at the previous Session, based on the thought that, taking wheat as an example, if we produce in excess of 25 per cent in this country of wheat over our needs, obviously one of two things will happen. If it stays in this country it will hang over the market, as a huge surplus, which will keep the price of wheat away down. If it goes out of the country, the price of wheat in this country will be exactly what the world price is, no greater and no less. Taking wheat again as an example, if we reduce the excess surplus -- of course we have got to have a small surplus always -- if you can reduce it to the point where the world market will not be the only controlling factor, undoubtedly the domestic prices will go up.

And, of course, that did happen before the drought. In other words, last March -- nobody could foresee the drought at that time -- the price of wheat had gone up very, very materially in this country and was, because of the control of the surplus, substantially above the world market, somewhere around 20 or 25 cents above the world market. Now that price presupposes -- I am going back to the pre-

--- [8] ---

drought period -- that we would keep this surplus down to a reasonable point, that we would try to maintain a reasonable surplus and prevent it from getting us back in the future to a point where wheat would be forced down again to 30 cents a bushel.

Actually, the drought has had the result of reducing the excess surplus in one year instead of perhaps two years or three years. So we go on at this time with the normal development of the policy which otherwise would not have gone into effect until a year or two years from now. In other words, there is no change in the plan even though that puts some people out on a limb. (Laughter)

Q: Mr. President, has there been any further thought about the Government granaries for establishing a yearly surplus?

THE PRESIDENT: On that again, we have to consider the control of the surplus one year earlier than we would have had to otherwise. What the actual machinery will be I don't know. We haven't got to it yet. But, undoubtedly, we will have to work out some kind of machinery that will prevent the speculative use of the normal and reasonable surplus, so that Mr. Cutten won't be able to -- leave out his name -- so that Mr. X won't be able to corner the wheat market and so that there will be a controllable, reasonable surplus big enough to prevent starvation and, at the same time, not so big that it can force down American prices the way it has in the past.

There is literally nothing new on this thing at all. It is all old stuff. The drought has merely pushed up the next step by one year or possibly two years.

Q:    To set up any machinery as that, such as, just for example, the ever-normal granary, would that take any additional legislation?

--- [9] ---

THE PRESIDENT:    I don't know; I haven't studied it enough to know.

Q:    Mr. President, have you had time to hear anything about the administration of the Jones-Costigan Sugar Bill? There seems to be some difficulty, particularly with Hawaii and Puerto Rico. Hawaii seems to think that as a result of your visit there they are likely to get an increase in their quota.

THE PRESIDENT:    In the Hawaii case there will be no change in the quota. They are taking in this year about four million dollars more than they took in last year. In the case of Puerto Rico, that came up late yesterday afternoon. We will probably get action on it today.

The only other thing I have heard is the demand from some of the refineries that under the Act the differential on Cuban refined be greatly increased -- no, I am wrong on that -- that the amount of the differential be greatly decreased so as to allow more sugar to be refined in this country than has been in the past. That comes under the Cuban Treaty.

Q:    Anything new on silver?

THE PRESIDENT:    No, I don't think so. I might just as well tell you a secret on silver. I have had three or four telegrams and four or five people come in to congratulate me on the marvelous timing of the Green Bay speech and the nationalization of silver, that it was within three minutes the two appeared on the Stock Exchange ticker. The actual story was this; if anybody had read the law they would have known exactly what was going to happen two months beforehand. The law provided that we were to go ahead and buy silver with the ultimate objective of getting 25 per cent of silver and 75 per cent of gold as bullion reserves. We started in to carry out that law in good faith and bought a good deal of silver. Before I went away

--- [10] ---

about a week before, I had a talk with the Secretary of the Treasury and others and it was obvious that if we were going to buy silver on a fairly good scale the price would go up, the world price. Now, the law also says that the silver in this country which is speculatively held, somewhere around 200 to 250 million ounces, can be bought by us at 50 cents an ounce if we are going to take it over. Now, suppose the world price of silver goes to 55 cents an ounce. We would be in the position of offering less than the public market for all of that silver. Therefore, we must make provisions to take over the American stocks of silver before silver reaches 50 cents an ounce.

Before I went away I signed all the papers, a complete set of papers, which were to go into effect merely by sending me a radio if I had been on the boat or a telegram if I had been on the train, saying that silver has gone to 49 3/4 cents an ounce, "Do you authorize your orders going into effect?" All that was done before I left and the price set was 49 3/4 cents an ounce. Silver struck that the morning of the Green Bay speech. That was the careful timing.

Q:   Can you explain, Mr. President, why on June 14, five days prior to the silver purchase act going into effect, there was an authorization to Mr. Morgenthau to coin up all the silver he had on hand? Why was it June 14?

THE PRESIDENT:   I don't know why. I think he came in and said to me, "You know, I have discovered we have a lot of silver on hand, 100 million ounces or something like that. We have never issued currency against it." I said, "Why didn't we?" He said, "It just accumulated and everybody forgot about it." I said, "Go ahead and issue currency against it."

--- [11] ---

Q:   Did you have the silver purchase act in mind?

THE PRESIDENT:   I think it was absolutely coincident in this case that he discovered the silver lying around loose.

Q:   Is there a plan to remove the duty on Canadian hay?

THE PRESIDENT:   I don't know; I cannot answer that question today. Do you mean buying Government hay in Canada? Now, whether that means removal of the duty or not I don't know, but I don't think there is an intention of removing the duty for other people, other than the Government.

Q:   Would an extention of that plan perhaps affect other commodities later on?

THE PRESIDENT:   I don't know. I have not considered it.

Q:   What will you do with the three grains of corn which are being presented to you when you get them?

THE PRESIDENT:   I will give them to the cook. (Laughter)

Q:   When do you expect to go to Hyde Park?

THE PRESIDENT:   I don't know. I will probably go a week from tonight.

Q:   Anything on N.R.A.?

THE PRESIDENT:   I don't know; not yet.

(The Press Conference adjourned at 11:10 A.M.)

Press Conference #136
Executive Offices of the White House
August 17, 1934, 4:15 P.M.


THE PRESIDENT:  I do not think there is a blessed bit of news.

Q:  Any news in our department [referring to the District of Columbia]?

THE PRESIDENT:  There was a piece of news -- I do not know if it is ready to
    announce yet, it ought to be -- about your Engineer Commissioner, Colonel
    Dan Sultan.

Q:  That is Colonel?

THE PRESIDENT:  Colonel -- I think it is Colonel.

Q:  What is the status of the trade negotiations with Cuba?

THE PRESIDENT:  I do not know at the precise moment but I hope within a week or
    ten days to have something.

Q:  Can you tell us anything about the Cabinet meeting this afternoon?

THE PRESIDENT:  Nothing happened; just received about a dozen different items --
    no particular item -- just discussed a great many things that we have not
    talked about for a long time.

Q:  Anything definite on reports that the Government or the R.F.C. may take
    over a number of railroads, including the Southern Pacific and the Denver
    and Rio Grande?

THE PRESIDENT:  Sounds like a ghost story; I never heard of it.  Why should we?

Q:  They are going into complete receivership.

THE PRESIDENT:  Are they as badly off as that?  I had not heard at all.

Q:  Anything new on the drought?

THE PRESIDENT:  No.  They has some rains in Missouri yesterday.

Q:  Are you going to be in town over the week end?

THE PRESIDENT:  I think I will go down on the yacht.

--- [13] ---

Q:  On the SEQUOIA?

THE PRESIDENT:  On the SEQUOIA.  I am going back to the old days.

Q:  Can you tell us anything about the textile strike?  The labor leaders say
    you are the only one to prevent it.

THE PRESIDENT:  I do not think we are ready to talk about it at all.  I think I
    should say this -- off the record, because we cannot print anything from

this end, we don't know enough about it yet -- it is one of those things not sufficiently clear to say yet. There are certain what might be called inter-union political troubles there and it is complicated by the old differences between the northern textile people and the southern textile people and we are very hopeful that the thing is going to be worked out. The thing has not crystalized yet so that you can characterize it or define it in any one way.

Q: Any further monetary plan, Mr. President?

THE PRESIDENT: Well, let us see -- you mean in September, 1935, we are going to do this, that or the other thing? Or something immediate?

Q: A little more in the present.

Q: Does that mean something in September, 1935?

THE PRESIDENT: Pick your own date, Stevie (Mr. Stephenson), it is all right.

Q: That textile strike was off the record?

THE PRESIDENT: Yes, off the record, because, frankly, we do not know enough about all the internal complications to comment on it in any way at this time and there are a lot of internal complications. We do not know what they are after, in the first place. We do not know the demands.

Q: Have you anything to say as to what your intentions are with respect to the carrying out of the new National Labor Relations Board attacks

--- [14] ---

on other Government agencies, particularly with reference to the Chicago Motor Bus case, where the Board [the National Labor Relations Board] made a ruling and asked that the Blue Eagle be removed and the N.R.A. has failed to act? The N.R.A. is seeking, according to General Johnson, to make an investigation of its own.

THE PRESIDENT: I haven't the faintest idea how to reply to that. I do not know anything about it at all. I will have to ask about it. What is the particular case?

Q: The Chicago Motor Coach case. The Company refused to appear before the Regional Labor Board. The Regional Labor Board ruled against the Company and that ruling was afterwards reviewed by the whole [National Labor Relations] Board. There has been handed down [by the National Labor Relations Board] a final ruling [against the Company] and they referred the thing to the N.R.A. Compliance Board for action. This was two weeks ago. General Johnson said he is going to propose, or has proposed, that they send an investigator out there and make a study in the field. The Board maintains that General Johnson has no authority to review its findings. The Board cannot force the Company to take action but the N.R.A. can remove its Blue Eagle.

THE PRESIDENT: What is the name of the company?

Q: The Chicago Motor Coach Company which operates about 150 miles of bus lines in the City of Chicago. The Board found that they had discharged some twenty workers for union activity.

THE PRESIDENT:  I am taking this down and will look into it.

Q:   In recent months there have been some thoughts expressed in certain quarters about the Civil Service system.

THE PRESIDENT:  What about it?

Q:   These quarters have expressed concern over what they call the gradual

--- [15] ---

increase in the blanketing in of the Soldiers Home attendants down there.

THE PRESIDENT:  Well, on that specific case of Johnson City -- there is no
point in talking about it as a general situation -- as I remember it, and
this recollection goes back a couple of months, a very large percentage
of the employees in that Veterans' Home and never taken any examination.
Probably the great majority are perfectly competent but they had never
taken any Civil Service examination and, therefore, they had been covered
in by Executive Order.  The question of politics does not come in;  I do
not know whether they are Republicans or Democrats or anything else.  It
was simply that they had never gone into Civil Service in the regular way.
The Johnson City Order provided that all of those people and anybody else
were to take an examination and if they pass it, they will continue in the
employment.  I think that cannot be considered as weakening the Civil
Service; I should call in strengthening the principle of Civil Service.

Q:   There have been a lot of inconsistent views expressed about political
activity [by Government employees].  The Homw Owners' Loan Corporation
ordered their employees to refrain but two or three other departments have
announced that they do not intend to and do not see any need.

THE PRESIDENT:  Which ones?

Q:   A couple have said that they do not contemplate and do not see any need.

THE PRESIDENT:  Which ones?

Q:   A.A.A. and N.R.A. have issued no policy as far as --

THE PRESIDENT:  (interposing)  I don't see why they should not go along.

Q:   -- and Ickes said he was not going to issue any instructions.

THE PRESIDENT:  The general policy is that they are not supposed to engage

--- [16] ---

in political activities and the same rule would apply to all Government
employees.

Q:   At the Wednesday Conference I believe you told us that you had not heard
the results of the Tuesday primaries.  Have you -- (Laughter)

THE PRESIDENT:  What primaries?

Q:   Last Tuesday's, in Nebraska and Ohio.

THE PRESIDENT:  Oh, did they have primaries there?  You will have to tell me
about it afterwards.

Q:   It is my recollection that Colonel Sultan was Engineer Officer at Chicago.
Has there been any replacement there?

THE PRESIDENT:  I do not think so; only decided on it yesterday afternoon, late.

Q:   What color do you want this tweed suit to be?

THE PRESIDENT:  I think an inoffensive gray, one of those drab colors.

Q:   Thank you, Mr. President.

Press Conference #137
Executive Offices of the White House
August 24, 1934


Q:     Have you any plans for fall?

Q:     Anything you can say on the formation of the American Liberty League?  Anything to say about it?

THE PRESIDENT:  The only thing I can do is to talk to you informally the way I told you on the train that I was going to do.  Naturally, I have no formal statement.  In anticipating another of Fred's (Storm) questions, "Did Jouett Shouse speak to me about it?" -- he did and he came in here and pulled a piece of paper out of his pocket and read me the two objectives which I think all the papers have printed, and I told him that both of the objectives could be subscribed to by every American citizen; that they were what might be called axiomatic, [un-] equivocally acceptable to all Americans, and when he asked me whether there were any objections to the formation of the private organization, I said of course not, it is none of my business and I wouldn't have any objections anyway to a private work which had as its principles working for axiomatic principles of American life.  Well, that's about all that happened.  He said, "Thank you very much" and went out.  So that is literally all that happened when Jouett came in.  Next, Fred?

Q:     Then you are for the Constitution?

THE PRESIDENT:  I won't say "still" because somebody will say that was too passive, I'll say "actively."  Of course, again talking just between us, really I suppose you can use this for background, the

--- [18] ---

thing to note about an organization of this kind -- of course there are a great many of them, with all kinds of names -- you will find in history organizations of this kind that are fraternal and semi-religious, and everything else.  Personally, my own feeling is this:  that when you come down to the definition of American principles you want to go the whole hog; you want to go all the way, instead of stopping short.  An organization that only advocates two or three out of the Ten Commandments, may be a prefectly good organization in the sense that you couldn't object to the two or three out of the Ten Commandments, but that it would have certain shortcomings in having failed to advocate the other seven or eight Ten Commandments.  To put it again in a Biblical way, it has been said that there are two great Commandments -- one is to love God, and the other to love your neighbor.  A gentleman with a rather ribald sense of humor suggested that the two particular tenets of this new organization say you shall love God and then forget your neighbor, and he also raised the question as to whether the other name for their God was not "property."  Now as a matter of fact these two things are worth reading.  One is that the organization will designate officials that will teach the necessity of respect for the rights of persons and property as fundamental to every successful form of government, and will teach that government to encourage enterprise.

Going back again, there isn't much said about your neighbor, and if you

analyze certain things in the Declaration of Independence which helped
opportunity -- life, liberty and the pursuit of happiness -- there are
quite a number of other things that the

--- [19] ---

average, and more than average human, gets out of government besides these
two things.  There is no mention made here in these two things about the
concern of the community, in other words the Government, to try to make it
possible for people who are willing to work, to find work to do.  For
people who want to keep themselves from starvation, keep a roof over their
heads, lead decent lives, have proper educational standards, those are the
concerns of government, besides these two points, and another thing which
isn't mentioned, and that is the protection of the life and the liberty of
the individual against elements in the community that seek to enrich or
advance themselves at the expense of their fellow-citizens.  They have
just as much right to protection by government as anybody else.  I don't
believe that any further comment is necessary after this, what would you
call it -- a homily?  Except that in The Times this morning -- I lay in
bed and laughed for ten minutes -- if you will turn to the financial page
of The Times, "Topics in Wall Street;" that has a short paragraph -- one
that appealed to me.  Darned good too, most of them, because they give you
a real highlight on what's going on, and there was one paragraph that
started off like this -- I forget the exact phraseology -- The speculative
fraternity in Wall Street regards the new American Liberty League as a
direct answer from Heaven to their prayer."

Q:    Do you subscribe to the view of Secretary Ickes that this will draw lines
      pretty sharply between liberals and reactionaries?

THE PRESIDENT:   I don't want to say anything about it.

Q:    Did Mr. Shouse invite you to become a member?

--- [20] ---

THE PRESIDENT:   I don't think he did.  Must have been an oversight.

Q:    Senator Schall made a speech last night in which he said that there were
      indications that the Administration was thinking of setting up its own
      press services and that the U.P., A.P., and the I.N.S. are going to be
      scrapped in favor of this governmental agency?

THE PRESIDENT:   I will have to tell you that I was so much interested in that
      statement and so utterly opposed to putting the U.P., A.P., and I.N.S. out
      of business that I sent word to Senator Schall asking for his information,
      because a thing like that ought to be run down and stopped right away.  Of
      course he must have had definite and certain information on which to base
      a statement of that kind.

Q:    Did you talk with General Johnson today?  Have you anything to say about
      N.R.A. organization?

THE PRESIDENT:   No, we are just going ahead.  Of course on N.R.A., if I were
      writing a story I didn't think could be overdrawn -- at this time the
      actual situation is this:  The National Recovery Act, as I remember it,
      lapses -- goes out of existence, I think -- in June next.  I think, ob-

viously, before then, we have to get some kind of legislation if any portion of it, or portions of it, are to be made permanent -- and obviously
a great many portions of it will be made permanent -- just to take some
one controversial thing, for instance child labor, minimum hours, certain
provisions relating to unfair practices -- but between now and January we
have got to decide to work up a decision, or come to a decision, as to
what legislation will be asked in Congress, and I think about all that can
be said today is that we are in a position, and will be for

--- [21] ---

the next two or three months, of studying what kind of recommendation will
be made to the Congress. And General Johnson is working on that Triple A.
There are several dozen people who are all giving a certain amount of consideration to that problem. And in the meantime N.R.A. per se -- we have
already lifted certain features out of it, like National Labor Relations
-- will probably continue to function. Probably General Johnson, who is
off on a holiday now, will devote most of his time to it, but not to the
actual details of administration, but will certainly continue as Administrator of National Recovery. In other words, we are beginning to look for
a proposal to come up next winter in Congress and we are getting ready to
meet it before it comes.

Q:  Is price fixing one of those questions still to be determined?

THE PRESIDENT:  Oh my, yes.

Q:  Has anything been discussed about the possibility of recommended changes
in anti-trust laws?

THE PRESIDENT:  No, we haven't got to it -- the question of the relationship
between price fixing and the anti-trust laws are all being worked on and
at the present time we haven't got to any point.  If I were writing your
story I wouldn't say anything except that we are working on it and would
not even give a suggestion as to any determination on it.

Q:  Do you know anything about what General Johnson referred to as a plan you
would have ready to announce in about two weeks at Hyde Park?

THE PRESIDENT:  That would be so that in the interim we would have administrative handling of N.R.A. problems.

--- [22] ---

Q:  Will you tell us when you will proclaim the Cuban Treaty?

THE PRESIDENT:  This afternoon about five o'clock -- they told me that this
morning -- does anybody know?

MR. EARLY:  That's correct.

Q:  Will you proclaim it immediately afterwards -- you have to make it effective?

THE PRESIDENT:  I suppose so -- I don't know, nobody mentioned it.

Q:  It was slipped to us for of course there is a lot of talk about what is and
isn't going to be done.

THE PRESIDENT: I don't know. I haven't heard about it. I think it was a story
to Stevie of the A.P.'s credit, one of those Timbuktu stories, that ...
was going to come out immediately and have the government taken over.

Q: Have you conferred with Mr. Frederick H. Prince in that connection?

THE PRESIDENT: No, I thought he was busy racing.

Q: Getting back to N.R.A., do you have anything to say now about his "interim"
organization?

THE PRESIDENT: No, of course we have been talking about it for two weeks or
more.

Q: May I get back to the Constitution for a moment. Have you given any thought
to the possible connection between conditions in the State of Louisiana today and certain clauses in the Constitution which make it mandatory on the
Federal Government to maintain a republican form of government in every
state?

THE PRESIDENT: That's a new one -- of course there again on this Louisiana
situation, obviously we want to maintain a republican form of government,
but at the same time, under the republican

--- [23] ---

form of government, a municipality is definitely a creature of a state
government. Now a state government -- for instance, when I was Governor
of New York when New York City's finances were getting into such a jam,
there were a lot of very hoity-toity Senators who were strict constitution-
alists, who came to me and said, "Take over the government of the City of
New York," because all of their city bonds were in jeopardy. I met prominent businessmen and lawyers from New York City who wanted me as Governor
to take over the City of New York, but I had to tell them I couldn't do
it. I told them, however, that the Legislature of the State of New York,
having been the body which granted the charter to the City of New York,
had the right to take away the charter from the City of New York and set
up any form of municipal government that the Legislature thought should
apply to that municipality. In this Louisiana case the Legislature of the
State of Louisiana has the inherent, constitutional right to govern a
municipality within that State as it sees fit, provided it does not violate the right of franchise and certain rights of self-government. That
is about as far as you can go.

Q: Are you satisfied they have not violated those certain rights?

THE PRESIDENT: They haven't done it up until today.

Q: You are satisfied then that there is a republican form of government?

THE PRESIDENT: In the City of New Orleans?

Q: No, in the State.

THE PRESIDENT: I should say that if there was a free franchise in the State of
Louisiana, the questions would come up as to whether a

--- [24] ---

free franchise was being exercised or not, and we haven't gotten to that
yet. Here's a nice point. Let me ask you a question. Is it a republican
form of government for the State of Rhode Island to confine the franchise
only to people who have a certain amount of property?

Q:   They had a revision of that one time.

THE PRESIDENT:   That's a nice question -- there is a very restrictive franchise
in the State of Rhode Island today.

Q:   In other words the clause is all wide open.

THE PRESIDENT:   No.

Q:   Do you have any comment to make on threatened textile strikes?

THE PRESIDENT:   I haven't heard anything about it in the last couple of days.
There is only one other thing, for the benefit of the Hearst papers, and
there may be others which may copy the idea. I horrified the Secretary of
Agriculture coming back on the train, by suddenly announcing out of a
clear blue sky, that I was very glad that he had said what he did about
the theory, the economic theory of foreign ships carrying some American
goods. If you will read his letter, it is a rather interesting thing, and
shows why it is necessary to always give the whole story instead of part
of the story. Representative Bland wrote him a letter in June and he answered it about July fifteenth, and in effect he said that while there were
many considerations, such as national defense, etc., in regard to our
Merchant Marine, one should also at the same time consider certain other
things, which were not always considered. And in effect what he said was
absolutely true from the point of view of economics. One reason why American manufac-

--- [25] ---

turers and American farmers can't sell more goods to ·other countries is
because other countries can't buy. It is obvious if they could pay they
could buy more. If other countries were able to pay a portion of that
cost in the form of services, they could buy more American goods. There
is apparently no question that if every time our American exports were
carried on foreign ships foreigners could buy more American exports. But
that is only one side. Hearst papers take notice. There are other factors
to which the Secretary of Agriculture referred. He didn't outline them
but they are very simple. There are three other factors they forgot to
counterbalance against the facts he mentioned. One is the fact that from
the point of view of national defense we obviously need a certain number
of American merchantmen which could be used for national defense in time
of war. That's perfectly clear. Number two, in the event of a war in
which we were not a party, let us say, a general European war or a Far
Eastern War, foreign shipping might be finally eliminated because of that
war and then we would have no bottoms to carry our American goods and we
would be out of luck. So that is another case of the necessity for having
American ships. And there is a third factor. We know that when we didn't
have American ships on certain runs in certain lanes of world trade, foreign ships and foreign shipowners have had an unfortunate tenacity in getting together and squeezing American exporters on rates. In other words,
in having control of the ships and using it against American trade, and in

favor of their own trade, you have a third insurance factor that makes it
necessary for us to have an American Merchant Marine, and all the Secretary
of Agriculture did was

--- [26] ---

to call attention to the obvious economic factor on the other side of the
insurance question; that the more we make it impossible for foreign ships
to carry some of our goods, the more difficult it makes it for them to buy
our goods. There is the whole story, not just a part of it. And if the
whole story is written the answers are perfectly obvious.

Q: Now that Hopkins is back will you have a conference with him on the Pennsylvania relief situation before you go to Hyde Park?

THE PRESIDENT: I am going to see him tomorrow, but I don't believe Harry knows
anything about the Pennsylvania situation.

Q: Have you had any recent indications what is to be done up there?

THE PRESIDENT: Two weeks, or about a week ago, I was told by Aubrey Williams
that Pennsylvania would be asked by the Federal Government to do its
share, which they are not doing at the present time, and the only way out
is to call an extra session. We are in favor of an extra session.

NOTE:

In keeping a numerical record of the Press Conferences, the reporter allowed for three Press Conferences which he had been informed were held during his absence on a brief vacation.  Actually, however, only one Press Conference (No. 137) had been held during that period.  Unfortunately, this error was not discovered until after some two hundred subsequent Press Conferences had been held and it was therefore decided to skip Nos. 138 and 139.

Press Conference #140
Held in the President's Study at Hyde Park, N. Y.
August 29, 1934, 11:15 A.M.


THE PRESIDENT: I do not think I could even invent news and that is saying a
    lot. Somebody wrote a new song [referring to the stack of papers in front
    of him]; somebody had a Golden Wedding; somebody was 102 years old. That
    is all.

Q: We can't use any of it.

THE PRESIDENT: Several towns had One Hundredth Anniversaries.

Q: Can you comment on Henry Morganthau's statement?

THE PRESIDENT: I have not read it.

Q: He announced last night that this $2,800,000,000 of gold profit would ul-
    timately be used to curtail the public debt.

THE PRESIDENT: That is a hope, isn't it?

Q: He said it wasn't;he made it very definite. What is worrying most people,
    but is the only way to do it, is to turn it into currency in exchange for
    Government securities, which would mean increasing the Budget $5,000,000,000
    to $7,800,000,000 which would be a very real inflation and which would
    serve at once to make the dollar worth only about sixty cents in this
    country.

THE PRESIDENT: Say, he is good, you know!

Q: He rehearsed that before the mirror.

Q: Give us that again. (Laughter)


                (Mrs. Roosevelt entered the room at this point.)


THE PRESIDENT: How are you? How is Sis?

MRS. ROOSEVELT: She is fine. We had dinner together and I put her on the
    train.

                        --- [29] ---

THE PRESIDENT: It is too early but Henry [Secretary Morgenthau) did, I think,
    use the word "ultimately."

Q: We ought to get the paper.

THE PRESIDENT: Just between us, if I make a speech and say I am going to do
    something ultimately, what does it convey to you? It means some unan-
    nounced time pretty far distant. If I were going to do it tomorrow, I
    would not say "ultimately." Well, that is about the size of it. In other
    words, it is just another of those things where I suppose he is perfectly

correct in saying "ultimately" that money will be used.  It is there.  It is -- I do not know what the word for it is -- it is a nest egg.  Ultimately, one uses one's nest egg.  I think that is about all that one can say about it.

Q:  Mr. President, have you any comment this morning on the textile situation?

THE PRESIDENT:  No, anything I say would be purely speculative.

Q:  At this meeting where they adopted this resolution the day before yesterday in connection with your Order 23, at that time they appointed one man who was supposed to convey all that to you and it was not quite clear whether that was going to be by telegram or whether he would come up to see you.

THE PRESIDENT:  I do not think so.  I have not had anybody ask to see me.

Q:  You haven't had any requests?

THE PRESIDENT:  Have we, Mac (Mr. McIntyre)?

MR. McINTYRE:  No, sir.

Q:  There was a story appearing in the Washington papers, I think it was Monday, that General Johnson put a letter of resignation on your desk.  Is there anything?

--- [30] ---

THE PRESIDENT:  I think he said something, didn't he?

Q:  He said, "I have not resigned."

THE PRESIDENT:  Well, I haven't anything further to say than what he said.

Q:  He did not categorically say that he had not made an attempt to resign at one time or another, did he?

THE PRESIDENT:  Well, he made a statement.  I guess it was all right.

Q:  How are you enjoying it up here?

THE PRESIDENT:  Fine.  I have not started to work yet.

Q:  Neither have we.

Q:  We have got you working hard in the daily press.

THE PRESIDENT:  I forget who is coming to lunch.

Q:  Norman Davis.

THE PRESIDENT:  Right, in fact he is coming at 12:00 o'clock and then this afternoon Felix Frankfurter and his wife are coming to spend the night.  I have not seen him for nearly a year.

Q:  What had we better make him?

THE PRESIDENT:   It will be an awful shock to Mark Sullivan and others that I have not seen Felix for nearly a year.

Q:   He saw you at Groton?

THE PRESIDENT:   Is that it?  Well, that was in September; it was early.  Oh, no, you are thinking about the campaign and that was 1932.  I saw him up here last September before he went to spend his college [sabbatical] year on the other side.

Q:   We are putting him on the Supreme Court this afternoon.

THE PRESIDENT:   I suppose that probably Felix and his wife will talk mostly about things on the other side.

Q:   What school?  It is not Cambridge or Oxford?

--- [31] ---

THE PRESIDENT:   He was exchange professor at Oxford for a year and now he is going back, I take it -- I have not heard anything to the contrary -- to Harvard Law School and I take it he will tell me much about things on the other side.  I do not think he knows much about things on this side.  That is literally all I could write about it.

Q:   Davis will do the same thing?

THE PRESIDENT:   Yes; I have not seen him since he got back.

Q:   There were always rumors about Woodin resigning.  Are you going to get out a statement to reassure people about something?

THE PRESIDENT:   About what, Russell (Mr. Young)?

Q:   (Mr. Young)  About confidence.  (Laughter)

THE PRESIDENT:   I think the best thing to do on that will be to get hold of Bill Dewart and Mrs. Ogden Reed and get them up to lunch and give them a lot of personal reassurances.

Q:   Mr. President, please let us not get personal.  (Laughter)

THE PRESIDENT:   That was off the record.

Q:   Have you invited them to lunch?

THE PRESIDENT:   If you get me a list of names of the people that want these reassurances, we will have a picnic for them.

Q:   How about Henry Fletcher [Chairman of the Republican National Committee]?

THE PRESIDENT:   People outside of the political arena.

MRS. ROOSEVELT:   Would you serve frankfurters?  (Laughter)

THE PRESIDENT:   Yes.

Q:   In place of the Count [Rudolph de Zapp], may I ask you whether the matter of the new [Public] Health Officer [for the District of Columbia] has been brought to your attention?

THE PRESIDENT: I never heard of it. I did not know there was a vacancy.

--- [32] ---

Q: I think the Commissioners [of the District of Columbia] make the appointment.

THE PRESIDENT: I think they do. Whom do they generally appoint?

Q: I think they pick out some local doctor.

Q: Mr. President, I wasn't quite clear about the cotton garment situation -- what you said a few minutes ago.

THE PRESIDENT: There isn't any news.

Q: That will come before you directly because that is your Executive Order that they are defying?

THE PRESIDENT: I don't know.

Q: What is the next step?

THE PRESIDENT: I do not know. Frankly, I do not know what the next step is in either the textile or the garment.

Q: Of course, if they go ahead and refuse to abide by that Order, there must be some enforcement agency to take up the problem in due time, either an N.R.A. agency or the Department of Justice. I am wondering what machinery --

THE PRESIDENT: (interposing) I am wondering too.

Q: Are you awaiting the return of General Johnson to get further information on the subject?

THE PRESIDENT: No; nothing to do with it. Frankly, I do not know a thing about it. I just get a few high spots here and there.

Q: There were reports from Washington that in order to build up or increase employment during the winter it may mean taking off the restrictions on production and let them increase production and at the same time take measures to increase consumption. Have you heard anything about it?

THE PRESIDENT: No; it is over my head.

--- [33] ---

Q: Is this Garment Code, Executive Order on the garment thing, against which they are protesting, being relaxed in any way?

THE PRESIDENT: I do not know anything about. If I did I would not tell you but it is true that I do not know anything about it. (Laughter)

Q: Can you tell me anything about the Governor's [Governor Lehman] visit yesterday?

THE PRESIDENT: No, just ordinary conversation, that is all. In other words, even for a speculative story it is too damned early. I would not know what to write. We talked over all sorts of things.

Q: He intimated to the boys up in Albany that he discussed with you chiefly his State campaign and things up here [in New York].

THE PRESIDENT: We did not talk campaign at all, not a bit.

Q: (Mr. Storm of the U.P.) Make that record off the record, please. (Laughter)

Q: (Mr. Francis Stephenson of the A.P.) I can deny your story.

THE PRESIDENT: We will make that off the record. Really, Herbert [Governor Lehman] and I talked about a whole lot of things but it was just conversation, mostly at the table with the family there.

Q: Have you any comment to make on the outcome of the California primary?

THE PRESIDENT: No -- no more than on any other primary -- that should be added to it.

Q: Anything of special interest in Dr. Pearson's [Professor Alfred J. Pearson] visit here?

THE PRESIDENT: No. The only reason that most of these people come -- just for information and not for quotation or anything like that -- is that people tell me about people who have just come back from the

--- [34] ---

other side. I had never heard about this man before and somebody said that he was an extraordinarily interesting man and it would be worth my while to see him when he came back. He came back and told me the same thing he told you. He is tremendously interested in Sweden.

Q: I think it is going to be in his new book.

THE PRESIDENT: New book, probably. (Laughter)

Q: What did you say about never having heard of him before? (Laughter)

THE PRESIDENT: A lot of people coming to Hyde Park are people who have been on the list for two or three months as having been highly recommended as being interesting people. Now we are cleaning up on them, going over the old lists. They are people we said we would see a long time ago. It would not be polite to send them a cordial invitation and say that we have never heard of them before.

Q: Just use that as background?

MRS. ROOSEVELT: The Press is beginning to believe that Dr. Pearson enjoyed his visit more than you did.

THE PRESIDENT: He was very interesting. He told me all about his visit to

Hitler.

Q:  And Russia?

THE PRESIDENT:  Yes.

Q:  For public use, are you going to the Fair [the County Fair at Rhinebeck]
    tomorrow?

THE PRESIDENT:  This afternoon or tomorrow, I don't know which yet.

MR. McINTYRE:  That isn't for publication.

THE PRESIDENT:  There again, the Fair has been trying to advertise for their re-
    ceipts that I would get there on a certain afternoon and I refuse to be ad-
    vertised.

--- [35] ---

Q:  It has been publicly advertised that you will be there today or tomorrow.

Q:  They [referring to two of the reporters] were "taken" on the Midway.  They
    are city slickers.

THE PRESIDENT:  Did you ever see that game where they have a little shell that
    goes over -- (Laughter)

Q:  (Mr. Roddan, interposing)  It wasn't that; it was a black and red wheel and
    it would never stop on the one you bet it was going to stop on.

THE PRESIDENT:  Of course, I am very anxious to have this Dutchess County Fair
    of ours put on a paying basis so I hope you will all go and see all the
    exhibits.

MR. McINTYRE:  Mr. President, with respect to your remarks about the little shell
    game, Charlie Hurd says that we have seen it played without shells in some
    of these Press Conferences.  (Laughter)

Q:  I wonder if you would add anything more about Dutchess County for the lo-
    cal newspapers?  I just noticed that Jim Townsend --

THE PRESIDENT:  (interposing)  There again, I have not seen Jim since I do not
    know when -- last fall.

Q:  There is a water project down in the town of Hyde Park?

THE PRESIDENT:  I heard about it yesterday from Henry Hackett and have not
    heard about it any more.

Q:  I thought probably you might be interested; you are a taxpayer of course.

Q:  (Mr. Roddan)  Is he paid up?

THE PRESIDENT:  I do not know enough about it to comment on it.  I haven't any
    idea of the details.

Q:  Did you know that you were pretty nearly blacklisted and posted up at the
    Press Club?

THE PRESIDENT: Didn't I pay my dues?

--- [36] ---

Q: You did finally. (Laughter)

THE PRESIDENT: They were damned lucky to get paid at all.

MR. McINTYRE: Missy [Miss LeHand] rushed a check over to them.

Q: Are we going to see Norman Davis?

MR. McINTYRE: I imagine he will stop off at the Hotel [The Nelson House] on his way down.

THE PRESIDENT: Now I will tell you why not. He stopped down last time at the Nelson House and believe me -- (interrupted by laughter). I think he is going right back to Stockbridge.

Q: He has already said almost everything he had to say on the European situation down in Washington, so there is no reason in having him stop.

Q: You will be surprised what we can get out of him.

MR. McINTYRE: This is a purely personal visit anyhow.

THE PRESIDENT: This is a purely personal visit.

MR. McINTYRE: Will you let the Secret Service men notify us in advance as to when you are going to the Fair because we have to --

THE PRESIDENT: (interposing) I don't think it will be until tomorrow but I don't think it is quite the right thing to use it for advertising.

Q: Have the boys arrived?

THE PRESIDENT: Not yet. John [Roosevelt] won't get here until Saturday night and Franklin [Roosevelt] is still so far off on the coast of Maine, cruising, that he cannot get back in time.

MR. McINTYRE: Are your plans definite enough about the yacht races to tell the boys now?

THE PRESIDENT: I will tell you what you can do. You can put it this way, which is strictly true, that if everything is all quiet I may go on the NOURMAHAL on the fourteenth around to Newport and see the races.

--- [37] ---

Of course I am awfully keen on those races; I have seen a great many in the past. I will then come back here. It is only a matter of three or four days but it is purely tentative because, as you know, when I came up here the question of plans was absolutely open. I might go back to Washington -- any one of a dozen different things.

Q: Would you get on the NOURMAHAL here?

THE PRESIDENT: Yes.

Q:   They are betting six to five on the ENDEAVOR this morning.

THE PRESIDENT:  So I see.  They must have seen her sail alongside the old boat.

Q:   Have you a destroyer for us?

MR. McINTYRE:  Would there be any objection to going aboard the destroyer to see the races?

THE PRESIDENT:  I think it is all right to keep it within our own group.  I think if I do go around it is a devil of a trip to make you take.  The best thing would be for you to go to Newport from here, motor over and, if you cannot get accommodations in Newport, then just get them in Jamestown.

MR. McINTYRE:  We are also trying to borrow a yacht.  It won't be as big as the NOURMAHAL.

Q:   Thank you, Mr. President.

Press Conference #141
In the Study of the President's Home at Hyde Park, N. Y.
September 5, 1934, 10:50 A.M.


THE PRESIDENT: Where is the Captain? [Referring to the captain of the ball team which had played Lowell Thomas' team at Pawling the Sunday previous.]

Q:  On the way.

Q:  We have discovered a way to beat them. We are going to put two left fielders out there with gloves.

Q:  I will say you have to have gloves.

MR. McINTYRE: The best of that strategy is having Fred (Mr. Storm) in the box. He can't hit.

Q:  I think we will play Stevie (Mr. Stephenson) on the fence all the time.

THE PRESIDENT: You are certainly good, getting over the fence.

Q:  (Mr. Stephenson) Wasn't I? And with my eye on the ball all the time. That eighteenth time is what wrecked me.

THE PRESIDENT: There is only one way we can be sure of winning and that's like in the old Harvard -- the Crimson Lampoon games. You never had a keg [of beer] on first; you had to earn that. But we did have a keg on second and one on third.

Q:  How did you get anybody back to the home plate?

THE PRESIDENT: Oh, we had two kegs there. (Laughter)

Q:  Speaking of kegs, what did you feed Upton Sinclair?

THE PRESIDENT: Do you know what I fed him? Two long glasses of iced tea.

Q:  You must have had something in them.

Q:  He was babbling when he came back [to the Nelson House].

--- [39] ---

Q:  Well, he traveled a long way.

Q:  Mr. President, can you tell us anything more than Sinclair told us yesterday in five thousand well chosen words?

Q:  He promised that you were going to tell us; that you would tell us what happened here.

THE PRESIDENT: Did he, really?

Q:  Yes.

THE PRESIDENT: Then he must have had something on the way to Poughkeepsie.

Q:    There is nothing that you can say about it, Mr. President?

THE PRESIDENT:  No.

Q:    Cannot you discuss the Epic Plan along purely nonpolitical lines?

THE PRESIDENT:  No.

I do not think there is any news.  I am going to possibly have a story this afternoon.  I think I can give you the background on it now so that if the thing does break you will know about it.  It is the appointment of one of those special boards of three for the cotton textile.  For heaven's sake, do not use the story until I give you the release on it.  The Garrison Board which, of course, might be called the Court of Appeals, feels, I think very rightly, that they should not take original jurisdiction over the strike settlements, that it should go to one of the courts of first instance and they recommended that instead of having any question of settle- ment come before the cotton textile mediation board, of which Robert Bruere is the chairman, that we should carry it out by a special board.  There is a provision, you know, in the law for the appointment of a special board. As I remember it, wasn't that San Francisco board one of those special boards?  I think it was.

--- [40] ---

Q:    Yes, sir.

THE PRESIDENT:  Well, this will be exactly the same kind.  I have not got the third man yet because I cannot locate him.  Two of them will be Governor Winant of New Hampshire and one Mr. Smith of Atlanta.

Q:    Who is he?

THE PRESIDENT:  A prominent attorney and has been the chairman of the Regional Labor Board with very great success.  He is a sone of old Hoke Smith.  This is all subject to release.  The third man they could not get so we have to get a third man.

Q:    Garrison is the chairman?

THE PRESIDENT:  This [indicating] is the Labor Relations Board Letter:  (Read- ing)

"My dear Mr. President:

"This Board, as you know, has tried through mediation to avert the textile strike.  We wish to report the circumstances which brought us into the situation; the steps which we took in en- deavoring to avert the strike; and our recommendations for a course of action which we hope may bring about a prompt and just settlement of the controversy.

"One of the duties imposed upon the Board by the Executive Order which created it is a study of the work of industrial relations boards established under the Codes.  Because of com- plaints made to us that the machinery for handling violations of section 7 (a) in the cotton textile industry was inadequate, we gave special attention to this matter.  During the past

month we sought, by conferences with the Cotton Textile National
Industrial Relations Board, the Code Authority, members of the
Cotton Textile Institute, and officials of the United Textile
Workers Union, to establish agreement upon a procedure which
would provide more adequate handling of 7 (a) cases in the cotton textile industry.  In the course of these discussions it became apparent that no action which our Board might take with
respect to these cases would in itself prevent the strike.  The
Board concluded, therefore, that nothing would be gained by any
final action on its part until the strike was either averted
or terminated.

"Our inquiries and discussions in connection with the 7 (a)
cases merged into the causes of the present strike, one of
which is the handling of these cases.  These circumstances
led us inevitably into the role of mediator, particularly
since the offer of the Cotton Textile National Industrial
Board to

--- [41] ---

mediate had been rejected by the Union.  This rejection occurred
last Friday, August 24, and the Union requested our Board to
act.  The Board immediately called in the Union Committee and
conferred with it throughout the week-end.  On Monday the Board
dispatched invitations to the Cotton Textile Institute, the
Cotton Textile National Industrial Relations Board and the
Union Committee to attend a round table conference.  On Wednesday the President of the Cotton Textile Institute declined the
invitation.

"The Board being unable to bring about a joint conference, which
the Board believed held out the only real possibility of avert-
ing the strike, separate conferences were held with representatives of the Cotton Textile Institute and the Union.  In these
conferences the Board made every possible effort to find some
formula for avoiding the strike, but without success.

"As a matter of policy we doubt the wisdom of the Board's acting
as mediator in this or any other strike situation.  Mediation
is frequently carried on by the regional labor boards, which are
under the jurisdiction of this Board; but it has been our con-
viction that the purposes of Public Resolution 44 and the Executive Order establishing this Board could best be served if the
Board kept itself clear of mediation activities.  It is evident
that the  Public Resolution and the Executive Order intended
our Board to serve as a quasi-court for interpreting in terms
of particular cases the meaning and intent of section 7 (a).

"As a semi-judicial body it is desirable that we be as far removed as possible from direct participation in controversies
over some aspects of which we may at a later date be asked to
sit in judgment.  The Board ought not to be placed in a position
which might hamper respect for its judicial activities and
hinder its effectiveness as a body for building up public
opinion in support of disinterested interpretations of the
law.  It is true that under the Public Resolution and the
Executive Order the Board is authorized to investigate issues

in controversies which are burdening interstate commerce, but
in our judgment this power should be exercised sparingly, and
rather for the purpose of ascertaining the facts prior to a
strike situation, than for the purpose of settling it after it
has occurred.

"In deference to the important function which we have been
created by you to discharge, we believe that the public interest would best be served by our immediate withdrawal from
further mediation efforts in the textile strike.  From our
knowledge of the situation we are satisfied that mediation
looking toward a termination of the strike can best go forward
by your creating a special board under Public Resolution 44,
with full authority to investigate the causes of the strike
and to propose a just basis of settlement.

"We shall be glad to assist such a board in whatever ways
seem appropriate and in conformity with the general purposes

--- [42] ---

which it is our duty under the statute and the Executive Order
to discharge.

"Respectfully submitted,

"Lloyd K. Garrison, Chairman."

Q:   Is that to be released?

THE PRESIDENT:  If you want to carry that letter and the fact that this board
    will be announced very soon, that is all right.

Q:   But not to use the names?

THE PRESIDENT:  Not the names yet.  I have to get all three at the same time and
    I will probably get the third name this afternoon.

Q:   Late enough for the morning papers?

Q:   Early enough for the evening papers?  (Laughter)

THE PRESIDENT:  That will give you a grand story.

Q:   In connection with the textile strike, did you have a telegram from Senator
    Kean, of New Jersey?

MR. McINTYRE:  Got it this morning.

THE PRESIDENT:  What does the old boy want?

Q:   I think he has had a tip it was going to be done and he wanted to get in
    on the band wagon quick.  It has all the earmarks.

Q:   Somebody told him.

THE PRESIDENT:  He would not have done it of his own accord.

Q:   Somebody told him it was going to be done.

Q:   Is there anything to say about Mayor LaGuardia's visit here?

THE PRESIDENT:  No, I don't know what he is going to talk about.  I suppose in
general it will be about the City financial problems and relief problems.

There is one thing you boys could ask about and get an awfully good story.
About three months ago there appeared an editorial in the

--- [43] ---

London Times which, of course, people over here still regard as the bail-
wick of Toryism, and as I remember it, I have filed it away, the editorial
ran something like this.  That we in England are somewhat surprised, somewhat amazed at the resistance, the objections being offered by certain
elements in American industry to Article 7-A, which reads as follows --
and then it quoted Article 7-A which, as you know, is very short.  Then it
goes on to say, "Our surprise is based on the fact, which every Englishman
knows, that its principle has been accepted in England since" -- when was
the general strike?

Q:   1926.

THE PRESIDENT:  " -- since 1926, and the acceptance of the principles of 7-A
since that time has prevented any serious labor difficulties in the British
Isles, and therefore, perhaps, it is interesting to note that conservative
old England has been for so many years several steps ahead of so-called
radical young America in its dealing with social problems and labor problems."  I wish you [addressing Lord Illiffe, who was attending the Press
Conference] could talk to these good people and tell them something about
how you have worked out some of your labor problems, except that you are
just about three jumps ahead of us.

LORD ILLIFFE:  (Joint owner of the London Telegraph and other papers)  Of course,
labor has had its experiences in England for a very much longer time than
it has in the United States, has it not?

THE PRESIDENT:  Taking it by and large, yes.

LORD ILLIFFE:  We have a responsible union system now but, as you know, we have
had very considerable troubles.  But I think the same thing is going to
apply to the United States.  You have unions here that

--- [44] ---

have only just begun to feel their power and when a man gets power at first
he does not know how to use it, but he does after a bit.  I am perfectly
certain it is going to turn out right in the end.

THE PRESIDENT:  Some of our unions are going to work out really well.

LORD ILLIFFE:  The result of the general strike in England in 1926, I think, is
that it gave unions a greater feeling of responsibility than they feel before.  They really thought that it was possible for them to do anything and
they did not consider the interest of the Nation as a whole.  Before 1926
they played their own hand; after 1926 they realized that they have to consider the general good of the public.  In the United States, as soon as

they realize that, you will find that the union system works all right.

In these days, when you have organized capital you have to have organized labor, and each side has to realize its responsibility for the public good as a whole.

Q: Does England realize the principle of collective bargaining?

LORD ILLIFFE: Oh, yes; it does.

THE PRESIDENT: Did the bill pass the present House of Commons that was pending away back in June before I went off on my trip? It was a bill which would give the government enforcement authority in the case of agreements which had been made in any particular industry between labor and capital. As I recall it, there was some bill pending of that kind and it was a government measure.

LORD ILLIFFE: I don't remember it. Was it just recently?

THE PRESIDENT: It was in June before I went on my trip.

LORD ILLIFFE: I don't remember that. You mean to enforce agreements that have been arrived at voluntarily between capital and labor, that they should be enforced by government?

--- [45] ---

THE PRESIDENT: Yes.

LORD ILLIFFE: I don't remember that.

THE PRESIDENT: There was something of that kind. I saw it in a newspaper story. It might not have been entirely accurate.

One thing -- and this is off the record completely, just conversation between us -- thinking people are beginning to realize certain elements in the situation. This brings in California again, but I have to keep it off the record becuase there is no use talking about things like that out loud.

In the San Francisco strike a lot of people completely lost their heads and telegraphed me, "For God's sake come back; turn the ship around." Stephenson and Roddan and Fred (Storm) would not let me turn the ship around. They insisted on Hawaii. Everybody demanded that I sail into San Francisco Bay, all flags flying and guns double shotted, and end the strike. They went completely off the handle.

Well, I kept in pretty close touch, which I would not admit to the Three Musketeers. It appeared very clear to me that just as soon as there was talk about a general strike, there were probably two elements bringing about that general strike. One was the hot-headed young leaders who had had no experience in organized labor whatsoever and said that the only thing to do was to have a general strike, and, on the other side was this combination out there on the Coast of people like the editor of the Los Angeles Times, for instance, who was praying for a general strike. In other words, there was the old, conservative crowd just hoping that there would be a general strike, being clever enough to know that a general strike always fails. Hence there was a great deal of encouragement for a general strike.

--- [46] ---

That is why I have to say this off the record because, if you put me in court, I could not prove it from the legal point, but it was there. For instance, this Hearst man operated among some of the newspapers in San Francisco and along the Coast, and they all agreed to work together, all the editors of all the papers, for a general objective, and the objective was to encourage the general strike. That is the fact, as I say, although I could not produce legal proof of it in court. But the fact remains that they did discuss and encourage it among themselves. In other words, they baited the other fellows into it, not by offering him money but by baiting him into it.

The general strike started and immediately the strikers, being young, did the silly thing of saying to the inhabitants, "You cannot eat in that restaurant, but you can eat in that restaurant." Naturally, the public resented it.

Of course they learn by things of that kind. They have got to go through the actual processes, actual examples, and not interference from the Federal Government or the President or the United States troops. People will learn from a certain number of examples. We have to conduct the country and essentially to conduct labor to their responsibility.

LORD ILLIFFE: We realized in England that there would be a general strike on before 1926, but, until the thing occurred, we were frightened of it. But I am inclined to agree that no general strike can succeed and that it did a lot towards making the labor element realize its responsibility in Great Britain.

THE PRESIDENT: As a matter of fact, this textile strike, off the record, would not have occurred at all if it had not been for a gentleman named Norman Thomas. He is an idealist but, when it comes down to practical

--- [47] ---

things, he is not there at all. There is nothing. He got up and made a speech in this meeting, a meeting which was completely in hand, well in hand. They were not going to go out on the third of September until he made a speech and then they forced the thing on McMahon and others. It was against their will because these unfortunate textile people in the meeting did not realize what McMahon and the leaders knew, that there was a six-weeks supply of cotton goods on hand, on the shelves, and the people running the factories were perfectly delighted.

LORD ILLIFFE: They wanted their stocks used up?

THE PRESIDENT: Yes.

Q: Mr. President, would it be possible for us to use this interview with Lord Illiffe, and bring in the fact that you questioned him a little bit about English labor conditions?

THE PRESIDENT: Submitting it to him first, submitting it to the editor.

I don't know that there is anything pending. I am nearly cleaned up. I was terribly far behind.

Q:   Mr. President, would you care to make any comment on the decline in Government bonds and the effect on new financing?

THE PRESIDENT:   I didn't know that they had any.

Q:   There are five new lows.

THE PRESIDENT:   What did it amount to?

Q:   Just a little bit below par.

THE PRESIDENT:   No, the only comment would have to be off the record.  It is regarding the attitude of certain newspapers and therefore I want to make it off the record.  But it is an interesting thing, the number of people who have come to me, not in political life or government life at all, and said -- readers of these papers -- "Why are

--- [48] ---

people trying to destroy the credit of their own Government?"  Now, that is the fact.  Why are newspapers trying to destroy the credit of their own Government?  It is just one of those things.  It is a little bit like that front page of the Sun that came out two weeks ago Saturday that I wrote to Will Dewart (N. Y. Sun) about.  The average layman, reading that sort of thing, says, "My God, is the Government going to have trouble in financing a small amount of $1,700,000,000 on September 15th and October 15th?"  That is the impression he would gain from reading the financial pages and the front pages.  And, of course, there is nothing to be done about it.  You cannot do anything against it, that would be silly.

Some day I am going to read to you, off the record, my letter to Bill Dewart which he got two weeks ago and to which he has not replied.  If I do say so, I think it is good.

Q:   I should think it would be.  (Laughter)

THE PRESIDENT:   There is one line which you cannot use because I am going to use it later on, and that was that I would have to amend what I said in my Inaugural Address when I said that the greatest thing that America has to fear is fear itself.  I would now say that there is a greater thing that America needs to fear, and that is those who seek to instill fear into the American people.

Q:   A number of the papers have been carrying stories recently to the effect that the budget would not be balanced.

THE PRESIDENT:   Oh, Stevie, (Mr. Stephenson) send this damn thing down to your office in Washington.

Q:   (Mr. Stephenson)  What date line is that?

THE PRESIDENT:   Send it down.  $500,000,000 -- this is off the record -- it is an A.P. story that a five hundred million dollar tax bill is

--- [49] ---

planned.  It is an assertion -- a lie.  It says that the Administration is to ask new relief from Congress. Paragraph one, lead, "A five hundred million dollar tax bill is one of the chores to be asked of Congress in January." That is a lie.  It says that it is also reported to it that they are going to ask for relief and for other purposes.  Of course we are going to ask for relief, et cetera.  Tell your office in Washington that that is the kind of thing --

Q:  (Mr. Stephenson)  I will take this so you won't see it again.  (Laughter)

THE PRESIDENT:  Otherwise we are feeling very well this morning.

(The Press Conference adjourned at 11:10 A.M.)

CONFIDENTIAL
Press Conference #142
In the Study of the President's Home at Hyde Park, N. Y.
September 7, 1934, 4:15 P.M.

(Senator McAdoo was present at the Press Conference)

Q: He [Senator McAdoo] told us he would tell all.

Q: He said he would tell all if he were free to do so but, of course, everybody who ever sees the President is free to do so.

THE PRESIDENT: Then what he said was perfectly true.

Q: We have an important matter to take up before the Conference. We have a return game scheduled on Sunday [return game at Lowell Thomas']. Will we be able to play or are you having a busy day?

Q: We were a little curious whether General Johnson would be here Monday?

THE PRESIDENT: He is coming Monday or Tuesday.

Q: Will you be able to ride over?

THE PRESIDENT: I think I have somebody coming over on Sunday -- only neighbors, no visitors.

Q: We will be safe?

THE PRESIDENT: Absolutely.

Q: We are hoping it may be called off.

Q: Just immediate neighbors or Hyde Park?

THE PRESIDENT: Just a few people from up the river and around here.

Q: In connection with Johnson's [General Johnson] visit, who else is coming with him?

THE PRESIDENT: Nobody I know of.

Q: Not Richberg?

THE PRESIDENT: No.

Q: Is there anything you can tell us about Senator McAdoo's visit?

--- [51] ---

THE PRESIDENT: We talked about everything, including the kitchen stove.

Q: How is the kitchen stove?

Q: His kitchen stove or yours?

THE PRESIDENT:  It is becoming an electric stove very rapidly.

Q:  That comes under the housing program?

THE PRESIDENT:  Yes.

What we are trying to do is to build up the business of the private companies.  That is off the record.  (Laughter)

Q:  Mr. President, is there anything you can tell us in connection with the textile strike?  Have you received any word?

THE PRESIDENT:  I don't know a thing.  I have not had a word today.

Q:  Mr. President, anything you can tell us about California -- what Senator McAdoo thinks about it, perhaps?

THE PRESIDENT:  He has not been back for so long that he did not mention anything firsthand.

Q:  We will be glad to have a secondhand view.

MR. McINTYRE:  If you get out soon enough you can ask him [indicating Senator McAdoo].

Q:  Did Mr. Cheney [Nelson Cheney], Mr. Pierre Flandin or Louis Donham know anything?

THE PRESIDENT:  Talked about everything including the kitchen stove.

Q:  His name is Wallace [Donham].

THE PRESIDENT:  I saw them together and separately.

Q:  Who is he [Mr. Donham]?

THE PRESIDENT:  He is Dean of the Harvard School of Business.

Q:  What was on Straus' [Mr. Percy Straus] chest?

THE PRESIDENT:  Nothing.  I just asked them all sorts of questions and

--- [52] ---

they asked me all sorts of questions.  We talked over general things.  In other words, nine out of ten of these people who come up, I am asking them questions: "What do you think about this and that?"  They are being sent for to give me their points of view on all kinds of things, no particular subject.  It is just to get their points of view.

Q:  All of them have been traveling and making observations?

(The President indicated in the affirmative.)

Q:  Donham is quite a fellow.

THE PRESIDENT: There will be quite a number of them over the next month or two.

Q: We can almost mimeograph a lead and fill in the blank spaces.

THE PRESIDENT: Yes, you can almost mimeograph a lead and fill in the blank spaces.

Q: When Mayor LaGuardia was here he indicated that a new formula for Federal relief in large cities was being drawn up. Anything you can tell us about that?

THE PRESIDENT: I don't know; I cannot tell you what that meant.

Q: We didn't either but we assumed that it would probably be a continuation of C.W.A. during the winter.

THE PRESIDENT: No, I do not think we have been talking about it at all.

Q: In that connection, there is a story carried by the United Press today out of Springfield, Illinois, saying that the Federal Government is going to take over all the relief to relieve the situation?

THE PRESIDENT: It is the Springfield situation? That is a U.P. story.

Q: (Mr. Stephenson of the A.P.) Yes, it is a U.P. story.

Q: (Mr. Storm of the U.P.) It is our turn to get it today. (Laughter)

Q: Mr. Donham (Wallace Donham) is quite a gentleman. Is there anything in particular?

--- [53] ---

THE PRESIDENT: No, I suppose we talked about thirty or forty different items we are all interested in.

Q: He isn't under consideration for any Federal appointment?

THE PRESIDENT: No. None of these people is under consideration for anything except I am pumping them dry to get their views.

Q: Any comment on the munitions investigation that is going on down in Washington? There seems to be --

THE PRESIDENT: (interposing) The only thing is that which you have already had out of Washington -- I announced it last June -- that any data they wanted from the Government, the Government would be only too glad to give to them. In other words, we would cooperate in every way possible with the Senate Committee. I think he announced that himself down there.

Q: Have you given any thought, outside of the impending visit of Mr. Johnson, to your temporary reorganization plans for N.R.A.?

THE PRESIDENT: Not any more than I have been doing every day for the last three months. I give a certain amount of thought to it every day. Norhing out of the ordinary.

Q: Have you received any reports or any data from Washington?

THE PRESIDENT: Nothing for about a week. Of course I get reports all the time in the way of suggestions and recommendations. There isn't anything. I couldn't write a story if I tried. None of those reports and recommendations are news.

Q: Has the program for reorganization taken any fairly definite shape yet that you can talk about?

THE PRESIDENT: I haven't got to that point yet but things are sort of shaping up. Certain aspects are becoming in my mind more and more clear. Now, as I think I told you before, the ultimate shaping up

--- [54] ---

is legislation for the next Congress. So it is not exactly a spot news story and it is very difficult to write it as a dope story because no program has been determined on and we are looking at all kinds of permanent administration. The trouble is that if I were to give you an example it would give that particular thing undue prominence in a very big program. That is why it is so difficult to do. There are a lot of things, like child labor. You cannot alleviate that unless you talk about minimum wages and hours of work, also the old-age pension and the interpretation of 7A. You have to have the individual authorities getting together and exchanging views. Then, how far can you go on the exchange of views before running afoul of the anti-trust law -- price fixing and things of that kind. You might say they all have an equal value in the entire picture and we are considering them all.

Q: While you are shaping that legislation, are you likely to have anybody from the Navy come up and talk, or from the Army?

THE PRESIDENT: No.

Q: Mr. President, do you expect that you will get an N.R.A. reorganization, a temporary one, well under way during this month or October, or are you going to wait until shortly before Congress?

THE PRESIDENT: There I think you can probably make a fairly good guess on that. If I were writing the story I would say that there will undoubtedly be a recommendation to the Congress for permanent legislation. It does not matter whether it goes up in January or does not go up until March, but something will have to be done before Congress adjourns that would be permanent legislation in the sense that it would at least tide over for one year. In other words, we

--- [55] ---

are feeling our way on all of these steps. You cannot at this time say that the permanent form of N.R.A. is going to be A, B, C or D. Child labor and collective bargaining, the collective principle of bargaining, are examples of those things which should have a permanent position in American life. Now, those things will have to be taken up by Congress, otherwise the whole thing will have to be renewed for another year.

Then you come to the borderline, it is partly administrative and partly a question of whether the thing has worked or not. If it has not worked, should it be modified or abandoned, such as price fixing. That is one of the items on which there is a question mark. We all know that. It runs afoul of the Sherman Anti-Trust Law and other things.

Then, on the administrative end, it is probably that there will be certain temporary changes in the purely administrative set-up which is more a matter of detail than anything else, before the legislation of the next Session goes into effect. Again we are feeling our way, feeling our way towards the ultimate goal. What we do may not be permanent; it may be changed a half dozen times. There have been changes in the past, quite a number of them. There probably will be more as we work towards a simplification of the whole procedure.

Q: You are not including price-fixing policy and price posting, things of that sort, in the category of things that might be changed? After all, you don't need new legislation to change that.

THE PRESIDENT: They might be modified in the meantime. We are trying it out. After all they were put in there to try out. But those things, as I said, are pretty vague and I would not go so far as to say that they are going to be done, because I don't know. They are among the

--- [56] ---

things that are open for discussion and have been right along; very much so.

Q: On administrative set-ups, will there be a change in that in the near fut- ure, say by the first of October?

THE PRESIDENT: Now you are getting too definite. I don't know. That is the trouble, you haven't a spot news story. You have an interpretative long- range story. I cannot tell you what will be done because I don't know. But we are working, gradually towards a simplification of N.R.A., throwing overboard or modifying the things that were not working -- putting in even- tually through perhaps a process of several changes a machinery that would seem to work better, with a more permanent and more simplified organiza- tion. It is hard to say anything categorically about it.

Q: Then there will be, in effect, no particular unit in N.R.A. which will be affected but, rather, a series of steps in the N.R.A., very gradually, as they appear workable?

THE PRESIDENT: Then again, suppose we decide this time that certain things in all the codes that require man power to administer should be either modi- fied or abandoned. Obviously, you have to modify your administration machinery by abolishing or consolidating personnel.

Q: Mr. President, one more question on relief. Is there any chance that Louisiana or some of those other states whose legislatures failed to make any appropriation will be cut off by the Federal Government?

THE PRESIDENT: I don't know. You will have to ask Harry Hopkins that. I think in most of those states they have taken care of their share legally where they have not had legislative appropriations.

Q: In Louisiana, I believe, the Legislature has not done anything?

THE PRESIDENT: Louisiana is, at the present moment -- I will say it off the

--- [57] ---

record -- a horrible example.

Q:   Did you see the reports from New Orleans where Huey (Senator Long) has moved in 3,000 National Guardsmen into New Orleans in order to enforce the laws passed by the special session of the Legislature?

THE PRESIDENT:   Three thousand -- God!

Q:   Do you think the Constitution has been violated there?

THE PRESIDENT:   We had a very funny thing.   Some of those people -- this is off the record entirely -- asked an opinion as to when the Constitution was violated.   I got the Attorney General's office to write an opinion, and, of course, there isn't anything to be done on the situation as it exists today, not a thing.   There isn't a precedent in history for it.

Q:   There probably wouldn't be a precedent before Election Day -- I mean if they were to have any interference with the balloting.

THE PRESIDENT:   Again, it is a primary election.

Q:   The Federal laws do not cover a primary?

THE PRESIDENT:   No, in no shape, manner or form.   We are all sorts of tied up and, of course, Huey Long knows it.

I do not believe there is any news except a few people coming tomorrow.

I had Monsieur Flandin, Minister of Public Works (France), he and his wife and daughter came in to lunch, and we talked about everything relating to the United States and France except public works.

Q:   Did you talk about the debt?

THE PRESIDENT:   No -- this has got to be off the record -- we spent most of the lunch hour talking about Germany.

Q:   What is the situation there?

THE PRESIDENT:   Off the record, the French are not very happy.

Q:   Are they worried?

--- [58] ---

THE PRESIDENT:   Oh, yes.

Q:   Why?

THE PRESIDENT:   What they are afraid of -- we will have to keep this entirely off the record; you know I cannot talk foreign affairs about so-called friendly nations.   The situation, -- all those fellows that have been coming back -- really what they are afraid of in Germany is that the German economic situation is breaking down.   In fact, as it is they have no gold, no foreign exchange, they cannot buy materials on the outside.   What are they going to do to keep the factories going?   They are turning out synthetic rubber, gasoline, synthetic cattle and horse fodder -- perfectly amazing -- and employing all those people to turn out synthetic substitutes for everything.

He (Mr. Flandin) says that a thing like that cannot go on, that you cannot use synthetic rubber and synthetic food for everybody and that it is bound to break down of its own weight. The question is, when?

Then, they are afraid in France that when the thing does get to the point of closing down their factories, with already a very large unemployment list, then one or two things will happen. Either they will have chaos inside of Germany, with all of these fellows fighting among themselves -- we got one report the other day from Dodd (Ambassador Dodd in Germany) describing how Hitler's Secret Service was being followed by Goebbel's Secret Service, which was being followed by Reichswehr's Secret Service, which was being followed by the Gestapo, all of them following each other around -- or else that the leaders over there, to retain their power, will start to march on something, to walk across the border. I suppose the easiest way would be to toss a coin to see which border they will have to walk across to retain the

--- [59] ---

present regime in power and the whole of Europe is scared pink of something like that.

Q: How can they get the money to buy the bullets to shoot at people?

THE PRESIDENT: Of course the French say they have an awful lot of it on hand. The French are convinced. They say big guns are the easiest thing in the world. When you are casting a stern tubing for a ship, for the shaft tubing, it is almost exactly the same process as casting the tube of a gun, of a 14-inch gun. It is exactly the same thing. You cast two and put one over in the corner. The French are convinced that they have all the small artillery, the 75's and the 155's, according to the French, and the French -- this did not take place today so don't think it is Flandin -- the French are prefectly sure that the Germans have more machine guns than the French Army. And they are also perfectly sure that they have as many airplanes available as France has.

Another lovely story is that the school children -- this is one of the silly ones, but it may be true; we do know that every factory worker in Germany works with a gas mask in a bag above his bench and every once in a while a whistle blows twice and everybody puts on his gas mask. I tell you the silly things because we get them all the time and only a few get printed.

The school children in Germany are now going through an education process. They have a box of matches and the head of the match is impregnated with the particular smell of the poisonous gases used in the World War. They gather around in the classroom and the children light a match and that is gas No. 3. They train them in knowing those different smells. It sounds crazy but we know there is a lot of that stuff going on. There are seven different smells and you have on the

--- [60] ---

gas mask seven different slides, each one against a different type of gas.

Then there is the story of the professor of foreign languages at Bryn Mawr, who went over there last fall and visited a German professor in Stuttgart. She went to his house -- she had stayed with him before. His family and workmen were working down in the basement. She said, "What is all this work that is going on?" "I am carrying out the orders of the Government. I am putting a bomb proof in the cellar. We are all doing it." She said, "What are you doing it for?" "We get a remission of half year's taxes if we prepare against airplane attack. They are doing it in France." She said, "They are doing it in France?" "Oh, yes; the papers say so. The English are doing it and they are doing it in the United States along the whole Atlantic Seaboard."

She said, "I have not been home for two months but I am sure I have not seen it." "You do not know. We know. Our Government tells us."

Now, there is a professor who swallows the whole thing, hook, line and sinker.

And then the little boy came down at night to say his prayers, his age eight or nine years, and he kneeled down at his mother's knee and said his prayers and ended up in good German, like a good German boy, and he said, "Dear God, please permit it that I shall die with a French bullet in my heart."

You get that sort of thing and that is what has got the French scared when ninety per cent of the German people are thinking and talking that way. If I were a Frenchman, I would be scared too. There are only 40 million Frenchmen and there are 70 million Germans.

Q: When is this war going to start?

THE PRESIDENT: I said last winter on that that as long as they are talking

--- [61] ---

war in Europe ther won't be a war.

Q: They might talk themselves into one, don't you think?

THE PRESIDENT: They are all saying there won't be a war.

Q: Isn't Italy going to collapse?

THE PRESIDENT: No; they have $240,000,000 of gold left.

Q: It is decreasing, though.

THE PRESIDENT: Oh, yes. Those things aren't so hot.

Q: Pretty bad in France?

THE PRESIDENT: Harry Hopkins talked to you about Italy?

Q: I wasn't there.

Q: He did.

THE PRESIDENT: He thought Italy was much worse off than any of the stories we

have been getting would indicate because he said out in the country the
average family did not have enough money for spaghetti. I said, "What do
they do?" He said, "I think most of them are using wheat chaff which they
boil into soup."

Q:   How much did the French Minister say about France's unemployment, econo-
     mically?

THE PRESIDENT:  He said they were not as well off as last year but still not
     serious. I think he said something like three or four hundred thousand.
     Of course, the French are very conservative. They do not put a man down
     as unemployed unless he really is, and we do.

Q:   Do those reports coming to you indicate there is a general slight reces-
     sion in world business, that is, abroad, as well as at home in the last
     month or two?

THE PRESIDENT:  Oh, undoubtedly, of course. England, we know, is off and I do
     not know whether Italy and Germany have gone off but they are coming to an
     end of their resources, which is just about as serious. They

--- [62] ---

have not got any foreign exchange to buy their raw materials with and, of
course, France is a little off from last year, but not as much off as they
were in the last three or four months. Our foreign trade is the only one
that has gone up. We have gone up pretty well on foreign trade.

Q:   And imports reduced?

THE PRESIDENT:  Imports reduced but exports up.

MR. McINTYRE:  Everything you said since talking about N.R.A. is off the record?

THE PRESIDENT:  Yes, everything is in the family. It is just to get a general
     picture. But the general world picture is not as good today as it was a
     year ago. There is no question about that.

Q:   In that connection, while we are talking unemployment here, off the record,
     I wonder if you would not tell us your own reactions to this big program
     of taking over idle factories and lands and putting men to work on "produc-
     tion for use?"

THE PRESIDENT:  Absolutely off the record. To be quite frank, I have never
     read the entire program. I know he (Upton Sinclair) has a State-wide pro-
     gram which, in all probability, is impossible, absolutely impossible, on a
     scale anything like that. Now, on the other hand, there is real merit and
     real possibility in the community plan based on the same principle, where
     you have your scrip or whatever you call it a purely local matter. The
     simplest thing I know is where you can get two families, one making shoes
     and clothes and socks, everything that a person wears, and the other family
     making everything that a person can eat. There you have a perfectly eco-
     nomic proposition. Those two families can swap both food and clothing.
     That is obvious. You can extend that, as they have been doing in Ohio, to
     a community basis. There are a number of these experiments which are work-
     ing awfully well

in Ohio. There are something like 200,000 people in the State of Ohio who are working in these community cooperatives and there is a certain amount of exchange between cooperatives. They have the entire support of the mayors and the business men in these smaller towns in Ohio. By trial and error during the past year -- they have made mistakes -- the thing is succeeding and they won't give them up in this kind of period for anything. They are taking care of 200,000 people and they are reducing their relief costs by doing that something like 65 or 70 per cent.

I said to Sinclair the other day, "That is perfectly fine if you can do it on a perfectly small community basis." But what happens to the needs for United States cash that a family has got to have? Suppose one of these families in Ohio wants a postage stamp? You cannot take two cents in scrip to a postmaster. He has to have real cash. That is why they are trying, on the Ohio plan, to employ them for cash a portion of the time, that being the percentage of relief money or public works money that goes into it. But it has to be very little, one day a week instead of four days a week because, with one day a week for actual cash, the average family can supply the cash needs that cannot be bought for scrip. How are they going to pay the rent? Well, they have to work that out on a community basis. They are trying out this exchange of work plan which tides over a large portion of their immediate human needs, making the cost of relief infinitely less. It cuts it way down. But I do not think it is a possible thing to put it on a State-wide basis.

I said to Sinclair the other day, "Suppose the landlord gets paid in this scrip, what does the landlord do with the scrip?"

--- [64] ---

"Oh," said Sinclair, "He would pay the State taxes."

I said, "What would the State do with the scrip, use it to employ the workers on the highway?" I said, "The difficulty there is how would you set up for the State of California an absolutely different currency system? You would have the two side by side and it won't work."

I think probably, if Sinclair has any sense in him, he will modify at least in practice this perfectly wild-eyed scheme of his and carry it on as a community experiment. It will do a lot of good work that way.

Q: May I ask your reaction to the opposition advanced to the community plan? The general reasoning is that even today these men have shoes and something resembling clothing on their backs manufactured by private industry at a profit and the minute you start putting these men to work for their own needs, the demand for products of private industry falls off and you have increased unemployment.

THE PRESIDENT: Well, let us take shoes, for instance. As I understand it some of these hides that have come off the cattle, about two-thirds or three-quarters of them, instead of being dumped on the market, are going to be sold so much a month for a year. The shoe manufacturers are perfectly happy about that. The other quarter they are going to take and divide in half and give half the hides to the present shoe companies on such a basis that the present shoe companies with these orders plus what they have will be insured full-time production. That will apply to every going shoe concern in this country. The other quarter of the hides will be used by the workers unemployed in idle plants to make shoes for the unemployed.

Now the question is, would they use shoes anyway?  No.  They would use shoes only to the extent that they would make one pair of shoes last through the entire year.  This way they will use two pairs of shoes.

--- [65] ---

Now let us take other needs such as mattresses.  There you have a problem of people who haven't got mattresses.  Around Warm Springs, taking that as an example, if you went to every house, negro and white, within ten square miles you will find that one family out of four has a mattress.  Now, that is an amazing statement but you take in North Dakota farmhouses -- I don't know but I think it was the Devils Lake section -- we have had surveys made and about half the families haven't mattresses, and those are nice-looking farmhouses.

Q:    What do they use?

THE PRESIDENT:  Corn husks and quilts and old rags and things like that.

Q:    How are they coming with this experiment down in Warm Springs on a new brand of liquor?

Q:    I hope you can put one of those new mattresses in my bed down there. (Laughter)

THE PRESIDENT:  But through the South I could not tell you how many million families absolutely lack mattresses.  Now those people are not going to buy from mattress manufacturers.  There are 18,000 people working in mattress factories in the United States and that is very nearly the normal. Hopkins is giving those people enough work to give them employment at full time for one year to come.  Every mattress factory in this country is guaranteed work for a year to come and, in addition to that, we are taking 200,000 bales of cotton and putting people to work on that and making mattresses to go in homes that never had them before.

Now, if people get accustomed to mattresses in homes that never had them before, they are going to buy mattresses if they have the money.

Q:    How about stockings?

--- [66] ---

THE PRESIDENT:  You know what Perkins (Secretary Perkins) said in the South.

Q:    I see how you can follow -- the objections to the scrip when you extend it beyond the community, but once you get into the manufacture of goods, in that case you have to go beyond scrip?

THE PRESIDENT:  That is a different thing.  On this Ohio thing they are keeping it in the community entirely.

Q:    They are keeping the scrip there, but if you are going to manufacture goods, as Sinclair (Upton Sinclair) is proposing to do with idle factories, you haven't the factories to distribute it properly.

THE PRESIDENT:  His thought is to make of California a complete economic unit and not go all around it.  You can't do it.  The scrip would circulate inside there and nowhere else in the world.  It is too damned big.

Q:   Thank you, Mr. President; it was very nice of you.

Q:   I have one query I have to put.  It probably will be answered off the
     record.  My boss has been bombarded with queries as to whether you will ask
     for taxes or wait until the Committee would make its report?

THE PRESIDENT:  I have not heard a word.  By the way, has Ingersoll accepted?

Q:   Yes, he has.  LaGuardia announced that this morning.

THE PRESIDENT:  No, I haven't heard a word, Charlie (Mr. Hurd).  (Referring to
     taxes.)

Q:   On that story the other day, the boss said that was based on some work be-
     ing done by the Ways and Means Committee down there, where they are doing
     it unofficially.

THE PRESIDENT:  But they do not every year appoint a special committee to look
     into new forms of taxation.  I guess there was nothing in it.  They might
     invent taxes that would bring in three billion dollars.  It is just survey.

Press Conference #143
In the President's Study at Hyde Park, N. Y.
September 12, 1934, 10:30 A.M.


THE PRESIDENT: How is everybody? I want to offer congratulations on Charles'
    (Mr. Hurd) very excellent editorial (in the Poughkeepsie paper). (Laugh-
    ter)

    I did not see yesterday's. Who wrote it?

Q:   Brother McCaffery.

THE PRESIDENT: He did! **Good.** I will have to dig him up.

Q:   I thought it was a very strong pro-Administration editorial.

THE PRESIDENT: I do not think there is any news. Do you know of anything?

MR. McINTYRE: That Straus matter.

THE PRESIDENT: Oh, yes. The only difficulty about giving out the letter is
    that I have not got to it yet. I have not had time. Look, why don't I
    dictate a little letter accepting his resignation with regrets and send it
    down? (Dictation)

        "My dear Nathan:

        "I am indeed sorry to have your resignation as State Director
        of the National Emergency Council. I fully understand the
        reasons which make it necessary at this time but I hope that
        you will come back to help the Government later on.

                            "Very sincerely yours,"

MR. McINTYRE: I will give out the text of the two letters.

Q:   Is there anything to add to the N.R.A. set-up as Secretary Early explained
    to us yesterday?

THE PRESIDENT: No, except that I would not, in the least bit, be categorical
    about any of it. Of course, it is still in the study stage, and personal
    animus does not enter into it at all.

                        --- [68] ---

    How we will take the N.R.A. and divide it up into three parts, I don't
    know. You cannot say categorically that three component parts will be made
    up out of N.R.A.

Q:   That is the word I was looking for all day yesterday, "component."

THE PRESIDENT: We are working on the theory that you got all right, that the
    easiest way to divide the functions is the normal Government way, into
    three branches, the policy branch, the judicial branch and the executive
    branch. If we do go ahead on that general broad plan, how we will tie them
    in, I don't know. In other words, I don't believe you would be on the right

track if you said that N.R.A. itself is going to continue as N.R.A. with
three functions. I will give you a simple illustration. When you come
down to enforcement, what we are trying to avoid as a general proposition
is having too many departments. That is going back to the old method of
having eleven departments of the Federal Government, each having its own
law department. We had the same thing in Albany when Al Smith reorganized
the State government. There were 122 departments in the State government
and, as I remember it, there were somewhere around forty legal divisions in
those departments. What he did was to reorganize those departments down to
eighteen and cut down the legal departments and put them all into the
Attorney General's office with the exception of one or two that were in
special fields.

So, with the legal end of N.R.A., on enforcement, what I would like to do
would be to work out a method by which the enforcement would be where it
properly belongs, under the Department of Justice, but not so separated
from N.R.A. or its activities that they would not know what was going on at
all times. What we would do would be to give the

--- [69] ---

responsibility to some organization, possibly a new division in the Department of Justice. If something like that were done it would mean that probably a good part of the personnel now doing enforcement work would be
transferred.

Q: Then this legal department of the N.R.A., as you were thinking of it, would
actually be in the Department of Justice entirely?

THE PRESIDENT: The responsibility for determining on prosecutions would rest
with the Attorney General. I can give you -- and this has to be off the
record because there is no use dragging it up again; just so you will understand what it is about, but off the record -- you will remember last
December or in the early Winter some of the legal people in Public Works --
I mean the Oil Administration -- decided on a method of settling the California oil trouble and they worked out what might be called an agreement
with the oil operators. They had the approval of 97% of the oil operators.
They were going gaily ahead with it and they did not know that the Attorney
General and the District Attorney were prosecuting an actual case and had
obtained indictments covering one of the practices which the oil administra-
tors' agreement actually legalized. There you had a case where there were
two branches of the Government, one was legalizing an operation by approval
and agreement, and the other one was prosecuting in the courts for the violation of that particular practice.

That is a very good illustration of how we have to prevent the crossing of
wires.

Q: In that connection, in relation to the Policy Board, as far as you have
gone now is it your idea that the Policy Board should be created or consist
solely of men in the N.R.A. or would some of its members be from outside
agencies to coordinate the work of the N.R.A. with the other

--- [70] ---

Recovery Administration?

THE PRESIDENT: Put it that way; it is all right. I would say that probably a majority of them would come from outside the N.R.A.

Q:   Mr. President, your suggestion that the principle of collective bargaining
was here to stay raises another question in view of the National Relations
Board ruling with respect to majority rule.  That differed a little bit
with the settlement on a proportional basis in the automobile strike.  Does
that indicate any change in your views?

THE PRESIDENT:  Those are pure details as I see it.  Those are things that have
to be worked out and depend on the industry.

Q:   Any further information on the textile strike?

THE PRESIDENT:  I have not heard a thing, Fred (Mr. Storm).

Q:   On the forthcoming investigation of the ocean mail contracts, in the event
any iniquities are shown in those contracts, will it be the policy of the
Administration to cut off all help?

THE PRESIDENT:  My policy is to continue helping the Merchant Marine.  I think
it might be made clear that this Post Office Department investigation does
relate primarily to the post office end of it.  They will, for instance,
bring out how much would be the commercial cost of carrying that many
pounds of freight in a completely safe way.  In other words -- I do not
know what you call it; special freight is what it comes down to -- that
would give approximately the proportion that the subsidy bears to the total
amount that is now being paid.  As I think I said last year, off the record,
I am very, very much in favor of calling a subsidy a subsidy.  If it is a
subsidy, let's call it a subsidy.

Q:   And you do favor a subsidy?

THE PRESIDENT:  Just the same way -- and this has to be off the record --

--- [71] ---

I am not at all certain we would not be justified in calling, using the word
"subsidy" for the large loss that the Federal Post Office makes today in
carrying newspapers and magazines.  (Laughter)

Q:   That is off the record.  (Laughter)

THE PRESIDENT:  That is off the record.  (Laughter)  I am a rough fellow.  It
all depends on whose baby has the measles.

Q:   That is right.  (Laughter)

Q:   Did you happen to see yesterday Dave Lawrence's column out of Washington?

THE PRESIDENT:  I did not get my Sun last night and that is the only one that
carried it.

Q:   As a matter of fact, it was a very interesting column.  He quoted the text
of the British Collective Bargaining Law, showing that while it does grant
to labor virtually everything that we have granted to labor under 7 (a),
it does impose on labor very rigid restrictions which we have never attempted to impose.

MR. McINTYRE: They did that years ago.

THE PRESIDENT: Years ago and, as I was saying the other day, that was evolutionary and that was twenty-five years ahead of us.

Q: It sounded like a good law, the way it ran.

THE PRESIDENT: I wish Dave Lawrence, who has lots of facilities for looking up
things, would look up the bill that I asked Lord Illiffe about the other
day, because I think there was something done in this Parliament or the
one previous.

Q: Dave (Mr. Lawrence) got the date, did he not?

Q: He said it was enacted in 1927.

THE PRESIDENT: In other words, it gave the British Government, in a sense, enforcing power after an agreement was made.

Q: That is perfectly true. It also prevented mass picketing on the grounds

--- [72] ---

that it was certainly designed to intimidate a worker who wanted to remain
at his post. There were also certain restrictions on the rights of labor
to strike.

THE PRESIDENT: Well, it is working pretty well; that is the answer and of course
they have much more responsible leadership than we have at the present time.

Q: We have an inquiry whether or not the Militia General has been selected?

THE PRESIDENT: Does the Chamber of Commerce want one?

Q: As a matter of fact, the Chamber of Commerce called me up. (Laughter) I
think they have a candidate.

THE PRESIDENT: The War Department, as I understand it, said that they did not
think they needed one.

Q: I think that is true but they seem to think that it was brought up again.

THE PRESIDENT: I do not think it carries any increase of pay.

Q: No pay at all. Just somebody who wants to be a general.

THE PRESIDENT: I think you can give them the low-down that if the War Department does not think they need a general, I won't appoint one, either for
social or political purposes.

Q: Getting back to ocean mail, do you favor a subsidy?

THE PRESIDENT: Oh, we have to have some kind of a subsidy, let us call it that,
if we are going to maintain a reasonably large number of sea-going ships
on foreign routes. Obviously the American ships, which cost anywhere from
25 to 50% more to build and a good deal more to operate because of our
shipping laws, the seamen's laws, cannot compete with other ships in foreign commerce unless they get some assistance from somewhere.

Then, of course, there are other things which -- oh, I don't know, I think you can use it because we were all appalled by that Morro

--- [73] ---

Castle catastrophe -- I am inclined to think that there will be a rather definite effort made by the next Congress to eliminate wood construction on passenger-carrying vessels of all kinds.

Q:   This is getting on page one, watch out.

Q:   How about tapestries and decorations?

THE PRESIDENT:   There you face the question, which would you rather be on, which would you rather do, cross the ocean or go to sea on a vessel that has a Louis Quinze dining room and a Roman bath and so forth, highly decorated in inflammable woodwork, or would you rather go to sea on a ship with modern steel, vanadium steel construction, which can be made perfectly pleasant to look at but it is not as luxurious but at the same time would not burn up? I would prefer to go on the ship which did not have the Louis Quinze dining room. Almost everything today can be constructed out of fireproof materials, including the tapestries and including rugs. We had a long session at the dinner table last night and the boys tried to get me. They said, "How about things like sofa pillows, you certainly cannot make those out of things that cannot burn up," and they thought they had me. I said, "Haven't you ever heard of asbestos wool?"

Q:   Isn't that pretty broad, to use that on passenger vessels?

THE PRESIDENT:   Well, why not?

Q:   Would that include these river ships?

THE PRESIDENT:   Why not? My Lord, we have had perfectly terrible disasters with river boats and Long Island Sound boats. They killed hundreds of people. There was the Slocum and there was a terrible disaster before that on Long Island Sound which killed six or seven hundred people.

Q:   Such a law would apply to ships hereafter built?

THE PRESIDENT:   Yes.

--- [74] ---

Q:   Are there any ships built now that are supposed to be fireproof?

THE PRESIDENT:   I do not know, Stevie (Mr. Stephenson). There are some ships pretty nearly fireproof. Well, take the cruisers we were on. They were not difficult to live on.

Q:   I have only one suggestion. Do not apply this steel wool to the mattresses.

THE PRESIDENT:   I think this will be a serious question for Congress to take up.

Q:   Will you favor it?

THE PRESIDENT: I will leave it up to the Congress for a while.

Q: You will not oppose? (Laughter)

Q: Is there any possibility that the Department of Justice will be called upon to investigate the origin of this fire (on the Morro Castle)?

THE PRESIDENT: If they have anything to go on, certainly.

Q: You will leave that up to Conboy (Martin Conboy, District Attorney in New York)?

Q: On that Department of Justice investigation, would they wait for a report from Conboy?

THE PRESIDENT: That I do not know. I do not know how it would originate. If it were a thing for J. Edgar Hoover's Bureau and if there was enough to go on, undoubtedly they would move.

Q: As soon as this is printed, Hoover will start moving. (Laughter)

THE PRESIDENT: As a matter of fact, and this has to be off the record, I have not seen enough in the paper yet to do anything about an explosive on board.

Q: The officers claimed that. They claimed also that there was another fire on the last voyage down in the hold and while it was being put out they found a lot of burnt paper in the cargo as though that paper had been there and ignited.

--- [75] ---

On this voyage, in this locker, there was some kerosene and gasoline.

Q: I think some of the engineers, regarding that earlier fire, said it was of accidental origin, that they had traced a cigarette butt on down through a crevice.

Q: If it was proved, it was said the ship's company is not liable to any damages. So Mr. Brisbane says, and he is always right.

Q: I never heard of him. (Laughter)

THE PRESIDENT: He is not entirely right. I used to be an admiralty lawyer and he was not. The company is not liable if it can be shown that it exercised reasonable care to prevent the setting of the fire.

Q: That is the law in everything, isn't it? (Laughter)

Q: The company is going to have a hard time proving that.

THE PRESIDENT: Arthur Brisbane -- of course he sounds like a million dollars but he always keeps beside him Ridpath's History of the World. (Laughter)

Q: Is Mr. Richberg coming up today?

THE PRESIDENT: After lunch.

Q:   Is he going to stay overnight?

THE PRESIDENT:   No.

Q:   Just a short time on N.R.A.?

THE PRESIDENT:   Nothing to do with N.R.A.  It is on Executive Council and Emergency Council and these reports he has been editing.

Q:   Will he go back on N.R.A. or continue along on this thing?

THE PRESIDENT:   That I do not know.  He gets through the first of October, I think.

Q:   Anything from a Dutchess County angle, particularly?  The NOURMAHAL is here now, I understand -- is it here now?

--- [76] ---

THE PRESIDENT:   I do not think so.  I have some people coming in this afternoon to talk to me about some additional water storage for the Hyde Park Fire Department.

Q:   By the way, Mr. Tugwell was up here yesterday?

THE PRESIDENT:   Yes.

Q:   What did he want?

THE PRESIDENT:   Jsut to say goodbye.

Q:   He is going to Europe?

THE PRESIDENT:   He was awfully worried.

MR. McINTYRE:   Some of the dope stories had him going away yesterday.

Q:   Where is he going?

THE PRESIDENT:   He is going to this Rome conference.  What time does the ship sail?

Q:   We don't know.

THE PRESIDENT:   Then I might tell you boys what he is worried about.  Don't, for the love of Pete, use it.  Don't telephone it to New York.  You can use it after he actually sails.  On this Hawaiian sugar suit, with respect to the quota for Hawaii, attacking it on the grounds that it is unconstitutional, the suit apparently has been filed.  Henry Wallace was going back to Washington the other night from New York and when he passed through Baltimore at 4:30 A.M., a hand came into his berth and shook him roughly and said, "Here is a subpoena."  Rex said that apparently it was the first time, since Henry Wallace is a perfectly mild man, the first time he completely lost his temper and he lost his temper all day.  Rex is scared perfectly pink that on the way to his boat today somebody is going to slap a subpoena on him and he and his wife will have to give up the European trip.  So be kind to him and don't flash it down because it may put ideas into their heads.

--- [77] ---

Q:  Would you care to comment on the criticism by Mr. Law of the American Bankers Association that the reason the bankers cannot extend their loans is
because the Federal examiners come along and make them "slow" if it is not
backed 100% by liquid collateral?

THE PRESIDENT:  There is something in it, no question.  Morgenthau has a committee at work on it.  I think they are leaving Washington today.  They are to
go into that whole method on the methods employed by the Federal bank examiners.  The story on that end will break from Washington.  Nelson Cheney
was down here the other day.  He is State Senator from out near Buffalo and
is the President of a little local bank.  What he said was the same thing,
that the small banks are all complaining that the Federal examiners throw
out what they consider perfectly good loans.  I think, if the Poughkeepsie
papers want a story on that, they ought to go and see the Poughkeepsie
Trust Company and ask them what their experience was.

I think I can give you a typical case.  It was not a Poughkeepsie case,
and although it was a bank not very far from here, it was not in this
County.  It is typical of what the Federal bank examiners are apt to do.
They are operating under the old rules when there were much fewer national
banks and when the country banks were state banks.  In the particular case
a man had started a very small clothing business.  He had made good at it
and he wanted to go into a little larger store and he needed eight hundred
dollars in cash.  He had always made money and this was a sort of a family
business.  He went to the bank and told them that he needed eight hundred
dollars.  The bank said yes, they would give him the money if he could get
two endorsers.  He got two endorsers, one a man worth half a million dollars and one a lawyer in this town, on the type of John Mack, and the both
went on

--- [78] ---

his note.  Of course the bank let him have the eight hundred dollars.  Then
the Federal examiner came along and said, "It is out."

In this county, this was not a trust company case, the bank had loaned
three thousand dollars on this farm.  It was a farm which I happen to know
very well, and if you gave me the job of selling it, I could get $6,000 for
it without any question inside of a couple of weeks, and if you gave me a
couple of months I would probably get $8,000.  There was $3,000 loaned on
this farm.  Well, the owner of the farm had paid his interest right along
but had not paid down on the mortgage for three years.  The Federal bank
examiner came along and said that it was out because he had not paid anything down on the mortgage.  Yet, if the bank had foreclosed, it would have
been able to get about $6,000 for that farm.

Q:  Is it up to the judgment of the bank examiners themselves, their individual
judgment, or do they have rules?

THE PRESIDENT:  You can only have general rules.

Q:  You think they have been too severe?

THE PRESIDENT:  I don't think they have used the rule of reason in a great many
cases.  You have the same thing on the Coast and the same kick on it out
there.  You see, one of their rules is that unless the amount of the debt

has been paid down so much each year, without fail, they have to throw it out. Now I say that anybody who has been able to pay the interest in the last three or four years is pretty lucky.

Q:    In other words, they are just following the rules out of the window.

THE PRESIDENT:  Yes.

Q:    What is Morgenthau going to do?

THE PRESIDENT:  He has a committee at work on it and they are checking the whole thing.  I don't know what their report is going to be, so I won't

--- [79] ---

even make a suggestion.

Q:    Mr. President, on this same line, when Walsh (Frank P. Walsh, of the New York Power Authority) came back from talking to you last week, he handed out a printed statement which had in it a sentence to the effect that the reactionary interests were fighting the recovery program all along the line.  Would you care to make any comment on that?

THE PRESIDENT:  It sounds like Mark Sullivan.  (Laughter)

Q:    Farley (Postmaster General Farley) told us yesterday, remembering what you said about politics in the relief work, he said it had been reported to him that there was a lot of politics through Republican control of relief, that they were using it for politics.  He said he had heard a lot of complaints about it.  I thought he might have taken it up with you?

THE PRESIDENT:  I think there are probably just as much Democratic politics in it as there are Republican.  It depends on what state, what county and what town, and who the leader is.

Q:    May we say that?

THE PRESIDENT:  I think so.  The one difficulty in the administration of relief has been, in a great many cases, the inefficiency of the local person who was responsible for picking out the people who want to go on relief.  That is a personal equation and every week that goes by we try more and more to eliminate, to get rid of the people who are using it for either personal purposes or political purposes or any other purposes.  Sometimes we catch a fellow who is grafting, but the purpose is to get the right people in the smaller units of government, in towns, villages, counties and cities.

Q:    Thank you, Mr. President.

Q:    Did you hear anything about the Main results?

--- [80] ---

THE PRESIDENT:  Maine?  Maine?  I think she sank in -- (Laughter)

Q:    Somebody must have raised it.  (Laughter)

Q:    It looks that way.

Q:   By the way, do you happen to know what ship Mr. Tugwell is sailing on to-day?

THE PRESIDENT:   I wouldn't tell you if I knew.  (Laughter)

Q:   I only wanted to check up on what time he is leaving.  We have to know.

Q:   Make it morning release.

THE PRESIDENT:   Either the MANHATTAN or the WASHINGTON.

Q:   They got plenty of news for the afternoon  Why not  make it a morning re-lease?  They have plenty for the afternoon.

THE PRESIDENT:   Why couldn't you hold it for morning release?

Q:   Because we want it for the afternoon.  (Laughter)

Q:   What is the Rome conference?

THE PRESIDENT:   It is the International Agricultural Institute.

MR. McINTYRE:   The Institute of Agriculture.

THE PRESIDENT:   That is the International Institute of Agriculture and it is an organization that was started a great many years ago by some very famous American.

Q:   Luden.

THE PRESIDENT:   By a man named Luden, who was one of our great experts on agri-culture about thirty-five or thirty years ago, wasn't it, Ernest?

MR. LINDLEY:   I think so.

THE PRESIDENT:   It antedated the League of Nations by years and years.  It was the first effort in the world to have a central organization which would be fact-finding and interchange information of all kinds on some particular thing.  On agriculture, they undertook to find out what the crop production would be, et cetera, and Luden started this thing and

--- [81] ---

I think it was after his death that the thing sort of began to die and the Italian Government got interested and kept it going.  It is only in the past year, since I started the Wheat Conference and the general interchange of information on world surpluses that the thing seems to have taken a new lease on life.  Also, we did not subscribe to it for years and I got through an appropriation of $50,000 a year ago so we are now members in good stand-ing and we are sending Tugwell over there.  We are sending, also, MacMurray, who is our Minister to one of the Baltic States down there, and he is the American delegate to the Wheat Conference, and also Bingham is a member of the Wheat Conference.  Tugwell is going to London to keep in touch with the wheat situation, and then, with Bingham and MacMurray he is going down to Rome.  We are very much interested in the success of the Institute.

Q:   Will there be any new efforts for world wheat control?

THE PRESIDENT:  Well, it is going on.

CONFIDENTIAL
Press Conference #144
In the President's Study at Hyde Park, N. Y.
September 21, 1934, 10:30 A.M.

THE PRESIDENT: What is the news?

Q: That is what we are here for.

THE PRESIDENT: It is another dull day.

Q: Oh, say it isn't so.

THE PRESIDENT: I don't think I have a blessed thing.

Q: What was the mayors' conference like?

THE PRESIDENT: They talked to me about the general subject of relief.

Q: Do they have a plan?

THE PRESIDENT: I don not know, unless they have drawn one in the last twenty-four hours.

Q: Are you seeing them this morning?

THE PRESIDENT: They are here now.

Q: Who besides Mayor LaGuardia?

THE PRESIDENT: I do not know.

Q: More for our own benefit than for publication, any idea as to when we leave for Washington?

THE PRESIDENT: I think probably Tuesday night, so far as I can tell now, but I might put it off until Wednesday night because they are still working on the elevator down there.

Q: Do you suppose you could persuade them to keep on working until Saturday?

THE PRESIDENT: The only definite appointment I have for next week, which is a perfect damned nuisance, is for Mrs. Maloney of the Tribune (New York Herald Tribune). She is pulling off one of her family conferences. I think I am supposed to be addressing it by long distance.

--- [83] ---

Q: The Herald-Tribune announced that you would do it from Hyde Park on the twenty-seventh of September.

THE PRESIDENT: I think I will have to get back Thursday morning anyway.

Q: Have you any other radio speeches? Do you think you will make another report to the country?

THE PRESIDENT: I suppose so; I have not a date. I did it last year about the first of October.  I haven't any date in mind and I have not any subject in mind.  I really have given it no consideration but we are about due for one.

Q:  Around the first?

THE PRESIDENT:  It may be before the first, or after.  You had better say "in the next few weeks."

Q:  When do you expect to announce the relief setup for the winter, Mr. President?

THE PRESIDENT:  Probably the third of January.  (Laughter)

Q:  But what are all these poor people going to do?

THE PRESIDENT:  The fourth of January.  One (the third of January) is the Annual Message and the other (the fourth of January) is the Budget Message.

Q:  Can you tell us anything about your talk with Harry Hopkins?

THE PRESIDENT:  I did not know he was coming in to see me.  When I heard he was here, I asked him to come to the picnic.

Q:  Will he sit in with you when you talk to the mayors?

THE PRESIDENT:  Is he here?

Q:  Yes, sir.

THE PRESIDENT:  I will have him sit in.

Q:  What was the report that the cities and states will have to bear a larger share?

--- [84] ---

THE PRESIDENT:  Anything you write on relief at the present time will be wrong.

Q:  That leaves us quite a wide field.

THE PRESIDENT:  That is a categorical statement.  Anything you write on relief will be wrong.  We have not any plan outlined -- we are still in the study period.

Q:  Can you make any comment on the organization of the railroads in Chicago yesterday to clean house among themselves?  To merge --

THE PRESIDENT:  (interposing) You mean the new association?  I do not thing it has any idea of cleaning house.  I gave out a statement from Washington, didn't I?

MR. McINTYRE:  I do not think you did.

THE PRESIDENT:  I am supposed to have.

MR. McINTYRE:  They have not made any announcement down there, but there will be a statement.

Q:   It was announced yesterday.

THE PRESIDENT:   Whenever the Pelley (J. J. Pelley) announcement comes out, there is waiting in the White House a statement from me to go out.

MR. McINTYRE:   I think that is coming out from Joe Eastman. Wasn't that the final decision that Eastman was going to issue the Administration statement?

THE PRESIDENT:   But anyway, we talked it over -- everybody knows that and everybody is in sympathy with this thing.

Q:   When is General Johnson coming down again?

THE PRESIDENT:   He isn't, so far as I know.

Q:   He was coming down before you went back to Washington?

THE PRESIDENT:   I do not think so. I do not think I have any particular business except the picnic and -- who is coming today?

--- [85] ---

MR. McINTYRE:   The forestry people.

THE PRESIDENT:   Oh, yes, the forestry people are coming today.

Q:   Any comment on the subject of a central bank? We hear a lot of talk about it lately.

THE PRESIDENT:   No comment.

Q:   Who are the forestry people?

THE PRESIDENT:   The people who comment on the experimental crops this year.

Q:   That is this local thing?

THE PRESIDENT:  Yes.

Q:   I note in the Times (The New York Times) the story that McCarl (the Comptroller General) has ruled against the use of the $15,000,000?

THE PRESIDENT:   Charlie (Mr. Hurd), I think the story -- I won't guarantee it but I think it is all cockeyed. (Laughter)

What happened, as I remember it, is this, and it ought to be checked up because it is just recollection on my part. The original project called for $15,000,000. It included in it quite a large amount for land purchases and the original proposal of the Department (of Agriculture) was to take out not merely the employment, that is, the wages of the people concerned, from relief, but also to take out for the land to be purchased to put the trees on. McCarl, when he went over that with me about four or five days before we went up on that, said, "I do not think we can take any purchase out of relief money." I said, "I agree with you one hundred per cent."

So, there wasn't any disagreement between us on that item. He said that obviously any money spent for wages for the unemployed is perfectly all right. In other words, I think it is a thing that came up as a result of the discussion in one of the departments, agriculture or relief, as to whether they could get land purchase money out of

--- [86] ---

relief money.

Q:    You have land purchase money anyway?

THE PRESIDENT:  Yes.

Q:    Where does that money for land purchase come in?  Do you recall offhand?

THE PRESIDENT:  I do not.  The Greeks had a name for it but I do not recall it. The Greeks bearing gifts.

Q:    I do remember that.

Q:    You are going ahead with this timber belt?

THE PRESIDENT:  Oh, heavens, no; lots of things have not been decided.  There is the method of acquiring the land, whether it will be built along the section lines or not.  We are going ahead with the appropriations for tree planting but the thing is very tentative as to the actual details.  Oh, we are going ahead with it, sure.

Q:    I noticed a story said that McCarl had approved $1,000,000 for this preliminary work.  Is that correct?

THE PRESIDENT:  Yes, that is correct.  Then, of course, the Government departments wanter five (million dollars) for the preliminary work and I cut that to one.

Q:    The only reason I brought it up was that it did get quite a play.

THE PRESIDENT:  I entirely approve of McCarl's stand that you could not buy land out of relief (money).

Q:    You do not mind if we quote you as saying the Times' story is cockeyed?

THE PRESIDENT:  All right, if the A.P. will guarantee to run it.  (Laughter)

Q:    That is safe.

Q:    I notice Frank Walker is here.  Are you trying to make him go to work again?

THE PRESIDENT:  I think so.

Q:    Back at the old job, or have you a new one?

--- [87] ---

THE PRESIDENT:  I don't know; I have not seen him.

Q:    Do you think they will drop the Bankhead Cotton Act as a result of the opposition?

THE PRESIDENT:   I have not heard a word except what I read in the paper about it and the only letter I had was on the constitutional question -- the controversy between two Democratic Senators.

Q:   Oscar Johnson is reported to have recommended that it be scrapped.  He is the A.A.A. Cotton Board Manager.  I wondered if that would have anything to do with it?

THE PRESIDENT:   I do not know; I do not know anything about it.

MRS. ROOSEVELT:   It seems to be sprinkling but it will be sprinkling on and off so it won't do you any harm.

THE PRESIDENT:   What is a little rain to us sailormen?

MRS. ROOSEVELT:   If it does rain we will have to have it (the picnic) indoors in all three rooms.

Q:   Mr. President, anything new in the textile situation?

THE PRESIDENT:   I don't know a thing.

Q:   You received no answer from them?

THE PRESIDENT:   No, I do not think we have had anything on the textiles.

Press Conference #145
Executive Offices of the White House
September 26, 1934, 10:30 A.M.


THE PRESIDENT: You little know what you escaped last night. We had it all
    planned on the train. I got Starling (Colonel Starling of the Secret Ser-
    vice) in and we had it all planned. We were going to let you fellows stay
    asleep and at one minute before midnight we were going to get off the train
    and go back home and all of you people would have waked up in Washington
    with no President.

Q:   And no job. (Laughter)

Q:   We would be down in Richmond by this time.

THE PRESIDENT: We came very near doing it. You little know what you escaped.

MR. DONALDSON: All in.

THE PRESIDENT: I do not think there is any news except the sartorial announce-
    ment that I am still wearing a high hat. Otherwise, I do not know a thing.

Q:   You put a hot one over on us last night.

THE PRESIDENT: What?

Q:   You gave us a big job up there last night -- General Johnson.

THE PRESIDENT: Why did you have to write so much?

Q:   Is there any further comment on it?

THE PRESIDENT: No, no further news at all.

Q:   Can we induce you to comment on the Russian debt situation?

THE PRESIDENT: I have not been in touch with it at all in the last week. You
    probably know a lot more than I do.

Q:   Are you a little disappointed over the results of recognition?

THE PRESIDENT: Oh, no.

Q:   You did not expect any more?

                          --- [89] ---

THE PRESIDENT: Oh, it will be worked out some way.

Q:   Mr. President, have you put out your answer yet to the Chamber of Commerce?

THE PRESIDENT: To the U. S. Chamber of Commerce? No, I think on that, the U. S.
    Chamber of Commerce -- I don't know whether to put it as off the record or
    background -- there are a great many organizations in the United States,
    probably several hundred that are national in scope similar to the Chamber
    of Commerce. Of course, obviously, if the President of the United States

starts answering questionnaires by all of them, it will create a perfectly impossible situation.  The Chamber of Commerce is merely one of many.

I think the only other suggestion I would have is that on reading the questionnaire which they did send to me I am very forcibly reminded of the lawyer who put his question in the form of "Have you stopped beating your wife?"

Q:   Mr. President, when will you announce the new N.R.A. setup?

THE PRESIDENT:   I do not know; I haven't any more idea that you have.  I will start taking it up today but we have, as you know, been talking about it for several months.  I don't think you can guess any particular day.

Q:   Who will see you on this?

THE PRESIDENT:   Again, as I said at Hyde Park, it will be evolutionary.  I could not tell you whether it will be today or next week.

Q:   Have you any appointments with anyone on this topic today -- Mr. Richberg?

THE PRESIDENT:   I will probably telephone to various people to talk to me about that and other things.  I do not think I have any appointments at all to-day.

Q:   Can you tell us when you may see Norman H. Davis?

THE PRESIDENT:   He is to be here, I think it is tomorrow.  I do not know

--- [90] ---

yet what date he is going to sail and I will talk with him about the time he is sailing. He is going over -- that we all know.  What the steamer will be, I don't know.  I think he is due tomorrow.

Q:   The Textile Union is complaining of the widespread discrimination against textile strikes instead of going back to work Monday.

THE PRESIDENT:   I will probably take that up this afternoon.

Q:   Any possibility of an appointment of the new Board this afternoon?

THE PRESIDENT:   I doubt it.

Q:   In connection with Davis' (Norman H. Davis) visit, have you any new ideas in mind concerning the naval disarmament situation?

THE PRESIDENT:   No; just the same thing.

Q:   Have you anything to say to Secretary Wallace's statement that the Hawaiian Islands were not an integral part of the United States in connection with the suit brought by the Hawaiian sugar planters to test the constitutional-ity of the Jones Export Act?

THE PRESIDENT:   I will bet he is a good lawyer.

Q:   The Hawaiians seem to think that is in variance with your remarks that the Islands were an integral part of the United States.

THE PRESIDENT:  That is a matter that has two phases.  We undoubtedly think of
     Puerto Rico, the Virgin Islands, the Canal Zone, Hawaii, Alaska, speaking
     in lay terms, as a part of the United States.  As to the constitutional
     side of it, as to whether under the Constitution they are an integral part
     of the United States as a matter of constitutional law, that is a thing I
     could not begin to pass on.  There are a great many decisions of the Supreme
     Court and it would take a very careful study of them to express any opinion
     as to the status of Hawaii in regard to this particular Act.  In other
     words, it is a legal question.

--- [91] ---

Q:   Mr. President, how is your railroad program coming along?

THE PRESIDENT:  I do not know.  I have not heard from Joe Eastman for a couple
     of weeks.  I have not heard anything about it.

Q:   Mr. President, have you any reactions on the business situation?

THE PRESIDENT:  I have not got as many reactions as some of the businessmen
     have.  (Laughter)  Nor as many inhibitions.

Q:   It is football season.  May we have something on the football game you once
     talked about?

THE PRESIDENT:  I do not know that you can get anything more except the fact
     that we still seem to be scoring.

Q:   What do you think of the RAINBOW (speaking of the sailing races at New-
     port)?

THE PRESIDENT:  Oh, Fred (Mr. Storm), don't ask me that question!  (Laughter)  I
     wish I had more news for you.  I literally haven't a single thing.  I am
     pretty well cleaned up and I suppose there will be a certain amount of news
     the next couple of days.

Q:   Thank you, Mr. President.

CONFIDENTIAL
Press Conference #146
Executive Offices of the White House
September 28, 1934, 4:15 P.M.


THE PRESIDENT:  What is the news?  I don't believe I have got a single thing.
    Everything is all quiet.  I am going to start in tonight or tomorrow and
    try to put down on paper what I am going to say on Sunday night.

Q:    What are you going to say, Mr. President?

THE PRESIDENT:  That is in line with what happened at a little dinner -- this is
    off the record -- a little dinner that was held in New York last night.
    There were about nine of ten very prominent gentlemen in New York and one
    of them said that he had just had a talk with a very close friend of his
    who had just finished reading the President's speech which the President
    was to deliver on Sunday night and that it was a very serious matter be-
    cause the President was coming out in complete and full endorsement of
    anything and everything that organized labor might be doing or might do in
    the future and that he had read this speech.  (Laughter)  So I see what
    you people are up against.

Q:    Mr. President, did the rumor you heard about last night get into print any-
    where or was it just a word-of-mouth rumor?

THE PRESIDENT:  The Post carried it and it was carried over the news wires too.
    Of course it was killed before it got here but I understand that it was
    carried over the wires.

Q:    Along that line, we have a report from San Francisco that you will send a
    message to the labor convention at San Francisco, endorsing the 35-hour
    week.

THE PRESIDENT:  I guess that is another one.  Don't I generally send just the
    usual every-year letter to the --

                        --- [93] ---

MR. EARLY:  The National but not the State Federations.

Q:    That is the American Federation of Labor?

MR. EARLY:  Yes, always.

THE PRESIDENT:  I suppose I nearly always send a letter of greetings; that is
    all.

Q:    Mr. President, have you taken up with anyone yet the note from China pro-
    testing our monetary policy?

THE PRESIDENT:  I am going to see Secretary Morgenthau and Secretary Hull about
    it in the course of the next two or three days.

Q:    We understand the communication which the Chinese Government has sent us
    complains that our silver policy is having a detrimental effect on the
    internal economic situation there.  That is, it is making it more difficult
    for them to send their silver abroad.  Was that anticipated by us?

THE PRESIDENT:   By Congress?

Q:   Yes.

THE PRESIDENT:   I do not know.  I have not seen the note yet.

Q:   I thought the general impression prevailed here that it would be helpful to
rather than hurt China?

THE PRESIDENT:   There are three different schools of thought and they are probably all wrong.  In other words, it is one of those things where one man's
guess is as good as another.

Q:   On labor:  This Order reducing working hours ten per cent in the garment
industry going into effect Monday, is there any possibility of a revision
of that?

THE PRESIDENT:   There is a possibility of a stay in it for two weeks in order
that a hearing may be held by a special committee, but that has not yet
been finally decided on.

--- [94] ---

Q:   Not finally decided whether there will be a stay?

THE PRESIDENT:   Yes.

Q:   Will that hearing be under N.R.A.?

THE PRESIDENT:   Well, it will be by one person or two people or three people,
whatever it might be, who have not had any part in the particular questions
arising up to that time.  In other words, it would be an impartial report.

Q:   You mean a group yet to be named?

THE PRESIDENT:   Yes.

Q:   On the two week's stay?

THE PRESIDENT:   If it is going to be, it will be a two week's stay, but it is
still being talked about.

Q:   Are you considering a judicial section in the reorganization of N.R.A.?

THE PRESIDENT:   Fred (Mr. Storm), that is awfully indefinite yet.  We have not
got to talking on it.  We have been merely talking about the theory of
separating the judicial functions which are really in three parts, the enforcement end of it, the labor settlements through judicial means, and the
code practices settlements through judicial means, and that is as far as
we have got.  I have stated the whole thing there.  We have not got ahead
of that discussion.  The labor settlement is actually in process of going
into effect.  We have the National Labor Relations Board, the Steel
Board, the Textile Board and other boards.

Q:   Do you have a new chairman for the National Labor Relations Board?  There
is a story from Wisconsin that Frank, (Glenn Frank of the University of
Wisconsin) wanted Garrison (head of the Labor Board) to come back?

THE PRESIDENT:  I wanted him to stay.

Q:  Have you settled the dispute yet?

--- [95] ---

THE PRESIDENT:  Not yet.

Q:  Concerning the new setup of N.R.A., can you tell us how you expect the new boards set up to organize down there?  It looks like there will be more time tracing things back from one board to the other --

THE PRESIDENT:  (interposing)  I don't believe there will.  One of the objectives is to cut red tape and speed up.

Q:  Can you give us any example as to how that might be effected?

THE PRESIDENT:  No, I don't know anything about it.

Q:  Any appointments to the Governorship of the Federal Reserve Board or the director of the Federal Reserve Board?

THE PRESIDENT:  Not yet.

Q:  When do you intend to meet with Secretary Hull and Secretary Morgenthau?

THE PRESIDENT:  Probably not until Monday.

Q:  Any other countries involved in that silver situation?

THE PRESIDENT:  Not that I have heard.

Q:  Did you discuss the Lindbergh case with the Attorney General?

THE PRESIDENT:  Oh, we have had mutual congratulations around the Cabinet table, that is all.

Q:  Have you seen Norman Davis on naval disarmament yet?

THE PRESIDENT:  I talked with him yesterday and he is coming -- I do not know if he is coming back today or next -- he is coming down next Tuesday or Wednesday for a final talk before he goes abroad.  He is sailing on the eighth or tenth on the MANHATTAN.

Q:  Is it pretty well worked out now?

THE PRESIDENT:  Oh, yes.

Q:  Can you tell us anything about the general aspects?

THE PRESIDENT:  Again, in this Naval Conference, we will pursue exactly the same methods we pursued heretofore when Davis first went over to the

--- [96] ---

other side.  There won't be any announcement from here of any kind and any announcement will be made by the American delegation over there -- it is not really a delegation -- the American conferees -- because this is not the conference itself. It is merely a perfunctory and informal meeting of the conferees of the three powers.

Q:   Any statement contemplated this far in advance?  It will depend on what the conferees have to say?

THE PRESIDENT:  Everybody has the say.

Q:   Will it be announced here as to who the conferees are to be?

THE PRESIDENT:  Yes.

Q:   Will that be ready this weekend?

THE PRESIDENT:  Probably not until next Wednesday.

Q:   Did you discuss in a general way the political situation in Maryland and Wisconsin, in which the Republican Party seems to be the New Deal Party and the Democratic Party the Conservative Party?

THE PRESIDENT:  No.  (Laughter)  What did they do in Maryland?

Q:   The Republican Party, in convention, has endorsed the New Deal.

THE PRESIDENT:  It is making it sort of unanimous, isn't it?

Q:   He has been reading the Sun (The Baltimore Sun), I guess.

THE PRESIDENT:  Fred (addressing Mr. Essary), I would not stand for it; take him out and drown him.

Q:   (Mr. Essary)  It is understood that Wisconsin reads the Chicago Tribune. (Laughter)

Q:   Thank you, Mr. President.

Q:   Did you say what you were going to talk about Sunday night?

THE PRESIDENT:  About twenty-two minutes.  (Laughter)

CONFIDENTIAL
Press Conference #147
Executive Offices of the White House
October 3, 1934, 10:45 A.M.


Q: (Mr. Lockett) Now people can see you that never have before. Fred Storm is on his vacation.

THE PRESIDENT: That is right too. (Laughter)

I will see if I can find some news in here (looking through a folder) for you.

MR. DONALDSON: All in.

THE PRESIDENT: I do not think there is any particular news. I am seeing Mr. Norman Davis and the Secretary of State at three o'clock this afternoon for a final talk before Mr. Davis sails for London. I am seeing Congressman Byrns in regard to the possibility of stopping at the Hermitage in November on the way to Warm Springs. I don't think I have got any others.

MR. EARLY: None others of news value.

Q: Have you given any consideration to the appointment of the Alley Dwelling Commission?

THE PRESIDENT: Yes, I will tell you the exact status of that. The final Order is now being drawn up. The delay was caused by a question over the Civil Service that had to go back and forth a couple of times to the Civil Service Commission and the Attorney General. That is all straightened out and the Order is being drawn up and will be signed probably today or tomorrow.

Q: Will be signed and the appointments will be announced?

THE PRESIDENT: Yes.

Q: At your last Press Conference you said you thought you usually sent a message of greeting to the A. F. of L. at this convention?

--- [98] ---

MR. EARLY: Not this year. Miss Perkins went out.

THE PRESIDENT: Miss Perkins went out.

Q: Have you given any thought to the successor of Lloyd Garrison?

THE PRESIDENT: No, I have not. We are awfully sorry to lose him. I will have to say this off the record -- no reason you should not know the truth of it -- Glenn Frank said he could not remain Dean (of the University of Wisconsin) and stay in Washington so it sort of put it up to him.

Q: Mr. President, on the labor truce proposition, does this involve the acceptance by both sides of arbitration?

THE PRESIDENT: I think probably the easiest thing to do is to read just what I

said and not draw any other conclusions. It means just what I said, nothing less and nothing more. I do not think it is useful at this time to
try to elaborate because what I said was as clear as I could make it at
that time and I cannot prognosticate as to whom I will see and when and
what we will talk about. I don't know.

Q: At your last conference you said you might be able to tell us today who
the naval experts would be that were to accompany Mr. Davis.

THE PRESIDENT: I think we will have that by tonight.

Q: There is another appointment in the Municipal Court -- in fact, two.

THE PRESIDENT: They keep coming up all the time. Count (Rudolph de Zappe), I
have not done a thing. I will have to ask the Attorney General for his
selections.

Q: The railroad situation seems to be shaping up very fast, particularly from
the standpoint of reorganizations. In view of that, do you have in mind
sending up railroad legislation early and making it "must" legislation?

THE PRESIDENT: I don't know. I could not say yes or no to that because,
frankly, it has not clarified in my own mind sufficiently. At the

--- [99] ---

Council meeting yesterday, the Railroad Administrator -- I will see if I
can find it here (looking among papers) -- he reported that three important reports -- four important reports are nearing completion. One is the
report of the extent to which the various transportation agencies are subsidized by the Government directly or indirectly. The second is a report
on wages and working conditions of transportation agencies other than railroads, including a comparison with railroad wages and working conditions.
The third is a report on the pooling of railroad freight cars in which it
is recommended that all box cars be handled on a pool basis. The fourth
is a report on the handling of railroad passenger traffic.

Until we get a little further I am not in a position to say anything yet.

Q: Can you tell us what you are doing about finding a successor for Lew
Douglas?

THE PRESIDENT: What?

(The question was repeated.)

THE PRESIDENT: Oh, heavens; the matter has not been considered yet. We have a
very satisfactory Acting Director of the Budget.

Q: He will carry on through the preparation of this year's budget?

THE PRESIDENT: Oh, yes; the budget is coming in a perfectly normal way. It has
every year before, in spite of stories.

Q: Are your plans for P.W.A. and relief work taking such shape that you care
to tell us about them?

THE PRESIDENT: No; that would be absolutely guesswork. I could not write a story on it myself if I were paid for it.

Q: Getting back to the labor truce for a moment, has William Green communicated with you? It was said that he would hurry to Washington to

--- [100] ---

confer with you.

THE PRESIDENT: I do not think we have had anything -- no.

Q: Any developments on the Chinese silver situation?

THE PRESIDENT: We had a talk about it the other day, the Secretary of the Treasury, the Secretary of State and I, and I think probably, as with most of these diplomatic matters, you will have to get information from the Secretary of State. I understood he was going to see the Chinese Minister and that is as far as I can say.

Q: Any plans for taking up the annual wage question referred to in your speech Sunday night?

THE PRESIDENT: The annual wage thing?

Q: Yes, sir.

THE PRESIDENT: You mean the annual wage to Government employees?

Q: Insuring workmen an annual income.

THE PRESIDENT: I don't think I mentioned that, did I, in the speech?

Q: Yes, sir; you spoke of the inadequacy or possible inadequacy of wage minimums for a given short length of time such as a week or an hour or two, to establish living standards.

THE PRESIDENT: That I merely mentioned as one of the things people are beginning to think about.

Q: Would you call it an immediate problem?

THE PRESIDENT: Frankly, I don't know. I just mentioned it as something people are thinking about. As a matter of fact, when I first dictated that speech the other day I had an example which would have made more clear that phase of the wage problem.

Last winter, as you will recall, the automobile workers were down here. They were a pretty young crowd, most of those fellows were about 35 years or along there. I said to one of them, "What are you

--- [101] ---

getting? What is your hourly wage?" He said, "A dollar and a quarter an hour." I said, "Eight hours?" He said,"Yes, sir." I said, "That is $10 a day?" He said, "Yes, sir; that is right." I said, "It seems to me that is a pretty good wage. What are you, a machinist?" "Yes, sir." I said, "I think that is a pretty good wage."

Then he said, "Mr. President, that is a pretty good wage, yes, but last year I only worked 65 days. My total gross income was $650."

I think that particular story emphasizes the thought better than anything else that you can use or I can use as to the reason for thinking in terms of how much a fellow gets by December 31 instead of how much he gets per hour. That is what I was driving at. We are beginning to orient ourselves a little bit differently.

Q:  Mr. President, you had a request to increase the cattle-buying program in the drought sections?

THE PRESIDENT:  To increase?

Q:  Yes, sir.

THE PRESIDENT:  No. I think that most of it is completed. If you will wait a minute I will check up here on the Council report yesterday.

Up to September twenty-fourth, the number of cattle purchased in drought areas totaled 6,074,808. The program contemplates a total purchase of 7,000,000. In other words, it is more than six-sevenths completed -- less than a million still to be purchased. And that was the original program.

Q:  Mr. President, have you arrived at any decision on filling the R.F.C. vacancy?

THE PRESIDENT:  I have not had time to talk about it yet.

Q:  Mr. President, have you had any estimate of the total cost of the drought to the Federal Government?

THE PRESIDENT:  Well, we know we have an appropriation of 525 million and,

--- [102] ---

naturally, we will stay within that. Whether there will be what might be called the aftereffects of the drought next spring, it is much too early to talk about. I doubt it, personally. If there are aftereffects, they would probably fall under the heading of relief rather than drought. In other words, they would be families we expect to get back on their feet before next spring and something might happen and they might not get back.

Q:  Are you satisfied with the way the housing program is coming along? Do you think it has been successful so far?

THE PRESIDENT:  I think that Moffett is really very much encouraged on the whole with the way it is getting along. One difficulty with the housing program is that the -- a lot of people connected with the financing of it, the private financing of it, have not taken the trouble to read the Act so that it is more a question of education than anything else. There are a lot of building and loan associations and banks which are a little slow in coming along but, on the whole, the pickup is very good. It takes time for them to find the time to read what it is all about and, when they do read it and get it explained to them, they come along. Considering the fact that it has been going a very short time, both Moffett and I believe it is making real progress.

Q:  In that connection, isn't it true that the Housing Administration is not particularly concerned with banks making loans under its own plan, just so they make loans?

THE PRESIDENT: Yes.

Q:  So the total number of applications to the Housing Administration or through the Housing Administration would not be a good index?

THE PRESIDENT: Before I attempted that, I would have to find out how many loans any given bank had made on their own plan.

--- [103] ---

Q:  Wouldn't the increase in building permits and for operations of that sort from the Bureau of Labor index be a better index over a period?

THE PRESIDENT: Only if you analyzed them. You could not take any table of figures because you might be taking a $10,000,000 office building.

Q:  I understand they are broken down into items.

THE PRESIDENT: Are they? Well, that is a helpful suggestion and I hope you are right.

Q:  Thank you, Mr. President.

Press Conference #148
Executive Offices of the White House
October 5, 1934, 4:15 P.M.


Q:   Mr. President, is there anything you can say on the progress of the Housing Administration so far?

THE PRESIDENT:  We talked about that the other day and I got a letter here from
Mr. Moffett that gives a great many figures.  I don't believe you all want
the figures.  Do you see any reason, Steve, why we should not take this
letter out to the Press Room and use the figures if the Press wants to?

MR. EARLY:  I don't see any reason why not.

THE PRESIDENT:  It is a two and a half page letter.  If you want the figures you
can have them.  Here are some of the high spots.  Moffett sent out contracts to all types of financial institutions, 23,300 institutions, and a
little over 8,000 have accepted the contracts -- in other words, about 35
per cent.  The average amount of existing loans made is $443 and the aver-
age amount of the makers' income is $2711.  The average maturity of the
loans is twenty-six months.  The loans have been made in forty-eight
states.

Moffett then goes on to say that the banks generally are unfamiliar with
the Personal Credit Installment Payment Plan and we (F.H.A.) are required
to carry on an extensive educational campaign.  (Reading)

> "The American Bankers Association have provided us with liaison
> officers for every state in the Union, who are helping us to
> carry on the educational program.  New banks are accepting our
> contracts at the rate of approximately fifty per day.  Loans
> reported each day show an increase of forty per cent over the
> corresponding day of the previous week,....  Considering the
> short period of time we have been operating, I think we have
> made rapid progress and, to my mind, the success of the oper-
> ation will equal our most optimistic expectations....  The
> pro-

--- [105] ---

> position is dependent on the public individuals' willingness
> to purchase, and the private financial institutions' willing-
> ness to lend.  The operation has shown a steady, natural
> growth since its inception, and will gather momentum as the
> educational and community campaign increase."

Then he quotes a telegram which I cannot give you the name of the sender because it would be advertising a private company.  It is addressed to him
and says that a countrywide survey of the progress of the private housing
program has just been completed and the results of this survey prove that
"you should be gratified with the excellent work your organization has
done.

> "I find business encouraged because Government is stimulating
> the flow of private capital by means of this Act.  Business
> will accept the opportunity to assist you in employing private

initiative to stimulate business and employment. My field
reports indicate that although a great many banks have
qualified, many are reluctant to furnish money. Although
this presents an important problem, I am not greatly discouraged by this fact and it is anticipated that, at the
outset, because of lack of understanding some banks would
not be willing to embrace these new ideas until thoroughly
educated. (Laughter) As to their profit possibilities,
several bankers have informed me personally that they have
found this new business profitable.

"As you have been informed, we have organized a credit
corporation and applied for the privilege of lending money
to home-owners to make improvements under the provisions
of the National Housing Act. We are supplying credit
facilities to those communities where such facilities are
not now available.

"Time payments: In the light of our experience with time
payment financing before the passage of the National
Housing Act, it showed only two per cent loss on such loans
and to offer this plan on a nationwide basis is not only a
sound business move but also a delightful contribution toward attaining the objectives of the Act. Our analysis shows
that no other industry has a greater potential market than
the building industry."

et cetera and so on, the rest being about their own company. That particular company believes that the goal of stimulating a billion, five hundred
million dollar's worth of business in the next fourteen months is an entirely possible achievement.

--- [106] ---

So much for that. This letter of Jimmy Moffett's, Steve will take it out
and you can read it.

Q:    Mr. President, on September twenty-fourth there was a Proclamation by which
the processing tax on sugar from Hawaii will go into the general treasury
of the Territory. Will you throw a little light on that?

THE PRESIDENT: I wish I could. I do not know enough about the details of the
plan.

Q:    It came out today when the State Department --

THE PRESIDENT: (interposing) I do not know. It is an accounting proposition,
I take it.

Q:    In view of the apparent ease with which prisoners are escaping from jails,
having in mind this recent Richmond break, is the Department of Justice
doing anything to try to counteract that?

THE PRESIDENT: I took that up with the Attorney General as soon as that Richmond jail escape occurred and asked him what the general policy was. Of
course the Richmond jail was a city or state institution. He wrote me
this (indicating memorandum) and gave it to me today. On account of the
poor conditions prevailing in many of the jails throughout the country,

the Department of Justice, partly for its own protection and partly to
stimulate improvement in such jails, make it a rule not to place Federal
prisoners in institutions which as a result of examination do not measure
up to a required standard. (Reading)

> "I think you might be interested to know that the Richmond
> jail did not come up to the Federal standards and in August,
> 1933 the United States Marshal was instructed to remove the
> Federal prisoners therefrom and to make no further commit-
> ments of any type of Federal prisoners to that jail."

That was the jail from which two desperate prisoners sentenced to death
recently escaped and the prisoners were not Federal prisoners.

[107] ---

In other words, we are trying to improve the standard of city and county
and state jails throughout the country.

Q:   Bigger and better! (Laughter)

Q:   As a result of your conversations with Ambassador Davis are you at all
     optimistic as to any possibility of achieving disarmament?

THE PRESIDENT:  That was close to an "if" question. (Laughter)

Q:   I wonder if we will concentrate on limitation rather than actual disarma-
     ment.

THE PRESIDENT:  I don't think you had better concentrate on anything. In other
     words, as I have said before -- this part has to be off the record -- we
     are very, very sincere in hoping that we are going to get a new Naval
     treaty next year. The more that is said by Government officials and the
     more that is said by the Press at this time, the more difficult, frankly,
     it becomes for these conferees -- I suppose they should be called "conver-
     sationalists" rather than conferees -- the more difficult it becomes for
     them to come to an agreement. That is why I am trying to say nothing
     about it and I hope very much that you good people won't do too much gues-
     sing or stating that our delegation is going to do this or that. What we
     are trying to do is to get an agreement and the less we talk about it, the
     more chance we have to encourage a reduction in Naval armaments.

It is not much of a secret that we are seeking to carry out the language
of the Washington Treaty, the preamble of the London Treaty that has the
whereas clauses in it that state as the objective of all of these conferences a progressive reduction in Naval armaments as being a very great contribution to modern civilization. I think it is worth noting that the
Washington Treaty of 1922 was the very first voluntary step that nations
took towards limitation or reduction of

--- [108] ---

armaments. Previous steps such as the Versailles Treaty could not properly
be called a voluntary step. The disarmament of the Versailles Treaty was
felt to be imposed by a number of the nations concerned.

What we are trying to do is to carry out the spirit of the previous conferences and seek a continuation of progressive reduction. I don't think it

is possible to go any further than that without making it difficult, more
difficult for the British delegates, the Japanese delegates and the American delegates -- they are not delegates, that is the wrong word to use --
to sit in a friendly way around the table and get somewhere.  Of course
things are not in the least bit helped -- this is off the record entirely
-- by the kind of statement that was made by our old friend Billy Mitchell
the other day at that hearing.  Billy Mitchell would be a much more useful
person to this country if he would not talk that way.

Q:   Do you not personally think that we would have to give a little way on
     such things as our existing ratios if we hope to get the Japs to agree to
     anything?

THE PRESIDENT:   That is entirely speculative.

Q:   We are not taking an adamant stand on that?

THE PRESIDENT:   I think the only way you can put it, the only thing I can say
     that is truthful, is that we are trying to carry out the objectives and
     purposes we have been seeking since 1922.  I cannot go any further than
     that.

Q:   Can you tell us, sir, who may be the next Chief of Staff?

THE PRESIDENT:   Fred (Mr. Essary), I won't know that until some time -- I think
     until about the first of November.

Q:   Mr. President, is there any change in the Government's price policies?

THE PRESIDENT:   Price policies?

--- [109] ---

Q:   Yes, sir; as reflected in the N.R.A. Codes?

THE PRESIDENT:   The only thing I can do is to ask you to read what I said on
     Sunday night.  That is about all there is we can say at the present time.

Q:   Mr. President, are you taking any personal interest in the dumping of
     Japanese Nationals in Arizona?  (Laughter)

THE PRESIDENT:   I decline to incriminate myself under advice of counsel.
     (Laughter)  I put in a plea of not guilty.  (Laughter)

Q:   Mr. President, what do you think of this idea of a permanent transporta-
     tion coordinator or a Cabinet Transportation Department?

THE PRESIDENT:   Well, you know, as I think I said about a week ago, there have
     been suggestions for new Cabinet officers for at least half a dozen things.
     They wanted a Cabinet officer for a new Department of Recreation the other
     day -- I have forgotten --

Q:   (interposing)  Golf player?

THE PRESIDENT:   Recreation, and of course from time to time there are lots and
     lots of new ideas that creep up.

Q:   Have you received a report of the Mississippi Valley Committee from Secretary Ickes?

THE PRESIDENT:  I have it here on my desk in two huge volumes and I have not
opened it yet.

Q:   You have not looked at it?

THE PRESIDENT:  I have not looked at it.

Q:   Have you a report that a group of industrial leaders are coming down to see
you tonight or tomorrow from New York?

THE PRESIDENT:  I do not know.  I see one or two industrial leaders or bankers
every day of my life.

Q:   This is to be a group.

--- [110] ---

THE PRESIDENT:  I am still pretty husky and will take on all comers.  Steve (Mr.
Early), do you know anything about it?

MR. EARLY:  No, sir.

Q:   Has any consideration been given to public works appropriations or possible
enlargement of the program?

THE PRESIDENT:  No.

Q:   There is quite a lot of speculation going on about it now.

THE PRESIDENT:  Again, off the record, for your own information, as you know the
method of handling unemployment divides up, so far as the activities we
have undertaken are concerned, roughly into three groups.  One is C.C.C.
camps, one the public works and the other is Harry Hopkins' relief organization which again divides itself into the C.W.A. type of work and the
grocery-store order or home relief.  Naturally, we have been considering
and will continue to consider until the fourth of January -- the second
or third of January -- the general problem of unemployment, as to how unemployment should be met.  Of course public works is one of the methods of
meeting unemployment.  Now, that is literally as far as we have got.  We
are discussing the whole subject at the present time rather than in sub-
divisions of methods.  Probably we won't get into the subdivision-of-
methods conversations until somewhere around the middle of November.  We
are looking at it first as a broad picture of unemployment as a whole.

Q:   The New York power authorities, the trustees, are coming down to visit
T.V.A. in the hope of bringing to the Northeast the same law?

THE PRESIDENT:  Frank Walsh, who is Chairman of the New York Power Authority,
came to see me about three or four weeks ago at Hyde Park and told me that
they are very much interested in what the T.V.A. is trying

--- [111] ---

to do and also what this new board that is studying the general plan for
large Federal public works -- I have forgotten the name of it, the planning
board or something like that --

Q:    National Resources?

THE PRESIDENT:  That's it, National Resources Board, what they are doing.  So I
    told Frank Walsh that I would be delighted if he would look at the work of
    the T.V.A. and furthermore I would be very glad if he would sit in at
    meetings of the National Resources Board without becoming actually a member
    because there is a local question that if he were to become a member he
    might forfeit the chairmanship of the New York Power Authority.

Q:    In that connection, how do the voluntary reductions which have been made by
    the privately-owned utilities affect that general situation?  For instance,
    the P.W.A. loans for municipal plants?

THE PRESIDENT:  The only thing that has come to me was a statement by -- I
    couldn't even tell you who it was -- but it was the people who put in cer-
    tain similar although perhaps not identical rate reductions in the terri-
    tory near Tupelo.  They had exactly the same experience as the T.V.A.
    people had had in greatly increased consumption of electricity and I am
    told that they are very well satisfied with the experiment.

Q:    Referring to the T.V.A. again, is there any intention of divorcing the
    power venture of the St. Lawrence Treaty from navigation in order to get
    the treaty through at the coming session?

THE PRESIDENT:  No.

Q:    The treaty will be submitted in the same form?

THE PRESIDENT:  It ties together.  I will have to make the rest of the answer
    off the record because we haven't, as far as I know, said anything to
    Canada about it at the present time.  It is possible we might talk with

--- [112] ---

Canada about certain rather minor modifications of the treaty as it was
submitted last year to the Senate but the general principle will remain.
You will remember the one question raised about American workmen on the
American operation of the project.  That is a thing that can be cleared up
very easily.  I have said that before so you can make it background.

Q:    The Chicago diversion is a point there; have you considered that matter?

THE PRESIDENT:  Yes.  I have considered it quite finally some time ago.

Q:    How about the appointment of a Governor on the Federal Reserve Board?

THE PRESIDENT:  No, I haven't thought of it at all nor the R.F.C. vacancies.

Q:    Is there anything you can say as to how this country might mitigate the
    effects of its silver program on China?

THE PRESIDENT:  I cannot talk about that.  The Secretary of State has talked to
    the Chinese Minister.  What the status of those conversations is I don't
    know.

Q:    Thank you, Mr. President.

                    (The Press Conference adjourned at 4:28 P.M.)

Press Conference #149
Executive Offices of the White House
October 10, 1934, 10:40 A.M.


Q:   Good morning, Mr. President.

THE PRESIDENT:  Well, I came across yesterday, Count (Rudolph de Zappe).

Q:   (Mr. de Zappe)  Thank you; that was very nice.

THE PRESIDENT:  I told Steve (Mr. Early) not to release it until he got hold of you.

Q:   (Mr. de Zappe)  That is very kind; thank you.

MR. DONALDSON:  All in.

THE PRESIDENT:  I have just been going over the schedule for Roanoke and Williamsburg with Steve (Mr. Early).  We will leave here a week from Friday and get to Williamsburg Saturday morning.  We get all through about a quarter past one and then I am going to motor over to Yorktown, get aboard the SEQUOIA nad cruise leisurely back to Washington.  Steve and I just wanted to suggest to you who are going with us, that being Saturday afternoon and nothing to do for the next thirty-six hours, that Old Point Comfort Virginia Beach are quite close to Williamsburg in case you want a week end.  We abandon the train at Williamsburg and there is no way of getting home.

Q:   Could you run the SEQUOIA down to Virginia Beach for us?  (Laughter)

THE PRESIDENT:  I will try to do that and we will put the lid on as soon as we leave Williamsburg.

Q:   Are you going to Hyde Park again?

THE PRESIDENT:  What happened on that was that we were going to attend the dedication of the Theodore Roosevelt Memorial on the Twenty-seventh of October in New York -- that is the new front of the Natural Museum (Museum of Natural History), but yesterday Professor Henry Fairfield

--- [114] ---

Osborn, the President Emeritus of the Museum, sent word to us that because there had been a good deal of delay in completing the work on the Memorial, they had decided to put off the dedication for at least six months.  So I am not going to New York on the twenty-seventh but, as I always prefer to vote in person instead of by mail, we are going to Hyde Park probably the Saturday before election and stay over Election Day for three days.  We are not taking any White House staff with us.  I think we will put the lid on completely.

Q:   Have you any fresh advices this morning as to the situation in Europe?

THE PRESIDENT:  I have not.  I just got down here this moment.  I haven't heard a thing.

Q:  Will you announce the appointment of the administrator to Archives soon, or the Archivist or the Archĩvist?

THE PRESIDENT:  I don't know; I have always said Archĩvist but do not know whether it is right.  I have not looked it up.

Q:  It will be announced today?

THE PRESIDENT:  Yes, today.

Q:  Anything you can tell us about your N.R.A. plans after the visit of the new Board?

THE PRESIDENT:  No, no announcement.  It will be an evolutionary process.

Q:  In his comments in Chicago on the Budget, was Richberg speaking for the Administration?

THE PRESIDENT:  I did not read his comments on the Budget so I cannot tell you.

Q:  Have you done anything about a successor for Garrison in the Labor Relations Board?

THE PRESIDENT:  I think so and I think it will come out either today or tomorrow.  No, I am wrong -- cancel that; that is another board.  (Laughter)

--- [115] ---

Q:  What board is that?

THE PRESIDENT:  That is the Cotton Textile Board, in the place of Judge Stacey.  Steve (Mr. Early) says that is still doubtful so do not say anything about it, but that is the one I had in mind.

Q:  Mr. President, it has been some time since you said anything on prices.  Have you any comment?  Do you still wish higher prices?

THE PRESIDENT:  Yes.  I cannot tell you the exact numbers of dollars and cents.  Let us put this as background, so that you can use it for background if you wish.

Over a year ago, after consulting with almost everybody in the world, industry and agriculture and finance, mortgagees, farm credit, etc., everybody was agreed and I think it was pretty nearly unanimous that there ought to be a rise in prices, a very substantial rise in prices, in order to relieve the general debtor-creditor situation.  It has been at least a year ago.

I don't know whether I talked on the record or off the record to the crowd but what I did point out at that time was something along this line:  that in the Spring of 1933 -- well, let us go back further, in 1929 before the crash, the total of the assets of the United States, the asset column was away over, away above the total of the liability column.  On that basis a great many debts had been created.  But, from the standpoint of values, according to those prices, the asset column was, taking your pick, anywhere from seventy-five to a hundred and fifty million dollars higher than the liability column.  Now, mind you, this is simply repeating what I said over a year ago.

After 1929 the country was confronted with the simple fact that the asset column, in terms of values and prices, was constantly sliding down and the debt column, the liability column, was remain-

--- [116] ---

ing constant, with the net result, as practically all the figures checked up, that by March 1933, the asset column had sunk down until it was actually lower than the liability column.

Obviously, at that time there were three methods of procedure. This is awfully old stuff, but it holds good today just as it did at that time. In order to bring those columns into a proper relationship so that the assets were greater than the liabilities, so that we would be back in the black again, we could have and many suggestions were made that we could cut the debt column, the liability column, by some rule of thumb procedure. The idea would be that if some fellow owed a thousand dollars by reason of some kind of debt, tell him that he only owed five hundred dollars. Cut the debt structure of the country. Of course that was thrown out as being impossible under our Constitution and law.

The second possibility was to make a very definite attempt to raise the asset column by increasing values. We accepted that, but we also used a part of the third method, which was to do both things at the same time; in other words, to raise values so that the asset column would increase, and at the same time cut down the debt column through various legal methods such, for example, as the Farm Credit organization which materially reduced interest rates to farmers. Of course, interest is a liability as well as principal so that helped to cut down the debt column. Then the loans to home owners, the refinancing of home loans through the various methods that were allowed, that also was a method of cutting down the debt column. The bill that allowed a corporation to go through a new form of receivership was a third method, and there were quite a lot of other methods of cutting down, in a perfectly legal way, the liability column of the

--- [117] ---

United States.

Now, to go back to the question of prices. We have raised them. It depends on whose figures you take. I won't give you the figures because immediately you get into the argumentative stage; but the fact remains that the values in the United States have advanced very, very materially.

The net result is that the asset column of the United States has gone up a great deal and the debt column has gone down a little bit. We don't think that the asset column has gone up enough yet, and it ought to be up some more.

Now, obviously, I cannot put that in figures of percentage or dollars and cents or indexes. Perhaps you will remember that I have been very, very careful never to accept the theory of the Press that we were seeking 1926 values although it has been very, very often said that that was the definite Administration policy. Of course, I have never said such a thing in my life. Some 1926 values are all right, some 1925 or 1924 values are all right. In the case of farm products, we have by common consent on the farm organizations at that meeting which they held here in the Spring of 1933, they all agreed that we would base what we call "parity" on the average of

1909 to 1914 prices.

In other words, there are a great many factors and you cannot be didactic and take one year for everything.

Of course, obviously, when I say that we want increased prices, it is only fair to put the other side of the picture. We don't want one-way prices or values. That is equally important.

Taking it by and large, the progress on prices and values, considering the comparative shortness of the time, has been pretty substantial, and it will go a little further and that is about as far as

--- [118] ---

you can go.

Then, of course, ther is one other factor in the situation. You haven't asked me this question but it is really on the same general subject, so I might just as well talk to you now. When I was in Newport, somebody brought on board a copy of the dear old Boston Transcript, which I love to see because it reminds me of my childhood days. It has changed very little and it is a splendid paper and always has been. On the financial page there was about a half column head, "Historic events," and "Historic events" consisted of listing the highs and lows of commodity prices of various kinds from 1920, I think, to 1934. Well, I read it, and I said to myself, "There must be something wrong with our finances and business to allow a condition such as shown in those highs and lows." The ordinary layman would say that if there were a rise or a fall of 25% in the price of something that he was interested in, it would be a pretty substantial change. And if it was a 50% rise or fall he would say that it is a whale of a change and he would get a little worried in the ordinary course of things. And yet, if you take the highs and the lows from 1920 to 1934 you will find that the changes were not 25% and not 50%, but they were 500% and 800% and a thousand per cent. It is perfectly amazing and it is well worth looking into the thing to see what the highs and lows have been just in the past few years.

How can anybody plan ahead, how can you have stabilization if prices vary 500 and 700 and 1000%? Look at the range of cotton, look at the range of wheat, look at the range of butter, look at the range of cattle, and so forth and so on. Take any 15 or 20 or 30 different articles in general use and you will find that the range has been, as I say, anywhere between 500 and 1000% just over a little period of

--- [119] ---

fourteen years.

What we are seeking, obviously for the good of my old friend the average individual, is to prevent fluctuations of that kind. Not "fluctuations," of course not, but fluctuations of that kind in the days to come. Wheat, for example, sold at 35¢ a bushel and then at $2.04 a bushel. Copper was selling at 5¢ a pound and at 32¢ a pound. Butter was selling at 15¢ a pound and 72¢ a pound. Those are not accurate figures but just to give you an example.

That is why we are very definitely trying to raise the price level some more, I don't say how much more and when we get it there to try to keep it within reasonable bounds for a reasonable length of time.

I think that covers that question pretty well.

Q:   Any immediate plans for doing that?

THE PRESIDENT:   No, it has just been the policy of the Administration for about a year and a half.

Q:   When you do get it high enough, how do you propose to stabilize?  What would the machinery be that you will use?

THE PRESIDENT:   The only way I can answer that is that we are learning every day.  In other words, we cannot say we are going to do this on the 30th of next month and that on the 30th of the following month we are going to do thus and so.  There has been a good deal of study given in the late months to the question not only of raising prices but when they get up there to prevent them from going through the roof.  We are getting interested in that phase as the price level goes up.

Q:   Would it have anything to do with the control of gold and the dollar?

THE PRESIDENT:   I don't know.  I am not enough of an expert on that.  (Laughter)  It might be a factor.

--- [120] ---

Q:   Richberg, in one of his reports, said that between June, 1933, and 1934 there was a drop of 10% in wages.  With the increase in prices, is it reasonably to suppose that this drop would be affected?

THE PRESIDENT:   It certainly ought to.  You mean real wages, actually dollars and cents?

Q:   The relationship between dollar volume --

THE PRESIDENT:   (interposing)  Let's put it a little more clearly.  Suppose prices went up 10%.  The dollar wages of labor certainly ought to go up at least 10%.  I think that is the easiest way of putting it.

Q:   You spoke a moment ago of the liability column coming down and the asset column going up.  Have they passed each other, in your judgment?

THE PRESIDENT:   I don't know, but I should say, offhand, that they have.  In other words, this is again subject to any number of kinds of figures, depending on the person who figures them.  But I should say, offhand, that a year and a half ago the liabilities of the country very definitely exceeded the assets of the country and I am inclined to think that today we see the assets up a little bit above the liabilities, but not sufficiently.

Q:   Mr. President, do you feel yet that the prices have yet reached the point where you could begin to put some sort of a brake on the upward speed?  You say you want to keep on raising them, but at some point you will want to slow the process down.

THE PRESIDENT:   Well, you cannot very well slow down a process that is crawling.

Q:   As you approach the thing, you have to gradually stop it?

THE PRESIDENT:  Yes, but that is for the future.

Q:   Comptroller General McCarl -- I mean, the Comptroller of the Currency, Mr.
O'Connor, has been a very frequent visitor up here and we have

--- [121] ---

frequent rumors that he is going to resign his job.  Can you comment on
that?

THE PRESIDENT:  I do not know a thing about it.  We have been trying to get as
many banks as we can, before the Congress meets, completely cleared up.
I cannot tell you the exact figures but I think of the nonlicensed banks
there were last January somewhere around 650 and they are now down to 36,
as I remember the figures.  We are trying to get every one of them cleaned
up with this new method that Jesse Jones has been working on.  We are trying to get every single bank cleaned up by the first of January, if we
can, one way or the other.

Q:   There are just 36 Federal receivers in charge of banks?

THE PRESIDENT:  Oh, my, no.  A bank which is definitely in receivership, with a
definite method of working out its deposits is not listed in this.  In
other words, it might be a bank which has got to the point where there is
nothing for it to do except to complete the receivership.  But that is a
decision made.  These 36 that I am talking about, as I understand it, are
banks which are in process of making a final determination.

Q:   Have you had a chance to look over the Mississippi Valley Committee's
report?

THE PRESIDENT:  I took it down on Sunday with me and I did not read it.

Press Conference #150
Executive Offices of the White House
October 12, 1934, 4:10 P.M.


MR. DONALDSON:  All in.

THE PRESIDENT:  Steve (Mr. Early) reminds me that this is our 150th Conference.
    I congratulate you on your powers of endurance.

Q:    The same to you, sir.

THE PRESIDENT:   I think the only news I have is that I signed today the Executive
    Order establishing the 36-hour week in the cotton garment manufacturing in-
    dustry, effective on December first.   (Reading)

        "...The action was taken on recommendation --"

I might as well read it in case there is any question -- (Reading)

        " -- of a special impartial committee which had been created
        under an agreement with the industry that the findings would
        be accepted as final.

        "Under the order, not only will the work week be shortened
        from the present 40 hours, but weekly wages will be kept at
        the present total, and piece rates will be increased by ten
        per cent.

        "In addition the order provides:

        "1.   That a committee of three shall be appointed by the
        National Industrial Recovery Board to investigate and report
        by December 1, 1934 on the competition faced by this indus-
        try from prison labor and sheltered workshops;

        "2.   That the existing impartial committee of three be author-
        ized to continue investigation and to report by November 15
        on the protests of the sheep-lined and leather garment sub-
        division of the cotton garment industry; and,

        "3.   That the Recovery Board, on or before January 15, 1935,
        report to the President on the opera-

                --- [123] ---

tion of provisions in the cotton garment code which govern
the granting of exceptions and exemptions.  The latter was
based on a recommendation of the committee that exemptions
should be allowed sparingly and only for good cause since
'anything resembling wholesale exemptions would undermine
the Code and the splendid enforcement results which the
Code Authority, as now set up, is accomplishing.'

"Today's order grew out of a provision in this code requiring that a study be made of its labor provisions in
operation.  Hearings were conducted in June at the instance

of two competitive industries, dress manufacturing and
the men's clothing industry.  They resulted in approval
by the President on August 21 of an order immediately
shortening the work week to 36 hours.  On representations
of the Cotton Garment Code Authority this order was
stayed until October 15 to allow for a new review of
the facts.

"The President directed the National Industrial Recovery
Board to name a committee of three neutral persons.  The
Board named Willard E. Hotchkiss, president of Armour
Institute of Technology, chairman of N.R.A.'s General
Code Authority; W. Jett Lauck, prominent Washington labor
attorney; and Donald M. Nelson, official of Sears, Roebuck
and Company, a member of N.R.A.'s Industrial Advisory
Board.

"This committee's report and recommendations signed by all
three, were approved and adopted in full by the President's
order.

"The reason for making the order effective on December 1
was that this would give the industry time to prepare
for the change and would not break into the middle of
its fall production schedule.

"Furthermore, the committee pointed out, increase of the
piece rates would require establishment by the code authority of machinery for the filing of these rates.

"The committee expressed the opinion that the increase in
labor costs would not cause any great increase in the
price of merchandise, but that this probably would amount
to no more than a five cent jump in the cost of a 49 cent
work shirt.

"Shortening the work hours was deemed especially desirable
by the committee in view of the fact that competing industries, such as dress and men's clothing

--- [124] ---

manufacturers, are already on the 36 hour week with generally higher wage scales.

"The code authority of the cotton garment industry was
commended for 'earnest and well directed effort' at enforcement of labor provisions of its code."

Put it on the mimeograph.

Q:   In that connection, can you give us a little more on the wage angle?  Did
you say that weekly wages would be kept at the present total?

THE PRESIDENT:   Yes.

Q:   Will there be any change in the wage rates?

THE PRESIDENT: Well, they get the same pay for thirty-six hours that they were getting for forty hours, after the first of December.

Q: That in effect is a raise in the hourly rate, which I suppose is made up in the piece work by that specific increase?

THE PRESIDENT: Yes.

Q: This cuts the Garment Code down to thirty-six hours. What is the next move? Do you look for a step of this kind in any of these other fields?

THE PRESIDENT: I do not know. You cannot figure out any general rule on it. These things come up from time to time.

Q: I wondered if there are any more coming?

THE PRESIDENT: I don't know.

Q: Pleading my own ignorance, wherein does this Order differ from the August twenty-seventh [August twenty-first?] one?

THE PRESIDENT: It does not differ from it except in requiring further study of certain items like sheep-lined garments and things like that and deferring it until the first of December.

--- [125] ---

Q: Is there any import competition?

THE PRESIDENT: On these things? I don't know.

Q: In this connection, would you comment on the resolutions by the American Federation of Labor for a 30-hour week?

THE PRESIDENT: No. To tell you the honest truth, I have not read them except what I read in the headlines.

Q: Have Secretaries Hull and Morgenthau agreed on what to tell the Chinese?

THE PRESIDENT: Yes. (Laughter)

Q: Can you tell us?

THE PRESIDENT: I think they will be ready to -- there is no reason why it should not be made public after they have talked with the Chinese Minister and have made arrangements so that when it does come out it will come out simultaneously both in China and here.

Q: Will it satisfy the Chinese?

THE PRESIDENT: I do not know. (Laughter)

Q: Is there anything you can tell us about the conflict between the National Labor Relations Board and the Department of Justice as to what should be done legally with reference to the Houde case? (The Houde Company had declined to abide by a ruling of the Labor Relations Board.)

THE PRESIDENT: I have not done a single thing. I never talked with anybody about it. I did not know there was a conflict.

Q: In the Houde case, the Labor Relations Board held there was a violation and ordered the Blue Eagle removed, also the majority recommended that the Department of Justice prosecute civilly

--- [126] ---

but not criminally and yesterday Mr. Cummings made it apparent they were not going to prosecute legally.

THE PRESIDENT: I don't know -- I did not know anything about it. I knew the decision in the Houde case but did not know the other thing.

Q: The Committee on Economic Security made a statement today stating that they had divided their work into eleven different phases of the social investigation and there are reports that the program is going to be limited because of difficulties in financing. Is that correct?

THE PRESIDENT: That is a new one on me. We gave them a generous allowance when the thing was set up.

Q: I do not know about the Committee itself but the difficulties of which I speak are those of financing any unemployment or insurance or old age pension plan.

THE PRESIDENT: You mean the problem of how they are to finance? Of course that is one of the problems they are to meet, to tell you how to finance it.

Q: Mr. President, a group of us talked with Richberg today and got the definite impression for the first time that there will be no judicial organization as such within the N.R.A. but that these functions for carrying out code enforcement and other matters of that sort will be exercised by the Federal Trade Commission, the Department of Justice, as they are now, but with probably some simplification of procedure. Can you give us any idea as to how that procedure will be simplified?

THE PRESIDENT: I cannot tell you the details because we do not know

--- [127] ---

the details of it yet. I think, Charlie (Mr. Hurd), that it is a mistake to use the word "judicial" in this connection. In other words, it is a perfectly natural error to make because about a month ago I talked about the examination of N.R.A. in regard to three functions, the executive function, the judicial function and the legislative function -- that is, policy making -- and I also explained that the judicial function, as a function, which is a matter of pure theory and not of organization, automatically divided itself into three parts: one portion of the judicial function related to the settlement of disputes between industry and labor. Of course we have made very distinct progress on that by setting up certain boards having quasi-judicial functions. Then the second component part of the function is the setting up of adequate quasi-judicial machinery to settle disputes between one manufacturer and the other. The third component part of the judicial function related to enforcement but it is not fair to refer to that as judicial because it is only one out of three parts. I think I would use the words "enforcement of codes" as being the more correct term.

As to that, the first thought -- and I think we talked up at Hyde Park about it -- was that we would make every effort to put enforcement into the enforcing branch of Government; in other words, the Department of Justice. But, on further study of it, it becomes perfectly clear -- I suppose the easiest way to put it is this: perhaps a hundred complaints of failure to live up to codes have come in. Every one of those has to be examined and probably out of one hundred, ninety-five of them

--- [128] ---

are straightened out without having to resort to the legal machinery of the Government. That would leave, let us say, five of them that would have to be turned over to the Department of Justice. Now, it seems probably better to leave the sifting of those hundred cases in N.R.A. rather than to make the Department of Justice a sifting instead of a prosecuting organization. Therefore, we will leave the investigation, sifting, settlement portion of enforcement in N.R.A.

When, however, you get down to, say, the five cases out of a hundred where you have to start the legal machinery of the Government working, we are trying to work out for that a practical and simple working organization between Justice and N.R.A. and the Federal Trade Commission so that there will be uniformity of policy with respect to all three of those organizations in dealing with actual enforcement cases. As I say, it might be only five out of a hundred -- what the actual details of them are, I do not know. It may be -- just to give you a lead -- that the Department of Justice would send a special Assistant Attorney General to sit with N.R.A. so that he would be familiar with those five cases out of a hundred when they are ripe, and another one over to the Federal Trade Commission to keep in touch with them and see whether the actual enforcement, just to give you an example, would be by the Department of Justice or the Federal Trade Commission.

Q:    What place has the Labor Relations Board in that judicial setup?

THE PRESIDENT:  Well, that is just one of the three operations or parts of the judicial function. It is a separate part; nothing

--- [129] ---

to do with enforcement.

Q:    These five cases, then, would be referred jointly to the Justice Department and the Federal Trade Commission or to one individual -- I mean, someone outside -- as to which it has to go to?

THE PRESIDENT:  The three decide it.

Q:    The three -- N.R.A., Federal Trade and Justice?

THE PRESIDENT:  Yes. In other words, that is a pure detail of administration. The principal purpose is to have constant watchfulness in order to accomplish quick enforcement in order that we may benefit by the results of such quick enforcement. One of our troubles has been, as you know, that if there was some chiseler somewhere who did not live up to the code, he might make enough money out of chiseling by the six months or a year before they caught him to make it worth while chiseling. Speed is of the essence in this kind of enforcement.

Q: In that connection, will some kind of liaison machinery be set up to function between these units?

THE PRESIDENT: Oh, that will be constant. That is the point -- it must be
automatic. In other words, every single case that comes to a head immediately is set upon, the same day, by these three organizations.

Q: This does clarify one thing. There has been a great deal of question,
there has been speculation as to whether some of the Federal Trade Commission or the Department of Justice work will be taken over by N.R.A., and it
will not be. There will only be a reference to the established channels?

THE PRESIDENT: Yes.

--- [130] ---

Q: Thank you.

Q: The labor boards are acting in violations under the present setup. I wonder if they will continue in that function?

THE PRESIDENT: What labor functions?

Q: The Garrison Board and the N.R.A. will sift the labor complaints while the
N.R.A. sifts trade practices?

THE PRESIDENT: I am merely referring to trade practices.

Q: This will not settle such difficulties as the Houde case, which involves a
labor question?

THE PRESIDENT: No, that is a different thing. These are violations of trade
practices we are talking about.

Q: Any comment to make on Professor Warren's visit yesterday?

THE PRESIDENT: No. (Laughter) Some of you people got a bum steer yesterday --
several bum steers.

Q: Mr. President --

THE PRESIDENT: (interposing) One of the best jokes was this: Old Roy Bulkley
came in. We talked about Charlie West and Vic Donahey and conditions in
Ohio and never mentioned finance or currency of inflation or deflation in
any shape, manner or form. However, we gave you a good story so it is all
right.

Q: In that connection, could we ask this: Will there be any immediate or near
future change in the gold policy? (Laughter)

THE PRESIDENT: I am neither a prestidigitator --

Q: (interposing) Yes, sir. (Laughter)

THE PRESIDENT: -- nor an astrologist. Let it go at that. (Laughter)

Q: In that connection, Senator Bulkley mentioned what he thought might happen,
using very particular care to call attention to

--- [131] ---

the fact that he thought it might happen and not necessarily you.  I think
that was probably the reason for these stories, and also brought up our
question.  He did not think there would be any change immediately but he
said he would not hesitate to use the power to use that nine cents difference in there if it became necessary, and he though it might become necessary.  Would you care to comment?

THE PRESIDENT:  It was an interesting glimpse into his mind.

Q:  Mr. President, was it his mind?

THE PRESIDENT:  You got a good story out of it, so it is all right.

Q:  Thank you, Mr. President.

CONFIDENTIAL
Press Conference #151
Executive Offices of the White House
October 17, 1934, 10:30 A.M.

THE PRESIDENT: I have not seen you for some time, Fred. You were not covering anything?

Q: (Mr. Frederick Storm) I went up (to New York) on a vacation.

THE PRESIDENT: Did you see any of the old crowd?

Q: (Mr. Storm) A few of them.

THE PRESIDENT: Most of them were away on the trip (referring to the campaign trip of Governor Lehman).

Q: (Mr. Storm) I was very homesick.

THE PRESIDENT: Oh, yes.

Q: (Mr. Storm) The objections are starting again.

THE PRESIDENT: To the size?

Q: (Mr. Storm) They say they can't see.

THE PRESIDENT: Fred, sit down in that chair. (Laughter)

Q: (Mr. Storm) This is great.

THE PRESIDENT: We solved a problem. Nobody could see around Fred Storm so from now on he is the only member of the Press that sits down at the Conference. We put him in a chair. (Laughter)

I do not think there is any news.

Q: Mr. President, do you favor Government contributions toward unemployment insurance?

THE PRESIDENT: Oh, gosh, I can't answer that at all. In other words, they are studying it now -- they are working on various plans. One of the plans, for instance, they are working on calls for Government -- no Government contribution but the Government pays for

--- [133] ---

the overhead for running the plan. I have no idea what recommendation will come out.

Q: Mr. President, is the committee from the Roper Council, the Business Advisory Planning Council, that committee on unemployment, working closely with your committee?

THE PRESIDENT: I have no idea. I told them to. (Laughter)

Q: Mr. President, there was a story appeared in the paper this morning that a

letter has been delivered to the State Department and also to you, request-
ing the recall of Ambassador Daniels in Mexico because of a speech he made
down there last July?

THE PRESIDENT: What has he done?

Q: He is supposed to have endorsed the Mexican policy of closing the churches
and --

THE PRESIDENT: (interposing) No, I never heard of it. It sounds fishy to me.
You had better ask the State Department.

Q: Mr. President, it has been some time since we had any general statement on
Government policy toward the railroads. Particularly at this time it might
be opportune to say something about Government policy on loans. Would you
care to mention that?

THE PRESIDENT: I do not think there is anything new on it that is coming up.
The only new case is the case of the Minneapolis and something --

Q: The Minneapolis and St. Paul?

THE PRESIDENT: That has been in receivership for eleven years and Jones (Mr.
Jesse Jones) is trying -- it is obvious they cannot put the road on its
feet as an independent operating unit. It would not pay either the banks
or the Government to lend them any

--- [134] ---

money on that basis -- that has been pretty abundantly proved for eleven
years -- and in that particular case Jones (Chairman Jesse Jones) is trying to get the nearby railroads to tide it over.

Q: I was particularly interested in a Government policy on loans to railroads
which are not earning their fixed charges?

THE PRESIDENT: Of course then it becomes a question of security. We have made
quite a lot of loans to railroads which are not earning their fixes charges,
but the Government has taken what it considered adequate security.

Q: A lot of roads are scraping bottom on securities, even?

THE PRESIDENT: Well, that is something that none of us have solved.

Q: Was there anything of interest in connection with your conference with Dr.
Morgan (Dr. A. E. Morgan, Chairman of T.V.A.) of the T.V.A.?

THE PRESIDENT: No. We went over the general question of what work they are
going to undertake next, how much it is going to cost this fiscal year and
how much money they will need for the next fiscal year. You might call it
a pre-budget survey of their needs for the coming year.

Q: Mr. President, would you comment on the fact that in certain states, about
twelve I believe, they have a constitutional provision with respect to
paupers and that in some of those counties an effort has been made to interpret that as including those on relief, and I think that in one or two
counties they have included those in the C.C.C. camps?

THE PRESIDENT: That came up in May a year ago. Also, some people made an effort along that line in 1933, before the Maine election. I

--- [135] ---

did not know there were twelve states. Are there as many as that?

Q: Yes, sir.

THE PRESIDENT: I think I talked about it quite frankly and freely at that time. Under no possible decent constitution could you regard a person who unfortunately happened to be out of work and willing to work, as a pauper. As a simple, straight answer, I don't believe that any court in the land would classify a person who is unemployed and wanted to work and getting relief -- I don't think any court in the land would classify him as a pauper. Furthermore, anybody suggesting it is suggesting a thoroughly un-American procedure. Let it go at that.

Q: Would you define a pauper?

THE PRESIDENT: That is a pretty difficult thing to do, off hand.

Q: Look around and describe them. (Laughter)

THE PRESIDENT: I sometimes feel that way myself.

Q: Can you tell us anything about your conversation with (Myron) Taylor, as to whether or not the steel situation was discussed?

THE PRESIDENT: I am trying to think of what we discussed. Yes, we talked about the general steel situation, all the phases, how much demand there was going to be for this, that or the other thing.

I think we were pretty thoroughly agreed -- I guess we had better keep this off the record because I cannot tell you about conversations with everybody I have seen. I think we are all in agreement that there has been a great deal of loose talk about heavy industries, the idea that it is possible for them to come back immediately if they got all the money and confidence in the world to come back to where they were in 1929. A very obvious

--- [136] ---

illustration is given by a very simple question. If you had a lot of money, would you build a skyscraper or office building in New York? You would not, because they are overbuilt. Would you build a new hotel in New York? Obviously not, for the same reason. Or an apartment house, I mean of the Park Avenue type? Again you would not, for the same reason. Well, those were the typed of construction which were going on in 1928 and '29. There was a great deal of overbuilding. They will serve most of the communities for a good many years to come.

You can take an example at the other end of the line, Poughkeepsie, New York. They have a couple of new office buildings which are not filled, apartment houses which are not filled. The Nelson House and the other hotels seem to have more than sufficient capacity for people. I won't say anything more, and, as I said, this is all off the record.

Now, let us take structural steel alone. I don't think any of them expect
structural steel to go back to what it was in 1928 and 1929, and that is a
major heavy industry. I don't think Taylor or Grace or any of them look
forward to it in any way.

Take another simple illustration, the big electric companies like G.E. and
Westinghouse. They were turning out in 1927 and 1928 and 1929 an enormous
volume of heavy machinery, turbines and generators, and during those years
almost every power plant in the country equipped itself with modern machinery, not only to take care of the needs of the moment but to take care of
20 or 25% excess needs. These power companies have been running along, and
just in this past year the total output has increased and in many cases

--- [137] ---

it is up to and even above the 1929 level. But they have machinery that
will last them five or ten years to come. They don't need any more, and
the turbines they turn out today are very nearly the same as in 1928 and
1929 -- very few improvements. That is another item of the so-called heavy
industries, and that probably won't pick up very much for the next five or
ten years.

Take the case of the famous rails we were talking about last spring. The
capacity of the four companies that make steel rails is about four million
tons a year and yet the railroads, even if they were not scraping bottom,
would probably not need more than about a million tons a year because
most of the bigger railroads have pretty good rails, heavy rails, and a
good many of them have got it even on their sidings. Probably a million
tons or a million and a half tons a year for the next few years would serve
their needs even if they had all the money in the world.

Most of these people, like Taylor and others that have been down, are in
complete agreement that the heavy industries in all probability -- again
speaking in generalities -- would not, as a whole, as a whole, go back to
100% production because there is no need for it. That is why I say there
has been an awful lot of loose talk about it, but that people who have
analyzed it, like the heads of those companies, will agree entirely with
me. They see the picture eye to eye.

That is all off the record because, as I say, that is a conversation with
one particular visitor.

Q: Could we make it general, that you have discussed things with various businessmen, bankers and what not, and leave the names out? This

--- [138] ---

is pretty good stuff.

THE PRESIDENT: I think it is better not to, and I will tell you why -- because
it is almost impossible to write a story of that kind without scaring
people. The reason for that is that there has been a lot of loose writing
and loose statements made by economists and others that the only way back
to prosperity is to immediately revive the heavy industries, and if you go
out with a story -- well, it won't be so good.

As a matter of fact, what we all do believe is that the heavy industries
are going to pick up very materially. In certain lines they won't go back

to anything like 1929 but, in other lines, they will pick up. And there again, you come to two other questions: the first is, what is a durable goods item? Is a refrigerator? Well, some people classify it as heavy goods and some people don't. The easiest way is to put it in the lighter type of heavy goods. Then there will be a big pickup.

Then the other item is the factor that invention is going on all the time. You have the streamlined trains. The railroad people don't know whether the streamlined train is going to be a success from the operating or the popular point of view. If it is a success and the railroads start on it, it is going to make for a big pickup in a new thing. Again it is one of those things you cannot write about unless you are awfully careful not to either over-encourage people or to scare people, and we don't want to do either.

I think, on the whole, we are getting along pretty well.

Q:  My request came because Governor Black pointed out to the boys around

--- [139] ---

here that the pickup in the heavy industries was not as great as might be desired and this is the answer to it.

Q:  Can you tell us anything about your talk with the bankers?

THE PRESIDENT:  What bankers?

Q:  Governor Black and Reynolds and Governor Harrison.

THE PRESIDENT:  Only to make a suggestion and that is this: I have been meeting them and others. Don't try, please, to forecast what I am going to say next Wednesday to the bankers. I not only have not written it but have not the vaguest idea of what I am going to say, and what I don't want to have happen is that I am going to do this or that or the other thing, because you will be getting yourselves out on a limb.

The difficulty is that you get yourselves out on a limb and then you have to come back and say that there was great disappointment because the President did not conform to what I guessed. (Laughter)

I haven't the faintest idea of what I am going to say to the bankers. It may be a few words of greeting or I may talk to them about something general or something specific, but I have probably a great deal less idea than most of you.

Q:  There are two more local appointments?

THE PRESIDENT:  Right.

Q:  And also a successor of General MacArthur?

THE PRESIDENT:  There is nothing on General MacArthur. There is nothing on the District because I do not know what they are -- there is a judge?

Q:  Yes, the Municipal Court.

--- [140] ---

THE PRESIDENT:  What is the other?

Q:  Two judges.

THE PRESIDENT:  Steve (Mr. Early), I told you to get me some names at least three weeks ago and you have done nothing about it.  (Laughter)

Q:  Mr. Jones (Chairman Jesse Jones) when he left here yesterday said he thought there was no need of extending the R.F.C. lending powers beyond January thirty-first except as to real estate mortgage and railroad lines. Does that represent your idea?

THE PRESIDENT:  I have not talked to him about it at all.

Q:  You haven't any ideas?

THE PRESIDENT:  I have to find out what he is lending money for and find out how much it should be extended.

Q:  Can you tell us anything with respect to relaxation of foreign exchange restrictions?

THE PRESIDENT:  What kind of foreign exchange restrictions?

Q:  That is general relaxation of the general restrictions which confine the purchase of exchange to commercial transactions and tourists.

THE PRESIDENT:  Is the Montreal silver market interested?  (Laughter)

Q:  There have been stories -- I think the U.P. carried the story.

Q:  Anything new on currency expansion?

THE PRESIDENT:  No.

Q:  It seems that the number of people on relief would be larger than last winter.  I wonder whether you have worked out any substitute for C.W.A. or any way of handling it?

THE PRESIDENT:  Not yet.

Q:  Did you have a report from Benedict Crowell on N.R.A. compliance?

THE PRESIDENT:  No.  What is he going to report on?

--- [141] ---

Q:  I understand he has made a study and report.

THE PRESIDENT:  No.

Q:  Is it likely that housing will fit into P.W.A. or that consideration will be given to more housing work for P.W.A.?

THE PRESIDENT:  I think so, without question.  On this question of housing -- well, my good friend, Paul Mallon, reminded me of it.  He wrote a quite

humorous story in the paper last night, Paul did, in regard to the incon-
sistency of killing little pigs and at the same time putting people out of
farms.

As a matter of fact, I think we ought to make certain things pretty clear
about housing. We happened to think of it, not on account of Paul Mallon,
but because Harry Hopkins brought several things to tell me about and among
them he had two projects to work out. One was down at Red House, West
Virginia -- you had better check on that, it may be Red Dock or Red Hook
or something like that. They are putting it through and there will be
about a hundred and fifty families who are going into these small farms
that run about an acre of land apiece -- very small. They are miners that
came from neighboring towns where they had been out of work for years and
had been on relief for the last two years. In order to save money and to
save human beings, they are putting them out on these small farms and giving them a chance to buy them. They hope to get a very small industry to
go into this community.

Of course, there is no relationship with that type of development on the
one side and the sub-marginal farmer on the other side. What we are trying
to do on this project of housing is to save humanity.

--- [142] ---

The other project was down in Arkansas, where they are putting people on
small farms, giving them a little house and a few acres at a cost of fourteen or fifteen hundred dollars. I said to the people who showed me the
photographs, when I got through looking at them, that it might be a good
place to go because I could own my own home in about fifteen years at about
one hundred dollars a year.

Then they are doing a grand thing in the development of sub-urban settlements in the same way. One purpose is to get rid of relief and the other
is to give them a chance -- people who have never had a chance.

So, undoubtedly, the housing program with a great many ramifications --
different types -- will be a part of next year's request on Congress, because it is working.

Q:  Thank you, Mr. President.


(The Press Conference adjourned at 10:45 A.M.)

Press Conference #152
Executive Offices of the White House
October 24, 1934, 10:45 A.M.


THE PRESIDENT: Stevie (Mr. Stephenson), you did not know about the new rule on Fred (Mr. Storn)?

Q:   (Mr. Stephenson)  I heard about it.

THE PRESIDENT:  Yes.  You must not get any bigger or they will be talking about you next.  The Count (Rudolph de Zapp) and I have passed the growing stage.

Q:   Groaning?

THE PRESIDENT:  Growing.

Q:   I am sorry.

THE PRESIDENT:  (indicating a pad with a cellophane top)  This is the most fascinating thing anybody has ever seen.  I take this pad and I write, "I owe you -- let us suppose it is Fred Storm -- $1,000," and I sign it, "F.D.R."  Now, Fred thinks that is perfectly grand and all I do is say, "You want it?"

> (The President was writing as he spoke and at the
> conclusion he handed the pad to Fred Storm, at the
> same time pulling a lever which obliterated the
> writing.)  (Laughter)

Q:   It does not show on the other side?

THE PRESIDENT:  Isn't it perfectly amazing?

Q:   What about the other page?

THE PRESIDENT:  It is all right.  (Indicating)  There is nothing incriminating.

MR. DONALDSON:  All in.

THE PRESIDENT:  I am showing the crowd a little gadget by which you can

--- [144] ---

write something that you do not want anybody to see and then you lift up the leaf and the writing is gone.  It is very useful for politicians.

Q:   (Mr. Stephenson)  For politicians and poker players.

Q:   Mr. President, have you received a telegram this morning from Upton Sinclair in which he points out to you that he has been grossly misrepresented by the newspapers in California in claiming Administration support for his campaign?

THE PRESIDENT:  Not that I know of.  Have I had one?

MR. McINTYRE: Yes, there is one.

THE PRESIDENT: Mac says there is one outside. I haven't seen it yet.

Q: Earlier he said that while up in Hyde Park he quoted you as saying that if you showed a statement dealing with certain public policies, he was sure to be elected.

THE PRESIDENT: What? I do not know what that is. You have me. That is a little too vague. Did it refer to the Central Valley or something like that?

Q: He did not specify.

THE PRESIDENT: I do not know; I have not seen it.

Q: No comment at all on the California gubernatorial test?

THE PRESIDENT: No.

Q: Would you care to outline your views on the central banking system?

THE PRESIDENT: Who raised that ghost? (Laughter)

Q: It has been raised --

THE PRESIDENT: (interposing) I only know what I have read about it in the papers. (Laughter) That is a mean question.

Q: Mr. President, yesterday Olson, Chairman of the Democratic State

--- [145] ---

Committee in California, said it might be necessary for the Federal Government to step in and prevent disorders at the polls resulting from the attempt to disenfranchise and he intimated that he would ask the Department of Justice to intervene. Has any plea been made to you for any Federal --

THE PRESIDENT: (interposing) No. Of course, as you know, in any national election there come in pleas from half a dozen or a dozen states and I don't know -- I do not think the Federal Government has ever intervened in state elections.

Q: Guffey here told us about a week ago that arrangements had been made for supervision by Justice agents in Pennsylvania.

THE PRESIDENT: They have a Senatorial committee on Senatorial campaigns.

Q: They told us that this equality demand (on naval disarmament) is a take-it-or-leave-it proposition with them, that if they do not get it at London they will go home and get what they want. Any position --

THE PRESIDENT: (interposing) I have not had any dispatches from the other side from Norman Davis. I do not think they have had any meetings, the American delegation, except that one courtesy call on Sir John Simon. So far as I know, that is the only thing that our people have done.

Q: I think there is a meeting with the Japs today.

THE PRESIDENT:  Is there?

Q:  Did you promise Sinclair (Upton Sinclair) you would make a statement at any time?

THE PRESIDENT:  No.

Q:  Ambassador Bingham in London made a speech yesteday in which he

--- [146] ---

said that stabilization between the United States and Great Britain would be a great thing.  Would you say anything on that?

THE PRESIDENT:  The only thing I can tell you is off the record because I did not know anything about it until I read the Times (the New York Times). Mac (Mr. McIntyre) called me up at midnight and told me there was a Times report.  If I have any connection with it, the thing will be that the President repudiates the Ambassador, or something like that.  I know absolutely nothing about it.

Q:  Does that mean you are going to repudiate?  (Laughter)

THE PRESIDENT:  No, but if I dignified it by comment in any way, if I even said out loud that I did not know anything about it, somebody would say that I repudiated the Ambassador.

Q:  Is the appointment of a governor of the Federal Reserve Board imminent?

THE PRESIDENT:  I hope so; it is overtime.  I do not think anything will be done for a few weeks.

Q:  How about the Federal Board, the National Labor Relations -- Garrison?

THE PRESIDENT:  There again I hope we will get something in the next few weeks.

Q:  How about the R.F.C.?

THE PRESIDENT:  I have not given any consideration to it.  I told Joe Robinson before he went abroad that I would not do anything about it until he came back.  When he was here the other day we did not have a chance to talk about it.

Q:  Has Sultan's place been decided upon?

THE PRESIDENT:  No.

Q:  Is he a Democrat, do you happen to know?

--- [147] ---

THE PRESIDENT:  I have no idea at all.  I never asked him and I probably won't.

Q:  What do you think of the idea of building equipment and leasing it to the railroads on cheap terms under P.W.A. arrangements?  As it is, they have to put up their family jewels to get a loan.  Do you think it would be possible to make some easier arrangements for getting these funds as a possible aid to the industries?

THE PRESIDENT: There again it follows too general a question. It depends a little bit on the railroad. We do want to help and we have helped a good deal. We helped on steel rails last year at a pretty low rate of interest. This year, if we help again on steel rails it will be at a lower rate. As I remember, last year it was four and a half per cent. I am inclined to think this year we will be able to cut it down to three and a half per cent.

Q: How about security requirements?

THE PRESIDENT: They will have to be adequate; that depends on what security they have.

Q: That seems to be the hitch right now; they cannot bring up any more security.

THE PRESIDENT: Yes.

Q: Have you anything to say in regard to the oil situation -- the impending price cuts in the mid-continent field?

THE PRESIDENT: No because, frankly, I do not know enough about the details -- they change from day to day. It is a very disturbing situation.

Q: Have you given any assurances that the Government is going to prosecute as fully as possible?

--- [148] ---

THE PRESIDENT: They have sent an attorney down there with several assistants with the thought that if the theory of preventing an enormous surplus is to be carried out we have to have some kind of adequate enforcement, which we have not yet got.

Q: Mr. President, have you anything to say about the report from various parts of the country that the Democratic leaders are using the argument that there has been a large Republican leak in contributions in their state?

THE PRESIDENT: It depends entirely on which paper you are writing for. (Laughter)

Q: That is pretty generally.

THE PRESIDENT: Well, you know what politicians are. At various places Democrats will claim certain credits and the Republicans will say, "You are trying to buy the election because you are feeding the people." You pays your money and takes your choice according to the paper you read and the candidate you are listening to.

Q: Anything for us (the District of Columbia)?

THE PRESIDENT: Didn't you get something yesterday? Didn't they appoint somebody in the Juvenile Court? I think they appointed a lady, or something.

Q: Steve (Mr. Early) has forgotten me entirely.

THE PRESIDENT: Steve (Mr. Early), will you do something about it?

Q:   On this oil enforcement, do you care to say how that will be brought about?
Any specific plan?

THE PRESIDENT:   I do not know enough about it.  What we are trying to get is
enforcement.

Q:   On your speech tonight, will that be ready soon?

--- [149] ---

THE PRESIDENT:   It hasn't been written.

Q:   What are you going to say?

THE PRESIDENT:   I am cutting out all appointments this afternoon.  I am going
to start on it at two or three o'clock and when you will get it the Lord
only knows.

Q:   Have you reached any determination on price-fixing and production control
policies of the N.R.A.?

THE PRESIDENT:   No -- that is too big a subject.  I can talk about it for an
hour.

Q:   The N.R.A., about two or three months ago, recommended that all P.W.A.
funds be held from the State of Georgia until the State complied with the
code requirements on the highway work of its own.  I wonder if anything
has been done?

THE PRESIDENT:   I have not heard a word since a month ago.

Q:   Any representation made from the White House to the N.R.A., if you remember?

THE PRESIDENT:   On the Georgia highways?

Q:   Yes, sir.

THE PRESIDENT:   That was Federal Emergency Relief, wasn't it?

Q:   No, sir; the State took over the contracts when the contractor there lost
his Blue Eagle and proceeded to pay the same wages he had been paying.  The
Policy Committee of the N.R.A. recommended that they receive no further
funds until they complied.

THE PRESIDENT:   Frankly, I have not heard a word about it.

Q:   Thank you, Mr. President.

THE PRESIDENT: I will get you one of those big, deep, leather chairs, if you wish.

Q: (Mr. Storm) I find this very nice, Mr. President.

Q: (Mr. Stephenson) You are trying to put the opposition to sleep for us.

Q: I see the bankers came up here begging today.

THE PRESIDENT: Yes. Who loaned them the quarter?

Q: I did; somebody has to have pity on them.

Q: You know the real story on that is that there was a reporter out there with a quarter.

THE PRESIDENT: That is the real story. When he came in here, I had the thing off the ticker. It was on the ticker in about three minutes, well covered.

MR. DONALDSON: All in.

THE PRESIDENT: I do not think I have any news at all. There is a complete vacancy.

Q: We will have to see about that.

Q: Have you been told about Mr. Davis' report in London from the Japanese?

THE PRESIDENT: Has one come in? I have not seen it, unless it is this (indicating). There it is; I have just got it. I have not read it yet.

Q: Read it aloud. (Laughter)

Q: Have you received the second telegram from Upton Sinclair?

--- [151] ---

THE PRESIDENT: I don't know. Have I, Mac?

MR. McINTYRE: I do not think so.

Q: He makes the statement that every statement made concerning you was in rigid conformity with an understanding with you. Will you please tell us if there was an understanding?

THE PRESIDENT: I cannot take part in any state campaign.

Q: Are you going to see Professor Moley any time soon?

THE PRESIDENT: Not that I know of; I haven't any date.

Q: Mr. President, can you tell us about your talk with the bankers (Messrs.

Hecht, Law and Fleming) this morning?

THE PRESIDENT:  Did I see any bankers this morning?  Oh, they just came in to start their year, the new officers.

Q:    Mr. Hecht told us that they came in and offered their services on your all-American team.  We asked them what positions they had been assigned and they said that had been left to you.  Have you any positions in mind?

THE PRESIDENT:  Well, I had hoped to put them out on end.  On the other hand, I do not know that they rate being center.

Q:    Can they carry the ball?

THE PRESIDENT:  It is rather difficult.  If I called them only a half-back, they would probably be insulted.

Q:    Do you think they can carry the ball?

THE PRESIDENT:  They will all take turns carrying the ball.

Q:    May I ask one more California question?  George Creel said you promised to make another survey of the Central Valley Project.  Will you tell us the purpose of another survey?

THE PRESIDENT:  Well, the National Resources Board had made a preliminary

--- [152] ---

survey and I think they were actually engaged last week in making a more detailed survey of it and I think that also brought up the question of the watershed up there.  They are going to do that at the same time.

Q:    Does that mean recommending the project to Congress?

THE PRESIDENT:  Well, only in the sense that we are looking them all over.  We do not know which ones are going to be listed.

Q:    The survey will be made by the National Resources Board?

THE PRESIDENT:  Just like all their other surveys.

Q:    Any comment on the action of the Legion with respect to the bonus?

THE PRESIDENT:  I had not seen it until three minutes ago when Louis Johnson brought in a copy of the resolution and remarked, off the record, that the headlines in the paper did not exactly describe what they had done.  According to him, they "recommended."  In other words, Louis Johnson -- this will have to be off the record because you have to get it from Louis Johnson -- told me that in the committee they defeated the language, whatever it was, that "demanded" it and they changed it to "recommended."

Q:    Mr. President, is there to be a new Comptroller of the Currency?

THE PRESIDENT:  Not that I know of.  Why, we have a perfectly good Comptroller of the Currency, haven't we?

Q:    The Comptroller said he had been offered a position as governor of the bank at San Francisco.

THE PRESIDENT: I do not know whether he is going to accept or not. I do not know whether he has made up his mind.

Q: Is that governor or agent?

THE PRESIDENT: Agent.

--- [153] ---

Q: Has he been offered the post?

THE PRESIDENT: So I was told by the Federal Reserve Board that you had better check with them because it only came to me third-hand.

Q: Mr. President, would you care to reiterate or give us a little amplification of your present views on the Government ownership of railroads? It is quite a timely topic.

THE PRESIDENT: Didn't we talk about it a week ago?

Q: Last spring we did.

THE PRESIDENT: I do not think there is any more on that that can be said. As you know, there are a number of railroads in a weak position at the present time and we are trying to see them through and that is about as far as we have got. I think it is rather important that the names of the weak railroads should be left out. You know which ones they are, but it is just as well not to talk about it out loud.

Q: With the Automobile Code expiring next week, do you know of any steps taken to extend it?

THE PRESIDENT: I do not, but they are working on it. The N.R.B. and the Department of Labor; I think they are both working on it.

Q: The N.R.A.?

THE PRESIDENT: Yes.

Q: Mr. President, has the Budget reached such stage yet that you can say what the funds will be for public works or relief?

THE PRESIDENT: Oh heavens, no; it won't reach that stage until the first of January.

Q: Thank you, Mr. President.

Press Conference #154
Executive Offices of the White House
October 31, 1934, 10:40 A.M.


MR. DONALDSON:  All in.

THE PRESIDENT:  I have a lot of stuff this morning.  By special request of the
      Count (Rudolph de Zapp) and Russell (Mr. Russell Young), there is no reason
      why you should not know that the Budget estimates, as they are being made
      up, will include the elimination of the five per cent reduction on Govern-
      ment salaries.  In other words, they will be five per cent more than they
      were this year, than is being paid now.

Q:    There is still five per cent of the original to go?

THE PRESIDENT:  No, it brings it all back.

Q:    On what basis are you taking that action?

THE PRESIDENT:  On the basis that the cost of living has gone up sufficiently
      by the first of July next year to justify it.

Q:    Make the newspaper publishers do the same thing.  (Laughter)

THE PRESIDENT:  By Jove, I think that is a good idea.  Let me get after them.

Q:    Mr. President, have you had your preliminary figures from the Labor Depart-
      ment?

THE PRESIDENT:  No, not yet.  They have not come in.  I did this on general
      estimates, that is all.

      This will apply the first of July next year, the fiscal year 1936.  The
      figures certainly will not show any justification for changing it the
      first of January.  No question about that.

Q:    (Mr. Stephenson)  Do you think that other businesses can do the same?

--- [155] ---

THE PRESIDENT: Ask the A.P. yourself.  Why ask me to do your dirty work for you.
      (Laughter)

Q:    Mr. President, can we take it, then, that you expect a continuing increase
      in the cost of living between January first and July first?

THE PRESIDENT:  It will go up substantially, without much question.  But, at
      the same time, couple something with that -- it is not fair to use just
      one-half of it.  Couple increases in values thereby lessening the diffi-
      culty of paying debts.

Q:    That is a story for us.

Q:    Mr. President, do you think then that the October trend in the wholesale
      price averages, which has been down, will be very shortly reversed?

THE PRESIDENT: October trend? I don't know. It is not out yet, is it?

Q: The averages for the first three weeks show rather surprising declines.

THE PRESIDENT: Whose chart are you going by?

Q: The National Fertilizer Association. (Laughter)

THE PRESIDENT: It will be interesting to see how that compares with the National Perfumeries Association. (Laughter)

The next order of business is an Executive Order which merges the Executive Council into the National Emergency Council. They have been in large part similar in membership and this order merely makes them one body which is simpler and gets rid of one organization. They are practically the same people that are now on the National Emergency Council. We have added the Chairman of the

--- [156] ---

Securities and Exchange Commission and the Governor of the Federal Reserve Board. They were neither of them on before.

Q: Will there be an executive officer of that Council?

THE PRESIDENT: Just as it is today, Richberg.

Q: Is there anything you can tell us on the public works program for the next year or the following year?

THE PRESIDENT: Only what I have read in the papers. (Laughter)

Q: The papers say 12 billion dollars.

THE PRESIDENT: Some say 12 and some say 10 and some say 5. You pays your money and takes your choice. In fact, it depends entirely on which paper you read. That reminds me. One man came in the other day and said, "I hear you have a very ambitious public works program, self-liquidating on a 20-year basis." I said, "That is absolutely true. They are planting some black walnut trees in certain areas and it takes them that long to mature."

So far as all these stories go, I think I would avoid guessing for the very reason that final responsibility will be mine and I haven't the vaguest idea at the present time and I probably won't have any until the end of December. We are asking all kinds of departments for all kinds of information so that we will have the whole thing in alignment, relief, public works, soil erosion, planning, and so forth and so on. We are just gathering information, that is all. There isn't another thing to do at the present time.

Q: In view of the recent developments and the interest being shown, are you going to recommend that the Costigan-Wagner Bill be passed?

THE PRESIDENT: You will have to give me about twenty-four hours because I will have to check up and see what I did last year. I

--- [157] ---

have forgotten.

Q:   You endorsed it.  You spoke several times, gave out interviews here after the Rolph thing in California.

THE PRESIDENT:  Just give me a chance to see what I said.

Q:   Will you have to hold back your tax program until you know what the total (expenditures) is?

THE PRESIDENT:  Yes, absolutely.  The two go together.

Q:   Can you make any comment on the present status of the naval discussion?

THE PRESIDENT:  No, I will have to refer you to London.

Q:   Have you read the interview given by Ambassador Saito (of Japan) here yesterday?

THE PRESIDENT:  No, I just read the headlines.

Q:   Can you tell us anything about your visit with Stimson (Harry Stimson)?

THE PRESIDENT:  As you know, he is a very, very old friend of mine and I have not seen him since he went abroad.  He came in and we talked about general world conditions, people he had seen on the other side.  There was nothing specific.  There was no object to it, just to say, "How do" again.  He comes to lunch with me every few months.

Q:   Mr. President, as a practical matter, can all the trucks be brought under regulation?

THE PRESIDENT:  All the trucks in the country?

Q:   Yes, sir; I mean this idea of regulating carriers by trucks.

THE PRESIDENT:  I hesitate to talk on the record on that because I do not know what has been found out so far by the various people

--- [158] ---

working on it.

My own general slant is that you cannot, as a practical matter, regulate every truck in the United States.  On the other hand, you probably can regulate trucks engaged in regular trucking business.  For example, there is a farmer up my way who has a perfectly good truck and when not using it himself he will occasionally take a load down to New York City, if anybody wants to take it down there.  He will make $2 or $3 out of it.  Now, is he a common carrier?  I doubt it.  He may do it four or five times a year, but he is not in the business.  As to him, there are great difficulties.  But as to regularly established trucking lines, that is a different thing.

Q:   Can you tell us about your talk yesterday with Secretary Morgenthau and the gentlemen from the State Department?

THE PRESIDENT:  The State Department was just talking about reciprocity and trade agreements -- nothing specific.

Q:  Did you discuss the most favored nation --

THE PRESIDENT:  (interposing)  No, it was not mentioned; it did not come out at all.

Q:  Have you any comment to make on the Labor Board's handling of the A.P. strike in Cleveland which, at this point, it appears will probably have a successful conclusion?

THE PRESIDENT:  I hope it will have a successful conclusion; that is about all we can say.

Q:  Have your studies with regard to relief needs for this winter come to where you can discuss them at all?

THE PRESIDENT:  Not until the end of December.  I could not begin to.

--- [159] ---

I do not know anything about them.  The information is flowing in here and will continue to flow for another couple of months.  Yesterday, at the Council meeting, we got a report from the Federal Emergency Relief that is so clear and interesting that I asked Steve (Mr. Early) to have the thing mimeographed for you.  It related to the farm surpluses.  You will find it outside.  It points out that in the previous winter we had fairly large surpluses with depressed farm prices.  A large number of people on relief at that time needed food so the Federal Surplus Relief Corporation purchased these various items of food, thereby reducing the surplus and at the same time feeding the hungry people.

It has all the figures in here and it gives also the figures with respect to the purchase of cattle and the processing of them into food.  It also points out that this handling of the problem has saved all those cattle from dying on ranges, and that all the meat was used for relief families. It took 58,000 pounds of tin plate, 128,000 carloads of freight and they used unemployed people to actually can a large amount of food which otherwise would not have been canned.

You can read it yourself; it is one of the clearest statements made yet. It was the report to the Council.

Q:  Mr. President, sometime ago you said that you were considering the problem of handling surpluses through a national granary.  Does this report mention the plans?

THE PRESIDENT:  That is still very much in the study stage.

Q:  Thank you, Mr. President.

THE PRESIDENT: I thought that this would be a small Conference, that most of you had gone home to vote. I am afraid very much that there is a lack of interest in the ballot.

Q: Most of us live here and cannot vote. Can't you fix that for us? (Laughter)

THE PRESIDENT: I am going home tonight and there is no reason why I should not give you the following which I wrote down three minutes ago. It is quite short but if you don't want to take it Steve (Mr. Early) will give you copies. (Reading)

> "I am returning to my home to cast my ballot as a citizen of the State of New York. I have no hesitancy in making it known that I expect to vote for Governor Lehman and that I hope he will be re-elected.

> "In the first place, New York is my home State.

> "In the second place, Herbert Lehman served as my Lieutenant Governor for four years and in that capacity earned my admiration as a public official and my warm regard as a man."

Only one more paragraph:

> "In the third place, as Governor he has made good. He has shown courage, energy, fine administrative and executive qualities and, above all, a deep interest in and understanding of the welfare and needs of the citizens of our State."

Das ist alles.

Q: Do you expect to see Governor Lehman at Hyde Park before Election Day?

THE PRESIDENT: No, I cannot. He is in the middle of a campaign.

--- [161] ---

Then I have one other piece of news. I have just signed an Executive Order extending the Automobile Manufacturing Code to February one.

Q: As it stands, Mr. President?

THE PRESIDENT: Yes. The Executive Order is long but it changes the date and that is all. I received the request from the Automobile Manufacturing Association, asking for an extension without change.

No. 2, Steve (Mr. Early) will give you afterwards -- we haven't had time to get it typewritten and mimeographed, you can get it in about fifteen minutes -- a statement -- I will read it to you hurriedly so you can get an idea of it.   (Reading)

> "With the extending of the Automobile Manufacturing Code,
> it is my purpose to institute a study which may contribute
> toward improvements in stabilizing employment in the in-
> dustry and reducing further the effects of the seasonal
> factors.  The manufacturers themselves have taken important
> steps since I first discussed the subject with them some
> months ago.
>
> "In addition to what they have done and are doing in
> omitting their national shows and staggering the intro-
> duction of new models, I believe that we should develop
> further facts on the seasonal peaks and valleys of pro-
> duction in their bearing upon employment.
>
> "I have not asked the manufacturers to agree that such an
> inquiry should be made.  I have thought it better to bring
> the inquiry about under my executive powers.
>
> "The manufacturers have cooperated in supporting the
> Administration's program in the past.  I am confident
> that they will also cooperate with the Administration
> in this way in serving the purposes of Recovery and will
> consider with an open mind any practical suggestions that
> may arise out of the inquiry.  And I am also confident
> that in this I shall have the interest and cooperation
> of labor."

Then, in addition to that -- does this go out too?

--- [162] ---

MR. EARLY:  No, sir.

Q:   What is it?

THE PRESIDENT:   There is no reason why the fact of it going out should not be
known.  Do you see any reason why we should not give out the whole letter?

MR. EARLY:   You never give out a letter in advance of its being sent.

THE PRESIDENT:   Steve says I cannot give it out until it is sent.

MR. EARLY:   You can tell them what you are doing.

THE PRESIDENT:   I am sending a letter to Mr. Green (William Green, President of
the A.F. of L.) and the same letter to Mr. Alan Macauley, who is secretary
(President) of the Automobile Manufacturers' Association.  The same letter
goes to him and to Mr. Green, telling them that I am going to start this
study and pointing out that there are a good many examples which make it
very advisable for this study to be made on the question of annual earnings as against the mere question of day rates, and saying that after such
investigations it will be possible for me to determine definitely on a
factual basis as to whether it will be necessary to arrange for a public
hearing, and that I will arrange for a conference with them as soon as I
get back.

I give out the letter as soon as it is sent.

Q:   A conference with labor or manufacturers?

THE PRESIDENT:  With me.

Q:   Is it a labor conference?

THE PRESIDENT:  I will have them all in to confer with me.

Q:   When are you coming back, Mr. President?

THE PRESIDENT:  Tuesday night or Wednesday night, I do not know which.

--- [163] ---

It depends on how much snow we have up there -- I said, "snow."

Q:   Mr. President, in your statement regarding Governor Lehman in New York
there is no mention of Senator Copeland.  Was that an oversight?

THE PRESIDENT:  No, I am not taking up anybody else on the ticket.

Q:   Mr. President, you are voting the straight Democratic ticket?  (Laughter)

THE PRESIDENT:  Well, Stevie (Mr. Stephenson), it would be amusing if anybody
knew how often I have voted for individual Republicans.

Q:   Mr. President, what, if any, recourse is left to us if any one of the
signatories to the Nine-Power-Pact completely disregards the obligations
under it?

THE PRESIDENT:  Say it again.

Q:   What, if any, recourse is left to us, if any one of the signatories to the
Nine-Power-Pact completely disregards the obligations under it?

THE PRESIDENT:  I will get out my library on that subject.  I think there have
been twelve volumes written on it so far.

Q:   You haven't given any thought to it yet?

THE PRESIDENT:  No.

Q:   Mr. President, any comment to make on the improved condition in the oil
industry as the result of your Board's operation in Texas?

THE PRESIDENT:  No.  Secretary Ickes lunched with me today and was very happy
over what he believed to be the fact that this new method seems to be
working and that the bootlegging of oil, at least for the moment, has come
to an end.  He was very much pleased because, as you know, the situation
got down to a critical point ten days

--- [164] ---

ago -- it was touch and go as to whether the thing would blow up in our
face or not.

Q:   Now that you have seen Davis' (Norman Davis) report on the London conference, can we induce you to tell us whether -- or at least comment on it?

THE PRESIDENT:   Which report?

Q:   The report you had on your desk last Wednesday.

THE PRESIDENT:   There have been six or eight since then.  That (report you
mention) is entirely out of date.

Q:   Anything you can tell us?

THE PRESIDENT:   Nothing we can say except that we are still hoping for a favorable outcome.

Q:   Any comment on Harriman's (Henry Harriman) statement regarding his plea
for a housing program?

THE PRESIDENT:   Who is that, Averill Harriman?

Q:   No, the Chamber of Commerce man.

THE PRESIDENT:   No.  Has he a plan?

Q:   It was described this morning in the papers.

THE PRESIDENT:   I did not know it.

Q:   He advocated putting some $15,000,000,000 into housing, principally smaller
houses.

THE PRESIDENT:   Is that all?

Q:   It is a rather large sum.

THE PRESIDENT:   That is almost worthy of a New York Times headline.  (Laughter)
That is a dirty crack on my part but, Charlie (Mr. Hurd of the New York
Times), it is well merited.

Q:   Mr. President, while we are on housing, has there been any reaction

--- [165] ---

to plans announced last night for 5 per cent interest on mortgage bonds?

THE PRESIDENT:   Not yet.  Of course I have given a great deal of thought to that
question and Moffett is right that probably in certain areas of the country
that have 8 or 10 or 12 per cent interest it is going to prevent or slow up
private capital going into mortgages on a lower basis, but it is a part of
the general plan throughout the country looking toward the reduction of
exorbitant and usurious rates, and the principle is more important than
anything else at this time.  We have to educate people that if they get a
sound, insured mortgage under present conditions 5 per cent is quite
enough for money to earn.  I am sure that there will be plenty of people
glad to put out their money for 5 per cent even in those sections of the
country that charge 10 or 12 per cent.  I feel very strongly on that subject.  One of the things that has prevented progress is usury.

Q:   Senator-Elect Bilbo is coming in to see you?

THE PRESIDENT:  He is coming in to see me in about twenty minutes.

Q:   Thank you, Mr. President.


(The Press Conference adjourned at 4:20 P.M.)

Press Conference #156
Held in the President's Study at Hyde Park
November 7, 1934, 1:10 P.M.


THE PRESIDENT: I commend to your attention -- you can take it away and read it
    if you want -- last night's editorial written in the Brooklyn Daily Eagle.
    It is probably one of the best things that has been said about Government
    in a long, long time. I do not know that there is anything more to say
    about it than that, but it is an awfully good editorial. I will let you
    have it if you will give it back to me.

Q: Was that in yesterday's paper?

THE PRESIDENT: Yes, written before the polls closed.

Q: Does it meet with your hearty approval?

THE PRESIDENT: It meets with my very hearty approval as a statement about
    Democratic government, that it still lives. If you carry anything about
    it, you ought to carry the whole editorial and not a part of it because
    it ties in together.

Q: If you were in our position, called upon to write an interpretive piece,
    would you interpret the verdict as an approval of what had happened or as
    a mandate to proceed further?

THE PRESIDENT: You must have got to bed early to talk about interpreting
    stories today. He has a very strong mind.

Q: I think it was a slug at gin this morning. (Laughter)

THE PRESIDENT: It must be hell to have to interpret.

Q: It speaks for itself.

Q: It is, at times.

THE PRESIDENT: It must be terrible. But you know, that is one reason

--- [167] ---

why -- this is a severe thing to say and I just say it strictly in the
    family and off the record -- why the American public today are paying less
    and less attention to news stories because so many of them have become
    interpretive. That really is true. You pays your money and takes your
    choice. Now, the press associations have got away from it pretty well and
    most of the individual papers are demanding interpretive stories. I know
    how hard it is and I must say it is hell to write them and I think it is a
    mistake for newspapers to go over into that field in the news stories.
    They are beginning to lose public confidence in news. I have a sort of
    sixth sense about the public and they are beginning to lose it more and
    more.

Q: You cannot fool the public.

THE PRESIDENT: It is a very serious question for the future of the American newspaper. I really, honestly believe that.

Q:   As I understand it, give people the facts and let them judge for themselves.

THE PRESIDENT:   That is the point, give them the facts and nothing else. In
other words, reductio ad absurdum. That is the substance, because if I
take Henry Morgenthau from Washington back to Dutchess County, there
isn't anything behind the fact. But the story that says, " In all probability this means that foreign debt was discussed," or something like
that, that is not news, that is just a wild stab in the dark, which is
wrong, 99 per cent wrong at times. But, on the other hand, your own
offices call for that sort of thing and what the hell are we going to do
about it? Do you think that is wise? I know you don't agree with that.

--- [168] ---

Q:   If we had some inkling about what Morgenthau talked about, we would be
justified in intimating that.

MR. McINTYRE:   His argument is that anybody who reads it does his own interpreting.

Q:   If we actually knew --

THE PRESIDENT:   Yes, if we talked debts, yes.

Q:   That is the way I feel about it. It is the feeling of the newspapers themselves.

THE PRESIDENT:   It is not the feeling of any of your people, I am thinking about
the general policy of the people who run individual newspapers in this
country in going into the interpretive features of it rather than the
news.

Q:   Do you think there is a public demand for that sort of thing or is it because they have been educated up to it?

THE PRESIDENT:   I think there is a big demand. It goes along to the extreme
of the Drew Pearson and the Walter Winchell -- that is the extreme of
it -- and of course it has been aided and abetted by the popularity,
quite frankly, of people like Mark Sullivan.

Q:   May I say something and put yourself in our place --

THE PRESIDENT:   (interposing) I do all the time; that is just it.

Q:   We get a query on it from twelve up to two at night that a fellow says
this about it --

THE PRESIDENT:   (interposing) And so you have to say something?

Q:   We don't have to but nevertheless it is what we are here for.

THE PRESIDENT:   Of course it puts an awful burden on the Government end of it.
For example, as a concrete case, the other day, last Friday, somebody
said, "Are you including Copeland in this?" I

should have gone into a long explanation when I said I was going to vote for Lehman. I said, "No, I am not including anybody but Lehman." I should have gone ahead and explained it but I did not do it because I forgot to.

Q: That did leave (room for) an interpretation there but I think the average fellow knew you didn't mean it that way.

THE PRESIDENT: I was so simple that I did not think of it at the time.

MR. McINTYRE: That is one case where he did not blame the boys.

THE PRESIDENT: Not a bit -- that was my fault.

Q: Mr. President, do you think the ordinary -- I won't say the ordinary but the intelligent reader of a newspaper is in a position to form, to judge on a bare presentation of the facts?

THE PRESIDENT: Pretty close to it, yes.

Q: I should say so.

Q: It is not from lack of intelligence but merely because they are out of the atmosphere in which it is occurring. I personally think that the reason the newspapers are going in for more interpretive writers is because there is an overwhelming demand for it.

Q: There is a demand for gossip.

Q: I am not referring to gossip so much. I am speaking of interpretation. They want the best opinion they can get, even if they read three or four in order to get different interpretations, on the ground that they want it from competent observers, particularly at a time like this when there is so much doubt.

THE PRESIDENT: Again you get into the difficulty of any person writing inter-pretive stories. For instance, Mark Sullivan -- a great friend of mine -- if Mark wrote once a week he would be much more

--- [170] ---

effective than if he wrote once a day. No human being can write a story once a day. He has to write a whole lot of pure bunk in order to fill his space.

Q: I believe that a lot of the papers are demanding interpretive stories simply on a competitive basis with Time Magazine and so on. They all want their readers to believe that they have the same sources of inside information, whether they have or not. The others purport to have and do not have.

THE PRESIDENT: I think it is one of the most difficult problems we have and the only reason I am talking about this at all is that I do sense that newspapers have a lot less influence than they had fifteen or twenty years ago.

MR. McINTYRE: Of course, if I were on that side of the fence instead of this, I could make a very interpretive --

THE PRESIDENT: How?

MR. McINTYRE: Give the boys that write those stories a little more leads.

THE PRESIDENT: By God, I give them all the leads I can think of. I don't want to get into the dissertation stage.

Q: Of course, Mr. President, our job is always finding out what you are going to do.

THE PRESIDENT: About two-thirds of the time I do not know.

Q: Mr. President, do you expect any change in the relief policy before Congress meets?

THE PRESIDENT: No. Well, there I can give you something but we will have to make it off the record. I have to keep it off the record because we don't know what the thing is going to develop into.

--- [171] ---

Q: Do you mean off the record or just background?

THE PRESIDENT: Absolutely off the record so you will know what we are talking about. It has not got to the stage of background because you cannot write about it without giving the slant that we are going to do something one way or the other. It is almost impossible.

You take this morning, I was talking to Jim Townsend, who is County Chairman here. He knows this county extremely well. I was talking to him about the people on relief in this county. Of course this was not from a political angle at all. I said, "How many of them do you think are chiselers?" "Well," he said, "I should say somewhere between 15 and 20 per cent." I said, "So where are they?"

He said, "Here is where they come in: you will find in the relief office at Poughkeepsie that three or four of the girls employed there come from families who have plenty of money to get by with. The girls don't need relief. Then, they hired fourteen engineers and of the fourteen engineers only about three of them were engineers who were absolutely up against it." I said, "Are there any more engineers up against it around here?" He said, "Yes, there are lots of them."

He told me about the eleven who could get by.

Then you get out into the towns and the human element comes into it. It does not make any difference whether it is a Democratic township or a Republican township. It comes through the supervisor and naturally they pick their friends first. It is a very difficult problem to handle as at present constituted.

--- [172] ---

Now, if that is true in Dutchess County, it is true in every state of the Union. It is not all Democratic and Republican politics, personal favoritism enters into it too. A great deal is personal favoritism. You will help your friends and build yourself up. The local fellow wants to be known as the man who hands out the jobs.  It is perfectly natural.

Now, how can we avoid that?

I said, "What is happening to the mental slant of those people on relief?"
"Well," he said, "it is bad, for the reason that if it is home relief,
a grocery store order or cash, they will barely get by in their families;
nobody works and they just bum around all day.  There is nothing to do.
It is very bad for them, obviously.  We ought, if we can, to give them
work."

I said, "How about work?  A lot of them are on some kind of work."  "Well,"
he said, "I will give you an illustration.  In the back part of the Town
of Pleasant Valley here, they are putting in a mile of road and they have
150 people, work relief people, on that mile of road.  They are supposed
to work 8 hours a day.  Most of them work 3 days a week.  But there is a
general feeling on the part of everybody who sees that work that the
people who are in charge of them almost give the order, 'Do not exert yourselves.  Do not push yourselves.  Spread it out as long as you can.'"

Now, that is a waste of money.  They probably waste at least 50 per cent of
the money spent for labor on that road.  It is inefficient.

They had a lot of people this summer around here.  They were at work
cleaning and cutting grass on the highways.  That does

--- [173] ---

not bring in anything.  It is not constructive.

Now, that applies to almost every county in the United States.  The result
is that most of the relief money spent -- of course part of it is local
money and part state and part Federal but the great bulk of it will never
come back, not alone to the Government but it won't come back to the Nation
in the form of permanent improvements.

Therefore, we are trying to find some method by which all this relief money
will be made to do one of two things, either make a practical contribution
to the wealth of the Nation such as, for instance, if you take a valley, a
little valley, and go in for soil erosion, to prevent the topsoil from
running off, to prevent flood damage and to use the land in the best way
possible by planting trees and things like that.  That is work which, if
it is efficiently performed, will give wealth to the Nation.  The other
thing we are trying to do is to get this money, as far as we can, returned
to the Government so that we can pay off the debts.  You see, we have to
borrow it therefore we are trying to find more and more self-liquidating
projects.

The objective, therefore, is twofold -- threefold: first, to eliminate --
don't call it graft -- but to eliminate the 10, 15 or 20 per cent of the
people who are on relief and who ought not to be on relief.  The second
thing is to put the money either into the kind of thing that will add to
the national wealth even if it does not come back to the Government or,
secondly, into the kind of public works that will liquidate themselves and
have the money returned to the Government so that it can pay off the debt

--- [174] ---

incurred when it was borrowed.

Now, that involves a tremendous search -- you might call it such at the present time -- a tremendous search problem and everybody is working on it. The idea is to see whether, with next year's relief money that is to be divided up between three organizations, really, the C.C.C. camps, public works, and Harry Hopkins, to see whether we cannot use all of that expenditure to take people off what we call home relief, that is cash and grocery orders, and put them on useful work instead.

Now, that is the thing we are groping for and we are only in the groping stage. We have no idea how much money it will cost. And, as I said the other day, you can put the figures anywhere from 2 billion to 100 billion. We have no idea of figures but we have an objective. We don't want to come out with new ideas and the objective of spending money in line with objectives unless we know the amount involved and unless we feel fairly certain that if Congress gives us so much money to relieve unemployment for the following year that we will be able to spend all of that money. In other words, unlike public works, the money will have to be put to work quickly.

One trouble with public works at the present time is that you have to plan each project very carefully in order to prevent waste and, when we do allocate the money, we do not have the assurance that it will go to work even that fiscal year. When we do a job, we want to do a 100 per cent job, and that is a difficult thing.

That is, really, the only way I can explain the whole situation to you, the present situation. We have to have something by

--- [175] ---

the third of January on it. What it will be, I don't know.

Q:   You expect to present a program, then?

THE PRESIDENT:  For example, in looking over all of these 150 or 200 different suggestions to carry out that objective, we must decide that this particular thing looks darn good and lift it out of the general pile and say that that is something we can accept. It is a process of weeding out those things which are out of the question and accepting the things that look pretty good.

Q:   Is there any indication as yet, any tangible figure at all, on the amount of absorption from these Government rolls into active private industry or business?

THE PRESIDENT:  I would say that there is a constant absorption. The only figures we have got are these C.C.C. figures which were given out two weeks ago and which show that of the last batch of the C.C.C. boys who finished their six months or a year in a camp, a larger percentage got jobs than the previous crowd. One reason for it is that the average employer thinks that these C.C.C. fellows are pretty good. They have some training and know how to work and have the right mental attitude and they are glad to employ them.

Now, if we can develop that idea -- not the C.C.C. camps but the theory of developing jobs for fellows that are really jobs and make them work at it, they stand a better chance of being taken back into employment.  I would not want to take this fellow on the road who have been cutting grass this summer in Hyde Park.  He has been working perhaps 3 days a week and out of every day he has been doing just about 1 hour and 10 minutes of useful work.  He has become a working bum.  I would not take him on my farm but I

--- [176] ---

would take the C.C.C. boy at the Staatsburgh Camp.

Q:   Then the general idea of the work you can put these people on and the way you can get this money out and give the workers a definite education and training and be able to build morale, et cetera, is a big part of the program?

THE PRESIDENT:  A big part of the program, and necessarily.  It does involve probably more concentrated work on larger projects rather than this absolutely diffused work at the present time of six men working here and ten men working there.  In order to make it more efficient we have to do it with infinitely better supervision and of course that calls for larger units, unquestionably.

Q:   Is there any danger in putting these men to work on definite work projects, instead of keeping them on the roads or on home relief as you call it, thereby -- this is a difficult question to frame -- thereby possibly removing some potential possibilities for construction or industrial work that may be done by industry?  In other words, is there any danger of going ahead and spending a great deal of money on roads and buildings, even public buildings, and cutting down the amount of work which may be done by private industry?  Must all the work that is being done to give relief, must all that work be non-competitive with private industry?

THE PRESIDENT:  Of course building roads does not represent competition.  That does not interfere with private business.  Putting up a public building does not interfere with private industry.  I will give you an illustration. I got a long letter from Joseph P. Day, who is tremendously interested and who is a very old friend of mine.  We are carrying on correspondence at the present time trying to

--- [177] ---

develop ideas.  He feels that if we go in for slum clearance in New York City it is going to hurt private enterprise.  That is very possible.  Well, I wrote him back and I dictated the letter this morning.  I told him, "I want you to think about two things before you come down to Washington.  The first is this:  The cost of a properly financed building is made high because it is very difficult to get private money in" -- he wrote me that he is very much against limited dividend corporations -- "at less than the reasonable expected return of 6 per cent, 5 or 6 per cent.  But if you charge 5 or 6 per cent it is almost impossible to provide really cheap housing and that brings up the second question:  The objective in New York City is to provide rooms that will rent for $5 per room for a month or say $6 maximum.  If it is properly financed, it is almost impossible to turn anything out at less than $11 or $12 a room a month.  Now, who are the people we are trying to help in the City of New York?  Who are the people living in the slums?  They are people having a family income of less than

$1,000 a year and there are several hundred thousand families. Those are
the people who inhabit the slums. They cannot pay that rental. Of course,
you have Fred French's Knickerbocker Village. That eliminates a lot of
old tenements but the people there in Fred French's district are mostly
financial district workers who are able to pay $13 or $14 a month, which he
charges."

Q:    Do you know what the charges were before?

THE PRESIDENT:  Around $6 under terrible conditions.

MR. McINTYRE:  Your luncheon has been waiting for you, Mr. President.

THE PRESIDENT:  Then, the other thing which I said to Joe Day:  "I want

--- [178] ---

you to think about another thing. It will be an awful shock to you. New
York City has seven million people in it. Can it give work to more than
six million?" That is a question mark and is an awful shock to, let us
say, the real estate people in New York. There are a million people too
many. Suppose we could come back to the 1929 level of industry? Wouldn't
we still have a million people on relief in the City of New York? A lot
of people think we would.

Q:    What is the answer to that?

THE PRESIDENT:  Decentralization of population.

Q:    Who is going to do that?

THE PRESIDENT:  Planning. We will have to invent a new word that is different
      from "planning." For instance, we are talking with the automobile industry,
      with General Electric and Westinghouse and the steel corporations about
      the possibility of their taking small units and putting them away from the
      big centers, putting them in small towns. The same thing is going on in
      England and on the Continent. There are probably too darn many people in
      the big centers.

Q:    But, if you take a million people out of the City of New York won't you
      still have a problem? In other words, that won't solve the problem because
      you will have a million people less consumption there and it will only re-
      duce your unemployment from a million to say 750,000 or 500,000.

THE PRESIDENT:  No, because with people living on relief consumption is terribly
      low. That brings up just one more point which is just a rule of thumb.
      Suppose I have got an unemployed individual in

--- [179] ---

the City of New York with a family of three or four, with a wife and several children, on home relief. It would probably cost the Government as a
whole, city, state and Federal, about $500 to support him and his family
for a year, to pay the rent, buy the food and buy the clothing. That is
all that goes to encourage consumption in this country, that $500. Sup-
pose I give him work, useful work, the kind of work I am trying to find,
and pay him $1,000 a year in wages. I have doubled his consumption.

MR. McINTYRE:  I think we ought to have a distinct understanding before we get
out that this is off the record.

THE PRESIDENT:  This has got to be off the record.  None of it should be printed
yet because, as I say, we are merely groping toward an ideal.  How far we
can get to it by practical recommendations we don't know yet.

MR. McINTYRE:  The most important matter has not come up yet.  When do you
think the pool ought to be split?  I am not sure about Vermont yet; that
is the reason I am holding out.

THE PRESIDENT:  I think Vermont is overboard and I am afraid Michigan is overboard this morning.

MR. McINTYRE:  I think about half and half; I think Vandenberg is elected.

THE PRESIDENT:  I think so too.

Q:  Here are some figures but there is nothing about the various states.

THE PRESIDENT:  I probably have as good information as anybody this morning.

Q:  I think you have better information than any of us.  Of course, we were
up all morning studying this.

THE PRESIDENT:  There is no question about this.  I lose very badly.

--- [180] ---

Q:  Every one of us has studied.  I do not know who wins.

MR. McINTYRE:  I think Grace (Miss Tully) does; she put "D" all along the line.

THE PRESIDENT:  Grace started in by saying, "How am I going to vote?  I do not
know any of these people; I do not know any of these states; I am going to
put a 'D' after every name."

Q:  Then I know who wins.

THE PRESIDENT:  That is all right.

Q:  Did you hear whether Governor Ritchie won in Maryland?

THE PRESIDENT:  I asked Charlie Michelson and Charlie did not know.

Q:  Have you heard about Wyoming?

THE PRESIDENT:  It is all right.

Q:  Did the Governor come through?

THE PRESIDENT:  Yes, the whole ticket.

Q:  Not wanting to do any interpreting, does your statement that you lost on
the pool mean that the Democratic landslide was a surprise to you?
(Laughter)

THE PRESIDENT:  I wasn't going to pass up twenty-eight or thirty dollars, you know.  (Laughter)

Q:   You do not mind if we print that, do you?  (Laughter)

THE PRESIDENT:  I talked to Jim (Mr. Farley) this morning -- and that is also
    off the record.  He said that Rhode Island came through by thirty thousand
    for Green, which again, off the record, surprised me very much because I
    thought that labor would have it in for Green ordering out militia and
    trying to get me to get out the troops.

MISS LeHAND:   I am going to eat, Mr. President.

--- [181] ---

Q:   Is there anything we can write about the election from the White House?

THE PRESIDENT:  I do not know how you can, Fred (Mr. Storm), because, heavens,
    what can I say?

Q:   We can begin by saying that you are obviously cheerful, but where do we go
    from there?  (Laughter)

Q:   Are you going to see anybody later today?

THE PRESIDENT:  I do not know of anybody.  I am going to see an awful lot of
    people between tomorrow and Next Thursday, flocks of people including, I
    think tomorrow, Bob LaFollette.

Q:   Is Phil coming too?

THE PRESIDENT:  Yes.  (Laughter)

MR. McINTYRE:  Don't you think he had his fill of LaFollette?  (Laughter)

THE PRESIDENT:  I will see lots of people over the weekend,  just trying to
    clean up before we go down.

Q:   Have you had any late reports on Georgia, whether that corn is aged suffic-
    iently for us to tackle it again?  (Laughter)

THE PRESIDENT:  Ambassador Long has an appointment, Prime Minister Steinhardt
    of Norway also has an appointment.

Q:   That is tomorrow?

THE PRESIDENT:  Long is tomorrow and I think Steinhardt is the next day.

Q:   He is Sweden?

THE PRESIDENT:  Yes.  I really don't know that there is anything at all to say.

MR. McINTYRE:  We will notify you of the returns.

THE PRESIDENT:  I think Grace is going to win.

Q:   I picked four or five Republicans there.  I know I should have gone right
    down the line.

Press Conference #157
Executive Offices of the White House
November 9, 1934, 4:15 P.M.


Q:   Did you win the pool?

THE PRESIDENT:   No; I was next to the worst.

Q:   I heard that Mac (Mr. McIntyre) is leading, Mr. President?

THE PRESIDENT:   Yes, Mac is leading.  We have got to hear from Cutting first.

Q:   It looks like he is licked.

THE PRESIDENT:   Cutting is licked?  Mac wins then.

MR. DONALDSON:   All in.

THE PRESIDENT:   We are trying to find out which member of the Press won the
Hyde Park pool.

There isn't any news.  You are all written out and I am all talked out, so
there we are.

Q:   Mr. President, would it be a good guess --

THE PRESIDENT:   Now, wait!  (Laughter)  Do rephrase it.

Q:   Might we speculate on the probability -- (Laughter)

THE PRESIDENT:   I will give you a third guess.

Q:   Well, to put it politely, is General MacArthur still going to be Chief of
Staff after the seventeenth?

THE PRESIDENT:   I do not know; I do not know anything about it.

Q:   Is Farley going to continue as Democratic National Chairman?

THE PRESIDENT:   I have done nothing about it.

Q:   Anything you can tell us about Governor Ritchie's defeat?

THE PRESIDENT:   No.  Now do not go and say that I declined to say anything about
it and therefore my silence was fraught with implica-

--- [183] ---

tions.  I am not saying anything about individuals, either defeated or
elected.

Q:   Can you tell us anything about a budget, Mr. President?

THE PRESIDENT:   It is coming along pretty well.  I had a nice talk with Congressman Buchanan yesterday and he is going to ask some members of his subcommittee to come up here -- he told you about it -- early in December and we

will have a number of the principal tentative estimates ready for those subcommittees. He felt he could not call all (of the members) of his sub-committees together, because the membership of some of the others has practically disappeared -- it has disintegrated or members are serving on the other subcommittees so could not handle both jobs, but I think he said there were four or five or those subcommittees that would be able to go through those estimates early in December. I have very nearly finished; I have only three more departments to go through.

Q:    Did you reach a total?

THE PRESIDENT:  Oh, heavens, no.

Q:    Could you indicate which subcommittees were --

THE PRESIDENT:  (interposing) He (Buchanan) did tell me but I would be afraid -- you had better get it from him. One was the Treasury-Post Office Bill; another was a bill that had four departments, State, Commerce, Justice and Labor. Is that right?

Q:    That is right.

THE PRESIDENT:  I have forgotten the other two.

Q:    The Great Lakes-St. Lawrence Tidewater Association seems to indicate that there has been some change in the St. Lawrence Treaty since the last ses-sion. Has there been any change in that up to date?

--- [184] ---

THE PRESIDENT:  I suppose there is no particular -- that sort of puts me in a hole because I do not know whether I want to answer that on the record or for background. Suppose you put it this way: I think it is perfectly all right because, naturally, I do not want to step on anybody's toes. When Under Secretary Phillips was in Ottawa, he spoke informally with the Prime Minister in regard to one or two small changes which he hoped that we could discuss. That is, really, as far as it has got.

Q:    Do you recall what the Prime Minister said, Mr. President?

THE PRESIDENT:  What?

Q:    Do you recall what the Prime Miniester said, Mr. President?

THE PRESIDENT:  Well, he has taken it under advisement.

Q:    Did you hear of Buchanan's hope of a short session in the Seventy-Fourth Congress?

THE PRESIDENT:  I always do.

Q:    Could you tell us whether those one or two small changes had reference to Lake Michigan?

THE PRESIDENT:  I can give you this as background, simply repeating what I have said so often to the Chicago papers. They might just as well get it through their heads once and for all and then you won't have to ask ques-tions again. Under common law, if I am a property owner on a stream, I can use the water of that stream for drinking purposes, for feeding cattle, for running a mill wheel, but I have got to put that water back into the stream.

Now, that is common law and if it is the common law between two people that our civilization is founded on, it is certainly common law between nations. The United States has not the right

--- [185] ---

and never will have the right to divert water from one watershed into another watershed to the detriment of somebody that lives downstream. Furthermore, the Supreme Court has said that it would not be reasonable to divert more than the amount provided for by treaty. And, number three, the Army states in absolutely categorical terms that that amount of water is sufficient for navigation from Lake Michigan out to the Mississippi.

They might just as well get that through their heads in Chicago; they have enough water and they won't get any more water.

Q: The power company is keeping up its fight against the Alcorn County Power Plant. After losing in the State courts, they have gone into the Federal courts and asked for an injunction on the ground that it is illegal constitutionally.

THE PRESIDENT: I haven't anything on that.

Q: Can you tell us whether you have anything on the Newspaper Code or the Special Newspaper Code?

THE PRESIDENT: Only that I had Heywood Broun and some of your other members at Hyde Park the other day. I promised two things and that is since the hearing was held in December I would take the matter up immediately, and number two, that I hope very much that the Press Associations will take part in these hearings on the general theory that a press association is a news collecting agency and not a country club. That is off the record, that part of it. That is merely for Stevie (Mr. Stephenson). (Laughter)

Q: Mr. President, I did not say the Newspaper Code -- I meant to say the Newsprint Code.

THE PRESIDENT: I do not know what has happened on that.

--- [186] ---

Q: I understand it has come to you.

THE PRESIDENT: I haven't it and Mac (Mr. McIntyre) hasn't it and I haven't got it.

Q: Any plans over the weekend?

THE PRESIDENT: No, except to clean up a lot of things before we go away Thursday. Everything else is all quiet. Lots of conferences.

Q: Can you tell us anything about a naval pact in London?

THE PRESIDENT: I will have to tell you this off the record. After I read this morning's papers, I got a bit worried and I called up Bill Phillips and I said, "What is the news from London?" He said, "None," and told me that up to an hour ago there hadn't been anything from Norman Davis, not a thing.

Q:   What were you worried about?

THE PRESIDENT:   It looked quite serious.  One or two of the dispatches had it that the British and Japs got into a jam.  This is off the record because I haven't any news.

Q:   There is a report around town that the present Minister to Norway may be replaced.

THE PRESIDENT:   That is a report around town.  It had not got here until you mentioned it.

Q:   Is there anything to the report that the Department of Agriculture will give up the Forestry Service, to be transferred to the Interior Department?

THE PRESIDENT:   No.

Q:   Do you contemplate any radio speeches in the near future?

THE PRESIDENT:   I suppose when I get back from Warm Springs.  In the last radio talk I had I did not talk about relief and lots of things.

--- [187] ---

Q:   It will be on the state of the Nation?

THE PRESIDENT:   Sometime early in December.

Q:   Are you planning to go down to Arlington Sunday (on Armistice Day)?

THE PRESIDENT:   Yes, Sunday at eleven o'clock.

Q:   Have you a telegram from the Acting Director of Housing in San Francisco asking for more money?

THE PRESIDENT:   Mac (Mr. McIntyre) says I have got a telegram; I have not seen it yet.  It will probably go to Secretary Ickes.

Q:   They want more housing.

THE PRESIDENT:   As I understand it, the Federal Housing Administrator out there reached his quota and wants to get more money.

MR. McINTYRE:   He wants to get a quota increase because it has gone over the top.

THE PRESIDENT:   Good; fine.

Q:   Will you make a speech (at Arlington)?

THE PRESIDENT:   The one minute of silence, just the way it was last year.

Q:   Will you say anything about a relief program?

THE PRESIDENT: We are still working on it awfully hard. We have been talking about it once a week every week in the evening. We have had different groups of people.

Q: Any tentative figure?

THE PRESIDENT: No.

Q: Is the new Federal Reserve Governor in sight yet?

THE PRESIDENT: You are getting warm. Pretty soon.

Q: What did you tell the Executive Committee of the railroad executives?

THE PRESIDENT: They were just in to tell me that they were organized

--- [188] ---

and ready and I told them any time they wanted to see me to let me know.

Press Conference #158
Executive Offices of the White House
November 14, 1934, 10:35 A.M.


MR. DONALDSON: All in.

THE PRESIDENT: Russell (Mr. Young) asked a question about a story that was giv-
en out about the publication of the volume of naval documents and thereby
hangs a tale. I do not think there is any particular news in it but a
great many years ago, in 1913, when I first went to the Navy Department I
started a tour of inspection and I got up under the eaves in the old State,
War and Navy Building and I found a place full of old war records and I
went into them to find out what records they were and I found that they
were all the Captains' letters from the Captains of the early frigates.
They were in awful condition, just all falling apart. They had been loose-
ly bound together somewhere between 1830 and 1840 and bookworms had got in
and they were being eaten. We rescued those and shortly after that we
started the Naval Records Division in the Navy Department, putting Dudley
Knox in charge and this past year I started an experiment which I hope
will extend to a lot of other Government publications. We have in the Navy
an enormous amount of very valuable historical manuscript material. In
the past, the custom has been to print it at a very large expense and hand
it out through members of the Administration and members of the Congress
free of charge. Last year we got from the Congress an appropriation which
I hope will become a revolving fund. It is only $10,000 but it is to be
used for the printing of these old Navy records and people will subscribe
to them and we will only

--- [190] ---

print the number of volumes that are subscribed to. They will be printed
on better paper than the ordinary Congressional document and will therefore
last. We hope to get the revolving fund and we hope to get back the cost
of each volume into that revolving fund. In other words, you might say
that with that cash capital of $10,000,if the congress grants this revolv-
ing fund, we will be able, eventually to print all the old historical
records.

Q:    Can you tell us what the price will be?

THE PRESIDENT: It won't be a popular book; it will be a book for libraries,
for students, for historians, et cetera. It depends on what it costs. If
it costs $5,000 to print and 500 people subscribe, it will be $10 a volume.

Q:    Have you heard anything from Davis (Norman H. Davis)?

THE PRESIDENT: No, not a word and nothing came in yesterday.

Q:    Mr. President, would you care to comment on reports that a plan for greatly
increased Government control over public utilities is being formulated
under your direction?

THE PRESIDENT: Absolutely nothing I know of. There is a report -- isn't there
some kind of a power board under the Secretary of the Interior, under his
chairmanship, that is working on a report on power? I think so. I am a

little vague as to who is on it (the committee) but in any event there is
nothing new. It is just coordinating activities.

In that connection, I have one more story that has some merit in it. As
you know, with all the old departments and new activities, we have been
studying the last few months the desirability of coordinating them and
tying them in together and there have been

--- [191] ---

various interdepartmental boards, committees -- they were informal, most of
them -- they were interdepartmental committees appointed to study and
report on this, that or the other thing. So the other day -- I think you
had better leave this off the record because it is on me -- somebody came
in and said, "What about the report of such and such an interdepartmental
board?" I said, "I never heard of it." They said, "Yes, you established
it six months ago." I had to go back to my files to remind myself that I
had established it.

Under those conditions you are very apt to get lost in the shuffle and so
se decided, in the Council meeting yesterday, that we would examine into
the number of these boards, how many there are, how many have completed
their work -- a good many have already completed their work -- and as to
which ones could properly be tied in in such a way that their existence
will not be forgotten by the President.

The first step we took was to make the Interdepartmental Committee on
Merchant Marine, which was merely a studying committee and which has
nearly completed its work, to make that a subcommittee of the Emergency
Council, and at each meeting of the Emergency Council the chairman of that
subcommittee will be required to report his existence, at least his existence. He may have something interesting to tell us but in any event he
will report through the secretary of the Emergency Council, Mr. Richberg.
It might be only a report that they are still alive and making progress.

Q: Who is the chairman, can you tell us?

THE PRESIDENT: I don't know; it is merely a good example.

--- [192] ---

Then we created another interdepartmental committee which we have had in
mind for some time, but we have created it as a subcommittee of the Emergency Council. Steve (Mr. Early) will give you the names of the people on
it afterwards -- it is too long to take it down -- but the object is to
tie in all of the Government lending agencies so that the lending agencies
will not be doing an overlapping business. Obviously, all of that ties up
into finance, therefore the Secretary of the Treasury was appointed the
chairman of this subcommittee, which will consist of the Secretary of the
Interior, who makes loans to municipalities and extends Government credit;
the Farm Credit Administration; the R.F.C.; the H.O.L.C.; The Home Loan
Bank Board; the Emergency Administrator of Public Works; the Public Housing Corporation; the Federal Housing Administration; the A.A.A.; the
president of the Export-Import Banks; the Commodity Credit Corporation;
the governor of the Federal Reserve Board and others.

As I say, that committee will meet from time to time and report back to
the Emergency Council on coordinating all of the work of lending by all

the departments of the Government concerned.

Now, there may be other committees and as we discover them, they will be made subcommittees of the Emergency Council.

Q:   Is it likely that the action taken yesterday with regard to the Home Loan Corporation, the Home Owners' Loan Corporation, in closing off all applications because the emergency is over can be duplicated soon in connection with the Farm Credit Administration?

THE PRESIDENT:   I do not know; you are a little previous.   I cannot tell you that until around the first of January.

--- [193] ---

Q:   Are we to assume also that the action in regard to the H.O.L.C. indicates a desire on your part to close up these emergency agencies or to restrict them in their scope as rapidly as recovery permits?

THE PRESIDENT:   I do not know.   I would not write too much about that because we won't know definitely at all until around the first of January.   Of course, in the case of the H.O.L.C., as I understand it, the number of applications they have got in, when reduced to terms of those that will pass, those that will be accepted, will use up the whole $3,000,000,000.   Well, they have only got $3,000,000,000 at the present time.   What we will do later, I do not know.

Q:   Can you give us any hint of the status of Dr. Hutchins?   There are reports that he is no longer under consideration.

THE PRESIDENT:   There has been nothing new on it at all.

Q:   Mr. President, is there anything new about the Chief of Staff of the Army?

THE PRESIDENT:   No and I told Steve (Mr. Early) this morning that I doubt whether there will be until I get back from Warm Springs.

Q:   Will there be some strengthening of the foreign trade activities of the Department of Commerce in view of the reciprocal arrangements?

THE PRESIDENT:   Do you mean more commercial attachés and things like that?

Q:   I mean the whole activities.

THE PRESIDENT:   I doubt it.

Q:   General MacArthur's term would expire before you got back, would it not?

THE PRESIDENT:   I think it expires tomorrow.

--- [194] ---

MR. McINTYRE:   That is the four-year usual term but there is no definite time limit on the appointment of Chief of Staff.   He can continue.

THE PRESIDENT:   It is just the same way in the Army and the Navy.   Any bureau chief stays on until his successor is appointed.

Q: Is there any likelihood of asking Congress for more H.O.L.C. funds?

THE PRESIDENT: I was just saying that I do not know. I cannot tell you anything on that until January.

Q: Would you care to comment on Chairman Jones' suggestion for modification of the Triple A?

THE PRESIDENT: You mean Marvin Jones? I do not know; I have not heard anything about it. What did he do?

Q: He suggested that the benefit be paid on the portion of the crop raised for domestic consumption and that individual restrictions be loosened.

THE PRESIDENT: That is going back to one of the old theories. I do not know; I have not read it.

We are leaving tomorrow afternoon, sometime. I do not know whether you know the schedule. Is there any reason why it should not be given out soon?

(Mr. Early indicated a negative.)

Anybody interested can stay behind and they can see the schedule.

Q: What Cabinet officers --

THE PRESIDENT: (interposing) Secretary Hull is going with me and Secretary Ickes. Secretary Ickes leaves after Chipley and Secretary Hull leaves at Knoxville to come back to Washington.

Q: How about Senator Norris?

--- [195] ---

THE PRESIDENT: He could not come because he had a date arranged about six months ago. I am awfully sorry he could not come.

Q: So is he.

Q: What time do you leave?

THE PRESIDENT: Four o'clock, standard time.

CONFIDENTIAL
Press Conference #159
In the President's Cottage on the Georgia
  Warm Springs Foundation, Warm Springs, Georgia
November 21, 1934, 10:30 A.M.


THE PRESIDENT: Drape yourselves around. Sit on the sofa, Russell (Mr. Young).
    Fred (Mr. Storm) does not have to sit down today; he is a little in the
    light, otherwise he is all right.

    Well, I asked the Trustees (of the Georgia Warm Springs Foundation) to come
    here today because we have been working on this thing for about a couple
    of weeks now, on the subject of a Birthday Ball. The easiest way to des-
    cribe it is to give you the letters all about it. Henry L. Doherty suggest-
    ed another Birthday Ball and we put it up to the Trustees and the Trustees
    made a recommendation which, really, is in two parts. You will get this
    thing (indicating mimeographed release). The first is: (reading)

        "to encourage, coordinate and enlarge the present established
        orthopaedic facilities and services wherever possible so that
        those already handicapped by Infantile Paralysis may be helped:

        "Second - to secure money for the continuance of scientific
        research which aims at preventing the disease itself and which
        must be carried on until successful if thousands of our chil-
        dren are to be spared its devastating aftermath.

        "For these reasons we feel that the willingness of Colonel
        Doherty again to place at the disposal of this humanitarian
        cause the National Committee for the Birthday Ball of the
        President is a magnanimous action which comes at a most op-
        portune time, and it is our hope that you will again lend the
        Committee your birthday, not for the benefit of the Georgia
        Warm Springs Foundation, but for a further effort toward the
        solution of the problem as a whole.

        "At a meeting of the Trustees of Georgia Warm Springs Founda-
        tion held today I was authorized to inform you that the
        Trustees, therefore, recommend to you that Colonel Doherty's
        offer of service be accepted and that a second Birthday Ball

                    --- [197] ---

        be held on the occasion of your next birthday in January 1935.

        "Furthermore, we recommend, in keeping with the two main
        phases of the problem as stated above, that

            "Seventy per cent of the funds raised through
            and by the American public on the anniversary
            of your next birthday be used directly to help
            those committees, individuals, doctors, hospi-
            tals and other organizations struggling with
            the task of providing care and treatment in
            their communities, counties or states for those
            afflicted with Infantile Paralysis, such funds
            to be expended within the community or within

                    [Volume 4:196-197]

the nearest geographical unit of which the
community is a part; and that

"Thirty per cent of the funds raised be
used to maintain and intensify the efforts
of medical research to develop preventives
of and immunization against Infantile
Paralysis with the purpose of eradicating
this scourge exactly as medical science
has successfully combatted and brought
under control smallpox, diphtheria, typhoid
fever, yellow fever and other similar maladies."

It means that the money would go, 70 per cent locally and 30 per cent for
research and none of it to the Foundation.

And then I wrote to Colonel Doherty yesterday and said: (Reading)

"My dear Colonel Doherty:

"Your generous offer of November 8th is most
gratifying to me.

"The Trustees of Georgia Warm Springs Foundation have acted on my request for their recommendation
in this matter and their suggestions which have my
hearty approval are transmitted to you herewith.

"It gives me much happiness to lend my next
birthday, January 30th, 1935, to the National Committee
for the Birthday Ball for the President for this purpose, in the hope that this effort will bring us nearer
to the goal of forever ending the tragic consequences
of Infantile Paralysis.

"May I again express, through you, my grati-
tude to all those who are making my birthday the occasion
for serving in this humanitarian cause.

Always sincerely,"

--- [198] ---

Well, there is the whole thing. Mr. Kannee has copies for you. I think
that covers it all right. We have been working on it quite hard for two
weeks at various meetings of the Trustees.

Q:  Mr. President, can you give us the names of the Trustees here today?

THE PRESIDENT:  Mr. Leighton McCarthy, Dr. Hoke, Mr. Keith Morgan, Mr. Arthur
Carpenter.  Then we have the regular meeting of the Trustees the day after
Thanksgiving.

MR. CARPENTER:  Thanksgiving day, the afternoon.

THE PRESIDENT:  I think this will be a great thing because it means that a
great many communities -- and this is not for quotes at all -- a great many
communities have not facilities and will now be able to either start their

own facilities for orthopaedic work of all kinds or to coordinate their
work with the next community that has got it and improve and build up
that community. It does not mean every little village will have a hospital
but they will be able to get together on a geographical basis.

Q: Is that broad enough in certain cities so that if they wanted to pick up
children they could use it that way for individual cases?

THE PRESIDENT: If the town has its own hospital, certainly.

Q: Do you recall the total raised?

MR. MORGAN: One million, 330 thousand --

THE PRESIDENT: (interposing) and 61 cents.

MR. MORGAN: Sixty-one dollars and eight cents.

THE PRESIDENT: I am wrong. (Laughter)

Q: Who got that eight cents?

THE PRESIDENT: I think Cary Grayson kept it; I do not know.

MR. McINTYRE: I think that went for postage.

Q: Any other news?

--- [199] ---

THE PRESIDENT: I do not believe there is any other thing. I have been studying
all kinds of reports and as a result there will be all sorts of interesting
things coming out in the course of the next two or three weeks. Nothing
startling. I have been studying this morning a tremendously interesting
report on the tying in together of all the map-making facilities of the
United States Government. We found that there are several dozen agencies
that are making maps and we are going to tie them in together as a first
step toward a greater consolidation. It does not mean that one organization will do it but it eliminates a good deal of duplication and will save
money.

At the same time, we hope to be able to start the standard key map of the
United States. A certain amount of work has already been done on that but
it ought to go on for the benefit of all kinds of services, states, municipalities, counties and the Federal Government work. I just use that as
an example of the kind of studying that we have been doing.

Q: Are you planning consolidations on a larger scale in any of the Departments?

THE PRESIDENT: No, these are minor.

Q: What is a key map?

THE PRESIDENT: Why don't you wait and let me give you a good story on this?
Well, it is a standard topographic map, all on the same scale. We find,
for example, that the Government has been doing mapping work on two or
three different scales which have no relationship to each other and this

standard map of the entire country would take a good many years to complete but would cover every portion of the country.

Q:   It has been started?

THE PRESIDENT:   It has been started.

--- [200] ---

Q:   Under what one of these agencies?

THE PRESIDENT:   I couldn't tell you; I do not know.   The Topographic Survey, I think.

Q:   Mr. President, in the absence of Joe Smith, I will ask this question:   Is there anything new from London.   I cannot put the accent to it -- (Laughter)

THE PRESIDENT:   No, I haven't had a thing.

Q:   Mr. President, in the absence of the Count (Rudolph de Zappe), I might ask you --

THE PRESIDENT:   (interposing)   Have we appointed anybody in Washington.   No. They did appoint somebody the other day.

MR. McINTYRE:   That got quite a play, so did the power story.

Q:   In that connection, on power, do you care to amplify --

THE PRESIDENT:   (interposing)   Why don't we wait until Friday and let me talk off the record?   Everybody gather around here and let me talk off the record because there are very few of you who are here now who were here two years ago and you will remember that two years ago we had a perfectly grand informal off-the-record talk about T.V.A., what it was all about, and I think perhaps it will help to do it again.

MR. McINTYRE:   I think on part of it you might just give them background and not all of it off the record.

THE PRESIDENT:   Most of it will be off the record.

MR. McINTYRE:   Yes, I appreciate that.

Q:   We are for you, Mac (Mr. McIntyre); talk that background.   (Laughter)

Q:   Can you tell us about the new relief plans?

THE PRESIDENT:   Nothing on it.   There won't be until the third of January.   I am just thumbs down on it until the third of January.

Q;   Did you read Donald Richberg's speech in Atlanta?

--- [201] ---

THE PRESIDENT:   No, did he speak yesterday?

MR. McINTYRE:   The day before yesterday.

THE PRESIDENT: No, I have not seen it.

MR. McINTYRE: They say he made a speech.

Q: Yes, he did.

Q: Governor Talmadge had some suggestions for you the other day. Did he have them up last night?

THE PRESIDENT: No.

MR. McINTYRE: Off the record, we certainly had Gene (Governor Eugene Talmadge of Georgia) on the spot last night.

THE PRESIDENT: We did not talk about the sovereign State of Georgia at all last night.

Q: Was there anything in the conference last night?

THE PRESIDENT: No. We talked about the unemployment insurance thing and then here is the thing I have got to give you off the record. I did talk with him a little bit about the idea of a Southeastern Council corresponding with the New England Council and told him what had been the actual experience of the New England Council. It (the New England Council) started off very well and it has lately become, primarily, an organization of the bigger businessmen. It does not have any of the other aspects, the Government officials or the citizenship represented on it and it has tended, in New England, to be a body which passes resolutions and fires them at the heads of individual governors and gets a great deal of the limelight -- has a hotblooded executive secretary, and things like that. In other words, it made the mistake of the United States Chamber of Commerce.

On the Southeastern thing, if they want to develop it, the Governors ought to be a little bit careful.

--- [202] ---

Q: They did organize last night in Georgia Hall, and invited Governor Laffoon (of Kentucky) and Governor McAlister (of Tennessee) and Conner (of Mississippi) to join them on the tenth of December.

THE PRESIDENT: That is exactly the difference. In other words, the New England Council is an association primarily of businessmen and the governors haven't any kind of say in it at all. The New England Council shoots things at Governors' heads.

I told the Governors last night that I thought as a result of my long experience in the big Governors' Conference -- I was on the Executive Committee for four years -- that if they would start a regional conference, all governors and nobody else, it would be an awfully good thing for the Southeast.

Q: That is what they did last night.

THE PRESIDENT: There is one very effective local governors' conference and that is the western governors -- that is the Rocky Mountain States and the Coast -- but only the governors attend them and they do not have any outsiders in at all. When I was in Albany we had a conference up there that related to the industrial Northeast to study unemployment insurance, old age pensions and things like that. That was a very effective instrument. But the general thought that I told them about last night was that if we could have five or six regions in this conference -- five or six governors covering the region, that if anything came up between them and the Federal Government we could get them up to Washington, getting five or six governors instead of forty-eight.

Q:  I think last night they decided to hold quarterly meetings and the governor of the state that holds the particular meeting becomes the governing officer for the succeeding quarter. That gives everybody

--- [203] ---

a chance to become president of the Governors' Conference.

Q:  There are reports in Birmingham this morning that Governor-elect Bibb Graves is coming here to see you this morning?

THE PRESIDENT:  He is sitting outside.

Q:  He was going to ask that the Government purchase $100,000,000 worth of State bonds in order to promote a subsistence home project to care for the unemployed.

THE PRESIDENT:  That is a new one to me.

Q:  Will you send him down to our cottage?

THE PRESIDENT:  It depends on what he says. He may sneak home over the mountain (Pine Mountain).

Q:  Mr. Wilkie of Commonwealth and Southern said in a statement in New York that he was sure you would give the utility people a chance to give you the facts on T.V.A. Do you expect to receive any of them?

THE PRESIDENT:  That was kind of him. (Laughter)

Q:  Thank you, Mr. President.

MR. McINTYRE:  May we have the Conference (the next Press Conference) at two o'clock, with the understanding that it is for the morning paper release?

Q:  I might report that we had a meeting last night for the redistribution of wealth.

THE PRESIDENT:  Did it circulate?

Q:  We might also add that I have petitioned the White House Correspondents' Association officials to name a receiver in bankruptcy for some of the boys.

THE PRESIDENT:  Are you a creditor?

Q:  Much obliged.

THE PRESIDENT:  Then you do need a receiver in bankruptcy.

Press Conference #160
Held at the President's Cottage
Georgia Warm Springs Foundation, Warm Springs, Georgia,
November 23, 1934, 2:17 P.M.


(Mrs. Roosevelt and Mr. Rexford G. Tugwell were present at the Conference.)


THE PRESIDENT: Now, first of all, have you any questions before we talk about
    other things off the record?

Q: Are you encouraged by the outlook for foreign trade?

THE PRESIDENT: Oh; I think it is generally picking up. All the figures show
    that it is picking up. If you want, I will talk to you for a minute off
    the record on foreign trade because there has been such a lot of perfect
    nonsense. As a perfect example, take cotton. We are down in the cotton
    country now and it is something we use all the time. There are definite
    efforts being made by -- what is the name of that firm in Atlanta? Ander-
    son Clayton (?) -- that type of businessman, who is a dealer in buying and
    selling cotton -- mind you, this is off the record, every bit of it --
    there is a real effort being made by the dealers in cotton to maintain
    the total volume of cotton. In other words, if they get a fifteen million
    bale crop to sell, they obviously, as commission men, make more money than
    if they only sell ten million bales of cotton. It is a little like the
    stock market operations. If you have an average of fifteen million shares
    a day, you can support three hundred brokerage firms, but if you only
    have an average of five hundred shares a day, you cannot support as many
    brokerage firms. Obviously, they want more and more shares dealt in on
    the Stock Exchange. Obviously, firms like Anderson Clayton like to see
    fifteen and twenty million bale crops because it is money in their pock-
    ets. Now, those people are spreading the rumor

--- [205] ---

that our cotton exports are falling off for the reason that the price is so
much above the world price that other countries cannot buy our cotton.
Therefore, they are in favor of cheaper cotton.

Their general -- I won't say "theory," becuase they know better -- their
general effort is to seel the idea to the public that if we have six-cent
cotton European countries would buy a good deal more of our cotton. Of
course, that is about 98% nonsense. There is about 2% truth. If we do
have cheaper cotton, probably we would sell a little more, but only a
little more.

Why is the export sale of American cotton decreasing? There are two very
simple reasons. The first is that on the other side they are going more
and more to substitutes. If you can get that thing out of the State
Department when you get home, there is no reason why you should not have
a story about it. Breck Long sent home about a month ago a very interesting story from Italy showing that Italy, with government help, had been
experimenting on a new cloth made out of 10% cotton and 90% wood fibre.
This year they manufactured out of that substitute cotton cloth about two
million kilos, which is a lot of cotton. It is roughly about five million
pounds of this new cloth. It is a process akin to the rayon process. They

take the wood fibre with 10% of cotton and stick it into the rayon process
and then they take it out after about half hour through the rayon process
and put it into a new process of their own.  Probably Italy will be able
to get the cost of that new cloth down sufficiently in the course of the
next year or two so that they will buy very little of our cotton.  Today,
Italy takes about a million bales a year.  Assuming that this new cloth is
a success, it means they will take only one hundred thousand bales instead
of a million.

--- [206] ---

Now, that is only one country that would be  doing it.  But why is Italy
doing it?  For all sorts of reasons, the first being that Italy has no
exchange with which to buy cotton.  She hasn't any money to send out of
Italy.  Obviously, she wants to keep her money home.

The same thing applies to Germany.  Hitler is wearing today a suit made of
90% fibre and 10% cotton.  It is a damn' good-looking suit and he points
it out with pride to every American that comes.

The most important reason for these substitutes is lack of exchange, because all of those countries have been importing more than they have been
exporting and therefore they haven't the money to buy goods on the outside.

Then, there is another reason, and that is that a very large number of nations today who have been buying British cotton cloth and American cotton
cloth and so forth, also Czechoslovakian cloth, have now started their own
factories.  Take Brazil, for example.  After the war, in 1920 or 1921,
Brazil imported all of its cotton goods.  Today Brazil is making somewhere
around 55 or 60% of its cotton goods.  They are making their own shoes in
Brazil for the first time.

Of course, while they are establishing their factories, it means we will
be exporting a good deal of machinery, but once that new machinery is set
up in Brazil and the Argentine, or any other country, as soon as that is
set up and they have begun manufacturing, they will buy less and less of
our own goods.

Now, what we are trying to do is to offset that by trying to get special
agreements with different countries which are essentially on a barter
basis.  The thing has only been going for a few months and

--- [207] ---

it is helping in the sense that it is preventing the situation from getting
worse.

I don't think we can look forwad to a vast volume of foreign trade, exports
or imports, but at least, through these agreements, we can keep the situation from getting any worse, and on some special lines we may be able to
add a little here, there and some other place.  Of course the total will
amount to a gread deal, but, so long as the other nations are headed for
a self-sufficiency program, we are not likely to go back to the old
figures unless there is an entire change of feeling all over the world.

Now, let us take it from another point of view.  That was on manufactured
goods.  On foodstuffs, the European nations have almost all, up to quite
recently, except Hungary and the Balkans, been importers of foodstuffs.

Now, as you know, there has been an intensive drive all over Europe and
England to raise their own foodstuffs. Why? There are a lot of reasons.
In the first place, they don't want to export the capital. In the second
place, they want to be self-sufficient in case of war. They don't want to
be caught as Germany was caught in 1914. The German population nearly
starved to death. Of course, all that means less demand for our food crops.

It is not our fault. It is not because of our high prices. Not a bit. It
is entirely because those nations have a definite policy to become self-
sufficient, both in agriculture and industry. We are just up against it
and we are doing the best we can to save what is left. I think that is the
easiest way to explain the general foreign trade situation.

Q:   Before you go on to the off the record you were speaking about, may I ask a
     question about Mr. O'Connor? Is he going out? Has he resigned?

                    --- [208] ---

THE PRESIDENT:  Which Mr. O'Connor?

Q:   J. F. T. O'Connor.

THE PRESIDENT:  I thought you meant Basil. Has he resigned? No.

Q:   He has not? The reason I asked was becuase there was a question as to
     whether he had been asked to resign.

THE PRESIDENT:  I haven't heard a word about it since I left. He still has
     everything under advisement.

Q:   Mr. President, is there anything you can tell us on the record concerning
     the visit of your various power officials here today?

THE PRESIDENT:  They are members of some kind of committee, I could not tell you
     the name of it, that has on it somebody from the Federal Trade Commission,
     somebody from T.V.A., somebody from Interior and one or two from the Power
     Commission, and they were just working and have been working -- I think
     the whole thing came out last Spring -- working on a general survey of the
     power situation, and they are going to talk with me about that tonight.

Q:   Is that your National Resources Committee?

THE PRESIDENT:  No, it is separate from that. It relates only to power.

MR. TUGWELL:  Manly can tell them about it. I have forgotten the name of the
     committee too.

THE PRESIDENT:  It is one of the inter-departmental committees to report on the
     general situation.

Q:   With recommendations for legislation?

THE PRESIDENT:  Yes, and policy.

Q:   Still on the record, does that visit here mean that you have in mind any
     new moves of a concrete nature in the immediate future in connection with
     what you were telling us the other day?

THE PRESIDENT: This has nothing to do with the trip or T.V.A. or anything

--- [209] ---

like that, except in so far as it relates to general power policy.

Q: To get back just for a moment to foreign trade, when you were talking about cotton, was that off the record?

THE PRESIDENT: Yes. I don't think the time is ripe. I just gave you that in order that you might understand the thing in case somebody talks to you.

MR. TUGWELL: We have in the Department of Agriculture samples of that stuff if the boys want to see it.

THE PRESIDENT: There is no reason why you shouldn't get a good story on it. The Department of Agriculture is getting it tested by the Bureau of Standards. Breck Long told me that the stuff feels like cotton and wears like cotton and the only catch is that if you send it to the laundry, they had better not boil it. If it boils it disintegrates into pulp. You can wash it in water up to 200 degrees but not to 212 degrees.

Q: On one of our $35-suits, what would it cost in that material?

THE PRESIDENT: They haven't got it down below the cost of a cotton suit, but expect to in the next year on large scale production.

Any old fibre mixed with wood pulp does it. There is an outlet, perhaps, in the future, for Georgia pine in addition to newsprint paper.

Q: Do the engineers think that one is a good equivalent of the other?

THE PRESIDENT: They think it is.

Q: What sections of the United States would be affected?

THE PRESIDENT: It means -- this is off the record -- it means, quite frankly, that instead of exporting six or seven million bales a year we will have a very large portion of that export cut off and a large portion of the cotton-growing states will have to turn to other things.

--- [210] ---

Cason Galloway takes pride in saying that he has thoroughly investigated agriculture in Georgia. You could grow anything in Georgia except corn and cotton, and yet those are the two things that the state grows. There is a lot of that.

Q: Do you think that European countries can be self-sustaining and self-sufficient?

THE PRESIDENT: Well, of course it depends a little bit on the country. I will give you two examples: Austria and England cannot grow enough foodstuffs to maintain their population. Without any question, I think that is true. There are forty million people in England, which is more than the acreage will support. It is the same way in Austria. On the other hand, countries like Hungary produce more than sufficient to support their population. But they have practically no manufactures. Taking Europe as a whole, they can

come pretty close to being self-sustaining. With the surplus of wheat in
the Balkan States you would come very close to making up for the deficien-
cies of wheat in England and Austria and certain parts of Germany.

Q:   Where are we going to export our surplus, then?

THE PRESIDENT:  This is still off the record.  That brings up a thing which is
going to appear this Winter.  George Peek believes in the old McNary-
Haugen Bill and many other people do.  It, in effect, would say to the
cotton growers and to the wheat farmers of the country, "Go ahead and
waste -- go ahead and plant all the wheat you want and we will fix a price
for the domestic consumption.  We will fix a price for the portion of your
crop consumed in this country."

Let us say, in the case of cotton, it will run to fifteen million bales
with unrestricted growing.  We can use nine million bales in this country.
They would be paid a fixed price for the nine million

--- [211] ---

bales.  We would pick some figure and pay them that much for the nine
million bales.  The other six-fifteenths we will take and dump on the rest
of the world.  That is the McNary-Haugen theory and, as I said, George
Peek still believes in it.

Now, of course, that brings up the difficulty of saying to the other nations, "We are going to dump these six million bales of cotton on you at
any old figure."  You see the implications?  It is a little risky to say
that to the rest of the world.  They may put up barriers against it.

Q:   It means, then, intensifying the crop production program?

THE PRESIDENT:  It means carrying it along on a definite, orderly procedure.  In
other words, the first year we plowed under 25% of the crop in 1933.  The
next year, this year, we restricted it by 40%.  This coming year we will
restrict it by 25%, probably.  Probably that will be enough.

Q:   Can we write that?

THE PRESIDENT:  No, you cannot write that.  It has to come out of Washington.

The following year, we cannot tell.  If our exports fall off, we may have
to go back to 40%, and eventually we may have to cut the unlimited acreage
down to 50%.  But probably not.  Probably the domestic consumption in this
country will be sufficient to take care of 60% of a fifteen million bale
crop, as far as you can tell for a number of years ahead.  You take this
State and any other cotton-growing state, and if they get twelve or fifteen cents a pound for a 60% crop, they are pretty well of financially.
All you have to do is to see the South today compared to what it was two
years ago.  It seems to work from the standpoint of economics.

Q:   I fell I am doing a lot of talking here, but the other day you spoke of
power and there are a lot of interpretations on it.  Purely --

--- [212] ---

THE PRESIDENT:  (interposing)  Oh, the interpretations are all pure.  (Laughter)

Q:    Do you mind telling us what your ideas are regarding the private power
      companies?

THE PRESIDENT:  All right, I will give you something on that, but this has to
      be off the record because I don't want to be in the position of interpret-
      ing what I said.  (Laughter)

      It is a perfectly simple thing.  Two years ago, in this room, you were
      here Fred --

MR. STORM:   I was here.

THE PRESIDENT:  We spent an hour and a half.  I think it was in January, 1933,
      and we had been down with Norris to see the Norris Dam.  (Perhaps the Pres-
      ident should have said Wilson Dam.)  And I had said up there publicly
      that we were going ahead with the development of Muscle Shoals.  That is
      all I said at that time publicly.  We came down here and we had this talk
      in which I outlined what developed into T.V.A.

      The easiest way of putting it is this:  Any of you who live in, let us
      say, a prosperous rural section of the State of New York, if you come down
      here into the average rural section of any of the Southern states, you are
      immediately struck by what looks like poverty, real poverty.  You cannot
      get away from it.  In the first place, you have the Negro problem.  In the
      second place, you have what they used to call the "poor white" problem.
      The standard of living is absolutely and totally different from what it
      is in the prosperous areas of the West or of the North.  That is very well
      illustrated by the survey that Harry Hopkins made of one or two counties
      where he found that three out of four families in these counties have never
      slept on a mattress.  That is almost unbelievable.  I told that last
      Summer to somebody in New York and he said, "I don't believe it!"  I said,
      "It is

                        --- [213] ---

true; you don't know the conditions in the South."  Now, that applies because of the fact that the average family in the South only sees, in the
way of cash, perhaps a couple of hundred dollars a year and a great many
don't see that.  The result is that the taxing power is almost nil.  This
State cannot raise money for education because there is nothing to tax.  Am
I right on that?

MR. TUGWELL:   Do you want to tell them about the future population?

THE PRESIDENT:  Now, right along with that is something we have been talking
      about and it will come out probably in the course of the next couple of
      weeks.  The figures show that in the course of the next fifty years the
      majority of the people of the United States will be descended from South-
      ern stock.  That is an extraordinarily interesting fact.  In other words,
      in the North and in the cities, the increase in population has stopped.
      It practically has stopped.  Practically all the increase in population
      in this country today is in the South.  Now, a couple of generations of
      that means that the majority of people will have Southern blood.  That is
      an interesting fact and we have got to consider what that population is
      going to be in fifty years.

      We have got to raise the standard of education; they are perfectly terrible.
      The standards of living are low.  Yet here is probably as fine a stock,

human stock, as you can find anywhere in the United States. It is going to
dominate the United States in the course of a couple of generations and
what is it going to be like? That is looking at it from a national point
of view.

Now for the T.V.A. I can put it this way: Power is really a secondary
matter. What we are doing there is taking a watershed with about three
and a half million people in it, almost all of them rural, and we are
trying to make a different type of citizen out of them, not

--- [214] ---

what they would be under their present conditions. Now that applies not
only to the mountaineers, we all know about them, but it applies to the
people around Muscle Shoals. Do you remember that drive over to Wheeler
Dam the other day? You went through a county of Alabama where the standards of education are lower than almost any other county in the United
States, and yet that is within twenty miles of the Muscle Shoals Dam. They
have never had a chance. All you had to do was to look at the houses in
which they lived. Heavens, this section around here is 1000% compared with
that section we went through. The home through here are infinitely better.

So T.V.A. is primarily intended to change and to improve the standards of
living of the people of the Valley. Power is, as I said, a secondary consideration. Of course it is an important one because, if you can get
cheap power to these people, you hasten the process of raising the standard
of living.

The T.V.A. has been going ahead with power, yes, but it has been going
ahead with probably a great many other things besides power and dam building. For instance, take fertilizer. You talk about a "yardstick of
power." Harcourt Morgan is running the fertilizer end of it and at Muscle
Shoals he is turning out, not a nitrate -- the plast was originally built
for a nitrate plant -- but he is turning out a phosphate. He is conducting
a very fine experiment with phosphate of lime. They believe that for this
whole area around here, and that would include this kind of soil around
here, phosphate of lime is the best thing you can put on land in addition
to being the cheapest.

Now, at once the fertilizer companies, the National Fertilizer Association
that gets out figures, I believe (laughter), they say, "Are you going into
the fertilizer business?" The answer is a very

--- [215] ---

simple one. The plant is primarily an experimental plant. That is the
primary purpose. Therefore, they are going to take this year a thousand
acres of Government land, which is worn out land, typical of the locality,
and they are going to use this phosphate of lime on this thousand acres
and show what can be done with the land. They are going to give a definite demonstration. They will compare it with the other fertilizers, putting them in parallel strips, and they will see which works out best and
at the lowest cost and, by having the large plant which they have, they
will be able to figure out what is a fair price for the best type of
fertilizer.

Having done that and having figured out the fair price, it becomes a process of education and if the farmers all through that area can be taught

that that type of fertilizer at X number of dollars a ton is the best thing
for them to use, then it is up to the National Fertilizer Association and
its affiliated companies to meet that price. Now, that is the real answer,
and we hope that they will meet that price, adding to it, to the cost of
manufacture, a reasonable profit. We will know what the cost of manufacture is, and it is very easy to say what a reasonable profit is. Now, if
those gentlemen fail to avail themselves of this perfectly magnificent
opportunity to conduct a sound business and make a profit, well, it is
just too bad. Then somebody will get up in Congress and say, "These fellows are not meeting their opportunities and the farmers will have to have
the fertilizer and of course we will have to provide it." But I, for
one, hope that that day will never come. Now, that is not holding a big
stick over them at all. It is saying to them, "Here is your opportunity.
We go down on our knees to you, asking you to take it."

Q:    Just a little guiding light.

--- [216] ---

THE PRESIDENT:   In other words, what we are trying to do is something constructive to enable business --

MRS. ROOSEVELT:   An intimation.  (Laughter)

THE PRESIDENT:   No, it is not even an intimation.  No, it is a generous offer.

Now, coming down to power. You take the example of Corinth we went through
the other day. In Corinth, without Government assistance -- they did it
themselves -- they had a county electric power association and they used to
buy their juice from the Mississippi Power Company. The T.V.A., because
they were on a through line to Tupelo, the T.V.A. came along and stepped
in as a middleman, and still bought the power from the Mississippi Power
Company, at a lower cost per kilowatt, but on the agreement with the
Mississippi Power Company that they would take more juice. The result was
that the Mississippi Power Company gets the same gross profit as they were
getting before, but selling more power. Then the T.V.A., merely acting as
middleman, without any profit to itself, turns around and sells it to the
county electric power association. That part of it does not change the
existing situation at all. The Mississippi Power Company merely gave a
lower rate to the Alcorn County people, but they did it via the T.V.A.
instead of direct. It was merely a bookkeeping matter. It does not cost
the T.V.A. anything and they do not receive anything.

Now the Alcorn County people, that is the Alcorn County Electric Power
Association, did a very interesting thing. There they had Corinth, which
is a good-sized town, and they found they could distribute in Corinth --
these are not accurate figures -- they found they could distribute house-
hold power at about two cents a kilowatt hour. But if they were to run an
electric line out to a farm, they would

--- [217] ---

have to charge three cents. In other words, the farmer would have to pay
more.

What did the Corinth people do? They said, "We can get cheaper power than
the farmer, but we think he should have the same rates we are getting."
Voluntarily they agreed to take and to pay for two and a half cent power

which enabled the farmer to get two and a half cent power. That is an extraordinary thing. That is community planning. Now, there was no reason in God's world why the Mississippi Power Company could not have gone to Corinth and said the same thing, no reason in the world. They just never thought of it. They could have done the same thing. But it was the T.V.A. that went down and sold the idea to the people in that county and said, "Let us have a uniform power rate for the man next to the powerhouse and the same rate for the man who lives twenty-five miles up the Valley. We don't want to concentrate any more people in Corinth. We want to increase the rural population."

The result of that operation is that they are increasing -- they have more nearly doubled the consumption of power. Furthermore, they have gone ahead and formed another association, tied up with this county one, by which people can buy refrigerators and electric cook-stoves and all the other gadgets at a figure which is somewhere around 60 or 70% of what they are paying before.

Now, the process behind what they were paying before amounted to this: A subsidiary of the Mississippi Power Company in the business of selling refrigerators, generally owned -- I am just saying this as a mean aside -- generally owned by the son of the president of the power company -- there is a lot of that nepotism -- would go around and say, "We will sell you a refrigerator. The cost is two hundred

--- [218] ---

dollars. You can pay for it over thirty months. The total cost to you at the end of thirty months will be three hundred dollars." In other words, it was a hundred dollars extra. They did not say that, but that is what it amounted to. In other words, they were selling them the thing at two hundred dollars and they were making an average of 18 to 20% on that sale during this thirty months.

Now, who else profits? That selling corporation of course made not only its 15 or 20%, but also made quite a lot on what they had paid for the machine. They had probably paid a hundred and seventy-five dollars for the machine. Now, who did they buy it from? They did not buy it from the General Electric of the Westinghouse. They bought it from the middleman and he also made a twenty-five dollar profit on it, and the General Electric Company only got a hundred and fifty dollars for the machine. Therefore, when the consumer paid three hundred dollars, it was just one hundred percent more than the General Electric Company got for the machine.

We went to the General Electric Company and said, "Will you give us your wholesale rate on machines?" They said, "Sure." And we went to all the other refrigerator manufacturers so as to have a complete line, and then we said to these householders, "You can buy this for a hundred and fifty dollars plus a five dollar handling charge, paying for it over thirty months at 5% interest instead of 18%." The net result is that instead of paying three hundred dollars, he pays a hundred and seventy-five or a hundred and eighty dollars. His installment cost is at 5% instead of 18%. He gets it at the wholesale price, which the Mississippi River Company could have done exactly as well as the T.V.A. In other words, we are teaching them something.

--- [219] ---

Q:   Who is Corinth getting its power from now?

THE PRESIDENT:   Mississippi Power Company.

Q:   I don't quite understand the power company getting its same profit.  Mr. Ruble, who runs a department store down there, told us that the building had its bill cut from sixty dollars a month to forty dollars and he doubled his consumption.

THE PRESIDENT:   That is the point; what do they do?  Suppose they were selling -- well, let us put it in algebra.  Suppose they were selling X kilowatt hours times Y cents per kilowatt hour.  The total receipts of the company amounted to Z.  Now, we come in and tell these local people that if they will buy 2X kilowatts times $\frac{1}{2}$Y -- in other words, half the price -- you will still have Z.  In other words, if he sells twice as much power at half the cost, the gross will be exactly the same at the end of the month.  Now, that is what we have been trying to do.

I don't know the consumption back in Corinth, but in Tupelo we estimated it would take a year at a three-cent rate running down to one, instead of a rate starting at six cents and running down to three, we figured it would take a year for the consumption power to double.  Actually, it took only four months.  The consumption of power in Tupelo has doubled in four months.

The result is that the local company has an even bigger gross in way of receipts than it had before, and yet the consumers of that power, whether shopkeepers or farmers or householders or anything else, they are getting their electricity for less than half the price, about 45%, of what they were paying before.

Q:   Isn't there a considerable change in the cost of having to step up its power production to meet a demand like that?

THE PRESIDENT:   Very little.  The only overhead is when you get an extension

--- [220] ---

of rural lines.  There you have a larger inspection force to watch the lines.  That is about all.

Then we are doing a third thing along the same lines.  The Power Companies did a perfectly silly thing for them to do when it came to rural electrification.  They put out all kinds of specifications for rural lines that were perfectly out of the question.  Well, there was a certain rural line we wanted here in Warm Springs, and the specifications of the Power Company called, as I remember it, for 35-foot poles, white oak, that had to come from North Georgia.  They had to be hauled here by railroad.  Then I think they charged eighty dollars for the transmission line into the farmhouse.  The net result is that a line for five or six farmers would cost somewhere on the average of four or five hundred dollars.  That is a pretty big debt for a farmer to assume.  Then they said to him, along the same line as the refrigerator "You can pay that over a number of years with a small charge for interest."  The interest ran from 18 to 20%.

What we are trying to do is to build a rural line which will be substan-

tial. We will put in transformers actually at cost from the electric supply company, the General Electric Company or the Westinghouse, and then let
the farmer pay for his power line at five percent instead of 18 or 20%.
It means that on the average he can put in his power line for about 60% of
what it costs the other way.

Now, we come back to the old simile we used before. I hope the the proper
power company officials will accept this free education that the Government
is giving them. It is a fine offer and a grand chance. If they come in
and do it right with a reasonable profit on their actual cost, that is all
we are asking. No threat, no intimadation.

--- [221] ---

Q:    Or else?

THE PRESIDENT:  No "or else."

Q:    This association which is furnishing the current, buying it from the Mississippi Power Company, is it a paying proposition?

THE PRESIDENT:  Sure.  And there was no reason in God's world why the Mississippi Power Company could not have done the same thing and have gotten the
same results. Listen to the results:  In three months, June, July and
August, the operating revenues were $17,847. That was in three months so
you see what a small proposition it is. The expenses for operating, maintenance and expense, including energy purchase -- that is what they paid
the Mississippi Power Company for it -- was $5,826.00, or exactly 33% of
the gross revenues. Then, in addition to that, they had general administrative expenses and new business expenses -- that meant pushing it and
pushing the commercial end -- of $2,094, or 12%. Then they had taxes and
of course, as I remarked the other day, some people do not admit taxes.
They are paying to the City $1,508 in taxes, or 8% of their gross. Then
they charged to depreciation $1,232, or 7%. They had to pay on interest,
interest on the money they borrowed to get this thing going, $964 or 5%.
They paid 5% interest.

Their total expenses and deductions came to $11,625 or 65% of their gross
receipts. Well, that looks like a good picture. It left them a balance
available for new construction and retirements to be applied on the debt,
35% of the gross. Now, that is as pretty a financial set-up as I know of
anywhere. In fact, it is so pretty that if it keeps up and they use some
of that 35% right along to retire the money they borrowed, they will be in
a position to reduce their rates below what they are today. There is no
question about it, and

--- [222] ---

they will still have some left for new construction.

Q:    In Atlanta the Georgia Power Company runs its auxiliary plant in Atlanta
with gas. It buys gas from Mississippi, makes electricity from the gas --
converts the gas into electricity -- and sells it at a profit. They use
twenty million cubic feet a day.

THE PRESIDENT:  Do you know, about gas -- Ickes told me this on the train the
other day -- there is going to waste every year in the Texas oil fields
$72,000,000 worth of gas. It is just escaping into the air. Now, if that

gas were turned into electricity, think what it would mean to Texas. That is $6,000,000 worth of gas a month.

Q:  They pipe the gas into Atlanta from Mississippi.

Q:  If that much is going to wast in Texas, what is the gas wasted on Capitol Hill?  (Laughter)

THE PRESIDENT:  That would run the District, anyway. It might cut the District tax rate.

Q:  The trouble is that that is non-convertible gas.

THE PRESIDENT:  Now, coming back to the point, this statement shows a balance available for construction and retirement of 35% of the gross. If you were to analyze the financing of most of the private power companies, you will find that in the majority of cases they have been following the pernicious rule of the railroads. They get out a twenty or thirty-year bond issue and they don't start a sinking fund, but when the bonds mature they don't pay them off. For example, in the paper yesterday morning, there is one company that is seeking to refund an issue of bonds which were issued twenty years ago. That is what has hurt the railroads. The railroads never paid off a single bond when it matured. They never set up a sinking fund.

The New York Central Railroad, which runs through our place at

--- [223] ---

Hyde Park, issued in 1842 some 7% gold construction bonds with which they built the railroad from New York to Albany. My great-grandfather was so keen to see that railroad built, so that he would not have to go by steamboat from Hyde Park to New York, that he took five of those bonds. My mother owns them today, owns the lineal descendants of those five bonds. To be sure, they are only 3½'s now, but it is the first mortgage bond that has never been paid off and it is 92 years since my great-grandfather bought them. That is why railroads go broke. On the last bond issue the maturity date was put at the year 2001. How silly. That is why it is time to teach Wall Street some very simple elementary lessons in finance. It is true, isn't it?

Q:  Do you think Wall Street can learn?

THE PRESIDENT:  Oh, yes, but it will take some time. They will learn a lot in two years.

Q:  The logical question that that raises is, can the average private utility undergo the reorganization necessary to cut the rates and take advantage of the opportunity given them?

THE PRESIDENT:  Only if they reorganize. Of course, we all know they do a lot of talking about widows and orphans. Now, whose fault is it? I will give you an example: A certain friend of mine, who makes or perhaps saves two or three thousand dollars a year, started in about 1928 to put aside a savings fund, realizing that some day he would get old and could not work any more. Wanting a little more than 4%, he went to two banks in New York City, the most reputable, old-fashioned banks he could find. I was partly responsible and told him where to go. As a result, today he finds that the fifteen or twenty thousand dollars he put in is invested, about two-thirds,

in bonds of utilities, not stocks, but bonds.  What kind of utilities?
Holding companies, all

--- [224] ---

of them holding companies, none of them operating companies.  He was advised to buy the bonds of these holding companies as the best form of investment he could get.  They were 6% and 7% bonds and he bought them at
102,103 and 104.  He bought them above par.  Today the average of those
bonds is about 40.  The result is that he has lost over half of the savings
that he put into those bonds.

Now, why are they selling at 40?  For the simple reason that you have to
find out what is behind them.  That starts you back over a chain.  Let us
take Associated Gas & Electric, as an example, of Commonwealth & Southern,
or any of the big holding companies.  They followed the same principle
that Insull did, exactly the same thing, and it was considered honest in
those days by a lot of people.  Those bonds have printed on them that behind them is so much stock.  Let us call the first company the A Company,
and their bonds state that they have so much stock of B Company, C Company, D Company, in the treasury of the A company, as security of those
bonds.  Then you analyze and you ask, what is the common stock of B, C and
D Companies?  You will find that they are holding companies.  And you will
also find that they have outstanding certain bonds which are backed by the
common stocks of E, F, G, H and I Companies.  And then you will come down
to those companies and perhaps they are operating companies or perhaps
they are holding companies too.  Sometimes you get the pyramid of the
holding company principle up to the fourth dimension.  You come down to the
fact that even the first holding company has as security for its bonds the
common stock of, let us say, the Meriwether County Electric Light Company
organized in the year 1900.  Now, when the Meriwether County Electric
Company was organized, how did they do that?  They got Mr. Peters (?), of
the bank in Manchester, and Dr. Peters (?) and Judge

--- [225] ---

Revell, of Greenville, all of them, to put in, in cash, $1,000 apiece.
For that $1,000 they received a thousand dollar bond.  In addition to that
they received ten shares of common stock.  And then, later on, when they
were merged into the Georgia Railway Power and Light Company -- these are
all fictitious --

Q:   You couldn't follow them all out?

THE PRESIDENT:  No, you couldn't, they went through six or eight different processes.  So each of them has a bond and also ten shares of common, and the
common were not represented by property since it was merely a possible
equity, because they had raised enough by bonds to build this local plant
entirely.  In other words, the ten shares were water in the first instance.
In the first reorganization he got a new bond, also ten shares of preferred and ten shares of common, which was water, and on the next reorganization with a holding company he got his bond and twenty shares of preferred and twenty shares of common.  There is one man who put in a thousand
dollars into one of these little local electric light companies about 1900,
and today his thousand dollars is twenty thousand dollars, although he has
never done a damn thing to make it worth twenty thousand dollars.

The banker who does the merging gets a lot of common stock and dumps it off on the market. Now what Charlie (Mr. Hurd) said was right. I don't like the expression "squeezing the water out," but if the utility companies in this country could recapitalize on the basis of the money put into them, every one of them would be making a profit today and every one of them could reduce the rates.

Q: You mean the money spent on plant?

THE PRESIDENT: Yes. I don't mean the money spent by Consolidated Gas in New York.

--- [226] ---

Q: But a lot of people have taken their money and gotten out.

THE PRESIDENT: And a lot of widows and orphans are holding the bag, having been persuaded by the best banks in New York City to buy that kind of bonds, which is not at all honest.

Q: The answer is that they hold the bag anyway, so that in reorganization it would not make any difference.

THE PRESIDENT: In a reorganization it is just too bad about people badly advised. It is not the Government's fault. In other words, somebody is bound to get hurt. There isn't any question about it.

It is a very simple proposition. Suppose, for the sake of argument, you can save the consumers of power one hundred million dollars at the rate of two hundred dollars a year. That would be five million people who would actually benefit in a year. They would benefit from that kind of saving through cheaper power. You would hurt a lot of people. You might hurt twenty or thirty or forty thousand people in benefitting five hundred thousand of five million. But, after all, that is one thing that Government cannot do, and that is to protect widows and orphans against bum advice they have had on investing.

Q: As a matter of opinion, how long do you think it is going to take to accomplish this reorganization?

THE PRESIDENT: I think it will come gradually. I think a great many of them will do it voluntarily.

Q: How would they go about it? Would there be a receivership?

THE PRESIDENT: People are not going to be as badly hurt as they think. Most of them are listed on the Curb. Well, Electric Bond & Share, for instance -- there are an awful lot of people who own that. Here are the quotations: Of course, it is all water, Electric Bond & Share is all water. It represents nothing but equities. The common stock is sell-

--- [227] ---

ing at seven or eight dollars a share. The 5% preferred is selling at 31. The 6% preferred is selling at 37.

Let us take Associated Gas & Electric, which an awful lot of people bought. It is selling at fifty cents a share. You can see that the loss is already established for most of these holding companies. Take Niagara

Hudson. That is practically all water. It is selling at $3.75 a share. In other words, the loss is there already.

Q:     What is Commonwealth & Southern?

THE PRESIDENT:  Commonwealth & Southern is selling at $1.12 a share. The high for the year has been $3.75. As you can see, the people who bought that have had their loss already.

Q:     They could not lose anything much?

THE PRESIDENT:  Take Cities Service, it is selling at $1.60 and the preferred is selling at $13.75. The 7% preferred is selling at $14 a share. There you are.

Q:     The widows and orphans can use that for wallpaper.

Q:     They have used lots of other things for wallpaper in the past too, haven't they?

THE PRESIDENT:  To give you a thought, what we are after primarily is to improve the standard of living for the country as a whole.

Q:     And power is merely one of the things?

THE PRESIDENT:  Merely one of the things. Better homes, slum clearance, better roads, they all tie in together. Better education is very, very important.

I think I told you the story about the first year I was down here, when a young man came up to the porch with his cap in his hand and said, "Can I speak to you, Mr. Roosevelt?" I said, "Yes, come up, son. What can I do for you?" He said, "Will you do a great favor for us?" I

--- [228] ---

said, "What do you want?" He said, "We are having our school commencement next week and we would be awfully glad if you would come over and give the prizes." I said, "Delighted to. Are you the president of the graduating class?" He said, "No, sir; I am the principal of the school." I said, "My God, man, how old are you?" He said, "I am nineteen." "Have you been to college?" "Oh, yes; I finished my Freshman year at Athens, Georgia."

There was a fine boy who got enough money to finish his Freshman year and then he had to go back to get money for the next term. It would take him eight years to get through college. I said to him, "How much are you being paid?" He told me that he had 150 children and that he was getting paid, as principal, board and lodging and $400 a year. He told me that he had three people teaching with him and that they were just local girls, which meant that they had never had anything, probably, except a local high school education.

Think of the enormous population being brought up that way, and yet, off the record, the Governor of Georgia is still in favor of the one-room teacher, the one-room school.

Q:     Do you think it is necessary to go ahead with the Tennessee Valley experiment on a national scale to bring about the plans you have outlined?

THE PRESIDENT:  Not the same kind of governmental power development if the other fellows will do it.  They have every chance in the world to do it.

You take a simple example:  Eight miles over here to the eastward is a place called the Cove where they make the best corn liquor in Georgia.

Q:  The best is none too good.  (Laughter)

THE PRESIDENT:  Throw him out.  (Laughter)  Now, in the Cove the Georgia Power Company owns one of the most favorable power sites in the State.

--- [229] ---

They can turn out at that power site something between forty and fifty thousand kilowatts at a cost of less than half a cent.  They have owned it for fifteen years and they bought the whole power site for a total of fifteen thousand dollars.  In other words, the bought it as a farm lot. They have sought in other years to carry it on their books for a million dollars.  It is an undeveloped power site and I think the old Public Service Commission of this State allowed them to do it for a while.

Further up, where we are going to picnic, is a place where they can develop 30,000 KW and I think they paid fifteen or eighteen thousand dollars for all the land comprising that site.  They have a grand chance to make cheap electricity for the whole region and we are just giving them the opportunity as well as showing them how.

Q:  None of this, I take it, is on the record.

THE PRESIDENT:  No, it is just so that when you talk about it in the future you will know all about it.

Q:  Can't we write this as background?

THE PRESIDENT:  I think not.  You had better keep it.  If you write anything at all it will look like trying to explain something.

Q:  We don't have to write it that way.

MRS. ROOSEVELT:  You would have to go back to foreign trade.  When you go back to foreign trade you are faced with the question of restricting production, which is practically what it comes down to, and when you face that, you face the fact that we are coming down to being self-supporting, eventually.

THE PRESIDENT:  Not necessarily; what I said was that we are trying to prevent it by agreement.

Q:  That is in the off-the-record?

--- [230] ---

THE PRESIDENT:  There are certain things we cannot produce and certain things that Brazil cannot produce.

MR. TUGWELL:  There are certain things on which we will always have an exchange.

MRS. ROOSEVELT:  But, with all this before us, what are we basing that whole thing on is our old theory of scarcity, because if everybody had everything he wanted, we could utilize all we can produce.

THE PRESIDENT: Yes?

MRS. ROOSEVELT: Isn't it again a question of how we are going to accomplish it? Isn't it the medium of exchange that would make it possible?

THE PRESIDENT: All of this is based on the assumption that consumption remains at the same level. On the other hand, if you can give a bigger purchasing power to the country --

MRS. ROOSEVELT: (interposing) How are you going to do that?

THE PRESIDENT: It's a very simple explanation. If you take the farmer who lives under such conditions that he gets one hundred dollars cash in the year, and if you can put him in a place where he will find decent living conditions and give him small factories to work in part of the time, so that he will get five hundred dollars cash a year, he has four hundred dollars more buying power. If you improve his condition, you improve his purchasing power.

MRS. ROOSEVELT: Hasn't the medium of exchange got to be changed in some way, because there isn't enough money in the world at the present time?

THE PRESIDENT: What you mean by "money" is cash and credit. At the present time we have almost unlimited credit in this country.

MRS. ROOSEVELT: What I am getting at is a thing called the Douglas (?) credit scheme, which says that if you have faith enough in human integrity, you can have unlimited credit, that nobody is back of anything,

--- [231] ---

really, on its face value.

THE PRESIDENT: You have plenty of credit in this country at the present time.

Q: Why isn't it being used?

THE PRESIDENT: Lots of reasons. The first is that a lot of them don't want to put it up. They are afraid to put it out. The second is that people have been afraid to borrow. The third is that purchasing power has not gone up sufficiently as yet.

MRS. ROOSEVELT: Of course, you are teaching them a lesson that they should not put money into anything which actually does not purchase anything or represent a service. But I don't think anyone knows just how to get credit. I think that is part of what is holding people up.

THE PRESIDENT: It is educational. It takes years and years to do it. If I could take Bill Jones and say, "Look, Bill, you have a rotten farm. You ought to improve it. It will cost you two thousand dollars to improve that farm, but when you do you will be able to live off it, get everything you need, and make yourself a self-sustaining unit and you will get five hundred dollars a year in cash out of it." Bill Jones will say, "No, I don't want to do that." It will take two or three years to educate Bill Jones.

Q: Don't you think, Mr. President, that there has been a little more borrowing since election?

THE PRESIDENT: It depends on what paper you are reading.

Q: Can't we use this, what you said this afternoon about Tennessee Valley and before -- can't we use that?

THE PRESIDENT: Instead of using it right now, jot your notes down and let me give you a hint. The National Resources Board preliminary report is coming out, and it ties right in with it. Let me dig that up for you. Don't use it today -- use it for a Sunday story or a Monday story.

--- [232] ---

Q: These notes are worth a thousand dollars at least, minimum.

THE PRESIDENT: Wait until you learn more about it. You don't know enough about it to write a story.

Q: If Georgia goes into raising things for which her soil is suited, we might have an overproduction of things in the West?

THE PRESIDENT: Not necessarily, because your consumption goes right up.

MRS. ROOSEVELT: In other words, one of the biggest things is decentralization of industry into farm districts.

THE PRESIDENT: Let me give you an illustration. The Department of Agriculture has three diets, "A," "B" and "C." "A" is the diet that people ought to have. "B" is the diet that they can get along on all right. "C" is the insufficient diet. "C" is the diet they have. Now, check me on these figures. If we were on a "B" diet instead of a "C" diet, we would be using in this country thirty-five million more acres a year. That would be just on the improvement of the diet from "C" to "B." If the whole nation lived on an "A" diet we would have to put in sixty million more acres into agri-culture. That answers that.

Q: Mr. President, if you were going to write a story today for the morning papers, what would you write?

THE PRESIDENT: I would write that the power people were all down here and were discussing power policy and legislation, just a preliminary talk.

MR. STORM: Thank you, Mr. President.

(The Press Conference adjourned at 3:00 P.M.)

CONFIDENTIAL
Press Conference #161
Held in the President's Cottage on Georgia Warm Springs
 Foundation, Warm Springs, Georgia,
November 28, 1934, 11:00 A.M.


THE PRESIDENT:  I do not know -- I haven't the vaguest idea of any news this
    morning.  There are various people coming down before we leave next Wed-
    nesday.  You can carry the story that we are probably leaving here next
    Wednesday, a week from today.  That is the fifth, is it not?  What time, I
    do not know, but we will be in Washington Thursday.

Q:   Mr. President, has Secretary of State Hull referred to you an invitation
    of the League of Nations to collaborate with the Chaco Peace Movement?

THE PRESIDENT:  No, I  have not heard anything about that at all in over a
    month.

Q:   Mr. President, can you tell us just who is coming down besides Farley,
    Walker and Moffett and Harry Hopkins?

THE PRESIDENT:  Harry Hopkins, Henry Morgenthau.  We have not heard from Ickes,
    by the way.

MR. McINTYRE:  No, sir.

THE PRESIDENT:  And we have not heard from Tugwell.  He may come down again.

Q:   Will Hopkins and Morgenthau be here together?

THE PRESIDENT:  I do not know; I have no idea.  I think Hopkins is coming Satur-
    day.  In other words, there is no object of their all coming together.

Q:   Mr. President, there was a dispatch out of Dublin day before yesterday --
    there were reports there that one of the Drexel Biddles, I forget whether
    it was the older or the son, would be Minister to the Irish Free State.
    Was that a rumor?

--- [234] ---

THE PRESIDENT:  What do we call it?

Q:   An "S.C.S."

Q:   Speaking for Mr. Duer of the Post and myself, have you any comment to make
    on that petition received for a more equitable agreement on the fiscal re-
    lations (between the Federal Government and the District of Columbia)?

THE PRESIDENT:  I will give you a Washington story, to the two of you.  Since
    1913, when I first came to Washington, I have been tremendously interested
    in the relationship between the Federal financing of the District of Col-
    umbia and the local financing of the District of Columbia, in other words,
    their taxes, and so far the relationship has been more or less hit or miss.
    We all know why.  It depended a little bit on who the District Commission-
    ers were and it depended a little bit on how the Congressional committees
    on the District were constituted.  There has been no more or less regular
    policy.  I have been talking -- I have not done it yet but I have been

thinking the thing over the last three or four days.  I do not know who I
will ask but probably I will ask the tax experts of the Treasury Department
to make a study of the cities that are larger than the District of Columbia -- I do not know how many there are but call it X number of cities that
have a bigger population than the District of Columbia -- and the same
number of cities that are smaller than the District of Columbia -- in other
words, enough cities of each size so that Washington will be right in the
middle as far as population goes, and then try to get from all of those
cities, the bigger ones and the smaller ones, what they call an evaluated
tax rate, in other words, how much the citizens of those cities have to pay
on real estate which, of course, is the principal form of city revenue
everywhere.  Then we will also find out what they have to

--- [235] ---

pay in other forms of city revenue which, of course, fall mostly into the
license class.

Now, an evaluated tax rate, of course, ought to be explained to the average
citizen but it is a perfectly simple thing.  If one city assesses values
on its real estate at 50 per cent of its true value, that is to say, its
selling price, and has a tax rate of four dollars, the people are not paying any heavier taxes than the city which assesses its real estate at full
value and the tax rate is two dollars.  You see how simple that really is?

Now, an evaluated tax rate simply means that they find out what relationship the assessed value is to true value, and then the fix the actual tax
rate of that particular city on the basis of true value to find out what
it will be.  That is the evaluated tax rate.

Now, the reason for this study is that nobody in the District has ever
agreed on whether the citizens of the District, the owners of real property,
are paying a higher rate of taxation or a lower rate of taxation than other
cities of similar size -- that is to say, bigger or smaller.  After that
study is made, we will know pretty well where in this list of cities the
District stands.  If the tax rate on the District shows that the owners of
real estate in the District are paying below the average of other cities,
there isn't very much kick coming from the owners of real estate in the
District of Columbia.

If, on the other hand, the study shows that they are paying above the average of the other cities, it probably means one of two things:  either that
the District Government is not as efficient as it ought to be or that the
Federal Government is not paying its share of the necessary expenses for
maintaining the District.  We will have to await the outcome of those
figures.  If the District people are paying more

--- [236] ---

than the average, we then proceed to find out whether the Federal Government should pay more or whether we can save in the cost of Government by
putting in more efficient methods.

Now, that is the first time, so far as I know, that a definite study of
that kind will have been undertaken and it ought to do a great deal to prevent this everlasting, year in and year out, squabbling between the people
in the District of Columbia, the real estate people, the newspapers, et
cetera and so on, seeking additional funds from the Federal Government.

Q:   Why wouldn't it be helpful to extend that survey to all cities?  Not as a
     tax rate of $1.50.

THE PRESIDENT:  What is that based on, 100 per cent?

Q:   Sixty per cent.  Of course it is based on --

THE PRESIDENT:  (interposing)  There are various organizations that have those
     figures already.  You will find quite a number of organizations that have
     already worked out figures showing how much -- what the relative tax is on
     the larger cities.

Q:   Presumably those figures are gathered for selfish purposes?

THE PRESIDENT:  A great many are.

Q:   What if the survey were extended to all cities and sanctioned by the Govern-
     ment?

THE PRESIDENT:  The difficulty is this, that the Federal Government hans't any
     authority to offer them to any other government.  In other words, all
     cities are creatures of the State.  I will say this, off the record, that
     it would be a perfectly practical thing for the Governors' Conference to
     take up.

Q:   There are two more points:  Irrespective of what the tax rate is, large or
     small, could you tell us whether you think the Federal Government is paying
     fairly for what it receives in the District of Columbia?

--- [237] ---

THE PRESIDENT:  I do not know.  Nobody has any idea, newspapers to the contrary
     notwithstanding.  Nobody knows.  You will find an editorial a week in the
     Star and often in the Herald, et cetera, stating facts and nobody knows
     whether they are facts or not.  They say the Federal Government ought to
     take over this and ought to bear this and ought to bear the other thing.
     I do not know.

Q:   Do you think that Congress ought to put through a law putting it on a 60-40
     basis?

THE PRESIDENT:  I don't know whether it ought to be done or not.  It might be
     less and it might be more.  We just plain don't know.

Q:   You are going to look into it?·

THE PRESIDENT:  Yes.

Q:   Is there any possibility of a release of that power material you gave us
     the other day?

THE PRESIDENT:  I do not think so.

Q:   The Edison Electrical Institute, as you saw, of course, is going to test
     the constitutionality of the T.V.A.

THE PRESIDENT:  Yes, McCarter (Thomas N. McCarter of the Public Service Corpora-
     tion of New Jersey ) and so on.  Mac (Mr. McIntyre), we got a request from

McCarter for an appointment, did we not?

MR. McINTYRE: I do not think it was McCarter.

Q: Down here?

THE PRESIDENT: Yes, but I cannot see him down here. And we got a request from Floyd Carlisle and (Wendell) Wilkie.

MR. McINTYRE: I do not think we have had any from McCarter.

Q: Mr. President, could you tell us about your plans for tomorrow and Thanksgiving day?

THE PRESIDENT: I do not know. You had better check up with Carp (Arthur

--- [238] ---

Carpenter) on it. They are having something planned for -- a fellow is coming down to give an exhibition to all the patients.

In the afternoon we have a Trustees' meeting. Right after lunch we all go down to dedicate two new buildings, up to the present time referred to as Unit A and Unit B. They will be christened tomorrow.

Q: Are you going to christen them any other name besides Unit A and Unit B?

THE PRESIDENT: Oh, yes; we are going to give them names.

Q: Who will decide what they are going to be?

THE PRESIDENT: We have decided already. And then after that, off the record, a cocktail party and then dinner.

Q: How many turkeys have you?

THE PRESIDENT: I do not know. I think we have been given about five. I have eaten one already. I am getting another one too, a wild turkey.

MRS. ROOSEVELT: When are you going to use that large one?

THE PRESIDENT: That is the one to be used tomorrow night. You better not put that down because there are four or five going to be used tomorrow night.

Q: Mr. President, would you care to tell us about the dispute between Moffett and Ickes over housing? That all came out of Washington. We didn't get anything here at all.

THE PRESIDENT: Do you want me to talk, off the record?

Q: That will be fine.

THE PRESIDENT: This has to be off the record because again there is no use of injecting me into it, because somebody will say it is denial and some will say it is affirming and some will say it is settling a row.

Apparently, what happened was this: Last Thursday Ickes had his press conference, and he talked about one form of housing plan, having that in mind perfectly clearly himself.  But the fellows in the

--- [239] ---

conference did not get what he had in mind.  He was talking about slum elimination and rural housing, the thing we were talking about the other day,
which of course cannot be done by private capital.  He said, "Why, of
course, private capital won't go into this thing.  We cannot rely on private
capital for it."  It was perfectly true.  The Post story was darned good
and made it perfectly clear.  But one or two of the other stories gave the
distinct impression that what he was referring to was housing in general.
Whereupon Moffett, on reading this, went up through the roof, thinking that
Ickes is going into the kind of housing that he is doing.  Thereupon the
hell hounds of the Press got around Moffett in the afternoon and worked up
a controversial story which, of course, was in large part Moffett's fault
because he thought that Ickes had been referring to general housing, which
he hadn't at all.  Finally, on Saturday, they had a meeting and put the
onus of the whole thing on the Press and said that they were in complete
accord and that their two programs did not conflict.

Now, the real answer is a perfectly simple one.  Obviously the two things
do not conflict.  We have four and three-quarter million people on relief.
Probably half of them are living under very terrible conditions.  There are
probably another four and three-quarter million people who are not on the
relief rolls.  Now, that just does not mean people, that means that the
four and three-quarter million people on the relief rolls represent eighteen million people on relief.

Taking the two groups living under undesirable conditions, it means that
there are nearly forty million people who are of such low earning capacity
that they cannot get credit.  They cannot get credit and private capital
won't give them credit.  I am not saying improperly, because I think very
properly.  You take the ordinary person, if he hasn't

--- [240] ---

a job or any capacity, private capital isn't going in and lending him money
to build a house.  Obviously not.  Now, what are we going to do?  Are we
going to leave him where he is just because he hasn't security to offer for
a private loan?

If he falls into the higher class, he comes to Moffett.  Now the simplest
illustration is this:  That of all the loans made through this Housing
Administration today, the average earning capacity of the people getting
loans is $2,750 a year.  Now that figure of $2,750 a year is nearly three
times the average family income in the United States.  Therefore the Housing
Administration is taking care of people with sufficient earning capacity to
obtain a private loan and it is doing a grand job.  It is taking care of
what might be called the very large number of people, again millions of
people, who fall into the category of having an income of somewhere, let
us say, between $1,500 and $3,500 a year.  Those people have found it difficult to go to the bank and get a loan at a low rate of interest because
the bank was not certain of things.  Therefore Moffett's organization goes
to the bank and says, "If you put this thing through, it is your responsibility, but you will get Government insurance up to a certain point."

Now, that is going well for certain people, that group, (earning between
$1,500 and $3,500 a year) but it was never intended for and nobody had any

thought that the Housing Administration could persuade banks to lend people
with incomes of $750 a year. There was not enough security. Nor could
they do it for people on relief who haven't any income except what they are
getting from a Government job or through relief.

That raised the question, "Are we going to call ourselves licked?" Now, I
will give you the best illustration: It raises other complica-

--- [241] ---

tions. Joe Day in New York is a very old friend of mine, and one of the
best real estate men in the City of New York. He and I have been carrying
on a very interesting correspondence. He started off by telling me that it
was terrible for the Federal Government to go into slum clearance. I said,
"Joe, this is all very well, but you have not eliminated the slums in
New York." He wrote back, "Give us a chance, I think we can." I said,
"At what cost per room per month?" He said, "You have me there, we
cannot do it for less than $12 per room per month." I said, "How many
families are in the City of New York that cannot afford to pay that?" He
came back and said, "We hope that with the return of prosperity there will
be more." I said, "That isn't any answer to my question."

Now, the very simple fact is that in the City of New York there are probably a million people -- there are probably about two hundred thousand families alone -- that is probably a rough guess -- whose earning capacity
brings them under the thousand dollars a year class. They probably ought
not to pay, out of that thousand dollars or less, more, let us say, than a
hundred and fifty, a hundred and forty or a hundred and fifty dollars a
year for their rent. They cannot afford it because they have to eat and
clothe themselves.

Now, what does that mean if the cheapest rooms in the City of New York rent
for $12 a room? That means that the whole family can afford to live only
in one of those $12 rooms and no other room. They have to cook, to eat, and
everything else in one room. If, on the other hand, you can get them rooms
for $6 a month, the family can use two rooms.

What is the result? They are living today under most terrible conditions,
in old tenement flats, on the East Side, also on the West

--- [242] ---

Side, in the middle West Side and the middle East Side. We all know the
conditions they live under. They are able to get, on the average, perhaps
two rooms at $5 or $6 a room. There is no sanitation, no light, no nothing.
They are pretty terrible living conditions.

Now, Joe says, "We are licked. Private capital could not afford to build
for $5 or $6 a room. That is not enough." That is his answer, "We are
licked."

Q: Is he convinced?

THE PRESIDENT: Yes, but he says that the Government ought not to go in.

Q: Why?

THE PRESIDENT: He says it is not the prerogative of the Government. It is un-

constitutional. Like T.V.A. It is illegal. He says the thing, over a
period of years, will work itself out some way. Then he also says, "If you
go in and tear down these tenements, you are going to cut real estate
values very much." Well, that is true. The value of tenements in the
City of New York, including the City assessed valuations, is much too high.
They are being held at those high prices with the hope of the owners that
some Fairy Godmother is going to come along and take it off their hands at
this price.

And that is the great difficulty of the Government going in to remove slum
conditions in the big cities, the fictitious cost we would have to pay for
that land. Yet I suppose there are tens of thousands of parcels of land
in the City of New York which are only bringing in on the assessed value, which is higher than what they can sell them for, bringing a yield of
1½ or 2%. But there is always the hope on the part of the owner that
something is going to happen.

Q:    If the Government built these homes, who would own them?

THE PRESIDENT:   In the case of a tenant there are practically only two methods.

--- [243] ---

One is tenant ownership, which has been used in a great many buildings in
the City of New York, such as the Bronx buildings that the labor people put
up. The tenant, by making extra payments over and above the rent, eventually, in twelve or fifteen years, owns his apartment. That is tenant
ownership.

The other method, especially in those places where you have a floating
population that moves out and in a great deal, you make it a straight
Government proposition which, after the Government has been paid back,
could probably be sold to private people. In other words, it does not mean
that the Government would stay in forever.

Of course Joe Day has this other thought, and in another letter he talked
about the terrible socialism and what had been done in Germany and England
and Vienna in cleaning up slums. He said it was just straight socialism
and of course we couldn't do anything like that. But if you had knowledge
of what happened in Germany and England and Vienna, you would know that
"socialism" has probably done more to prevent Communism and rioting and
revolution than anything else in the last four or five years. Vienna has
practically cleaned out her slums and has done a grand job.

Then, of course, there are the other phases such as rural housing. We
talked about that the other day and you understand the whole objective of
it. There, again, we have got to put up houses that private capital cannot
put up. We have to reach an entirely different group in the community. It
is a secret at the present time, but there are two or three fairly good-
sized things we are working on, plans for a new type of house. Don't use
this, because they are not ready -- it would not be fair to them. It would
be a complete, fabricated house, with pre-fabricated steel as an essential
part of the construction.

--- [244] ---

The house would have all of the latest developments in it. It would have
heating and air-cooling system for the summer time. It would have all the

electrical equipment you could possibly put into a house and they believe
that then can sell a house of that kind for $3,800. Now, that is perfectly
magnificent. It is an important step ahead. I think it is a five-room
house.

Now, who can buy a $3,800 house? None of the people on relief. It is too
much. It will be taking too much of a chance for private capital to take
a fellow off the relief rolls and put him into that house. Now, there are
what I call the "marginal" people who are just out on the line, people who
have a job, a little bit of a job, making $20 a week as a family. Private
capital cannot afford to put them into a $3,800 house. They are too close
to the line. It is not a good risk. So, what we are trying to do is to
put up houses where these people can go in and, because of the much lower
monthly payments, there is a chance of getting the money back, but private
capital cannot do it. It is a field into which Government alone can go,
and Government only can do it.

Government cannot say, "We are licked." Other countries have done it and
have put up perfectly grand houses at $1500 and $1600. We can come pretty
close to doing it here and it does not interfere in any way with the outlet for private capital, not one bit, because they would not go into that
field at all.

Q: How much money does it cost the Government?

THE PRESIDENT: It depends on the program. In other words, when it comes down
to that, you can take your program and run it from $100 to a hundred bil-
lion. I mean, that becomes a matter of financing rather than a matter of
policy.

Q: Is this on the record?

--- [245] ---

THE PRESIDENT: No, this is all off the record.

Q: On this housing program we were just talking about, has that been decided
on at all?

THE PRESIDENT: In figures, no. In policy, yes.

Q: Could we use that fact?

THE PRESIDENT: Depends on what you use with it. In other words, if I were
writing the story today I think it would be perfectly all right to say
this, without putting it on me: It has been made increasingly clear by
people coming to Warm Springs to see the President (laughter), meaning the
Press (laughter), that the Government recognizes as a matter of policy its
obligation to those people in the United States whose standards of living
are so low that something has to be done about it, but whose pocketbooks
are so small that private capital cannot properly lend them money. And if
somebody asks the question, "Is Government going to consider itself licked
in its effort to take care of people who cannot otherwise be taken care
of?", the answer is, obviously, "No!" And further, as a matter of policy,
the Government is going to continue every reasonable effort -- that answers
Stevie's question, and I cannot give you any figures -- continue every
reasonable effort to give the lowest income group in the United State a
chance to live under better conditions, for the very simple reason that if

Government does not do it, nobody else will or can.

Now, of course, a Government program of that kind is not all one-sided. My "missus" suggests a very excellent addition to it, that it means a very definite lift to the heavy industries not only during the construction period but also means that after that period is over there will be an additional consumers' demand, because, once people get a better

--- [246] ---

standard of living, they are going to insist on maintaining it.

In other words, the policy story is all right, as long as you don't try to get too factual about it, because I haven't any more idea than you have as to the dollars and cents or whether it will be done or anything of that kind.  It is a philosophical policy story.

Q:    Mr. President, in this connection, stories have been printed that the Government's guaranty of 20% of any losses be extended to other fields so that private banks and private financial agencies could do this financing which they don't see how they can do today.  In other words, they could lend money to people in the lower income brackets.

THE PRESIDENT:  There you have to come down to practical cases.  This has to be off the record, too.  Probably private capital, in most cases, is not efficiently organized to carry through a very large operation.  Let us take a very simple example:  Suppose we were to start here in Georgia a new community with decent homesteads for people on relief -- decent homes for people on relief.  Nobody thinks much about it.  Should the community consist of a thousand people, in other words, two hundred families, or five thousand people, a thousand families, or should it consist of ten thousand people.  That immediately brings up a question that probably only the Government can plan for.  We would try several types of communities of that kind.

Incidentally, and you will have to leave this off the record too, I had an awfully interesting talk with Edsel Ford about it because old man Ford -- Edsel brought me quite a number of photographs -- as you know, went into the valleys above Detroit and took little villages and put in very small manufacturing plants, plants that ran anywhere from twenty or thirty people up to a couple of hundred people.  Well, a plant of a couple of hundred people probably supplies a community of

--- [247] ---

2500 to 3000 people because a lot of people have to run the grocery stores and the post offices and so forth and so on.  He pointed out that it was perfectly true that in the case of Ford doing it, it means a pretty good assurance that the plant will run because it is a great, huge corporation and you can assure a good income to the workers in the community.  Actually, he showed that the smaller plants of the companies are paying $1350 annual income to the employees in that community, which is pretty good and away above the average.

If you can get a factory to come in, a small factory of a big concern that has a fairly steady demand for its products, that is all right, but there is a limit.  They are all working on it, General Electric, Westinghouse, Steel, et cetera.  Decentralization, if you can get enough, will probably be all right, but you probably cannot get enough.

Then you come down to the next question, "What can you use as a substitute for a branch factory of a big corporation?" Probably not very much except by trying to make the community itself self-supporting. That means a fairly good-sized community, big enough to make its own dresses, clothes, shoes, shirts, besides its own food supply. If a community of that kind can be made somewhere around 80% self-sufficient, it probably can be made a go of. But the point is that private capital, obviously, won't go into that. Some of the big companies with fairly large capital will, but, as you know, the big corporations -- the corporations employing, say, over a hundred men -- they only employ 40% of the industrial workers of this country. 60% of the workers are employed by companies employing less than a hundred men. They are not big enough to go into this sort of thing. Government has to help them to do it.

--- [248] --

I think that is about the only answer you can give on that, that again private capital is not in as favorable a position to do it as Government would be, and that private capital won't do it because there is too much risk.

Q: That would make this a good story, Mr. President.

THE PRESIDENT: They never have before.

Q: Are you willing to insure up to that amount?

THE PRESIDENT: We cannot insure. Suppose we did. Suppose we said to the private capital, "You go ahead and do it." I don't know. I don't suppose, in the first place, that private capital would do it. They haven't been organized and don't know enough about it. In the second place, they would consider that 20% was too little insurance. I just plain think they would not come in if we extended it.

MR. McINTYRE: In connection with what you said about housing policy, would you have any objections to the use of that part in which you pointed out that there is no conflict between the two?

THE PRESIDENT: That is perfectly all right to us. There was absolutely no conflict. The private dollar won't go into the Government housing that we are going ahead on. If private dollars show any desire to come in, we will be willing to give them every opportunity to do so.

Q: I cannot say we haven't very much; you did pretty good.

THE PRESIDENT: You got a real Washington story.

Q: Yes. It is getting kind of late. Looks like you are trying to take me out of it. (Laughter)

Q: In the papers this morning there is a story that the Nye Committee is going to consider the complaints of investigators that Government officers are holding up the investigation into munitions.

THE PRESIDENT: I do not know; I have not heard anything about it because

--- [249] ---

all the Federal Government officers are very much willing to give them everything we have.

Q:   You stated that at Hyde Park.

THE PRESIDENT:   The last time I saw Gerald Nye (Senator Nye) he told me he was delighted with all the cooperation he was getting.  Did he say where that is?

Q:   No, he did not.

Q:   He is calling a meeting on Monday.

Q:   Does your Order still stand?

THE PRESIDENT:   Yes, on everything that is not a military secret.

Q:   Did you hear about the report on pine wood resources?  The Hearst papers are very much interested and New York is very much interested (showing the President a clipping).

THE PRESIDENT:   You know, I have been tremendously interested in this right along.  Herty (Dr. Herty) came down here six years ago and did that.

Q:   I knew you had in general.

THE PRESIDENT:   Why don't you get a story out of George Foster Peabody while he is here?

Q:   I would like comment from you.

THE PRESIDENT:   The only comment I have is that I have been interested in it for five or six years and have been following the progress they are making with the belief that there are real possibilities for many, many new uses to which the wood resources, the forestry resources of the South could be put. They have only scratched the surface on that.

Q:   This is a report merely on the resources and not on the possibilities.

THE PRESIDENT:   The resources can be increased too.

CONFIDENTIAL
Press Conference #161-A
In front of the Newspapermen's Cottage on
 Georgia Warm Springs Foundation, Warm Springs, Georgia
November 30, 1934, 3:00 P.M.


Q:     Mr. President, will you give us a slant on what your plans are over the
       weekend, who you are going to see and what you are going to discuss with
       them?

THE PRESIDENT:   I haven't the foggiest idea when they are coming down.

MR. McINTYRE:   Why don't you ask him something else?  That stuff is all avail-
       able.

THE PRESIDENT:   I don't know what is available and there isn't any conference,
       just ordinary talk.  There is no subject.  It is tough luck for you, but
       there isn't any subject.

Q:     Any news in your talk today with Moffett?

THE PRESIDENT:   No; we talked about his work.

Q:     I have a nice old question resurrected.  We have got from London and Wash-
       ington the rumor that there has been a note suggesting war debt settlement.

THE PRESIDENT:   "S.C.S."

       I really, honestly, do not believe there is the slightest bit of news.  I
       do not believe I could write a story myself.

Q:     We have got to.

Q:     Any plans for consolidating the housing industry?

THE PRESIDENT:   Not that I know of.

Q:     This idea you were telling us about the other day -- the Federal housing
       program for low income people?

THE PRESIDENT:   No; still very much in the study period.

Q:     Mr. President, is there anything to say about the relief plans for the

                              --- [251] ---

winter?

THE PRESIDENT:   Still in the study period -- third of January.  You will get a
       story on the third of January.  Anything you write before that will be
       wrong.  (Laughter)

Q:     We took copious notes of our long Press Conference, the one we had the
       other afternoon and it would make a swell story if we could release them
       sometime.

THE PRESIDENT:   I do not know how we can.  Which one do you mean, the housing or the T.V.A.?

Q:   Couldn't we write it?

THE PRESIDENT:   No, I will tell you why:  You will cramp my style.  I am think-
     ing, again off the record, I am thinking of using that when I go on the
     air in December.  I think it is a good thing to use.

Q:   There will be gnashing of teeth.

THE PRESIDENT:   I think it will make an awfully good thing to use.  Obviously,
     I have to talk about agriculture.  In other words, you do know this, that
     I am going to talk on some of the things I did not mention in the last
     one.  I did not talk on agriculture and T.V.A. and probably other things.
     You all know I am going to touch on some of the things I did not mention
     in September.

Q:   Have you decided just what time you will speak -- what day?

THE PRESIDENT:   No, I have no idea at all.

Q:   Are you having a good time down here?

THE PRESIDENT:   That is a silly question.  I am going to lunch with Cason
     Callaway on Sunday.  No reason why you should not know that.

Q:   Over in La Grange?

THE PRESIDENT:   It isn't his place, it is on top of the mountain.

     I do not think there is another blessed thing.

--- [252] ---

Q:   Any plans for today?

THE PRESIDENT:   No, I am going up to the farm, and I will talk about whether I
     want to sell my cows now or later on.

Q:   For sale?  Your cows?

THE PRESIDENT:   Forty for sale.  These are beef cattle.

Q:   Is your superintendent having any luck with his breeding experiments?  I
     talked with him last year.

THE PRESIDENT:   Getting along very well and of course in our own cattle we are
     getting much improved stock.

Q:   Did you get any drought cattle at all?

THE PRESIDENT:   No; I have practically all I can feed.  I have to get rid of
     forty, if I can.  I had fifty calves this year but, of course, the prices
     are terrible, awful.

Q:   About two cents?

THE PRESIDENT:   Two cents; two and a half cents.

Q:   Are you going to take that up with the Administration?  (Laughter)  The way the boys are eating at our cottage, you might send one down.

THE PRESIDENT:  I will do that; it would be very good business.  I will send down a young, tender, fat heifer.

Q:   A few bottles too.  (Laughter)

Q:   No, we are going on a program of more eating and less of that.

THE PRESIDENT:  Well, it was a good party last night.

Q:   Fine.

Q:   Mr. President, are you going out to the farm from here?

THE PRESIDENT:  No, I have to go back to the house.

Q:   About what time will you be going out?

THE PRESIDENT:  About half past four.

Q:   Would you mind if we go out?

--- [253] ---

THE PRESIDENT:  No, you had better not because the most of the time I am going to be talking to the farmer.

Q:   About that tax investigation you are going to make, will you talk to the Census Bureau?  They have already made that investigation.

THE PRESIDENT:  I am glad to know that, Russ (Mr. Young).  I did not know that they had done that.

Q:   Thank you, Mr. President.

Press Conference #162
At the Newspapermen's Cottage on Georgia Warm Springs
 Foundation, Warm Springs, Georgia
December 4, 1934, 3:00 P.M.

(The President had come down to visit the newspapermen in their
cottage.  No notice had been given to the office, consequently
the first few minutes of the Press Conference were not recorded.
It is understood that the President stated to the Press that
the Bankhead Bill, provided Congress voted for it, would be retained and that he would recommend to the Congress, at its next
session, the exemption from the act of those farmers making two
bales of cotton or less.)

THE PRESIDENT:  -- And in spite of $5\frac{1}{2}$ cent cotton, our exports were diminishing.
This is the answer to Anderson Clayton, only don't say that I said it.
Yet, in spite of that surplus of cotton and that price, foreign production
of cotton in India, Brazil and other places was increasing.  Therefore,
cheap cotton not only means starvation for the cotton grower but it does
not in any way guarantee increased exports or the stopping of a foreign
growth of cotton.  I think that is the thing that ought to be emphasized
and emphasized and emphasized.

Now, just as long as we have $13\frac{1}{4}$ million bales' carryover, obviously the
price wasn't going to go up.  In 1933, when we used the plow-under method,
instead of an even greater crop than 1932, which we would have had, we cut
the carryover to 11 3/4 million bales.  Rex, check me if I am telling any
awful lies here.

MR. TUGWELL:  I probably would not know it, Mr. President.

THE PRESIDENT:  In 1934, when we used acreage restrictions and the Bankhead Tax
Bill, we reduced it still further to $10\frac{1}{2}$ million bales -- that is this
year.

Q:  Ten and a half million bales?

THE PRESIDENT:  Ten and a half million.  That was before this crop came in.
That was before the crop.  We hope that by August, 1935, by continuing

--- [255] ---

the present reduction methods -- not "reduction," call it restriction
methods -- that the carryover will be only 8 3/4 million bales.

All of which means that if we have patience and keep on doing like we are
doing, we will get back to about a 4-million bale surplus.

Q:  When, Mr. President?

THE PRESIDENT:  In a couple of years after 1935.  In other words, about three
more crops.

Q:  Do you consider that a normal surplus?

THE PRESIDENT: That should be a normal surplus unless -- I am glad you asked the question -- unless one of two things should happen. One would be in the event that foreign demands should be greater by reason of their giving up their synthetic processes, which does not look likely. I told you about the wood pulp process they started in Italy and the one they have in Germany. The other is if increased buying power in this country creates a greater demand. We hope that the latter is not only possible by probable.

In other words, it is the same old story, that if every man in this country should wear two shirts a week, it will do an enormous amount to increase cotton consumption. Unfortunately, there are too many men in this country who cannot afford to wear two shirts a week. I am not looking at you, Fred (Mr. Storm). (Laughter)

Q: (Mr. Storm) I was just thinking of having my laundry sent out. With all these barbed-wire clotheslines around here, we will need ten shirts a week.

Q: Did you say clotheslines or fences? (Laughter)

Q: Mr. President, do you favor retention of the Bankhead excise?

THE PRESIDENT: I think undoubtedly it is far and away the best thing for us to do, to continue with the plan of controlled production in order

--- [256] ---

to reduce the surplus which is still too much, too large, until it gets to a controllable size. There you have the picture of that three years' constant decline in the surplus. Suppose we took off the restriction, there are two things which would happen. People would plant everything, including the land under the house, and your surplus would go right up again. It would come right straight back and you would get infinitely lower prices for the cotton. The second thing which would happen if we do not go on with this control, the money which the Government has advanced on a total of about nine million bales, if the price of cotton goes down, we are going to have the same terrific loss to the Government that happened in the case of the Farm Board of the previous Administration. The Government is going to be left with nine million bales on its hands.

MR. McINTYRE: Is this off the record?

THE PRESIDENT: This is not for quotation, it is background. You saw what happened with the old Farm Board. The Government undertook to buy surplus and buy surplus and buy surplus so that the surplus of both wheat and cotton just came into the hands of the Government on a declining price-scale so that the Government was left with in and had to take a tremendous loss. The only thing to do is to keep the price up and if the price is kept up the Government will be able to get back what it gave.

Q: Under the other, the farmer would also lose?

THE PRESIDENT: Oh, yes.

Q: On the exemption, would that exemption be the usual certificate they give now?

THE PRESIDENT:  No, I don't know.

Q:  I have heard that the farmers when they have any excess certificates left,

--- [257] ---

just pass them along to someone else.

THE PRESIDENT:  Yes, the Administration will have to work that out.

Q:  Do you know how much production is involved in the one and two bales?

THE PRESIDENT:  Roughly 700,000 bales of which probably the majority are already in on the plan.  At a very rough guess it probably means only a deduction of between 200,000 and 300,000 bales, if that.  It is a drop in the bucket.

Q:  Do you know how many farmers will be affected by that?

THE PRESIDENT:  Roughly, 600,000.

Q:  One other question that shows a great deal of ignorance but I will be darned if I can recall the message.  You spoke of a parity price last year of about 13 cents and parity today is about 15½ cents.  How does that come about?

THE PRESIDENT:  Through the increase of outside things.  The parity of farmers' prices of the things he sells to the things he buys.  Take the relation-ship of 1900 and this year.  Now of course, if the other things go up, his have to go up too but his are going up faster than what he has to pay for the things he buys.  Is that correct, Rex?

MR. TUGWELL:  Yes, I think the parity is 15 cents or a little over.

THE PRESIDENT:  Yes, 15½ and I think it was about 13.

Q:  If you do reduce the surplus to 4 million bales on the present program, does that mean a corresponding increase in price?

THE PRESIDENT:  I am glad you mentioned that, Stevie (Mr. Stephenson).  What we are seeking is not 20-cent cotton or 25-cent cotton.  The objective is a parity price.  Now, we have gone from 5½-cent cotton to 12½-cent cotton and we hope we can get it higher but nobody has an idea and no sensible person in the south thinks we ought to have immediately 20 or 25 cent cotton.

--- [258] ---

If we can maintain something pretty close to parity for three or four years more all though the cotton-raising area, and all through this country, it is going to do more for the south than has been done at any time before in our lifetime.

Q:  This broad principle applies also to the wheat growers and others who are under crop restriction?

THE PRESIDENT: Yes.

Q:  Is there any thought of extending the Bankhead process to any other commod-ities?

THE PRESIDENT:  No.

Q:  What is this we hear that you did to General Farley down there in the pool today?

THE PRESIDENT:  Did you see the bumps on his head?  Those are not bumps of wisdom.  (Laughter)  Stevie, who was it named the mules?

Q:  We names them here, one "Tug" and the other "Hop."  (Laughter)

THE PRESIDENT:  Well, I wish we were not going away.

Q:  We wish the same.

Q:  The thing we are look forward to now is Miami.

THE PRESIDENT:  Yes.

Q:  What are the prospects of Florida this year?

THE PRESIDENT:  I don't know; it depends on the Congress.  You know what happened last year when I went away.

Q:  Any other news?

THE PRESIDENT:  I have been going around with Carp (Arthur Carpenter) and Duncan Leverett and a man we have hired to clean blackjack out of the woods and showing them how to do it.

Q:  What is that?

THE PRESIDENT:  That is jack oak.  We had a demonstration on about an acre

--- [259] ---

and I showed them what trees to take out and what to leave in.

MR. McINTYRE:  Senator (Mr. Young), don't you think you ought to tip the President off on this C.C.C. Camp?

THE PRESIDENT:  When do we get down there?

MR. McINTYRE:  You ought to get down there tomorrow before we leave.  The Senator made a speech there yesterday.

THE PRESIDENT:  Did he, really?

MR. McINTYRE:  He made a great hit with them.  He prayed for a continuation of this program indefinitely.  You get him to tell you about it.  It was No. 17-A.

THE PRESIDENT:  What was that?

Q:  (Mr. Young)  Character building.

Q:  He said, "We are aiming to build men all through, not only through this depression but all through, to carry the country forward."

Q:   The Senator addressed the Manchester Kiwanis Club about ten days ago.

THE PRESIDENT:  We heard about it.

The only lucky thing is that old man Sherman came through about thirty miles north of here -- if he had come through this section, he would never have come through alive.

Q:   Is this blackjack oak bad oak?

THE PRESIDENT:  Yes, bad oak.  It is scrub oak.

Q:   It keeps the others from growing?

THE PRESIDENT:  Yes.

Q:   Is there anything to say about relief or the budget?

THE PRESIDENT:  January third.

Q:   Any guess will be a wrong guess?  (Laughter)

THE PRESIDENT:  I think that is true.  We are no further ahead than we were two days ago and that is not very far.

--- [260] ---

Q:   Any engagements when you get back Thursday?

THE PRESIDENT:  I do not think so.  I probably will be exploring the new office.

Q:   We have a couple of couches in ours and I understand it is going to help us a lot.

THE PRESIDENT?  They are going to make you pay for your new telephones?

Q:   We always had ours anyhow.

Q:   We had a meeting of the Board of Governors today and formally replied.

THE PRESIDENT:  Don't you think you ought to let them phone back to Warm Springs on us?

MR. McINTYRE:  We only have $25,000 for entertainment.

Q:   I am for it and so are several others.

THE PRESIDENT:  Last year Mac telephoned daily down to Warm Springs for about two weeks.

MR. McINTYRE:  There were a lot of things we did not clean up when we left here.

THE PRESIDENT:  It only lasted two weeks; he forgot at the end of that time.

Q:   They checked up on it when he got back and he had a lot of explaining to do.

(The President's attention was called to the fact that
the Prenosil family was present.)

THE PRESIDENT: Yes, I know both of them. Billy wishes to get that cotton
story to the financial paper and the A.P. in New York. It is very important.

Q: (Mr. Stephenson) You had better come over and check on us, Bill.

Q: Is there any chance of giving the corn planters the same break you are
giving the cotton planters?

THE PRESIDENT: Did you see the price of corn? Has the corn-hog program

--- [261] ---

been announced?

MR. TUGWELL: It has been announced.

Q: Are you taking up with Tugwell the price of cattle?

THE PRESIDENT: I have.

Q: What did he report?

THE PRESIDENT: Dr. Hoke knows more about cattle down here than either one of
us. He says we will have to cut out raising cattle on the top of a mountain or else plant trees. I can't get any decent pasturage up there.

MR. TUGWELL: I say cows grazing on fruit land. It was the first time in my
life.

Q: Do you have to buy feed?

THE PRESIDENT: I have enough feed to carry them over but I haven't enough
fattening stuff. They can live up there but I cannot fatten them and as
long as I do not, I cannot get a decent price.

MR. TUGWELL: Can't you let them get their growth up there and then bring them
down and fatten them?

THR PRESIDENT: Yes; I have a lot of land on the other side, I have about 400
acres, but I will have to revamp the farm somehow.

Q: It is bad enough for Tug and Hop as it is. (Laughter)

MR. TUGWELL: Yes, they live on very little.

THE PRESIDENT: They come high in the beginning but after that they do not cost
much.

Q: That is true too.

Q: Speaking of the mules, are they fractious?

THE PRESIDENT: Their names sound fractious, don't they?

MR. McINTYRE:  They are broken as a team.

THE PRESIDENT:  They are a good-looking pair of mules, though.  (Laughter)

Q:  Have you decided on your radio speech that you talked about just before

--- [262] ---

you left Washington?

THE PRESIDENT:  No, I have no idea.  Somewhere between the tenth and the twentieth.

Q:  Are you making a speech at the Camp (C.C.C. Camp) tomorrow morning?

THE PRESIDENT:  I do not believe so.

MR. McINTYRE:  When is the best time to go?

THE PRESIDENT:  Arrange it for about quarter of eleven, just before I go to the
pool.

Q:  Thank you, Mr. President.

Press Conference #163
Executive Offices of the White House
December 7, 1934, 4:00 P.M.


THE PRESIDENT: How do you like it? (Referring to the new White House offices.)

Q: One thing missing; we haven't any flowers in our room.

MR. McINTYRE: Nor a public phone either.

THE PRESIDENT: I told them that in Warm Springs. This (referring to the President's office) is going to look all right as soon as we get pictures hung.

Q: It does not look much larger?

THE PRESIDENT: It is two feet wider and two feet longer. Isn't that nice up there, that ceiling?

Q: I would like to get one of those (referring to the seal) myself.

THE PRESIDENT: Did you find everything all well when you got back?

Q: (Mr. Young) Yes, sir.

THE PRESIDENT: Is there room in the back? Can you see?

Q: There must be 300 here.

MR. DONALDSON: All in.

THE PRESIDENT: It does not look to me as though there is as much room as there used to be. I was just saying to Senator Young that this room is two feet longer and two feet wider than the old room but it does not seem to be so. Every inch is taken. Next time we build a new one we will add a few feet.

I do not think there is any news at all. I have been trying to orient myself since we got back and I don't believe there is any news you have not got.

Q: Have you set the date for your radio talk yet?

--- [264] --

THE PRESIDENT: I have not thought of it. It is sometime between now and Christmas.

Q: Do you share Ambassador Bingham's views that a great opportunity exists at the present time for Anglo-American cooperation?

THE PRESIDENT: Where did you get that?

Q: He expressed that in his speech in London last week.

THE PRESIDENT: I will have to get a copy of it. (Laughter)

Q: One of the Press Associations today is carrying a story to the effect that

you will ask for $4,000,000,000 next year as a general fund in which
everything will appear for your various emergency agencies.

THE PRESIDENT: Down at Warm Springs, Russell (Mr. Young) and I invented a
ditty, the first verse of which goes like this: "There will be an announcement on that on January third." And the second verse goes like this --
we are very good at it together -- "If you guess now, the chances are ten
to one you will be wrong."

Q: That still holds?

THE PRESIDENT: That still holds. And then we invented another phrase down
there -- you might just as well become familiar with it -- "S.C.S." and I
am going to use that a great deal. It means "Sewing Circle Story."
Next!

Q: Can you tell us anything of your talk with Senator La Follette and Governor
La Follette today?

THE PRESIDENT: Nothing in particular. We talked about a lot of things, including the general problem of relief and public works and the general problem
of everything that goes with it. We were just surveying it from every
angle.

Q: I have a new question to ask. There has been pending in the Senate since
1931 a treaty for the preservation of the beauty of Niagara Falls and

--- [265] ---

within the last year there have been two big slides up there and, really,
the people on the Niagara frontier are concerned about it. Canada did
ratify the treaty but our Government never did, the Foreign Relations
Committee turning it down. I am wondering if anybody did anything about
it?

THE PRESIDENT: I will have to check on that; I did not know there was a treaty.

Q: The operating companies -- there was a provision that the power companies
would get 10 per cent more water.

THE PRESIDENT: I remember that when I was Governor. Didn't I write a letter
opposing it?

Q: I do not know.

THE PRESIDENT: I think I did on the ground that if there was any more water to
be taken, the power companies should pay for it. As I remember it, they
were going to get the additional water for nothing and I think, as Governor
of the State of New York, I wrote a letter of opposition to it on that
ground.

Q: That would be sound opposition but I wondered, on the larger thing, whether
there was anything done on the preservation?

THE PRESIDENT: I think something should be done. It is a brand new thought.
I think I will take it up. It is a grand question. As I understand it
from geologists, the question is whether you can eat your cake and have
it -- in other words, whether you can have enough water go over the Falls

and, at the same time, prevent the crest of the Falls receding year by year. They have been doing it at the rate of several thousand years and, at the present rate, they will be getting back to Lake Erie well after we are dead. It is a question. And another suggestion that was made was that the Falls should be turned on every so

--- [266] ---

often for the benefit of sightseers and then turned off again. But I am glad you told me about it. I will take that up and find out what it is.

Q: Can you tell us for what purpose you are sending Ambassador Gibson to Europe?

THE PRESIDENT: Sending whom?

Q: Hugh Gibson.

THE PRESIDENT: I am not sending him to Europe. I did not know he was going until he told me he had a small boy over there who was sick. He is over in the mountains and Hugh is going over.

Q: I was just wondering whether you had asked him to go over?

THE PRESIDENT: No, he is going over to see his boy; nothing official in it.

Q: Can you tell us whether General MacArthur will be Chief of Staff after the fifteenth?

THE PRESIDENT: I cannot.

Q: Can we induce you to comment on the naval negotiations?

THE PRESIDENT: No. I think that as things stand you know about as much as I do. You read Norman Davis' speech and Cordell Hull talked to you off the record on it yesterday. I do not think there is any more can be said on it now.

Q: Any background on the situation in the Balkans?

THE PRESIDENT: Again, off the record, I did not know anything until I read the first edition of the Star. I talked to the Secretary of State and he has been telegraphing to various people of ours in the embassies and legations. We have not heard a word yet. Maybe the wires are down.

Q: Have you received any report on the automobile industry?

THE PRESIDENT: No.

Q: Mr. President, did your statement at Warm Springs constitute a further

--- [267] ---

endorsement of the Bankhead Act?

THE PRESIDENT: I did not say it constituted an endorsement of the Bankhead Act. What I did do was to give them some figures that they could use down there -- the boys down there -- with the statement that if the Bankhead

Act continued and was extended, I would recommend to the Congress a provision to take care of the small crop grower. If I were writing the story I would say that it was not an endorsement but **does** show the Administration is in favor of extending the Bankhead Act. In other words, it is not an official endorsement or anything else, but we are in favor of it because we do not know any better method of handling the situation.

Of course, that statement down there was made after a long telephone call -- this is background -- with the Secretary of Agriculture and we had a complete and absolute meeting of the minds on it. Therefore, do not write a story that there was dissension between the Secretary of Agriculture and the President, because there is not.

Q:    Thank you, Mr. President.

(The Press Conference adjourned at 4:10 P.M.)

Press Conference #164
Executive Offices of the White House
December 12, 1934, 10:30 A.M.


THE PRESIDENT:  I have got a lot of news this morning.

Q:  How about this survey you are going to make by the Treasury Department --
this survey of the taxes (of the District of Columbia)?

THE PRESIDENT:  We are starting on it.  I do not know whether they have actually
started but they have orders to do it.

Q:  (Mr. Storm, who had come in behind the others)  It is pretty bad when you
have to make that end run out there.

MR. DONALDSON:  All in.

THE PRESIDENT:  Lots of news today.

No. 1, I have sent a letter to the Secretary of War directing that General
Douglas MacArthur be retained as Chief of Staff until his successor has been
appointed.  I am doing this in order to obtain the benefit of General Mac-
Arthur's experience in handling War Department legislation in the coming
session.  I cannot give you any date because I have no more idea than you
have when that work up on the Hill will be finished.  Of course, obviously,
sometime before the end of Congress.

Q:  That order to keep him on -- that is an Order?

THE PRESIDENT:  Yes.

Q:  We assume from that that General MacArthur will not have an appointment for
four years now?

THE PRESIDENT:  That is right.

Q:  Does this necessitate a new Executive Order?

THE PRESIDENT:  The other was not an Order, it was a letter to the Secretary of
War.  The letter says:  (Reading)

--- [269] ---

"My dear Mr. Secretary:

"I desire you to issue the necessary order to the effect
that Douglas MacArthur will continue as Chief of Staff until
his successor has been appointed."

That is all.

I signed an Executive Order setting up the Federal Prison Industries, Inc.,
as authorized by the Act of June 23, 1934.  This is a long step in the
right direction.  This board, among other things, will determine to what
manner and to what extent industrial operations shall be carried on in
Federal Penal institutions.  It is a board of five, one representing indus-

try, one representing labor, one representing agriculture, one representing retailers and consumers and one representing the Attorney General.

That particular statute was the result of being able to iron out a conflict of long standing between people who run the prisons, the industries and organized labor. This was agreed to by everybody last spring and the people going are Sanford Bates -- Steve (Mr. Early) will give you the Order -- Thomas A. Rickert, John D. Miller, Dr. M. L. Brittain of Georgia Tech. and Sam A. Lewisohn of New York.

Q: Mr. President, is it time to ask you a question? You indicated that you had ordered this survey of the local tax situation. Will that be out in time to give it to the Appropriations Committee?

THE PRESIDENT: Yes; that is what is intended.

And now, number three, is a very short one and principally for Washington, D.C. I think it is my fault. I think I gave Clark Howell the wrong impression about the aviation field for Washington. I had been studying the thing with a good deal of care and there had been a report, I think, either from the National Capital Park Planning Board or from the Interior Department in favor of a new field on the other

--- [270] ---

side of the river, opposite Haines Point. And good old Clark came in the other day with his Commission and they talked about a field and they were talking about the Haines Point field and I was talking about the one on the Virginia side.

As a matter of fact, I don't think there is any possibility of using the park at Haines Point. It is not the proper place for it, it is too close to the city, and it also destroys the park. We are still studying the Gravelly Point site. There is nothing decided on it yet but I think you can say that at the present time the Gravelly Point site looks like the best site.

Now, most important of all, I am having a meeting at 2 o'clock today with -- you had better take these names down because I haven't any copies -- with Secretary Hull, Secretary Morgenthau, Secretary Dern, General Mac-Arthur, Secretary Wallace, Secretary Swanson and Harry Roosevelt, Secretary Perkins, Coordinator Eastman, George Peek and Bernard M. Baruch and General Johnson. (Laughter)

Now I have got you all intrigued. Isn't that a funny combination?

Q: Is it for tea? (Laughter)

THE PRESIDENT: It all goes back and is a long story. Those of us who served in the World War know that we got into the war in a great hurry. We had never been in a war on such a scale in our National history and, as a result of it, we muddled through the war and did a lot of things we should not have done.

After the war was over, there was a very large sentiment in the country for so ordering things by law that if we should unfortunately get into another war, we would eliminate some of the very great faults of the World War.

One of the principal students of that particular problem was Mr.

--- [271] ---

Baruch.  He and General Johnson worked very hard for a good many years on the possibility of legislation which, in a broad sense, could be legislation to take the profit out of war.

Probably no two people have done more work on that subject than Baruch and Johnson.  There were a number of Congressional hearings of various kinds, I don't recall just what they were, but I think both Baruch and Johnson did appear before the Senate and House Committees and the whole subject was pretty thoroughly canvassed.  Nothing was ever done about it.  There was no legislation passed.

We have decided that the time has come when legislation to take the profit out of war should be enacted.  We are meeting this afternoon in order to discuss such legislation.  It is with the idea that some time, fairly early in the session, I will be able to send a message to the Congress on this general subject.

Everybody in the country knows what munitions profits and other profits meant during the World War.  Not only our country, but the world as a whole, is pretty thoroughly alive to these profits of munitions makers in time of war and in time of peace.

Gerald Nye's investigation has helped very materially in making people conscious of it and there is another reason for doing it now and that is that the world is at peace and there does not seem to be any war that is pending.  That is another reason why it is an opportune time to take the subject up.

I imagine that we will discuss the whole range of the subject.  In other words, not merely the financial side of it but also the economic side of it, bearing in mind that as a result of the last war, the World War, a good many things happened that, perhaps, headed us for the unfortunate ten-year period that succeeded the was such as overproduction,

--- [272] ---

enormous salaries, enormous personal profits and a complete lack of coordination in our economic system.

Then there is the other phase of it which might be called the personnel phase of it.  During the World War we did more than in any other war to mobilize the human beings in the United States, and we did a very good job, on the whole.  But, as a result of what might be called "unequal" mobilization -- well, for example, the whole bonus question is in good part the result of unequal mobilization of human beings during the war.

So this conference is going to take up both sides of the broad problem of how the United States would run a war if we were to get into one.  I regard it as one of the very important things that will be laid before Congress this winter.

Q:  What do you mean by unequal mobilization?

THE PRESIDENT:  Well, just for a very simple example, the boys in the trenches got paid a dollar a day and the boy who was working in the munitions plant in Bridgeport got perhaps $8 or $10 a day. Naturally, the boy in the trenches, when he came back, asked for an equalization, which was the origin of the bonus.

Q:    Does that mean taking the profits out of our own war or taking the profits out of munitions?

THE PRESIDENT:   That is an entirely different subject and perhaps you had better treat that question as not having been asked, because I don't want to spoil a good story.  A little bit later on I do think that I will have something to tell you with respect to the position of the United States as a neutral in the event of war between other nations, but I am not ready for it yet. Treat it as off the record.

Q:    Would there be any possibility of this country entertaining conversations

--- [273] ---

with other countries so that other countries might do the same as we do for themselves?

THE PRESIDENT:   I hadn't thought of that.  Perhaps the force of example might be good.

Q:    Could we put quotation marks on that, "since the time has come to take the profits out of war?"

THE PRESIDENT:   Yes.

Q:    Would the question of compulsory military training come up in connection with this broad plan you speak of?

THE PRESIDENT:   Oh, no.  No, that won't come up.  Steve (Mr. Early) suggests that because there are a good many new faces, just to reiterate the old rule about quotes and also to way what "background" means and what "off the record" means.  Will you explain it to everybody who does not know?

Q:    That sentence I gave is okay?

THE PRESIDENT:   That sentence is all right.

Q:    The Nye Committee is running pretty low in funds and there seems to be some discussion --

THE PRESIDENT:   (interposing)  I thought you said, "fun."  (Laughter)

Q:    And I was wondering if you have any idea of recommending that their supply of money be added to when Congress opens for a continuation of the inquiry.

THE PRESIDENT:   No, I never recommend anything with respect to Senatorial Committees.

Q:    We could not describe this as preparedness, as discussed before the World War?

THE PRESIDENT:   No.  Really it would be of service if you all would leave out any suggestion of this being a question of preparedness.  It is a question of permanent national legislation looking to an event which

--- [274] ---

we hope will never happen, and I am bringing it up because there isn't any cloud on the horizon at the present time.

Q:  You have a complete report on this line as a result of the report of the War Planning Commission.  Will that serve as a basis?

THE PRESIDENT:  I don't know that.

Q:  They studied it here for about two years and brought out a very exhaustive report.

THE PRESIDENT:  I have got to confess, off the record, that I never heard of it.

Q:  Have you any idea as to how this should be done, whether it should be done through an excess profits tax or --

THE PRESIDENT:  I have no idea at all.  We are having our first talk at two o'-clock today.

Q:  Mr. President, can you tell us about water resources and land utilization? We understand you have the reports.

THE PRESIDENT:  The National Resources Board report is not ready yet.  I under-stand it is to be released tomorrow for Monday morning papers.  That will give you about a three-day opportunity to read it.

Q:  Mr. President, the Supreme Court yesterday made some observations about the fact that Executive Orders had not been made public.  Are you looking into that?

THE PRESIDENT:  Yes.  There is no reason why I should not go into that.  It brought up a very nice question.

The Supreme Court discovered something of great importance and that is that there has never been any machinery in the Government for the publication of Executive Orders and similar orders.  I am looking into the question.

It has always been the custom in the past for Executive Orders to be kept on file here in the White House and another file to be open

--- [275] ---

to anybody's inspection in the State Department, but there has never been any medium, any vehicle, for the publication of Executive Orders or, even, of proclamations.

Obviously, in view of the Supreme Court's calling our attention to the fact, it is a thing we should do something about.  There is no secrecy with respect to Executive Orders of any kind, whether they be from the White House or the N.R.A. or the A.A.A. or any other source.  A great many of them are not of sufficient interest for the Press to publish them in full and, at the same time, I don't want to start a Government newspaper in order to publish them.

At any rate, we are looking into it to see what can be done.

Q:   Have you thought of bringing Joe Broderick down here for an official post?

THE PRESIDENT:   I haven't given any thought to it.

Q:   He resigned yesterday.

THE PRESIDENT:   Did he?   I didn't know that.

Q:   Did you say the Executive Orders can be found in the State Department?

THE PRESIDENT:   They are open to everybody, but there is no method for what the law calls publication at the present time.   There isn't any official publication.

Q:   Recently the State Department has been posting them on the Bulletin Board in the Press Room.

Q:   Thank you, Mr. President.


(The Press Conference adjourned at 10:40 P.M.)

CONFIDENTIAL
Press Conference #165
Executive Offices of the White House
December 14, 1934, 4:05 P.M.


MR. DONALDSON: All in.

THE PRESIDENT: There are two good reasons why there is no news today: The first is that I talked myself out on Wednesday, and the other is that Steve (Mr. Early) has gone duck hunting and said that I could not give you anything.

Q:   Have you anybody in mind to replace Mr. Farrell (Patrick J. Farrell) on the Interstate Commerce Commission?

THE PRESIDENT: No.

Q:   His term expires this year?

THE PRESIDENT: I have not taken it up at all.

Q:   Can you tell us whether you discussed the cotton barter deal with Germany lately?

THE PRESIDENT: No, not yet.

Q:   Do you intend to fill the two places on the Federal Tariff Commission?

THE PRESIDENT: I have not thought of it at all.

Q:   Anything you can tell us about Conboy's (Martin Conboy) visit this morning?

THE PRESIDENT: No -- yes, I can. I can tell you this, that Martin Conboy reminded me that he had said that he wanted very much to stay (as District Attorney in New York) only for a year and that the year would be up in January and that he still held to that but that if I could not find anybody to take his place at the end of the year, he would be entirely willing to stay on for a month or two until I found somebody. So that is entirely satisfactory.

--- [277] ---

Q:   During the crime conference there were several suggestions of better coordination on the part of police organizations and there was an indication that a step of that sort might be under consideration. Can you tell us or express your views on general coordination of the various police departments and investigative agencies?

THE PRESIDENT: I could not because I have not done anything but read the headlines and I have not had a chance to talk to them about that yet.

Q:   Is there a plan like that in consideration?

THE PRESIDENT: Coordinating?

Q:   Yes, and centralization?

THE PRESIDENT:  I would not put it that way.  Yes, coordination of work but I would not call it centralization.

Q:  No centralization of control or anything like that?

THE PRESIDENT:  No.

Q:  Ambassador Dodd is returning from Germany and the rumor is that he is coming back permanently?

THE PRESIDENT:  I sincerely hope not.  I think he is coming home for the Christmas holidays and that is all.

Q:  William Green (President of the American Federation of Labor) told us this morning about the recommendations of Labor on N.R.A.  One of those was a recommendation that Government supervision be continued in the new setup over industry.  I was wondering if you would care to comment on that?

THE PRESIDENT:  That is pretty vague.  I do not know what you mean.

Q:  What I think he means is that under the new N.R.A., the Government would continue to administer the relations over industry somewhat as it is doing now.

THE PRESIDENT:  You mean on the labor end of things?

--- [278] ---

Q:  Yes.

THE PRESIDENT:  Well, I do not think there is any question about that.  We put our hand to the plow and undoubtedly, with respect to all of these labor problems, there is going to continue to be a great deal of interest and participation in them by Government.  In other words, the country is certainly not going to abandon the very great steps that have been taken during the past year and a half -- child labor, working conditions, minimum wages, et cetera.  I do not think anybody would suggest that they be thrown out of the window.

Q:  Have you found any way to persuade the bankers and insurance companies to cooperate with the Federal Housing Administration under Title II?

THE PRESIDENT:  Is that the one that requires additional state laws?

Q:  In some instances.  Mr. Sloan in New York indicated that the Administration is not pleased -- rather, that there had been lack of cooperation on the part of bankers.

THE PRESIDENT:  Not that I know of.  The only phase I know of is that Jimmy Moffett has sent me a letter and I am preparing a letter now to the governors, I think of the forty-four states that have legislatures meeting, sending them all Jimmy Moffett's recommendations in regard to removing certain restrictions on that type of loan which now exist by virtue of state law. Just to give you an example, a great many states confine the amount of a loan to 50 per cent of the value.  The State of New York last August, in a special session, passed what Moffett said is the proper kind of amended statute.  I am sending that letter to the governors and, after they have had a chance to get it, I will give you copies of it.

Q:  Have you any comment to make on the resolution of Clay Williams that Green
    (President Green of the A.F. of L.) presented to you today?  (Laughter)

--- [279] ---

Q:  In view of the action of the principal European nations in defaulting out-
    right, do you hope there will be any resumption of payments under existing
    agreements?

THE PRESIDENT:  I certainly do.  (Laughter)

Q:  Mr. President, can you tell us anything about your conference with the util-
    ity men yesterday and Mr. Carlisle today?

THE PRESIDENT:  Well, it is very difficult.  It is such a tremendous subject.
    I should say that probably there are two things that should be properly
    said.  The first is that the talks were entirely amicable and that there
    was a disposition  to work together rather than at cross purposes by run-
    ning into court on every possible occasion.  The other thing is that I made
    perfectly clear that on the general utility problem it is largely a ques-
    tion of fact and the fact relates to how much capital is necessary to pro-
    vide the generation of electricity and its transmission and its distribu-
    tion, and that when you arrive, if it is a possible thing to do, at a meet-
    ing of the minds on those figures, it is a comparatively simple thing to
    say what the net earnings should be and what rate is necessary to produce
    those net earnings.

    Now, of course, the corollary of it is that if existing capital is far and
    away above those figures, it is just unfortunate.

Q:  Well, Mr. President, in those calculations would you produce the actual or
    the reproduction cost?

THE PRESIDENT:  Now, you are getting into details which are matters for discus-
    sion.  I will give you an example, however.  If you take reproduction
    costs in a period of rising prices, say during the 1920's, are you going to
    allow recapitalization each year and if the prices go up without, at the
    same time, saying that in a period of decreasing prices, declining prices,
    that you are going to decrease your capitalization?

--- [280] ---

    Nobody has ever been willing to admit that among the old line power crowd.
    They say the rule works one way and not both ways.  Of course the prudent
    investment theory is the one that most people should come to in this
    country, there is no question about that.

Q:  The Supreme Court hasn't?

THE PRESIDENT:  Hasn't got to it yet.  (Laughter)

Q:  Did they agree with your statement?

THE PRESIDENT:  No, but they thought it was worth talking about.  They did not
    advocate it.  In fact, quite a number of them have said, quite frankly,
    that if there is water in utility companies, there ought to be cooperation
    in squeezing it out, and they have been quite frank in saying so.  In
    other words, I think we are getting somewhere.  If you can squeeze water

out by common consent, it would be a great thing.

Q:    Did they discuss T.V.A. and your proposal to extend T.V.A. all over the country?

THE PRESIDENT:  When did I say that?

Q:    I think you said something down in the Tennessee Valley district that eventually that yardstick will be applied everywhere in the Union.

THE PRESIDENT:  That wasn't what I said.   You had better read the language.

Q:    In that same connection, I noticed you said that they were pretty much agreed that they would not run to court, that there was a disposition to work together rather than to run to court in every controversy.  With respect to that, did you discuss the pending court fight of the Edison Electrical Institute?

THE PRESIDENT:  Yes, and the people I talked to, I gathered they were not in the least bit in favor of it.  That was my impression because they told me they had nothing to do with the suits brought in the Tennessee Valley.  They disclaimed any connection with them.

Q:    I take it you did discuss squeezing the water out of stocks?

--- [281] ---

THE PRESIDENT:  I did not put it just like that.  You know, I am a rough fellow, but I did not.  (Laughter)

Q:    To return to the debts, may I ask on what you base your hope that the payments might be made?

THE PRESIDENT:  Now, now.  (Laughter)

Q:    Has any progress been made since Wednesday to take the profits out of war?

THE PRESIDENT:  Not yet.  We are getting on all right.

Q:    Mr. President, what will be the next step in the endeavor to take the profits out of war?

THE PRESIDENT:  Well, I suppose the Committee will talk it over in the course of the next couple of weeks and come back here and talk to various people in the House and Senate and try to arrive at something that everybody will agree on.

Q:    Can you tell us anything on O'Connor (Comptroller of the Currency)?

THE PRESIDENT:  What?

Q:    The Comptroller of the Currency?

THE PRESIDENT:  Oh, no; we just talked generally about the examination of banks; that is all.

Q:    Anything on the question of his leaving?

THE PRESIDENT:  No.

Press Conference #166
Executive Offices of the White House
December 19, 1934, 10:35 A.M.


MR. DONALDSON: All in.

THE PRESIDENT: I do not believe there is going to be any news much before the
third of January.

Q: How about your radio speech?

THE PRESIDENT: Well, what happened on the radio speech was what you would call
one of those things. So many things came in when I got back that I never
got around to preparing it. I never found a minute to prepare it. It is
still possible but improbable. You know, in preparing a Message there is
a tremendous volume of stuff that comes in. You have to sort it and then
the position I am in, quite frankly, at the present time, is trying to
determine how much should go into the Message and whether there is enough
outside of it that ought to be talked about separately. I have not just
got to it.

Q: You probably would have what you would have said in reduced form?

THE PRESIDENT: What is that?

Q: You will try to include what you would have said in your radio talk in your
Message?

THE PRESIDENT: If it is still possible, I may work something out on the air,
but it is improbable.

Q: There has been a lot said about the new policy of abandoning the freedom
of the seas. Can you tell us something about it?

THE PRESIDENT: No; that is newspaper talk.

Q: In that respect, so much has been said about this question of neutrality in
the papers. Could you tell us what your objective is?

--- [283] ---

THE PRESIDENT: The objective is neutrality, which has always been difficult to
retain in the past. Some of you older people who were here in 1914, 1915
and 1916 and the first few months of 1917 know exactly the difficulty of
retaining neutrality.

Q: Mr. President, there has been a screwworm epidemic in the Southeast.

THE PRESIDENT: What?

Q: A screwworm. Georgia is very much alarmed and it is also said that Warm
Springs has been attacked. I wonder if they will get help from the
F.E.R.A.?

THE PRESIDENT: What is that?

Q:   Screwworm.  They say it has gone up as far as --

THE PRESIDENT:  (interposing)  What does it affect?

Q:   Animals -- cows and horses.

Q:   It works itself in and spreads through the flesh.  It is very bad.

THE PRESIDENT:  My Lord!  I hope it does not attack the two mules.  (Laughter)

Q:   It affects all warm-blooded animals.  (Laughter)

THE PRESIDENT:  Both sexes?  (Laughter)

Q:   You put creosote on it.

THE PRESIDENT:  Well, we will have to get hold of Tug and Hop and go after it.
     It is partly agriculture and partly relief.  I wish somebody would tell me
     something more about it.  I will look into it.  I never heard of it.

Q:   I beg your pardon.  (Laughter)

Q:   We are very much interested in following out the story that came up here
     from New York City with relation to LaGuardia, the Power Commission of New
     York and the naval officers at New York with respect to the power plant at
     the Navy Yard up there.  Is anything going forward on it today?

THE PRESIDENT:  Only that they are coming in.  I think it is a mistake to talk
     about it from the general utilities end of things.  It is a per-

--- [284] ---

fectly simple question.  Well, let us illustrate:  Away back when I was in
the Navy Department, we did put up a powerhouse because we found we could
save money by putting up our own powerhouse.  If you were starting a factory in New York City, one of the things you would ask you engineers would
be, "Is it cheaper for us to make our own power or buy it from the New
York Edison Company?"  That is all there is to it.  The Navy, I think, has
at the present time a study which either is being made or has been completed in regard to additional power for Federal purposes and the question is,
"Is it cheaper for the Federal Government to make power for its own use or
buy it?"  Now, the City of New York is apparently up against the same question.  It is merely a question of whether it will be cheaper for the city
to make its own power or buy it.

Q:   Does that mean having it in yards in the Navy?

THE PRESIDENT:  No, just the New York yard.

Q:   I thought they already had it?

THE PRESIDENT:  Yes, but they need more power and the thing has been going on
     for some months.  As a matter of fact, I did not know it until Floyd Car-
     lisle told me that the Navy had not paid its power bill since July and then
     I looked into it.

Q:   Why is that?

THE PRESIDENT:  As to whether the price is excessive.

Q:    Do you happen to know of any kick or protest on the part of the Government
      against rates here in this city?  The Navy makes its own power at the Navy
      Yard in the capital.

THE PRESIDENT:  We buy some.

Q:    We buy two-thirds and make one-third.

THE PRESIDENT:  The only thing I heard was last year some suggestion that we
      give up the Navy Yard power plant and we looked into it and decided it

--- [285] ---

was cheaper.

Q:    Does that mean that the local rate is lower?

THE PRESIDENT:  Somewhat.

Q:    It is very low here.

THE PRESIDENT:  Yes.

Q:    Can you tell us something about the Nicaraguan Canal?

THE PRESIDENT:  Only that when I was a very small boy, about 1890, my father was
      very much interested in it and my mother still has in a safe deposit box
      enough stock in that old Nicaraguan Canal Company to paper a whole room.

Q:    You ought to be in favor of it then.

THE PRESIDENT:  That has gone.  (Laughter)

Q:    Does the statement of Mr. McCarter represent the attitude of all the public
      utility men you have talked with?

THE PRESIDENT:  I should say no.

Q:    On that same subject, if you find from your talk today that it might be
      cheaper for New York City to manufacture its own power, would the Federal
      Government help them perhaps with P.W.A. funds?

THE PRESIDENT:  If it is a legitimate self-sustaining project, it certainly would
      be considered.

Q:    Has Carlisle taken a more conciliatory attitude?

THE PRESIDENT:  That is getting into very tricky ground, talking about concilia-
      tory.

Q:    Do you have any other Federal yardsticks definitely in mind?

THE PRESIDENT:  Other than what?

Q:    Muscle Shoals, Boulder and St. Lawrence?

THE PRESIDENT:  No.

Q:  Can you tell us whether the reports are correct that the cotton barter deal

--- [286] ---

with Germany has bogged down?

THE PRESIDENT:  Still in the discussion stage.

Q:  Can you tell us whether the State Department has advised you that as it stands now it is in conflict with our most-favored-nation treaty policy?

THE PRESIDENT:  I could not answer that question because I have a long memo and have not read it yet.  I don't know.  It is in the basket.

Q:  There is a report this morning that Senators Costigan and Wagner are con- templating a bill for a billion dollars more fund for the Home Owners' Loan Corporation?

THE PRESIDENT:  No.  That is still in the study stage by the Credit Agency Com- mittee.  You know there is that subcommittee of the Emergency Council that is composed of the heads of the different credit agencies.  They have not reported yet.

Q:  Can you tell us anything about the naval situation?

THE PRESIDENT:  That will have to come from London.

Q:  Will you comment on the Japanese Privy Council's action in renouncing the London-Washington Treaty?

THE PRESIDENT:  We have not been advised of any action.

Q:  I am very much concerned about a report that you are planning to tear down the Library of Congress.

THE PRESIDENT:  I do not know where that came from.  It shows how terribly care- ful you have to be about making remarks.  I was driving back from the Navy Yard with somebody and we were driving past the Library of Congress and I said, "I feel that that building is entirely out of keeping with the Capi- tol, the Senate and House office buildings and the Supreme Court."  That is as far as I have gone.  I never said another thing, but somebody took it up.

Q:  Was it Lynn (Architect of the Capitol) you said it to?

--- [287] ---

THE PRESIDENT:  No; that is all I ever said.

Q:  You have not given any directions?

THE PRESIDENT:  No, none at all.

Q:  Before you decide on that, will you give us an opportunity to present a case for preserving American and Italian architecture?

THE PRESIDENT: Would you include the old Post Office building? (Laughter) You know, there is a lot in it. Why should we make everything --

Q: (interposing) How about the State, War and Navy building?

THE PRESIDENT: I have lived in it for a number of years.

Q: What is going to be done about the State, War and Navy building?

THE PRESIDENT: Nothing is going to be done. As a matter of fact, we are not going to rebuild any buildings at the present time because, as a matter of fact we cannot spare the space. We need every available space, so that all the talk about rebuilding any building for a number of years is silly. We need the floor space and the money for other purposes.

Q: Does that hold good about the change down in the Library of Congress?

THE PRESIDENT: Of course, unless Congress itself decides on that action.

Q: The old Post Office building will stand?

THE PRESIDENT: We need the space; it has got to stand.

Q: In that connection, the Secretary of War recommended the construction of a new War Department building as distinguished from the present building?

THE PRESIDENT: Only this: Of course, the one thing which I will always go down on my knees and ask forgiveness for was my plea for the Navy and Munitions building during the war. I was responsible for it and I am terribly sorry I made them so permanent. Eventually they have got to be taken out of the park.

In regard to what building we will build next, the War Department or something else, we do not know yet. It is a simple problem. We need

--- [288] ---

a lot more space and we will undoubtedly build new buildings with the objective of getting more floor space. What department will get the new building, nobody knows. But, whatever department gets a new building, the present department space will have to be retained temporarily.

Q: Are you familiar with the row over the location of the new building that the War Department will have? One school of thought was for extending it out along Pennsylvania Avenue to Nineteenth Street?

THE PRESIDENT: It is not going along Pennsylvania Avenue; it is going along the Mall.

Q: Can you tell us anything about steel labor negotiations -- background or any other way?

THE PRESIDENT: You had the story yesterday and they are still talking about it. There were three points to the agreement and I think the papers carried that this morning. It is more a question of a formula of words than anything else.

Q: On this building problem, do you expect there will be more Government employees in Washington during the coming year?

THE PRESIDENT: I hope not.

Q: Can you tell us about your talk with Eastman on the railroad question?

THE PRESIDENT: It is still in the conversation state; nothing definite on it.

Q: On steel, on this formula, are you hopeful of an agreement there?

THE PRESIDENT: I hope so, yes.

Q: Very soon?

THE PRESIDENT: The quicker the better. There is no specific date on it.

Q: Reverting to the Messages to the Congress, is it your plan to have a cover-all Message or send individual Messages later on?

THE PRESIDENT: Long before I even went to Albany, I was appalled and I think most people were appalled by the length and detail of all Presidential

--- [289] ---

and Governors' Messages. I started the practice in Albany of cutting the Message from an average of about 5,000 words down to about 2500. The same way here, my general thought is on Messages to the Congress that they should talk about principles and objectives, the larger ones, just the way I did last year. If you read last year's Message, you will get a good line on what type of Message it will be this year. And then, when you come down to the details of legislation, they go into Special Messages. Again, I am going to try to keep it as short as I possibly can.

Q: Do you recall the length last year?

THE PRESIDENT: Do you remember last year? About 3,000 or 3500. Better check on that.

Q: Gene Black died this morning.

THE PRESIDENT: I know. It is too bad. I am awfully sorry about that. He was a grand fellow. And, off the record -- this has got to be off the record -- I always loved Gene Black because he would come in and I would say, "Don't you think we had better do this? I have made up my mind." And he would answer, "Now, Boss, just let me present the other side of the case to you." And he would do it in five minutes and, at the end of that time, he would say, "Now, listen; I have told you the other side of the case; I am a good soldier; I will do whatever you want."

It is really a great shock because I think he was one of the last men I thought would go quickly. He seemed to be in good health. I saw him at Warm Springs.

Q: Getting back to power, have you had presented to you any detailed figures on the amount of water which should be taken out of utility stocks?

THE PRESIDENT: No. Of course, as a matter of fact on that, there is one thing -- I think you had better keep this off the record; well, no, you

--- [290] ---

can use it for background.  There has been a general -- I won't say an effort, because perhaps that is rough, but perhaps we have fallen into the
error, which is perhaps a more polite way of putting it, of lumping utility
securities.  There have been stories written about the insurance companies
and the savings banks which, of course, hold utility securities.

But, if you begin to analyze, taking the savings banks of this country, the
bonds that they hold are in almost all cases underlying bonds of operating
companies, and the overwhelming proportion, 98 or 99% of those bonds are as
sound as a government bond, absolutely all right.

Where there is water, it is not in the financial structure of the operating
companies, it is in the financial structure of what you and I call the holding companies, where it is first, or second, or third, or fourth, or fifth,
or sixth or seventh.

Therefore, it is beclouding the issue to lump all utility stocks and bonds
into the same category.  As I say, I am not saying it has been deliberately
done; I think it is just one of those slips that people are apt to fall into.

Q:   Does the same thing apply to railroads?

THE PRESIDENT:   No.  In the general railroad picture there are very, very few of
what you and I would call "holding companies."  There are a few, but comparatively few.  Most of the railroads have built up their capital structure
through a policy which I think most of them wish now they had never pursued, which was of not building up sinking funds or amortization funds and
when the bonded indebtedness came due, instead of paying off, they have refunded it, which resulted in the original construction cost of a large proportion of the railroads in this country being still part of the structure
after 75 or 100 years.  It has never been paid off.

Q:   Insurance companies hold the same type of stocks and bonds as banks?

--- [291] ---

THE PRESIDENT:   A great number of them -- underlying securities.

(The Press Conference adjourned at 10:50 A.M.)

Press Conference #167
Executive Offices of the White House
December 21, 1934, 4:05 P.M.


Q:    (Mr. Storm)   What is in the bottle, Mr. President?

THE PRESIDENT:   I will tell you about that.   (Laughter)   I wish there was some-
     thing in it -- it would be worth money today if there were.

MR. DONALDSON:   All in.

THE PRESIDENT:   There is a unanimous demand in the front row that this (indicat-
     ing a green and dark brown bottle) be explained.   In the first place, there
     is nothing in it.   The Public Works people dug, pulled that out of the York
     River the other day on the exact site where a British frigate was sunk at
     the time of the siege of Yorktown.   It is a hand-blown bottle, was probably
     down there 150 years and is an interesting relic of the War of Independence.

     I do not think I have anything today at all.   Have you anything, Fred?

Q:    (Mr. Storm)   We are not in the market for much.   (Laughter)

Q:    Do the prospects of a cotton barter deal with Germany look any better?

THE PRESIDENT:   I will talk to you about it Wednesday morning.

Q:    How about a Christmas story?

THE PRESIDENT:   The best Christmas story I know of is to put the lid on about
     4:30 today and not take it off until Monday morning.

Q:    What did you say, Wednesday or Monday morning?

THE PRESIDENT:   On Monday there might be news, but I don't know.

Q:    Are you coming into the office?

THE PRESIDENT:   Tomorrow I think I will stay over at the Oval Room (of the White
     House) and work on Christmas things and packages and the Message.

                          --- [293] ---

Q:    You will put the lid on tomorrow?

THE PRESIDENT:   This afternoon.   Various (members of my) family begin driving in
     tomorrow and there won't be much doing on Monday.   I don't think I have any
     appointments at all either for Monday or tomorrow.

Q:    That reception you had last year to the employees, was that Christmas Day
     or Christmas Eve?

THE PRESIDENT:   Crhistmas Eve -- they are coming through at twelve o'clock noon,
     to shake hands.

Q:    On the Message to Congress, you are working on that tomorrow?

THE PRESIDENT: Yes. As a matter of fact, the Message to Congress is getting on singularly well. If you want to know how far it has got, I might say that the preliminary rough draft is about three-quarters finished.

Q: What was the last thing you wrote, so we can tell how far along? (Laughter)

Q: Do you plan to meet with the leaders in a general conference?

THE PRESIDENT: Not a general conference. I will be delighted to see any of them but I have not heard anything of a general conference.

Q: In that connection, have you had an opportunity to read the reports submitted by the White Sulphur Conference?

THE PRESIDENT: Not yet. I have it right in the basket to read over the week-end, at which time I will read five or six other reports from different organizations. As a matter of fact, every weekend I take back to the White House an average of half a dozen reports and suggestions and give them all careful consideration and all fair and equal treatment.

Q: Is your mother coming down?

THE PRESIDENT: Yes, either tomorrow afternoon or Sunday.

Q: Has the State Department brought your attention to any recent communications from China concerning the silver situation?

THE PRESIDENT: Not very recent. I have not had anything in two weeks;

--- [294] ---

nothing new.

Q: Have you decided to do anything about this agitation for an extra holiday for Government employees?

THE PRESIDENT: Didn't the Executive Order go out about two weeks ago?

Q: Yes.

THE PRESIDENT: There won't be any change in that. In other words, the situation is a very simple one. There are a good many departments of the Government that simply cannot be closed for three days. If you once start trying to differentiate as to what office could be closed without interfering with the public business, and which office could be closed, it makes too difficult a problem and the general rule before Christmas and New Years is a half holiday.

The only exceptions to that are the industrial establishments of the Government like the Navy Yard, where, obviously, it is practically impossible to put an industrial establishment to work for just four hours.

Q: Does your participation in this Community Tree call for a little talk? Didn't you make one last year for two or three minutes?

THE PRESIDENT: Yes, I think three minutes.

Q: The same thing this year?

THE PRESIDENT: Yes, the same thing this year.

Q: Any developments in the New York power situation?

THE PRESIDENT: I have not heard a word since the day before yesterday.

Q: Can you tell us anything for background with respect to the naval situation in London?

THE PRESIDENT: The only thing I can do would be to talk not for background but off the record on that, and this would have to be off the record because, obviously, there isn't anything that I can say, even as back-

--- [295] ---

ground. We are all very much disappointed that the conference over there -- there were not conferences but conversations -- did not get any further and we all hope that something will turn up in the course of the next year which will make possible a renewal of the limitation of naval armaments or a new treaty which will continue at an even greater speed the reduction of naval armaments.

I do think this: We should all, as Americans, bear this in mind: That we have done nothing in any way to adopt an antagonistic or hostile attitude. Our whole position has been that every nation is entitled to relative secur- ity and we have believed that the two previous treaties did give, in one case three nations and in the other case five nations, relative security which has continued for a good many years, from 1921 down to date. And we wanted a continuance of relative security.

The reason I am speaking especially to the Americans present, and speaking off the records, is that I do want to emphasize that every time that any American talks in belligerent terms, it is merely an invitation to somebody else to speak in more belligerent terms. I have regretted anything said by members of Congress, quite frankly, in regard to what we would do under both circumstances. I regretted reading today that somebody had talked about new naval bases anywhere because, as I say, the more we talk about that, the more we are going to get repercussions from other countries.

I am not speaking about any one particular country. It seems to me that our attitude should be to continue to hope that in the next year or two years, since we have two years, to effectuate something, to get a limitation on naval armaments. In the meantime, we should keep our mouths shut about it no matter what we may have personally thought of in regard to hypotheti- cal conditions. They are too hypothetical to

--- [296] ---

express them out loud at the present time. Everything that the Administra- tion will do will be along that line of trying not to antagonize by thought, word, or deed.

I think that is the easiest way of putting it.

Q: Also off the record, is there any reason to believe that with the passage of the year the cause of the present breakdown of negotiations will change?

THE PRESIDENT: I hope so. I hope so.

Q:   Mr. President, do you think it would do any harm if we were to use for
background just that part, that you do hope for a treaty?

THE PRESIDENT:   All right, Stevie, as a way out.


(Mr. Early spoke to the President.)


THE PRESIDENT:   Steve suggests that we let it be used without attribution to the
White House sources of any kind.   You use it on your own authority.   Is
that all right?

Q:   In that connection and on the same basis, is there anything to say about the
McCarran Act, the excluding feature of the McCarran Act?

THE PRESIDENT:   I don't think so; that is not one of the pending questions.

Q:   It might be a cause of a good deal of feeling?

THE PRESIDENT:   There again, if you get into the reasons assigned by every nation for some kind of change, it is an interminable subject.

Q:   Also on the same basis, how are we getting along with Great Britain on
this?   There has been some discussion that our relations are improved as a
result of the strain in every direction.

THE PRESIDENT:   I do not think that any human being could write a story one way
or the other.   They are always what they have been, friendly.

Q:   Thank you, Mr. President.

THE PRESIDENT:   Merry Christmas to you all!

Q:   (Chorus)   The same to you, Mr. President!

Press Conference #168
Executive Offices of the White House
December 26, 1934, 10:35 A.M.


MR. DONALDSON: All in.

THE PRESIDENT: I do not think there is any news. The people whose faces I see
seem to have survived in pretty good shape. Stevie (Mr. Stephenson) asked
me if I was all right myself. I am extremely well. I did not overeat for
the very simple reason that I had to carve the turkey myself and there were
so many second helpings that I did not have a chance. Steve (Mr. Early)
can prove it.

I do not think there is any news at all. Between now and the opening of
Congress there won't be any conferences, as such. Of course, I will be
talking to an enormous number of people, various departmental heads, the
Director of the Budget, the leaders of the Senate and House, but there are
not any regular conferences scheduled as such. It is too big a word.

Q: Do you anticipate a larger field of operation for the Electric Home and Farm
Authority? The Tennessee Valley subsidiary?

THE PRESIDENT: We are working on that at the present time. There is not much
to be said about it because we are still working on it. If we can be helpful to private utilities in setting up some similar method of financing,
I think the idea is that we will want to be helpful. But it is still very
much in the discussion stage. The whole thought is that if you can buy
large blocks of appliances in large quantities and get a reduced rate than
it is customary to finance them, you will bet more people to buy them.

Q: You are talking about private financing, however?

THE PRESIDENT: Private financing, and a good many of the utilities are doing

--- [298] ---

a very good job on that work already.

Q: Mr. President, is there anything you can tell us about the Federal Trade
Commission's steel basing point report?

THE PRESIDENT: No. Have they made a report or are they going to make a report?

Q: The Trade Commission has and the N.R.A. has not as yet.

THE PRESIDENT: That was something I have not taken up at all. I knew there was
a report due.

Q: Can you tell us anything about the billion dollars that Congress is going to
be asked for for the H.O.L.C.? Many Congressmen are talking about it.

THE PRESIDENT: No; haven't got to it at all. There is that Credit Committee
that covers all of the credit agencies. I think they have a meeting today.

Q: Representative Tinkham said that by joining the International Labor Organization we virtually became a member of the League of Nations.

THE PRESIDENT: No, except to say, off the record, "Good old George." That is strictly off the record. (Laughter)

Q: Some of the papers are saying that you plan to call the Cabinet in today to either discuss or read your Message to the Congress.

THE PRESIDENT: It is the regular Friday meeting.

Q: Have you decided whether you will read your Message in person?

THE PRESIDENT: I never decide that until the last moment. If I was writing the story, I would make a pretty good guess.

Q: When you wrote a letter to the Federal Housing Administration, citing a five per cent basic interest rate on insured mortgages, did you intend that the annual service charges should be added to that interest rate? That they should be imposed in addition?

THE PRESIDENT: I could not tell you the details. As I remember it, they had

--- [299] ---

a quarter of one per cent to cover something -- I do not remember the details but it was not an annual service charge, as I remember it. I think the whole thing was lumped into an additional percentage in the beginning. Well, the whole thing came out at the time but I do not remember the details.

Q: You do not intend that there will be an annual additional charge?

THE PRESIDENT: I had better not tell you because I do not know. My impression was that those were taken up as an additional amount when the law was made but I am not sure.

Q: Did you get a chance to look over that committee's report?

THE PRESIDENT: Which one?

Q: The White Sulphur Springs Report?

THE PRESIDENT: No; I have not looked at the basket.

Q: In the Mississippi Valley Committee's report today, it recommends power development and flood control and in every case the navigation project is recommended to be held up.

THE PRESIDENT: What is that? Is that this one? (Indicating)

MR. EARLY: Yes, sir.

Q: In most navigation cases, it recommends it be held up until it has reached a point where the shipping will be able to pay for the cost.

THE PRESIDENT: This particular report, being on a large special project, was made the field for a special committee under Morris L. Cooke and he, also, was on the National Resources Board. This might also be called the report of a subcommittee of the National Resources Board and any actual work under the National Resources Board report. I could not tell you the details of it.

Q:   Is the Administration formulating a policy that local states and com-

--- [300] ---

munities shall bear a part of the navigation control costs?  It is in that
report.

THE PRESIDENT:  I couldn't tell you because I haven't read it.  What is that
for, floods and things like that?

Q:   Yes, sir; flood control.  Those that benefit should pay part of the cost.

THE PRESIDENT:  Of course that brings up a very large subject.  Because it is
fairly new, we haven't a policy on it yet.  We are studying it.  If you
take city improvements -- in a good many cases in city improvements you
charge a portion of the improvement cost to the propetry that is benefitt-
ed.  On our large national projects, we have never done it.  It does raise
a question which has not been raised before.

It is a very large subject as to whether, if you build a national highway
and it greatly benefits adjoining property, whether that property should
bear some of the cost.  And it is the same way with flood control.  If you
have bottom lands that are inundated every year or every other year or
every third year and therefore aren't of very great value, if the Federal
Government or State Government or the County Government makes your land
free of floods, ought you not to pay some fair proportion so that you
would not be a beneficiary without cost to yourself?  It is a very big
problem and I think eventually we are going to have a rule of reason on it
by which, if you can show that private property is very definitely benefitt-
ed by a government project of any kind, it probably ought to bear a reasonable share of the cost of the project.

Q:   Would that contemplate state improvements, such as the Missouri River going through the State of Missouri and the state paying --

THE PRESIDENT:  (interposing)  No, I don't think so.

Q:   Last year, you suggested some sort of payment by boats using water highways?

--- [301] ---

THE PRESIDENT:  That we are trying to establish as a principle, making it a
very, very small payment.  In other words, to establish the principle of
paying something toward the cost of government where you are directly bene-
fitted by it.  There have been two reports from the War Department already.

Q:   I understand there is a Civil Service Commission report with respect to
covering the emergency employees into civil service.  Is there anything
progressing on that that you can speak of?

THE PRESIDENT:  Only the general effort we are making, where an emergency agency
looks to be fairly permanent, to begin giving people who work for that
agency, perhaps a small number of them, gradually giving them the same
rights of other Government employees.  No wholesale business, but gradually
working them into the Government service.

Q:   Did that mean by Executive Order or by examination?

THE PRESIDENT:   That I do not know.  We haven't got as far as that yet.

Q:   Have you any numbers of those affected?

THE PRESIDENT:   What?

Q:   How many would it affect; about how many?

THE PRESIDENT:   I do not know; I could not tell you the total.

Q:   A few hundred?

THE PRESIDENT:   Oh, I hope more than that.

Q:   Do you mean that local participation would apply to navigation as well as
     flood control?

THE PRESIDENT:   Navigation is a pretty broad word.  For instance, let us take
     two concrete examples:  On the straight navigation end, the vessels that
     use the lighted channel or the buoy channel get some benefit out of it --
     they always have -- and in some cases they pay port dues.  But they have
     never paid for going up the Hudson River, where it costs quite

--- [302] ---

a lot to maintain the channel, dredging, etc.  Any charges there would be
very, very small.  In other words, it would be so small that it would not
affect navigation at all, to speak of.

Q:   I meant the development cost.

THE PRESIDENT:   On the development end -- I am just thinking out loud now --
     suppose you build a new channel from Kingston to Albany.  The Government
     does it.  The question is, does Coxsackie and this city of Hudson -- ought
     they to pay for their own new wharves?  I should think, obviously, yes.

Q:   I mean the development of the channel, not of port facilities.

THE PRESIDENT:   Oh, no.  I don't think you can charge that against the commun-
     ity.

Q:   Thank you, Mr. President.

Press Conference #169
Executive Offices of the White House
December 28, 1934, 4:05 P.M.


Q:   (Mr. Storm)  All right, Henry (Mr. Kannee), I will run you a race.

THE PRESIDENT:  How is your shorthand, Fred?

Q:   (Mr. Storm)  Not so good.

THE PRESIDENT:  I think you ought to get Kannee to start a shorthand course for
    the Press.  That is one thing I have always been sorry I did not learn.

Q:   Just one of the lessons would do me.

Q:   I do not think there are more than thirty in this whole Conference.

THE PRESIDENT:  I always regretted I did not learn it in college and I have al-
    ways said my four boys would learn it, but they have not.

Q:   We have our own symbols, our own shorthand.

THE PRESIDENT:  Right.

MR. DONALDSON:  All in.

THE PRESIDENT:  No news.  (Laughter)  I do not know a thing and neither do you.

Q:   We are not going to ask any either.

THE PRESIDENT:  What is that?

Q:   How are you coming on the Messages, Mr. President?

THE PRESIDENT:  Oh, still in the scrap form -- many scraps being gradually glued
    together.

Q:   Mr. President, it would be very helpful to us if you could give us a little
    background on this matter of relief.

THE PRESIDENT:  What about it; what has happened?

Q:   There seems to be a lot about it that isn't so.

THE PRESIDENT:  Right you are; never was a truer word spoken.

                    --- [304] ---

Q:   Maybe it is so?

THE PRESIDENT:  I said on the third of January but I think probably you won't
    know until the fourth of January.

Q:   What do you know?

THE PRESIDENT:  I don't know.  I talked with various people as to when I am expected to have a Message (on relief) up there and I don't think anybody knows yet. We are waiting until the fourth.

Q: Is that because of the delay in the organization of the House?

THE PRESIDENT: The delay in organization. It is a new House. You see, last year they did not have to organize. I do not think there is anything to say about relief. Any guesses will be with the same accuracies and inaccuracies as usual.

Q: There is a report today that Mr. Hopkins has announced that they are going to turn back the unemployables to the states on February first and Darrow's outfit is saying that this is going to bring on a plan for old age pension.

THE PRESIDENT: No, I think all of that -- there is nothing particularly new in that. I think the Relief Administration discovered on checking up in the course of the summer that there were quite a lot of cases on relief that had previously been taken care of by local poor funds or churches and charities, et cetera, and we want, in so far as possible, to get them back to what they always did. I do not think there is anything new in it.

Q: Thank you, Mr. President.

THE PRESIDENT: Russell (Mr. Young) says, "Thank you, very much." I do not know what he is thanking me for; I wish I knew some news.

Q: Any New Year's resolutions? (Laughter)

Q: Must I apologize?

THE PRESIDENT: No; that is grand, perfectly fine.

# Complete Presidential Press Conferences of
# FRANKLIN D. ROOSEVELT

## Index to Volumes 3 and 4 (1934)

Meeting to be held to discuss enactment of legislation to take profits out of war. Nye investigation,
etc. "Unequal" mobilization, etc.
War Planning Commissions.          4:270-274

LEHMAN, HERBERT

Talk with Lehman about raising
money for relief in New York State.3:245-246

Talk with Lehman.                  4:33

Roosevelt's statement about voting
for Lehman.                        4:160

Included in example of interpretive
news story.                        4:169

LEVERETT, DUNCAN

Roosevelt went with Leverett and
Arthur Carpenter to show how to
clean blackjack out of the woods.  4:258

LEWISOHN, SAM A.

Member of Federal Prison Industries
Board.                             4:269

LIBERTY LEAGUE, AMERICAN

Jouett Shouse's visit. Roosevelt's
views on objectives of League, etc.4:17-20

LIBRARY OF CONGRESS

Report about plan to tear down.
Roosevelt's explanation.           4:286-287

LINDBERGH, CHARLES A.

Lindbergh case.                    4:95

LINDSAY, SIR RONALD

Story about R. Walton Moore and
Sir Ronald swapping a ham and
scotch.                            3:60

Visit to see Roosevelt.            3:359

LIPPMANN, WALTER

Views on monetary stabilization.   3:95-96

LIQUOR TAXES

Consideration in Budget.           3:21-22

Proposed increase in.              3:27-28

Not much possibility of reduction. 3:310

LITVINOV, MAXIM M.

Promises made by Litvinov on recognition of Soviet Government.      3:228

Proposal at Geneva.                3:381

LOGAN, MARVEL M.

Letter to Senator Logan about oil
situation.                         3:365-367

LONDON ECONOMIC CONFERENCE

London Agreement on Silver.        3:72

LONDON NAVAL CONFERENCE

Re preliminary talks. No statements concerning American Naval
policy.                            3:374

Preliminary conversations. Admiral Leahy.                       3:393

News about preliminary talks to
come from London.                  3:399

British discussion [preliminary
talks] of U. S. naval plans.
Nothing from Norman Davis. No
comment on British plans.          3:432

Methods to be pursued. Preliminary conversations. Announce-
ment of conferees to be made.      4:95-96

Hoping for new Naval Treaty.
Difficulties of conferees. What
U. S. is trying to do. Statement
of Billy Mitchell.                 4:107-108

Report about report from Norman
Davis about report from the
Japanese.                          4:150

Equality demand. No word from
Norman Davis.                      4:145

Press referred to London for news.
Interview given by Ambassador
Saito.                             4:157

Reports from Norman Davis; hopes
for outcome.                       4:164

Rumor about British and Japanese.
Statement from State Department
about.                             4:186

Nothing on.                        4:200

Cannot comment on negotiations.    4:266

Any information to come from
London.                            4:286

Disappointed that conversations
did not get far; hoping for a renewal of limitation of armaments.
Roosevelt's views on American
position and what attitude of
Americans should be. Hope for a
treaty. question about McCarran
Act.                               4:294-296

LONDON NAVAL TREATY

London Naval Treaty and London
Naval Conference.                  4:107

LONDON TELEGRAPH

Owned by Lord Illiffe.             4:43

PROPAGANDA

Tendency of foreign communications
companies to interfere in U. S.
communications with other countries.
Dissemination of news in South
America. Havas Agency.                3:244

PUBLIC SERVICE CORPORATION OF NEW
JERSEY

Thomas N. McCarter's request to
see Roosevelt.                        4:237

PUBLIC WORKS

Appropriations and expenditures,
Budgets of 1933-34 and 1934-35.       3:8-13;15-20

Public Works rebuilding the face
of the country. Housing, etc.         3:23-26

Purchases. Salaries, etc.             3:32

Effect of Budget.                     3:33

Comparatively small Budget recommendation. Large, long-range plan
of public works. Objectives.
Financing.                            3:38-39

To ask Congress for additional
amounts.                              3:57

Firing of Iowa Administrator.
District Attorney to talk to Department of Justice.                  3:81-82

Hope to put C.W.A workers to work
through operation of P.W.A. funds.    3:103

Form of legislation for recovery
agencies. Amount.                     3:111-112

Douglas "on the Hill" about bills
for emergency appropriations.         3:117

Amount to be given to Public Works.   3:129

Staying within limits of
1,166,000,000.                        3:130

Contributions to state highway
construction.                         3:145-146

Study of waterways a gradual conversion of public works, and elimination of rivers and harbor bills.
Public Works allotments. Trans-
Florida Canal.                        3:153-154

Taking on men in spring.              3:162

Roosevelt's views on question of
National Committeemen bidding on
municipal contracts where P.W.A.
funds are involved.                   3:194

Waterways projects, like Fort Peek
Dam, to come out of Public Works
appropriation.                        3:206

Sending request for $2,000,000,000;
Public Works included in that. Bud-
get figures.                          3:208-209

Question about National Committeemen getting contracts under P.W.A. 3:217

Suggestion of having Government
Buildings built by Public Works
decorated by artists on relief
rolls. Representative Vinson's
suggestion for using P.W.A. funds
for building new Navy.                3:301-302

Government's part in Lumber Code
to be partly carried out by P.W.A.
                                      3:305

Question about exempting P.W.A.
from application of municipal
bankruptcy bill. Ickes' view.
Roosevelt to take up.                 3:321

Relief appropriation Message.         3:329

Expenditures and appropriation.
Amounts.                              3:335-336

Amount available for additional
appropriation, etc. - with relief.
Recommendation for T.V.A. etc.        3:337-338

Transfer of certain unused appropriations to relief deficits.         3:339

Part of P.W.A. money to go for
housing projects.                     3:342

No more money for new projects.       3:365

Application of Chemical Foundation for funds to develop pine
pulp paper in Georgia. Views on
use of Public Works funds.            3:390-391

Plans for use of P.W.A. funds for
help in drought area. Upper
Missouri projects.                    3:392-393

Projected visit to Columbia River
projects and Fork Peek.               3:420

Identical bids on Fort Peek Dam
project, etc.                         3:437

Nothing on plans for.                 4:99

One method of handling unemployment.                                 4:110

Loans for municipal plants.           4:111

Likelihood of more housing work.      4:141

Question of using P.W.A. funds to
build equipment for lease to railroads.                                4:147

N.R.A. recommendation about P.W.A.
funds in Georgia.                     4:149

Stories current about program.
Gathering information on relief,
public works, soil erosion, planning, etc.                             4:156

Effort to get public works that
will liquidate themselves. Effort
to prevent waste.                     4:173-174

Study of waterways would include St. Lawrence merely as one of the watersheds. 3:149

Action on St. Lawrence Waterway need not depend on development of waterways plan. 3:151

Hopes to see Senate vote on Treaty. 3:161-162

Talked with Frank Walsh about Treaty. 3:197

Hopes they will take vote on Waterway. 3:208

Visit of mayors of Great Lakes cities. 3:220

Meeting with Great Lakes mayors. 3:228-229

Voting on Treaty. Roosevelt's views on certainty of Seaway being built, if not by joint action, then by Canada alone. Physical problems. Problem of diversion. Possibility of Canada discriminating against U. S. ships. Treaty to go back. 3:232-236

Question of inclusion in reports on water use. 3:364

St. Lawrence Seaway. Treaty. 3:389-390

Permission to write story in connection with watershed report. 3:392

Not to separate power venture from navigation in Treaty. Question raised by Canada. Chicago diversion. 4:111-112

Great Lakes-St. Lawrence Tidewater Association. Under Secretary Phillips' talk with Prime Minister Bennett about Treaty. Roosevelt's views on Chicago's diversion of water from Lake Michigan. 4:183-185

St. Lawrence Project referred to as a yardstick. 4:285

SAITO, HIROSHI

Interview given by. 4:157

SALVADOR

Reason for U. S. recognition. Central American policy. 3:114

SAN FRANCISCO

Telegram from Acting Director of Housing. 4:187

SAYRE, FRANCIS B.

To be at meeting on Foreign Trade. 3:198

SCHALL, THOMAS D.

Speech about a Government press service. 4:20

SCOTT, [ARMAND W.?]

Opposition to Scott's appointment as Municipal Judge, Washington, D. C. 3:320

SEAVEY, CLYDE L.

Appointment to Federal Power Commission. 3:414

SECURITIES EXCHANGE

Reason for purchase of Government securities. 3:71

Expects Dickinson's report on regulation of stock exchanges. 3:85

Secretary Roper bringing report on stock exchanges, also report on sale of securities by investment bankers, etc. 3:97

Has report on stock exchange regulations. To send it to Congressional Committees and afterwards talk over subject. 3:99

Cannot tell if Stock Exchange report includes Grain Exchange. Hope for Congressional action on stock exchange regulation. 3:101

James M. Landis working on control of stock exchanges, issuance of securities, etc. Department of Commerce reports. 3:113

Discussions of Stock Market bill. 3:122

No talks about stock exchange regulations. 3:127

Has not heard a word about Securities Act. Dickinson report. 3:132

Has not conferred with leaders on Hill about Stock Exchange regulation. Roosevelt's position. 3:133-134

No further conferences at White House on stock market regulation. Relation of Securities Act, etc. to Democratic Party Platform. Has not read Bill. 3:146-147

Roosevelt's views on Stock Exchange regulation. 3:156

Has not read Stock Regulation Bill. 3:165

Has not yet read Stock Market Regulation Bill. 3:187

Richard Whitney's idea of stock exchange regulation. 3:194-195

Cannot answer questions on Stock Exchange Bill. 3:209

Study being made of a federal incorporation law. Further study to be made. Members of committee studying it. 3:210-211

rails. Shoe industry, etc.     3:168-173

TEN COMMANDMENTS

In connection with American Liberty
League.                        4:18-19

TENNESSEE VALLEY

Amount in Budget for T.V.A.     3:15

Report by Huston Thompson on question on Muscle Shoals brought up
by Senator Norris. Question of
culpability of Army Engineers.   3:128-129

Recommendation in budget.        3:338

Tennessee River included in reports
on water use.                    3:363

TENNESSEE VALLEY AUTHORITY

Frank Walsh to study T.V.A. Rate
reductions of privately owned
utilities.                       4:110-111

Conference with Dr. A. E. Morgan
on pre-budget survey of needs of
T.V.A.                           4:134

Power company fight against Alcorn
County Power Plant.              4:185

To talk on Friday on T.V.A.      4:200

Wendell Willkie's statement about
T.V.A.                           4:203

Has member on Committee on power,
working on general power policy.  4:208-209

Beginnings of T.V.A. Conditions in
the South. Purpose of T.V.A.
Development of fertilizer. Power.
Alcorn County Power Association.
Rates. Electric equipment. Building of rural lines. Association's
financial operations.            4:212-222

Not necessary to have other power
experiments if power companies will
do it.                           4:228

Edison Electrical Institute to test
constitutionality of.            4:237

Press not to use story on T.V.A.
Roosevelt expects to talk on.    4:251

Repudiates statement that he proposed extension of T.V.A. all over
country. Pending court fight of
Edison Electrical Institute, etc.  4:280

Muscle Shoals as a yard stick.    4:285

Electric Home and Farm Authority,
and effort to help private utilities
set up similar method of financing. 4:297-298

TEXAS

Improved conditions in oil industry.
                                 4:163-164

Waste of gas in oil fields.      4:222

THOMAS, SENATOR [ELMER?]

Humorous remark about, in connection with Farm Credit bonds..    3:46

THOMAS, NORMAN

Roosevelt's views on Thomas'
practical ability, and activities
in textile strike.               4:46-47

THOMPSON, HUSTON

Report by Thompson on Muscle
Shoals.                          3:128-129

THORP, [WILLIARD L.?]

Resignation.                     3:333

THURSTON, ELLIOTT

Reference to in connection with
question on C.W.A.               3:132

News story about Chamber of
Commerce.                        3:309

TIME MAGAZINE

Newspapers competing with interpretive news stories.            4:170

TINKHAM, GEORGE H.

Remark about joining International
Labor Organization.              4:298

TOKUGAWA, PRINCE IYESATO

Talked with Roosevelt.           3:218

TOLEDO

Strike.                          3:372-374

TOWNSEND, JAMES

Has not seen Townsend since previous fall.                      4:35

Talk with Roosevelt about relief
problems in Dutchess County, N.Y. 4:171-173

TRANSPORTATION

Question about Rayburn Bill.
Commissioner Eastman not ready
to report on recommendations for
legislation on transportation -
control of all transportation.   3:85-86

Campaign promise to coordinate
all transportation. Salt Lake
City speech.                     3:116

Included in long-range planning
for waterways. Studying taxing
use of water highways.           3:150-151

Eastman report on regulation of
motor and water carriers transmitted to Congress.              3:231-232

WAR, DEPARTMENT OF

WAR DEBTS